ACTION PHILOSOPHERS!

The lives and thoughts of history's A-list brain trust

THE MORE-THAN-COMPLETE EDITION

by Fred Van Lente and Ryan Dunlavey

The More Than Complete Action Philosophers
is published by Evil Twin Comics, 262 Fifth Avenue,
2nd Floor, Brooklyn NY, 11215.

Most of the material in this book originally
appeared in periodical form as *Action Philosophers*
#1-9.

First Printing: November 2009

Printed in Canada

ISBN: 0977832937
ISBN-13: 978-0977832934

3629

ROLL CALL for ACTION!!

PART ONE: IT'S ALL GREEK TO YOU! (ANCIENT PHILOSOPHY)

PART TWO: THAT OLD TIME RELIGION! (MEDIEVAL PHILOSOPHY)

PART THREE: BLINDED ME WITH SILENCE!
(MODERN PHILOSOPHY)

PART FOUR: OUR STUPID AGE OF "ISMs"
(CONTEMPORARY PHILOSOPHY)

"PHILOSOPHY IS NOT A ***THEORY***, BUT AN ***ACTIVITY***."

--LUDWIG WITTGENSTEIN, *TRACTATUS LOGICO-PHILOSOPHICUS*

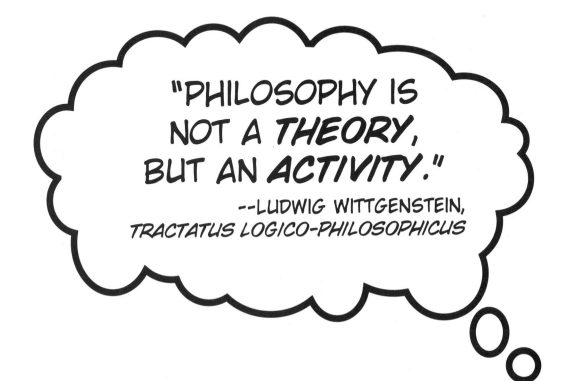

To Crystal,
who laughs at my jokes, and pretends I'm smart.
Not sure which one I like more...
-Fred V.

For my mom,
who taught me to always think for myself.
-Ryan D.

ACTION
PHILOSOPHERS!

PART ONE:

IT'S ALL GREEK TO YOU*
(ANCIENT PHILOSOPHY)

* Except where it's Chinese

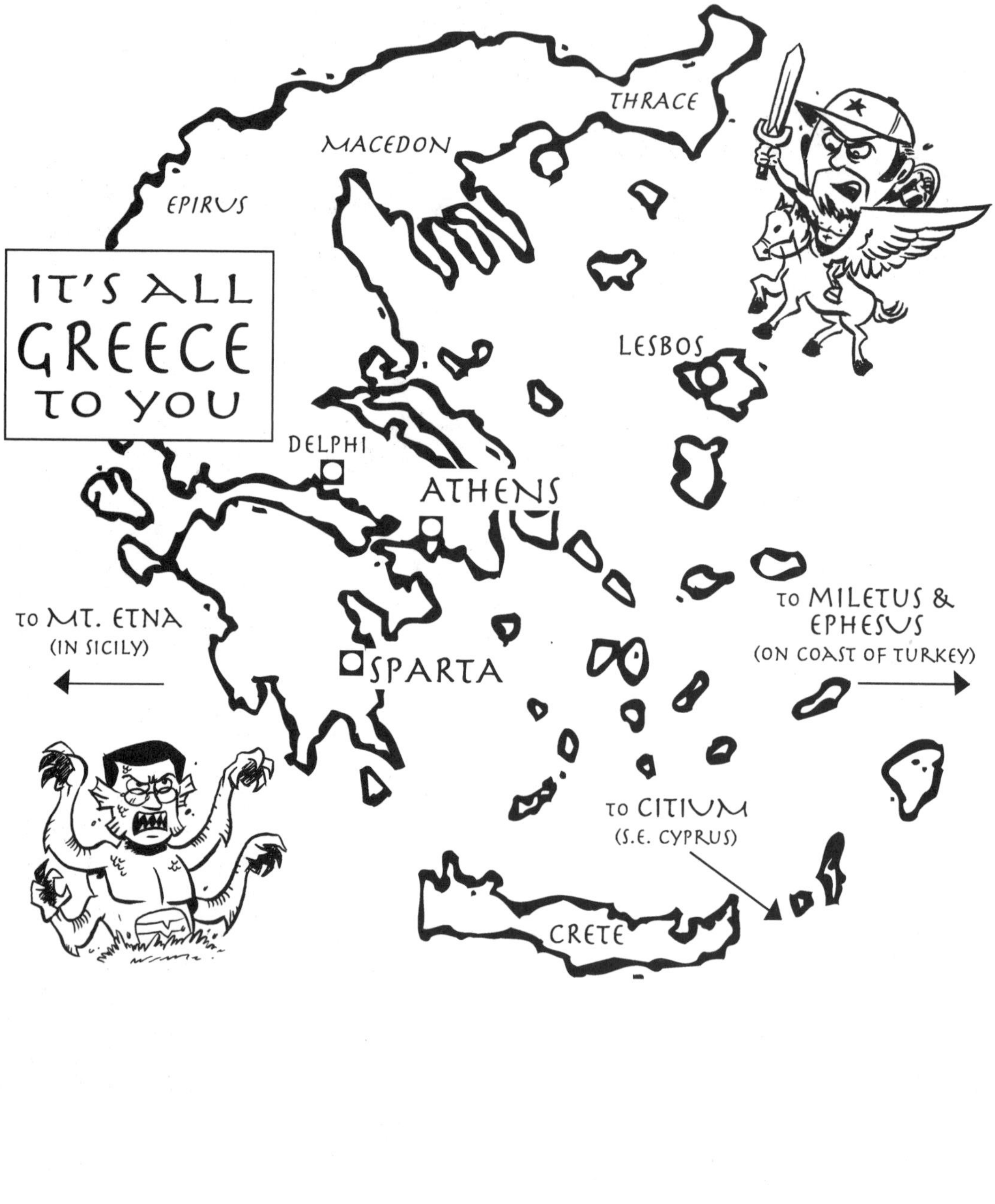

IT'S ALL
GREECE
TO YOU
THRACE
MACEDON
EPIRUS
LESBOS
DELPHI
ATHENS
SPARTA
TO MT. ETNA
(IN SICILY)
TO MILETUS &
EPHESUS
(ON COAST OF TURKEY)
TO CITIUM
(S.E. CYPRUS)
CRETE

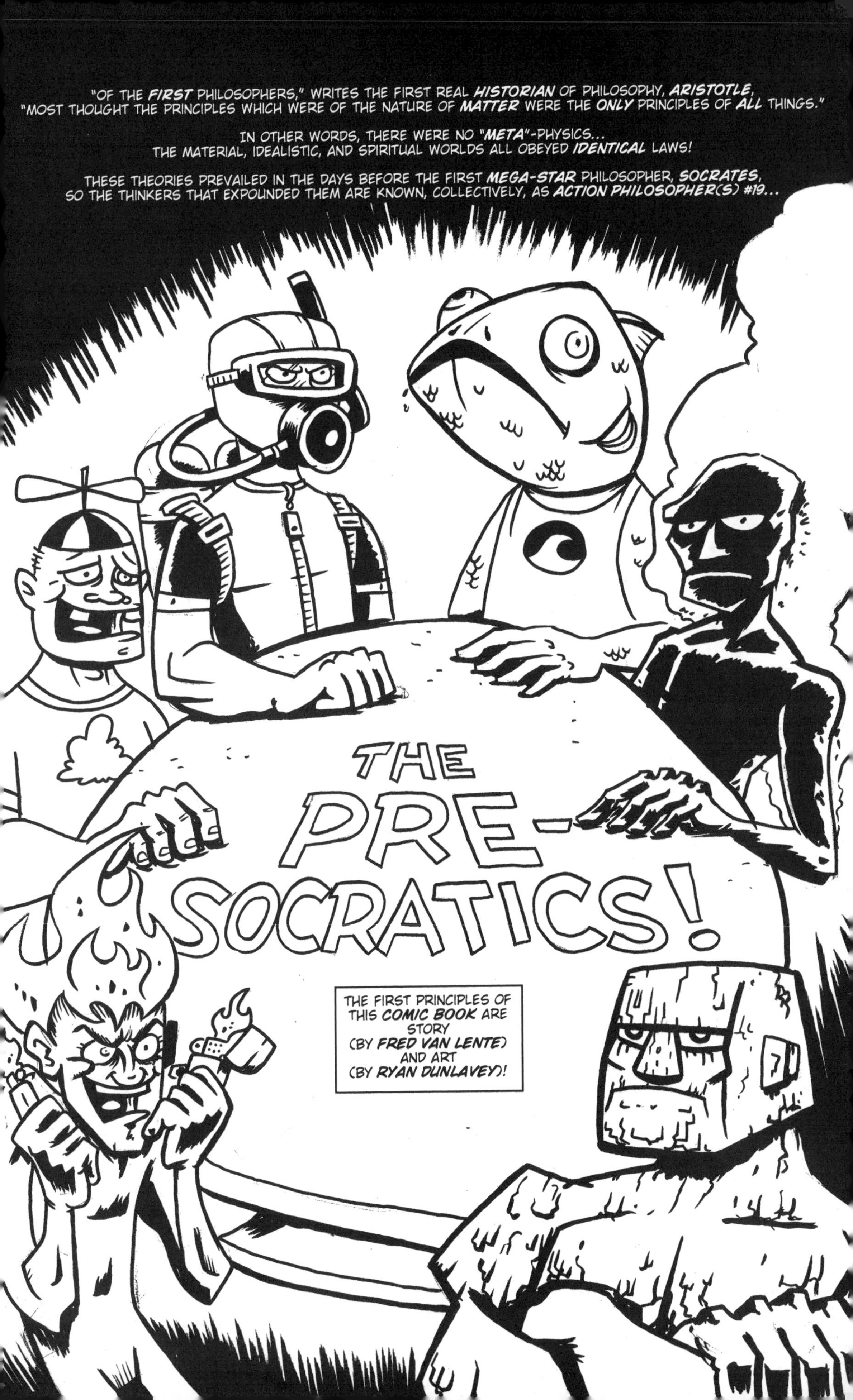
"OF THE FIRST PHILOSOPHERS," WRITES THE FIRST REAL HISTORIAN OF PHILOSOPHY, ARISTOTLE, "MOST THOUGHT THE PRINCIPLES WHICH WERE OF THE NATURE OF MATTER WERE THE ONLY PRINCIPLES OF ALL THINGS."
IN OTHER WORDS, THERE WERE NO "META"-PHYSICS... THE MATERIAL, IDEALISTIC, AND SPIRITUAL WORLDS ALL OBEYED IDENTICAL LAWS!
THESE THEORIES PREVAILED IN THE DAYS BEFORE THE FIRST MEGA-STAR PHILOSOPHER, SOCRATES, SO THE THINKERS THAT EXPOUNDED THEM ARE KNOWN, COLLECTIVELY, AS ACTION PHILOSOPHER(S) #19...
THE PRE-SOCRATICS!
THE FIRST PRINCIPLES OF THIS COMIC BOOK ARE STORY (BY FRED VAN LENTE) AND ART (BY RYAN DUNLAVEY)!

THALES OF MILETUS!

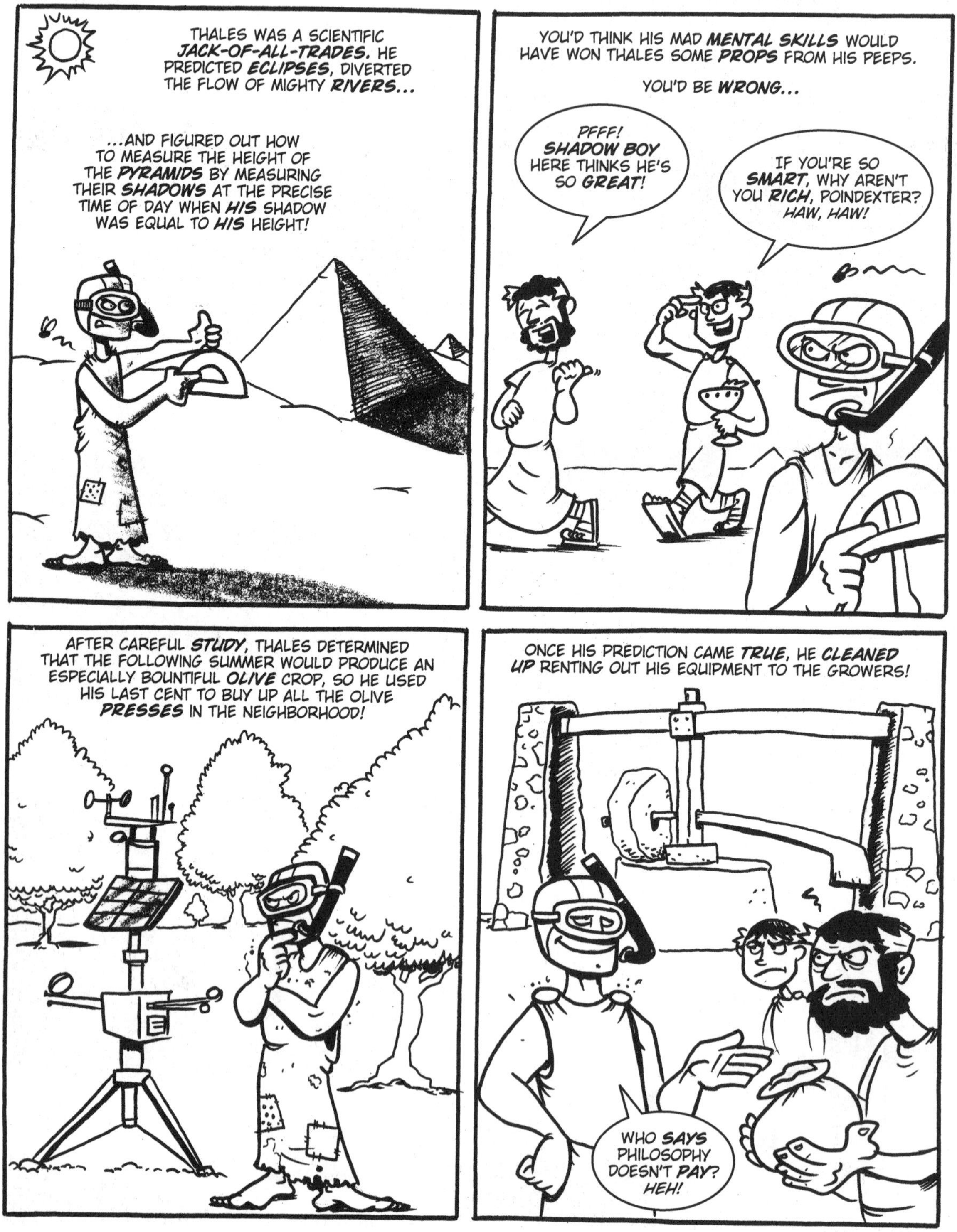

THALES WAS A SCIENTIFIC JACK-OF-ALL-TRADES. HE PREDICTED ECLIPSES, DIVERTED THE FLOW OF MIGHTY RIVERS...
...AND FIGURED OUT HOW TO MEASURE THE HEIGHT OF THE PYRAMIDS BY MEASURING THEIR SHADOWS AT THE PRECISE TIME OF DAY WHEN HIS SHADOW WAS EQUAL TO HIS HEIGHT!
YOU'D THINK HIS MAD MENTAL SKILLS WOULD HAVE WON THALES SOME PROPS FROM HIS PEEPS.
YOU'D BE WRONG...
PFFF! SHADOW BOY HERE THINKS HE'S SO GREAT!
IF YOU'RE SO SMART, WHY AREN'T YOU RICH, POINDEXTER? HAW, HAW!
AFTER CAREFUL STUDY, THALES DETERMINED THAT THE FOLLOWING SUMMER WOULD PRODUCE AN ESPECIALLY BOUNTIFUL OLIVE CROP, SO HE USED HIS LAST CENT TO BUY UP ALL THE OLIVE PRESSES IN THE NEIGHBORHOOD!
ONCE HIS PREDICTION CAME TRUE, HE CLEANED UP RENTING OUT HIS EQUIPMENT TO THE GROWERS!
WHO SAYS PHILOSOPHY DOESN'T PAY? HEH!

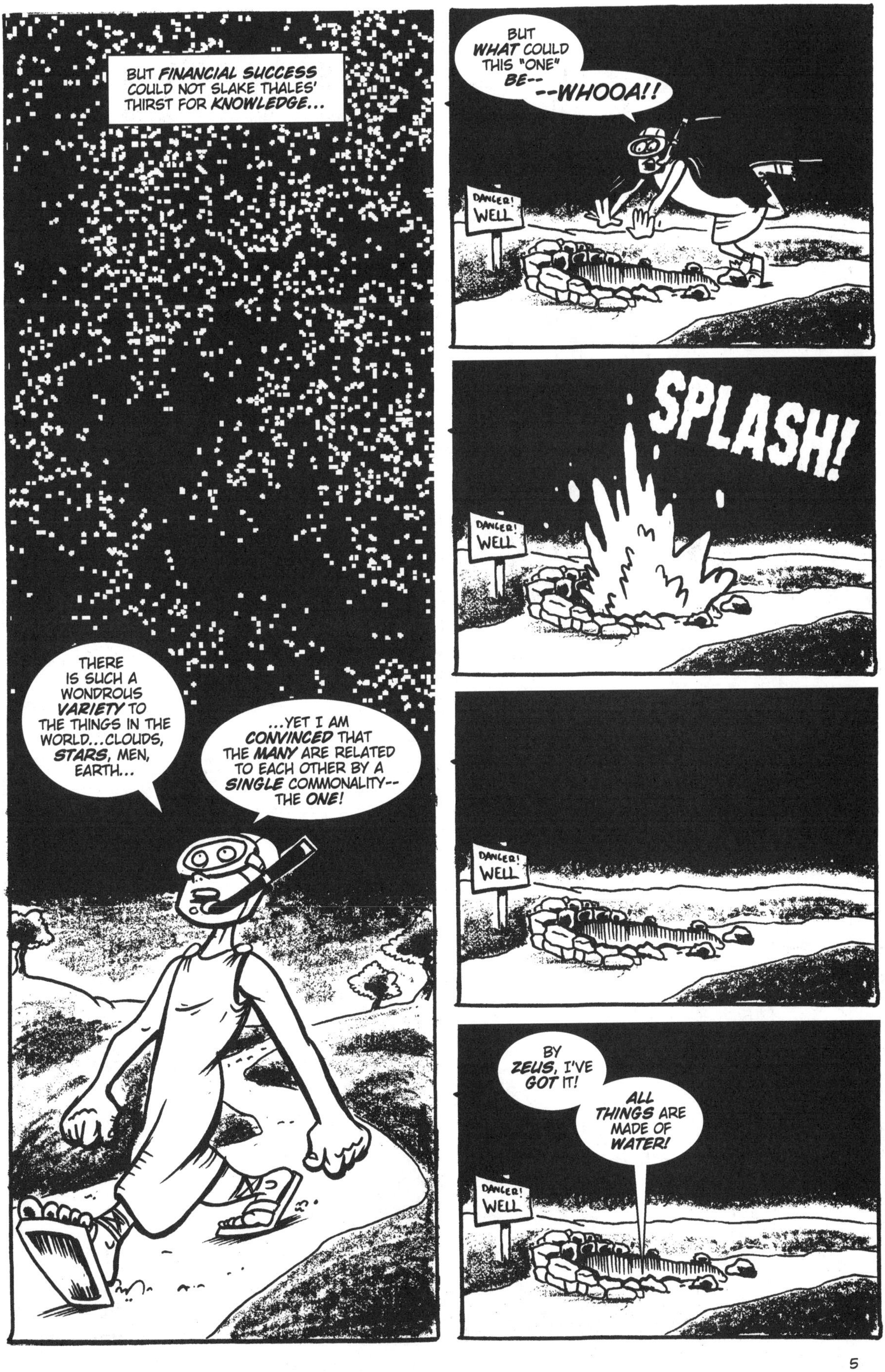
BUT FINANCIAL SUCCESS COULD NOT SLAKE THALES' THIRST FOR KNOWLEDGE...
THERE IS SUCH A WONDROUS VARIETY TO THE THINGS IN THE WORLD...CLOUDS, STARS, MEN, EARTH...
...YET I AM CONVINCED THAT THE MANY ARE RELATED TO EACH OTHER BY A SINGLE COMMONALITY-- THE ONE!
BUT WHAT COULD THIS "ONE" BE--
--WHOOA!!
DANGER! WELL
SPLASH!
DANGER! WELL
DANGER! WELL
BY ZEUS, I'VE GOT IT!
ALL THINGS ARE MADE OF WATER!
DANGER! WELL

ANAXIMANDER!

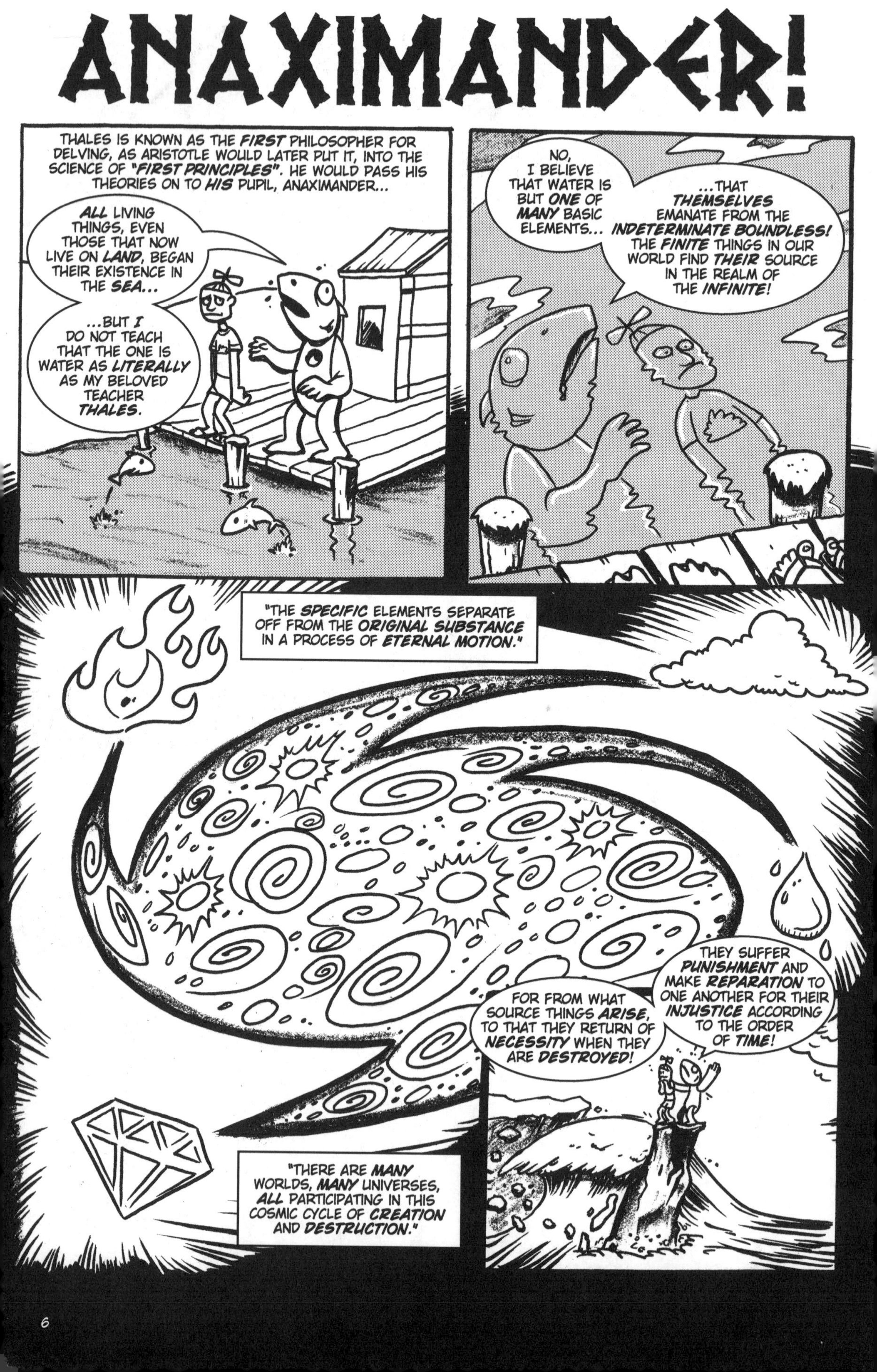
THALES IS KNOWN AS THE FIRST PHILOSOPHER FOR DELVING, AS ARISTOTLE WOULD LATER PUT IT, INTO THE SCIENCE OF "FIRST PRINCIPLES". HE WOULD PASS HIS THEORIES ON TO HIS PUPIL, ANAXIMANDER...
ALL LIVING THINGS, EVEN THOSE THAT NOW LIVE ON LAND, BEGAN THEIR EXISTENCE IN THE SEA...
...BUT I DO NOT TEACH THAT THE ONE IS WATER AS LITERALLY AS MY BELOVED TEACHER THALES.
NO, I BELIEVE THAT WATER IS BUT ONE OF MANY BASIC ELEMENTS...
...THAT THEMSELVES EMANATE FROM THE INDETERMINATE BOUNDLESS! THE FINITE THINGS IN OUR WORLD FIND THEIR SOURCE IN THE REALM OF THE INFINITE!
"THE SPECIFIC ELEMENTS SEPARATE OFF FROM THE ORIGINAL SUBSTANCE IN A PROCESS OF ETERNAL MOTION."
FOR FROM WHAT SOURCE THINGS ARISE, TO THAT THEY RETURN OF NECESSITY WHEN THEY ARE DESTROYED!
THEY SUFFER PUNISHMENT AND MAKE REPARATION TO ONE ANOTHER FOR THEIR INJUSTICE ACCORDING TO THE ORDER OF TIME!
"THERE ARE MANY WORLDS, MANY UNIVERSES, ALL PARTICIPATING IN THIS COSMIC CYCLE OF CREATION AND DESTRUCTION."

ANAXIMENES!

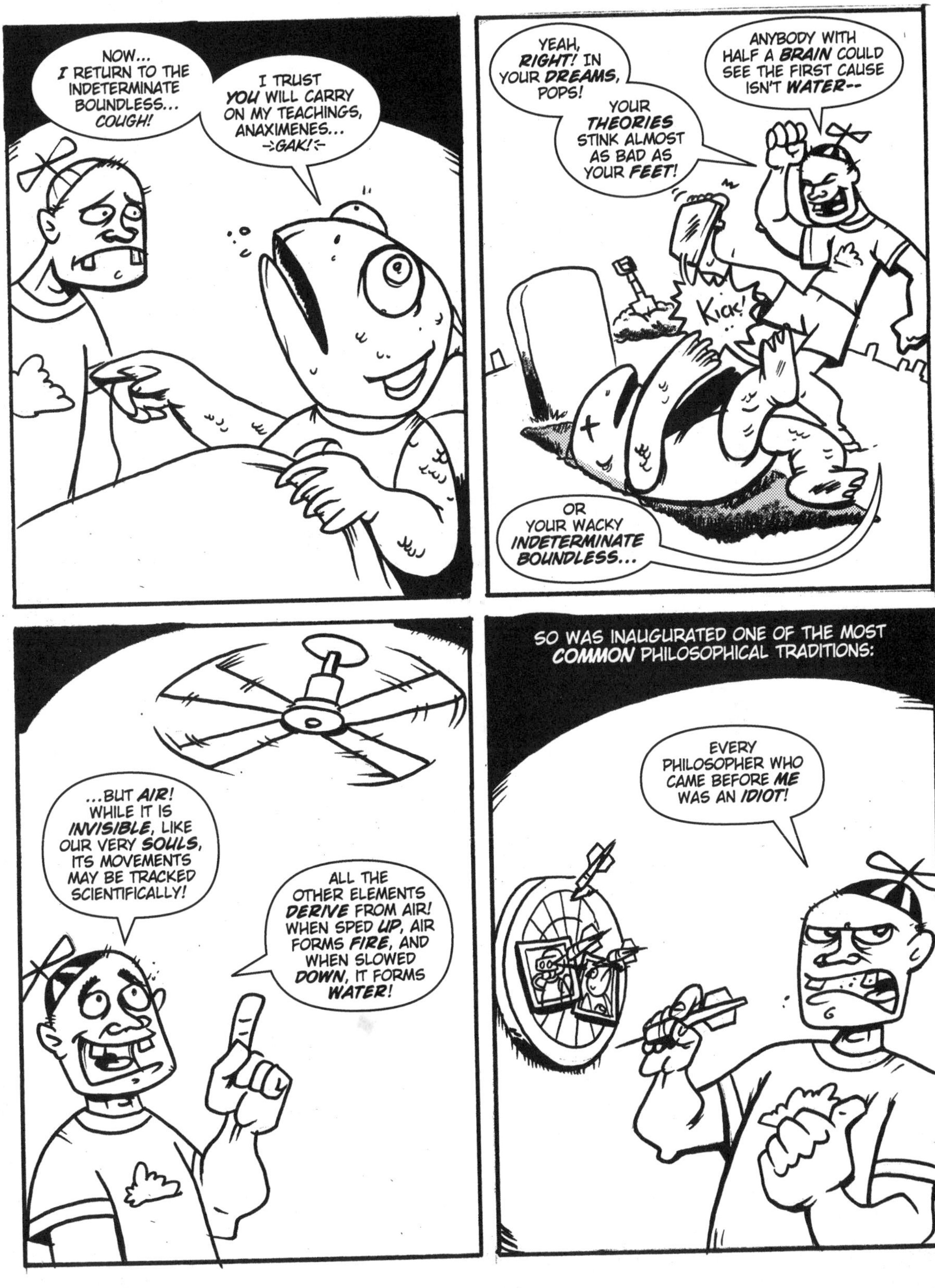
NOW... I RETURN TO THE INDETERMINATE BOUNDLESS... COUGH!
I TRUST YOU WILL CARRY ON MY TEACHINGS, ANAXIMENES... GAK!
YEAH, RIGHT! IN YOUR DREAMS, POPS!
ANYBODY WITH HALF A BRAIN COULD SEE THE FIRST CAUSE ISN'T WATER--
YOUR THEORIES STINK ALMOST AS BAD AS YOUR FEET!
KICK!
OR YOUR WACKY INDETERMINATE BOUNDLESS...
...BUT AIR! WHILE IT IS INVISIBLE, LIKE OUR VERY SOULS, ITS MOVEMENTS MAY BE TRACKED SCIENTIFICALLY!
ALL THE OTHER ELEMENTS DERIVE FROM AIR! WHEN SPED UP, AIR FORMS FIRE, AND WHEN SLOWED DOWN, IT FORMS WATER!
SO WAS INAUGURATED ONE OF THE MOST COMMON PHILOSOPHICAL TRADITIONS:
EVERY PHILOSOPHER WHO CAME BEFORE ME WAS AN IDIOT!

HERACLITUS!

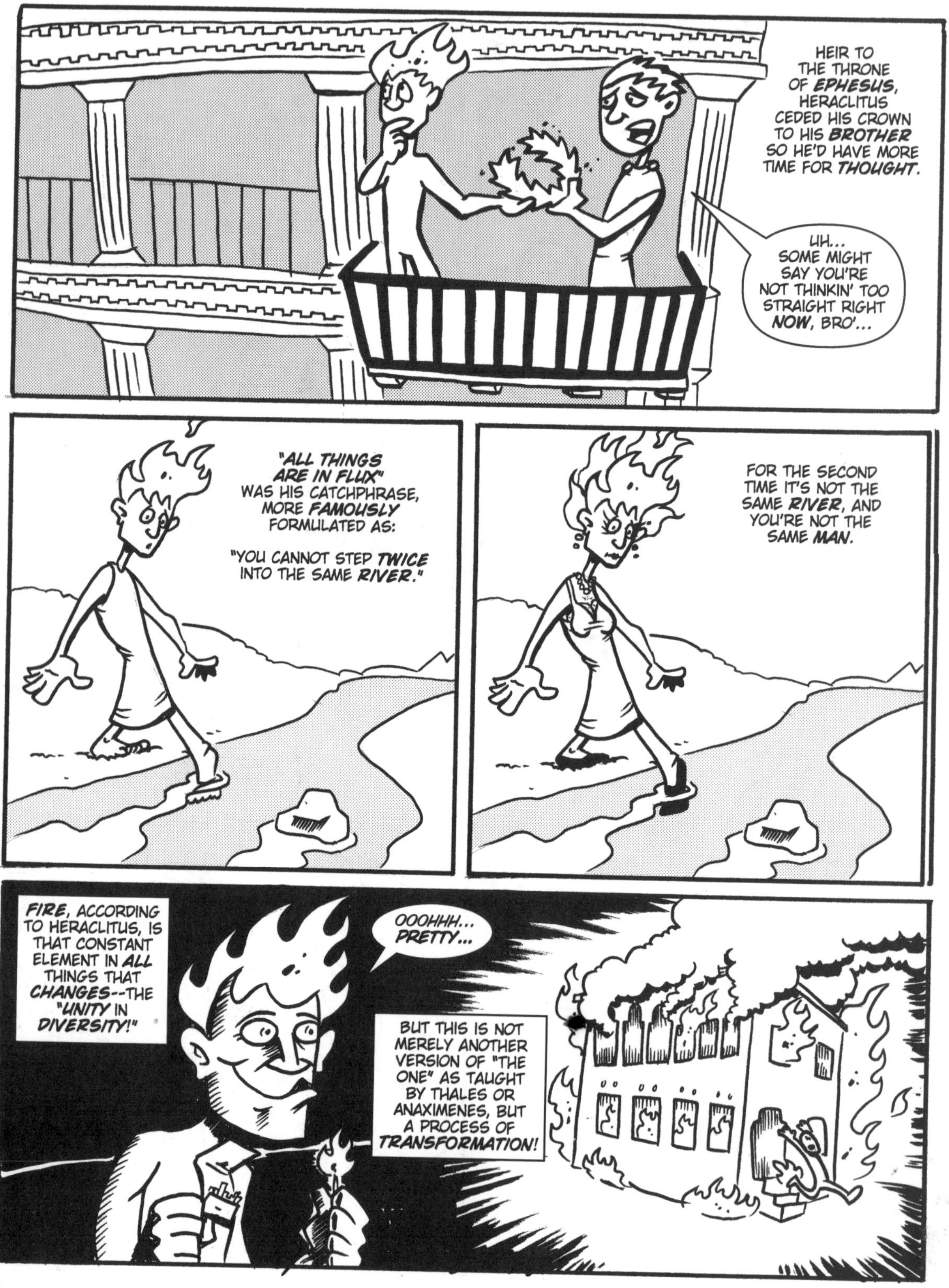
HEIR TO THE THRONE OF EPHESUS, HERACLITUS CEDED HIS CROWN TO HIS BROTHER SO HE'D HAVE MORE TIME FOR THOUGHT.
UH... SOME MIGHT SAY YOU'RE NOT THINKIN' TOO STRAIGHT RIGHT NOW, BRO'...
"ALL THINGS ARE IN FLUX" WAS HIS CATCHPHRASE, MORE FAMOUSLY FORMULATED AS:
"YOU CANNOT STEP TWICE INTO THE SAME RIVER."
FOR THE SECOND TIME IT'S NOT THE SAME RIVER, AND YOU'RE NOT THE SAME MAN.
FIRE, ACCORDING TO HERACLITUS, IS THAT CONSTANT ELEMENT IN ALL THINGS THAT CHANGES--THE "UNITY IN DIVERSITY!"
OOOHHH... PRETTY...
BUT THIS IS NOT MERELY ANOTHER VERSION OF "THE ONE" AS TAUGHT BY THALES OR ANAXIMENES, BUT A PROCESS OF TRANSFORMATION!

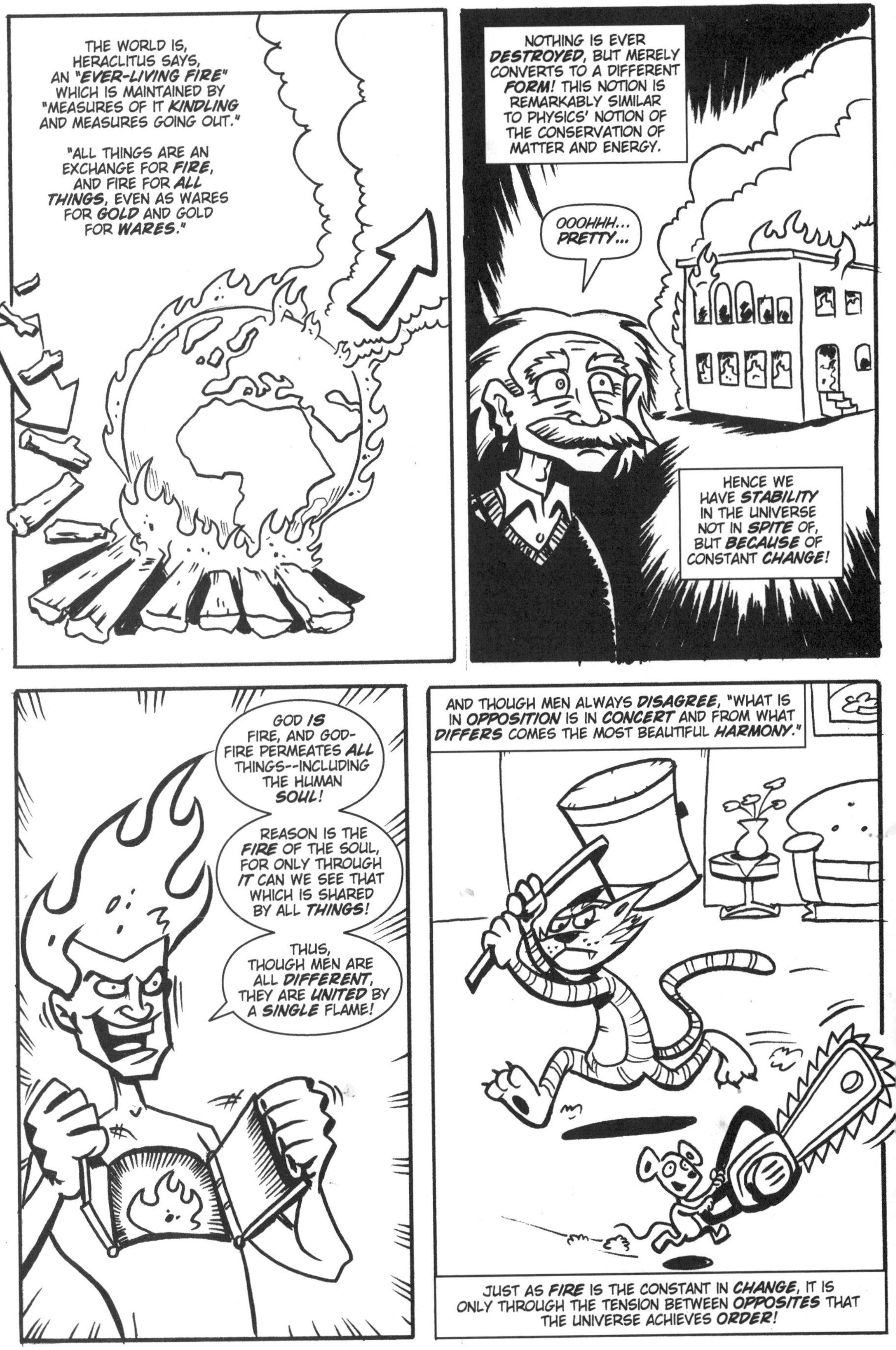
THE WORLD IS, HERACLITUS SAYS, AN "EVER-LIVING FIRE" WHICH IS MAINTAINED BY "MEASURES OF IT KINDLING AND MEASURES GOING OUT."
"ALL THINGS ARE AN EXCHANGE FOR FIRE, AND FIRE FOR ALL THINGS, EVEN AS WARES FOR GOLD AND GOLD FOR WARES."
NOTHING IS EVER DESTROYED, BUT MERELY CONVERTS TO A DIFFERENT FORM! THIS NOTION IS REMARKABLY SIMILAR TO PHYSICS' NOTION OF THE CONSERVATION OF MATTER AND ENERGY.
OOOHHH... PRETTY...
HENCE WE HAVE STABILITY IN THE UNIVERSE NOT IN SPITE OF, BUT BECAUSE OF CONSTANT CHANGE!
GOD IS FIRE, AND GOD-FIRE PERMEATES ALL THINGS--INCLUDING THE HUMAN SOUL!
REASON IS THE FIRE OF THE SOUL, FOR ONLY THROUGH IT CAN WE SEE THAT WHICH IS SHARED BY ALL THINGS!
THUS, THOUGH MEN ARE ALL DIFFERENT, THEY ARE UNITED BY A SINGLE FLAME!
AND THOUGH MEN ALWAYS DISAGREE, "WHAT IS IN OPPOSITION IS IN CONCERT AND FROM WHAT DIFFERS COMES THE MOST BEAUTIFUL HARMONY."
JUST AS FIRE IS THE CONSTANT IN CHANGE, IT IS ONLY THROUGH THE TENSION BETWEEN OPPOSITES THAT THE UNIVERSE ACHIEVES ORDER!

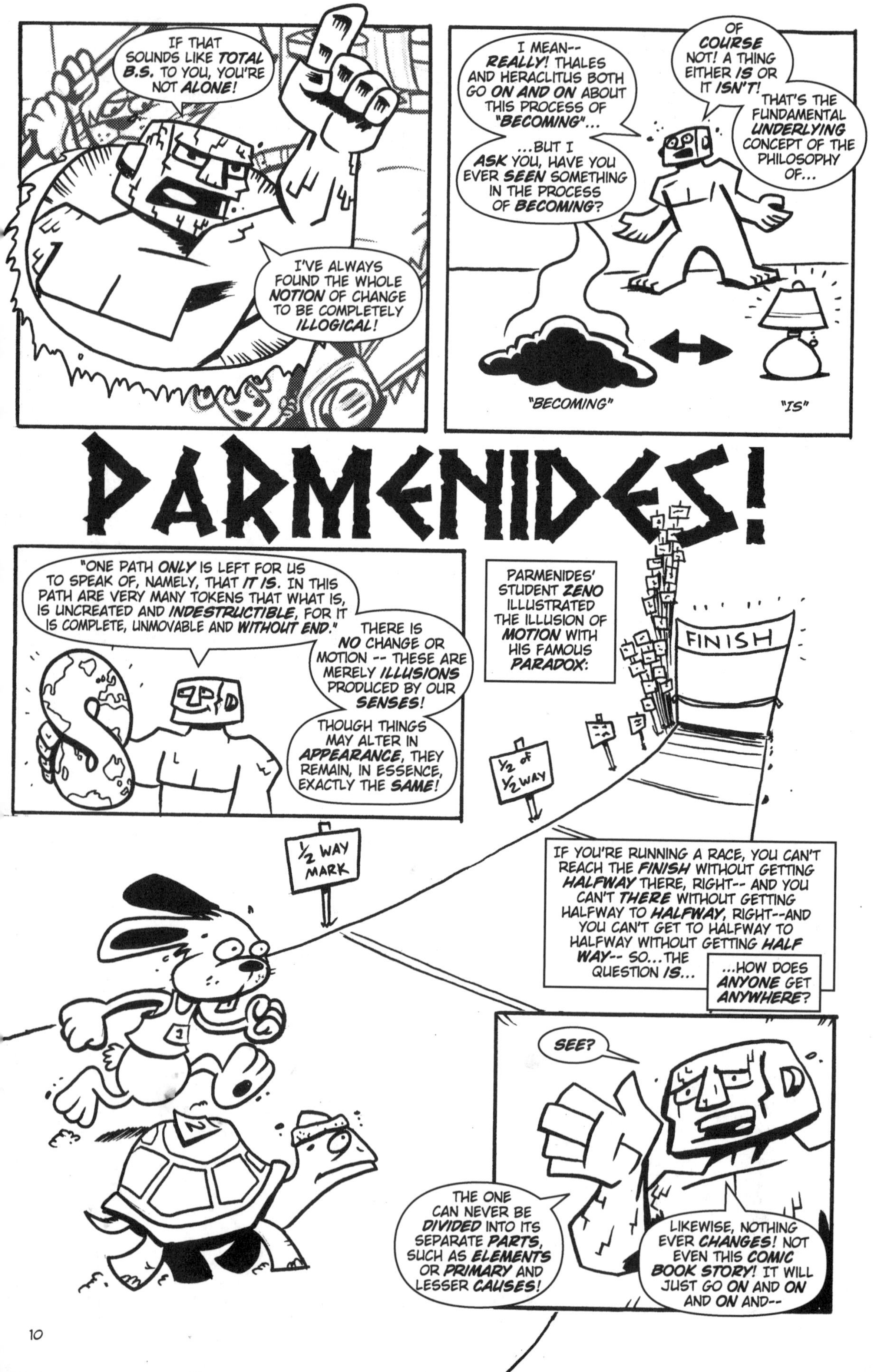
IF THAT SOUNDS LIKE TOTAL B.S. TO YOU, YOU'RE NOT ALONE!
I'VE ALWAYS FOUND THE WHOLE NOTION OF CHANGE TO BE COMPLETELY ILLOGICAL!
I MEAN-- REALLY! THALES AND HERACLITUS BOTH GO ON AND ON ABOUT THIS PROCESS OF "BECOMING"...
...BUT I ASK YOU, HAVE YOU EVER SEEN SOMETHING IN THE PROCESS OF BECOMING?
OF COURSE NOT! A THING EITHER IS OR IT ISN'T!
THAT'S THE FUNDAMENTAL UNDERLYING CONCEPT OF THE PHILOSOPHY OF...
"BECOMING"
"IS"
PARMENIDES!
"ONE PATH ONLY IS LEFT FOR US TO SPEAK OF, NAMELY, THAT IT IS. IN THIS PATH ARE VERY MANY TOKENS THAT WHAT IS, IS UNCREATED AND INDESTRUCTIBLE, FOR IT IS COMPLETE, UNMOVABLE AND WITHOUT END."
THERE IS NO CHANGE OR MOTION -- THESE ARE MERELY ILLUSIONS PRODUCED BY OUR SENSES!
THOUGH THINGS MAY ALTER IN APPEARANCE, THEY REMAIN, IN ESSENCE, EXACTLY THE SAME!
PARMENIDES' STUDENT ZENO ILLUSTRATED THE ILLUSION OF MOTION WITH HIS FAMOUS PARADOX:
FINISH
1/2 OF 1/2 WAY
1/2 WAY MARK
IF YOU'RE RUNNING A RACE, YOU CAN'T REACH THE FINISH WITHOUT GETTING HALFWAY THERE, RIGHT-- AND YOU CAN'T THERE WITHOUT GETTING HALFWAY TO HALFWAY, RIGHT--AND YOU CAN'T GET TO HALFWAY TO HALFWAY WITHOUT GETTING HALF WAY-- SO...THE QUESTION IS...
...HOW DOES ANYONE GET ANYWHERE?
1
2
SEE?
THE ONE CAN NEVER BE DIVIDED INTO ITS SEPARATE PARTS, SUCH AS ELEMENTS OR PRIMARY AND LESSER CAUSES!
LIKEWISE, NOTHING EVER CHANGES! NOT EVEN THIS COMIC BOOK STORY! IT WILL JUST GO ON AND ON AND ON AND--

EMPEDOCLES!

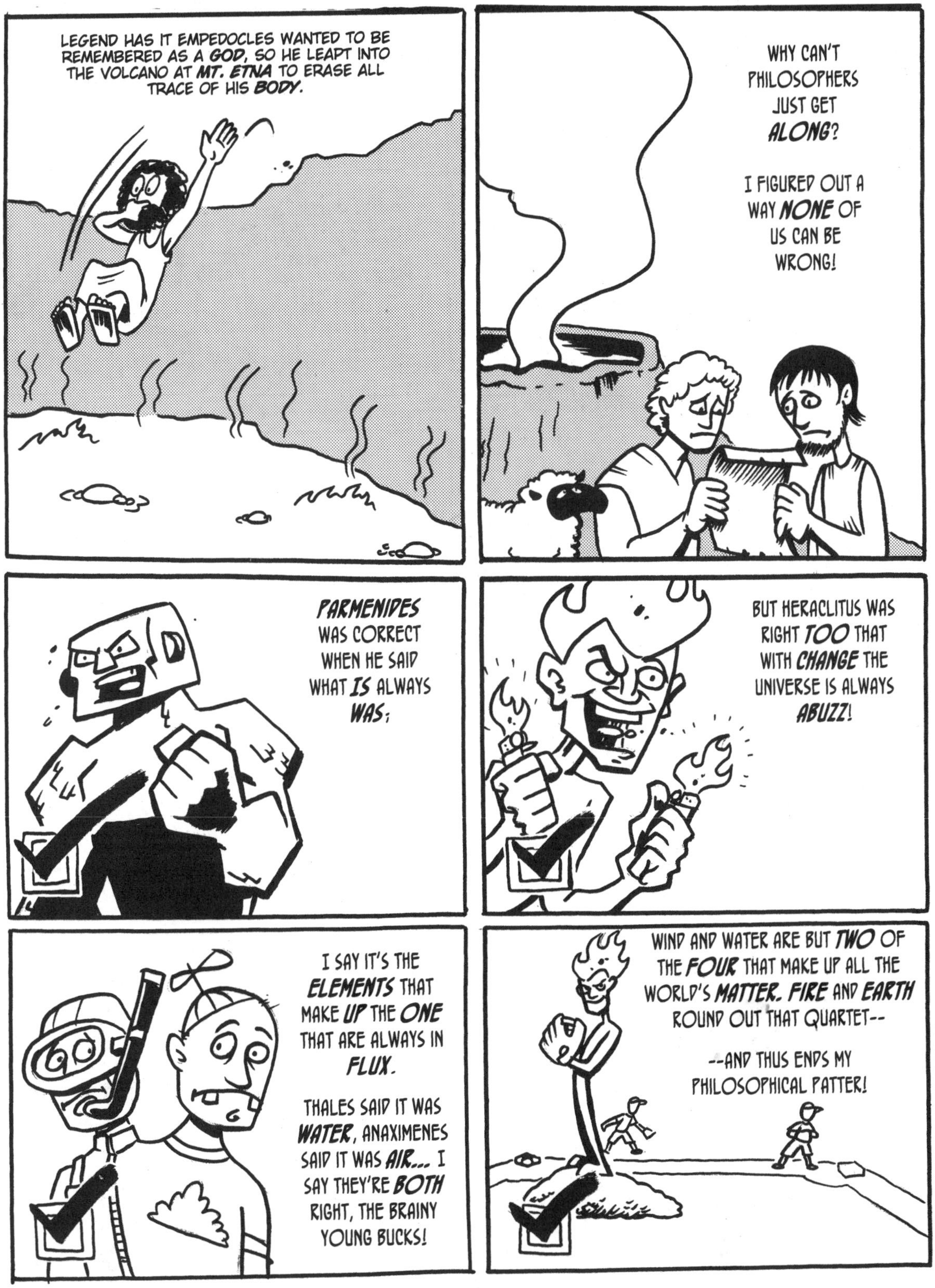
LEGEND HAS IT EMPEDOCLES WANTED TO BE REMEMBERED AS A GOD, SO HE LEAPT INTO THE VOLCANO AT MT. ETNA TO ERASE ALL TRACE OF HIS BODY.
WHY CAN'T PHILOSOPHERS JUST GET ALONG?
I FIGURED OUT A WAY NONE OF US CAN BE WRONG!
PARMENIDES WAS CORRECT WHEN HE SAID WHAT IS ALWAYS WAS;
BUT HERACLITUS WAS RIGHT TOO THAT WITH CHANGE THE UNIVERSE IS ALWAYS ABUZZ!
I SAY IT'S THE ELEMENTS THAT MAKE UP THE ONE THAT ARE ALWAYS IN FLUX.
THALES SAID IT WAS WATER, ANAXIMENES SAID IT WAS AIR... I SAY THEY'RE BOTH RIGHT, THE BRAINY YOUNG BUCKS!
WIND AND WATER ARE BUT TWO OF THE FOUR THAT MAKE UP ALL THE WORLD'S MATTER. FIRE AND EARTH ROUND OUT THAT QUARTET--
--AND THUS ENDS MY PHILOSOPHICAL PATTER!

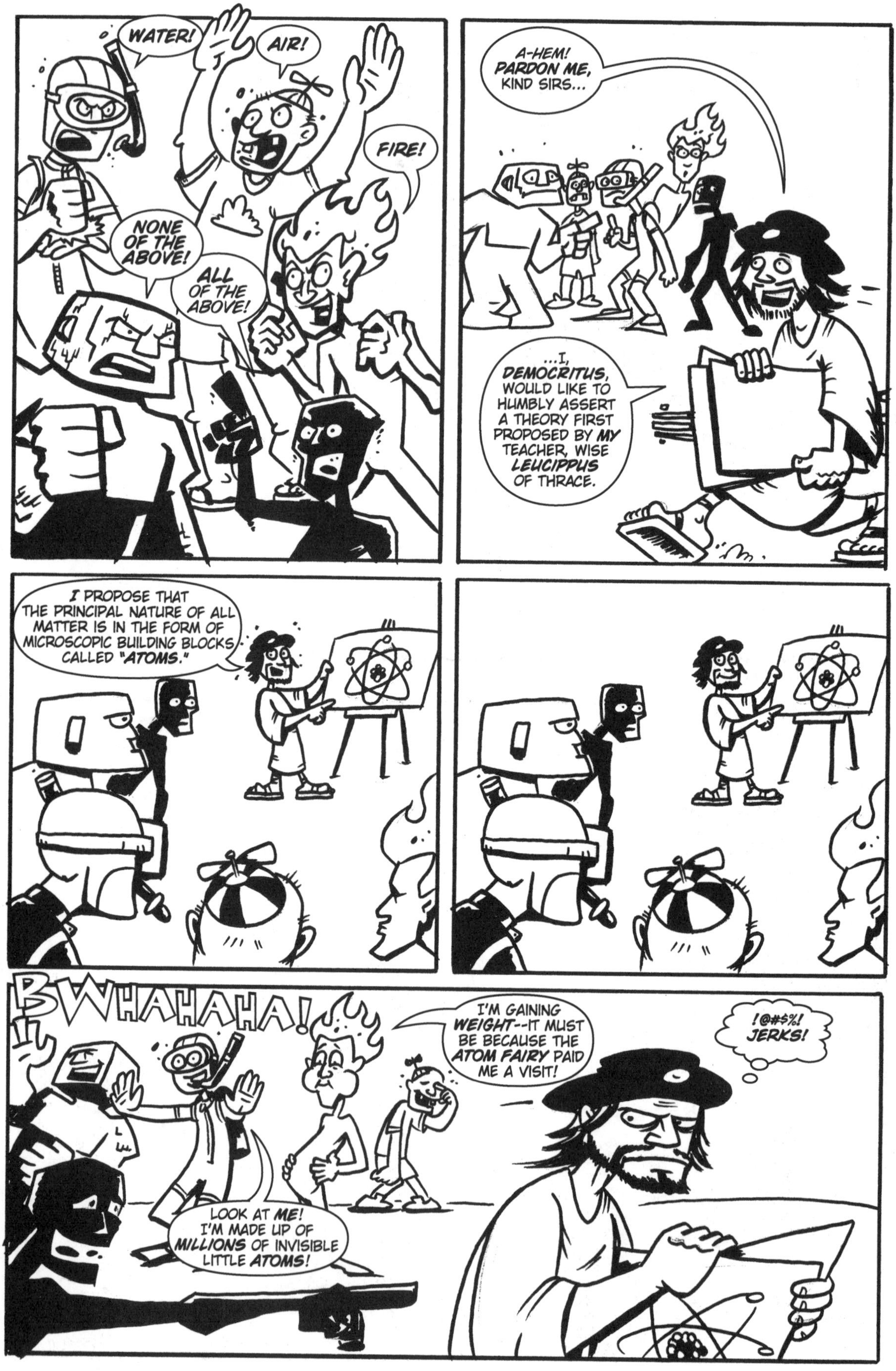
WATER!
AIR!
FIRE!
NONE OF THE ABOVE!
ALL OF THE ABOVE!
A-HEM! PARDON ME, KIND SIRS...
...I, DEMOCRITUS, WOULD LIKE TO HUMBLY ASSERT A THEORY FIRST PROPOSED BY MY TEACHER, WISE LEUCIPPUS OF THRACE.
I PROPOSE THAT THE PRINCIPAL NATURE OF ALL MATTER IS IN THE FORM OF MICROSCOPIC BUILDING BLOCKS CALLED "ATOMS."
BWHAHAHA!
I'M GAINING WEIGHT--IT MUST BE BECAUSE THE ATOM FAIRY PAID ME A VISIT!
!@#$%! JERKS!
LOOK AT ME! I'M MADE UP OF MILLIONS OF INVISIBLE LITTLE ATOMS!

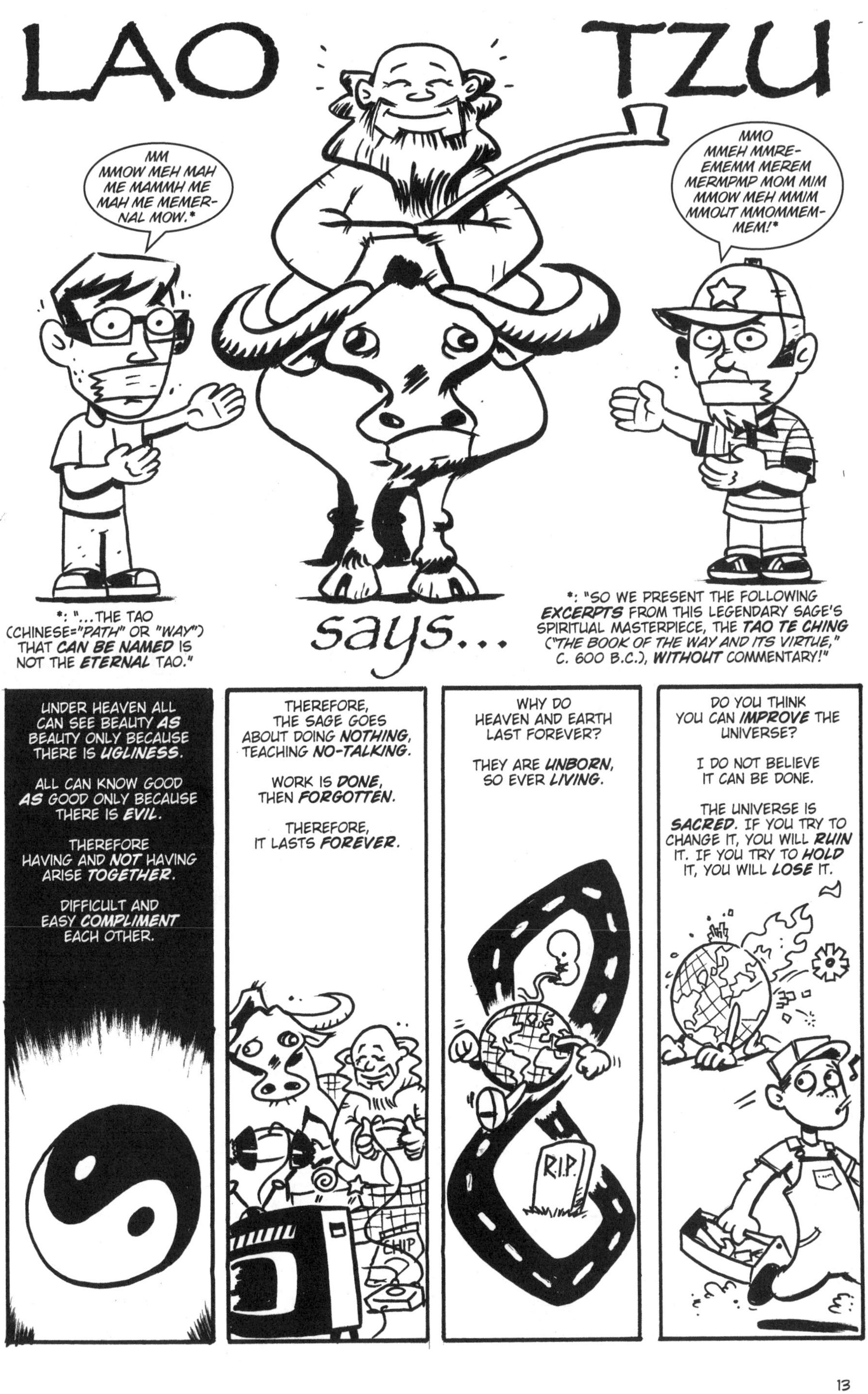
LAO TZU
MM MMOW MEH MAH ME MAMMH ME MAH ME MEMER-NAL MOW.*
MMO MMEH MMRE-EMEMM MEREM MERMPMP MOM MIM MMOW MEH MMIM MMOUT MMOMMEM-MEM!*
*: "...THE TAO (CHINESE="PATH" OR "WAY") THAT CAN BE NAMED IS NOT THE ETERNAL TAO."
says...
*: "SO WE PRESENT THE FOLLOWING EXCERPTS FROM THIS LEGENDARY SAGE'S SPIRITUAL MASTERPIECE, THE TAO TE CHING ("THE BOOK OF THE WAY AND ITS VIRTUE," C. 600 B.C.), WITHOUT COMMENTARY!"
UNDER HEAVEN ALL CAN SEE BEAUTY AS BEAUTY ONLY BECAUSE THERE IS UGLINESS.
ALL CAN KNOW GOOD AS GOOD ONLY BECAUSE THERE IS EVIL.
THEREFORE HAVING AND NOT HAVING ARISE TOGETHER.
DIFFICULT AND EASY COMPLIMENT EACH OTHER.
THEREFORE, THE SAGE GOES ABOUT DOING NOTHING, TEACHING NO-TALKING.
WORK IS DONE, THEN FORGOTTEN.
THEREFORE, IT LASTS FOREVER.
CHIP
WHY DO HEAVEN AND EARTH LAST FOREVER?
THEY ARE UNBORN, SO EVER LIVING.
R.I.P.
DO YOU THINK YOU CAN IMPROVE THE UNIVERSE?
I DO NOT BELIEVE IT CAN BE DONE.
THE UNIVERSE IS SACRED. IF YOU TRY TO CHANGE IT, YOU WILL RUIN IT. IF YOU TRY TO HOLD IT, YOU WILL LOSE IT.

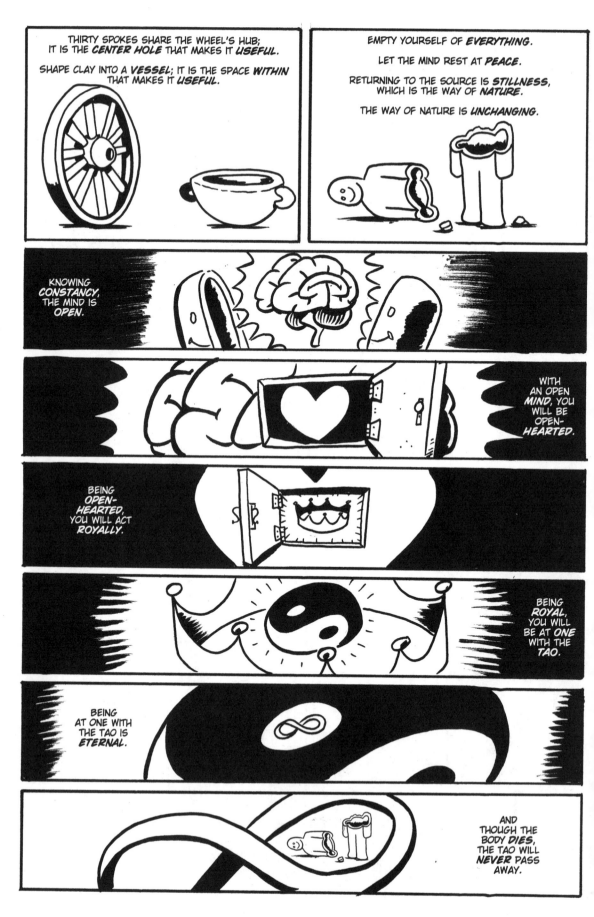

THIRTY SPOKES SHARE THE WHEEL'S HUB; IT IS THE *CENTER HOLE* THAT MAKES IT *USEFUL*.

SHAPE CLAY INTO A *VESSEL*; IT IS THE SPACE *WITHIN* THAT MAKES IT *USEFUL*.

EMPTY YOURSELF OF *EVERYTHING*.

LET THE MIND REST AT *PEACE*.

RETURNING TO THE SOURCE IS *STILLNESS*, WHICH IS THE WAY OF *NATURE*.

THE WAY OF NATURE IS *UNCHANGING*.

KNOWING *CONSTANCY*, THE MIND IS *OPEN*.

WITH AN OPEN *MIND*, YOU WILL BE OPEN-HEARTED.

BEING OPEN-HEARTED, YOU WILL ACT *ROYALLY*.

BEING *ROYAL*, YOU WILL BE AT *ONE* WITH THE *TAO*.

BEING AT ONE WITH THE TAO IS *ETERNAL*.

AND THOUGH THE BODY *DIES*, THE TAO WILL *NEVER* PASS AWAY.

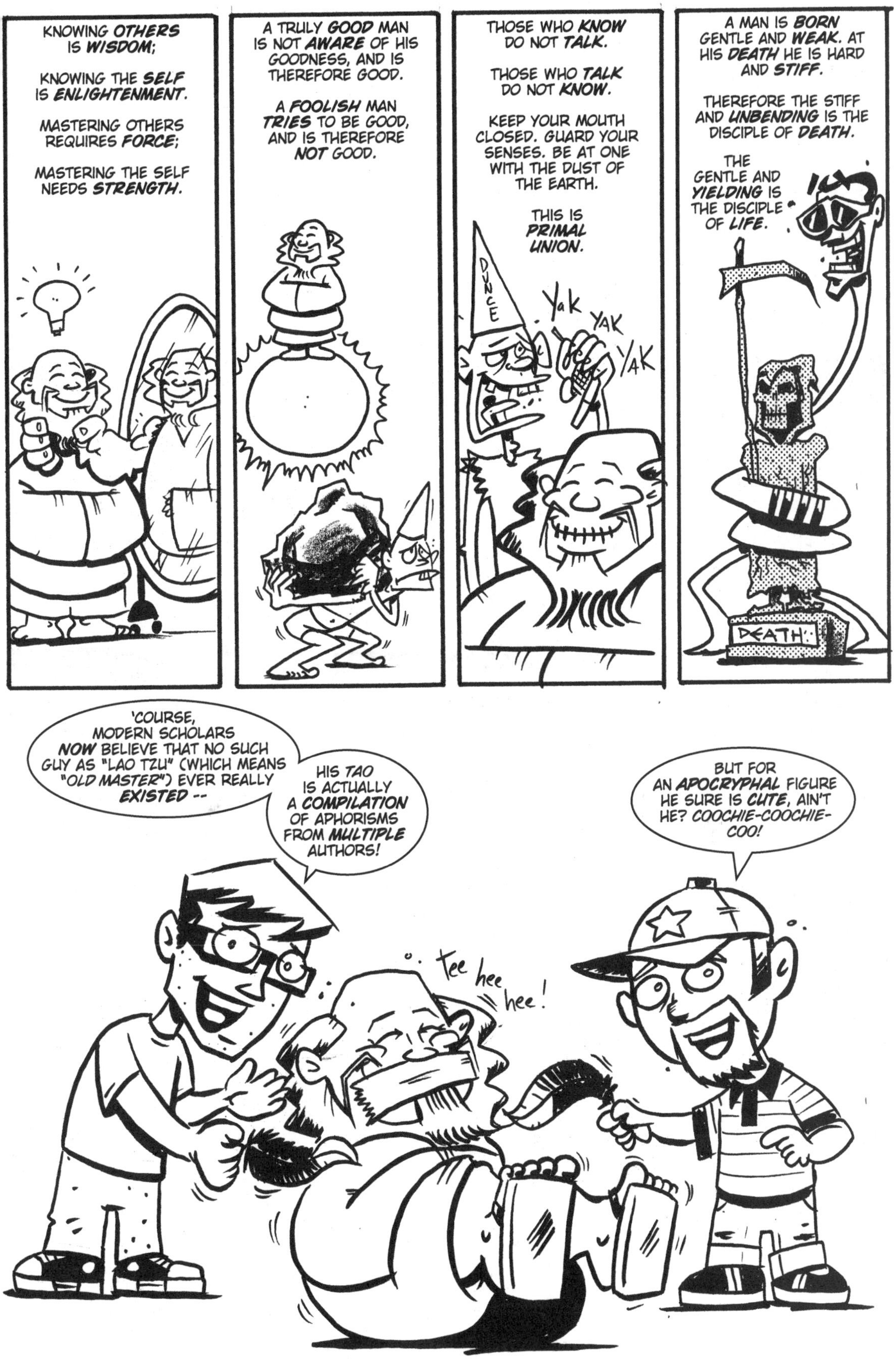
KNOWING OTHERS IS WISDOM;
KNOWING THE SELF IS ENLIGHTENMENT.
MASTERING OTHERS REQUIRES FORCE;
MASTERING THE SELF NEEDS STRENGTH.
A TRULY GOOD MAN IS NOT AWARE OF HIS GOODNESS, AND IS THEREFORE GOOD.
A FOOLISH MAN TRIES TO BE GOOD, AND IS THEREFORE NOT GOOD.
THOSE WHO KNOW DO NOT TALK.
THOSE WHO TALK DO NOT KNOW.
KEEP YOUR MOUTH CLOSED. GUARD YOUR SENSES. BE AT ONE WITH THE DUST OF THE EARTH.
THIS IS PRIMAL UNION.
DUNCE
YaK YAK YAK
A MAN IS BORN GENTLE AND WEAK. AT HIS DEATH HE IS HARD AND STIFF.
THEREFORE THE STIFF AND UNBENDING IS THE DISCIPLE OF DEATH.
THE GENTLE AND YIELDING IS THE DISCIPLE OF LIFE.
DEATH
'COURSE, MODERN SCHOLARS NOW BELIEVE THAT NO SUCH GUY AS "LAO TZU" (WHICH MEANS "OLD MASTER") EVER REALLY EXISTED --
HIS TAO IS ACTUALLY A COMPILATION OF APHORISMS FROM MULTIPLE AUTHORS!
BUT FOR AN APOCRYPHAL FIGURE HE SURE IS CUTE, AIN'T HE? COOCHIE-COOCHIE-COO!
Tee hee hee!

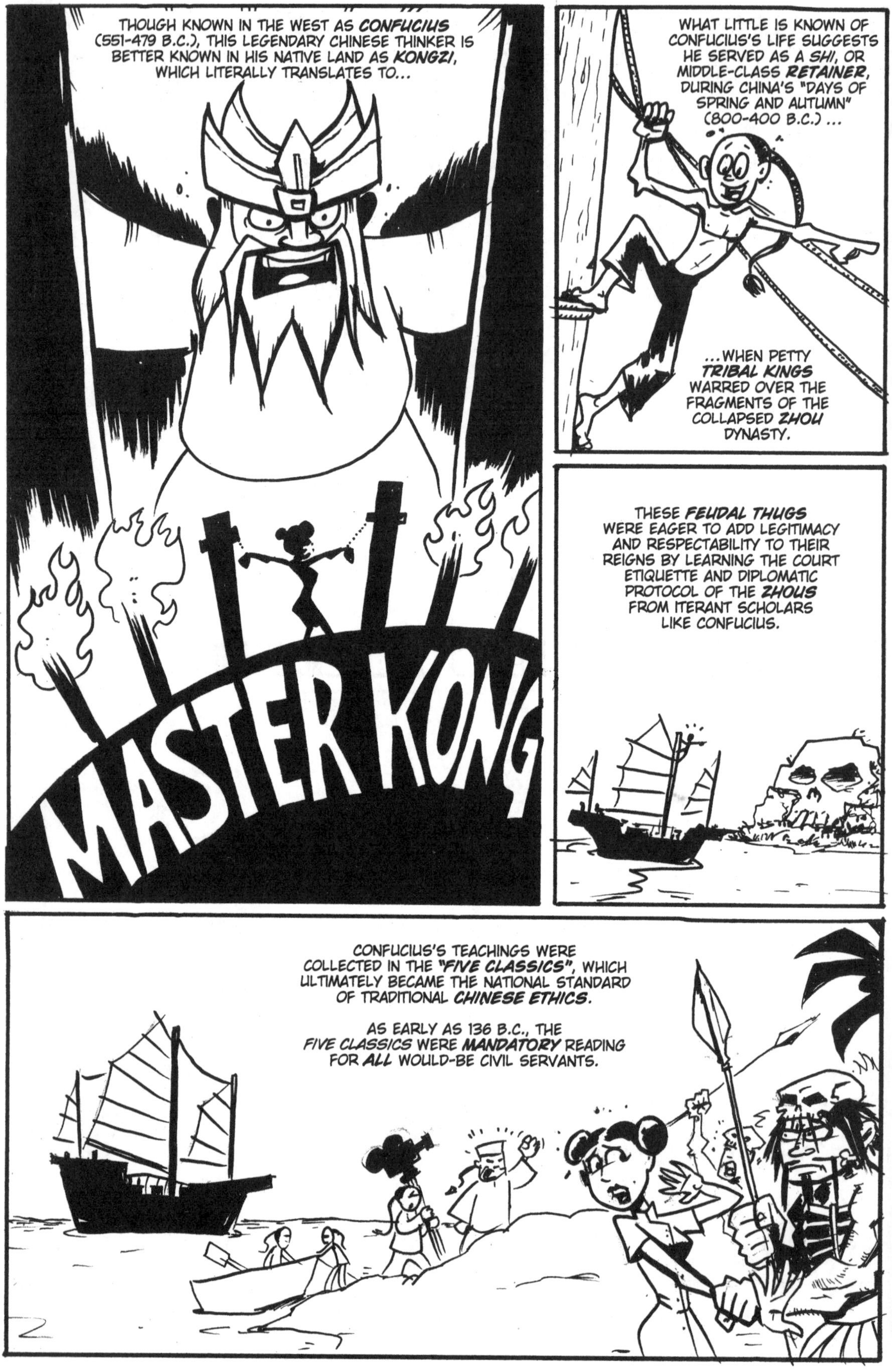
THOUGH KNOWN IN THE WEST AS CONFUCIUS (551-479 B.C.), THIS LEGENDARY CHINESE THINKER IS BETTER KNOWN IN HIS NATIVE LAND AS KONGZI, WHICH LITERALLY TRANSLATES TO...
MASTER KONG
WHAT LITTLE IS KNOWN OF CONFUCIUS'S LIFE SUGGESTS HE SERVED AS A SHI, OR MIDDLE-CLASS RETAINER, DURING CHINA'S "DAYS OF SPRING AND AUTUMN" (800-400 B.C.) ...
...WHEN PETTY TRIBAL KINGS WARRED OVER THE FRAGMENTS OF THE COLLAPSED ZHOU DYNASTY.
THESE FEUDAL THUGS WERE EAGER TO ADD LEGITIMACY AND RESPECTABILITY TO THEIR REIGNS BY LEARNING THE COURT ETIQUETTE AND DIPLOMATIC PROTOCOL OF THE ZHOUS FROM ITERANT SCHOLARS LIKE CONFUCIUS.
CONFUCIUS'S TEACHINGS WERE COLLECTED IN THE "FIVE CLASSICS", WHICH ULTIMATELY BECAME THE NATIONAL STANDARD OF TRADITIONAL CHINESE ETHICS.
AS EARLY AS 136 B.C., THE FIVE CLASSICS WERE MANDATORY READING FOR ALL WOULD-BE CIVIL SERVANTS.

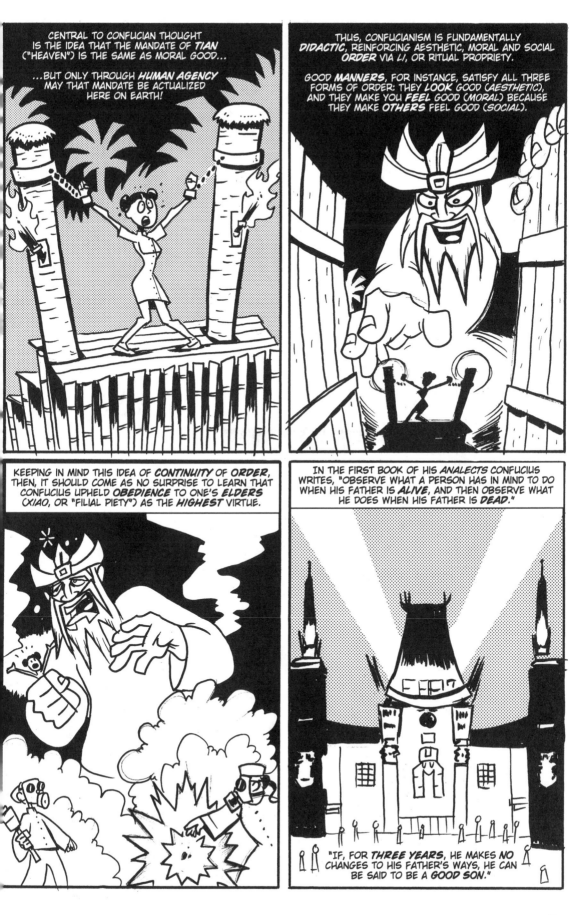

CENTRAL TO CONFUCIAN THOUGHT IS THE IDEA THAT THE MANDATE OF *TIAN* ("HEAVEN") IS THE SAME AS MORAL GOOD...

...BUT ONLY THROUGH *HUMAN AGENCY* MAY THAT MANDATE BE ACTUALIZED HERE ON EARTH!

THUS, CONFUCIANISM IS FUNDAMENTALLY *DIDACTIC*, REINFORCING AESTHETIC, MORAL AND SOCIAL *ORDER* VIA *LI*, OR RITUAL PROPRIETY.

GOOD *MANNERS*, FOR INSTANCE, SATISFY ALL THREE FORMS OF ORDER: THEY *LOOK* GOOD (*AESTHETIC*), AND THEY MAKE YOU *FEEL* GOOD (MORAL) BECAUSE THEY MAKE *OTHERS* FEEL GOOD (SOCIAL).

KEEPING IN MIND THIS IDEA OF *CONTINUITY* OF *ORDER*, THEN, IT SHOULD COME AS NO SURPRISE TO LEARN THAT CONFUCIUS UPHELD *OBEDIENCE* TO ONE'S *ELDERS* (*XIAO*, OR "FILIAL PIETY") AS THE *HIGHEST* VIRTUE.

IN THE FIRST BOOK OF HIS *ANALECTS* CONFUCIUS WRITES, "OBSERVE WHAT A PERSON HAS IN MIND TO DO WHEN HIS FATHER IS *ALIVE*, AND THEN OBSERVE WHAT HE DOES WHEN HIS FATHER IS *DEAD*."

"IF, FOR *THREE YEARS*, HE MAKES *NO* CHANGES TO HIS FATHER'S WAYS, HE CAN BE SAID TO BE A *GOOD SON*."

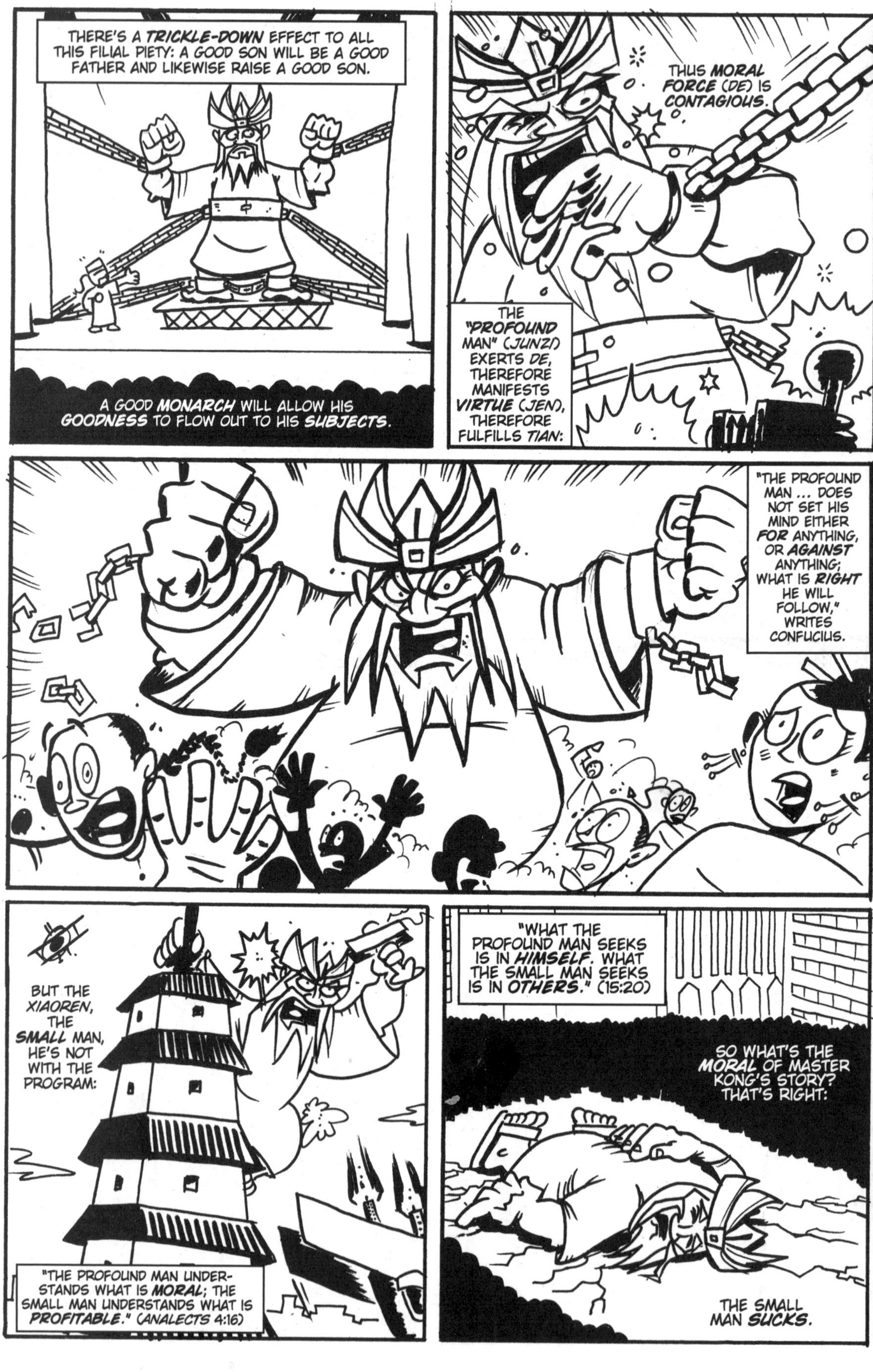
THERE'S A TRICKLE-DOWN EFFECT TO ALL THIS FILIAL PIETY: A GOOD SON WILL BE A GOOD FATHER AND LIKEWISE RAISE A GOOD SON.
A GOOD MONARCH WILL ALLOW HIS GOODNESS TO FLOW OUT TO HIS SUBJECTS.
THUS MORAL FORCE (DE) IS CONTAGIOUS.
THE "PROFOUND MAN" (JUNZI) EXERTS DE, THEREFORE MANIFESTS VIRTUE (JEN), THEREFORE FULFILLS TIAN:
"THE PROFOUND MAN ... DOES NOT SET HIS MIND EITHER FOR ANYTHING, OR AGAINST ANYTHING; WHAT IS RIGHT HE WILL FOLLOW," WRITES CONFUCIUS.
BUT THE XIAOREN, THE SMALL MAN, HE'S NOT WITH THE PROGRAM:
"THE PROFOUND MAN UNDERSTANDS WHAT IS MORAL; THE SMALL MAN UNDERSTANDS WHAT IS PROFITABLE." (ANALECTS 4:16)
"WHAT THE PROFOUND MAN SEEKS IS IN HIMSELF. WHAT THE SMALL MAN SEEKS IS IN OTHERS." (15:20)
SO WHAT'S THE MORAL OF MASTER KONG'S STORY? THAT'S RIGHT:
THE SMALL MAN SUCKS.

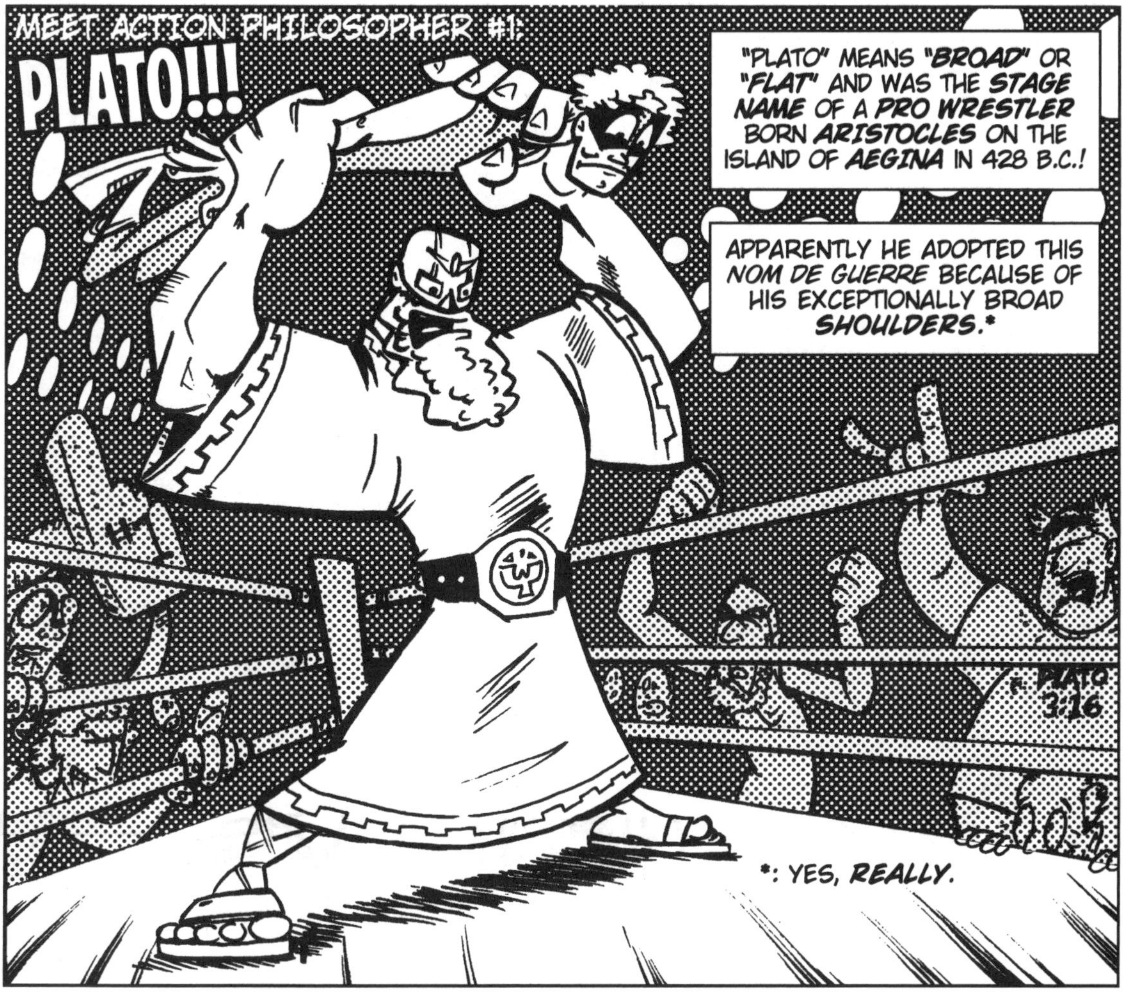
MEET ACTION PHILOSOPHER #1:
PLATO!!!
"PLATO" MEANS "BROAD" OR "FLAT" AND WAS THE STAGE NAME OF A PRO WRESTLER BORN ARISTOCLES ON THE ISLAND OF AEGINA IN 428 B.C.!
APPARENTLY HE ADOPTED THIS NOM DE GUERRE BECAUSE OF HIS EXCEPTIONALLY BROAD SHOULDERS.*
PLATO 3:16
*: YES, REALLY.

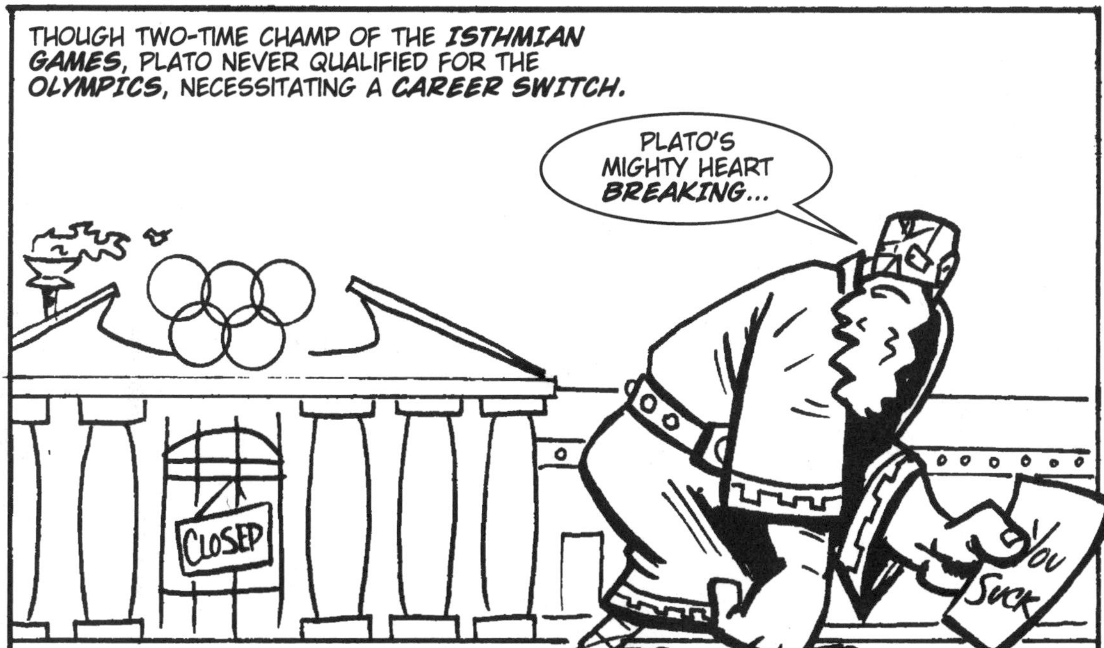
THOUGH TWO-TIME CHAMP OF THE ISTHMIAN GAMES, PLATO NEVER QUALIFIED FOR THE OLYMPICS, NECESSITATING A CAREER SWITCH.
PLATO'S MIGHTY HEART BREAKING...
CLOSED
YOU SUCK

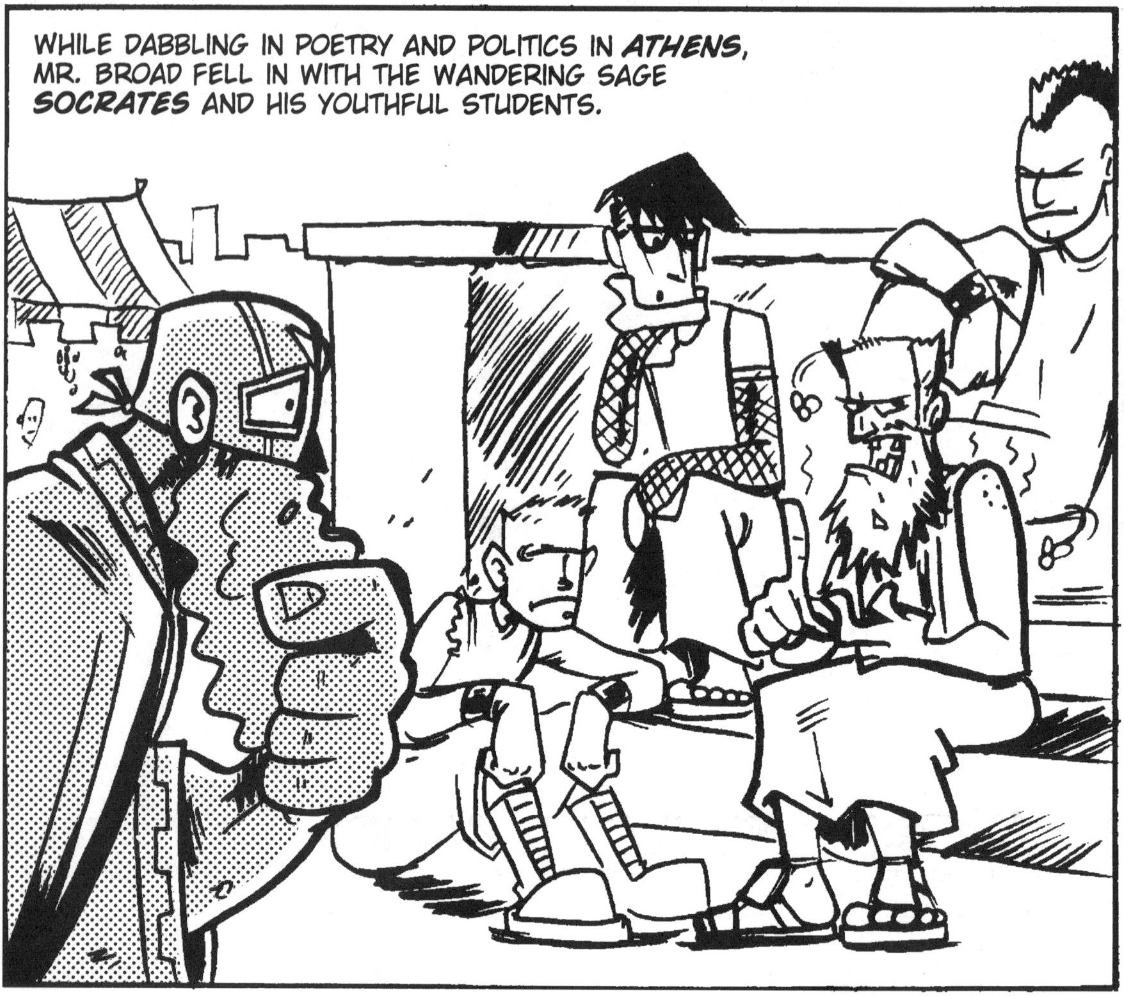
WHILE DABBLING IN POETRY AND POLITICS IN ATHENS, MR. BROAD FELL IN WITH THE WANDERING SAGE SOCRATES AND HIS YOUTHFUL STUDENTS.

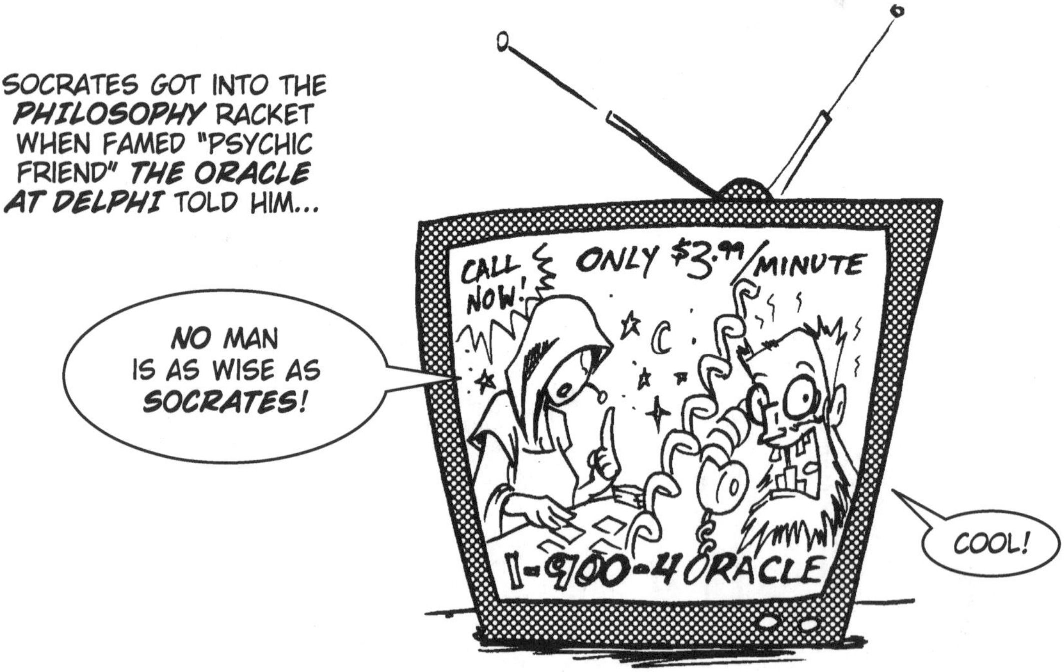
SOCRATES GOT INTO THE PHILOSOPHY RACKET WHEN FAMED "PSYCHIC FRIEND" THE ORACLE AT DELPHI TOLD HIM...
NO MAN IS AS WISE AS SOCRATES!
CALL NOW!
ONLY $3.99/MINUTE
1-900-4ORACLE
COOL!

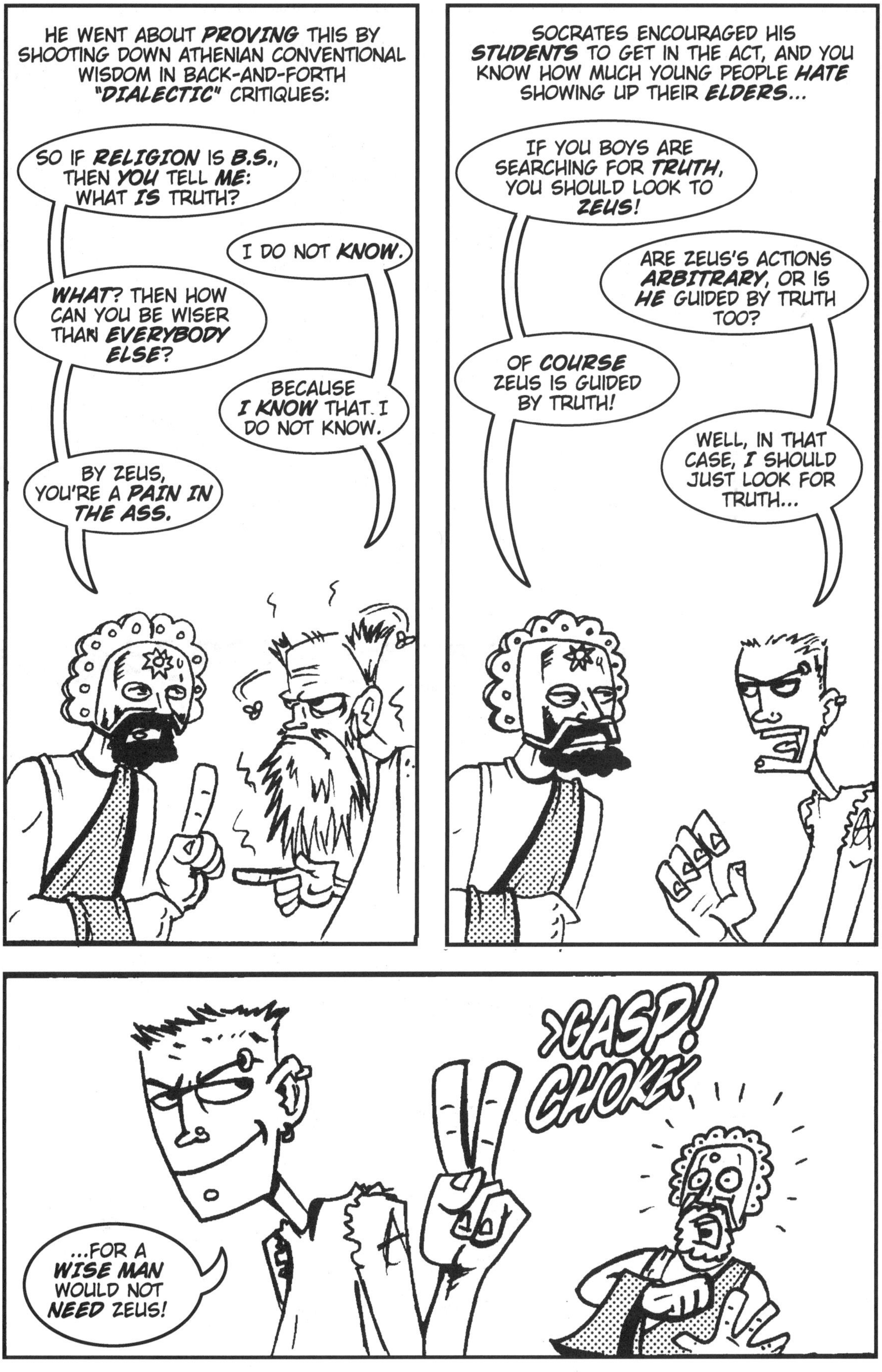
HE WENT ABOUT PROVING THIS BY SHOOTING DOWN ATHENIAN CONVENTIONAL WISDOM IN BACK-AND-FORTH "DIALECTIC" CRITIQUES:
SO IF RELIGION IS B.S., THEN YOU TELL ME: WHAT IS TRUTH?
I DO NOT KNOW.
WHAT? THEN HOW CAN YOU BE WISER THAN EVERYBODY ELSE?
BECAUSE I KNOW THAT I DO NOT KNOW.
BY ZEUS, YOU'RE A PAIN IN THE ASS.
SOCRATES ENCOURAGED HIS STUDENTS TO GET IN THE ACT, AND YOU KNOW HOW MUCH YOUNG PEOPLE HATE SHOWING UP THEIR ELDERS...
IF YOU BOYS ARE SEARCHING FOR TRUTH, YOU SHOULD LOOK TO ZEUS!
ARE ZEUS'S ACTIONS ARBITRARY, OR IS HE GUIDED BY TRUTH TOO?
OF COURSE ZEUS IS GUIDED BY TRUTH!
WELL, IN THAT CASE, I SHOULD JUST LOOK FOR TRUTH...
GASP! CHOKE!
...FOR A WISE MAN WOULD NOT NEED ZEUS!

THAT DIDN'T GO OVER WELL.

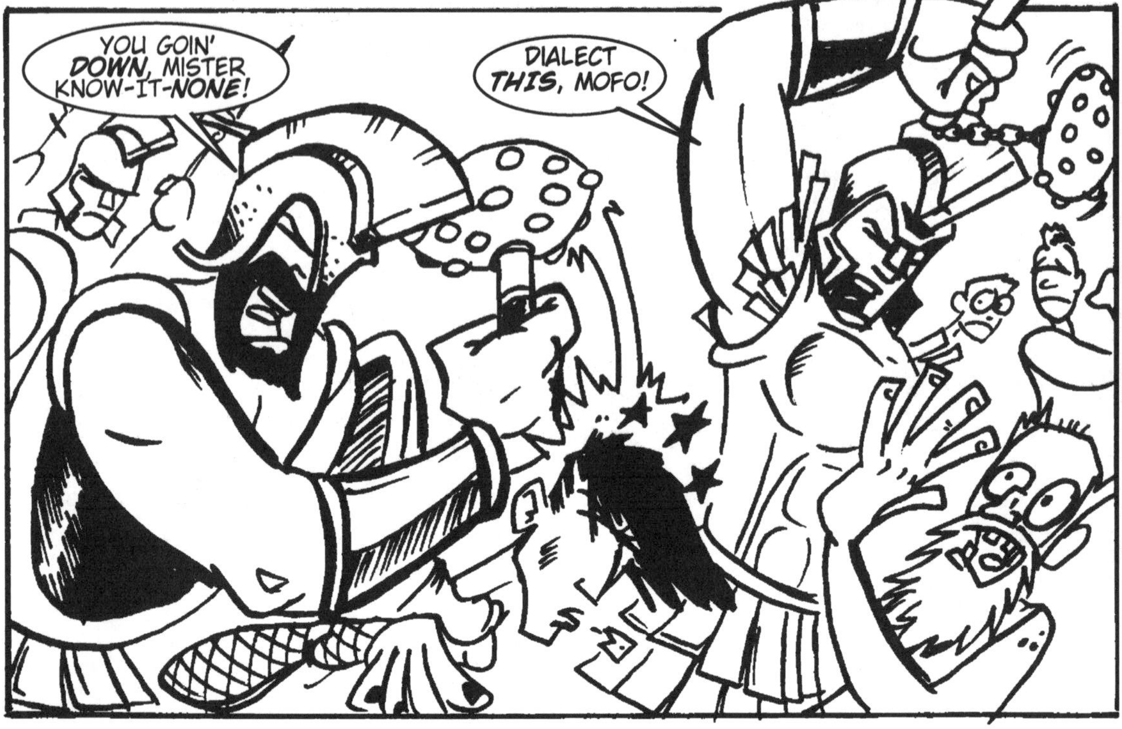
YOU GOIN' DOWN, MISTER KNOW-IT-NONE!
DIALECT THIS, MOFO!

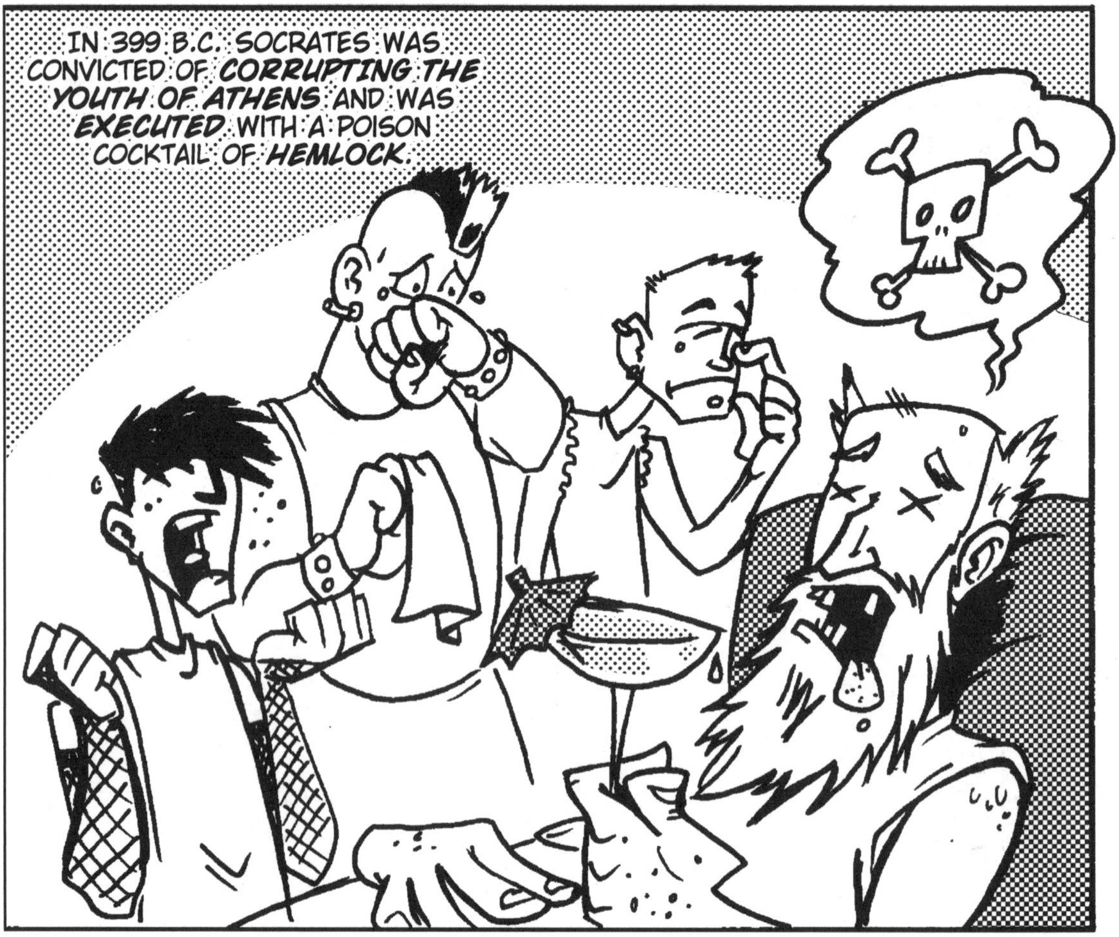
IN 399 B.C. SOCRATES WAS CONVICTED OF CORRUPTING THE YOUTH OF ATHENS AND WAS EXECUTED WITH A POISON COCKTAIL OF HEMLOCK.

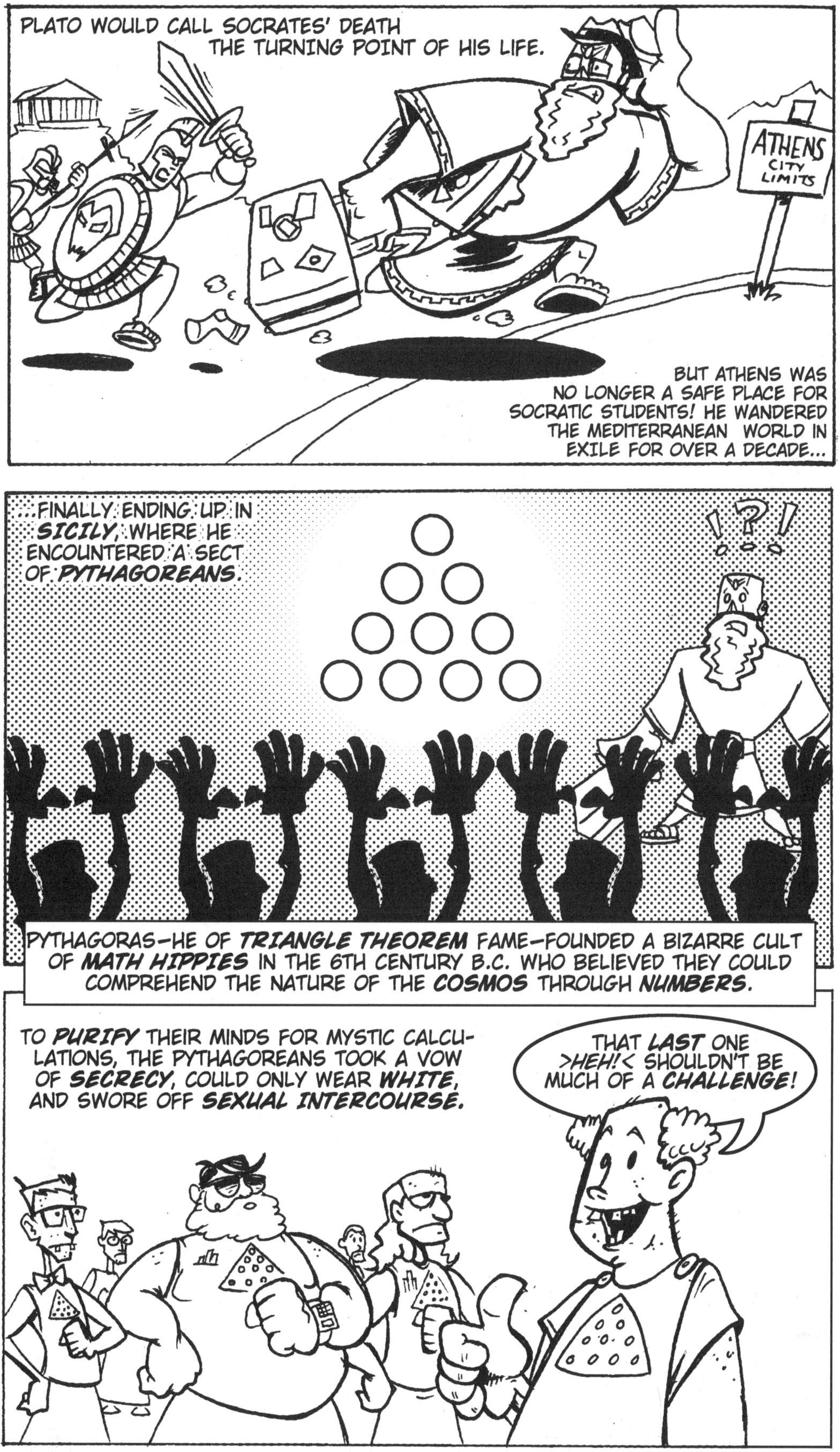

PLATO WOULD CALL SOCRATES' DEATH THE TURNING POINT OF HIS LIFE.
ATHENS CITY LIMITS
BUT ATHENS WAS NO LONGER A SAFE PLACE FOR SOCRATIC STUDENTS! HE WANDERED THE MEDITERRANEAN WORLD IN EXILE FOR OVER A DECADE...
...FINALLY ENDING UP IN SICILY, WHERE HE ENCOUNTERED A SECT OF PYTHAGOREANS.
!?!
PYTHAGORAS—HE OF TRIANGLE THEOREM FAME—FOUNDED A BIZARRE CULT OF MATH HIPPIES IN THE 6TH CENTURY B.C. WHO BELIEVED THEY COULD COMPREHEND THE NATURE OF THE COSMOS THROUGH NUMBERS.
TO PURIFY THEIR MINDS FOR MYSTIC CALCULATIONS, THE PYTHAGOREANS TOOK A VOW OF SECRECY, COULD ONLY WEAR WHITE, AND SWORE OFF SEXUAL INTERCOURSE.
THAT LAST ONE >HEH!< SHOULDN'T BE MUCH OF A CHALLENGE!

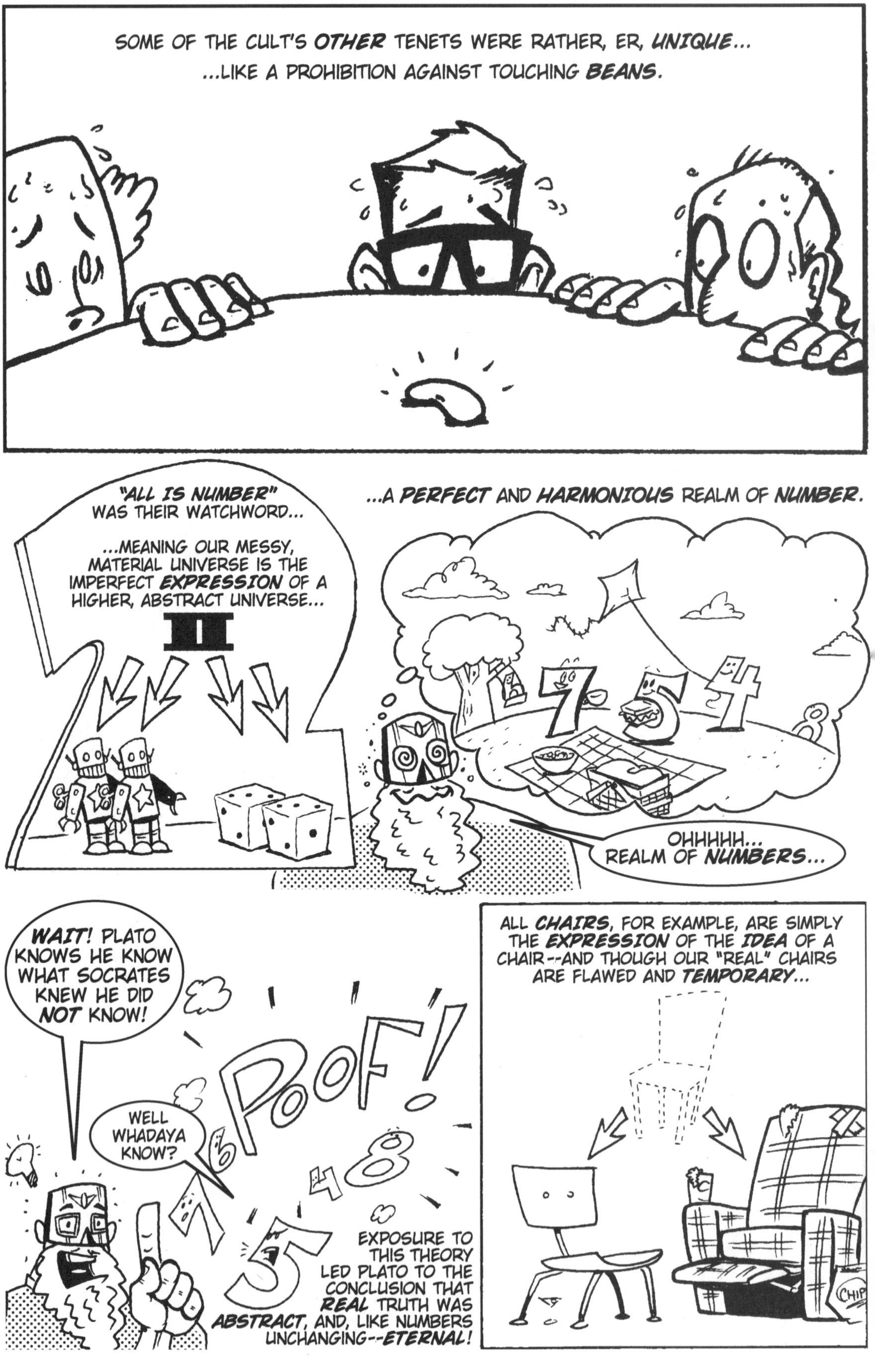
SOME OF THE CULT'S OTHER TENETS WERE RATHER, ER, UNIQUE...
...LIKE A PROHIBITION AGAINST TOUCHING BEANS.
"ALL IS NUMBER" WAS THEIR WATCHWORD...
...MEANING OUR MESSY, MATERIAL UNIVERSE IS THE IMPERFECT EXPRESSION OF A HIGHER, ABSTRACT UNIVERSE...
...A PERFECT AND HARMONIOUS REALM OF NUMBER.
OHHHHH... REALM OF NUMBERS...
WAIT! PLATO KNOWS HE KNOW WHAT SOCRATES KNEW HE DID NOT KNOW!
WELL WHADAYA KNOW?
POOF!
EXPOSURE TO THIS THEORY LED PLATO TO THE CONCLUSION THAT REAL TRUTH WAS ABSTRACT, AND, LIKE NUMBERS UNCHANGING--ETERNAL!
ALL CHAIRS, FOR EXAMPLE, ARE SIMPLY THE EXPRESSION OF THE IDEA OF A CHAIR--AND THOUGH OUR "REAL" CHAIRS ARE FLAWED AND TEMPORARY...
CHIP

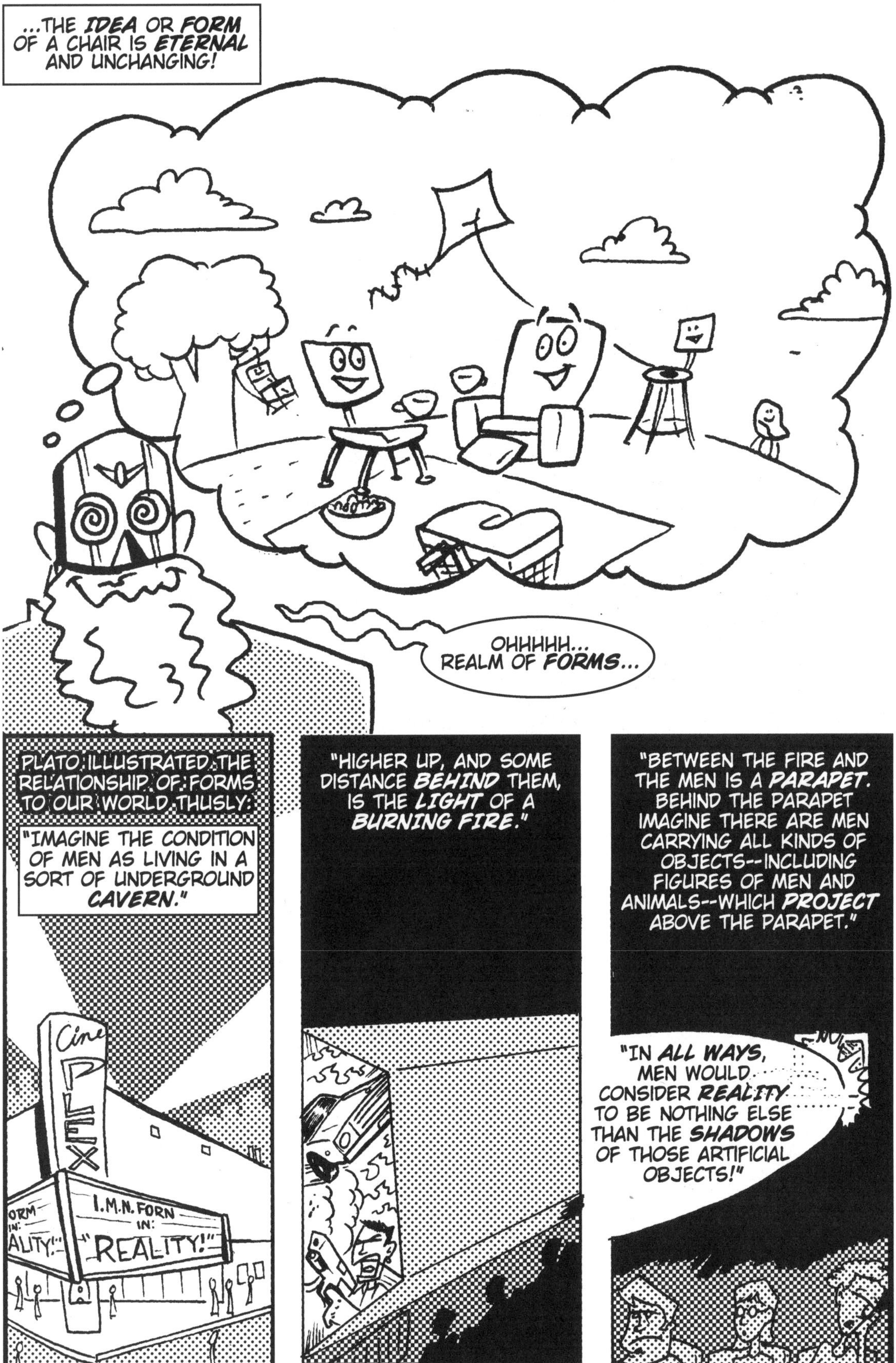
...THE IDEA OR FORM OF A CHAIR IS ETERNAL AND UNCHANGING!
OHHHHH... REALM OF FORMS...
PLATO ILLUSTRATED THE RELATIONSHIP OF FORMS TO OUR WORLD THUSLY:
"IMAGINE THE CONDITION OF MEN AS LIVING IN A SORT OF UNDERGROUND CAVERN."
CinePLEX
I.M.N. FORN IN: "REALITY!"
"HIGHER UP, AND SOME DISTANCE BEHIND THEM, IS THE LIGHT OF A BURNING FIRE."
"BETWEEN THE FIRE AND THE MEN IS A PARAPET. BEHIND THE PARAPET IMAGINE THERE ARE MEN CARRYING ALL KINDS OF OBJECTS--INCLUDING FIGURES OF MEN AND ANIMALS--WHICH PROJECT ABOVE THE PARAPET."
"IN ALL WAYS, MEN WOULD CONSIDER REALITY TO BE NOTHING ELSE THAN THE SHADOWS OF THOSE ARTIFICIAL OBJECTS!"

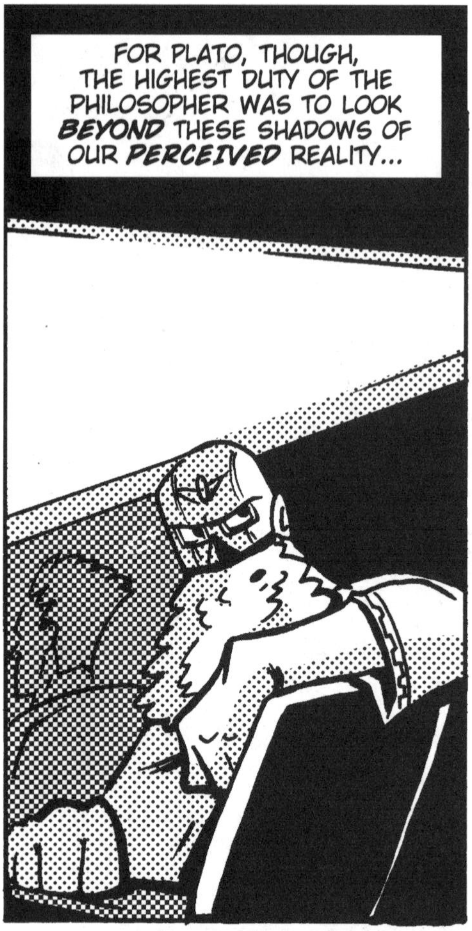
FOR PLATO, THOUGH, THE HIGHEST DUTY OF THE PHILOSOPHER WAS TO LOOK BEYOND THESE SHADOWS OF OUR PERCEIVED REALITY...

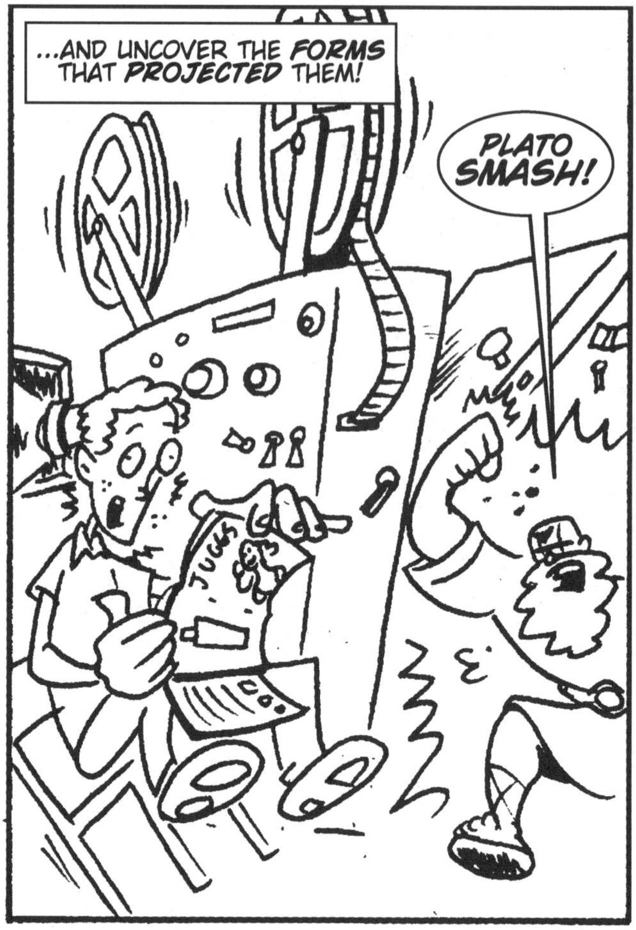
...AND UNCOVER THE FORMS THAT PROJECTED THEM!
PLATO SMASH!

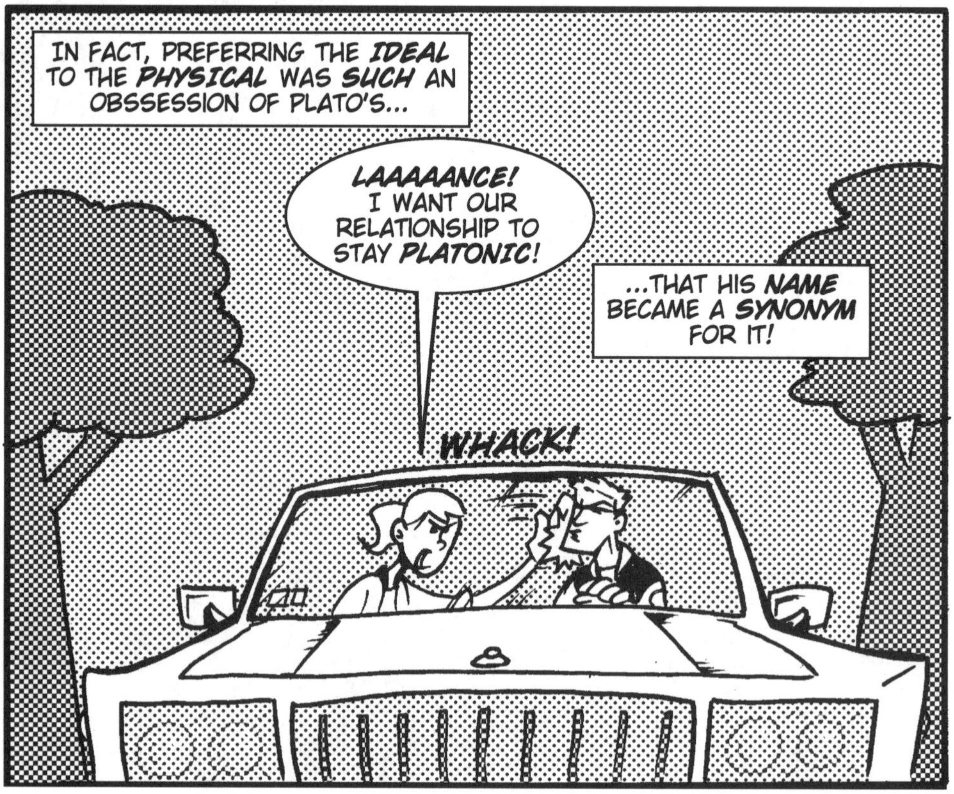
IN FACT, PREFERRING THE IDEAL TO THE PHYSICAL WAS SUCH AN OBSSESSION OF PLATO'S...
LAAAAANCE! I WANT OUR RELATIONSHIP TO STAY PLATONIC!
...THAT HIS NAME BECAME A SYNONYM FOR IT!
WHACK!

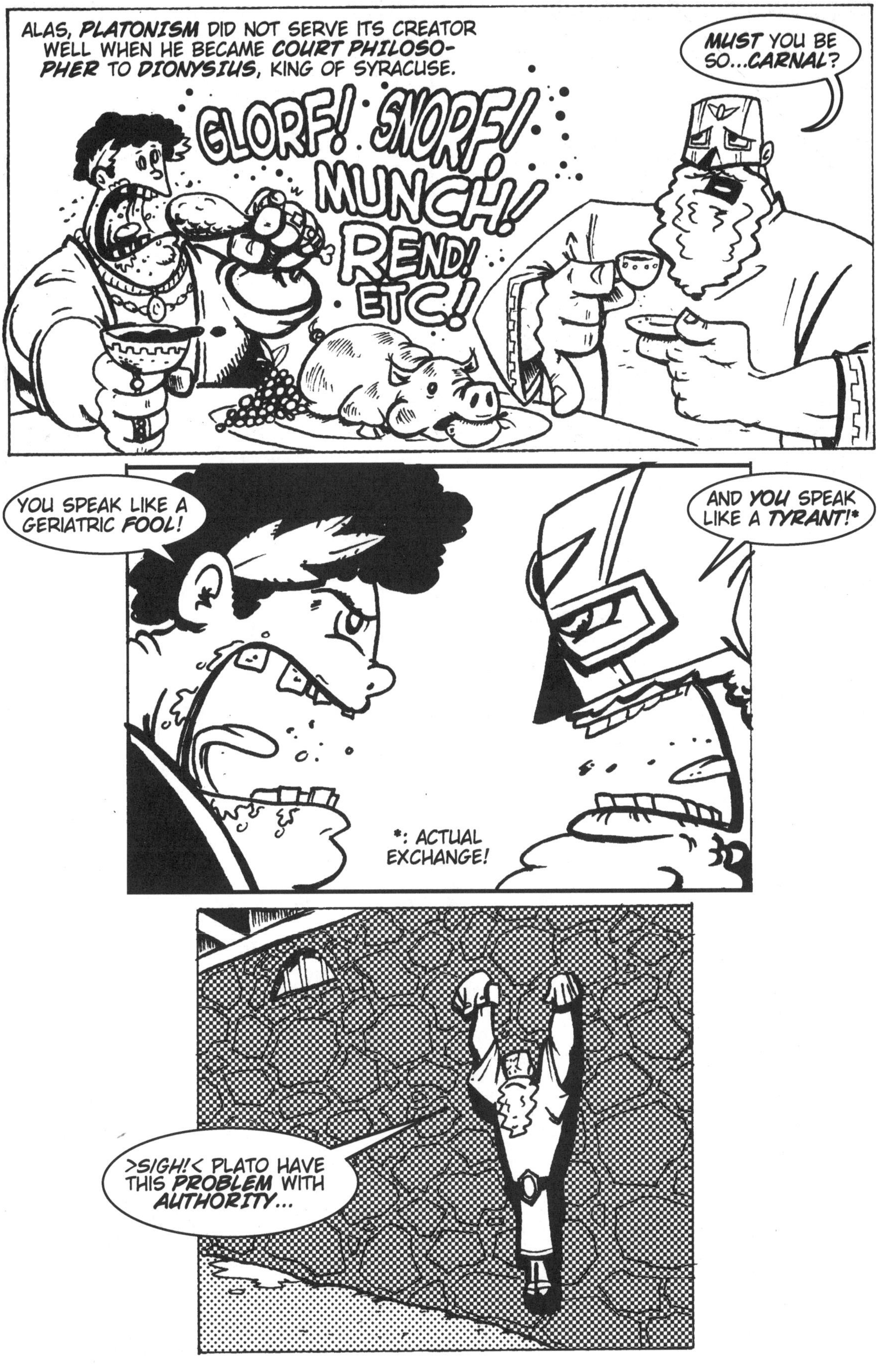
ALAS, PLATONISM DID NOT SERVE ITS CREATOR WELL WHEN HE BECAME COURT PHILOSOPHER TO DIONYSIUS, KING OF SYRACUSE.
GLORF! SNORF! MUNCH! REND! ETC!
MUST YOU BE SO...CARNAL?
YOU SPEAK LIKE A GERIATRIC FOOL!
AND YOU SPEAK LIKE A TYRANT!*
*: ACTUAL EXCHANGE!
>SIGH!< PLATO HAVE THIS PROBLEM WITH AUTHORITY...

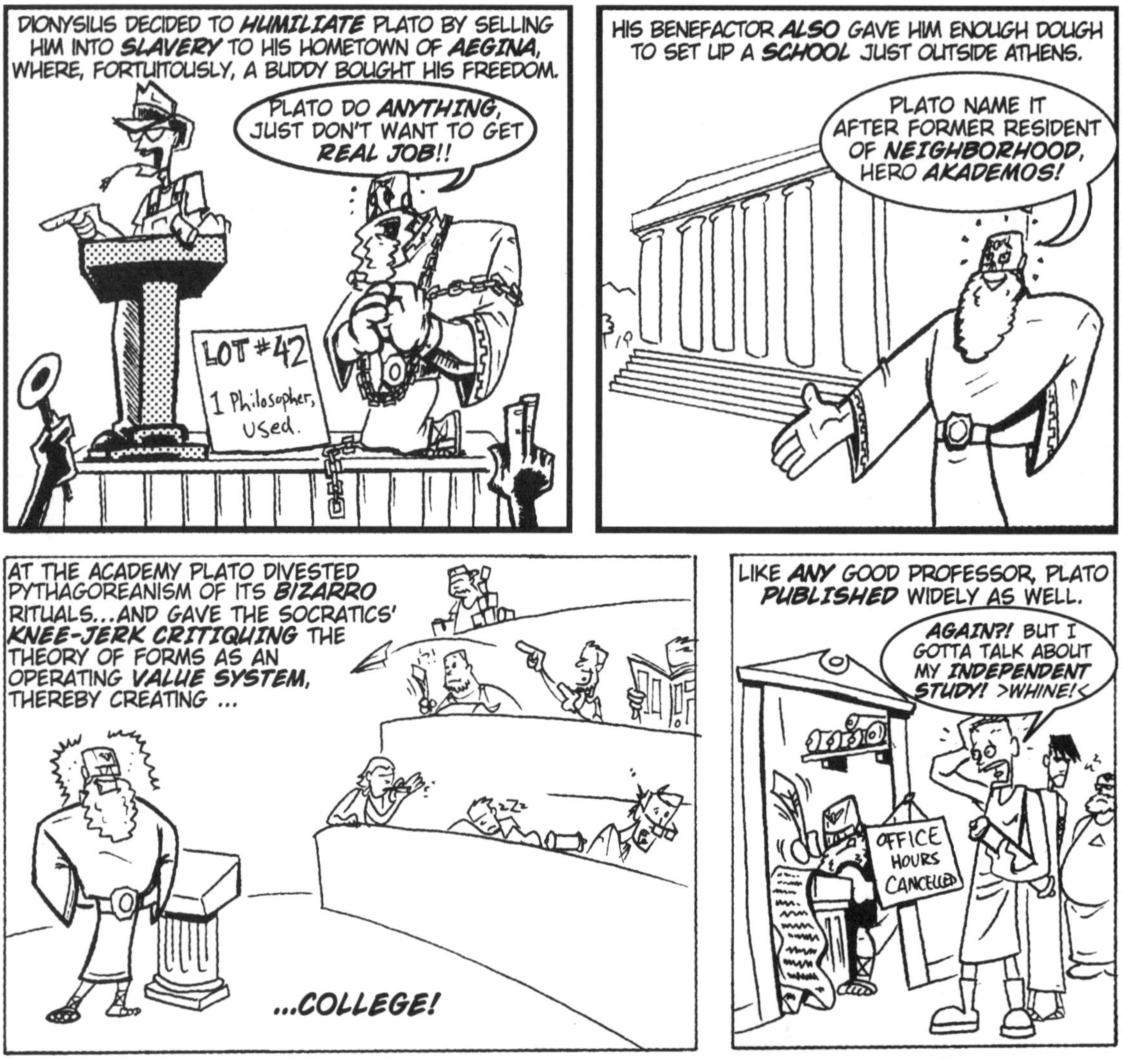
DIONYSIUS DECIDED TO HUMILIATE PLATO BY SELLING HIM INTO SLAVERY TO HIS HOMETOWN OF AEGINA, WHERE, FORTUITOUSLY, A BUDDY BOUGHT HIS FREEDOM.
PLATO DO ANYTHING, JUST DON'T WANT TO GET REAL JOB!!
LOT #42
1 Philosopher, Used.
HIS BENEFACTOR ALSO GAVE HIM ENOUGH DOUGH TO SET UP A SCHOOL JUST OUTSIDE ATHENS.
PLATO NAME IT AFTER FORMER RESIDENT OF NEIGHBORHOOD, HERO AKADEMOS!
AT THE ACADEMY PLATO DIVESTED PYTHAGOREANISM OF ITS BIZARRO RITUALS...AND GAVE THE SOCRATICS' KNEE-JERK CRITIQUING THE THEORY OF FORMS AS AN OPERATING VALUE SYSTEM, THEREBY CREATING ...
...COLLEGE!
LIKE ANY GOOD PROFESSOR, PLATO PUBLISHED WIDELY AS WELL.
AGAIN?! BUT I GOTTA TALK ABOUT MY INDEPENDENT STUDY! >WHINE!<
OFFICE HOURS CANCELLED

PLATO'S WORKS TAKE THE FORM OF ***DIALOGUES***, OR DISCUSSIONS BETWEEN TEACHER AND STUDENT. INVARIABLY THE ***TEACHER*** IS SOCRATES HIMSELF, ***RESURRECTED*** BY PLATO TO MOUTH ***HIS OWN*** THEORIES- AND GIVE THEM ADDED ***LEGITIMACY***!

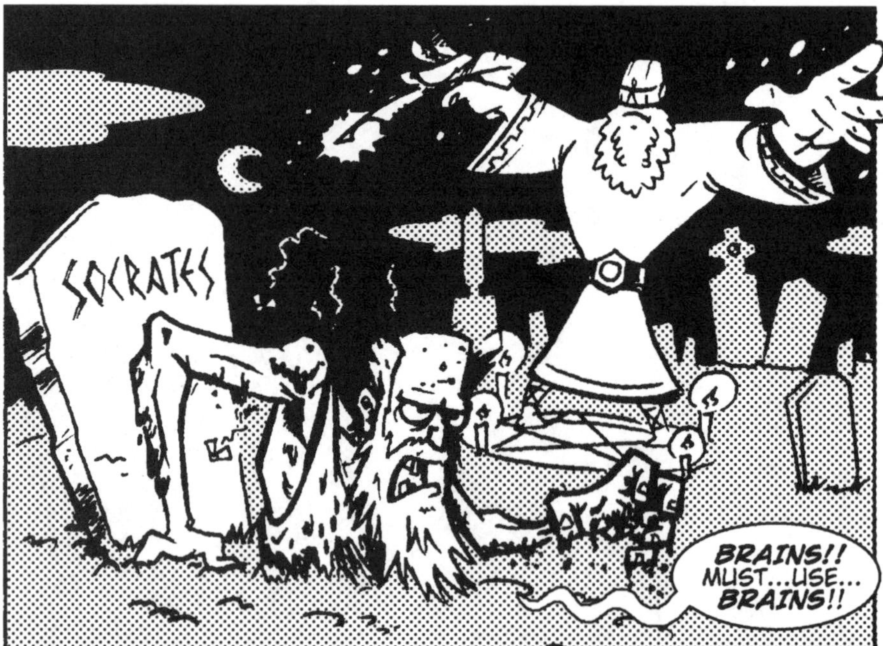
SOCRATES
BRAINS!! MUST...USE... BRAINS!!

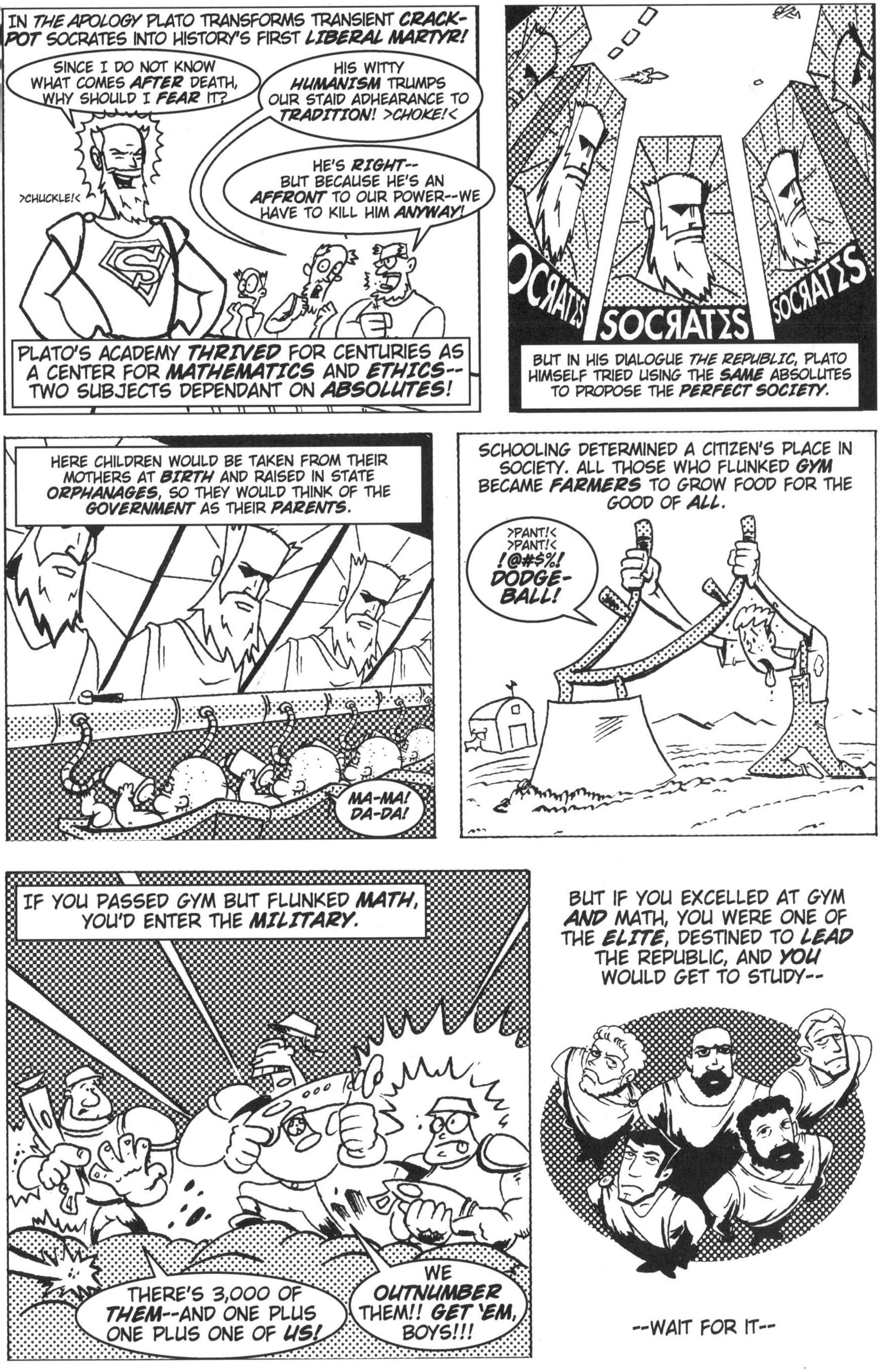
IN THE APOLOGY PLATO TRANSFORMS TRANSIENT CRACK-POT SOCRATES INTO HISTORY'S FIRST LIBERAL MARTYR!
SINCE I DO NOT KNOW WHAT COMES AFTER DEATH, WHY SHOULD I FEAR IT?
HIS WITTY HUMANISM TRUMPS OUR STAID ADHEARANCE TO TRADITION! >CHOKE!<
>CHUCKLE!<
HE'S RIGHT-- BUT BECAUSE HE'S AN AFFRONT TO OUR POWER--WE HAVE TO KILL HIM ANYWAY!
PLATO'S ACADEMY THRIVED FOR CENTURIES AS A CENTER FOR MATHEMATICS AND ETHICS-- TWO SUBJECTS DEPENDANT ON ABSOLUTES!
SOCRATES
SOCRATES
SOCRATES
BUT IN HIS DIALOGUE THE REPUBLIC, PLATO HIMSELF TRIED USING THE SAME ABSOLUTES TO PROPOSE THE PERFECT SOCIETY.
HERE CHILDREN WOULD BE TAKEN FROM THEIR MOTHERS AT BIRTH AND RAISED IN STATE ORPHANAGES, SO THEY WOULD THINK OF THE GOVERNMENT AS THEIR PARENTS.
MA-MA! DA-DA!
SCHOOLING DETERMINED A CITIZEN'S PLACE IN SOCIETY. ALL THOSE WHO FLUNKED GYM BECAME FARMERS TO GROW FOOD FOR THE GOOD OF ALL.
>PANT!< >PANT!< !@#$%! DODGE-BALL!
IF YOU PASSED GYM BUT FLUNKED MATH, YOU'D ENTER THE MILITARY.
THERE'S 3,000 OF THEM--AND ONE PLUS ONE PLUS ONE OF US!
WE OUTNUMBER THEM!! GET 'EM, BOYS!!!
BUT IF YOU EXCELLED AT GYM AND MATH, YOU WERE ONE OF THE ELITE, DESTINED TO LEAD THE REPUBLIC, AND YOU WOULD GET TO STUDY--
--WAIT FOR IT--

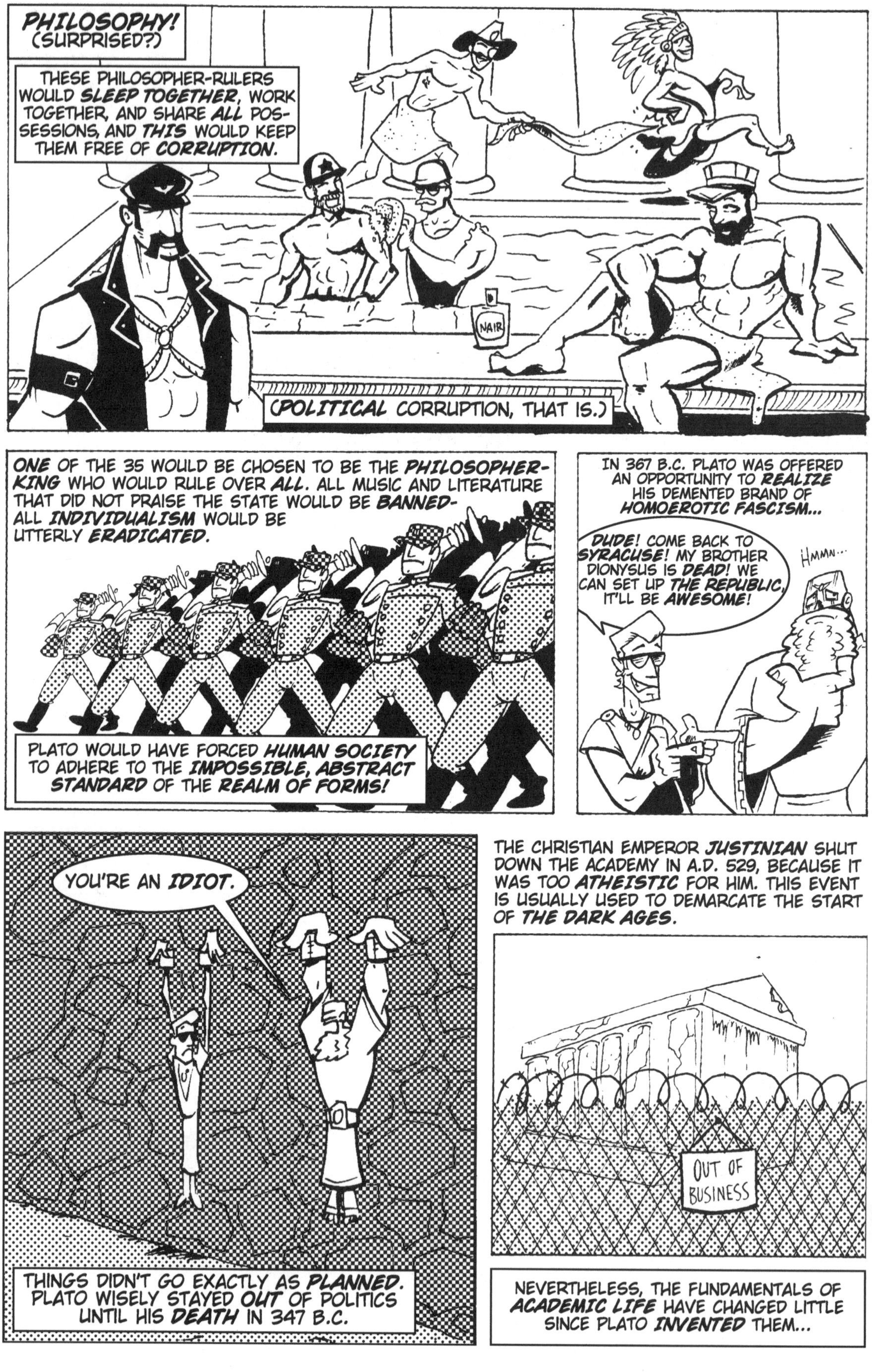
PHILOSOPHY! (SURPRISED?)
THESE PHILOSOPHER-RULERS WOULD SLEEP TOGETHER, WORK TOGETHER, AND SHARE ALL POSSESSIONS, AND THIS WOULD KEEP THEM FREE OF CORRUPTION.
NAIR
(POLITICAL CORRUPTION, THAT IS.)
ONE OF THE 35 WOULD BE CHOSEN TO BE THE PHILOSOPHER-KING WHO WOULD RULE OVER ALL. ALL MUSIC AND LITERATURE THAT DID NOT PRAISE THE STATE WOULD BE BANNED-ALL INDIVIDUALISM WOULD BE UTTERLY ERADICATED.
PLATO WOULD HAVE FORCED HUMAN SOCIETY TO ADHERE TO THE IMPOSSIBLE, ABSTRACT STANDARD OF THE REALM OF FORMS!
IN 367 B.C. PLATO WAS OFFERED AN OPPORTUNITY TO REALIZE HIS DEMENTED BRAND OF HOMOEROTIC FASCISM...
DUDE! COME BACK TO SYRACUSE! MY BROTHER DIONYSUS IS DEAD! WE CAN SET UP THE REPUBLIC, IT'LL BE AWESOME!
HMMN...
YOU'RE AN IDIOT.
THINGS DIDN'T GO EXACTLY AS PLANNED. PLATO WISELY STAYED OUT OF POLITICS UNTIL HIS DEATH IN 347 B.C.
THE CHRISTIAN EMPEROR JUSTINIAN SHUT DOWN THE ACADEMY IN A.D. 529, BECAUSE IT WAS TOO ATHEISTIC FOR HIM. THIS EVENT IS USUALLY USED TO DEMARCATE THE START OF THE DARK AGES.
OUT OF BUSINESS
NEVERTHELESS, THE FUNDAMENTALS OF ACADEMIC LIFE HAVE CHANGED LITTLE SINCE PLATO INVENTED THEM...

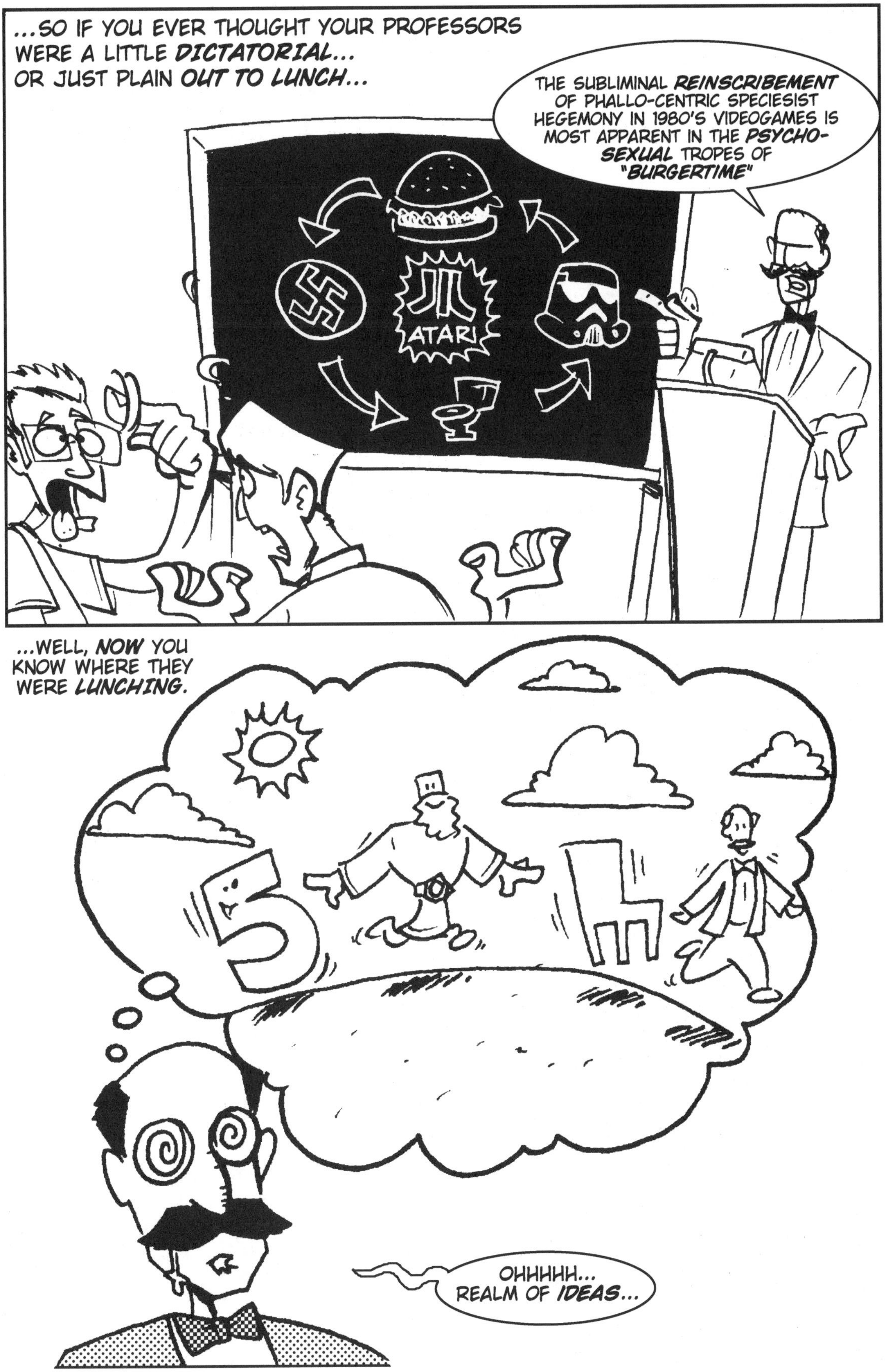
...SO IF YOU EVER THOUGHT YOUR PROFESSORS WERE A LITTLE DICTATORIAL... OR JUST PLAIN OUT TO LUNCH...
THE SUBLIMINAL REINSCRIBEMENT OF PHALLO-CENTRIC SPECIESIST HEGEMONY IN 1980'S VIDEOGAMES IS MOST APPARENT IN THE PSYCHO-SEXUAL TROPES OF "BURGERTIME"
ATARI
...WELL, NOW YOU KNOW WHERE THEY WERE LUNCHING.
OHHHHH... REALM OF IDEAS...

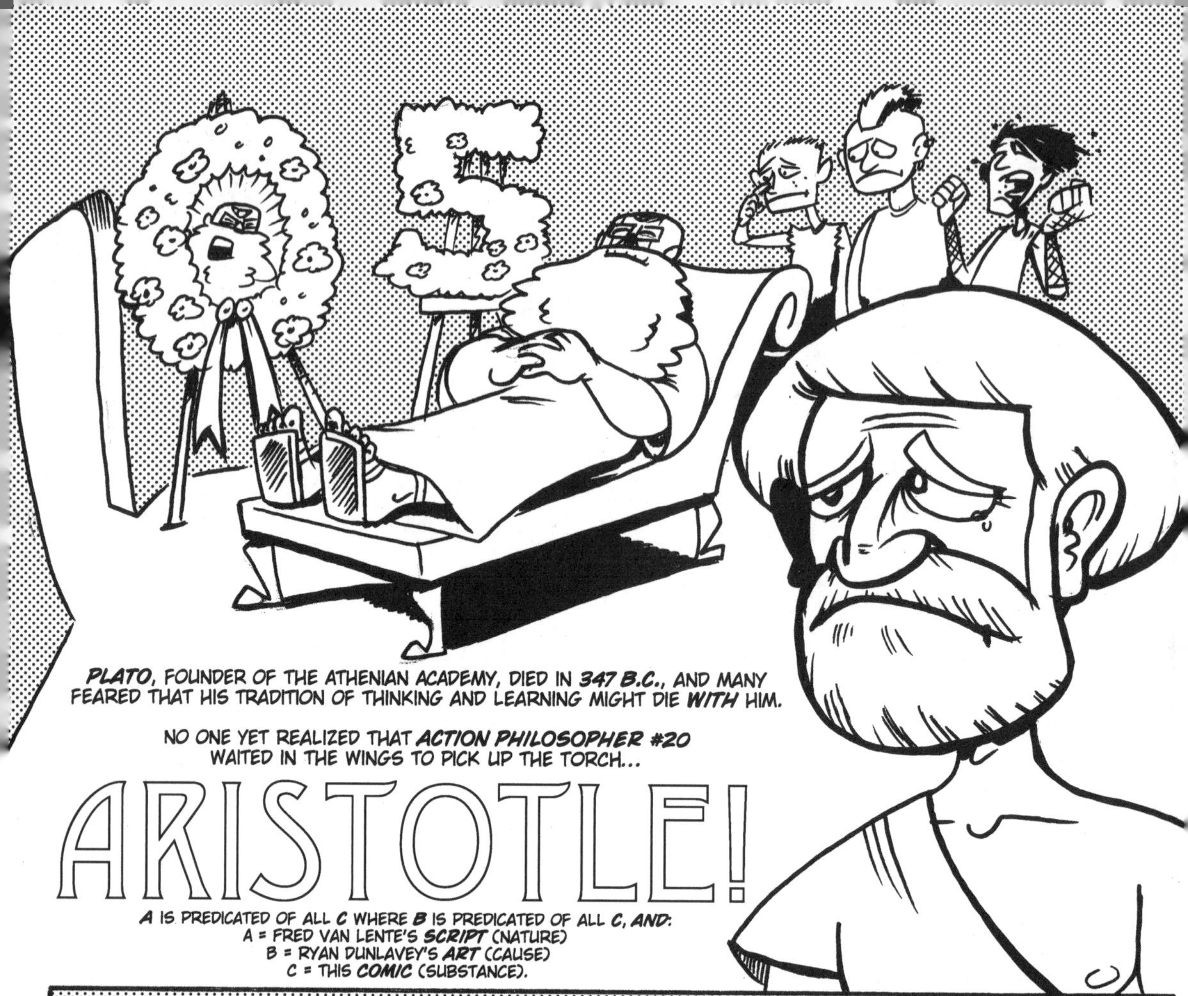
PLATO, FOUNDER OF THE ATHENIAN ACADEMY, DIED IN 347 B.C., AND MANY FEARED THAT HIS TRADITION OF THINKING AND LEARNING MIGHT DIE WITH HIM.
NO ONE YET REALIZED THAT ACTION PHILOSOPHER #20 WAITED IN THE WINGS TO PICK UP THE TORCH...
ARISTOTLE!
A IS PREDICATED OF ALL C WHERE B IS PREDICATED OF ALL C, AND:
A = FRED VAN LENTE'S SCRIPT (NATURE)
B = RYAN DUNLAVEY'S ART (CAUSE)
C = THIS COMIC (SUBSTANCE).

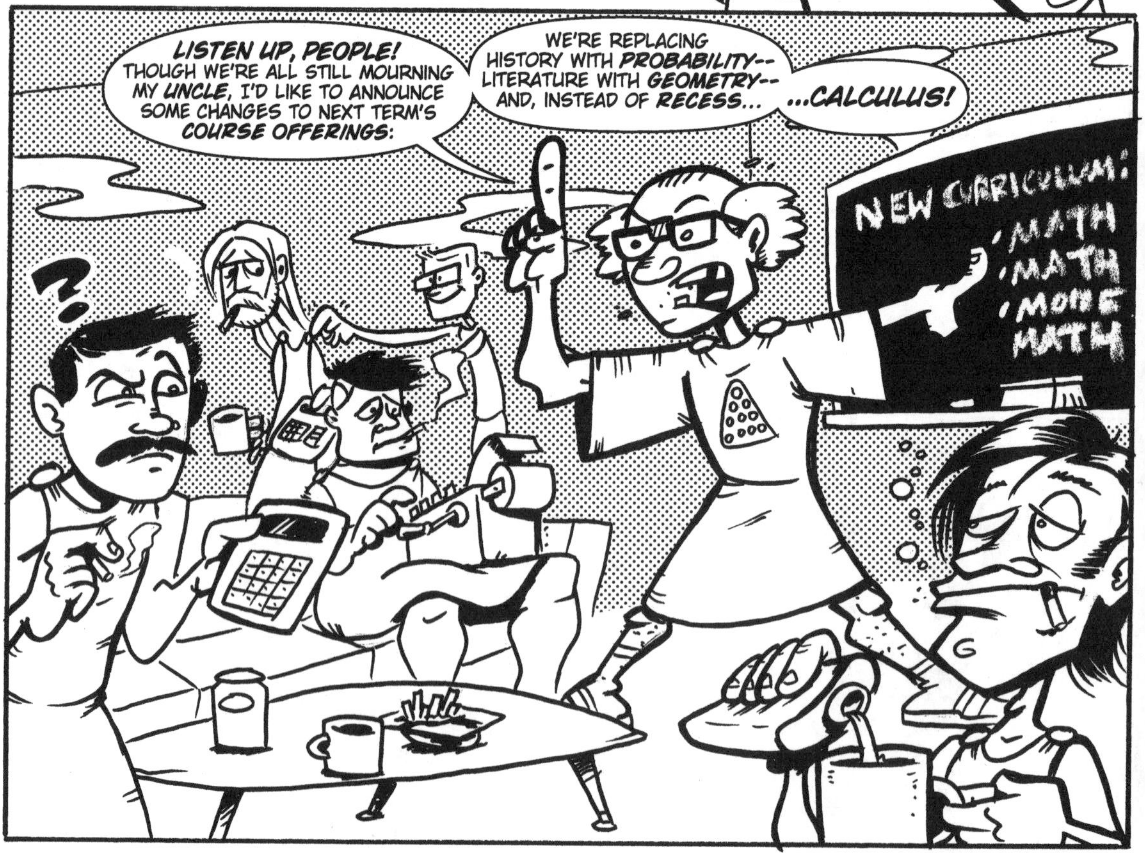
LISTEN UP, PEOPLE! THOUGH WE'RE ALL STILL MOURNING MY UNCLE, I'D LIKE TO ANNOUNCE SOME CHANGES TO NEXT TERM'S COURSE OFFERINGS:
WE'RE REPLACING HISTORY WITH PROBABILITY-- LITERATURE WITH GEOMETRY-- AND, INSTEAD OF RECESS...
...CALCULUS!
NEW CURRICULUM:
·MATH
·MATH
·MORE MATH

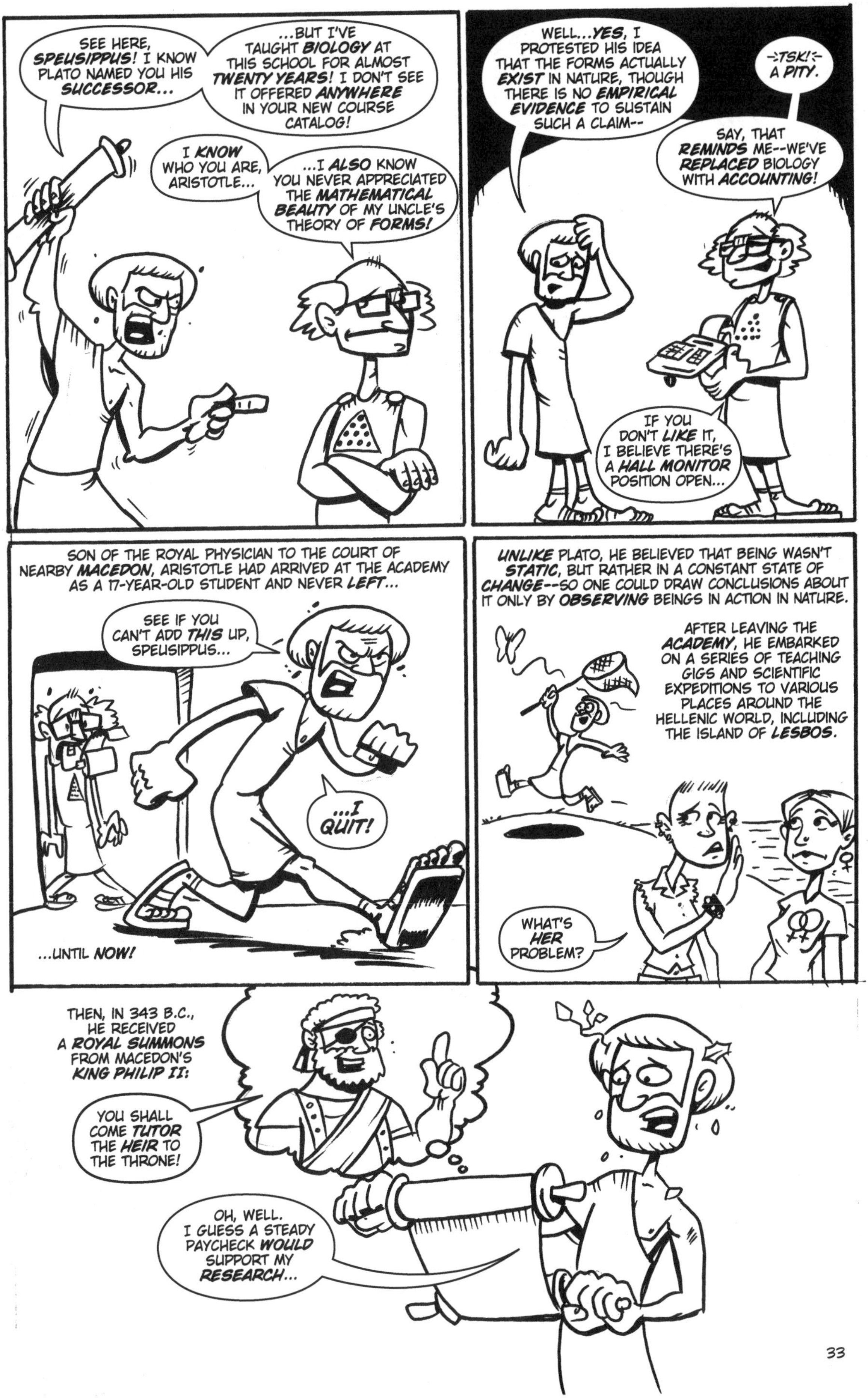
SEE HERE, SPEUSIPPUS! I KNOW PLATO NAMED YOU HIS SUCCESSOR...
...BUT I'VE TAUGHT BIOLOGY AT THIS SCHOOL FOR ALMOST TWENTY YEARS! I DON'T SEE IT OFFERED ANYWHERE IN YOUR NEW COURSE CATALOG!
I KNOW WHO YOU ARE, ARISTOTLE...
...I ALSO KNOW YOU NEVER APPRECIATED THE MATHEMATICAL BEAUTY OF MY UNCLE'S THEORY OF FORMS!
WELL...YES, I PROTESTED HIS IDEA THAT THE FORMS ACTUALLY EXIST IN NATURE, THOUGH THERE IS NO EMPIRICAL EVIDENCE TO SUSTAIN SUCH A CLAIM--
-TSK!- A PITY.
SAY, THAT REMINDS ME--WE'VE REPLACED BIOLOGY WITH ACCOUNTING!
IF YOU DON'T LIKE IT, I BELIEVE THERE'S A HALL MONITOR POSITION OPEN...
SON OF THE ROYAL PHYSICIAN TO THE COURT OF NEARBY MACEDON, ARISTOTLE HAD ARRIVED AT THE ACADEMY AS A 17-YEAR-OLD STUDENT AND NEVER LEFT...
SEE IF YOU CAN'T ADD THIS UP, SPEUSIPPUS...
...I QUIT!
...UNTIL NOW!
UNLIKE PLATO, HE BELIEVED THAT BEING WASN'T STATIC, BUT RATHER IN A CONSTANT STATE OF CHANGE--SO ONE COULD DRAW CONCLUSIONS ABOUT IT ONLY BY OBSERVING BEINGS IN ACTION IN NATURE.
AFTER LEAVING THE ACADEMY, HE EMBARKED ON A SERIES OF TEACHING GIGS AND SCIENTIFIC EXPEDITIONS TO VARIOUS PLACES AROUND THE HELLENIC WORLD, INCLUDING THE ISLAND OF LESBOS.
WHAT'S HER PROBLEM?
THEN, IN 343 B.C., HE RECEIVED A ROYAL SUMMONS FROM MACEDON'S KING PHILIP II:
YOU SHALL COME TUTOR THE HEIR TO THE THRONE!
OH, WELL. I GUESS A STEADY PAYCHECK WOULD SUPPORT MY RESEARCH...

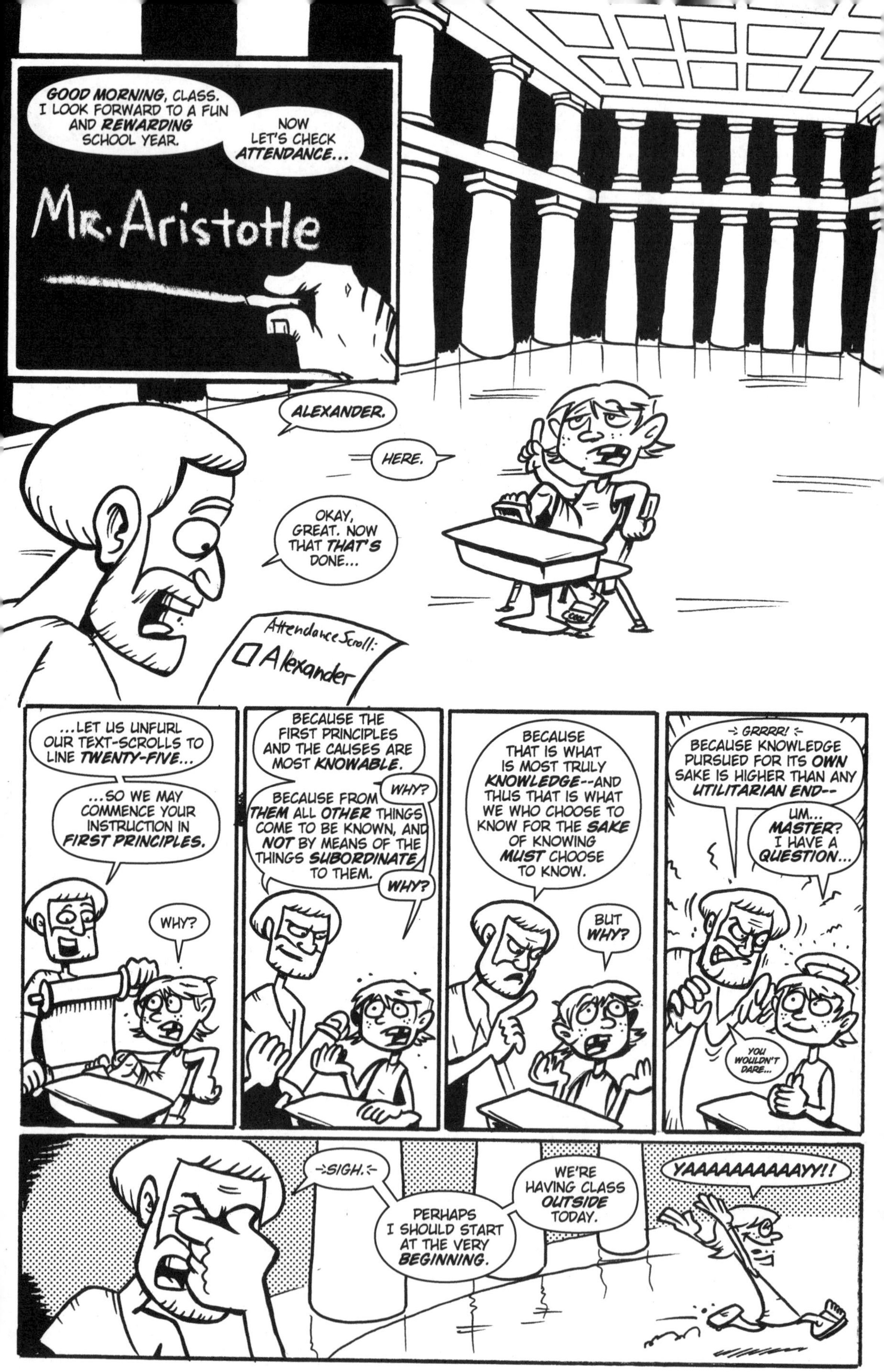
GOOD MORNING, CLASS. I LOOK FORWARD TO A FUN AND REWARDING SCHOOL YEAR.
NOW LET'S CHECK ATTENDANCE...
Mr. Aristotle
ALEXANDER.
HERE.
OKAY, GREAT. NOW THAT THAT'S DONE...
Attendance Scroll:
Alexander
...LET US UNFURL OUR TEXT-SCROLLS TO LINE TWENTY-FIVE...
...SO WE MAY COMMENCE YOUR INSTRUCTION IN FIRST PRINCIPLES.
WHY?
BECAUSE THE FIRST PRINCIPLES AND THE CAUSES ARE MOST KNOWABLE.
WHY?
BECAUSE FROM THEM ALL OTHER THINGS COME TO BE KNOWN, AND NOT BY MEANS OF THE THINGS SUBORDINATE TO THEM.
WHY?
BECAUSE THAT IS WHAT IS MOST TRULY KNOWLEDGE--AND THUS THAT IS WHAT WE WHO CHOOSE TO KNOW FOR THE SAKE OF KNOWING MUST CHOOSE TO KNOW.
BUT WHY?
GRRRR!
BECAUSE KNOWLEDGE PURSUED FOR ITS OWN SAKE IS HIGHER THAN ANY UTILITARIAN END--
UM... MASTER? I HAVE A QUESTION...
YOU WOULDN'T DARE...
SIGH.
PERHAPS I SHOULD START AT THE VERY BEGINNING.
WE'RE HAVING CLASS OUTSIDE TODAY.
YAAAAAAAAAAY!!

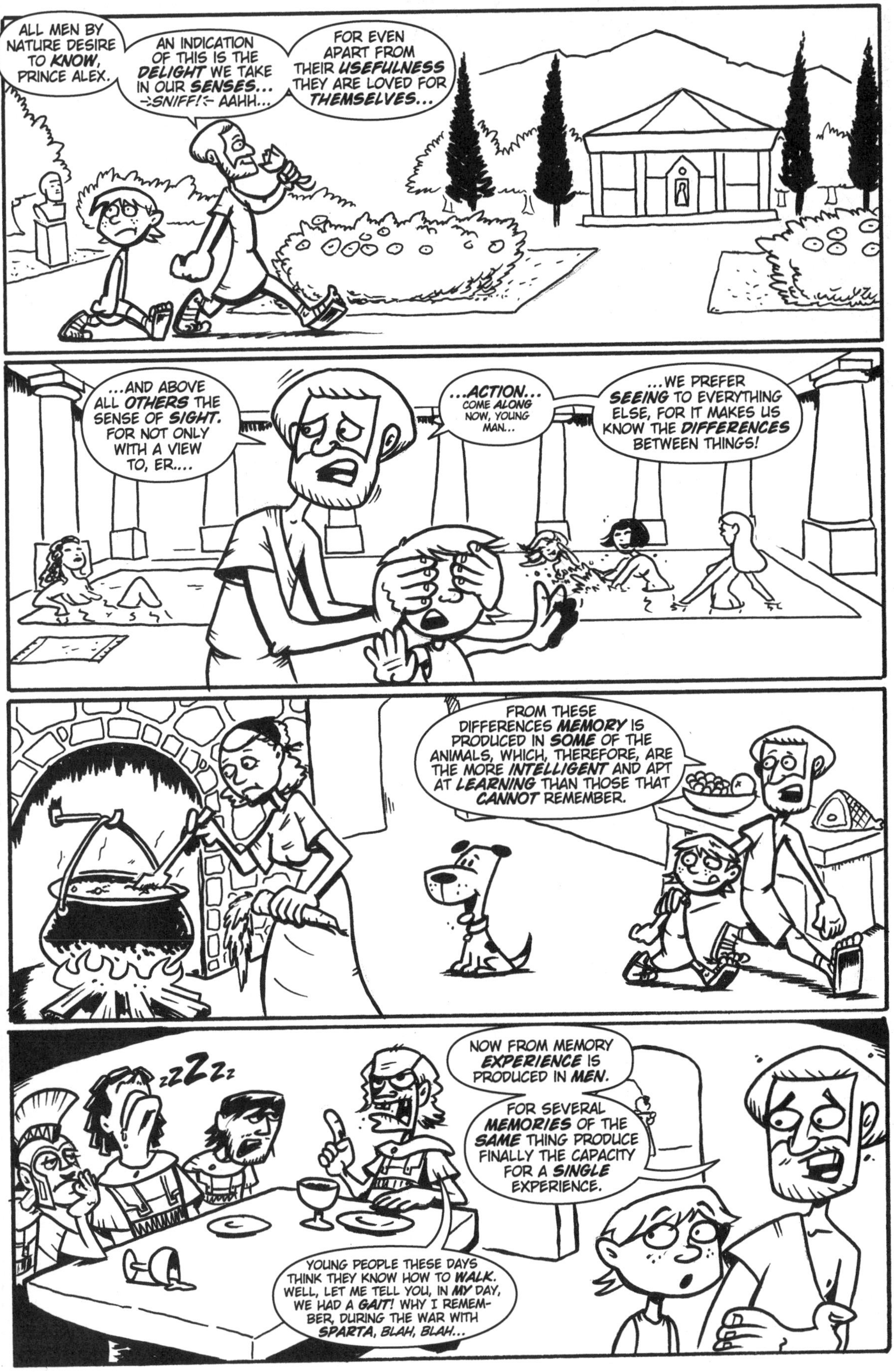

ALL MEN BY NATURE DESIRE TO KNOW, PRINCE ALEX.
AN INDICATION OF THIS IS THE DELIGHT WE TAKE IN OUR SENSES... SNIFF! AAHH...
FOR EVEN APART FROM THEIR USEFULNESS THEY ARE LOVED FOR THEMSELVES...
...AND ABOVE ALL OTHERS THE SENSE OF SIGHT. FOR NOT ONLY WITH A VIEW TO, ER....
...ACTION... COME ALONG NOW, YOUNG MAN...
...WE PREFER SEEING TO EVERYTHING ELSE, FOR IT MAKES US KNOW THE DIFFERENCES BETWEEN THINGS!
FROM THESE DIFFERENCES MEMORY IS PRODUCED IN SOME OF THE ANIMALS, WHICH, THEREFORE, ARE THE MORE INTELLIGENT AND APT AT LEARNING THAN THOSE THAT CANNOT REMEMBER.
zzZZzz
NOW FROM MEMORY EXPERIENCE IS PRODUCED IN MEN.
FOR SEVERAL MEMORIES OF THE SAME THING PRODUCE FINALLY THE CAPACITY FOR A SINGLE EXPERIENCE.
YOUNG PEOPLE THESE DAYS THINK THEY KNOW HOW TO WALK. WELL, LET ME TELL YOU, IN MY DAY, WE HAD A GAIT! WHY I REMEMBER, DURING THE WAR WITH SPARTA, BLAH, BLAH...

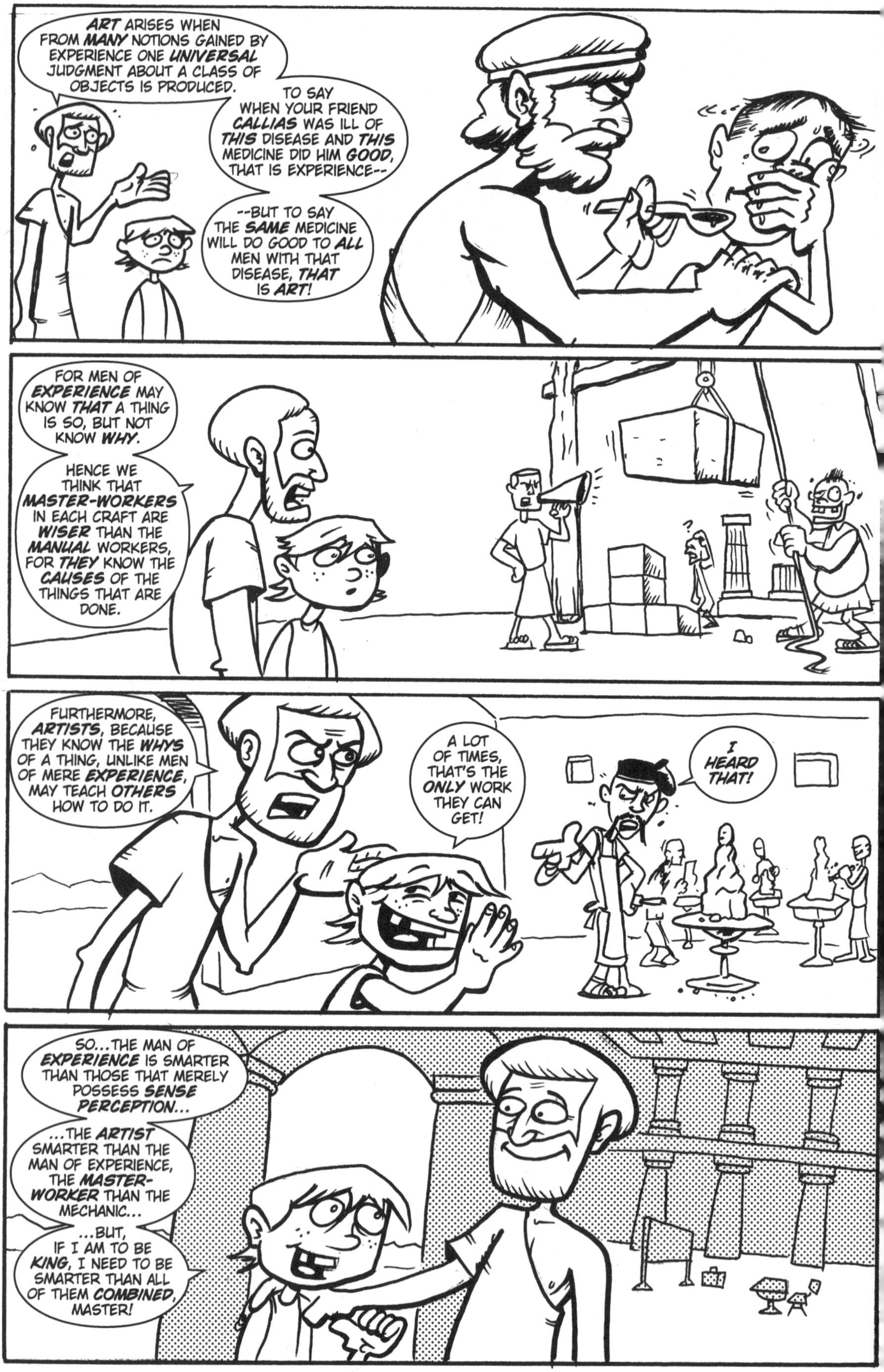
ART ARISES WHEN FROM MANY NOTIONS GAINED BY EXPERIENCE ONE UNIVERSAL JUDGMENT ABOUT A CLASS OF OBJECTS IS PRODUCED.
TO SAY WHEN YOUR FRIEND CALLIAS WAS ILL OF THIS DISEASE AND THIS MEDICINE DID HIM GOOD, THAT IS EXPERIENCE--
--BUT TO SAY THE SAME MEDICINE WILL DO GOOD TO ALL MEN WITH THAT DISEASE, THAT IS ART!
FOR MEN OF EXPERIENCE MAY KNOW THAT A THING IS SO, BUT NOT KNOW WHY.
HENCE WE THINK THAT MASTER-WORKERS IN EACH CRAFT ARE WISER THAN THE MANUAL WORKERS, FOR THEY KNOW THE CAUSES OF THE THINGS THAT ARE DONE.
FURTHERMORE, ARTISTS, BECAUSE THEY KNOW THE WHYS OF A THING, UNLIKE MEN OF MERE EXPERIENCE, MAY TEACH OTHERS HOW TO DO IT.
A LOT OF TIMES, THAT'S THE ONLY WORK THEY CAN GET!
I HEARD THAT!
SO...THE MAN OF EXPERIENCE IS SMARTER THAN THOSE THAT MERELY POSSESS SENSE PERCEPTION...
...THE ARTIST SMARTER THAN THE MAN OF EXPERIENCE, THE MASTER-WORKER THAN THE MECHANIC...
...BUT, IF I AM TO BE KING, I NEED TO BE SMARTER THAN ALL OF THEM COMBINED, MASTER!

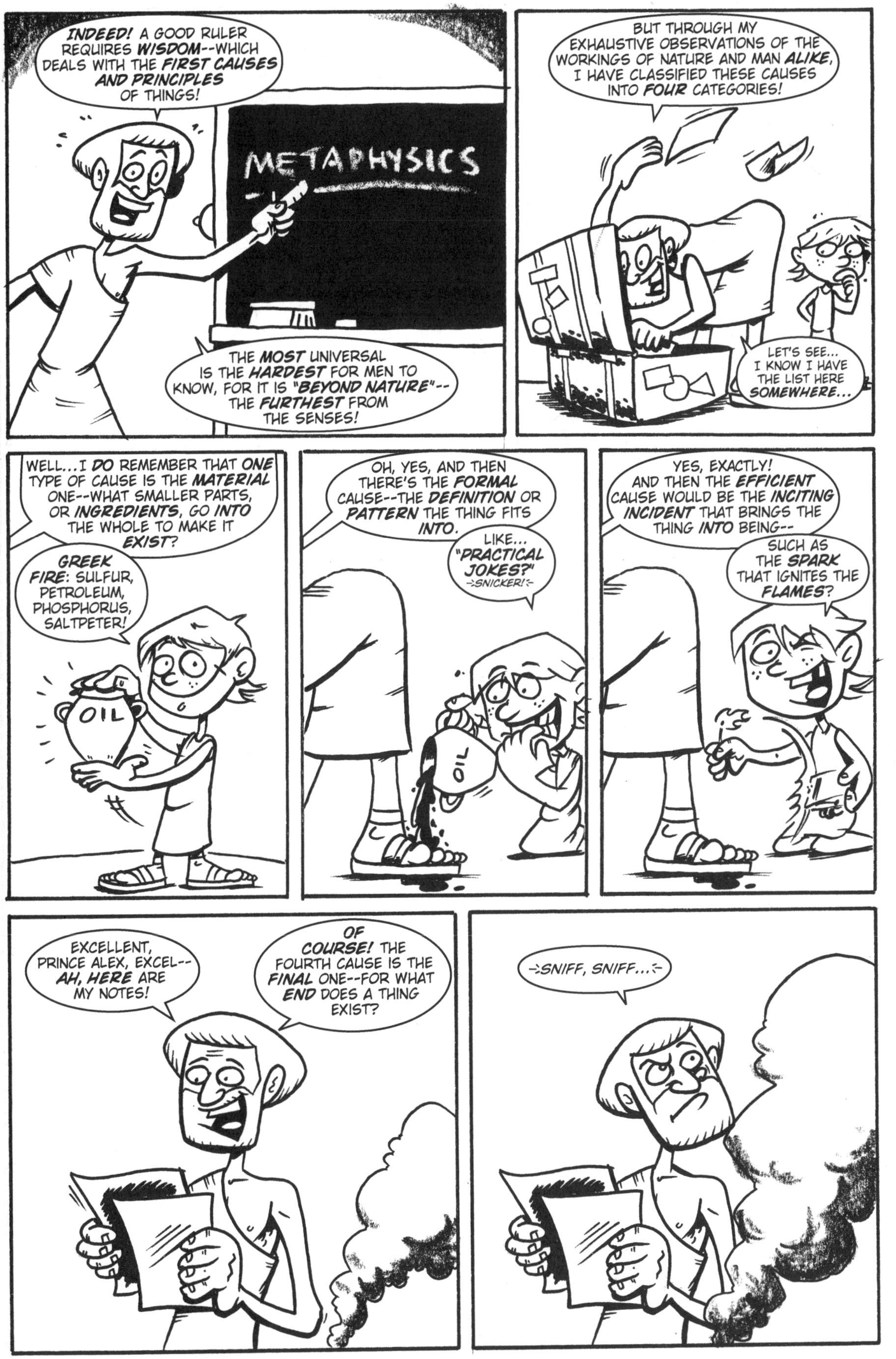
INDEED! A GOOD RULER REQUIRES WISDOM--WHICH DEALS WITH THE FIRST CAUSES AND PRINCIPLES OF THINGS!
METAPHYSICS
THE MOST UNIVERSAL IS THE HARDEST FOR MEN TO KNOW, FOR IT IS "BEYOND NATURE"--THE FURTHEST FROM THE SENSES!
BUT THROUGH MY EXHAUSTIVE OBSERVATIONS OF THE WORKINGS OF NATURE AND MAN ALIKE, I HAVE CLASSIFIED THESE CAUSES INTO FOUR CATEGORIES!
LET'S SEE... I KNOW I HAVE THE LIST HERE SOMEWHERE...
WELL...I DO REMEMBER THAT ONE TYPE OF CAUSE IS THE MATERIAL ONE--WHAT SMALLER PARTS, OR INGREDIENTS, GO INTO THE WHOLE TO MAKE IT EXIST?
GREEK FIRE: SULFUR, PETROLEUM, PHOSPHORUS, SALTPETER!
OIL
OH, YES, AND THEN THERE'S THE FORMAL CAUSE--THE DEFINITION OR PATTERN THE THING FITS INTO.
LIKE... "PRACTICAL JOKES?" -SNICKER!-
OIL
YES, EXACTLY! AND THEN THE EFFICIENT CAUSE WOULD BE THE INCITING INCIDENT THAT BRINGS THE THING INTO BEING--
SUCH AS THE SPARK THAT IGNITES THE FLAMES?
EXCELLENT, PRINCE ALEX, EXCEL--AH, HERE ARE MY NOTES!
OF COURSE! THE FOURTH CAUSE IS THE FINAL ONE--FOR WHAT END DOES A THING EXIST?
-SNIFF, SNIFF...-

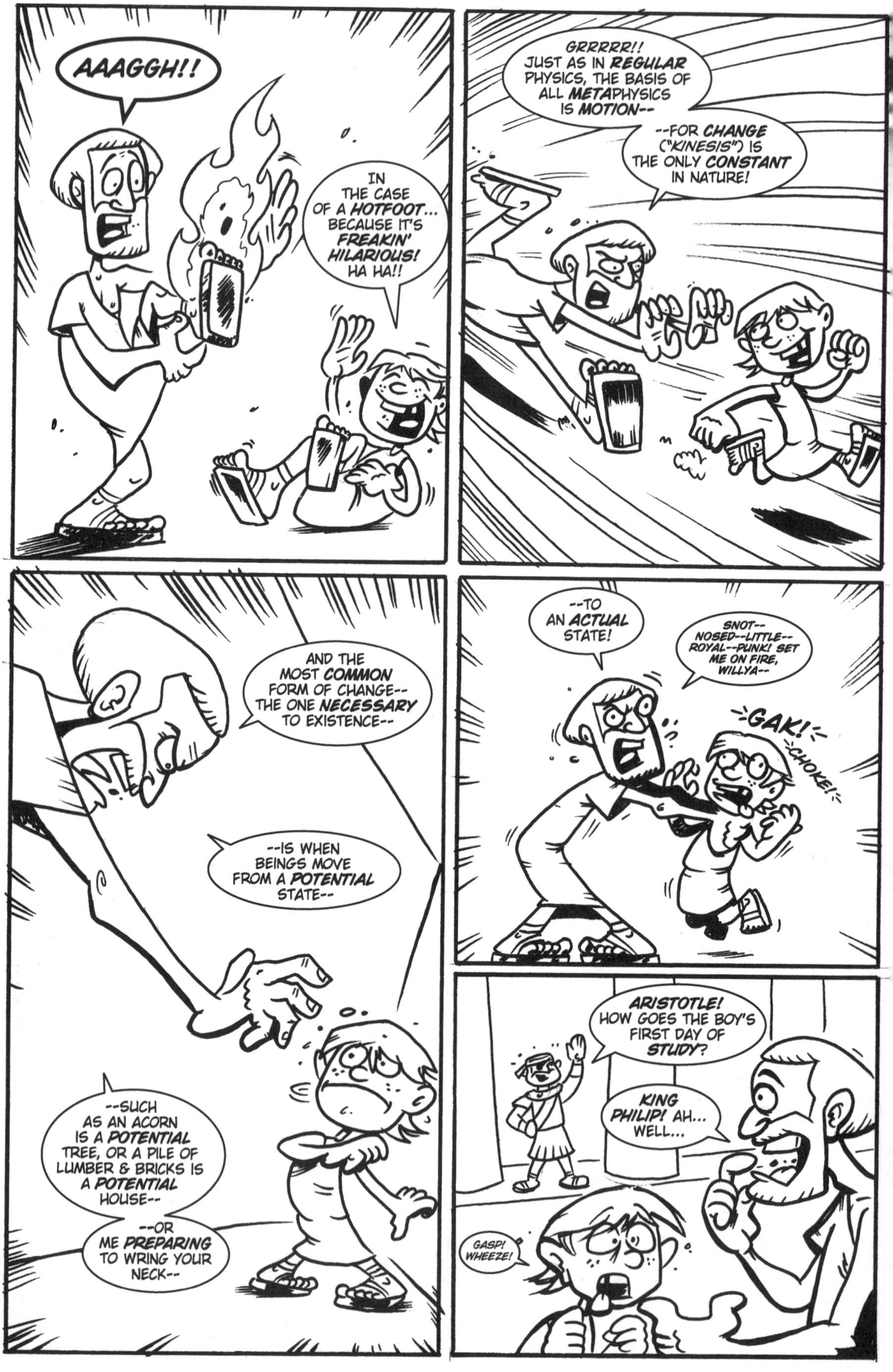
AAAGGH!!
IN THE CASE OF A HOTFOOT... BECAUSE IT'S FREAKIN' HILARIOUS! HA HA!!
GRRRRR!! JUST AS IN REGULAR PHYSICS, THE BASIS OF ALL METAPHYSICS IS MOTION--
--FOR CHANGE ("KINESIS") IS THE ONLY CONSTANT IN NATURE!
AND THE MOST COMMON FORM OF CHANGE-- THE ONE NECESSARY TO EXISTENCE--
--IS WHEN BEINGS MOVE FROM A POTENTIAL STATE--
--SUCH AS AN ACORN IS A POTENTIAL TREE, OR A PILE OF LUMBER & BRICKS IS A POTENTIAL HOUSE--
--OR ME PREPARING TO WRING YOUR NECK--
--TO AN ACTUAL STATE!
SNOT--NOSED--LITTLE--ROYAL--PUNK! SET ME ON FIRE, WILLYA--
GAK!
CHOKE!
ARISTOTLE! HOW GOES THE BOY'S FIRST DAY OF STUDY?
KING PHILIP! AH... WELL...
GASP! WHEEZE!

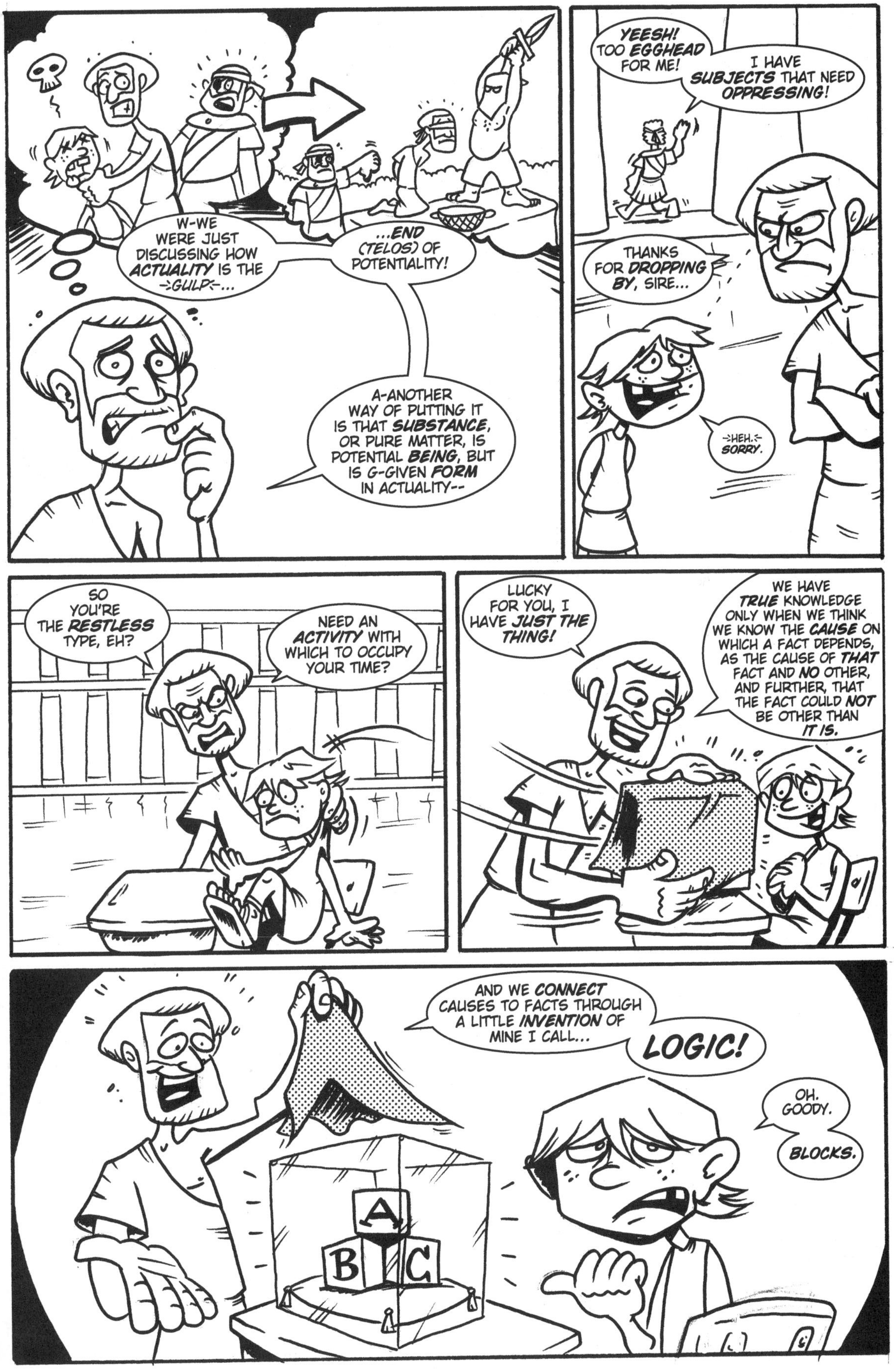
W-WE WERE JUST DISCUSSING HOW ACTUALITY IS THE ~GULP~...
...END (TELOS) OF POTENTIALITY!
A-ANOTHER WAY OF PUTTING IT IS THAT SUBSTANCE, OR PURE MATTER, IS POTENTIAL BEING, BUT IS G-GIVEN FORM IN ACTUALITY--
YEESH! TOO EGGHEAD FOR ME!
I HAVE SUBJECTS THAT NEED OPPRESSING!
THANKS FOR DROPPING BY, SIRE...
~HEH.~ SORRY.
SO YOU'RE THE RESTLESS TYPE, EH?
NEED AN ACTIVITY WITH WHICH TO OCCUPY YOUR TIME?
LUCKY FOR YOU, I HAVE JUST THE THING!
WE HAVE TRUE KNOWLEDGE ONLY WHEN WE THINK WE KNOW THE CAUSE ON WHICH A FACT DEPENDS, AS THE CAUSE OF THAT FACT AND NO OTHER, AND FURTHER, THAT THE FACT COULD NOT BE OTHER THAN IT IS.
AND WE CONNECT CAUSES TO FACTS THROUGH A LITTLE INVENTION OF MINE I CALL...
LOGIC!
OH. GOODY.
BLOCKS.
A
B
C

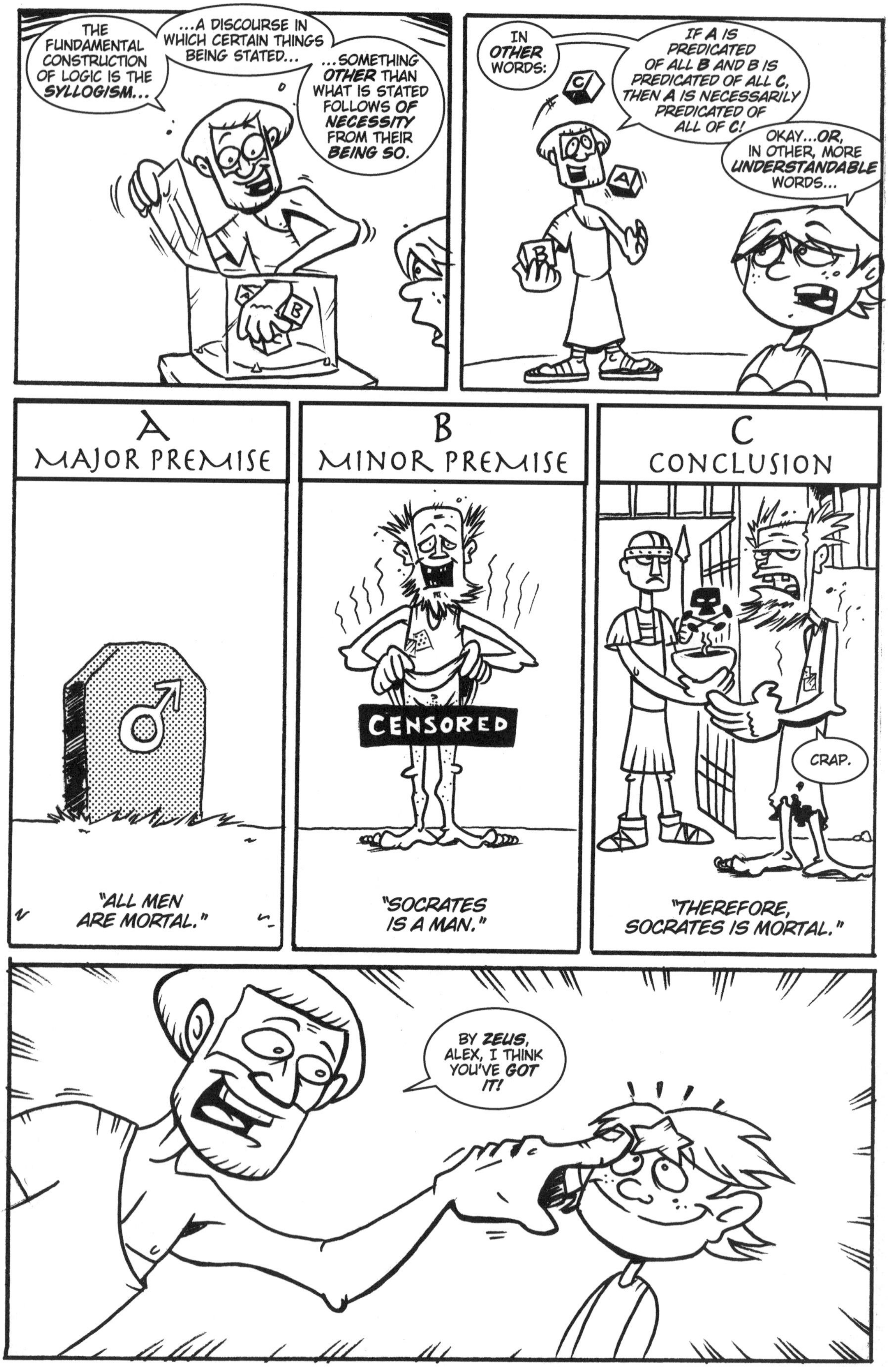
THE FUNDAMENTAL CONSTRUCTION OF LOGIC IS THE SYLLOGISM...
...A DISCOURSE IN WHICH CERTAIN THINGS BEING STATED...
...SOMETHING OTHER THAN WHAT IS STATED FOLLOWS OF NECESSITY FROM THEIR BEING SO.
IN OTHER WORDS:
IF A IS PREDICATED OF ALL B AND B IS PREDICATED OF ALL C, THEN A IS NECESSARILY PREDICATED OF ALL OF C!
OKAY...OR, IN OTHER, MORE UNDERSTANDABLE WORDS...
A
MAJOR PREMISE
B
MINOR PREMISE
C
CONCLUSION
"ALL MEN ARE MORTAL."
CENSORED
"SOCRATES IS A MAN."
CRAP.
"THEREFORE, SOCRATES IS MORTAL."
BY ZEUS, ALEX, I THINK YOU'VE GOT IT!

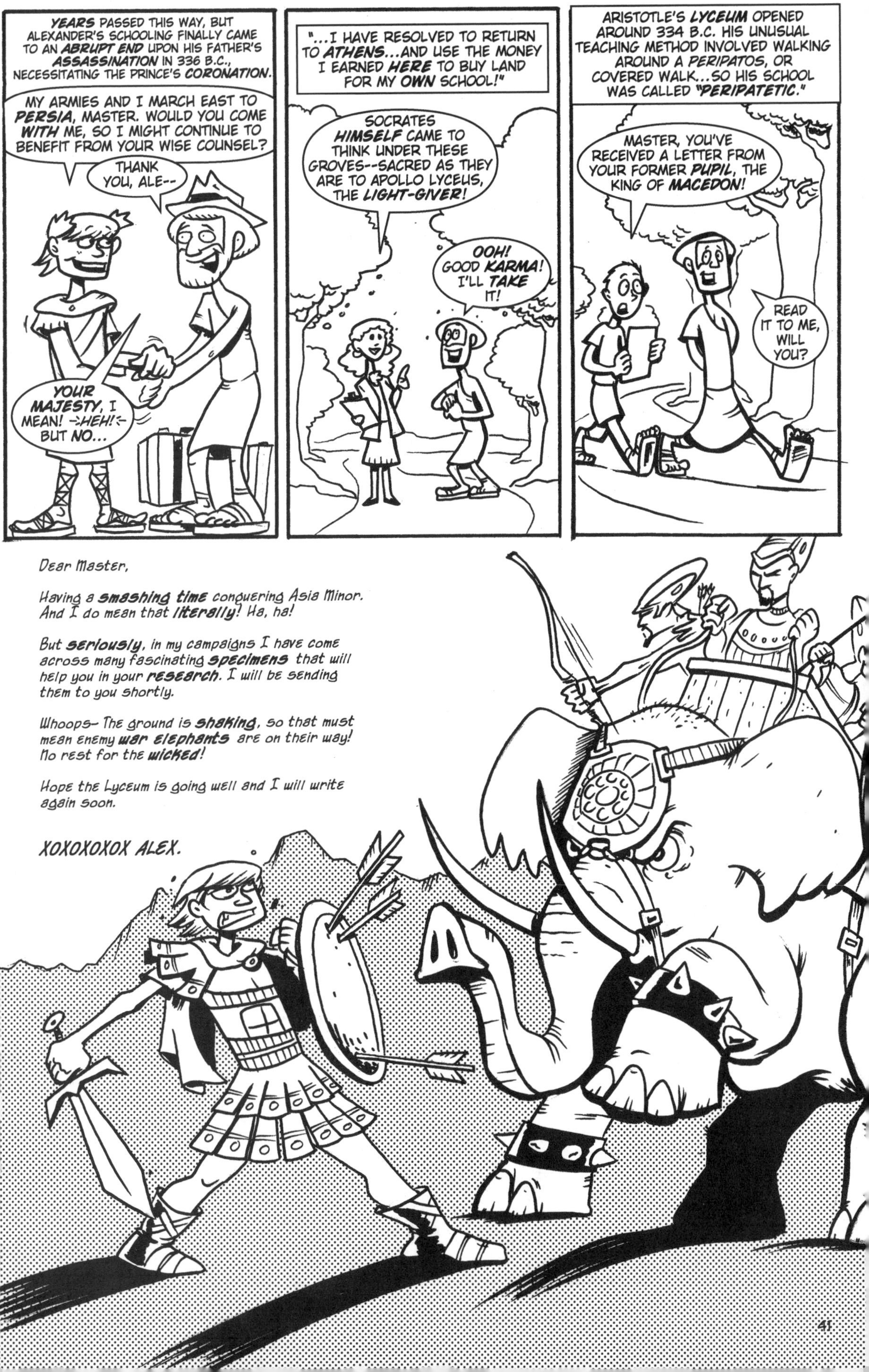
YEARS PASSED THIS WAY, BUT ALEXANDER'S SCHOOLING FINALLY CAME TO AN ABRUPT END UPON HIS FATHER'S ASSASSINATION IN 336 B.C., NECESSITATING THE PRINCE'S CORONATION.
MY ARMIES AND I MARCH EAST TO PERSIA, MASTER. WOULD YOU COME WITH ME, SO I MIGHT CONTINUE TO BENEFIT FROM YOUR WISE COUNSEL?
THANK YOU, ALE--
YOUR MAJESTY, I MEAN! -HEH!- BUT NO...
"...I HAVE RESOLVED TO RETURN TO ATHENS...AND USE THE MONEY I EARNED HERE TO BUY LAND FOR MY OWN SCHOOL!"
SOCRATES HIMSELF CAME TO THINK UNDER THESE GROVES--SACRED AS THEY ARE TO APOLLO LYCEUS, THE LIGHT-GIVER!
OOH! GOOD KARMA! I'LL TAKE IT!
ARISTOTLE'S LYCEUM OPENED AROUND 334 B.C. HIS UNUSUAL TEACHING METHOD INVOLVED WALKING AROUND A PERIPATOS, OR COVERED WALK...SO HIS SCHOOL WAS CALLED "PERIPATETIC."
MASTER, YOU'VE RECEIVED A LETTER FROM YOUR FORMER PUPIL, THE KING OF MACEDON!
READ IT TO ME, WILL YOU?
Dear Master,
Having a smashing time conquering Asia Minor. And I do mean that literally! Ha, ha!
But seriously, in my campaigns I have come across many fascinating specimens that will help you in your research. I will be sending them to you shortly.
Whoops- The ground is shaking, so that must mean enemy war elephants are on their way! No rest for the wicked!
Hope the Lyceum is going well and I will write again soon.
XOXOXOXOX ALEX.

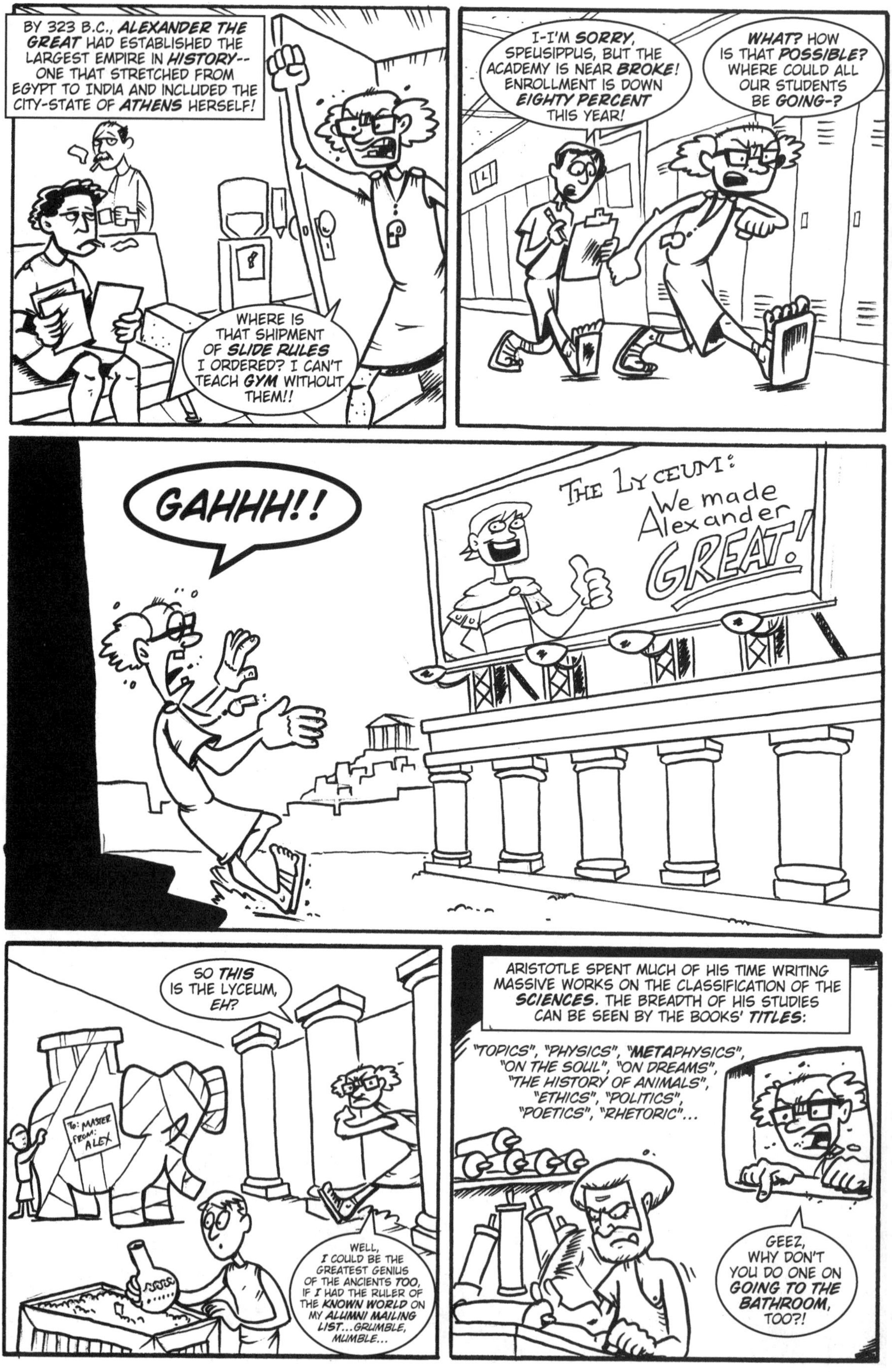
BY 323 B.C., ALEXANDER THE GREAT HAD ESTABLISHED THE LARGEST EMPIRE IN HISTORY-- ONE THAT STRETCHED FROM EGYPT TO INDIA AND INCLUDED THE CITY-STATE OF ATHENS HERSELF!
WHERE IS THAT SHIPMENT OF SLIDE RULES I ORDERED? I CAN'T TEACH GYM WITHOUT THEM!!
I-I'M SORRY, SPEUSIPPUS, BUT THE ACADEMY IS NEAR BROKE! ENROLLMENT IS DOWN EIGHTY PERCENT THIS YEAR!
WHAT? HOW IS THAT POSSIBLE? WHERE COULD ALL OUR STUDENTS BE GOING-?
GAHHH!!
THE LYCEUM: We made Alexander GREAT!
SO THIS IS THE LYCEUM, EH?
TO: MASTER FROM: ALEX
WELL, I COULD BE THE GREATEST GENIUS OF THE ANCIENTS TOO, IF I HAD THE RULER OF THE KNOWN WORLD ON MY ALUMNI MAILING LIST...GRUMBLE, MUMBLE...
ARISTOTLE SPENT MUCH OF HIS TIME WRITING MASSIVE WORKS ON THE CLASSIFICATION OF THE SCIENCES. THE BREADTH OF HIS STUDIES CAN BE SEEN BY THE BOOKS' TITLES:
"TOPICS", "PHYSICS", "METAPHYSICS", "ON THE SOUL", "ON DREAMS", "THE HISTORY OF ANIMALS", "ETHICS", "POLITICS", "POETICS", "RHETORIC"...
GEEZ, WHY DON'T YOU DO ONE ON GOING TO THE BATHROOM, TOO?!

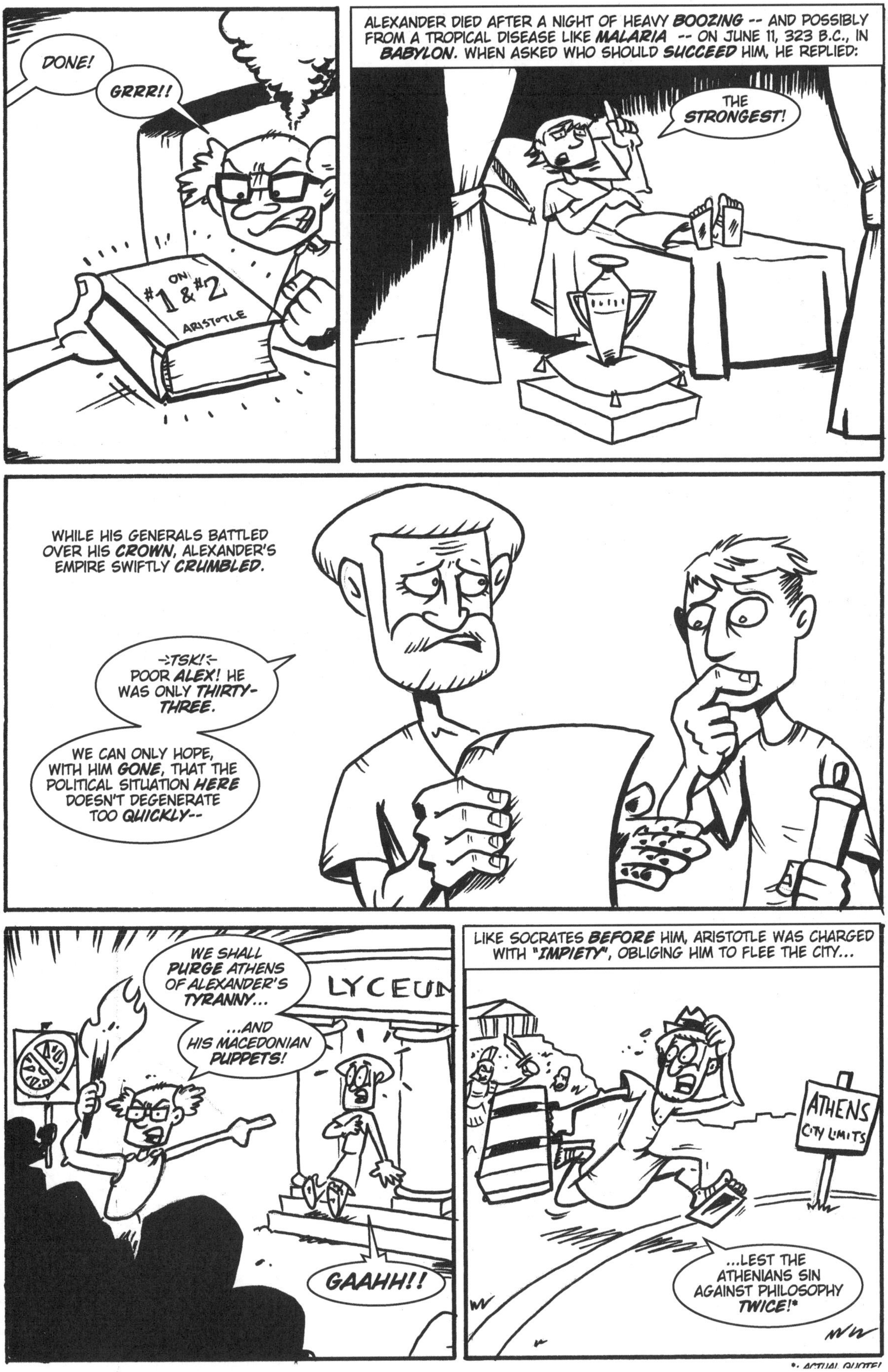
DONE!
GRRR!!
ARISTOTLE
ALEXANDER DIED AFTER A NIGHT OF HEAVY BOOZING -- AND POSSIBLY FROM A TROPICAL DISEASE LIKE MALARIA -- ON JUNE 11, 323 B.C., IN BABYLON. WHEN ASKED WHO SHOULD SUCCEED HIM, HE REPLIED:
THE STRONGEST!
WHILE HIS GENERALS BATTLED OVER HIS CROWN, ALEXANDER'S EMPIRE SWIFTLY CRUMBLED.
TSK! POOR ALEX! HE WAS ONLY THIRTY-THREE.
WE CAN ONLY HOPE, WITH HIM GONE, THAT THE POLITICAL SITUATION HERE DOESN'T DEGENERATE TOO QUICKLY--
WE SHALL PURGE ATHENS OF ALEXANDER'S TYRANNY...
...AND HIS MACEDONIAN PUPPETS!
LYCEUM
GAAHH!!
LIKE SOCRATES BEFORE HIM, ARISTOTLE WAS CHARGED WITH "IMPIETY", OBLIGING HIM TO FLEE THE CITY...
ATHENS CITY LIMITS
...LEST THE ATHENIANS SIN AGAINST PHILOSOPHY TWICE!*

*: ACTUAL QUOTE!

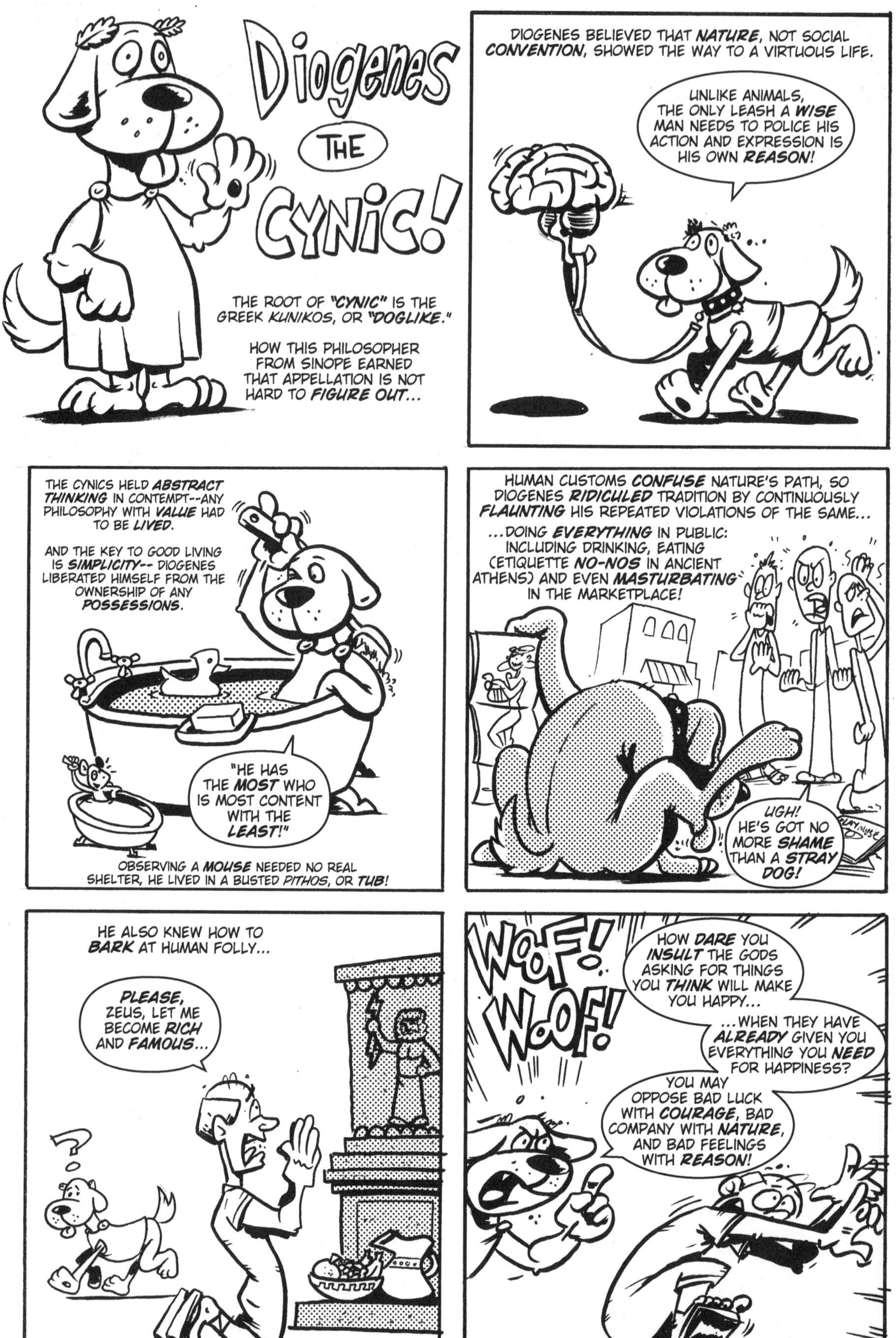
Diogenes
THE
CYNIC!
THE ROOT OF "CYNIC" IS THE GREEK KUNIKOS, OR "DOGLIKE."
HOW THIS PHILOSOPHER FROM SINOPE EARNED THAT APPELLATION IS NOT HARD TO FIGURE OUT...
DIOGENES BELIEVED THAT NATURE, NOT SOCIAL CONVENTION, SHOWED THE WAY TO A VIRTUOUS LIFE.
UNLIKE ANIMALS, THE ONLY LEASH A WISE MAN NEEDS TO POLICE HIS ACTION AND EXPRESSION IS HIS OWN REASON!
THE CYNICS HELD ABSTRACT THINKING IN CONTEMPT--ANY PHILOSOPHY WITH VALUE HAD TO BE LIVED.
AND THE KEY TO GOOD LIVING IS SIMPLICITY-- DIOGENES LIBERATED HIMSELF FROM THE OWNERSHIP OF ANY POSSESSIONS.
"HE HAS THE MOST WHO IS MOST CONTENT WITH THE LEAST!"
OBSERVING A MOUSE NEEDED NO REAL SHELTER, HE LIVED IN A BUSTED PITHOS, OR TUB!
HUMAN CUSTOMS CONFUSE NATURE'S PATH, SO DIOGENES RIDICULED TRADITION BY CONTINUOUSLY FLAUNTING HIS REPEATED VIOLATIONS OF THE SAME...
...DOING EVERYTHING IN PUBLIC: INCLUDING DRINKING, EATING (ETIQUETTE NO-NOS IN ANCIENT ATHENS) AND EVEN MASTURBATING IN THE MARKETPLACE!
UGH! HE'S GOT NO MORE SHAME THAN A STRAY DOG!
HE ALSO KNEW HOW TO BARK AT HUMAN FOLLY...
PLEASE, ZEUS, LET ME BECOME RICH AND FAMOUS...
?
WOOF! WOOF!
HOW DARE YOU INSULT THE GODS ASKING FOR THINGS YOU THINK WILL MAKE YOU HAPPY...
...WHEN THEY HAVE ALREADY GIVEN YOU EVERYTHING YOU NEED FOR HAPPINESS?
YOU MAY OPPOSE BAD LUCK WITH COURAGE, BAD COMPANY WITH NATURE, AND BAD FEELINGS WITH REASON!

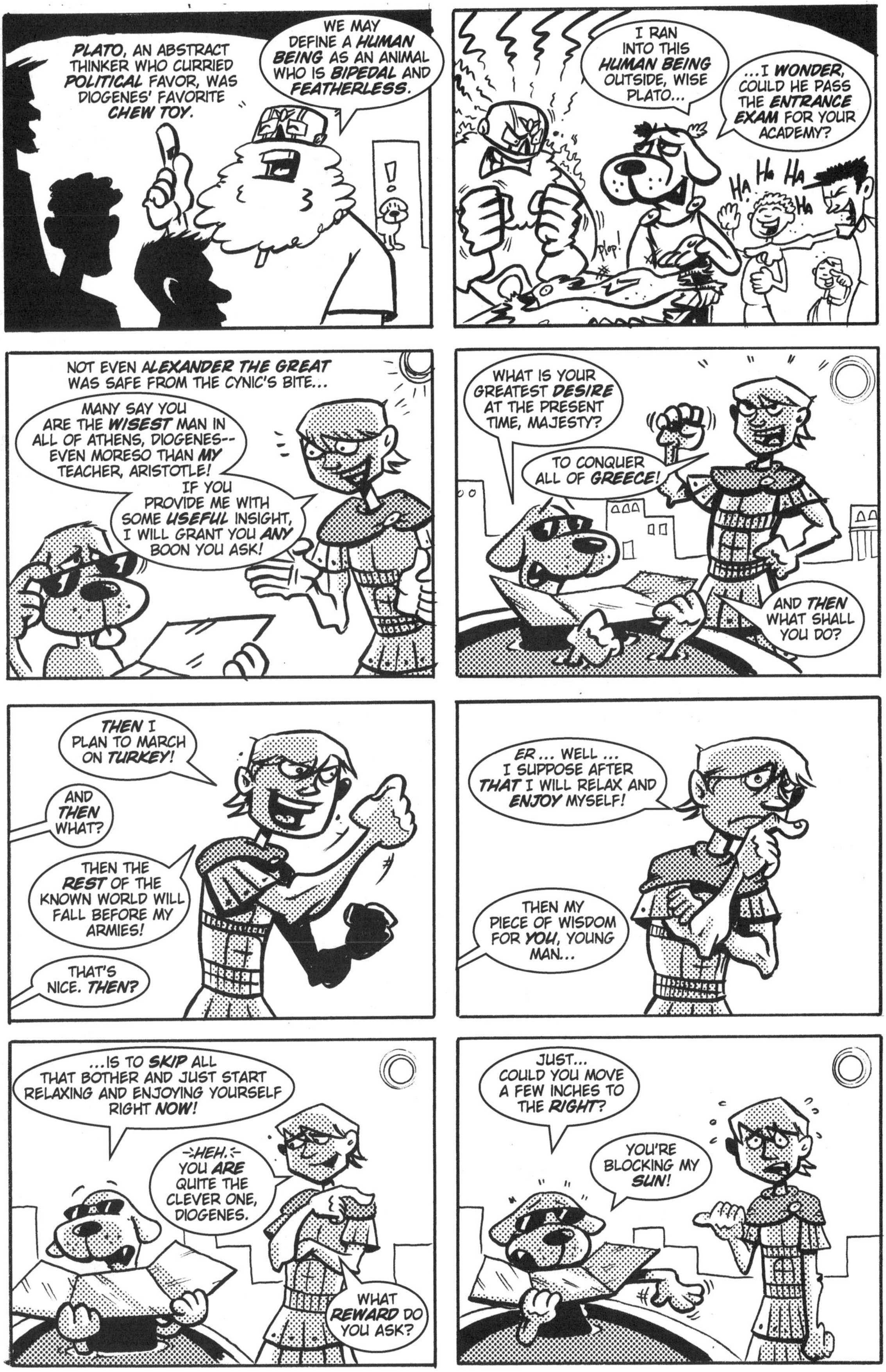
PLATO, AN ABSTRACT THINKER WHO CURRIED POLITICAL FAVOR, WAS DIOGENES' FAVORITE CHEW TOY.
WE MAY DEFINE A HUMAN BEING AS AN ANIMAL WHO IS BIPEDAL AND FEATHERLESS.
!
I RAN INTO THIS HUMAN BEING OUTSIDE, WISE PLATO...
...I WONDER, COULD HE PASS THE ENTRANCE EXAM FOR YOUR ACADEMY?
HA HA HA HA
PLOP!
NOT EVEN ALEXANDER THE GREAT WAS SAFE FROM THE CYNIC'S BITE...
MANY SAY YOU ARE THE WISEST MAN IN ALL OF ATHENS, DIOGENES-- EVEN MORESO THAN MY TEACHER, ARISTOTLE!
IF YOU PROVIDE ME WITH SOME USEFUL INSIGHT, I WILL GRANT YOU ANY BOON YOU ASK!
WHAT IS YOUR GREATEST DESIRE AT THE PRESENT TIME, MAJESTY?
TO CONQUER ALL OF GREECE!
AND THEN WHAT SHALL YOU DO?
THEN I PLAN TO MARCH ON TURKEY!
AND THEN WHAT?
THEN THE REST OF THE KNOWN WORLD WILL FALL BEFORE MY ARMIES!
THAT'S NICE. THEN?
ER... WELL... I SUPPOSE AFTER THAT I WILL RELAX AND ENJOY MYSELF!
THEN MY PIECE OF WISDOM FOR YOU, YOUNG MAN...
...IS TO SKIP ALL THAT BOTHER AND JUST START RELAXING AND ENJOYING YOURSELF RIGHT NOW!
HEH. YOU ARE QUITE THE CLEVER ONE, DIOGENES.
WHAT REWARD DO YOU ASK?
JUST... COULD YOU MOVE A FEW INCHES TO THE RIGHT?
YOU'RE BLOCKING MY SUN!

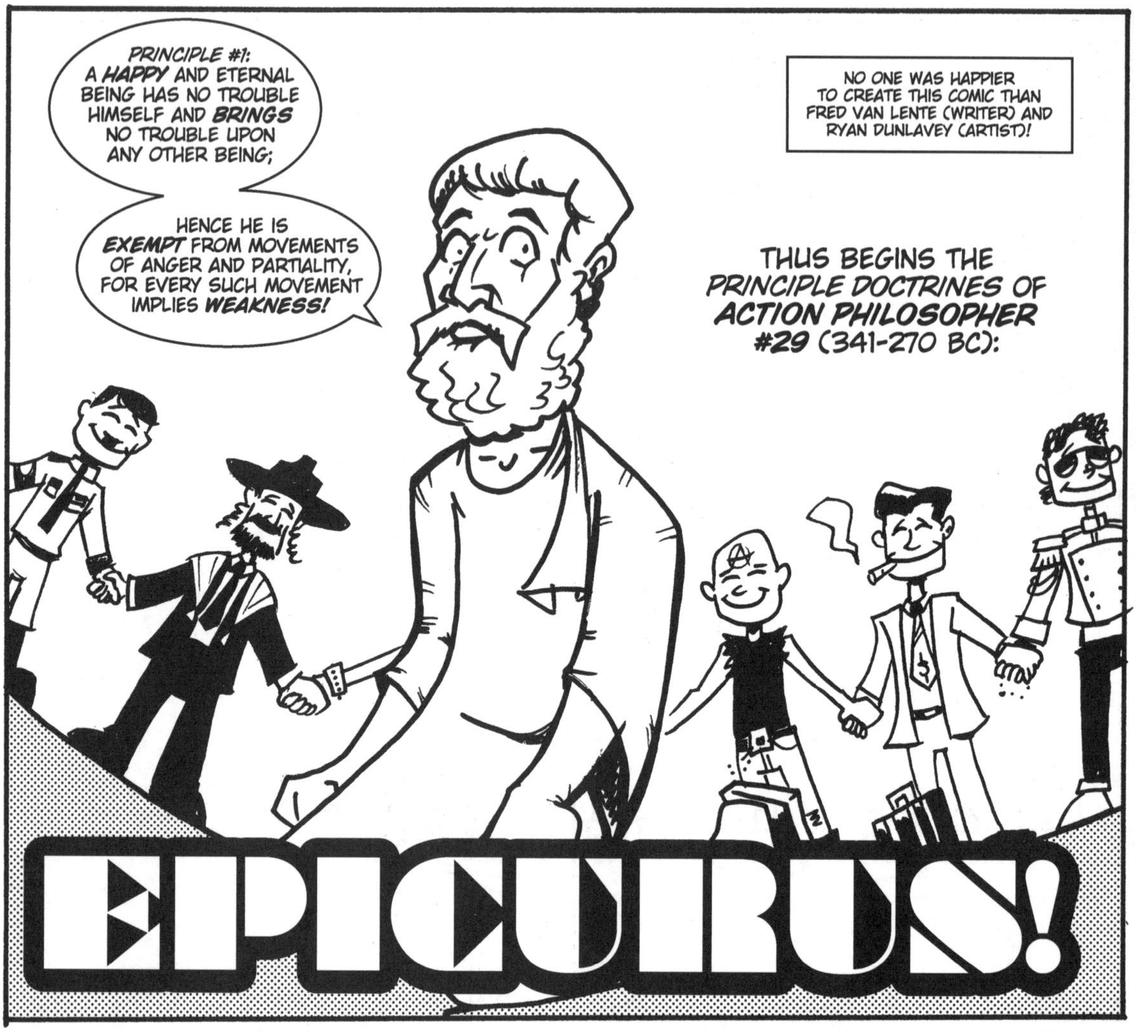
PRINCIPLE #1: A HAPPY AND ETERNAL BEING HAS NO TROUBLE HIMSELF AND BRINGS NO TROUBLE UPON ANY OTHER BEING;
HENCE HE IS EXEMPT FROM MOVEMENTS OF ANGER AND PARTIALITY, FOR EVERY SUCH MOVEMENT IMPLIES WEAKNESS!
NO ONE WAS HAPPIER TO CREATE THIS COMIC THAN FRED VAN LENTE (WRITER) AND RYAN DUNLAVEY (ARTIST)!
THUS BEGINS THE PRINCIPLE DOCTRINES OF ACTION PHILOSOPHER #29 (341-270 BC):
EPICURUS!

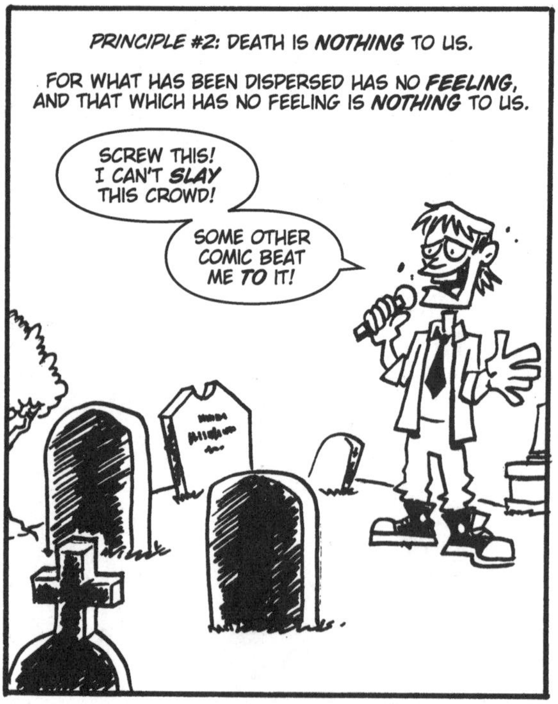
PRINCIPLE #2: DEATH IS NOTHING TO US.
FOR WHAT HAS BEEN DISPERSED HAS NO FEELING, AND THAT WHICH HAS NO FEELING IS NOTHING TO US.
SCREW THIS! I CAN'T SLAY THIS CROWD!
SOME OTHER COMIC BEAT ME TO IT!

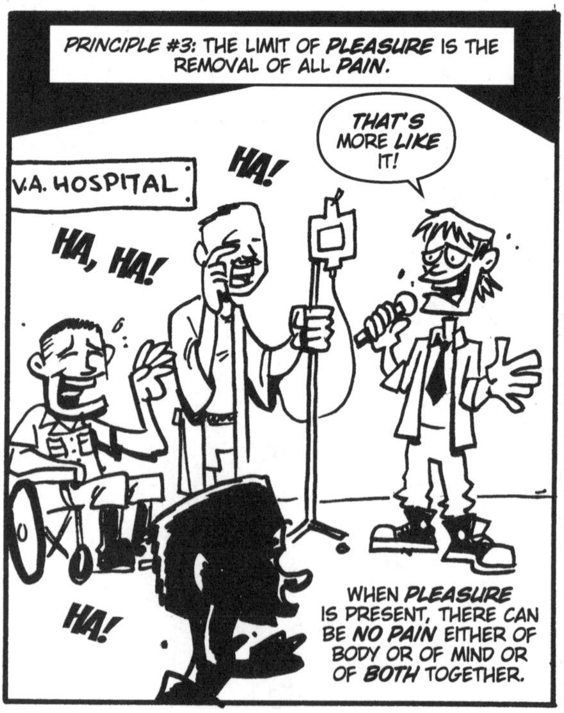
PRINCIPLE #3: THE LIMIT OF PLEASURE IS THE REMOVAL OF ALL PAIN.
V.A. HOSPITAL
HA!
THAT'S MORE LIKE IT!
HA, HA!
HA!
WHEN PLEASURE IS PRESENT, THERE CAN BE NO PAIN EITHER OF BODY OR OF MIND OR OF BOTH TOGETHER.

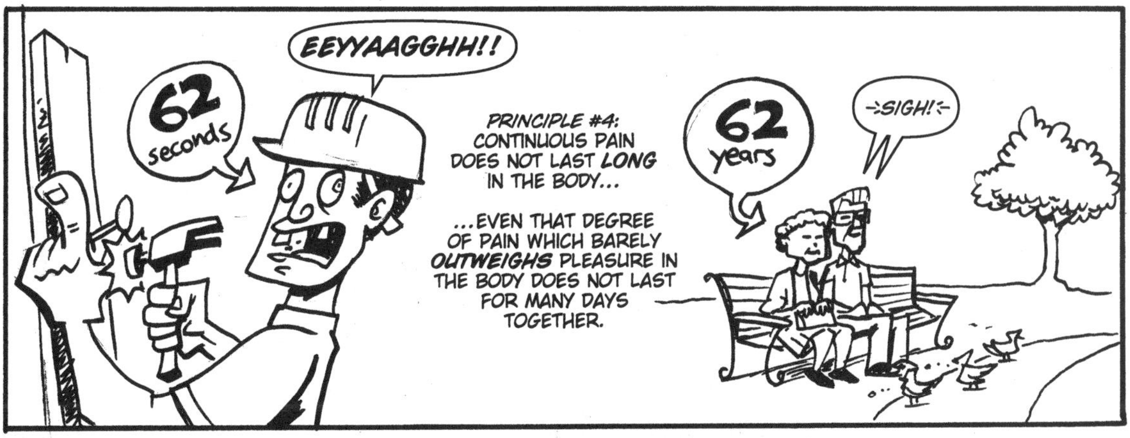
EEYYAAGGHH!!
62 seconds
PRINCIPLE #4: CONTINUOUS PAIN DOES NOT LAST LONG IN THE BODY...
...EVEN THAT DEGREE OF PAIN WHICH BARELY OUTWEIGHS PLEASURE IN THE BODY DOES NOT LAST FOR MANY DAYS TOGETHER.
62 years
-SIGH!-

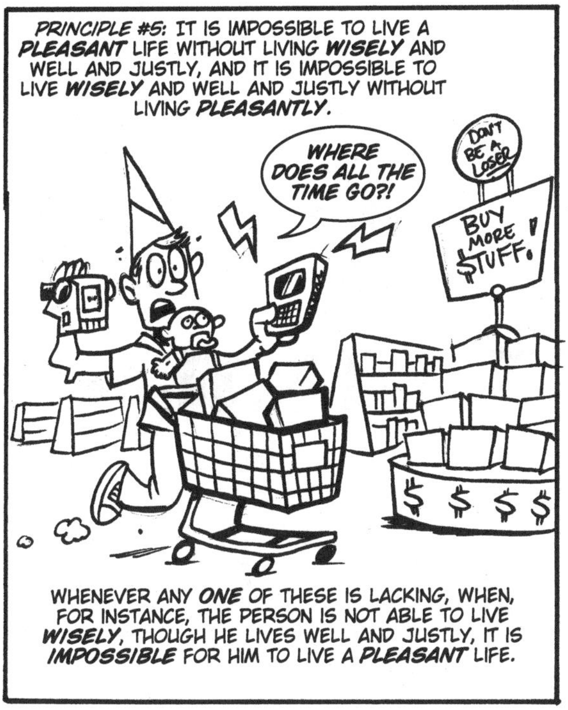
PRINCIPLE #5: IT IS IMPOSSIBLE TO LIVE A PLEASANT LIFE WITHOUT LIVING WISELY AND WELL AND JUSTLY, AND IT IS IMPOSSIBLE TO LIVE WISELY AND WELL AND JUSTLY WITHOUT LIVING PLEASANTLY.
WHERE DOES ALL THE TIME GO?!
DON'T BE A LOSER
BUY MORE $TUFF!
$ $ $ $
WHENEVER ANY ONE OF THESE IS LACKING, WHEN, FOR INSTANCE, THE PERSON IS NOT ABLE TO LIVE WISELY, THOUGH HE LIVES WELL AND JUSTLY, IT IS IMPOSSIBLE FOR HIM TO LIVE A PLEASANT LIFE.

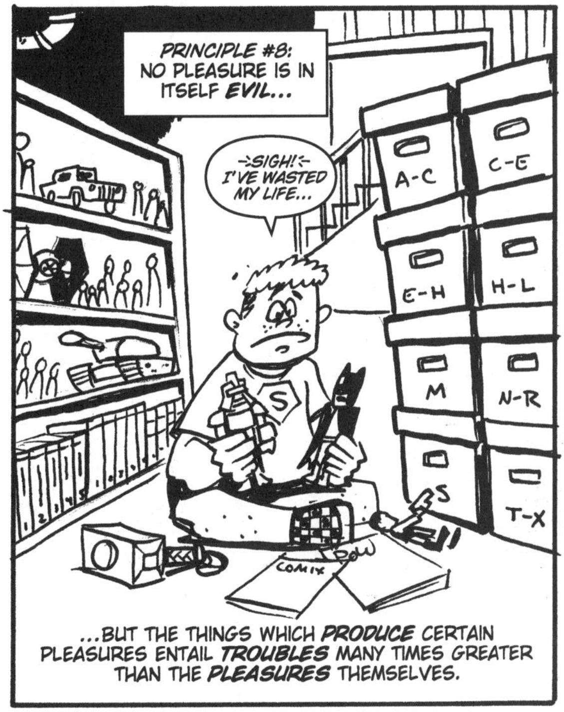
PRINCIPLE #8: NO PLEASURE IS IN ITSELF EVIL...
-SIGH!- I'VE WASTED MY LIFE...
A-C
C-E
E-H
H-L
M
N-R
S
T-X
COMIX
POW
...BUT THE THINGS WHICH PRODUCE CERTAIN PLEASURES ENTAIL TROUBLES MANY TIMES GREATER THAN THE PLEASURES THEMSELVES.

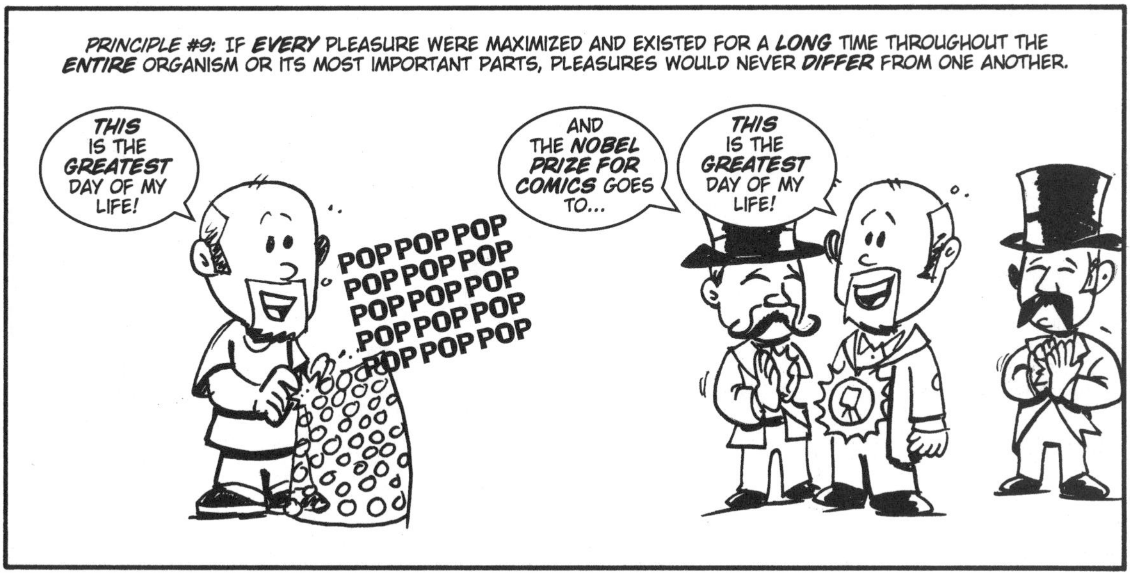
PRINCIPLE #9: IF EVERY PLEASURE WERE MAXIMIZED AND EXISTED FOR A LONG TIME THROUGHOUT THE ENTIRE ORGANISM OR ITS MOST IMPORTANT PARTS, PLEASURES WOULD NEVER DIFFER FROM ONE ANOTHER.
THIS IS THE GREATEST DAY OF MY LIFE!
POP POP POP POP POP POP POP POP POP POP POP POP POP POP POP
AND THE NOBEL PRIZE FOR COMICS GOES TO...
THIS IS THE GREATEST DAY OF MY LIFE!

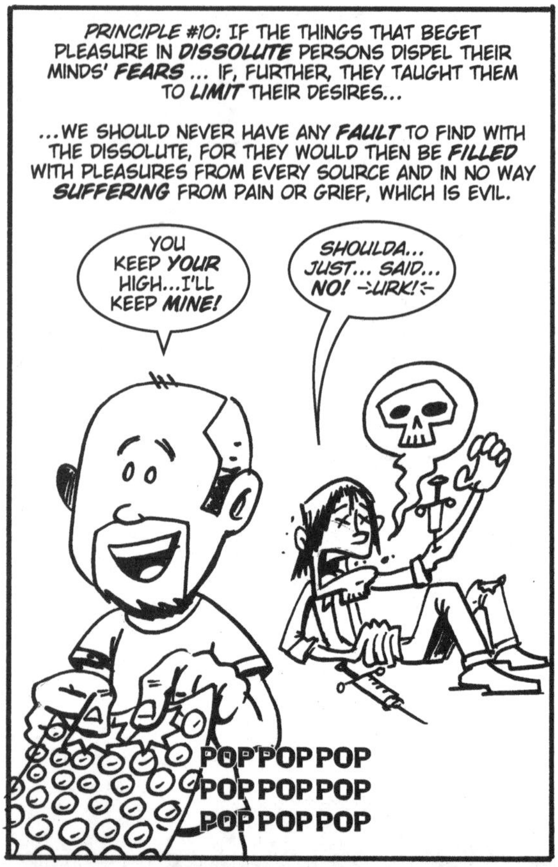
PRINCIPLE #10: IF THE THINGS THAT BEGET PLEASURE IN DISSOLUTE PERSONS DISPEL THEIR MINDS' FEARS ... IF, FURTHER, THEY TAUGHT THEM TO LIMIT THEIR DESIRES...
...WE SHOULD NEVER HAVE ANY FAULT TO FIND WITH THE DISSOLUTE, FOR THEY WOULD THEN BE FILLED WITH PLEASURES FROM EVERY SOURCE AND IN NO WAY SUFFERING FROM PAIN OR GRIEF, WHICH IS EVIL.
YOU KEEP YOUR HIGH...I'LL KEEP MINE!
SHOULDA... JUST... SAID... NO! -URK!-
POPPOPPOP
POPPOPPOP
POPPOPPOP

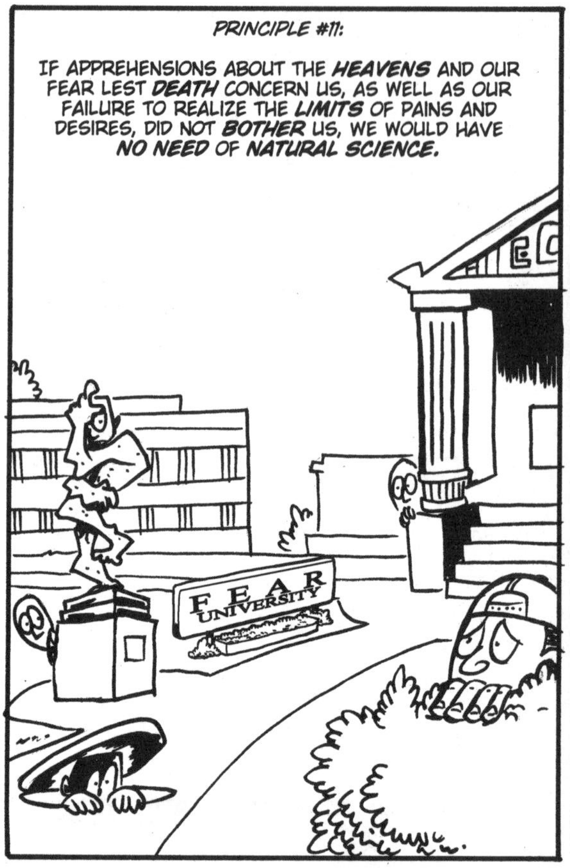
PRINCIPLE #11:
IF APPREHENSIONS ABOUT THE HEAVENS AND OUR FEAR LEST DEATH CONCERN US, AS WELL AS OUR FAILURE TO REALIZE THE LIMITS OF PAINS AND DESIRES, DID NOT BOTHER US, WE WOULD HAVE NO NEED OF NATURAL SCIENCE.
FEAR
UNIVERSITY

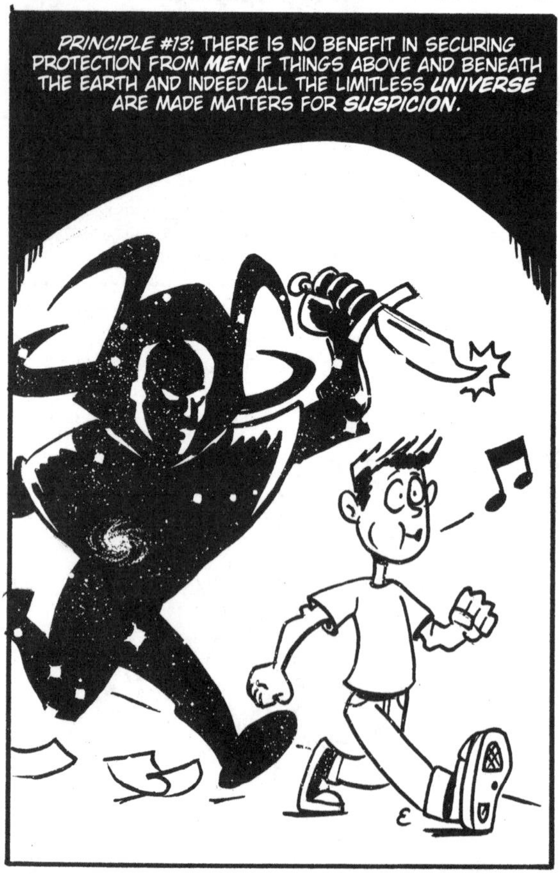
PRINCIPLE #13: THERE IS NO BENEFIT IN SECURING PROTECTION FROM MEN IF THINGS ABOVE AND BENEATH THE EARTH AND INDEED ALL THE LIMITLESS UNIVERSE ARE MADE MATTERS FOR SUSPICION.

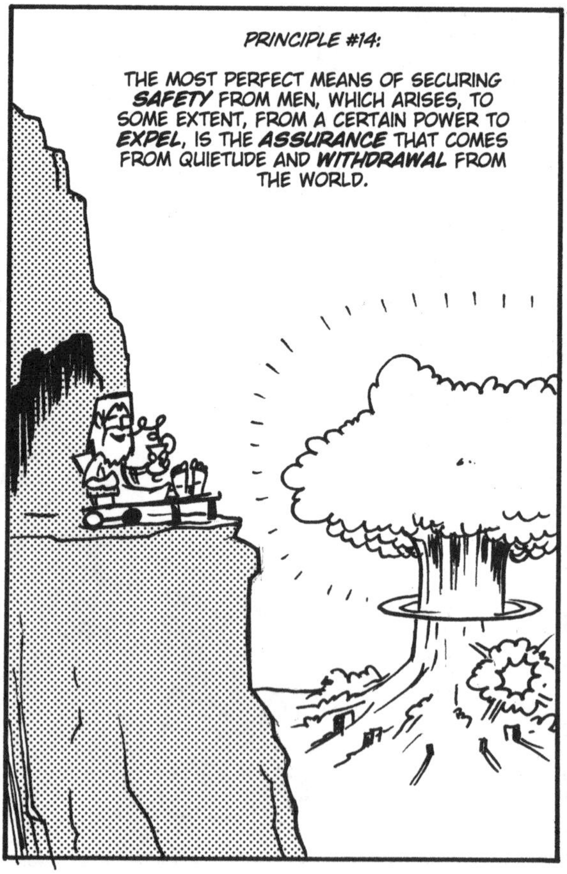
PRINCIPLE #14:
THE MOST PERFECT MEANS OF SECURING SAFETY FROM MEN, WHICH ARISES, TO SOME EXTENT, FROM A CERTAIN POWER TO EXPEL, IS THE ASSURANCE THAT COMES FROM QUIETUDE AND WITHDRAWAL FROM THE WORLD.

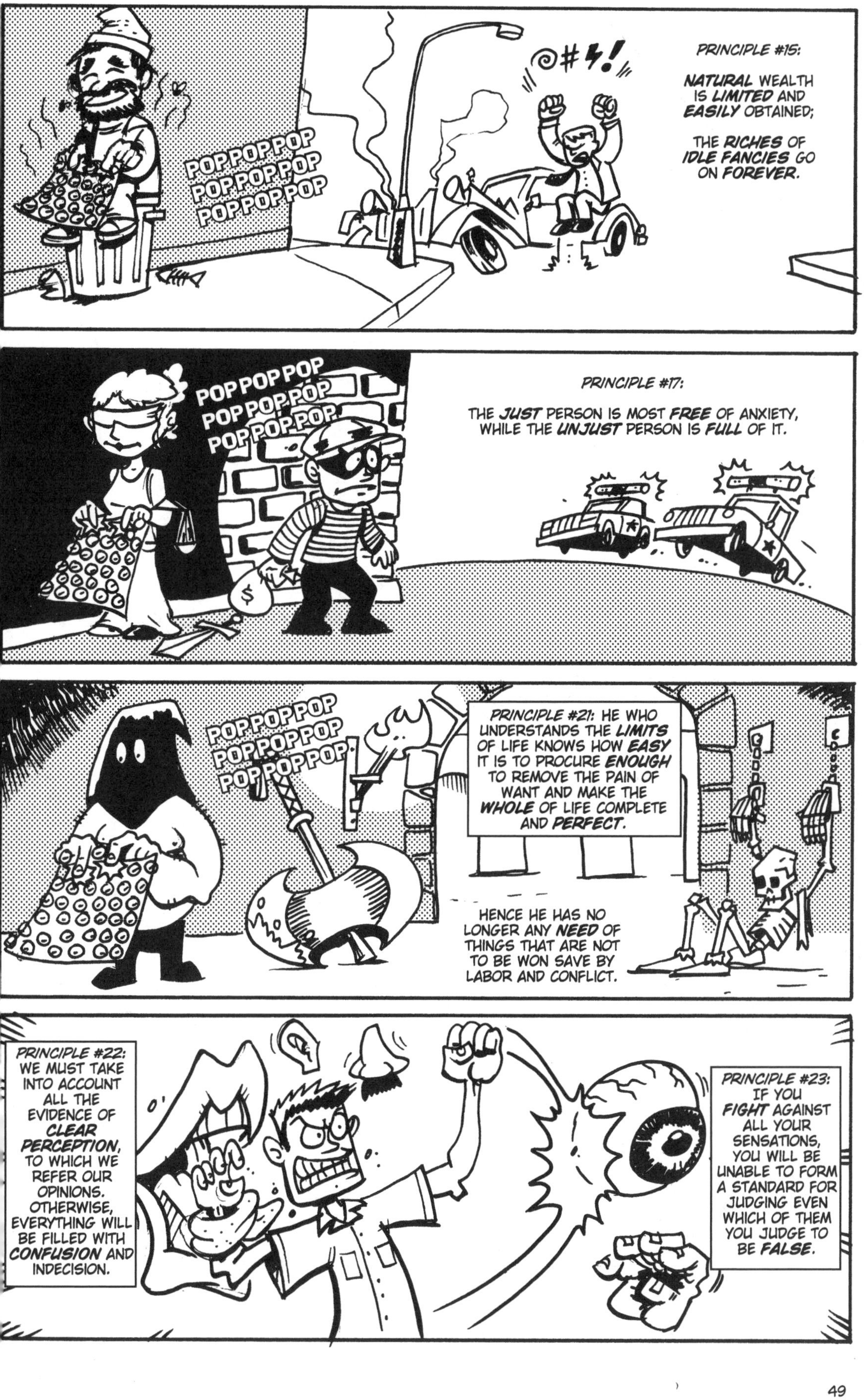

POPPOPPOP
POPPOPPOP
POPPOPPOP
@#ϟ!
PRINCIPLE #15:
NATURAL WEALTH IS LIMITED AND EASILY OBTAINED;
THE RICHES OF IDLE FANCIES GO ON FOREVER.
POPPOPPOP
POPPOPPOP
POPPOPPOP
PRINCIPLE #17:
THE JUST PERSON IS MOST FREE OF ANXIETY, WHILE THE UNJUST PERSON IS FULL OF IT.
$
POPPOPPOP
POPPOPPOP
POPPOPPOP
PRINCIPLE #21: HE WHO UNDERSTANDS THE LIMITS OF LIFE KNOWS HOW EASY IT IS TO PROCURE ENOUGH TO REMOVE THE PAIN OF WANT AND MAKE THE WHOLE OF LIFE COMPLETE AND PERFECT.
HENCE HE HAS NO LONGER ANY NEED OF THINGS THAT ARE NOT TO BE WON SAVE BY LABOR AND CONFLICT.
PRINCIPLE #22: WE MUST TAKE INTO ACCOUNT ALL THE EVIDENCE OF CLEAR PERCEPTION, TO WHICH WE REFER OUR OPINIONS. OTHERWISE, EVERYTHING WILL BE FILLED WITH CONFUSION AND INDECISION.
PRINCIPLE #23: IF YOU FIGHT AGAINST ALL YOUR SENSATIONS, YOU WILL BE UNABLE TO FORM A STANDARD FOR JUDGING EVEN WHICH OF THEM YOU JUDGE TO BE FALSE.

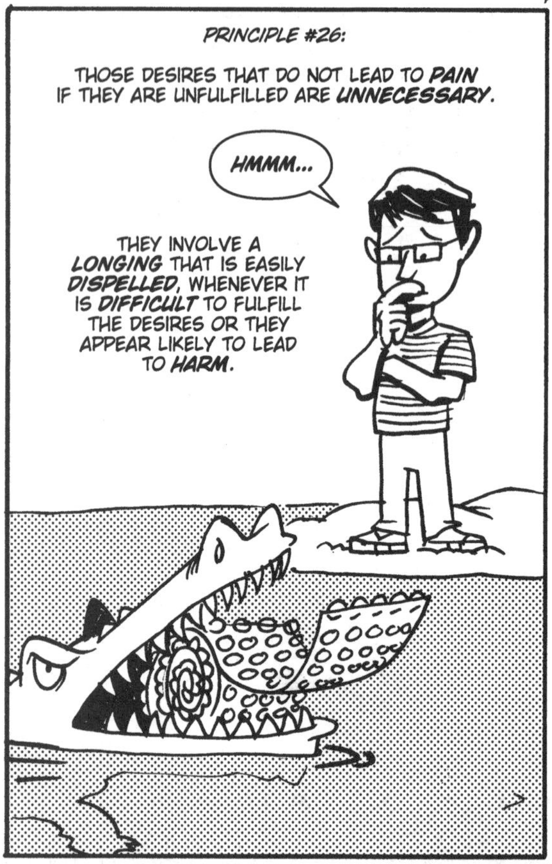
PRINCIPLE #26:
THOSE DESIRES THAT DO NOT LEAD TO PAIN IF THEY ARE UNFULFILLED ARE UNNECESSARY.
HMMM...
THEY INVOLVE A LONGING THAT IS EASILY DISPELLED, WHENEVER IT IS DIFFICULT TO FULFILL THE DESIRES OR THEY APPEAR LIKELY TO LEAD TO HARM.

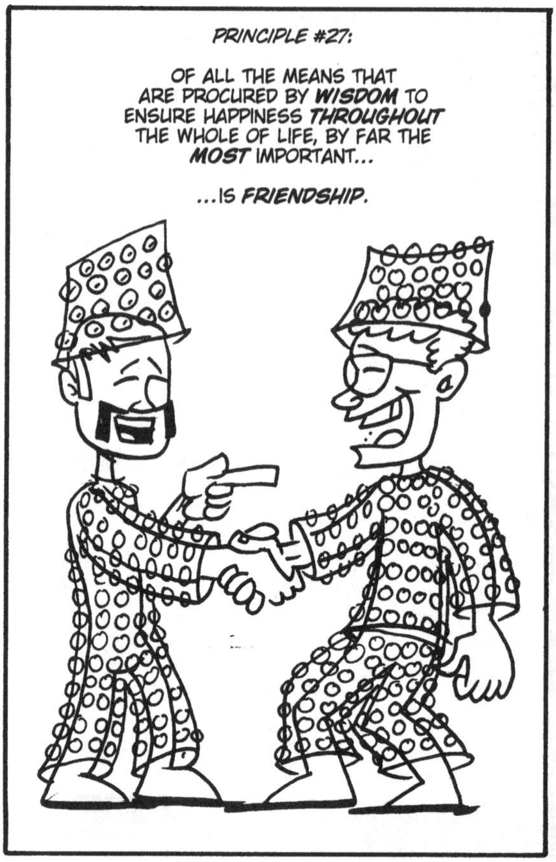
PRINCIPLE #27:
OF ALL THE MEANS THAT ARE PROCURED BY WISDOM TO ENSURE HAPPINESS THROUGHOUT THE WHOLE OF LIFE, BY FAR THE MOST IMPORTANT...
...IS FRIENDSHIP.

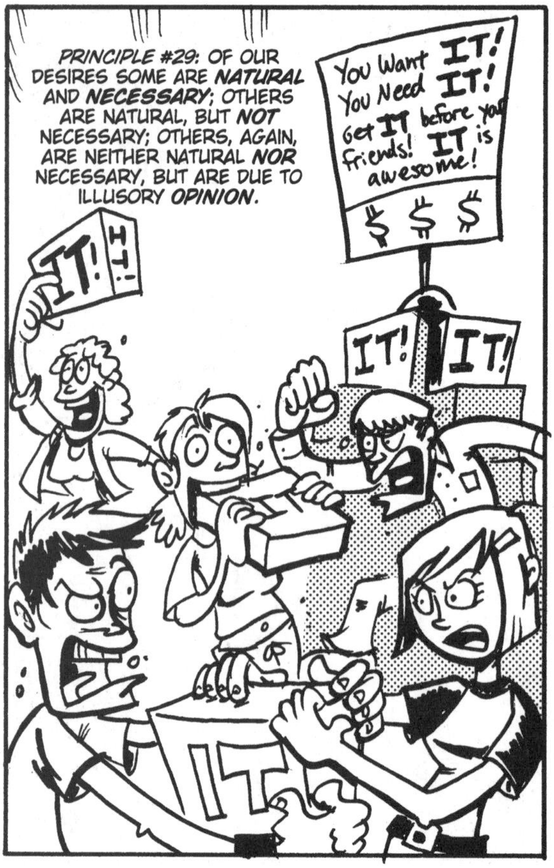
PRINCIPLE #29: OF OUR DESIRES SOME ARE NATURAL AND NECESSARY; OTHERS ARE NATURAL, BUT NOT NECESSARY; OTHERS, AGAIN, ARE NEITHER NATURAL NOR NECESSARY, BUT ARE DUE TO ILLUSORY OPINION.
You Want IT! You Need IT! Get IT before your friends! IT is awesome!
$ $ $
IT! IT!
IT! IT!
IT

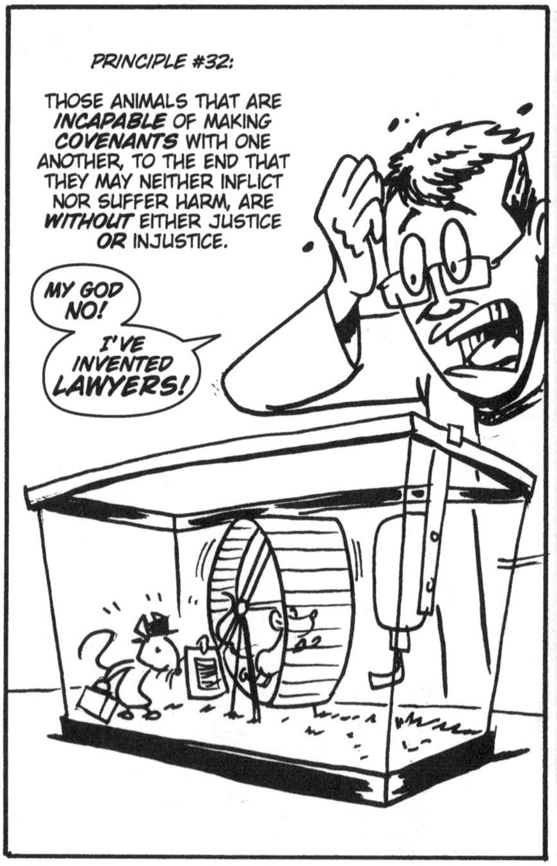
PRINCIPLE #32:
THOSE ANIMALS THAT ARE INCAPABLE OF MAKING COVENANTS WITH ONE ANOTHER, TO THE END THAT THEY MAY NEITHER INFLICT NOR SUFFER HARM, ARE WITHOUT EITHER JUSTICE OR INJUSTICE.
MY GOD NO!
I'VE INVENTED LAWYERS!

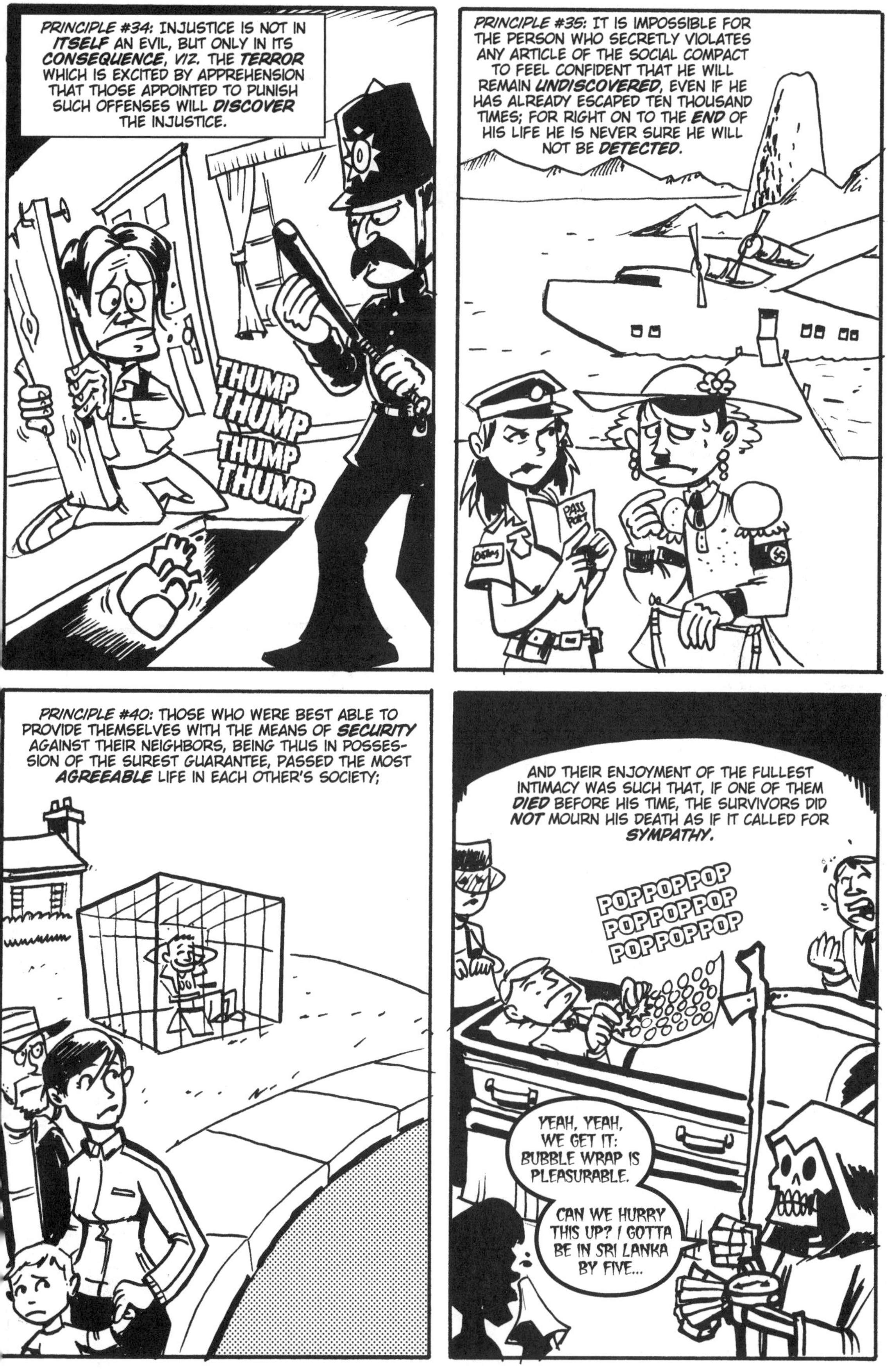
PRINCIPLE #34: INJUSTICE IS NOT IN ITSELF AN EVIL, BUT ONLY IN ITS CONSEQUENCE, VIZ. THE TERROR WHICH IS EXCITED BY APPREHENSION THAT THOSE APPOINTED TO PUNISH SUCH OFFENSES WILL DISCOVER THE INJUSTICE.
THUMP THUMP THUMP THUMP
PRINCIPLE #35: IT IS IMPOSSIBLE FOR THE PERSON WHO SECRETLY VIOLATES ANY ARTICLE OF THE SOCIAL COMPACT TO FEEL CONFIDENT THAT HE WILL REMAIN UNDISCOVERED, EVEN IF HE HAS ALREADY ESCAPED TEN THOUSAND TIMES; FOR RIGHT ON TO THE END OF HIS LIFE HE IS NEVER SURE HE WILL NOT BE DETECTED.
PRINCIPLE #40: THOSE WHO WERE BEST ABLE TO PROVIDE THEMSELVES WITH THE MEANS OF SECURITY AGAINST THEIR NEIGHBORS, BEING THUS IN POSSESSION OF THE SUREST GUARANTEE, PASSED THE MOST AGREEABLE LIFE IN EACH OTHER'S SOCIETY;
AND THEIR ENJOYMENT OF THE FULLEST INTIMACY WAS SUCH THAT, IF ONE OF THEM DIED BEFORE HIS TIME, THE SURVIVORS DID NOT MOURN HIS DEATH AS IF IT CALLED FOR SYMPATHY.
POPPOPPOP POPPOPPOP POPPOPPOP
YEAH, YEAH, WE GET IT: BUBBLE WRAP IS PLEASURABLE.
CAN WE HURRY THIS UP? I GOTTA BE IN SRI LANKA BY FIVE...

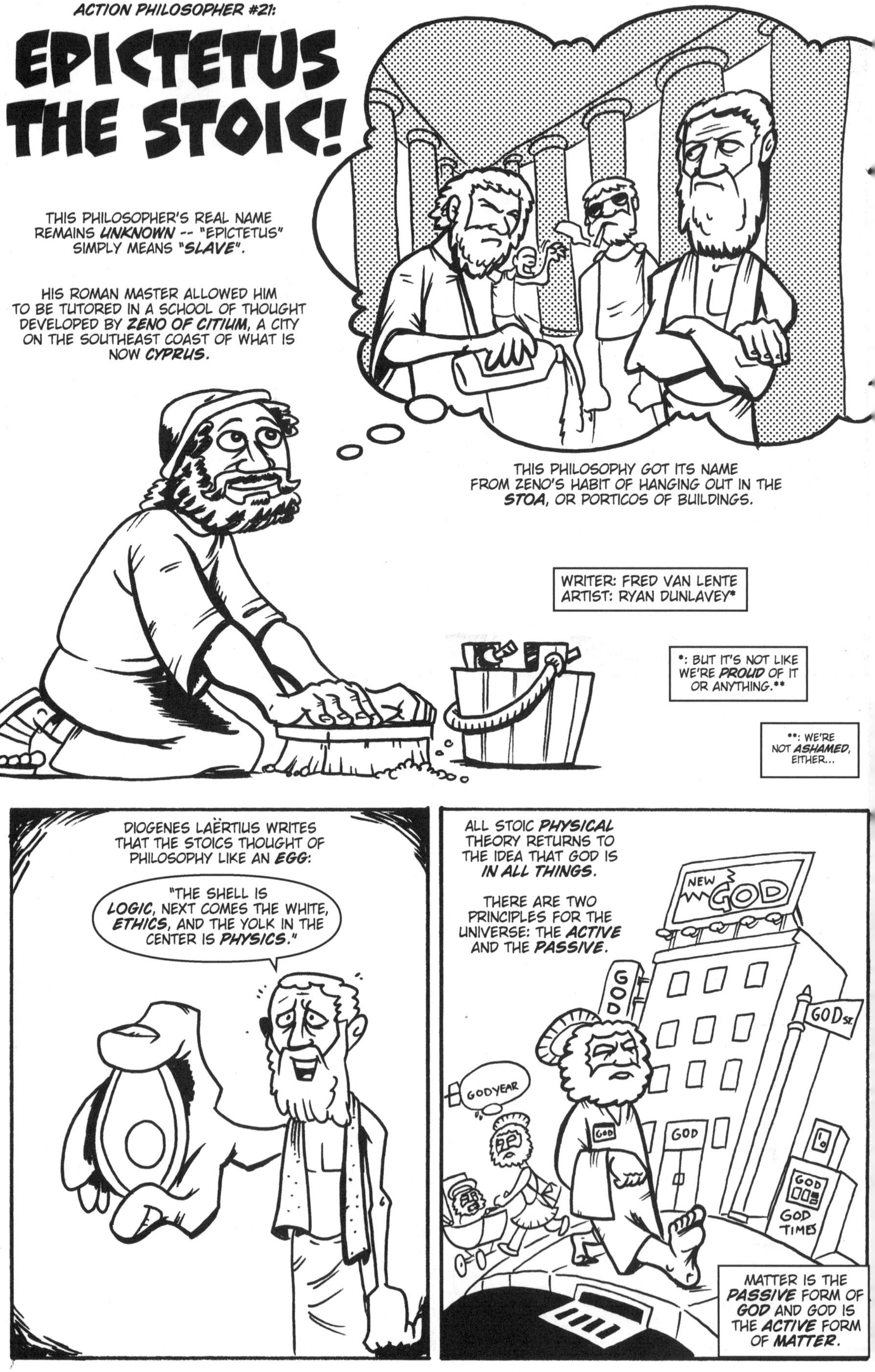
ACTION PHILOSOPHER #21:
EPICTETUS THE STOIC!
THIS PHILOSOPHER'S REAL NAME REMAINS UNKNOWN -- "EPICTETUS" SIMPLY MEANS "SLAVE".
HIS ROMAN MASTER ALLOWED HIM TO BE TUTORED IN A SCHOOL OF THOUGHT DEVELOPED BY ZENO OF CITIUM, A CITY ON THE SOUTHEAST COAST OF WHAT IS NOW CYPRUS.
THIS PHILOSOPHY GOT ITS NAME FROM ZENO'S HABIT OF HANGING OUT IN THE STOA, OR PORTICOS OF BUILDINGS.
WRITER: FRED VAN LENTE
ARTIST: RYAN DUNLAVEY*
*: BUT IT'S NOT LIKE WE'RE PROUD OF IT OR ANYTHING.**
**: WE'RE NOT ASHAMED, EITHER...
DIOGENES LAËRTIUS WRITES THAT THE STOICS THOUGHT OF PHILOSOPHY LIKE AN EGG:
"THE SHELL IS LOGIC, NEXT COMES THE WHITE, ETHICS, AND THE YOLK IN THE CENTER IS PHYSICS."
ALL STOIC PHYSICAL THEORY RETURNS TO THE IDEA THAT GOD IS IN ALL THINGS.
THERE ARE TWO PRINCIPLES FOR THE UNIVERSE: THE ACTIVE AND THE PASSIVE.
NEW GOD
GOD
GOD St.
GODYEAR
GOD
GOD
GOD
GOD TIMES
MATTER IS THE PASSIVE FORM OF GOD AND GOD IS THE ACTIVE FORM OF MATTER.

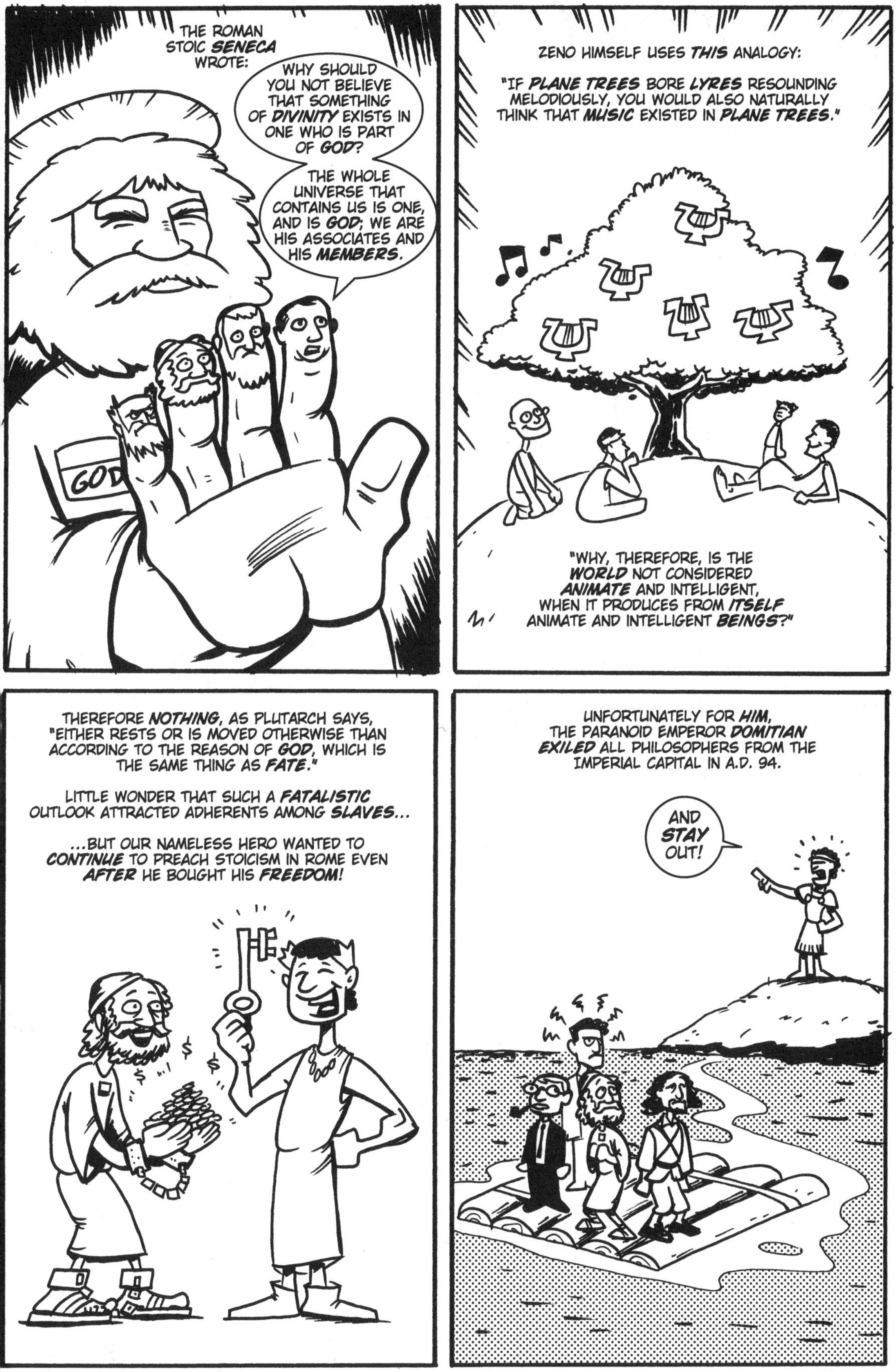

THE ROMAN STOIC **SENECA** WROTE:
WHY SHOULD YOU NOT BELIEVE THAT SOMETHING OF **DIVINITY** EXISTS IN ONE WHO IS PART OF **GOD**?
THE WHOLE UNIVERSE THAT CONTAINS US IS ONE, AND IS **GOD**; WE ARE HIS ASSOCIATES AND HIS **MEMBERS**.
ZENO HIMSELF USES **THIS** ANALOGY:
"IF **PLANE TREES** BORE **LYRES** RESOUNDING MELODIOUSLY, YOU WOULD ALSO NATURALLY THINK THAT **MUSIC** EXISTED IN **PLANE TREES**."
"WHY, THEREFORE, IS THE **WORLD** NOT CONSIDERED **ANIMATE** AND INTELLIGENT, WHEN IT PRODUCES FROM **ITSELF** ANIMATE AND INTELLIGENT **BEINGS**?"
THEREFORE **NOTHING**, AS PLUTARCH SAYS, "EITHER RESTS OR IS MOVED OTHERWISE THAN ACCORDING TO THE REASON OF **GOD**, WHICH IS THE SAME THING AS **FATE**."
LITTLE WONDER THAT SUCH A **FATALISTIC** OUTLOOK ATTRACTED ADHERENTS AMONG **SLAVES**...
...BUT OUR NAMELESS HERO WANTED TO **CONTINUE** TO PREACH STOICISM IN ROME EVEN **AFTER** HE BOUGHT HIS **FREEDOM**!
UNFORTUNATELY FOR **HIM**, THE PARANOID EMPEROR **DOMITIAN EXILED** ALL PHILOSOPHERS FROM THE IMPERIAL CAPITAL IN A.D. 94.
AND **STAY** OUT!

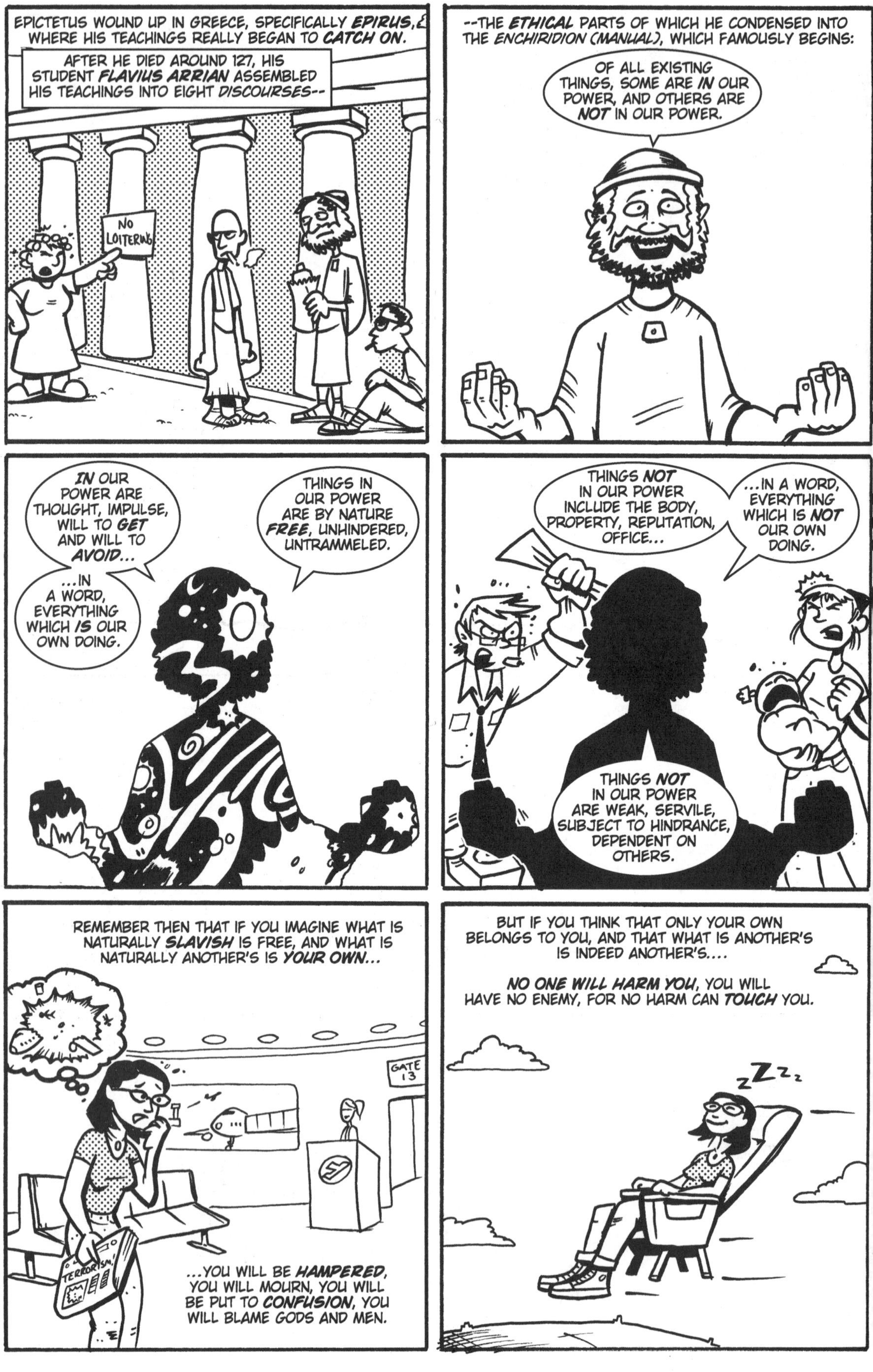
EPICTETUS WOUND UP IN GREECE, SPECIFICALLY EPIRUS, & WHERE HIS TEACHINGS REALLY BEGAN TO CATCH ON.
AFTER HE DIED AROUND 127, HIS STUDENT FLAVIUS ARRIAN ASSEMBLED HIS TEACHINGS INTO EIGHT DISCOURSES--
NO LOITERING
--THE ETHICAL PARTS OF WHICH HE CONDENSED INTO THE ENCHIRIDION (MANUAL), WHICH FAMOUSLY BEGINS:
OF ALL EXISTING THINGS, SOME ARE IN OUR POWER, AND OTHERS ARE NOT IN OUR POWER.
IN OUR POWER ARE THOUGHT, IMPULSE, WILL TO GET AND WILL TO AVOID...
...IN A WORD, EVERYTHING WHICH IS OUR OWN DOING.
THINGS IN OUR POWER ARE BY NATURE FREE, UNHINDERED, UNTRAMMELED.
THINGS NOT IN OUR POWER INCLUDE THE BODY, PROPERTY, REPUTATION, OFFICE...
...IN A WORD, EVERYTHING WHICH IS NOT OUR OWN DOING.
THINGS NOT IN OUR POWER ARE WEAK, SERVILE, SUBJECT TO HINDRANCE, DEPENDENT ON OTHERS.
REMEMBER THEN THAT IF YOU IMAGINE WHAT IS NATURALLY SLAVISH IS FREE, AND WHAT IS NATURALLY ANOTHER'S IS YOUR OWN...
GATE 13
TERRORISM
...YOU WILL BE HAMPERED, YOU WILL MOURN, YOU WILL BE PUT TO CONFUSION, YOU WILL BLAME GODS AND MEN.
BUT IF YOU THINK THAT ONLY YOUR OWN BELONGS TO YOU, AND THAT WHAT IS ANOTHER'S IS INDEED ANOTHER'S....
NO ONE WILL HARM YOU, YOU WILL HAVE NO ENEMY, FOR NO HARM CAN TOUCH YOU.
ZZZz

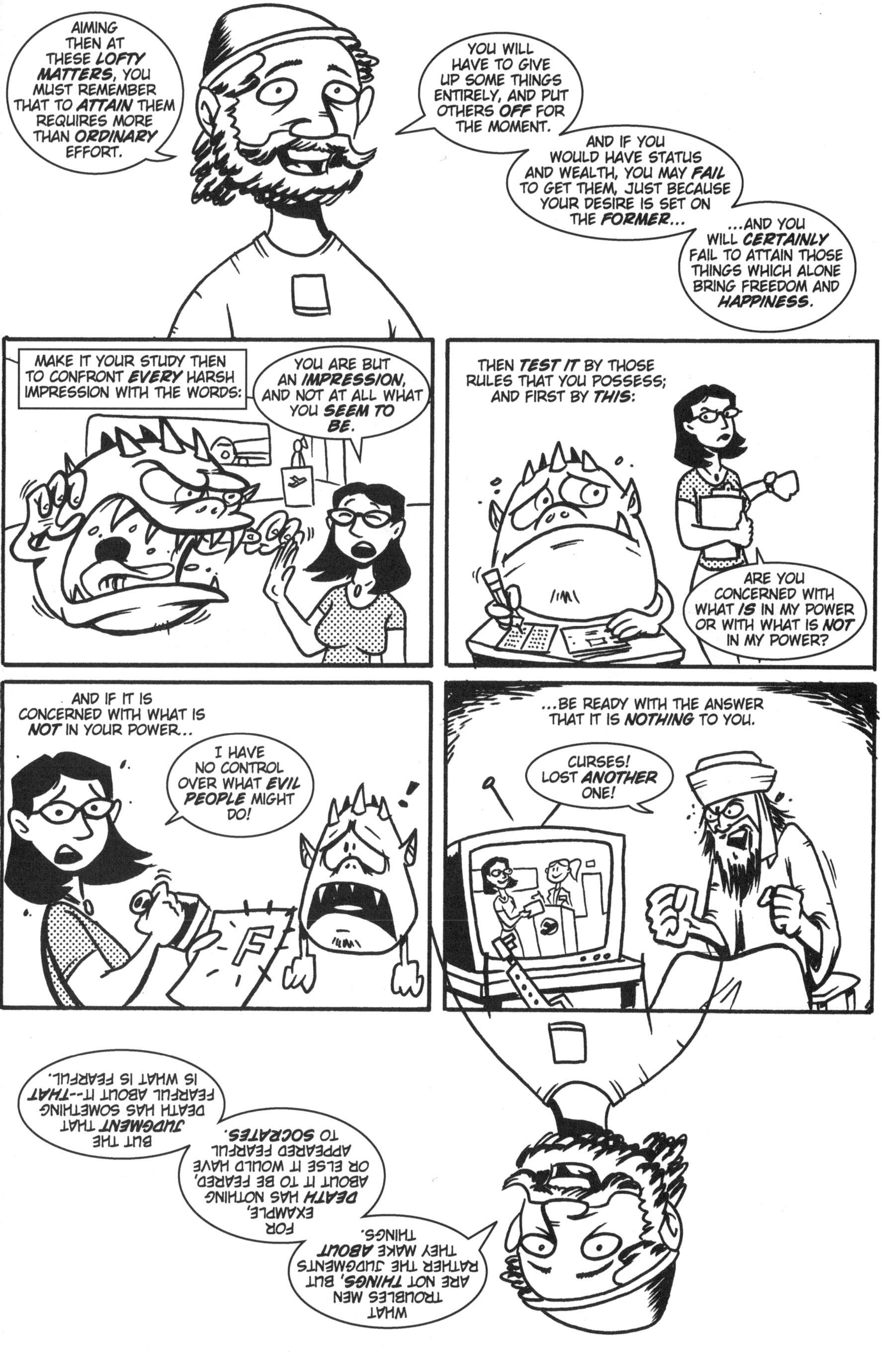

AIMING THEN AT THESE LOFTY MATTERS, YOU MUST REMEMBER THAT TO ATTAIN THEM REQUIRES MORE THAN ORDINARY EFFORT.
YOU WILL HAVE TO GIVE UP SOME THINGS ENTIRELY, AND PUT OTHERS OFF FOR THE MOMENT.
AND IF YOU WOULD HAVE STATUS AND WEALTH, YOU MAY FAIL TO GET THEM, JUST BECAUSE YOUR DESIRE IS SET ON THE FORMER...
...AND YOU WILL CERTAINLY FAIL TO ATTAIN THOSE THINGS WHICH ALONE BRING FREEDOM AND HAPPINESS.
MAKE IT YOUR STUDY THEN TO CONFRONT EVERY HARSH IMPRESSION WITH THE WORDS:
YOU ARE BUT AN IMPRESSION, AND NOT AT ALL WHAT YOU SEEM TO BE.
THEN TEST IT BY THOSE RULES THAT YOU POSSESS; AND FIRST BY THIS:
ARE YOU CONCERNED WITH WHAT IS IN MY POWER OR WITH WHAT IS NOT IN MY POWER?
AND IF IT IS CONCERNED WITH WHAT IS NOT IN YOUR POWER...
I HAVE NO CONTROL OVER WHAT EVIL PEOPLE MIGHT DO!
F
...BE READY WITH THE ANSWER THAT IT IS NOTHING TO YOU.
CURSES! LOST ANOTHER ONE!
WHAT TROUBLES MEN ARE NOT THINGS, BUT RATHER THE JUDGMENTS THEY MAKE ABOUT THINGS.
FOR EXAMPLE, DEATH HAS NOTHING ABOUT IT TO BE FEARED, OR ELSE IT WOULD HAVE APPEARED FEARFUL TO SOCRATES.
BUT THE JUDGMENT THAT DEATH HAS SOMETHING FEARFUL ABOUT IT--THAT IS WHAT IS FEARFUL.

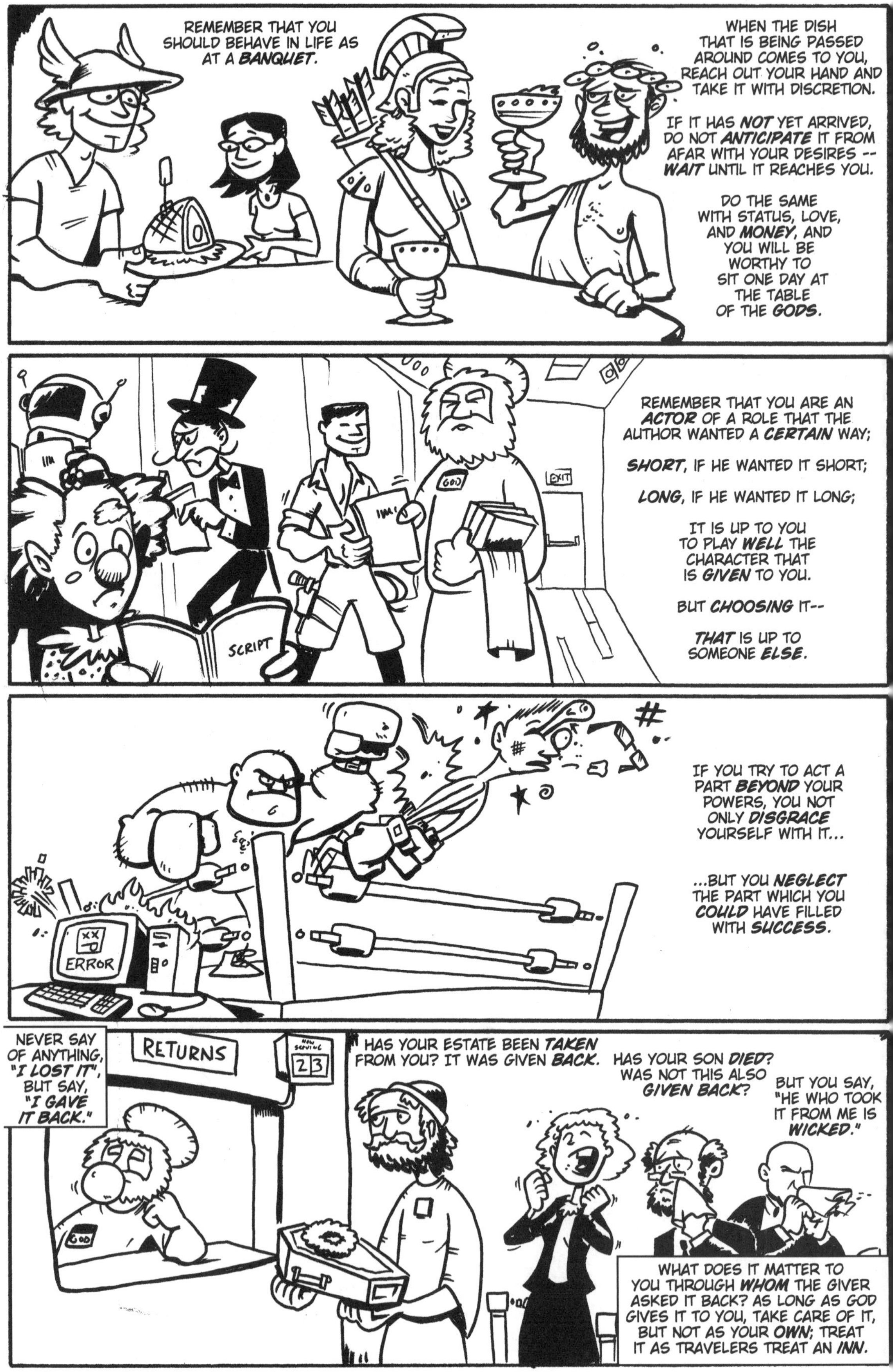
REMEMBER THAT YOU SHOULD BEHAVE IN LIFE AS AT A BANQUET.
WHEN THE DISH THAT IS BEING PASSED AROUND COMES TO YOU, REACH OUT YOUR HAND AND TAKE IT WITH DISCRETION.
IF IT HAS NOT YET ARRIVED, DO NOT ANTICIPATE IT FROM AFAR WITH YOUR DESIRES -- WAIT UNTIL IT REACHES YOU.
DO THE SAME WITH STATUS, LOVE, AND MONEY, AND YOU WILL BE WORTHY TO SIT ONE DAY AT THE TABLE OF THE GODS.
REMEMBER THAT YOU ARE AN ACTOR OF A ROLE THAT THE AUTHOR WANTED A CERTAIN WAY;
SHORT, IF HE WANTED IT SHORT;
LONG, IF HE WANTED IT LONG;
IT IS UP TO YOU TO PLAY WELL THE CHARACTER THAT IS GIVEN TO YOU.
BUT CHOOSING IT--
THAT IS UP TO SOMEONE ELSE.
GOD
EXIT
SCRIPT
IF YOU TRY TO ACT A PART BEYOND YOUR POWERS, YOU NOT ONLY DISGRACE YOURSELF WITH IT...
...BUT YOU NEGLECT THE PART WHICH YOU COULD HAVE FILLED WITH SUCCESS.
ERROR
NEVER SAY OF ANYTHING, "I LOST IT", BUT SAY, "I GAVE IT BACK."
RETURNS
NOW SERVING
23
GOD
HAS YOUR ESTATE BEEN TAKEN FROM YOU? IT WAS GIVEN BACK.
HAS YOUR SON DIED? WAS NOT THIS ALSO GIVEN BACK?
BUT YOU SAY, "HE WHO TOOK IT FROM ME IS WICKED."
WHAT DOES IT MATTER TO YOU THROUGH WHOM THE GIVER ASKED IT BACK? AS LONG AS GOD GIVES IT TO YOU, TAKE CARE OF IT, BUT NOT AS YOUR OWN; TREAT IT AS TRAVELERS TREAT AN INN.

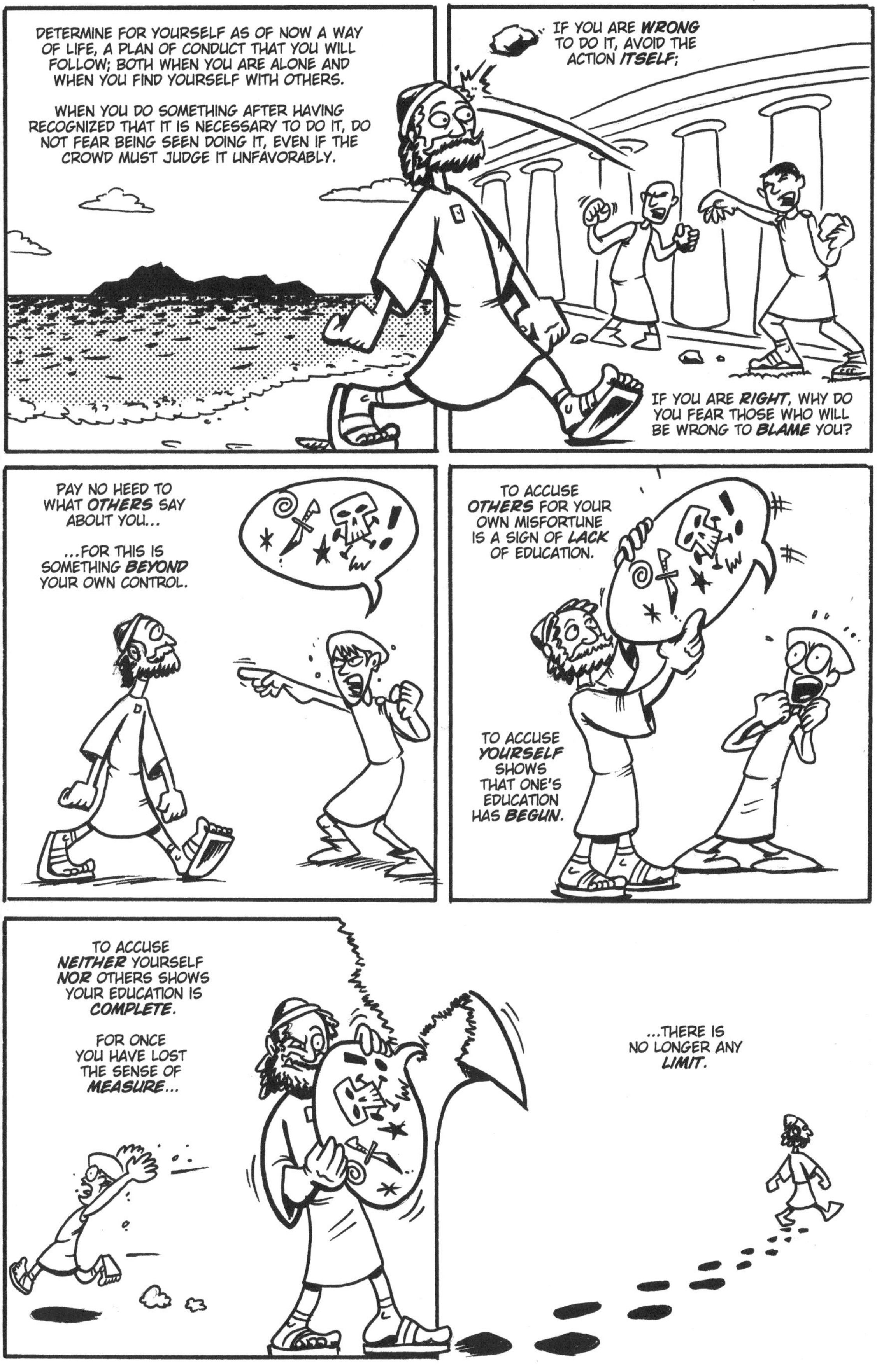
DETERMINE FOR YOURSELF AS OF NOW A WAY OF LIFE, A PLAN OF CONDUCT THAT YOU WILL FOLLOW; BOTH WHEN YOU ARE ALONE AND WHEN YOU FIND YOURSELF WITH OTHERS.
WHEN YOU DO SOMETHING AFTER HAVING RECOGNIZED THAT IT IS NECESSARY TO DO IT, DO NOT FEAR BEING SEEN DOING IT, EVEN IF THE CROWD MUST JUDGE IT UNFAVORABLY.
IF YOU ARE WRONG TO DO IT, AVOID THE ACTION ITSELF;
IF YOU ARE RIGHT, WHY DO YOU FEAR THOSE WHO WILL BE WRONG TO BLAME YOU?
PAY NO HEED TO WHAT OTHERS SAY ABOUT YOU...
...FOR THIS IS SOMETHING BEYOND YOUR OWN CONTROL.
TO ACCUSE OTHERS FOR YOUR OWN MISFORTUNE IS A SIGN OF LACK OF EDUCATION.
TO ACCUSE YOURSELF SHOWS THAT ONE'S EDUCATION HAS BEGUN.
TO ACCUSE NEITHER YOURSELF NOR OTHERS SHOWS YOUR EDUCATION IS COMPLETE.
FOR ONCE YOU HAVE LOST THE SENSE OF MEASURE...
...THERE IS NO LONGER ANY LIMIT.

PART TWO:

THAT OLD-TIME RELIGION

(MEDIEVAL PHILOSOPHY)

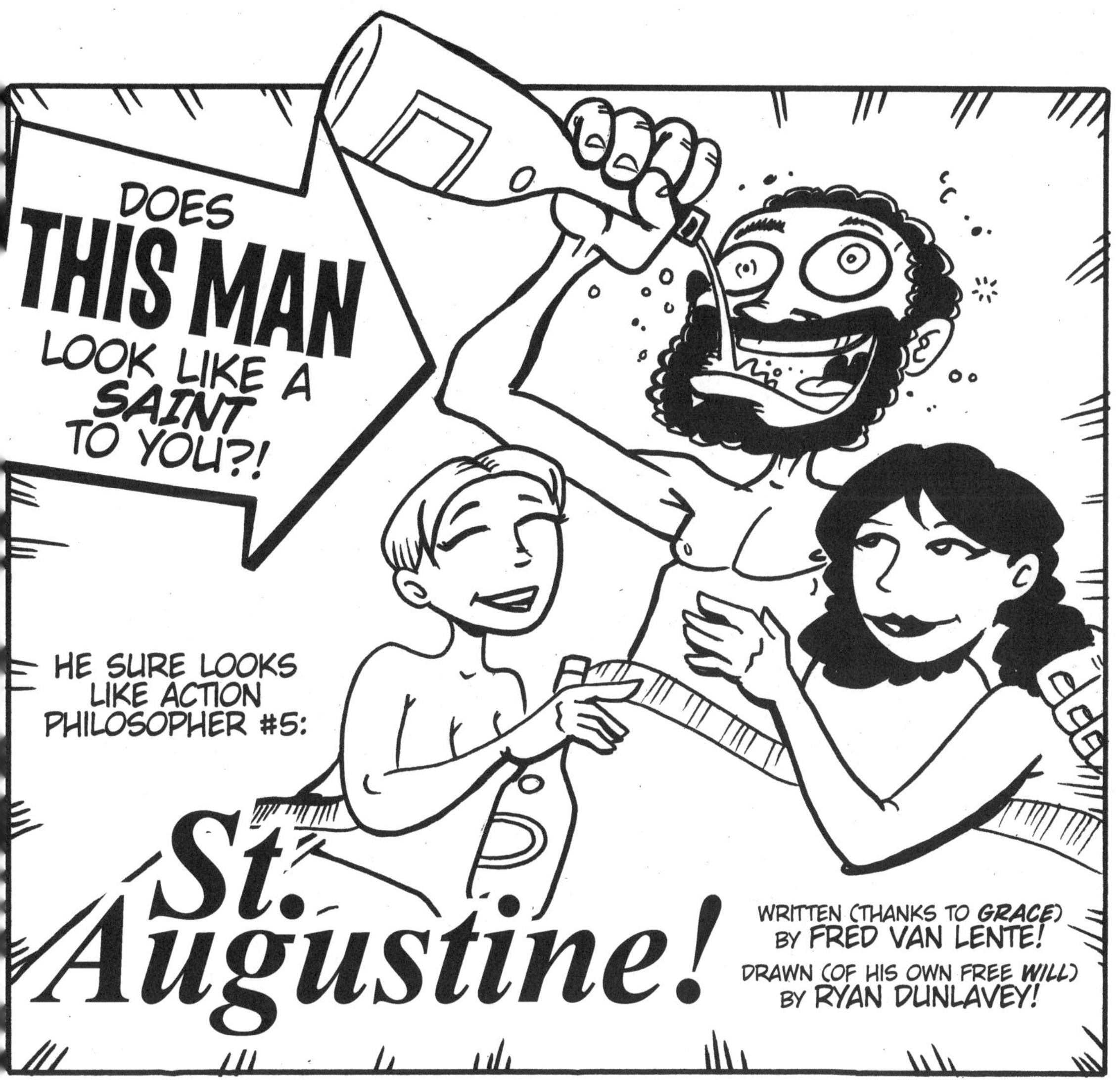
DOES THIS MAN LOOK LIKE A SAINT TO YOU?!
HE SURE LOOKS LIKE ACTION PHILOSOPHER #5:
St. Augustine!
WRITTEN (THANKS TO GRACE) BY FRED VAN LENTE!
DRAWN (OF HIS OWN FREE WILL) BY RYAN DUNLAVEY!

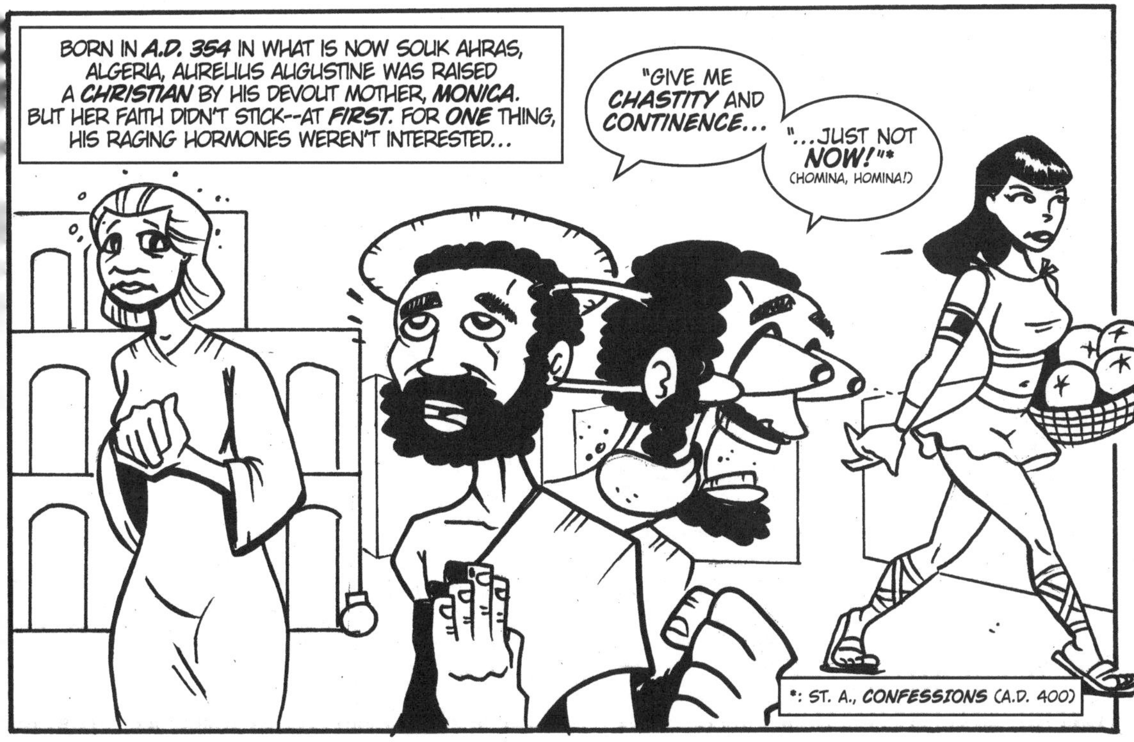
BORN IN A.D. 354 IN WHAT IS NOW SOUK AHRAS, ALGERIA, AURELIUS AUGUSTINE WAS RAISED A CHRISTIAN BY HIS DEVOUT MOTHER, MONICA. BUT HER FAITH DIDN'T STICK--AT FIRST. FOR ONE THING, HIS RAGING HORMONES WEREN'T INTERESTED...
"GIVE ME CHASTITY AND CONTINENCE...
"...JUST NOT NOW!"*
(HOMINA, HOMINA!)
*: ST. A., CONFESSIONS (A.D. 400)

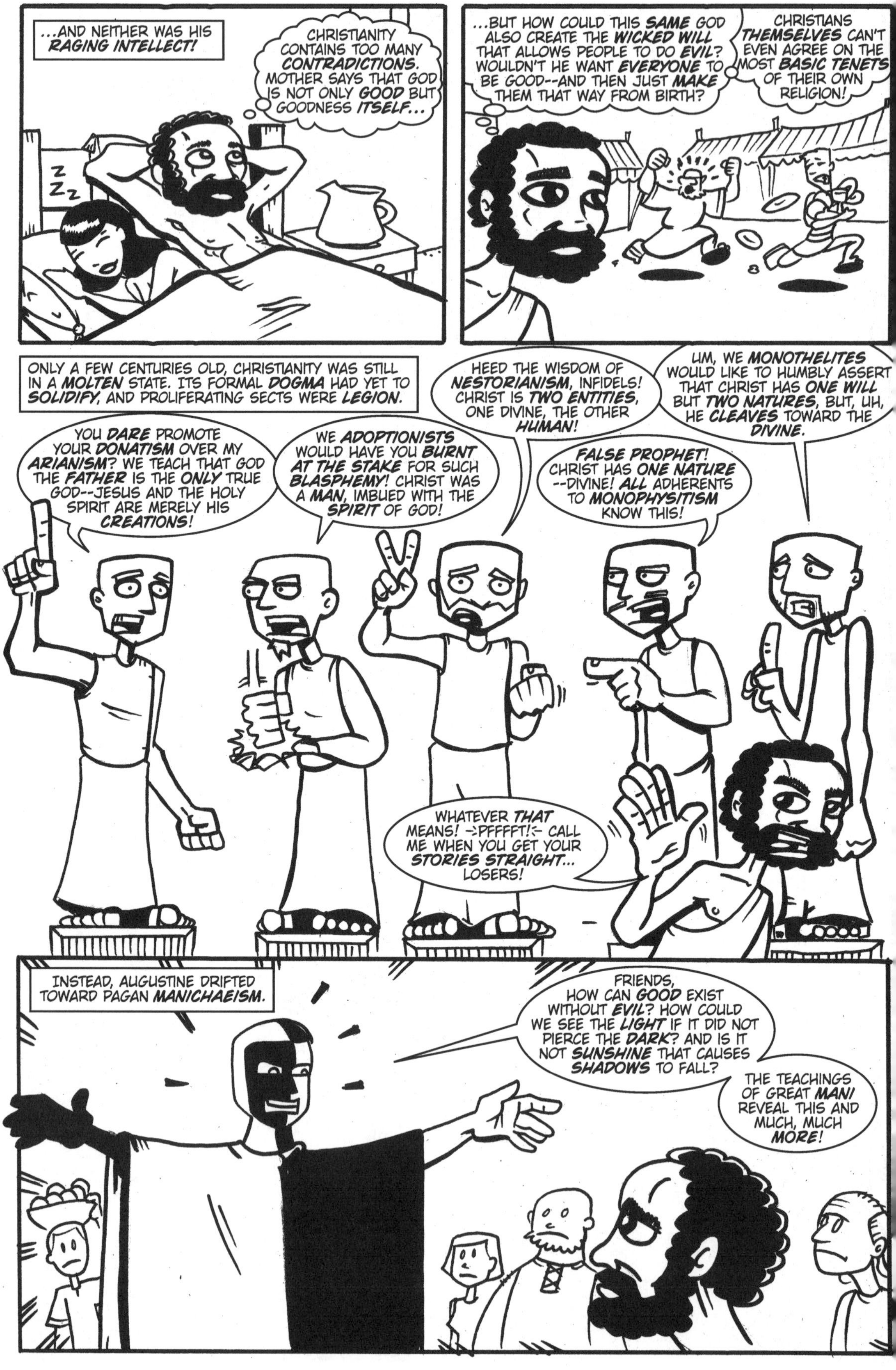

...AND NEITHER WAS HIS RAGING INTELLECT!
CHRISTIANITY CONTAINS TOO MANY CONTRADICTIONS. MOTHER SAYS THAT GOD IS NOT ONLY GOOD BUT GOODNESS ITSELF...
Z Z Z
...BUT HOW COULD THIS SAME GOD ALSO CREATE THE WICKED WILL THAT ALLOWS PEOPLE TO DO EVIL? WOULDN'T HE WANT EVERYONE TO BE GOOD--AND THEN JUST MAKE THEM THAT WAY FROM BIRTH?
CHRISTIANS THEMSELVES CAN'T EVEN AGREE ON THE MOST BASIC TENETS OF THEIR OWN RELIGION!
ONLY A FEW CENTURIES OLD, CHRISTIANITY WAS STILL IN A MOLTEN STATE. ITS FORMAL DOGMA HAD YET TO SOLIDIFY, AND PROLIFERATING SECTS WERE LEGION.
YOU DARE PROMOTE YOUR DONATISM OVER MY ARIANISM? WE TEACH THAT GOD THE FATHER IS THE ONLY TRUE GOD--JESUS AND THE HOLY SPIRIT ARE MERELY HIS CREATIONS!
WE ADOPTIONISTS WOULD HAVE YOU BURNT AT THE STAKE FOR SUCH BLASPHEMY! CHRIST WAS A MAN, IMBUED WITH THE SPIRIT OF GOD!
HEED THE WISDOM OF NESTORIANISM, INFIDELS! CHRIST IS TWO ENTITIES, ONE DIVINE, THE OTHER HUMAN!
FALSE PROPHET! CHRIST HAS ONE NATURE --DIVINE! ALL ADHERENTS TO MONOPHYSITISM KNOW THIS!
UM, WE MONOTHELITES WOULD LIKE TO HUMBLY ASSERT THAT CHRIST HAS ONE WILL BUT TWO NATURES, BUT, UH, HE CLEAVES TOWARD THE DIVINE.
WHATEVER THAT MEANS! →PFFFFT!← CALL ME WHEN YOU GET YOUR STORIES STRAIGHT... LOSERS!
INSTEAD, AUGUSTINE DRIFTED TOWARD PAGAN MANICHAEISM.
FRIENDS, HOW CAN GOOD EXIST WITHOUT EVIL? HOW COULD WE SEE THE LIGHT IF IT DID NOT PIERCE THE DARK? AND IS IT NOT SUNSHINE THAT CAUSES SHADOWS TO FALL?
THE TEACHINGS OF GREAT MANI REVEAL THIS AND MUCH, MUCH MORE!

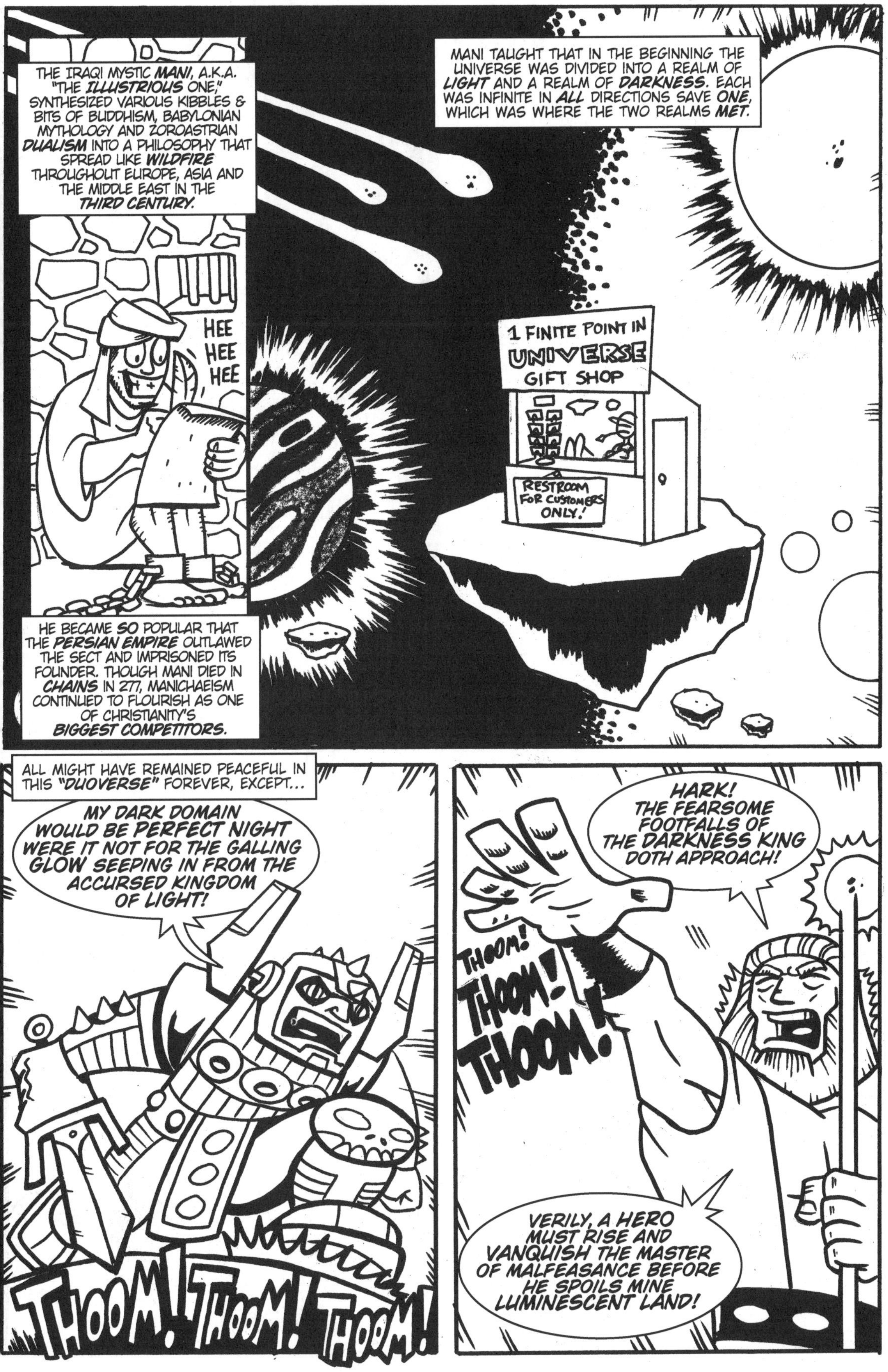
THE IRAQI MYSTIC MANI, A.K.A. "THE ILLUSTRIOUS ONE," SYNTHESIZED VARIOUS KIBBLES & BITS OF BUDDHISM, BABYLONIAN MYTHOLOGY AND ZOROASTRIAN DUALISM INTO A PHILOSOPHY THAT SPREAD LIKE WILDFIRE THROUGHOUT EUROPE, ASIA AND THE MIDDLE EAST IN THE THIRD CENTURY.
HEE HEE HEE
HE BECAME SO POPULAR THAT THE PERSIAN EMPIRE OUTLAWED THE SECT AND IMPRISONED ITS FOUNDER. THOUGH MANI DIED IN CHAINS IN 277, MANICHAEISM CONTINUED TO FLOURISH AS ONE OF CHRISTIANITY'S BIGGEST COMPETITORS.
MANI TAUGHT THAT IN THE BEGINNING THE UNIVERSE WAS DIVIDED INTO A REALM OF LIGHT AND A REALM OF DARKNESS. EACH WAS INFINITE IN ALL DIRECTIONS SAVE ONE, WHICH WAS WHERE THE TWO REALMS MET.
1 FINITE POINT IN UNIVERSE GIFT SHOP
RESTROOM FOR CUSTOMERS ONLY!
ALL MIGHT HAVE REMAINED PEACEFUL IN THIS "DUOVERSE" FOREVER, EXCEPT...
MY DARK DOMAIN WOULD BE PERFECT NIGHT WERE IT NOT FOR THE GALLING GLOW SEEPING IN FROM THE ACCURSED KINGDOM OF LIGHT!
THOOM! THOOM! THOOM!
HARK! THE FEARSOME FOOTFALLS OF THE DARKNESS KING DOTH APPROACH!
THOOM! THOOM! THOOM!
VERILY, A HERO MUST RISE AND VANQUISH THE MASTER OF MALFEASANCE BEFORE HE SPOILS MINE LUMINESCENT LAND!

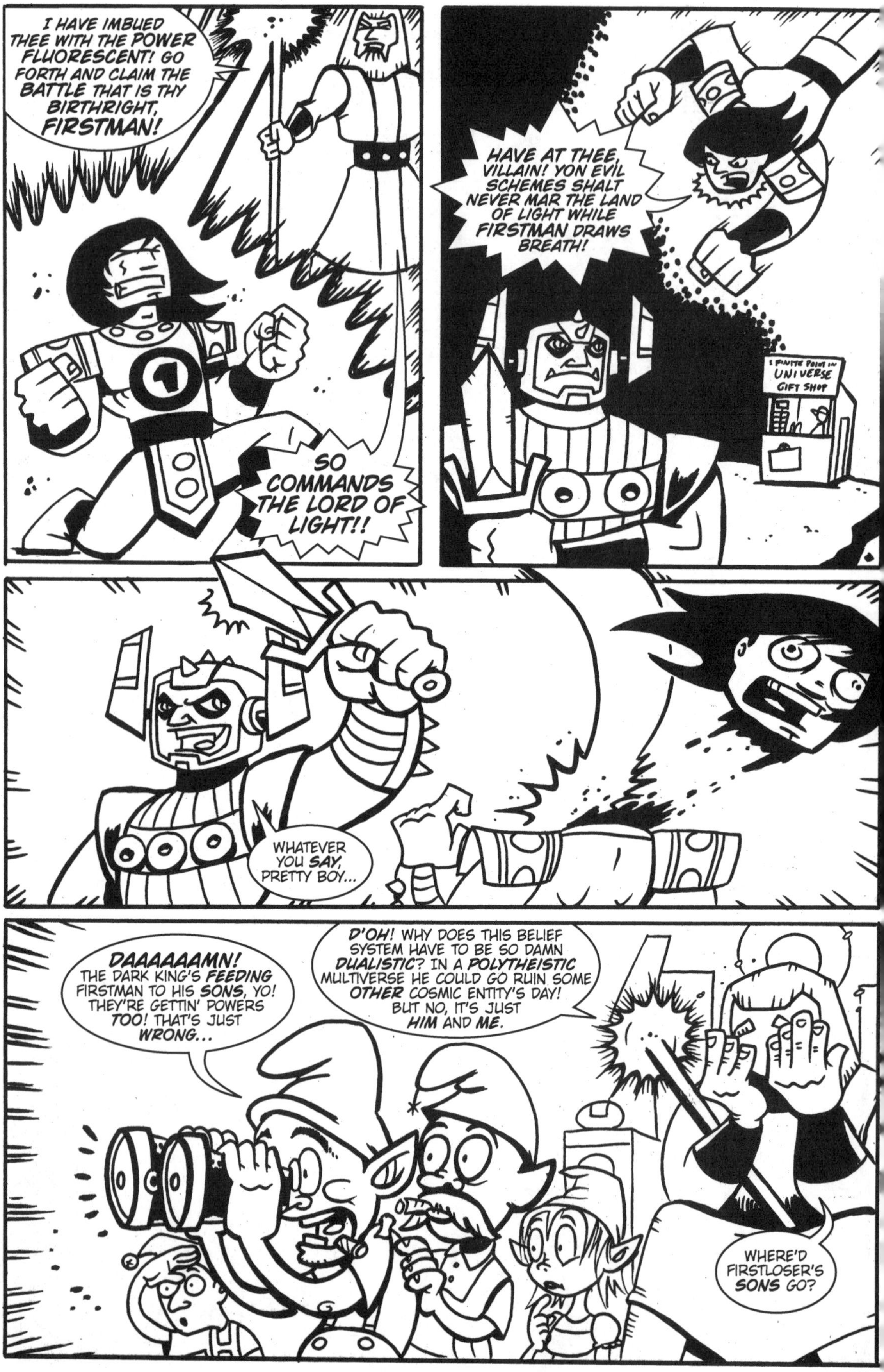
I HAVE IMBUED THEE WITH THE POWER FLUORESCENT! GO FORTH AND CLAIM THE BATTLE THAT IS THY BIRTHRIGHT, FIRSTMAN!
SO COMMANDS THE LORD OF LIGHT!!
HAVE AT THEE, VILLAIN! YON EVIL SCHEMES SHALT NEVER MAR THE LAND OF LIGHT WHILE FIRSTMAN DRAWS BREATH!
UNIVERSE GIFT SHOP
WHATEVER YOU SAY, PRETTY BOY...
DAAAAAAAMN! THE DARK KING'S FEEDING FIRSTMAN TO HIS SONS, YO! THEY'RE GETTIN' POWERS TOO! THAT'S JUST WRONG...
D'OH! WHY DOES THIS BELIEF SYSTEM HAVE TO BE SO DAMN DUALISTIC? IN A POLYTHEISTIC MULTIVERSE HE COULD GO RUIN SOME OTHER COSMIC ENTITY'S DAY! BUT NO, IT'S JUST HIM AND ME.
WHERE'D FIRSTLOSER'S SONS GO?

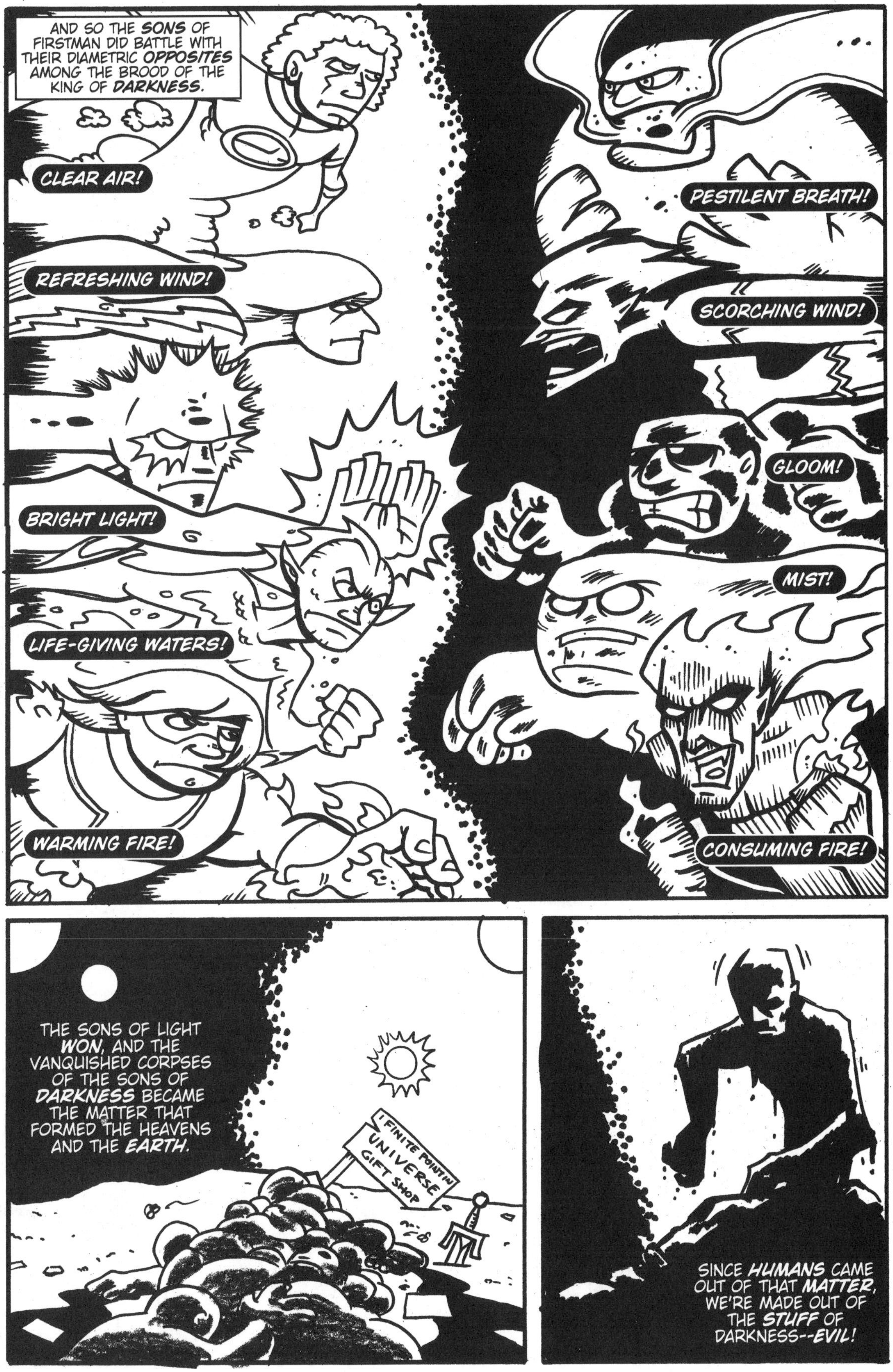
AND SO THE SONS OF FIRSTMAN DID BATTLE WITH THEIR DIAMETRIC OPPOSITES AMONG THE BROOD OF THE KING OF DARKNESS.
CLEAR AIR!
PESTILENT BREATH!
REFRESHING WIND!
SCORCHING WIND!
BRIGHT LIGHT!
GLOOM!
LIFE-GIVING WATERS!
MIST!
WARMING FIRE!
CONSUMING FIRE!
THE SONS OF LIGHT WON, AND THE VANQUISHED CORPSES OF THE SONS OF DARKNESS BECAME THE MATTER THAT FORMED THE HEAVENS AND THE EARTH.
I FINITE POINT IN UNIVERSE GIFT SHOP
SINCE HUMANS CAME OUT OF THAT MATTER, WE'RE MADE OUT OF THE STUFF OF DARKNESS--EVIL!

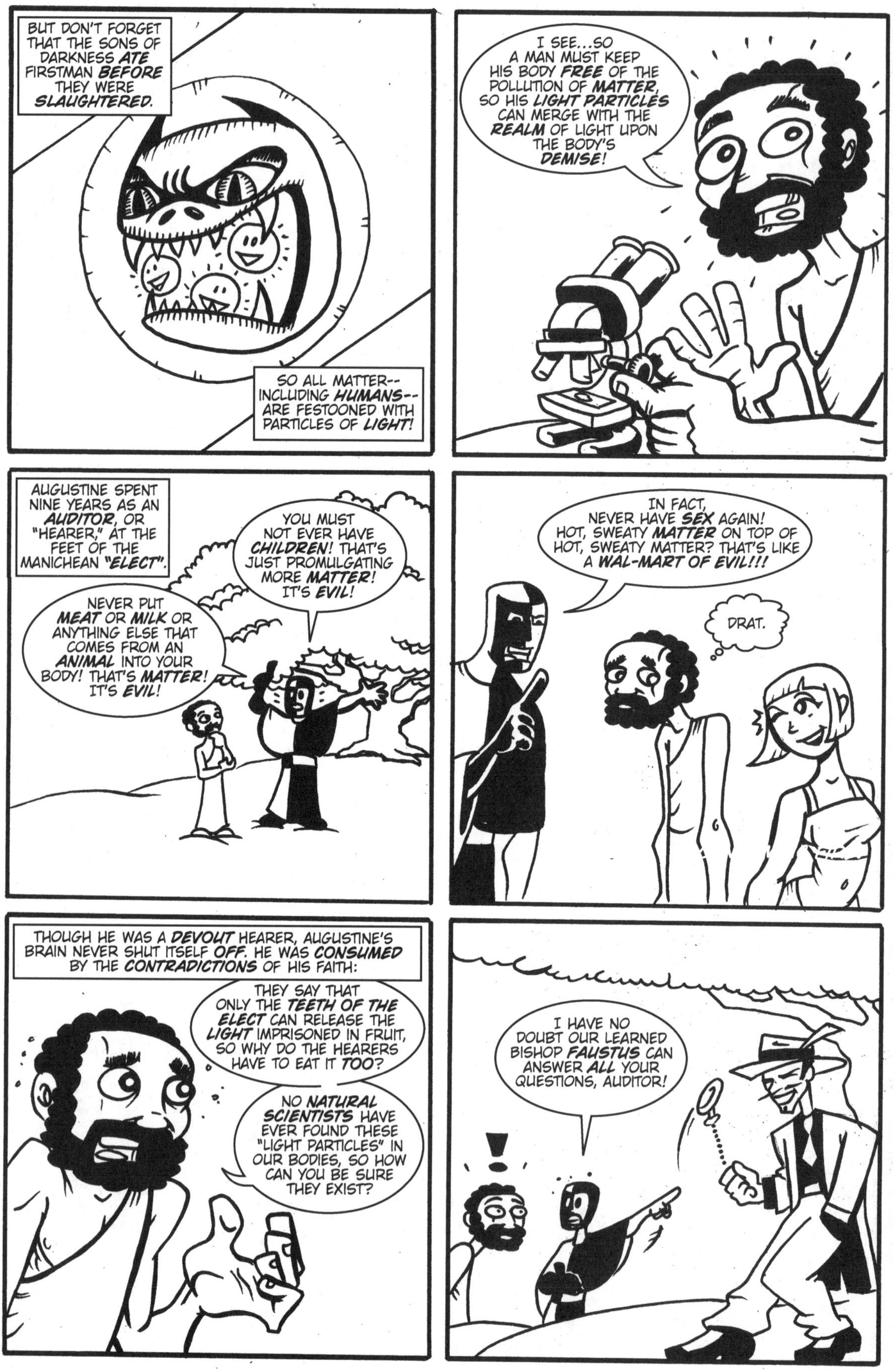
BUT DON'T FORGET THAT THE SONS OF DARKNESS ATE FIRSTMAN BEFORE THEY WERE SLAUGHTERED.
SO ALL MATTER-- INCLUDING HUMANS-- ARE FESTOONED WITH PARTICLES OF LIGHT!
I SEE...SO A MAN MUST KEEP HIS BODY FREE OF THE POLLUTION OF MATTER, SO HIS LIGHT PARTICLES CAN MERGE WITH THE REALM OF LIGHT UPON THE BODY'S DEMISE!
AUGUSTINE SPENT NINE YEARS AS AN AUDITOR, OR "HEARER," AT THE FEET OF THE MANICHEAN "ELECT".
YOU MUST NOT EVER HAVE CHILDREN! THAT'S JUST PROMULGATING MORE MATTER! IT'S EVIL!
NEVER PUT MEAT OR MILK OR ANYTHING ELSE THAT COMES FROM AN ANIMAL INTO YOUR BODY! THAT'S MATTER! IT'S EVIL!
IN FACT, NEVER HAVE SEX AGAIN! HOT, SWEATY MATTER ON TOP OF HOT, SWEATY MATTER? THAT'S LIKE A WAL-MART OF EVIL!!!
DRAT.
THOUGH HE WAS A DEVOUT HEARER, AUGUSTINE'S BRAIN NEVER SHUT ITSELF OFF. HE WAS CONSUMED BY THE CONTRADICTIONS OF HIS FAITH:
THEY SAY THAT ONLY THE TEETH OF THE ELECT CAN RELEASE THE LIGHT IMPRISONED IN FRUIT, SO WHY DO THE HEARERS HAVE TO EAT IT TOO?
NO NATURAL SCIENTISTS HAVE EVER FOUND THESE "LIGHT PARTICLES" IN OUR BODIES, SO HOW CAN YOU BE SURE THEY EXIST?
I HAVE NO DOUBT OUR LEARNED BISHOP FAUSTUS CAN ANSWER ALL YOUR QUESTIONS, AUDITOR!
!

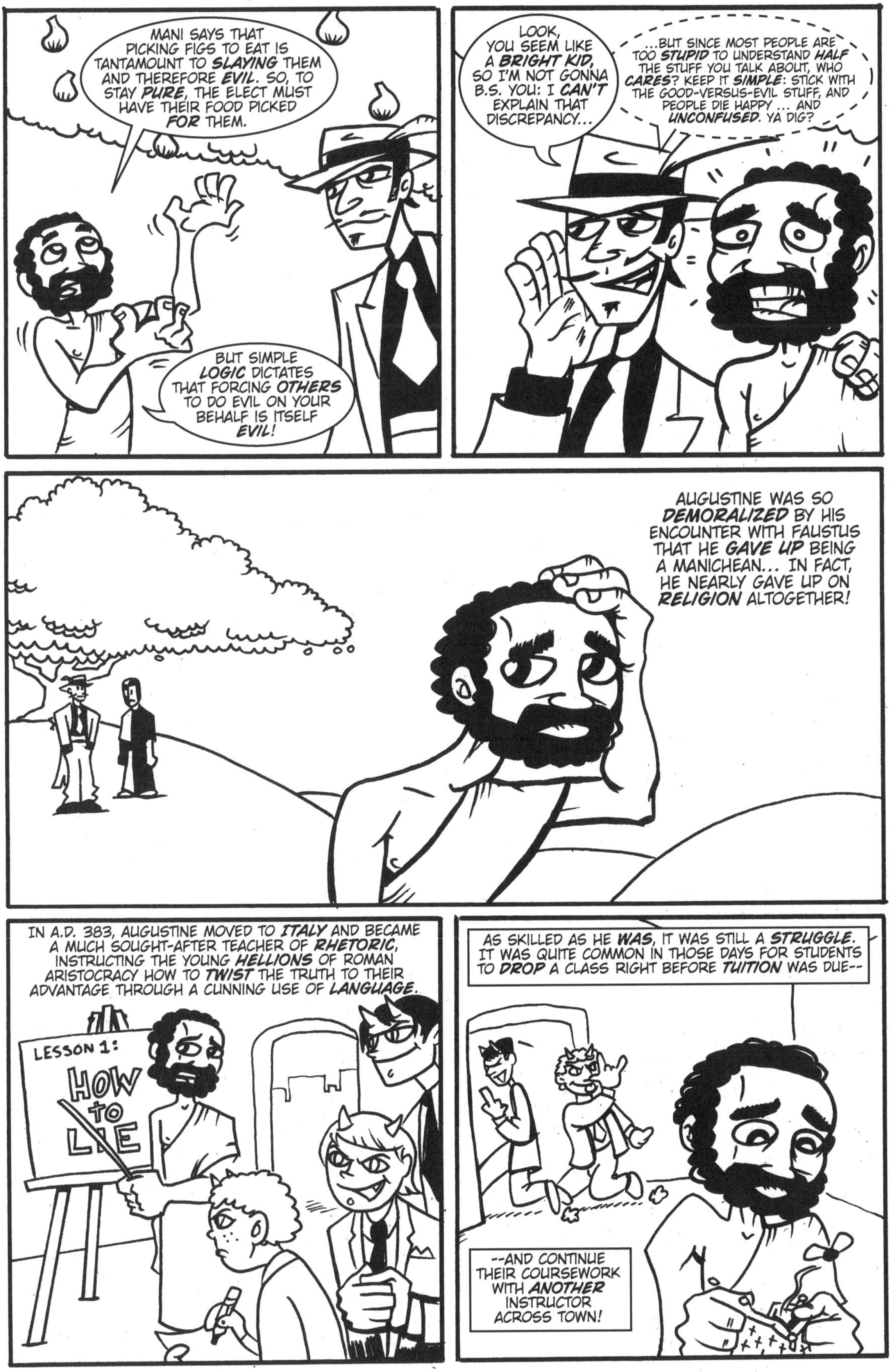
MANI SAYS THAT PICKING FIGS TO EAT IS TANTAMOUNT TO SLAYING THEM AND THEREFORE EVIL. SO, TO STAY PURE, THE ELECT MUST HAVE THEIR FOOD PICKED FOR THEM.
BUT SIMPLE LOGIC DICTATES THAT FORCING OTHERS TO DO EVIL ON YOUR BEHALF IS ITSELF EVIL!
LOOK, YOU SEEM LIKE A BRIGHT KID, SO I'M NOT GONNA B.S. YOU: I CAN'T EXPLAIN THAT DISCREPANCY...
...BUT SINCE MOST PEOPLE ARE TOO STUPID TO UNDERSTAND HALF THE STUFF YOU TALK ABOUT, WHO CARES? KEEP IT SIMPLE: STICK WITH THE GOOD-VERSUS-EVIL STUFF, AND PEOPLE DIE HAPPY ... AND UNCONFUSED. YA DIG?
AUGUSTINE WAS SO DEMORALIZED BY HIS ENCOUNTER WITH FAUSTUS THAT HE GAVE UP BEING A MANICHEAN... IN FACT, HE NEARLY GAVE UP ON RELIGION ALTOGETHER!
IN A.D. 383, AUGUSTINE MOVED TO ITALY AND BECAME A MUCH SOUGHT-AFTER TEACHER OF RHETORIC, INSTRUCTING THE YOUNG HELLIONS OF ROMAN ARISTOCRACY HOW TO TWIST THE TRUTH TO THEIR ADVANTAGE THROUGH A CUNNING USE OF LANGUAGE.
LESSON 1: HOW TO LIE
AS SKILLED AS HE WAS, IT WAS STILL A STRUGGLE. IT WAS QUITE COMMON IN THOSE DAYS FOR STUDENTS TO DROP A CLASS RIGHT BEFORE TUITION WAS DUE--
--AND CONTINUE THEIR COURSEWORK WITH ANOTHER INSTRUCTOR ACROSS TOWN!

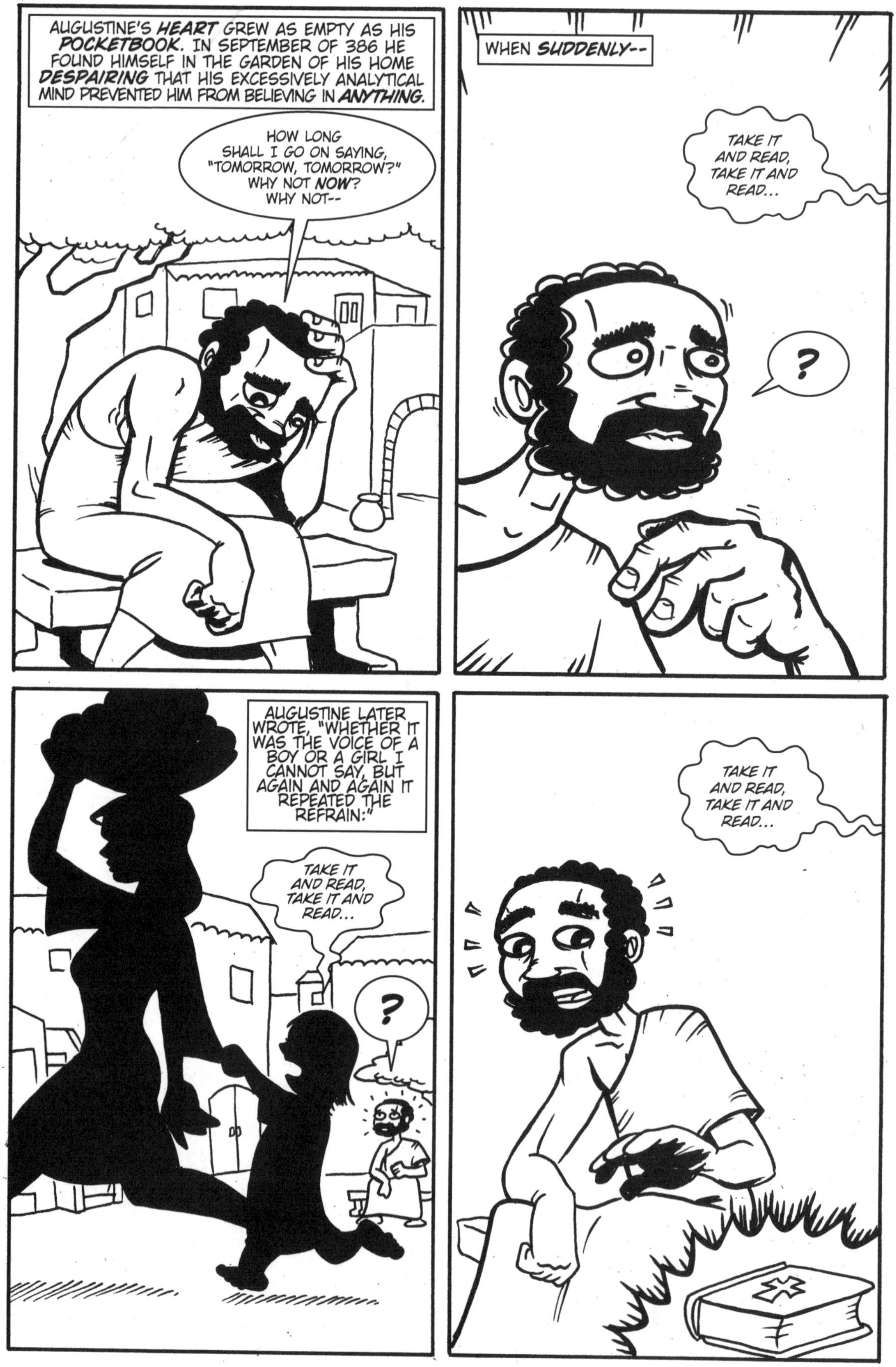
AUGUSTINE'S **HEART** GREW AS EMPTY AS HIS **POCKETBOOK**. IN SEPTEMBER OF 386 HE FOUND HIMSELF IN THE GARDEN OF HIS HOME **DESPAIRING** THAT HIS EXCESSIVELY ANALYTICAL MIND PREVENTED HIM FROM BELIEVING IN **ANYTHING**.
HOW LONG SHALL I GO ON SAYING, "TOMORROW, TOMORROW?" WHY NOT **NOW**? WHY NOT--
WHEN **SUDDENLY**--
TAKE IT AND READ, TAKE IT AND READ...
?
AUGUSTINE LATER WROTE, "WHETHER IT WAS THE VOICE OF A BOY OR A GIRL I CANNOT SAY, BUT AGAIN AND AGAIN IT REPEATED THE REFRAIN:"
TAKE IT AND READ, TAKE IT AND READ...
?
TAKE IT AND READ, TAKE IT AND READ...

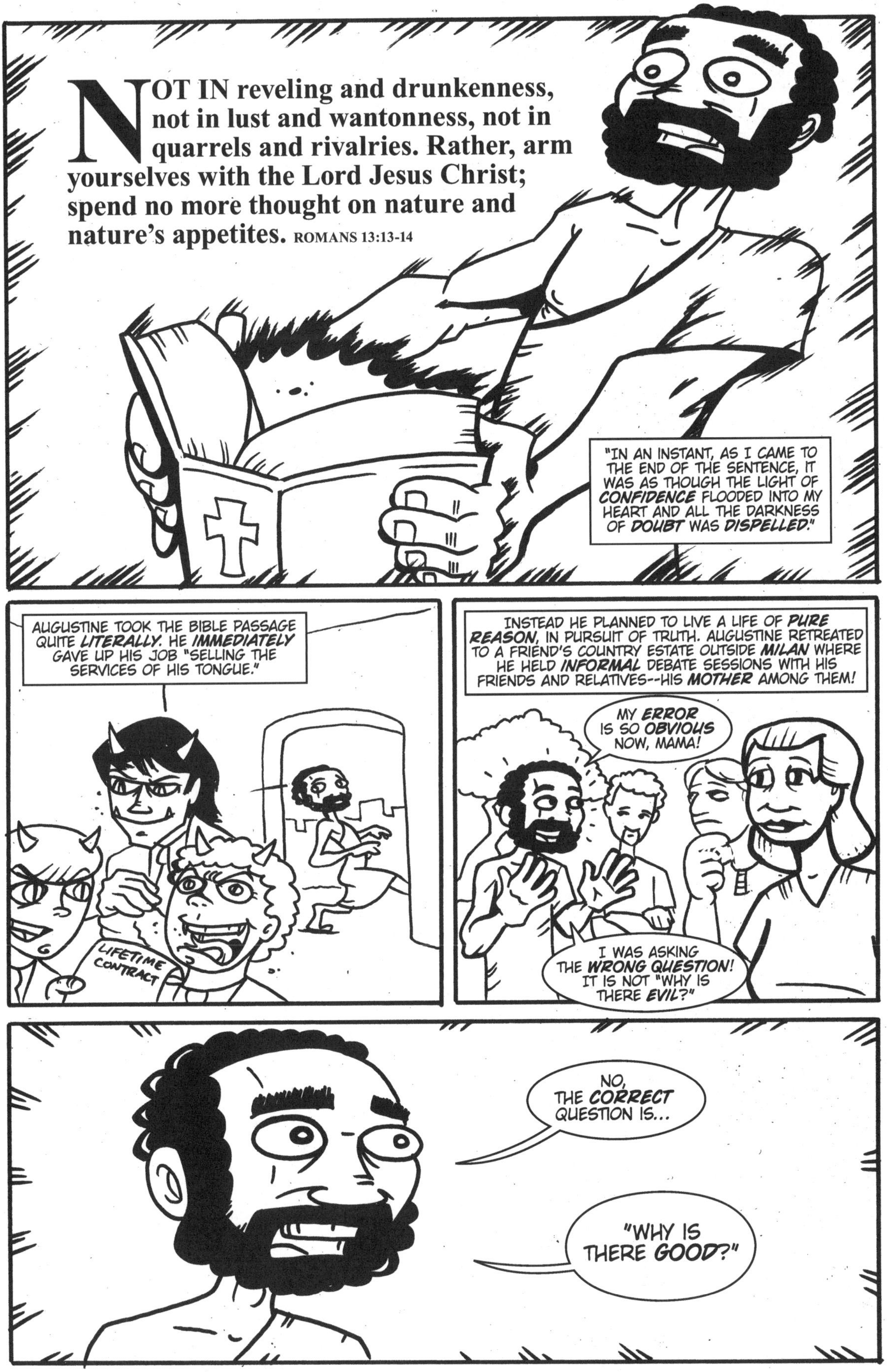
NOT IN reveling and drunkenness, not in lust and wantonness, not in quarrels and rivalries. Rather, arm yourselves with the Lord Jesus Christ; spend no more thought on nature and nature's appetites. ROMANS 13:13-14
"IN AN INSTANT, AS I CAME TO THE END OF THE SENTENCE, IT WAS AS THOUGH THE LIGHT OF CONFIDENCE FLOODED INTO MY HEART AND ALL THE DARKNESS OF DOUBT WAS DISPELLED."
AUGUSTINE TOOK THE BIBLE PASSAGE QUITE LITERALLY. HE IMMEDIATELY GAVE UP HIS JOB "SELLING THE SERVICES OF HIS TONGUE."
LIFETIME CONTRACT
INSTEAD HE PLANNED TO LIVE A LIFE OF PURE REASON, IN PURSUIT OF TRUTH. AUGUSTINE RETREATED TO A FRIEND'S COUNTRY ESTATE OUTSIDE MILAN WHERE HE HELD INFORMAL DEBATE SESSIONS WITH HIS FRIENDS AND RELATIVES--HIS MOTHER AMONG THEM!
MY ERROR IS SO OBVIOUS NOW, MAMA!
I WAS ASKING THE WRONG QUESTION! IT IS NOT "WHY IS THERE EVIL?"
NO, THE CORRECT QUESTION IS...
"WHY IS THERE GOOD?"

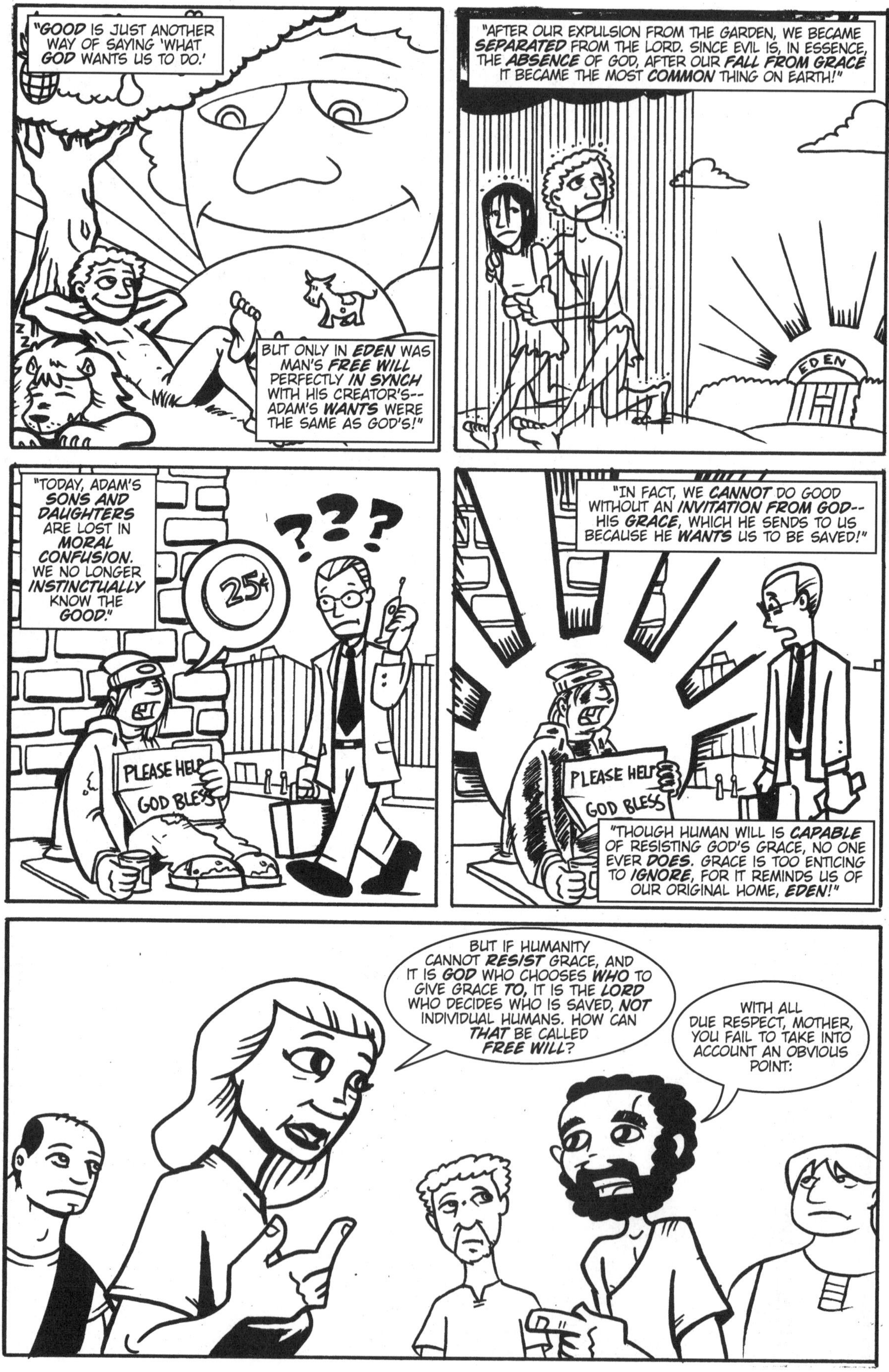
"GOOD IS JUST ANOTHER WAY OF SAYING 'WHAT GOD WANTS US TO DO.'
BUT ONLY IN EDEN WAS MAN'S FREE WILL PERFECTLY IN SYNCH WITH HIS CREATOR'S-- ADAM'S WANTS WERE THE SAME AS GOD'S!"
"AFTER OUR EXPULSION FROM THE GARDEN, WE BECAME SEPARATED FROM THE LORD. SINCE EVIL IS, IN ESSENCE, THE ABSENCE OF GOD, AFTER OUR FALL FROM GRACE IT BECAME THE MOST COMMON THING ON EARTH!"
EDEN
"TODAY, ADAM'S SONS AND DAUGHTERS ARE LOST IN MORAL CONFUSION. WE NO LONGER INSTINCTUALLY KNOW THE GOOD."
25¢
???
PLEASE HELP
GOD BLESS
"IN FACT, WE CANNOT DO GOOD WITHOUT AN INVITATION FROM GOD-- HIS GRACE, WHICH HE SENDS TO US BECAUSE HE WANTS US TO BE SAVED!"
PLEASE HELP
GOD BLESS
"THOUGH HUMAN WILL IS CAPABLE OF RESISTING GOD'S GRACE, NO ONE EVER DOES. GRACE IS TOO ENTICING TO IGNORE, FOR IT REMINDS US OF OUR ORIGINAL HOME, EDEN!"
BUT IF HUMANITY CANNOT RESIST GRACE, AND IT IS GOD WHO CHOOSES WHO TO GIVE GRACE TO, IT IS THE LORD WHO DECIDES WHO IS SAVED, NOT INDIVIDUAL HUMANS. HOW CAN THAT BE CALLED FREE WILL?
WITH ALL DUE RESPECT, MOTHER, YOU FAIL TO TAKE INTO ACCOUNT AN OBVIOUS POINT:

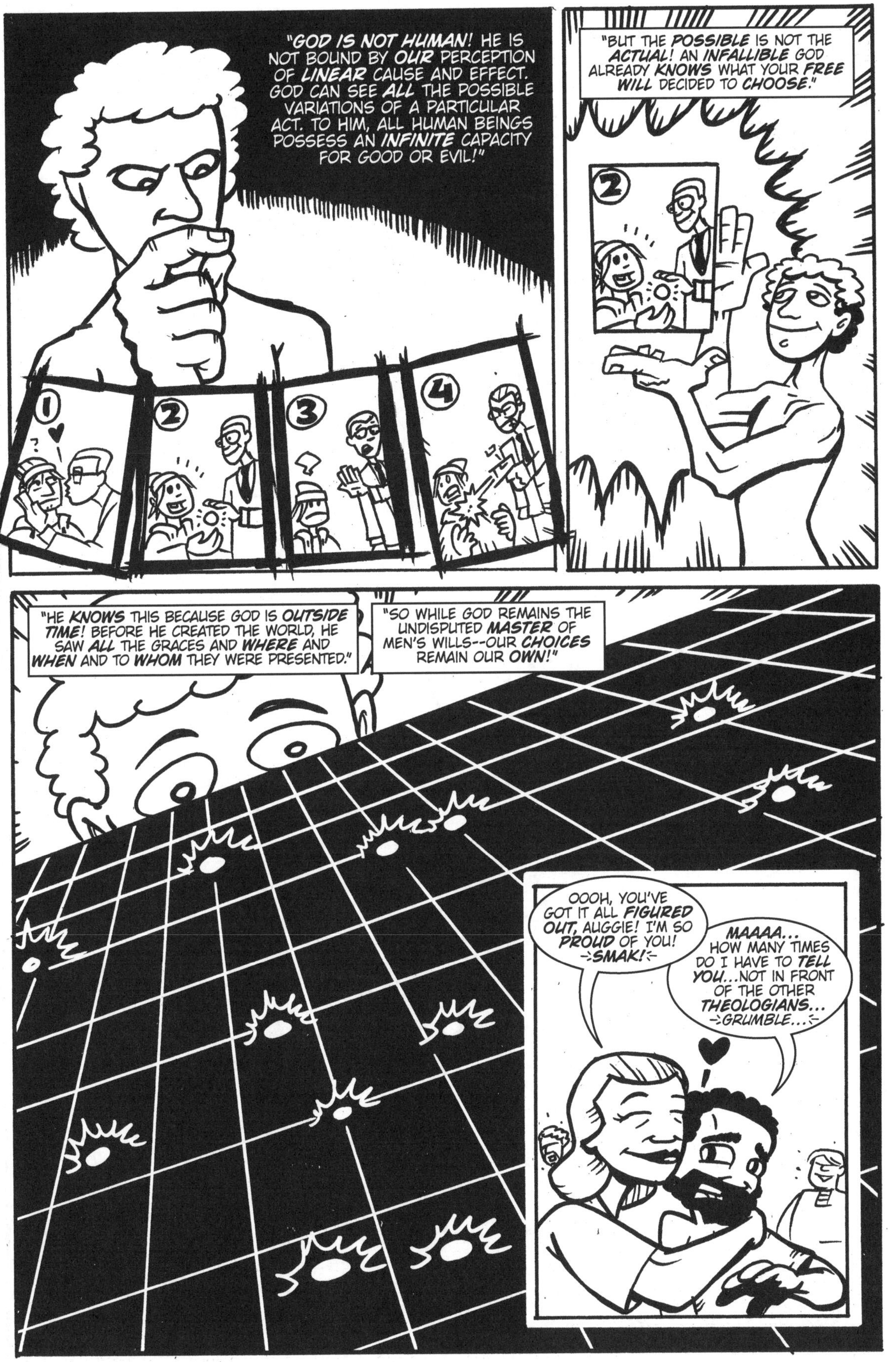
"GOD IS NOT HUMAN! HE IS NOT BOUND BY OUR PERCEPTION OF LINEAR CAUSE AND EFFECT. GOD CAN SEE ALL THE POSSIBLE VARIATIONS OF A PARTICULAR ACT. TO HIM, ALL HUMAN BEINGS POSSESS AN INFINITE CAPACITY FOR GOOD OR EVIL!"
1
2
3
4
"BUT THE POSSIBLE IS NOT THE ACTUAL! AN INFALLIBLE GOD ALREADY KNOWS WHAT YOUR FREE WILL DECIDED TO CHOOSE."
2
"HE KNOWS THIS BECAUSE GOD IS OUTSIDE TIME! BEFORE HE CREATED THE WORLD, HE SAW ALL THE GRACES AND WHERE AND WHEN AND TO WHOM THEY WERE PRESENTED."
"SO WHILE GOD REMAINS THE UNDISPUTED MASTER OF MEN'S WILLS--OUR CHOICES REMAIN OUR OWN!"
OOOH, YOU'VE GOT IT ALL FIGURED OUT, AUGGIE! I'M SO PROUD OF YOU! -SMAK!-
MAAAA... HOW MANY TIMES DO I HAVE TO TELL YOU...NOT IN FRONT OF THE OTHER THEOLOGIANS... -GRUMBLE...-

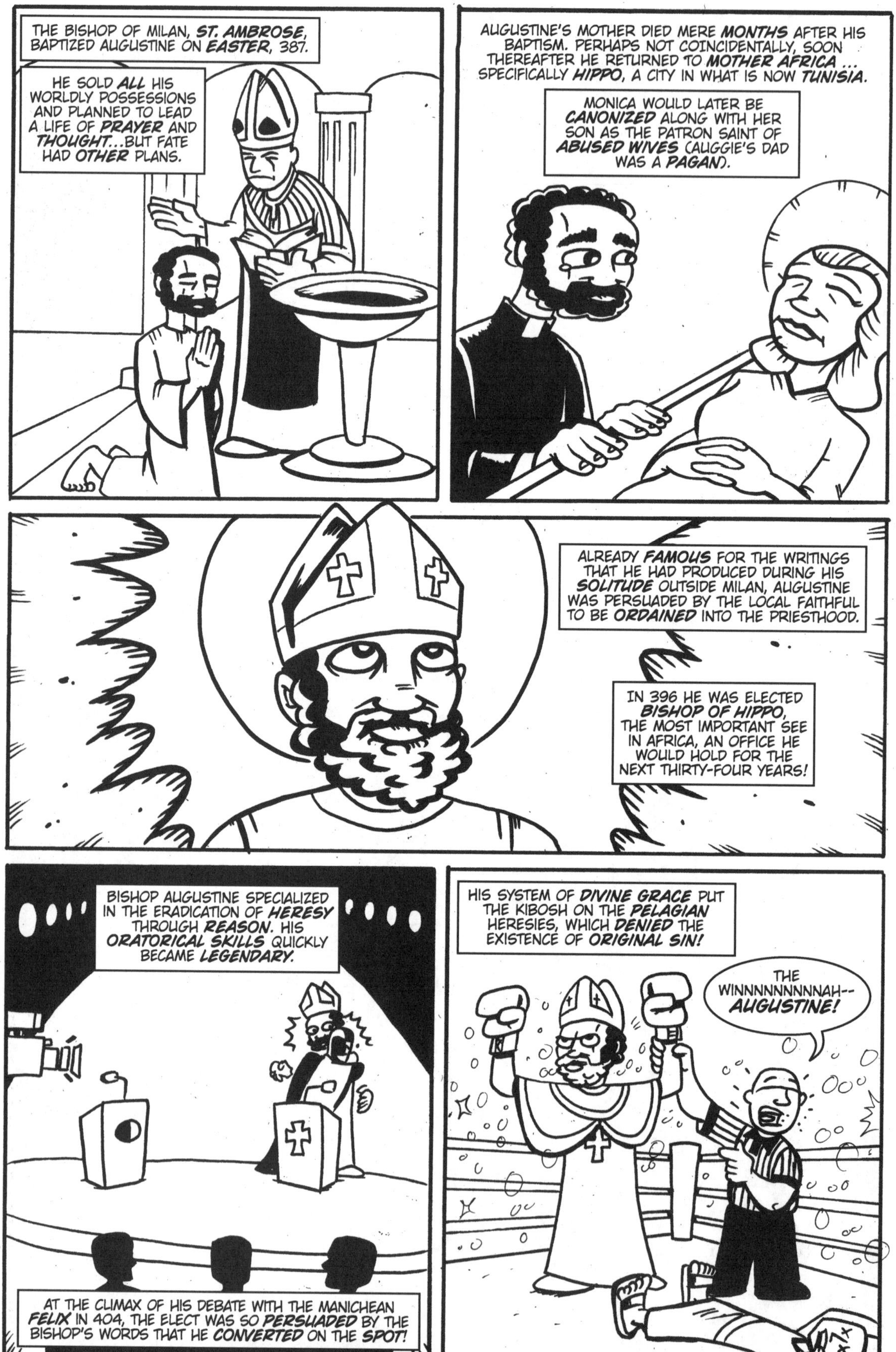

THE BISHOP OF MILAN, ST. AMBROSE, BAPTIZED AUGUSTINE ON EASTER, 387.
HE SOLD ALL HIS WORLDLY POSSESSIONS AND PLANNED TO LEAD A LIFE OF PRAYER AND THOUGHT...BUT FATE HAD OTHER PLANS.
AUGUSTINE'S MOTHER DIED MERE MONTHS AFTER HIS BAPTISM. PERHAPS NOT COINCIDENTALLY, SOON THEREAFTER HE RETURNED TO MOTHER AFRICA ... SPECIFICALLY HIPPO, A CITY IN WHAT IS NOW TUNISIA.
MONICA WOULD LATER BE CANONIZED ALONG WITH HER SON AS THE PATRON SAINT OF ABUSED WIVES (AUGGIE'S DAD WAS A PAGAN).
ALREADY FAMOUS FOR THE WRITINGS THAT HE HAD PRODUCED DURING HIS SOLITUDE OUTSIDE MILAN, AUGUSTINE WAS PERSUADED BY THE LOCAL FAITHFUL TO BE ORDAINED INTO THE PRIESTHOOD.
IN 396 HE WAS ELECTED BISHOP OF HIPPO, THE MOST IMPORTANT SEE IN AFRICA, AN OFFICE HE WOULD HOLD FOR THE NEXT THIRTY-FOUR YEARS!
BISHOP AUGUSTINE SPECIALIZED IN THE ERADICATION OF HERESY THROUGH REASON. HIS ORATORICAL SKILLS QUICKLY BECAME LEGENDARY.
AT THE CLIMAX OF HIS DEBATE WITH THE MANICHEAN FELIX IN 404, THE ELECT WAS SO PERSUADED BY THE BISHOP'S WORDS THAT HE CONVERTED ON THE SPOT!
HIS SYSTEM OF DIVINE GRACE PUT THE KIBOSH ON THE PELAGIAN HERESIES, WHICH DENIED THE EXISTENCE OF ORIGINAL SIN!
THE WINNNNNNNNNAH-- AUGUSTINE!

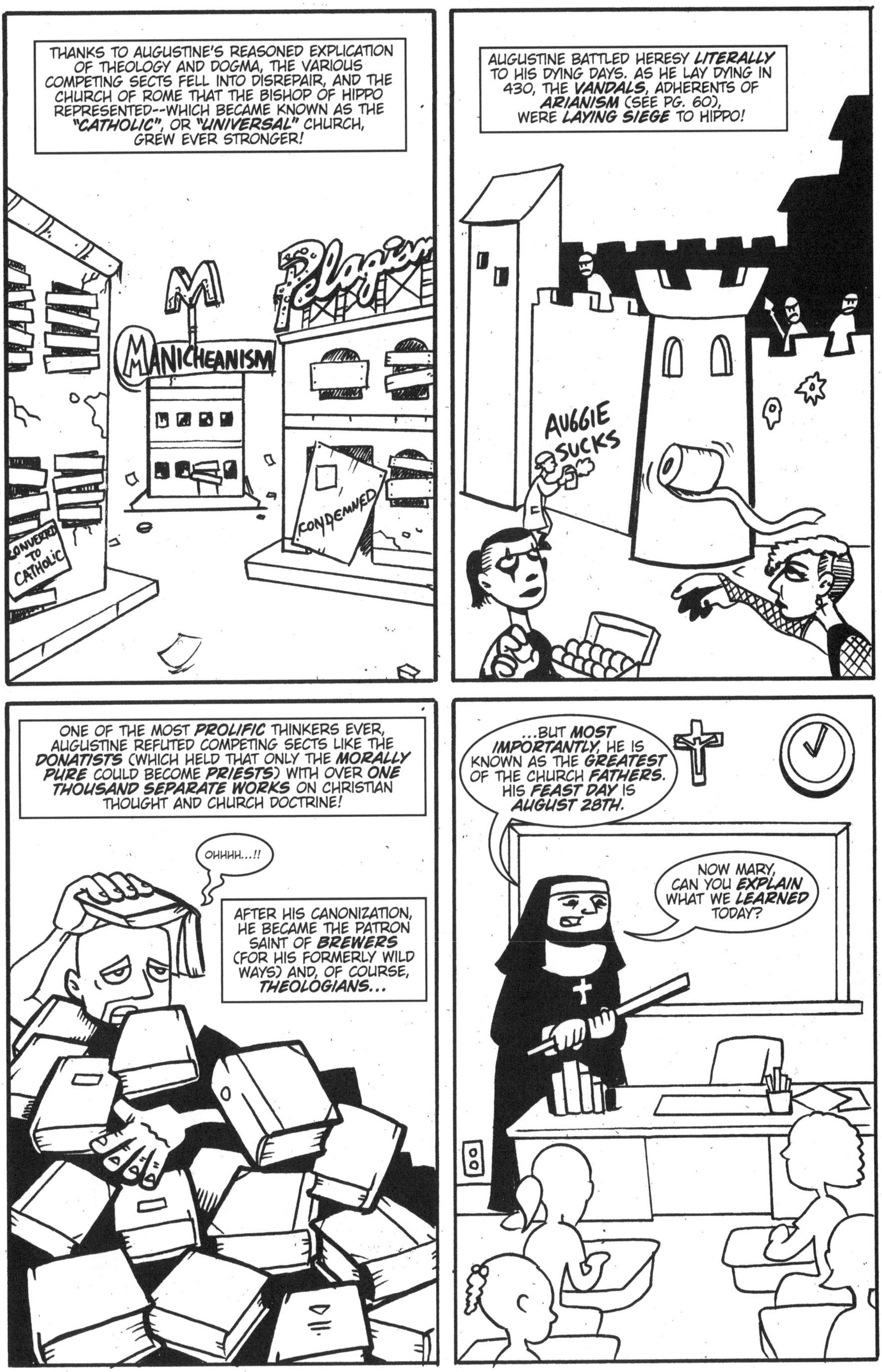
THANKS TO AUGUSTINE'S REASONED EXPLICATION OF THEOLOGY AND DOGMA, THE VARIOUS COMPETING SECTS FELL INTO DISREPAIR, AND THE CHURCH OF ROME THAT THE BISHOP OF HIPPO REPRESENTED--WHICH BECAME KNOWN AS THE "CATHOLIC", OR "UNIVERSAL" CHURCH, GREW EVER STRONGER!
MANICHEANISM
CONDEMNED
CONVERTED TO CATHOLIC
AUGUSTINE BATTLED HERESY LITERALLY TO HIS DYING DAYS. AS HE LAY DYING IN 430, THE VANDALS, ADHERENTS OF ARIANISM (SEE PG. 60), WERE LAYING SIEGE TO HIPPO!
AUGGIE SUCKS
ONE OF THE MOST PROLIFIC THINKERS EVER, AUGUSTINE REFUTED COMPETING SECTS LIKE THE DONATISTS (WHICH HELD THAT ONLY THE MORALLY PURE COULD BECOME PRIESTS) WITH OVER ONE THOUSAND SEPARATE WORKS ON CHRISTIAN THOUGHT AND CHURCH DOCTRINE!
OHHHH...!!
AFTER HIS CANONIZATION, HE BECAME THE PATRON SAINT OF BREWERS (FOR HIS FORMERLY WILD WAYS) AND, OF COURSE, THEOLOGIANS...
...BUT MOST IMPORTANTLY, HE IS KNOWN AS THE GREATEST OF THE CHURCH FATHERS. HIS FEAST DAY IS AUGUST 28TH.
NOW MARY, CAN YOU EXPLAIN WHAT WE LEARNED TODAY?

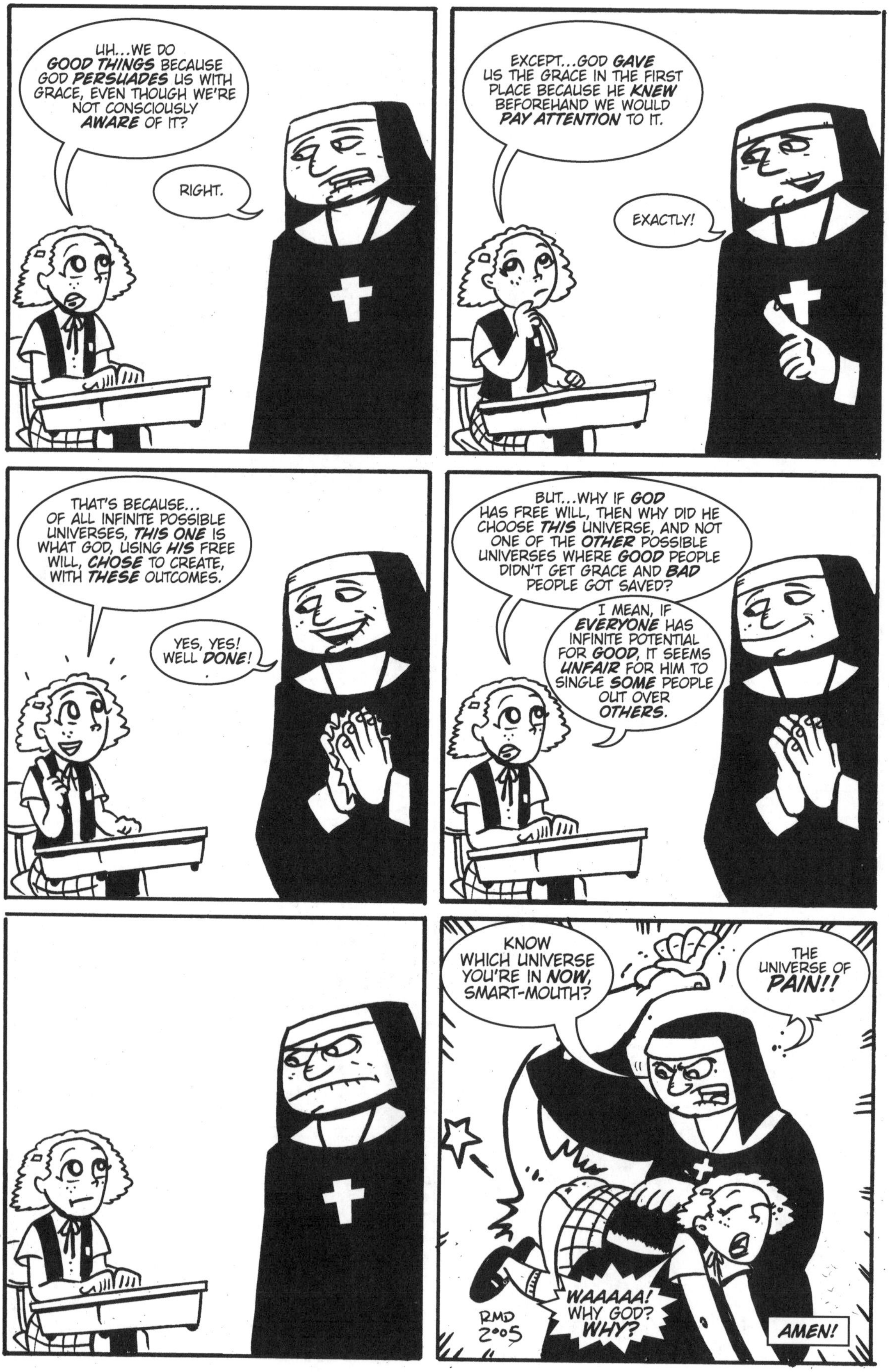
UH...WE DO **GOOD THINGS** BECAUSE GOD **PERSUADES** US WITH GRACE, EVEN THOUGH WE'RE NOT CONSCIOUSLY **AWARE** OF IT?
RIGHT.
EXCEPT...GOD **GAVE** US THE GRACE IN THE FIRST PLACE BECAUSE HE **KNEW** BEFOREHAND WE WOULD **PAY ATTENTION** TO IT.
EXACTLY!
THAT'S BECAUSE... OF ALL INFINITE POSSIBLE UNIVERSES, **THIS ONE** IS WHAT GOD, USING **HIS** FREE WILL, **CHOSE** TO CREATE, WITH **THESE** OUTCOMES.
YES, YES! WELL **DONE**!
BUT...WHY IF **GOD** HAS FREE WILL, THEN WHY DID HE CHOOSE **THIS** UNIVERSE, AND NOT ONE OF THE **OTHER** POSSIBLE UNIVERSES WHERE **GOOD** PEOPLE DIDN'T GET GRACE AND **BAD** PEOPLE GOT SAVED?
I MEAN, IF **EVERYONE** HAS INFINITE POTENTIAL FOR **GOOD**, IT SEEMS **UNFAIR** FOR HIM TO SINGLE **SOME** PEOPLE OUT OVER **OTHERS**.
KNOW WHICH UNIVERSE YOU'RE IN **NOW**, SMART-MOUTH?
THE UNIVERSE OF **PAIN!!**
WAAAAA! WHY GOD? **WHY?**
RMD 2005
AMEN!

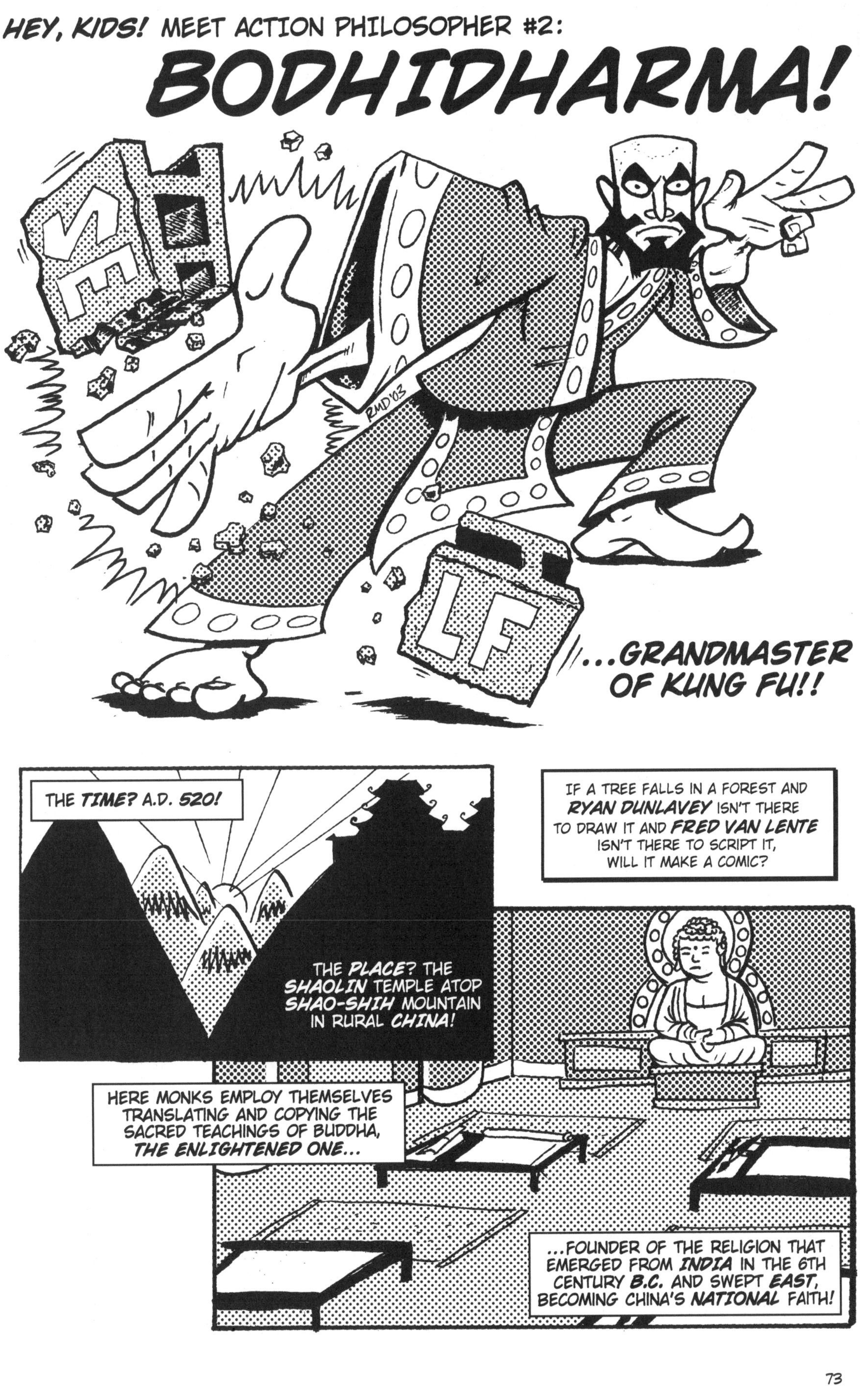
HEY, KIDS! MEET ACTION PHILOSOPHER #2:
BODHIDHARMA!
SE
LF
...GRANDMASTER OF KUNG FU!!
THE TIME? A.D. 520!
THE PLACE? THE SHAOLIN TEMPLE ATOP SHAO-SHIH MOUNTAIN IN RURAL CHINA!
IF A TREE FALLS IN A FOREST AND RYAN DUNLAVEY ISN'T THERE TO DRAW IT AND FRED VAN LENTE ISN'T THERE TO SCRIPT IT, WILL IT MAKE A COMIC?
HERE MONKS EMPLOY THEMSELVES TRANSLATING AND COPYING THE SACRED TEACHINGS OF BUDDHA, THE ENLIGHTENED ONE...
...FOUNDER OF THE RELIGION THAT EMERGED FROM INDIA IN THE 6TH CENTURY B.C. AND SWEPT EAST, BECOMING CHINA'S NATIONAL FAITH!

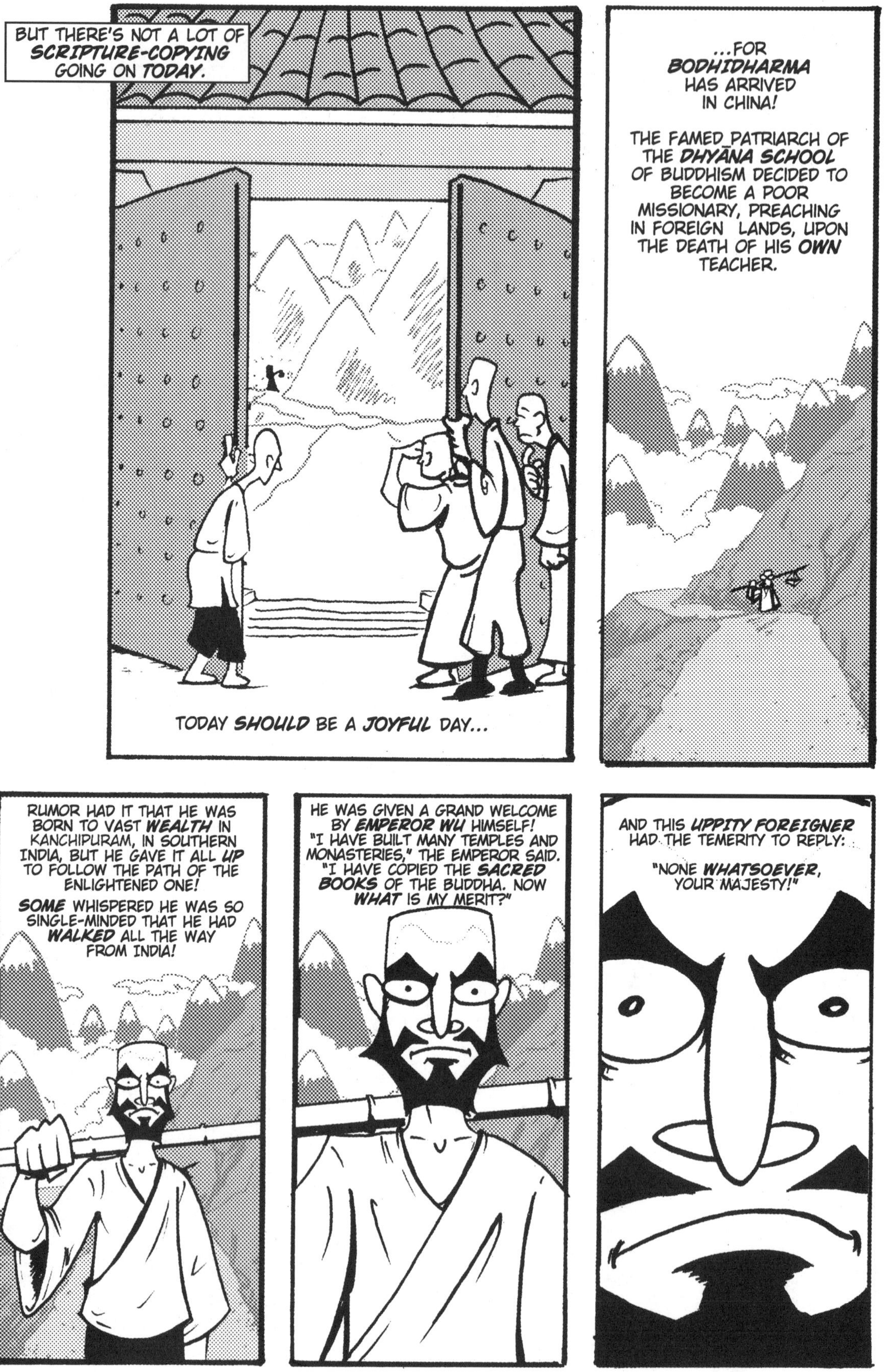

BUT THERE'S NOT A LOT OF SCRIPTURE-COPYING GOING ON TODAY.
TODAY SHOULD BE A JOYFUL DAY...
...FOR BODHIDHARMA HAS ARRIVED IN CHINA!
THE FAMED PATRIARCH OF THE DHYĀNA SCHOOL OF BUDDHISM DECIDED TO BECOME A POOR MISSIONARY, PREACHING IN FOREIGN LANDS, UPON THE DEATH OF HIS OWN TEACHER.
RUMOR HAD IT THAT HE WAS BORN TO VAST WEALTH IN KANCHIPURAM, IN SOUTHERN INDIA, BUT HE GAVE IT ALL UP TO FOLLOW THE PATH OF THE ENLIGHTENED ONE!
SOME WHISPERED HE WAS SO SINGLE-MINDED THAT HE HAD WALKED ALL THE WAY FROM INDIA!
HE WAS GIVEN A GRAND WELCOME BY EMPEROR WU HIMSELF! "I HAVE BUILT MANY TEMPLES AND MONASTERIES," THE EMPEROR SAID. "I HAVE COPIED THE SACRED BOOKS OF THE BUDDHA. NOW WHAT IS MY MERIT?"
AND THIS UPPITY FOREIGNER HAD THE TEMERITY TO REPLY:
"NONE WHATSOEVER, YOUR MAJESTY!"

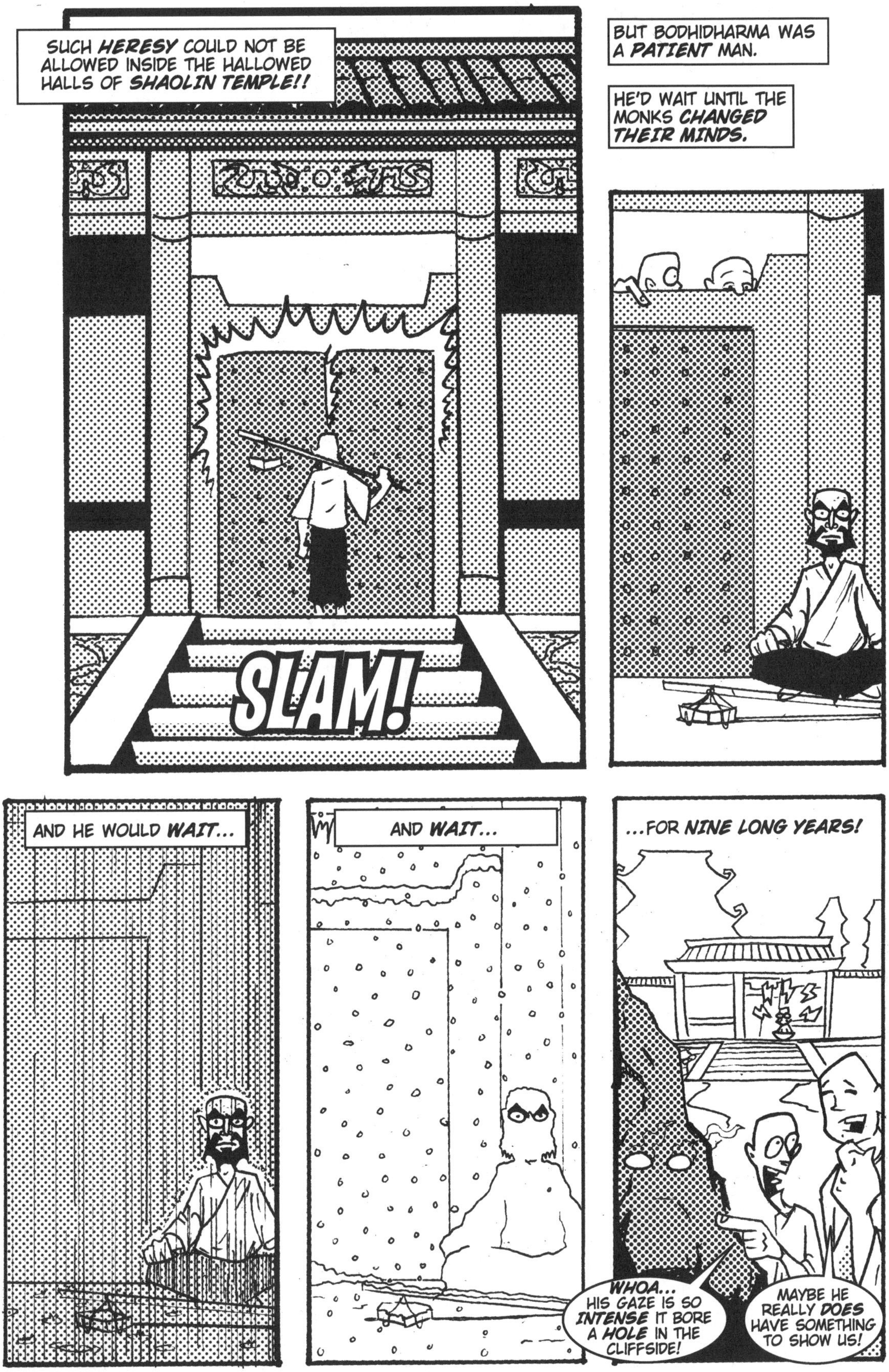
SUCH HERESY COULD NOT BE ALLOWED INSIDE THE HALLOWED HALLS OF SHAOLIN TEMPLE!!
SLAM!
BUT BODHIDHARMA WAS A PATIENT MAN.
HE'D WAIT UNTIL THE MONKS CHANGED THEIR MINDS.
AND HE WOULD WAIT...
AND WAIT...
...FOR NINE LONG YEARS!
WHOA... HIS GAZE IS SO INTENSE IT BORE A HOLE IN THE CLIFFSIDE!
MAYBE HE REALLY DOES HAVE SOMETHING TO SHOW US!

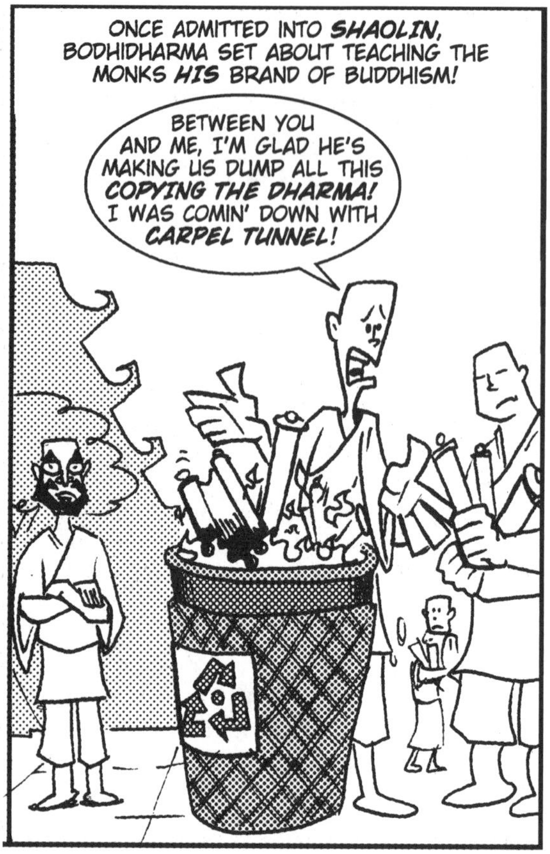
ONCE ADMITTED INTO SHAOLIN, BODHIDHARMA SET ABOUT TEACHING THE MONKS HIS BRAND OF BUDDHISM!
BETWEEN YOU AND ME, I'M GLAD HE'S MAKING US DUMP ALL THIS COPYING THE DHARMA! I WAS COMIN' DOWN WITH CARPEL TUNNEL!

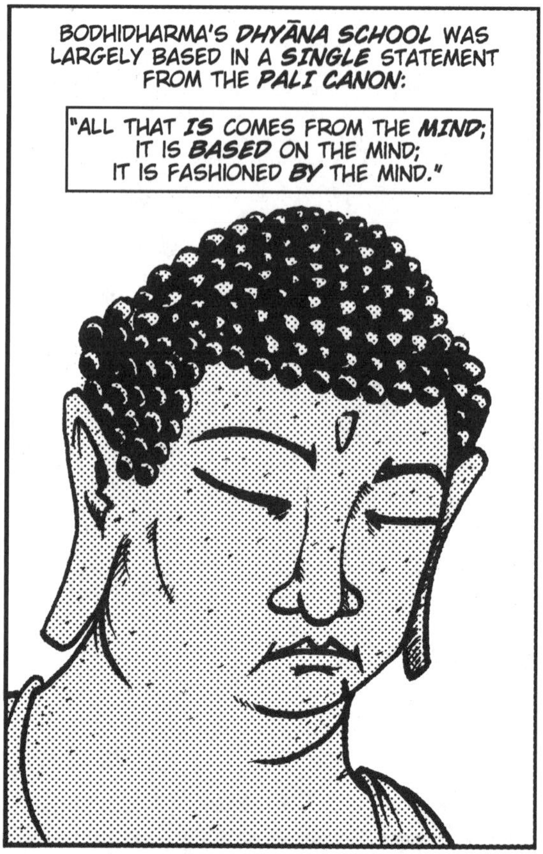
BODHIDHARMA'S DHYĀNA SCHOOL WAS LARGELY BASED IN A SINGLE STATEMENT FROM THE PALI CANON:
"ALL THAT IS COMES FROM THE MIND; IT IS BASED ON THE MIND; IT IS FASHIONED BY THE MIND."

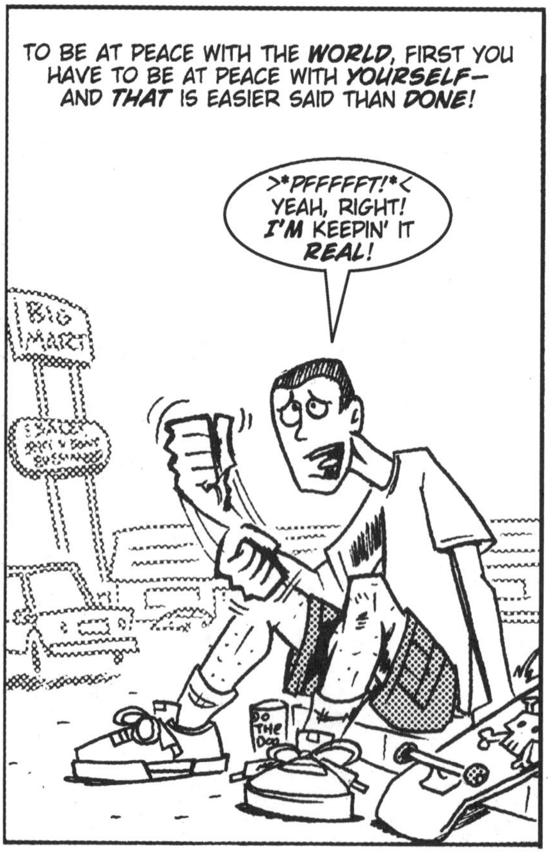
TO BE AT PEACE WITH THE WORLD, FIRST YOU HAVE TO BE AT PEACE WITH YOURSELF— AND THAT IS EASIER SAID THAN DONE!
>*PFFFFFT!*< YEAH, RIGHT! I'M KEEPIN' IT REAL!
BIG MART

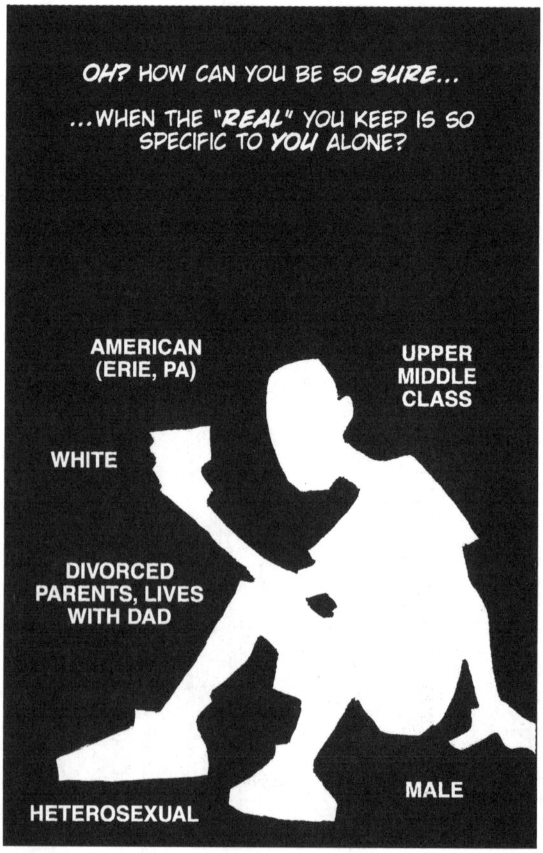
OH? HOW CAN YOU BE SO SURE...
...WHEN THE "REAL" YOU KEEP IS SO SPECIFIC TO YOU ALONE?
AMERICAN (ERIE, PA)
UPPER MIDDLE CLASS
WHITE
DIVORCED PARENTS, LIVES WITH DAD
HETEROSEXUAL
MALE

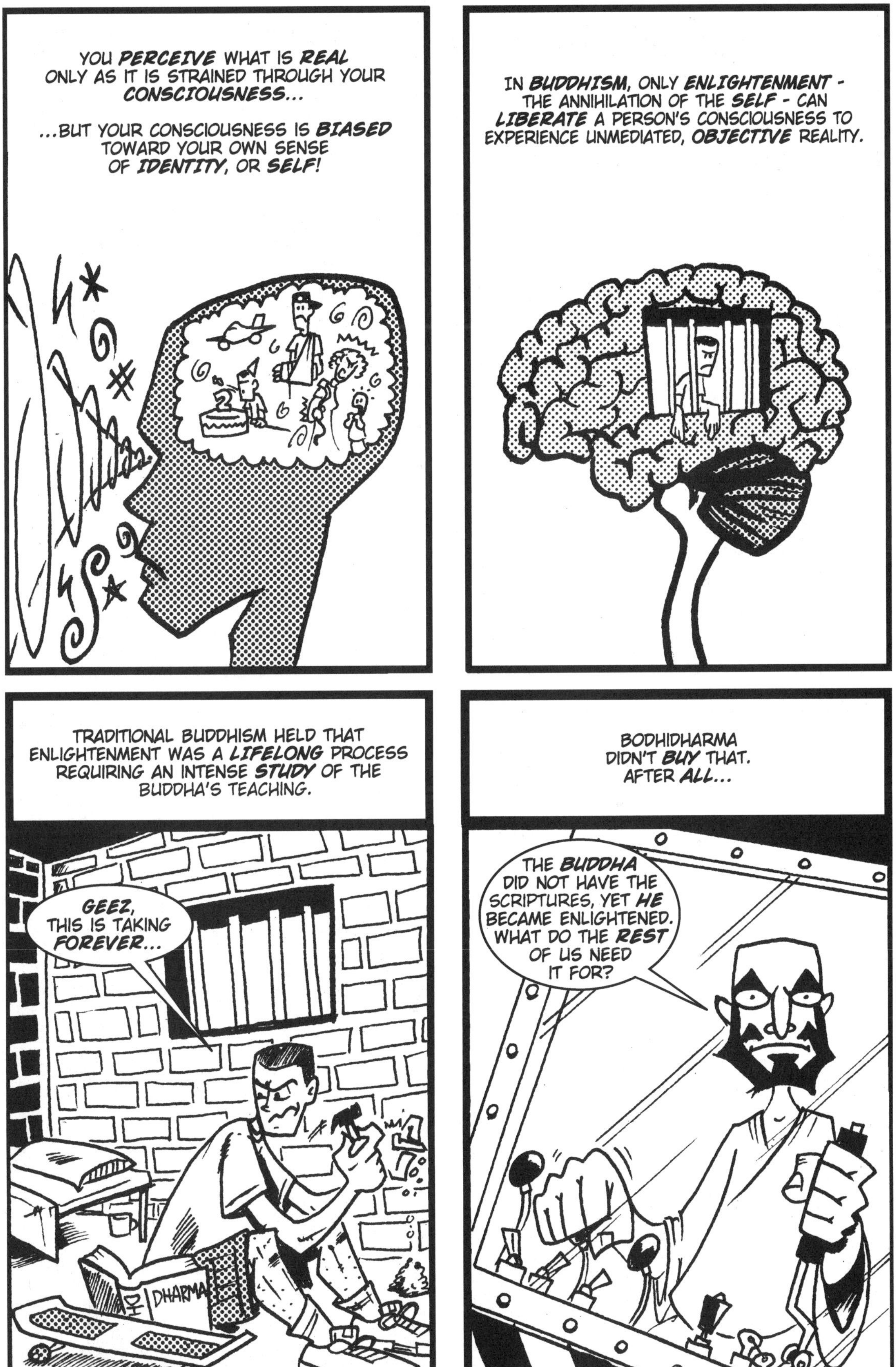
YOU PERCEIVE WHAT IS REAL ONLY AS IT IS STRAINED THROUGH YOUR CONSCIOUSNESS...
...BUT YOUR CONSCIOUSNESS IS BIASED TOWARD YOUR OWN SENSE OF IDENTITY, OR SELF!
IN BUDDHISM, ONLY ENLIGHTENMENT - THE ANNIHILATION OF THE SELF - CAN LIBERATE A PERSON'S CONSCIOUSNESS TO EXPERIENCE UNMEDIATED, OBJECTIVE REALITY.
TRADITIONAL BUDDHISM HELD THAT ENLIGHTENMENT WAS A LIFELONG PROCESS REQUIRING AN INTENSE STUDY OF THE BUDDHA'S TEACHING.
GEEZ, THIS IS TAKING FOREVER...
DHARMA
BODHIDHARMA DIDN'T BUY THAT. AFTER ALL...
THE BUDDHA DID NOT HAVE THE SCRIPTURES, YET HE BECAME ENLIGHTENED. WHAT DO THE REST OF US NEED IT FOR?

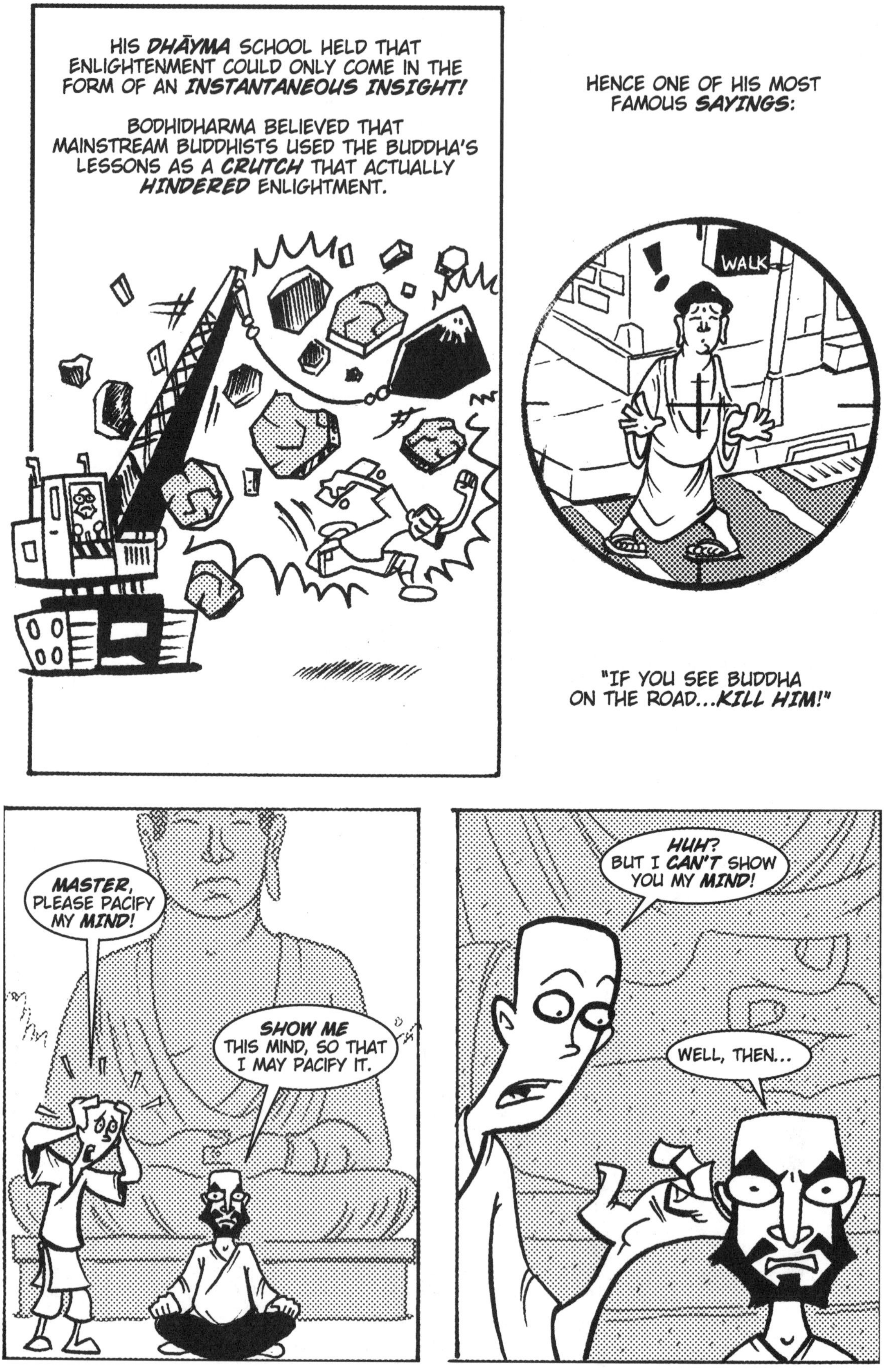
HIS DHĀYMA SCHOOL HELD THAT ENLIGHTENMENT COULD ONLY COME IN THE FORM OF AN INSTANTANEOUS INSIGHT!
BODHIDHARMA BELIEVED THAT MAINSTREAM BUDDHISTS USED THE BUDDHA'S LESSONS AS A CRUTCH THAT ACTUALLY HINDERED ENLIGHTMENT.
HENCE ONE OF HIS MOST FAMOUS SAYINGS:
WALK
"IF YOU SEE BUDDHA ON THE ROAD...KILL HIM!"
MASTER, PLEASE PACIFY MY MIND!
SHOW ME THIS MIND, SO THAT I MAY PACIFY IT.
HUH? BUT I CAN'T SHOW YOU MY MIND!
WELL, THEN...

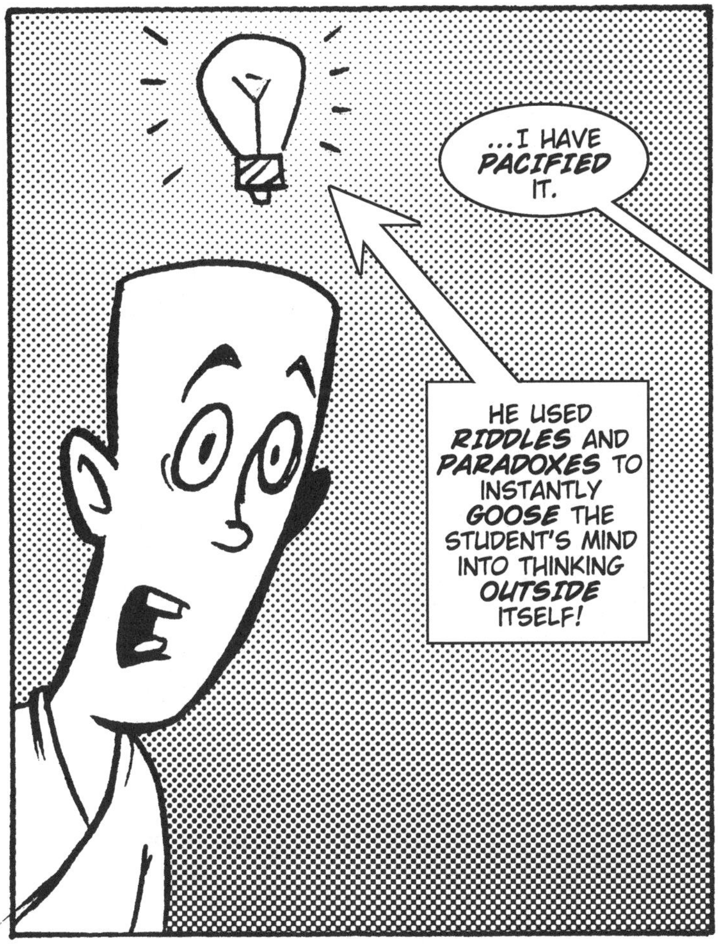
...I HAVE PACIFIED IT.
HE USED RIDDLES AND PARADOXES TO INSTANTLY GOOSE THE STUDENT'S MIND INTO THINKING OUTSIDE ITSELF!

THESE RIDDLES, CALLED "**KŌANS**," DEMONSTRATE THE ***ABSURDITY*** OF TRUTH, AT LEAST INASMUCH AS IT IS UNDERSTOOD BY THE SUBJECTIVE SELF:

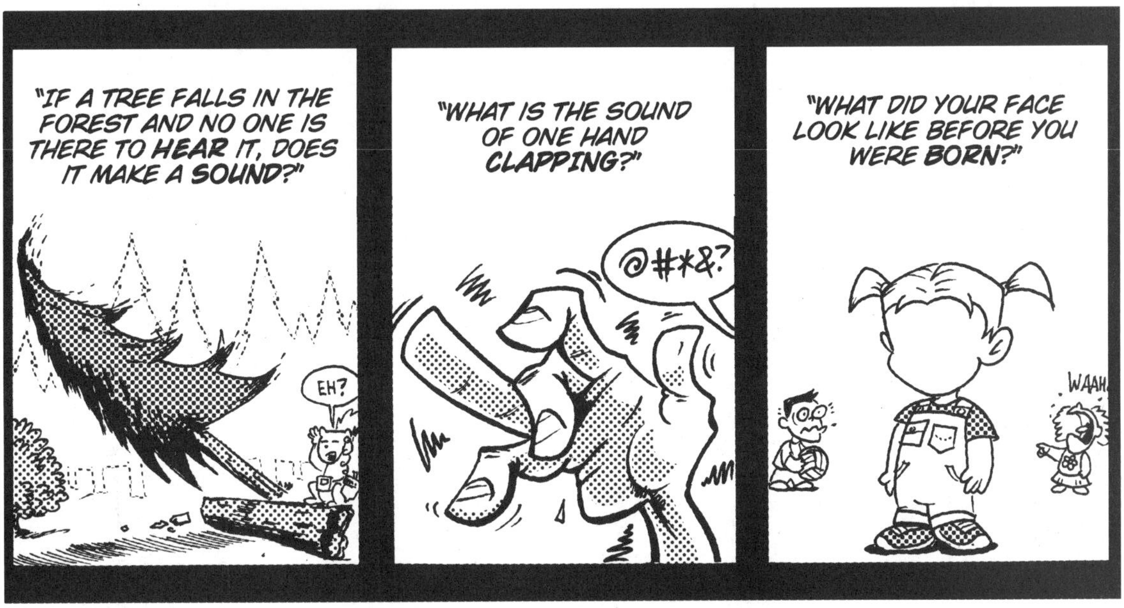
"IF A TREE FALLS IN THE FOREST AND NO ONE IS THERE TO HEAR IT, DOES IT MAKE A SOUND?"
EH?
"WHAT IS THE SOUND OF ONE HAND CLAPPING?"
@#*&?
"WHAT DID YOUR FACE LOOK LIKE BEFORE YOU WERE BORN?"
WAAH

THE POINT ISN'T TO ***ANSWER*** KŌANS, BUT TO CONTEMPLATE WHY THEY ***CAN'T*** BE ANSWERED!

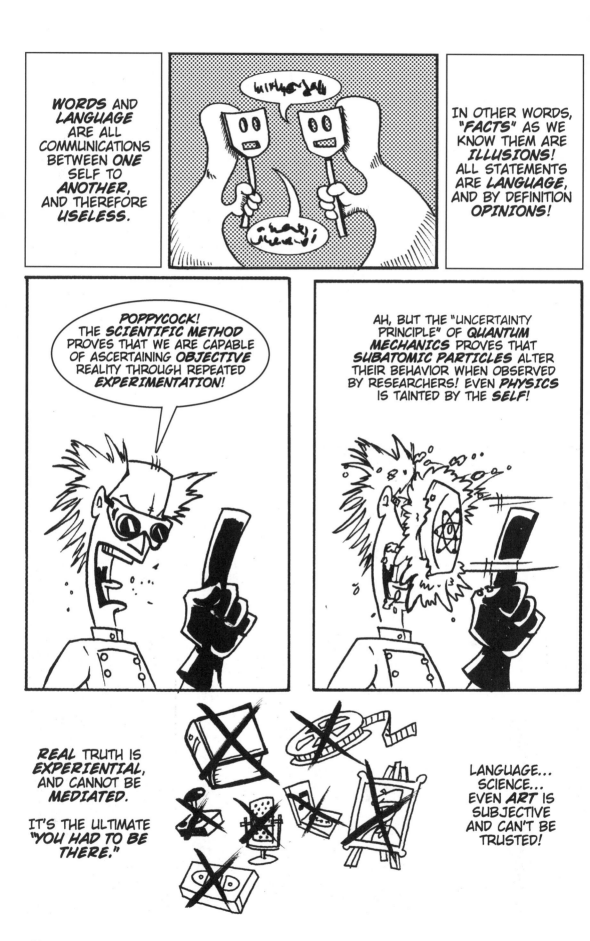

WORDS AND LANGUAGE ARE ALL COMMUNICATIONS BETWEEN ONE SELF TO ANOTHER, AND THEREFORE USELESS.

IN OTHER WORDS, "FACTS" AS WE KNOW THEM ARE ILLUSIONS! ALL STATEMENTS ARE LANGUAGE, AND BY DEFINITION OPINIONS!

POPPYCOCK! THE SCIENTIFIC METHOD PROVES THAT WE ARE CAPABLE OF ASCERTAINING OBJECTIVE REALITY THROUGH REPEATED EXPERIMENTATION!

AH, BUT THE "UNCERTAINTY PRINCIPLE" OF QUANTUM MECHANICS PROVES THAT SUBATOMIC PARTICLES ALTER THEIR BEHAVIOR WHEN OBSERVED BY RESEARCHERS! EVEN PHYSICS IS TAINTED BY THE SELF!

REAL TRUTH IS EXPERIENTIAL, AND CANNOT BE MEDIATED.

IT'S THE ULTIMATE "YOU HAD TO BE THERE."

LANGUAGE... SCIENCE... EVEN ART IS SUBJECTIVE AND CAN'T BE TRUSTED!

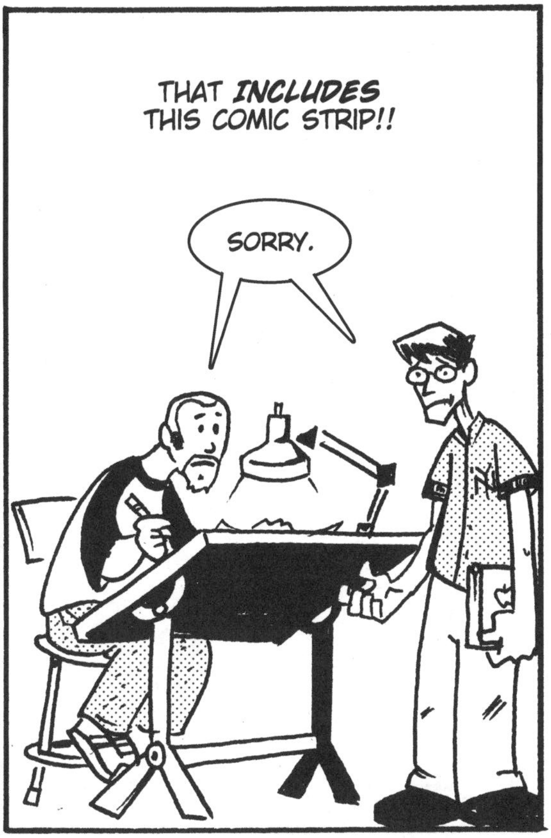
THAT INCLUDES
THIS COMIC STRIP!!
SORRY.

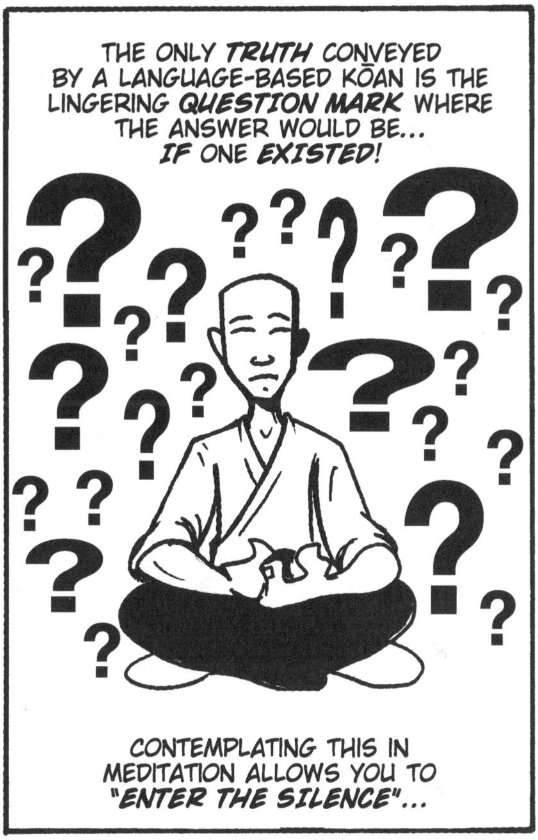
THE ONLY TRUTH CONVEYED BY A LANGUAGE-BASED KŌAN IS THE LINGERING QUESTION MARK WHERE THE ANSWER WOULD BE... IF ONE EXISTED!
CONTEMPLATING THIS IN MEDITATION ALLOWS YOU TO "ENTER THE SILENCE"...

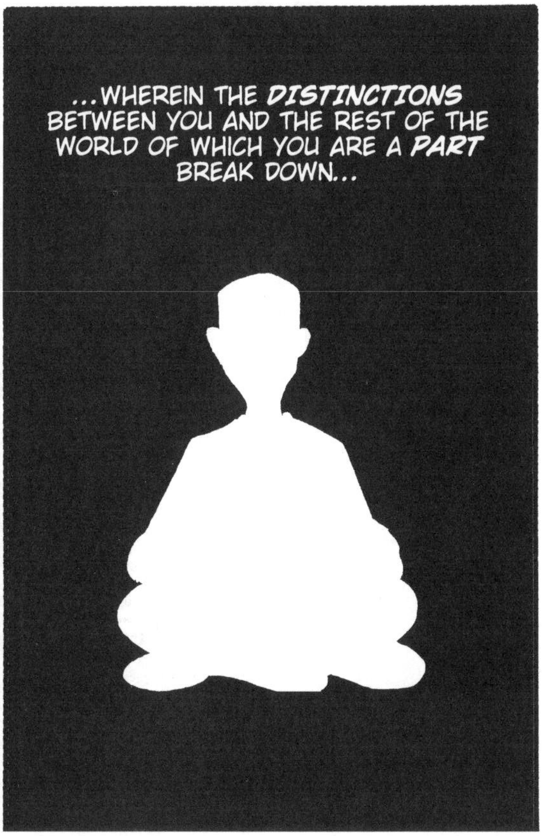
...WHEREIN THE DISTINCTIONS BETWEEN YOU AND THE REST OF THE WORLD OF WHICH YOU ARE A PART BREAK DOWN...

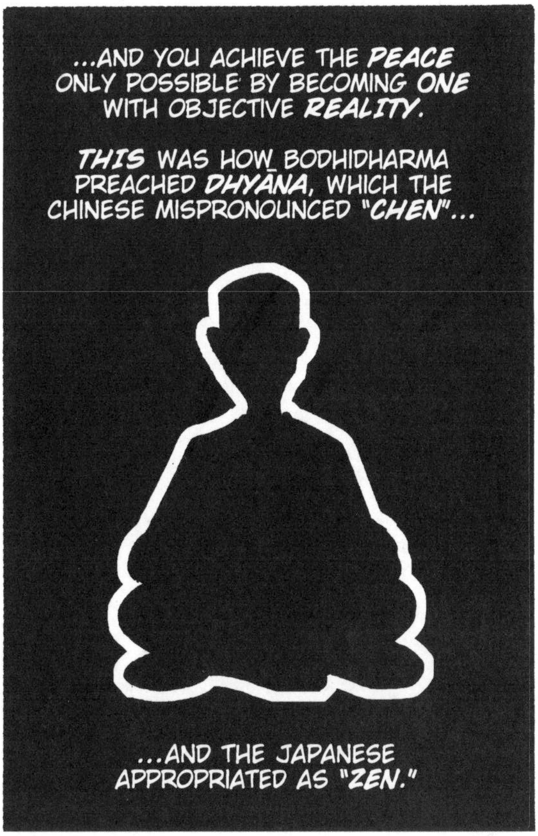
...AND YOU ACHIEVE THE PEACE ONLY POSSIBLE BY BECOMING ONE WITH OBJECTIVE REALITY.
THIS WAS HOW BODHIDHARMA PREACHED DHYĀNA, WHICH THE CHINESE MISPRONOUNCED "CHEN"...
...AND THE JAPANESE APPROPRIATED AS "ZEN."

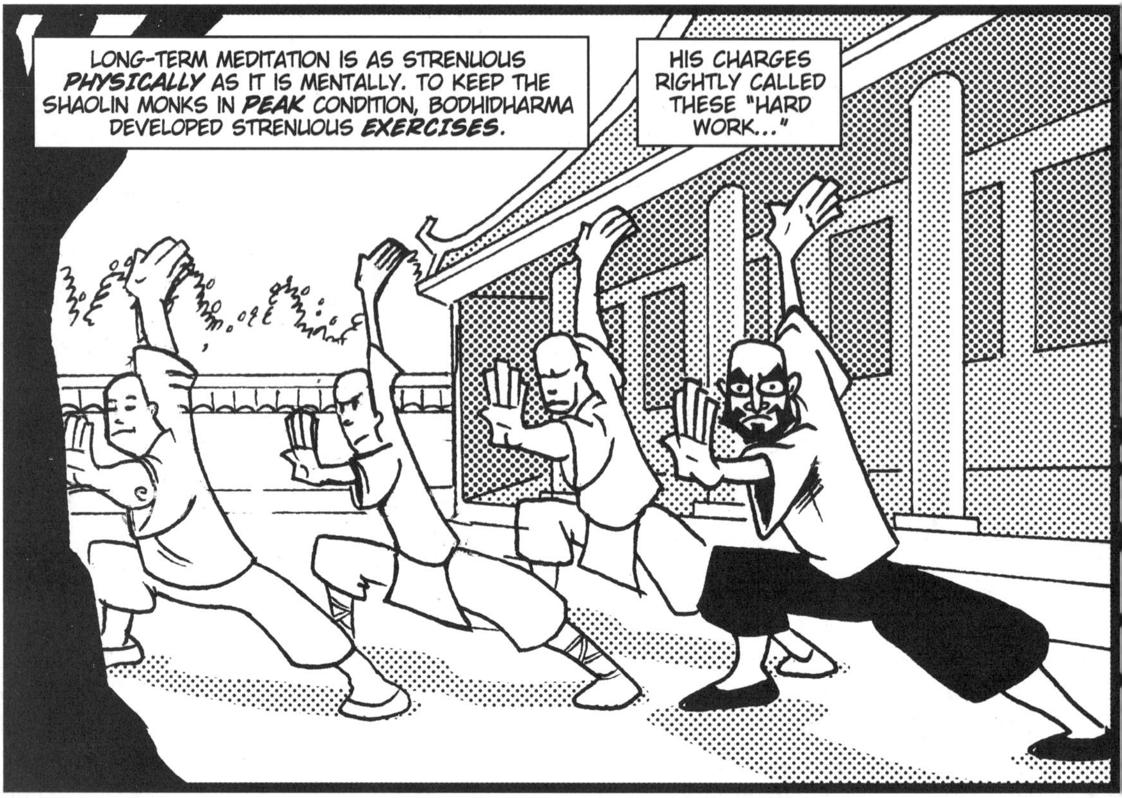
LONG-TERM MEDITATION IS AS STRENUOUS *PHYSICALLY* AS IT IS MENTALLY. TO KEEP THE SHAOLIN MONKS IN *PEAK* CONDITION, BODHIDHARMA DEVELOPED STRENUOUS *EXERCISES.*
HIS CHARGES RIGHTLY CALLED THESE "HARD WORK..."

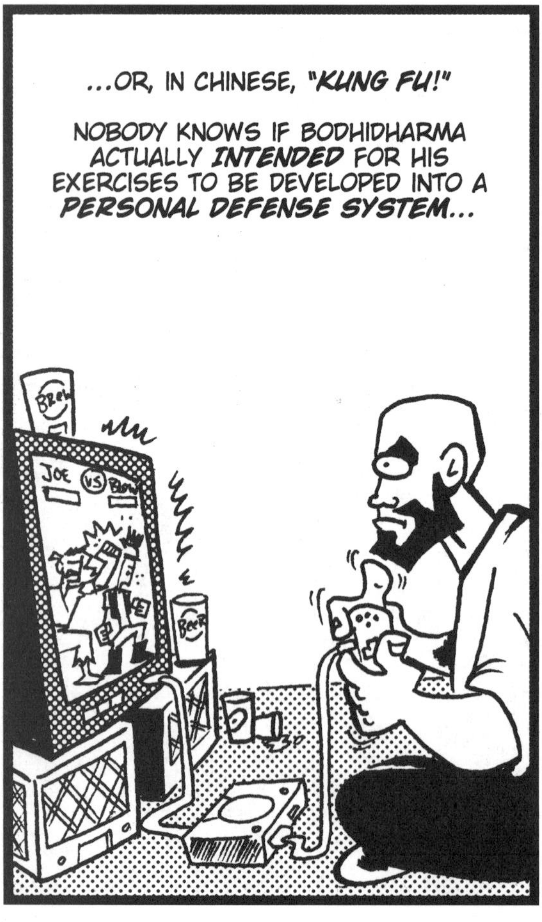
...OR, IN CHINESE, "*KUNG FU!*"
NOBODY KNOWS IF BODHIDHARMA ACTUALLY *INTENDED* FOR HIS EXERCISES TO BE DEVELOPED INTO A *PERSONAL DEFENSE SYSTEM...*
JOE VS BLOW
BEER

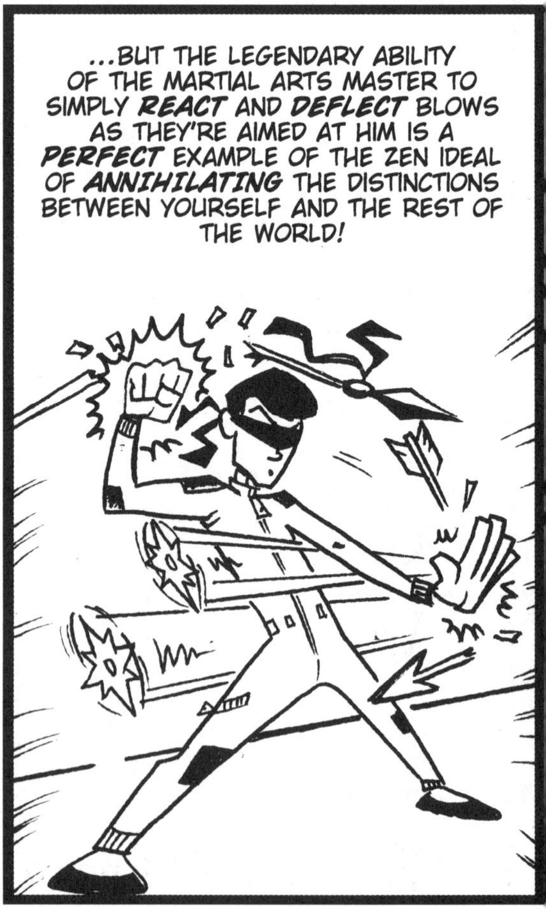
...BUT THE LEGENDARY ABILITY OF THE MARTIAL ARTS MASTER TO SIMPLY *REACT* AND *DEFLECT* BLOWS AS THEY'RE AIMED AT HIM IS A *PERFECT* EXAMPLE OF THE ZEN IDEAL OF *ANNIHILATING* THE DISTINCTIONS BETWEEN YOURSELF AND THE REST OF THE WORLD!

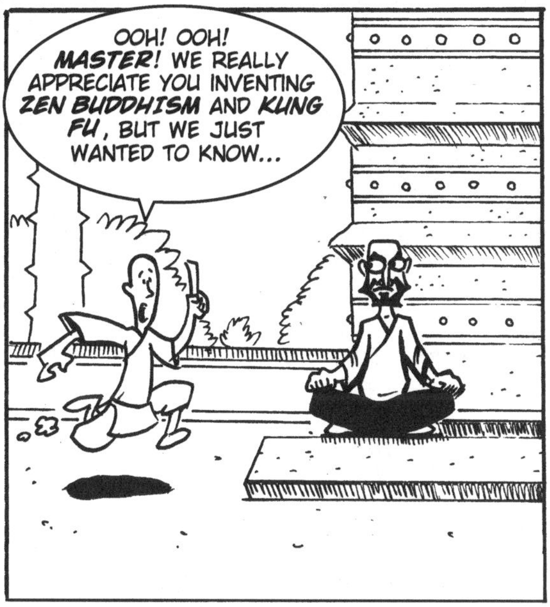
OOH! OOH! MASTER! WE REALLY APPRECIATE YOU INVENTING ZEN BUDDHISM AND KUNG FU, BUT WE JUST WANTED TO KNOW...

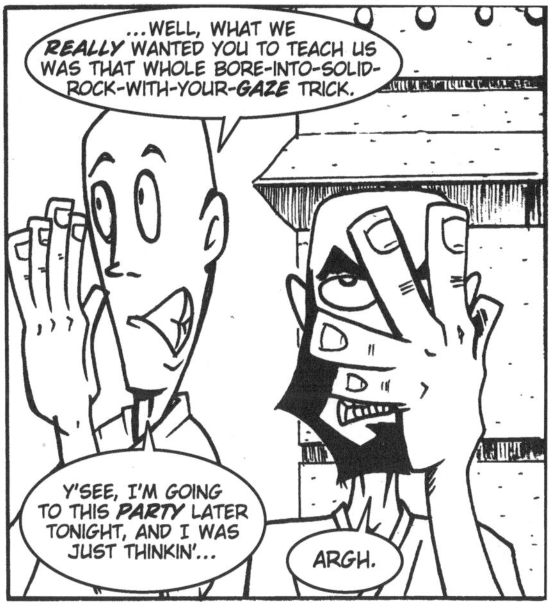
...WELL, WHAT WE REALLY WANTED YOU TO TEACH US WAS THAT WHOLE BORE-INTO-SOLID-ROCK-WITH-YOUR-GAZE TRICK.
Y'SEE, I'M GOING TO THIS PARTY LATER TONIGHT, AND I WAS JUST THINKIN'...
ARGH.

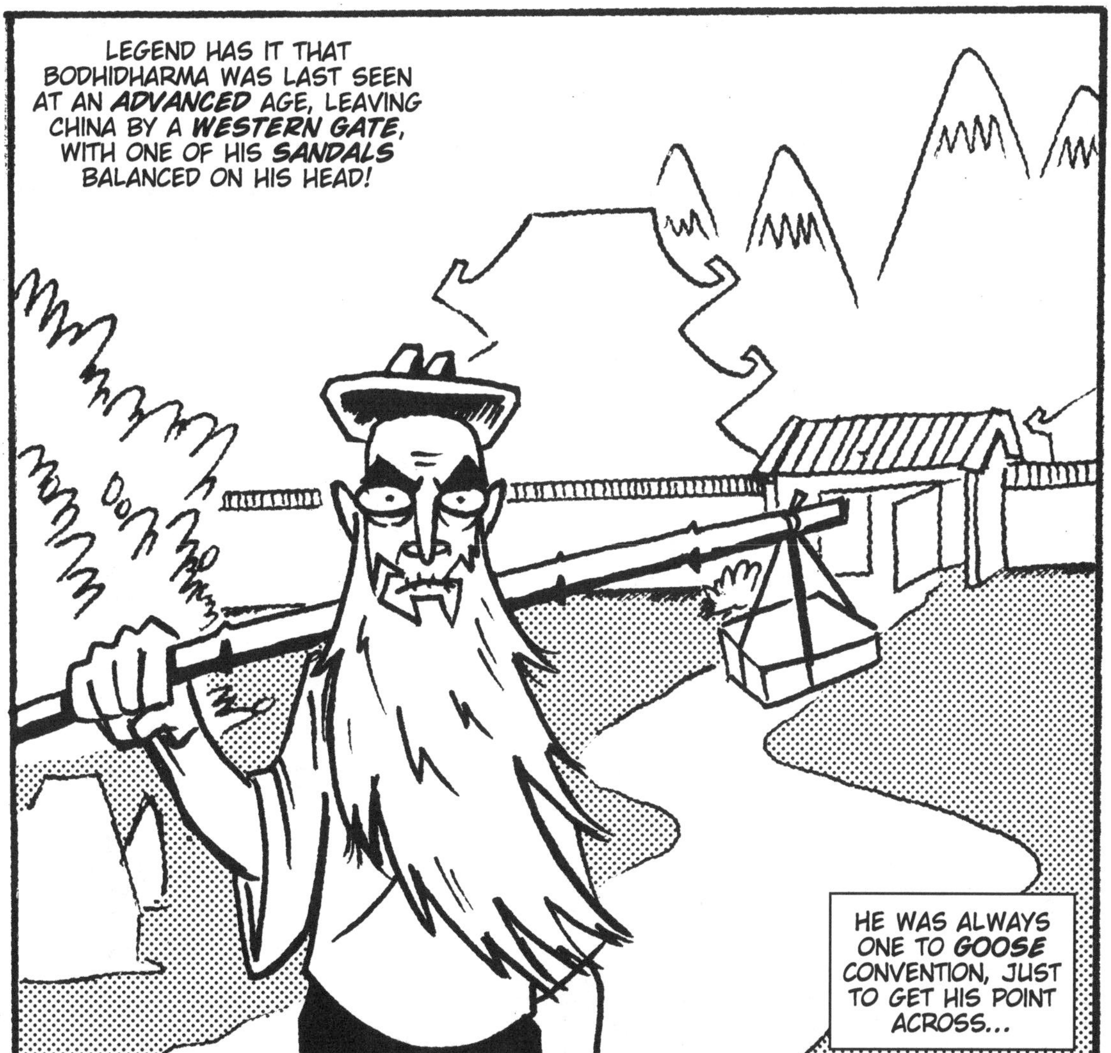
LEGEND HAS IT THAT BODHIDHARMA WAS LAST SEEN AT AN ADVANCED AGE, LEAVING CHINA BY A WESTERN GATE, WITH ONE OF HIS SANDALS BALANCED ON HIS HEAD!
HE WAS ALWAYS ONE TO GOOSE CONVENTION, JUST TO GET HIS POINT ACROSS...

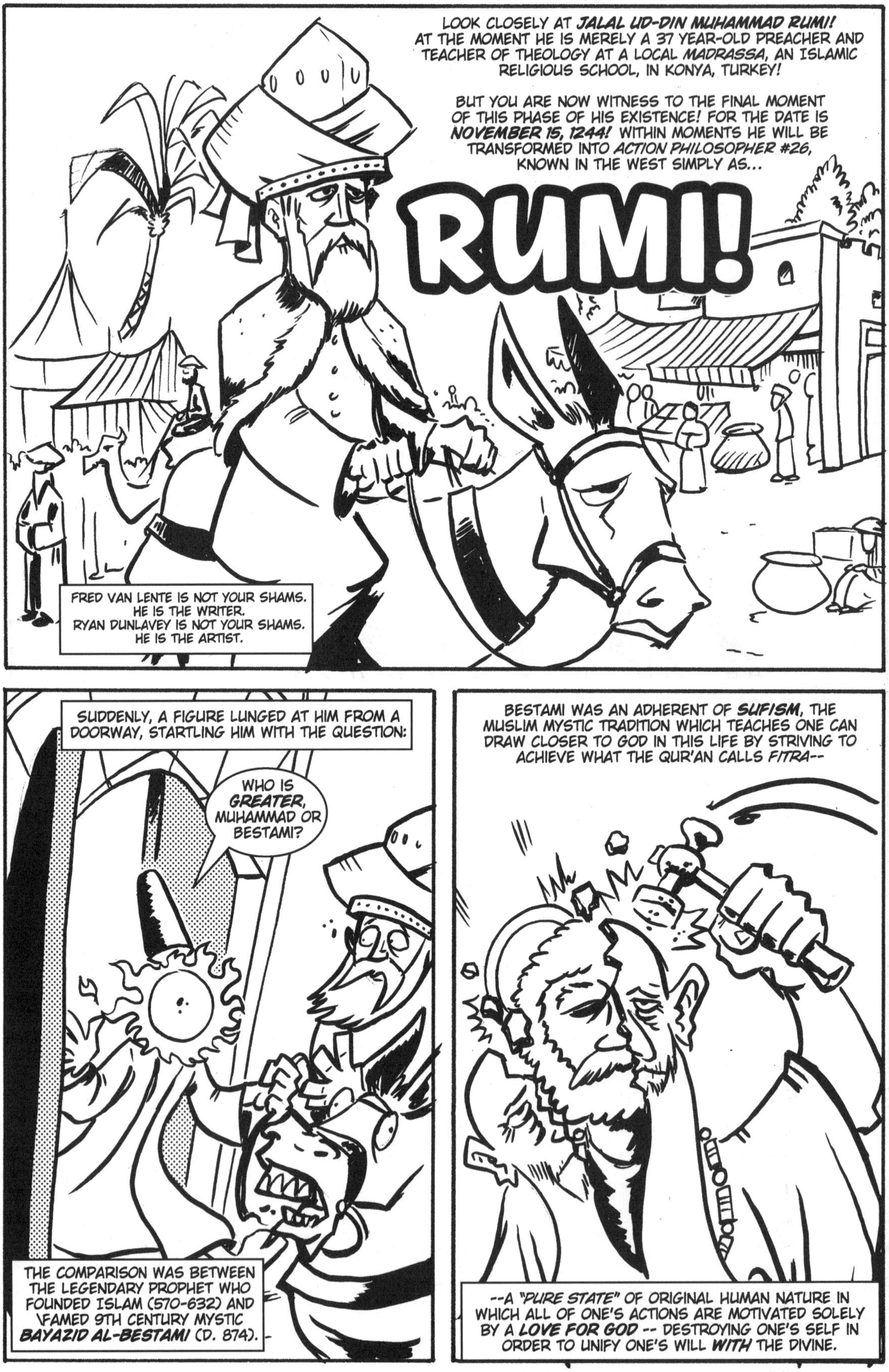
LOOK CLOSELY AT JALAL UD-DIN MUHAMMAD RUMI! AT THE MOMENT HE IS MERELY A 37 YEAR-OLD PREACHER AND TEACHER OF THEOLOGY AT A LOCAL MADRASSA, AN ISLAMIC RELIGIOUS SCHOOL, IN KONYA, TURKEY!
BUT YOU ARE NOW WITNESS TO THE FINAL MOMENT OF THIS PHASE OF HIS EXISTENCE! FOR THE DATE IS NOVEMBER 15, 1244! WITHIN MOMENTS HE WILL BE TRANSFORMED INTO ACTION PHILOSOPHER #26, KNOWN IN THE WEST SIMPLY AS...
RUMI!
FRED VAN LENTE IS NOT YOUR SHAMS. HE IS THE WRITER. RYAN DUNLAVEY IS NOT YOUR SHAMS. HE IS THE ARTIST.
SUDDENLY, A FIGURE LUNGED AT HIM FROM A DOORWAY, STARTLING HIM WITH THE QUESTION:
WHO IS GREATER, MUHAMMAD OR BESTAMI?
THE COMPARISON WAS BETWEEN THE LEGENDARY PROPHET WHO FOUNDED ISLAM (570-632) AND FAMED 9TH CENTURY MYSTIC BAYAZID AL-BESTAMI (D. 874).
BESTAMI WAS AN ADHERENT OF SUFISM, THE MUSLIM MYSTIC TRADITION WHICH TEACHES ONE CAN DRAW CLOSER TO GOD IN THIS LIFE BY STRIVING TO ACHIEVE WHAT THE QUR'AN CALLS FITRA--
--A "PURE STATE" OF ORIGINAL HUMAN NATURE IN WHICH ALL OF ONE'S ACTIONS ARE MOTIVATED SOLELY BY A LOVE FOR GOD -- DESTROYING ONE'S SELF IN ORDER TO UNIFY ONE'S WILL WITH THE DIVINE.

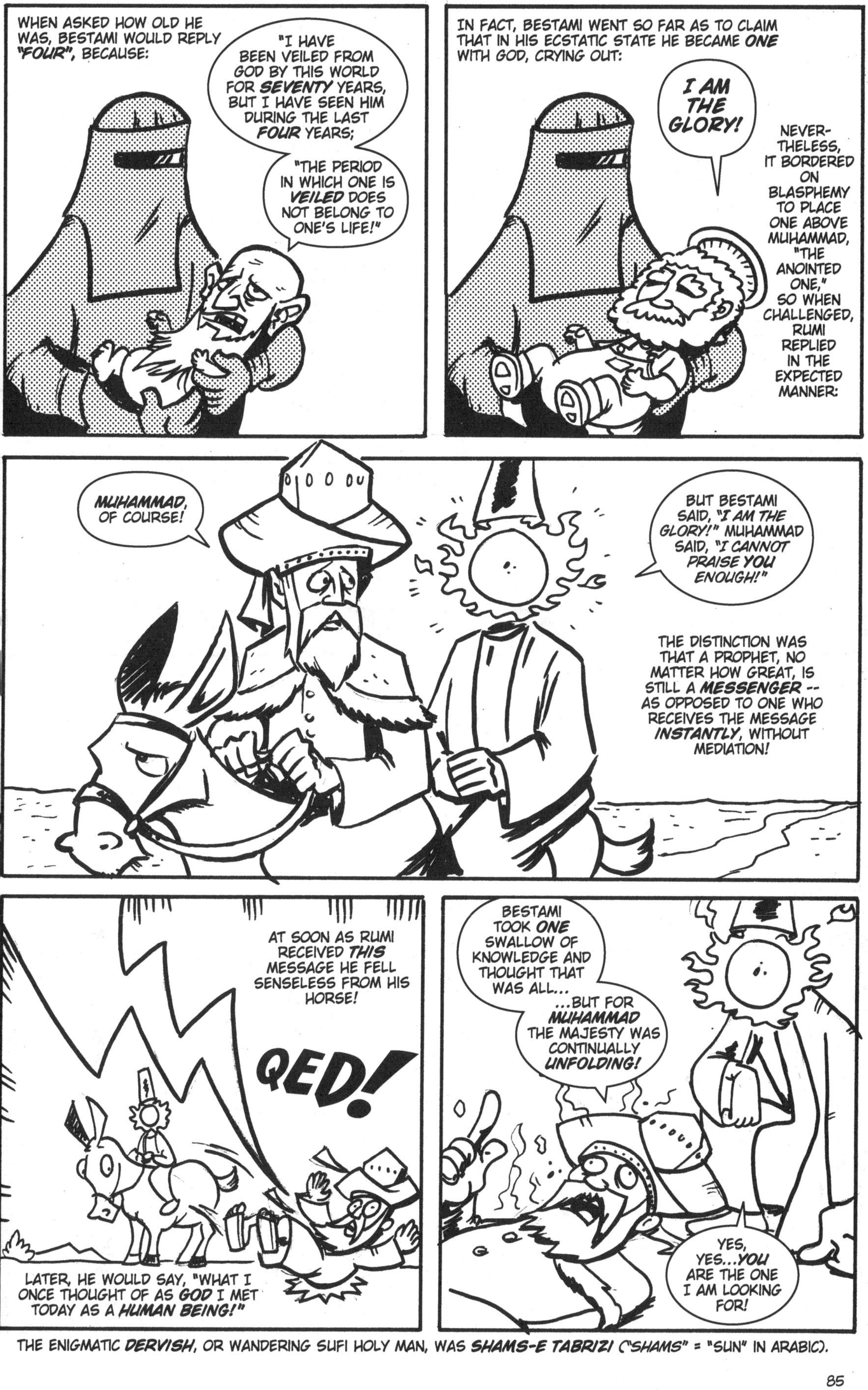
WHEN ASKED HOW OLD HE WAS, BESTAMI WOULD REPLY "FOUR", BECAUSE:
"I HAVE BEEN VEILED FROM GOD BY THIS WORLD FOR SEVENTY YEARS, BUT I HAVE SEEN HIM DURING THE LAST FOUR YEARS;
"THE PERIOD IN WHICH ONE IS VEILED DOES NOT BELONG TO ONE'S LIFE!"
IN FACT, BESTAMI WENT SO FAR AS TO CLAIM THAT IN HIS ECSTATIC STATE HE BECAME ONE WITH GOD, CRYING OUT:
I AM THE GLORY!
NEVER-THELESS, IT BORDERED ON BLASPHEMY TO PLACE ONE ABOVE MUHAMMAD, "THE ANOINTED ONE," SO WHEN CHALLENGED, RUMI REPLIED IN THE EXPECTED MANNER:
MUHAMMAD, OF COURSE!
BUT BESTAMI SAID, "I AM THE GLORY!" MUHAMMAD SAID, "I CANNOT PRAISE YOU ENOUGH!"
THE DISTINCTION WAS THAT A PROPHET, NO MATTER HOW GREAT, IS STILL A MESSENGER -- AS OPPOSED TO ONE WHO RECEIVES THE MESSAGE INSTANTLY, WITHOUT MEDIATION!
AT SOON AS RUMI RECEIVED THIS MESSAGE HE FELL SENSELESS FROM HIS HORSE!
QED!
LATER, HE WOULD SAY, "WHAT I ONCE THOUGHT OF AS GOD I MET TODAY AS A HUMAN BEING!"
BESTAMI TOOK ONE SWALLOW OF KNOWLEDGE AND THOUGHT THAT WAS ALL...
...BUT FOR MUHAMMAD THE MAJESTY WAS CONTINUALLY UNFOLDING!
YES, YES...YOU ARE THE ONE I AM LOOKING FOR!

THE ENIGMATIC ***DERVISH***, OR WANDERING SUFI HOLY MAN, WAS ***SHAMS-E TABRIZI*** ("*SHAMS*" = "SUN" IN ARABIC).

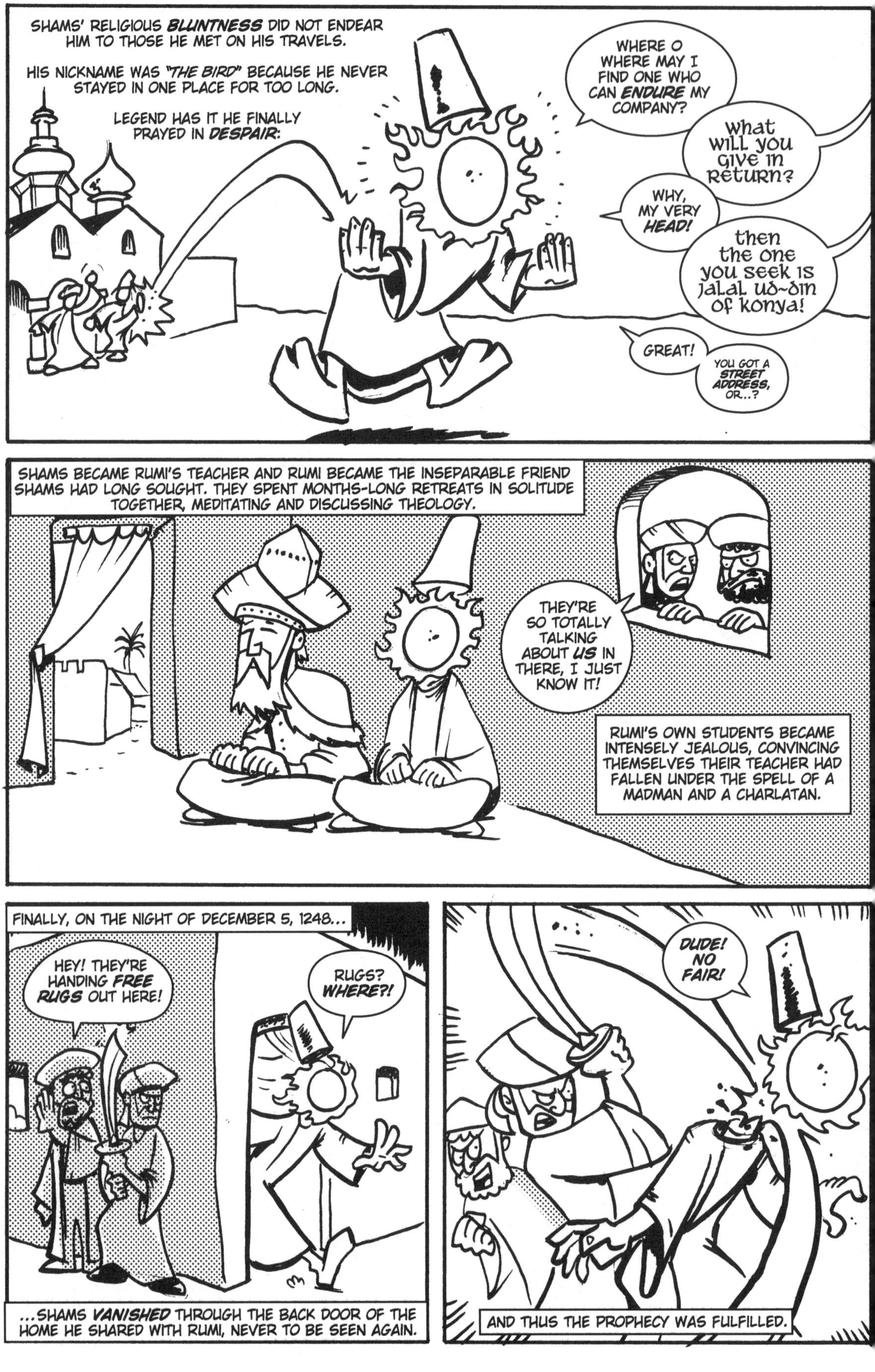
SHAMS' RELIGIOUS BLUNTNESS DID NOT ENDEAR HIM TO THOSE HE MET ON HIS TRAVELS.
HIS NICKNAME WAS "THE BIRD" BECAUSE HE NEVER STAYED IN ONE PLACE FOR TOO LONG.
LEGEND HAS IT HE FINALLY PRAYED IN DESPAIR:
WHERE O WHERE MAY I FIND ONE WHO CAN ENDURE MY COMPANY?
What will you give in return?
WHY, MY VERY HEAD!
then the one you seek is Jalal ud-din of konya!
GREAT!
YOU GOT A STREET ADDRESS, OR..?
SHAMS BECAME RUMI'S TEACHER AND RUMI BECAME THE INSEPARABLE FRIEND SHAMS HAD LONG SOUGHT. THEY SPENT MONTHS-LONG RETREATS IN SOLITUDE TOGETHER, MEDITATING AND DISCUSSING THEOLOGY.
THEY'RE SO TOTALLY TALKING ABOUT US IN THERE, I JUST KNOW IT!
RUMI'S OWN STUDENTS BECAME INTENSELY JEALOUS, CONVINCING THEMSELVES THEIR TEACHER HAD FALLEN UNDER THE SPELL OF A MADMAN AND A CHARLATAN.
FINALLY, ON THE NIGHT OF DECEMBER 5, 1248...
HEY! THEY'RE HANDING FREE RUGS OUT HERE!
RUGS? WHERE?!
...SHAMS VANISHED THROUGH THE BACK DOOR OF THE HOME HE SHARED WITH RUMI, NEVER TO BE SEEN AGAIN.
DUDE! NO FAIR!
AND THUS THE PROPHECY WAS FULFILLED.

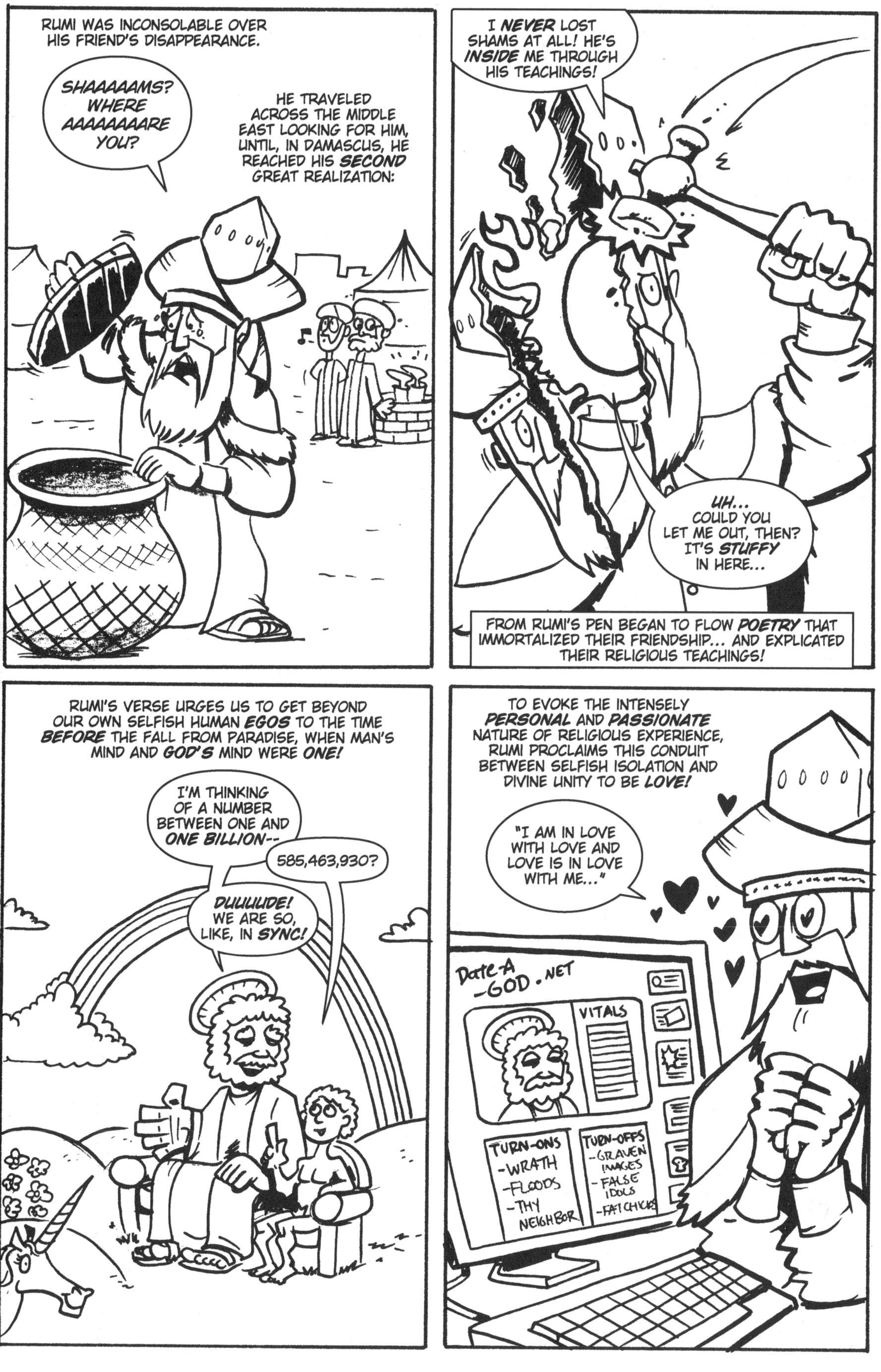

RUMI WAS INCONSOLABLE OVER HIS FRIEND'S DISAPPEARANCE.
SHAAAAAMS? WHERE AAAAAAAARE YOU?
HE TRAVELED ACROSS THE MIDDLE EAST LOOKING FOR HIM, UNTIL, IN DAMASCUS, HE REACHED HIS SECOND GREAT REALIZATION:
I NEVER LOST SHAMS AT ALL! HE'S INSIDE ME THROUGH HIS TEACHINGS!
UH... COULD YOU LET ME OUT, THEN? IT'S STUFFY IN HERE...
FROM RUMI'S PEN BEGAN TO FLOW POETRY THAT IMMORTALIZED THEIR FRIENDSHIP... AND EXPLICATED THEIR RELIGIOUS TEACHINGS!
RUMI'S VERSE URGES US TO GET BEYOND OUR OWN SELFISH HUMAN EGOS TO THE TIME BEFORE THE FALL FROM PARADISE, WHEN MAN'S MIND AND GOD'S MIND WERE ONE!
I'M THINKING OF A NUMBER BETWEEN ONE AND ONE BILLION--
585,463,930?
DUUUUDE! WE ARE SO, LIKE, IN SYNC!
TO EVOKE THE INTENSELY PERSONAL AND PASSIONATE NATURE OF RELIGIOUS EXPERIENCE, RUMI PROCLAIMS THIS CONDUIT BETWEEN SELFISH ISOLATION AND DIVINE UNITY TO BE LOVE!
"I AM IN LOVE WITH LOVE AND LOVE IS IN LOVE WITH ME..."
Date-A-GOD.NET
VITALS
TURN-ONS -WRATH -FLOODS -THY NEIGHBOR
TURN-OFFS -GRAVEN IMAGES -FALSE IDOLS -FAT CHICKS

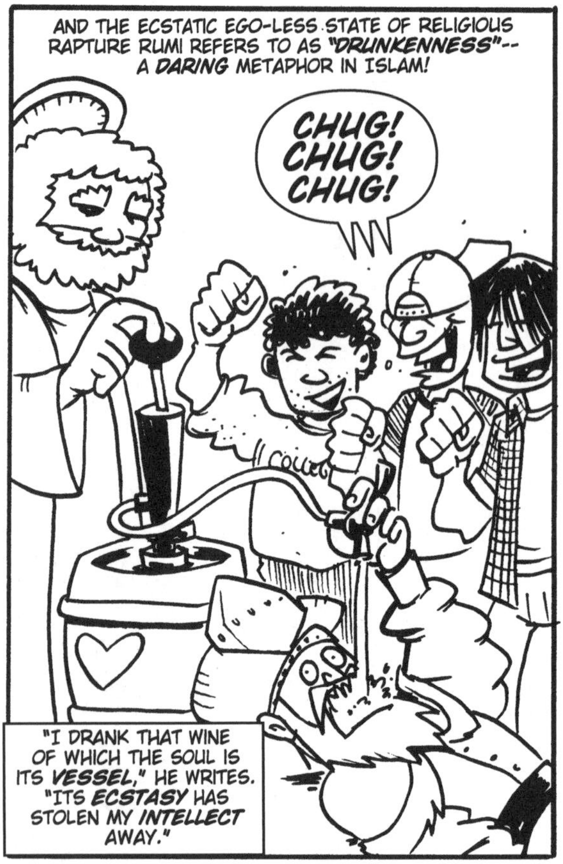
AND THE ECSTATIC EGO-LESS STATE OF RELIGIOUS RAPTURE RUMI REFERS TO AS "DRUNKENNESS"-- A DARING METAPHOR IN ISLAM!
CHUG! CHUG! CHUG!
"I DRANK THAT WINE OF WHICH THE SOUL IS ITS VESSEL," HE WRITES. "ITS ECSTASY HAS STOLEN MY INTELLECT AWAY."

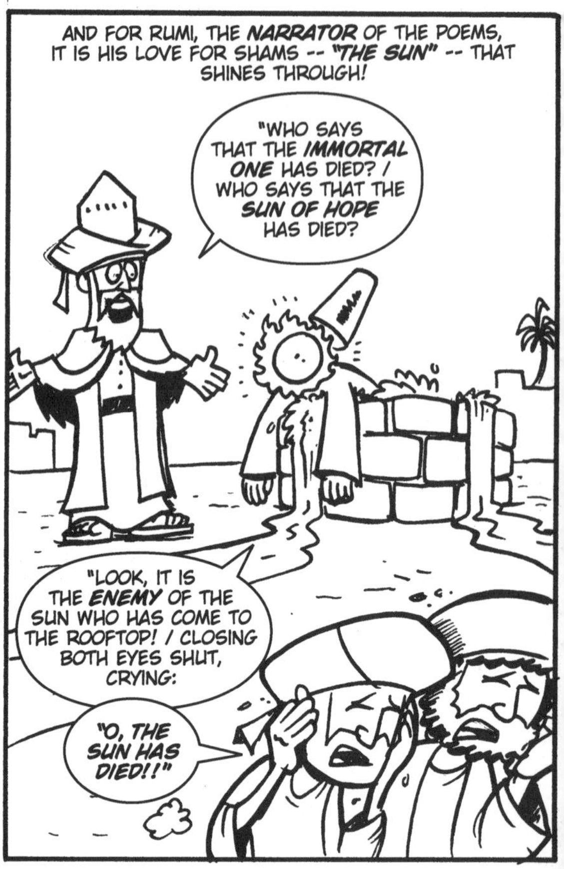
AND FOR RUMI, THE NARRATOR OF THE POEMS, IT IS HIS LOVE FOR SHAMS -- "THE SUN" -- THAT SHINES THROUGH!
"WHO SAYS THAT THE IMMORTAL ONE HAS DIED? / WHO SAYS THAT THE SUN OF HOPE HAS DIED?
"LOOK, IT IS THE ENEMY OF THE SUN WHO HAS COME TO THE ROOFTOP! / CLOSING BOTH EYES SHUT, CRYING:
"O, THE SUN HAS DIED!!"

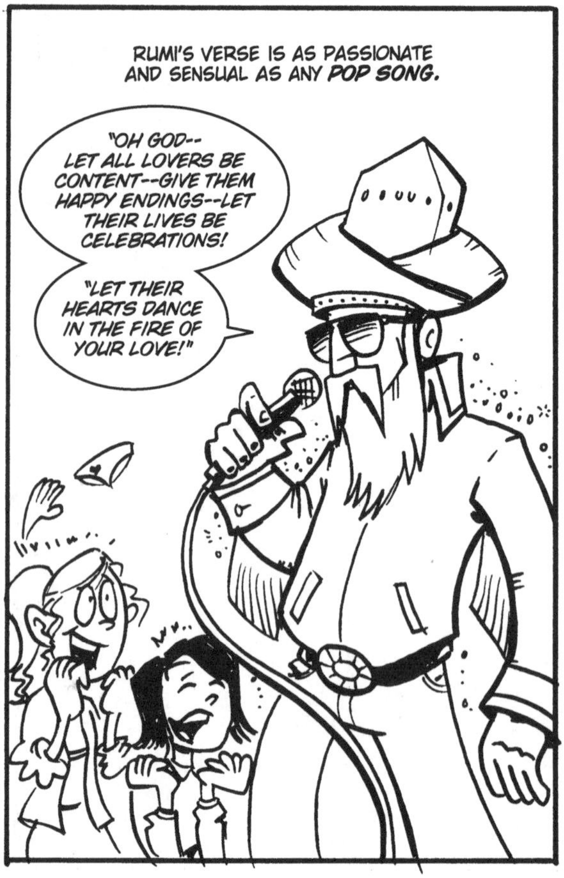
RUMI'S VERSE IS AS PASSIONATE AND SENSUAL AS ANY POP SONG.
"OH GOD-- LET ALL LOVERS BE CONTENT--GIVE THEM HAPPY ENDINGS--LET THEIR LIVES BE CELEBRATIONS!
"LET THEIR HEARTS DANCE IN THE FIRE OF YOUR LOVE!"

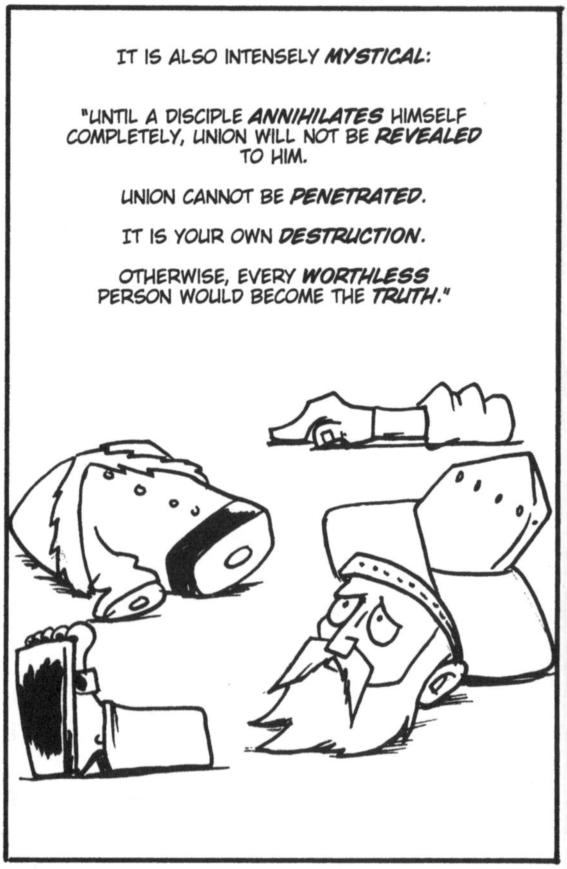
IT IS ALSO INTENSELY MYSTICAL:
"UNTIL A DISCIPLE ANNIHILATES HIMSELF COMPLETELY, UNION WILL NOT BE REVEALED TO HIM.
UNION CANNOT BE PENETRATED.
IT IS YOUR OWN DESTRUCTION.
OTHERWISE, EVERY WORTHLESS PERSON WOULD BECOME THE TRUTH."

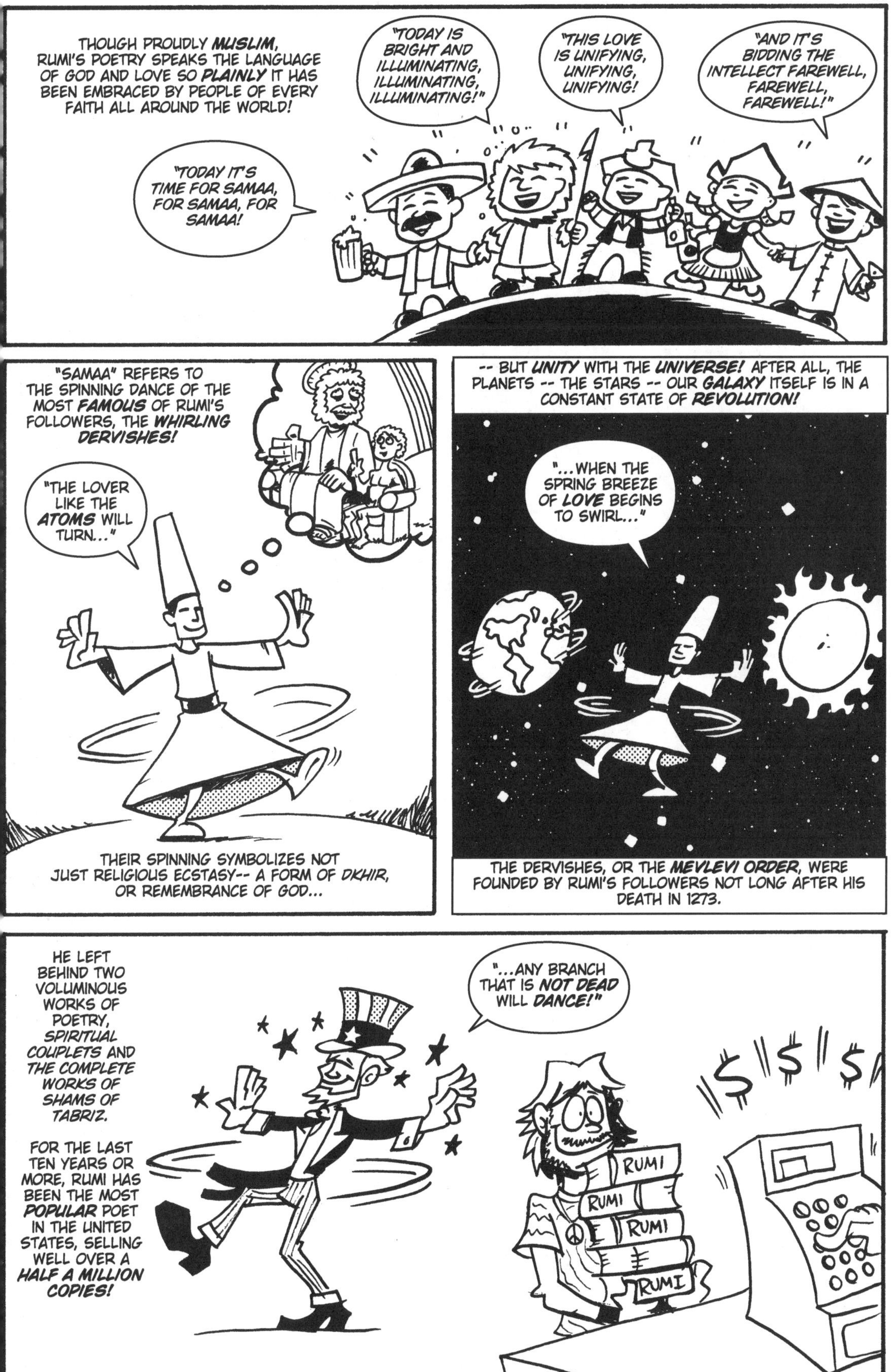

THOUGH PROUDLY MUSLIM, RUMI'S POETRY SPEAKS THE LANGUAGE OF GOD AND LOVE SO PLAINLY IT HAS BEEN EMBRACED BY PEOPLE OF EVERY FAITH ALL AROUND THE WORLD!
"TODAY IT'S TIME FOR SAMAA, FOR SAMAA, FOR SAMAA!
"TODAY IS BRIGHT AND ILLUMINATING, ILLUMINATING, ILLUMINATING!"
"THIS LOVE IS UNIFYING, UNIFYING, UNIFYING!
"AND IT'S BIDDING THE INTELLECT FAREWELL, FAREWELL, FAREWELL!"
"SAMAA" REFERS TO THE SPINNING DANCE OF THE MOST FAMOUS OF RUMI'S FOLLOWERS, THE WHIRLING DERVISHES!
"THE LOVER LIKE THE ATOMS WILL TURN..."
THEIR SPINNING SYMBOLIZES NOT JUST RELIGIOUS ECSTASY-- A FORM OF DKHIR, OR REMEMBRANCE OF GOD...
-- BUT UNITY WITH THE UNIVERSE! AFTER ALL, THE PLANETS -- THE STARS -- OUR GALAXY ITSELF IS IN A CONSTANT STATE OF REVOLUTION!
"...WHEN THE SPRING BREEZE OF LOVE BEGINS TO SWIRL..."
THE DERVISHES, OR THE MEVLEVI ORDER, WERE FOUNDED BY RUMI'S FOLLOWERS NOT LONG AFTER HIS DEATH IN 1273.
HE LEFT BEHIND TWO VOLUMINOUS WORKS OF POETRY, SPIRITUAL COUPLETS AND THE COMPLETE WORKS OF SHAMS OF TABRIZ.
FOR THE LAST TEN YEARS OR MORE, RUMI HAS BEEN THE MOST POPULAR POET IN THE UNITED STATES, SELLING WELL OVER A HALF A MILLION COPIES!
"...ANY BRANCH THAT IS NOT DEAD WILL DANCE!"
RUMI
RUMI
RUMI
RUMI
$ $ $

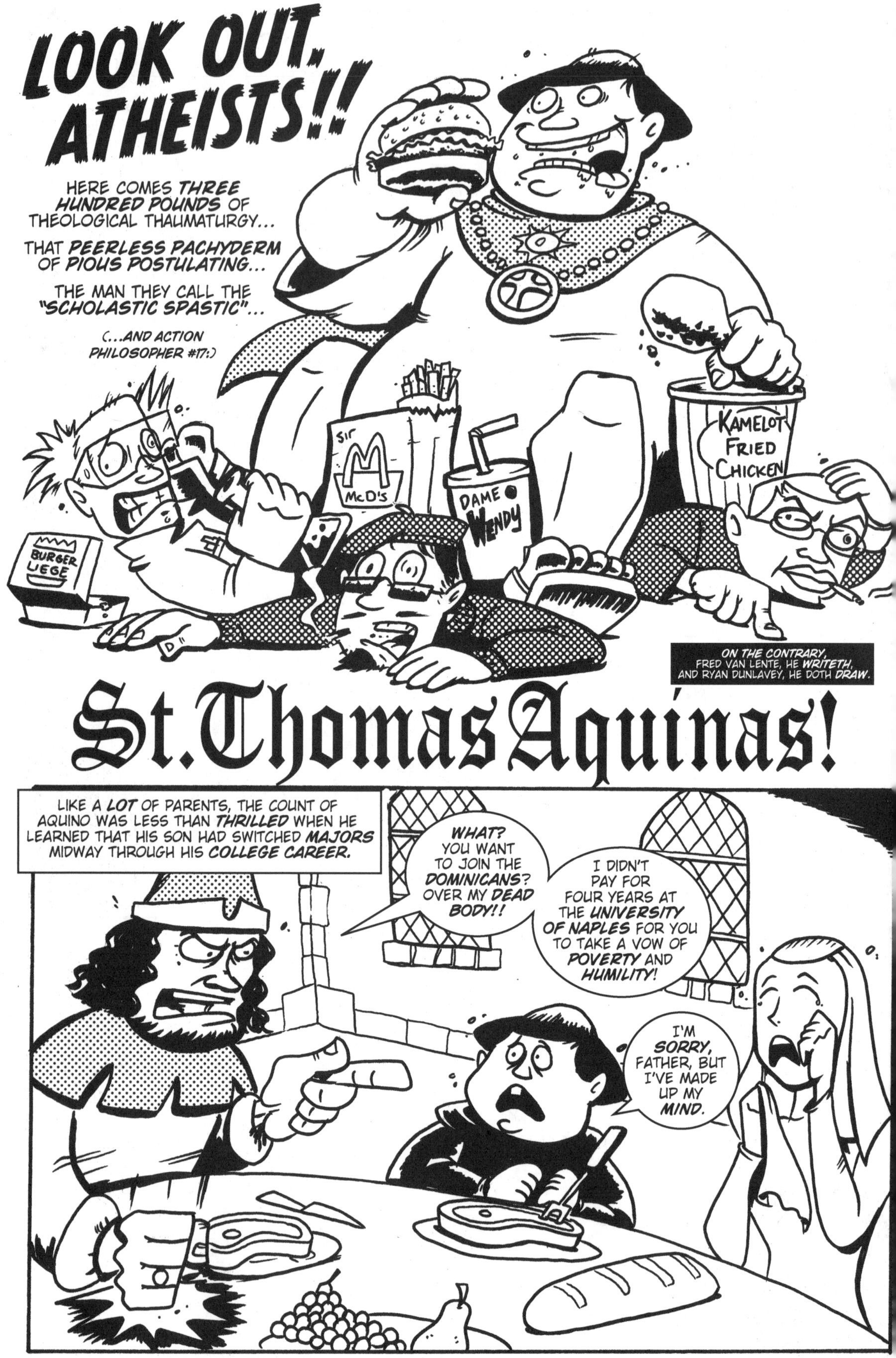
LOOK OUT, ATHEISTS!!
HERE COMES THREE HUNDRED POUNDS OF THEOLOGICAL THAUMATURGY...
THAT PEERLESS PACHYDERM OF PIOUS POSTULATING...
THE MAN THEY CALL THE "SCHOLASTIC SPASTIC"...
(...AND ACTION PHILOSOPHER #17:)
SIR McD'S
DAME WENDY
KAMELOT FRIED CHICKEN
BURGER LIEGE
ON THE CONTRARY, FRED VAN LENTE, HE WRITETH, AND RYAN DUNLAVEY, HE DOTH DRAW.
St. Thomas Aquinas!
LIKE A LOT OF PARENTS, THE COUNT OF AQUINO WAS LESS THAN THRILLED WHEN HE LEARNED THAT HIS SON HAD SWITCHED MAJORS MIDWAY THROUGH HIS COLLEGE CAREER.
WHAT? YOU WANT TO JOIN THE DOMINICANS? OVER MY DEAD BODY!!
I DIDN'T PAY FOR FOUR YEARS AT THE UNIVERSITY OF NAPLES FOR YOU TO TAKE A VOW OF POVERTY AND HUMILITY!
I'M SORRY, FATHER, BUT I'VE MADE UP MY MIND.

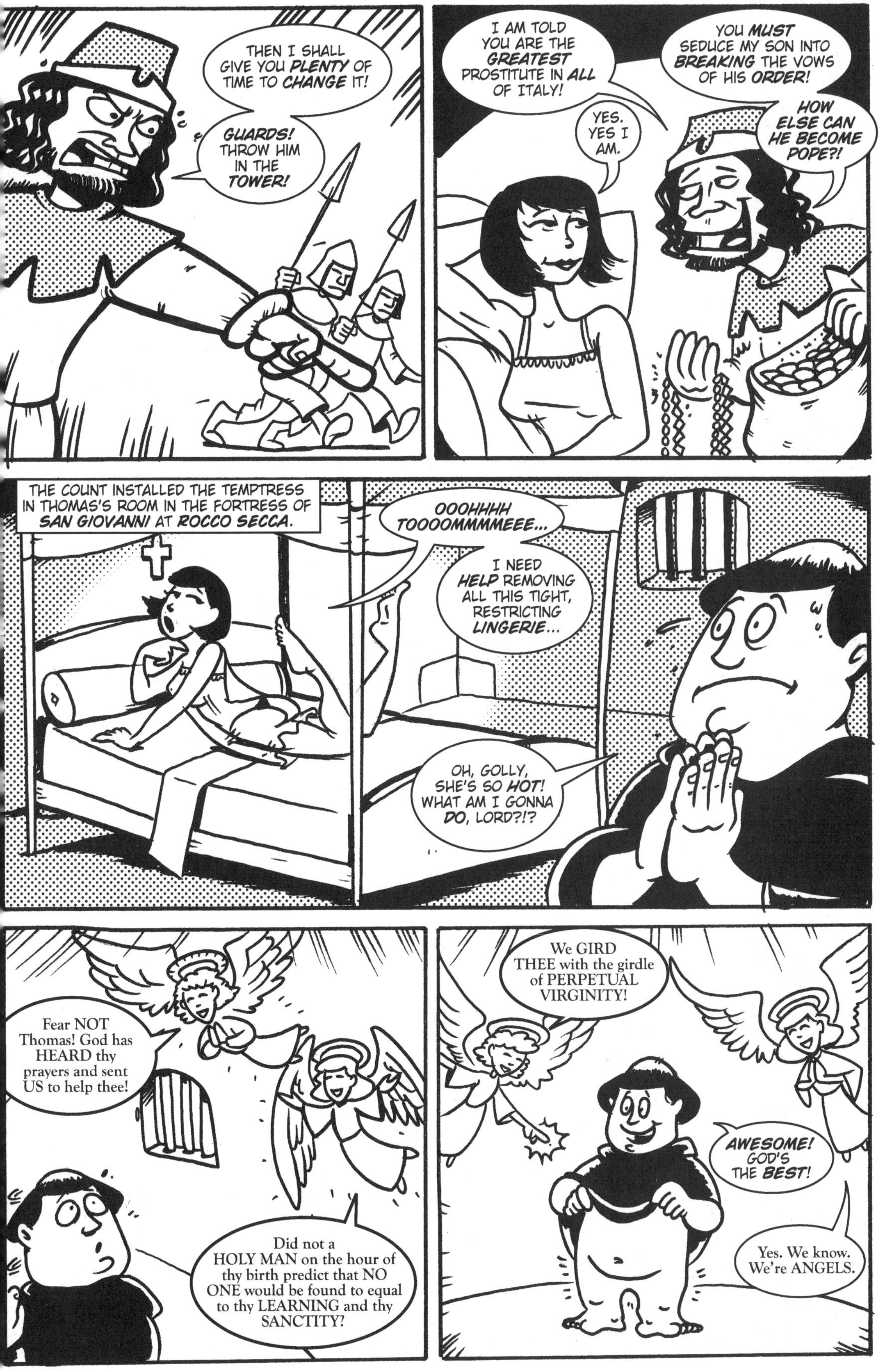
THEN I SHALL GIVE YOU PLENTY OF TIME TO CHANGE IT!
GUARDS! THROW HIM IN THE TOWER!
I AM TOLD YOU ARE THE GREATEST PROSTITUTE IN ALL OF ITALY!
YES. YES I AM.
YOU MUST SEDUCE MY SON INTO BREAKING THE VOWS OF HIS ORDER!
HOW ELSE CAN HE BECOME POPE?!
THE COUNT INSTALLED THE TEMPTRESS IN THOMAS'S ROOM IN THE FORTRESS OF SAN GIOVANNI AT ROCCO SECCA.
OOOHHHH TOOOOMMMMEEE...
I NEED HELP REMOVING ALL THIS TIGHT, RESTRICTING LINGERIE...
OH, GOLLY, SHE'S SO HOT! WHAT AM I GONNA DO, LORD?!?
Fear NOT Thomas! God has HEARD thy prayers and sent US to help thee!
Did not a HOLY MAN on the hour of thy birth predict that NO ONE would be found to equal to thy LEARNING and thy SANCTITY?
We GIRD THEE with the girdle of PERPETUAL VIRGINITY!
AWESOME! GOD'S THE BEST!
Yes. We know. We're ANGELS.

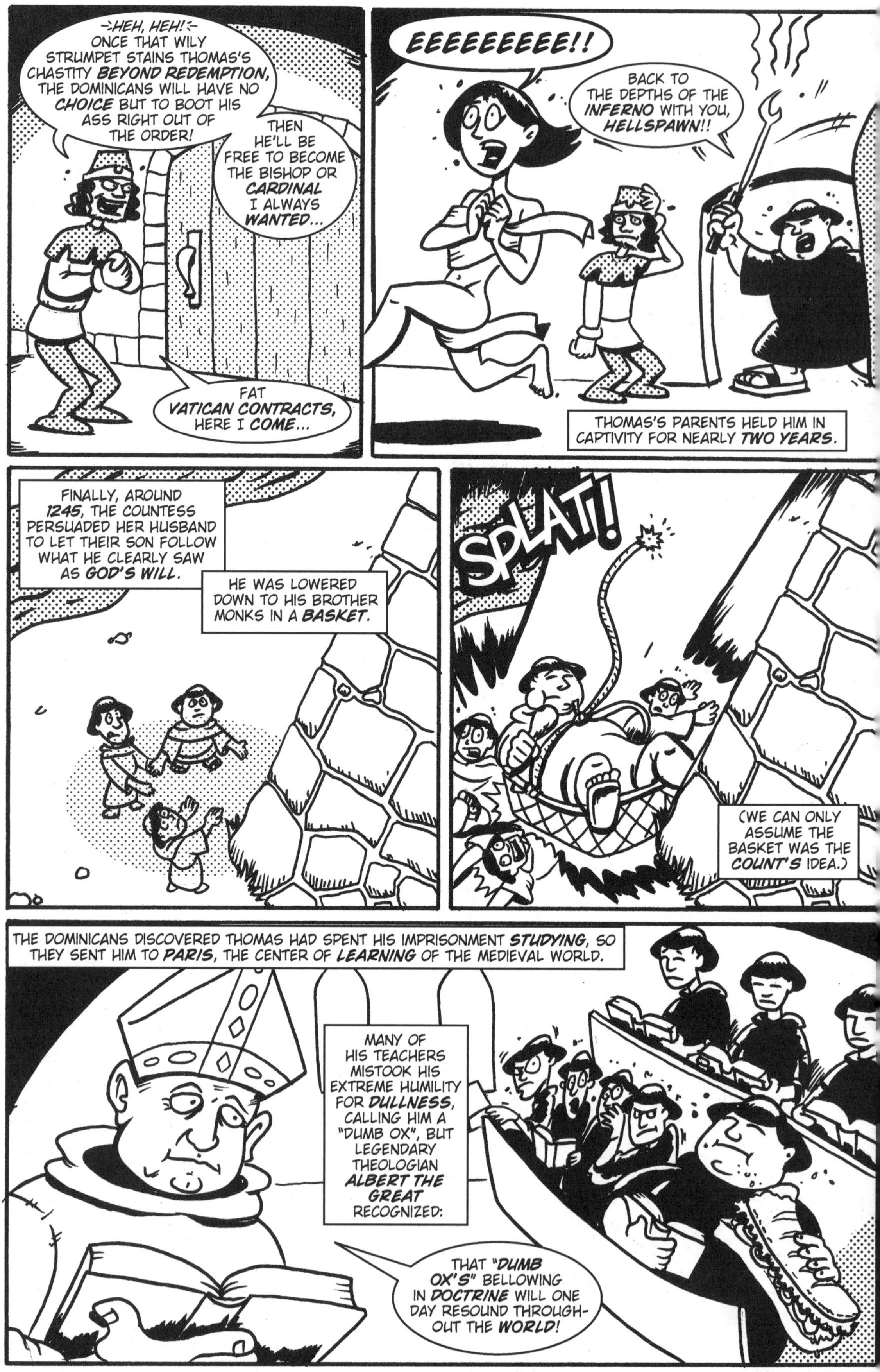
HEH, HEH!
ONCE THAT WILY STRUMPET STAINS THOMAS'S CHASTITY BEYOND REDEMPTION, THE DOMINICANS WILL HAVE NO CHOICE BUT TO BOOT HIS ASS RIGHT OUT OF THE ORDER!
THEN HE'LL BE FREE TO BECOME THE BISHOP OR CARDINAL I ALWAYS WANTED...
FAT VATICAN CONTRACTS, HERE I COME...
EEEEEEEEE!!
BACK TO THE DEPTHS OF THE INFERNO WITH YOU, HELLSPAWN!!
THOMAS'S PARENTS HELD HIM IN CAPTIVITY FOR NEARLY TWO YEARS.
FINALLY, AROUND 1245, THE COUNTESS PERSUADED HER HUSBAND TO LET THEIR SON FOLLOW WHAT HE CLEARLY SAW AS GOD'S WILL.
HE WAS LOWERED DOWN TO HIS BROTHER MONKS IN A BASKET.
SPLAT!
(WE CAN ONLY ASSUME THE BASKET WAS THE COUNT'S IDEA.)
THE DOMINICANS DISCOVERED THOMAS HAD SPENT HIS IMPRISONMENT STUDYING, SO THEY SENT HIM TO PARIS, THE CENTER OF LEARNING OF THE MEDIEVAL WORLD.
MANY OF HIS TEACHERS MISTOOK HIS EXTREME HUMILITY FOR DULLNESS, CALLING HIM A "DUMB OX", BUT LEGENDARY THEOLOGIAN ALBERT THE GREAT RECOGNIZED:
THAT "DUMB OX'S" BELLOWING IN DOCTRINE WILL ONE DAY RESOUND THROUGH-OUT THE WORLD!

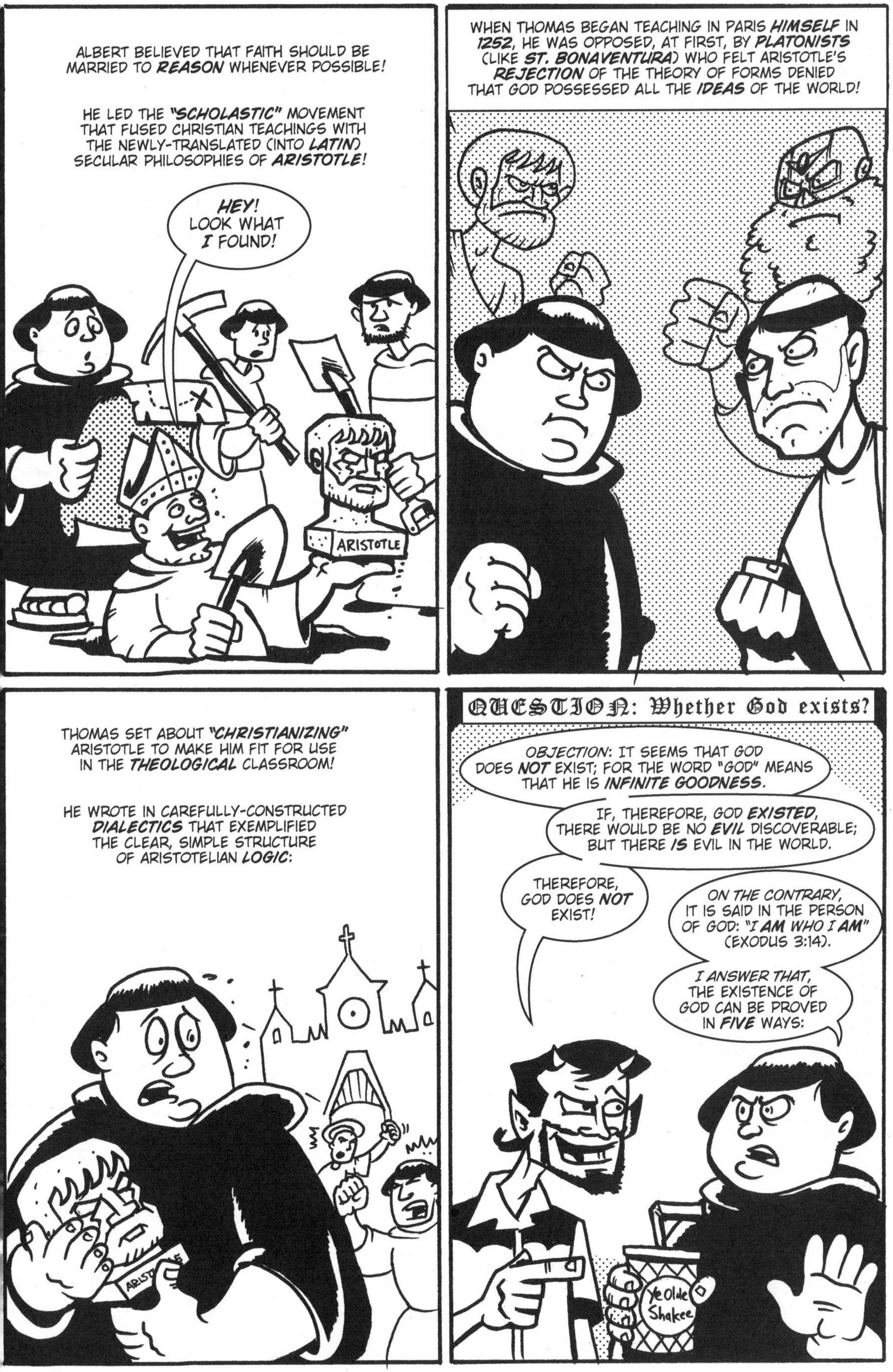
ALBERT BELIEVED THAT FAITH SHOULD BE MARRIED TO REASON WHENEVER POSSIBLE!
HE LED THE "SCHOLASTIC" MOVEMENT THAT FUSED CHRISTIAN TEACHINGS WITH THE NEWLY-TRANSLATED (INTO LATIN) SECULAR PHILOSOPHIES OF ARISTOTLE!
HEY! LOOK WHAT I FOUND!
ARISTOTLE
WHEN THOMAS BEGAN TEACHING IN PARIS HIMSELF IN 1252, HE WAS OPPOSED, AT FIRST, BY PLATONISTS (LIKE ST. BONAVENTURA) WHO FELT ARISTOTLE'S REJECTION OF THE THEORY OF FORMS DENIED THAT GOD POSSESSED ALL THE IDEAS OF THE WORLD!
THOMAS SET ABOUT "CHRISTIANIZING" ARISTOTLE TO MAKE HIM FIT FOR USE IN THE THEOLOGICAL CLASSROOM!
HE WROTE IN CAREFULLY-CONSTRUCTED DIALECTICS THAT EXEMPLIFIED THE CLEAR, SIMPLE STRUCTURE OF ARISTOTELIAN LOGIC:
QUESTION: Whether God exists?
OBJECTION: IT SEEMS THAT GOD DOES NOT EXIST; FOR THE WORD "GOD" MEANS THAT HE IS INFINITE GOODNESS.
IF, THEREFORE, GOD EXISTED, THERE WOULD BE NO EVIL DISCOVERABLE; BUT THERE IS EVIL IN THE WORLD.
THEREFORE, GOD DOES NOT EXIST!
ON THE CONTRARY, IT IS SAID IN THE PERSON OF GOD: "I AM WHO I AM" (EXODUS 3:14).
I ANSWER THAT, THE EXISTENCE OF GOD CAN BE PROVED IN FIVE WAYS:
Ye Olde Shakee

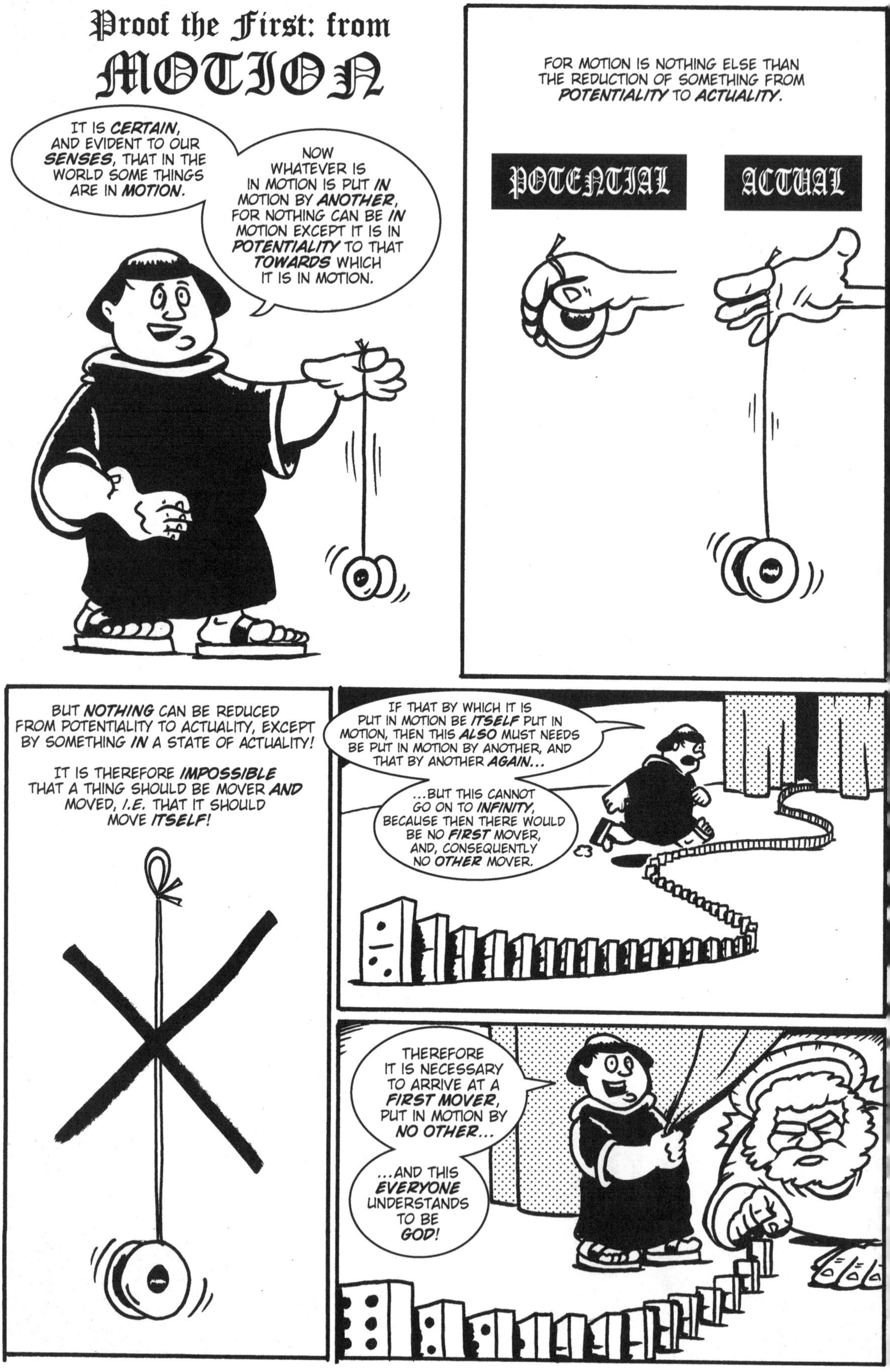
Proof the First: from
MOTION
IT IS CERTAIN, AND EVIDENT TO OUR SENSES, THAT IN THE WORLD SOME THINGS ARE IN MOTION.
NOW WHATEVER IS IN MOTION IS PUT IN MOTION BY ANOTHER, FOR NOTHING CAN BE IN MOTION EXCEPT IT IS IN POTENTIALITY TO THAT TOWARDS WHICH IT IS IN MOTION.
FOR MOTION IS NOTHING ELSE THAN THE REDUCTION OF SOMETHING FROM POTENTIALITY TO ACTUALITY.
POTENTIAL
ACTUAL
BUT NOTHING CAN BE REDUCED FROM POTENTIALITY TO ACTUALITY, EXCEPT BY SOMETHING IN A STATE OF ACTUALITY!
IT IS THEREFORE IMPOSSIBLE THAT A THING SHOULD BE MOVER AND MOVED, I.E. THAT IT SHOULD MOVE ITSELF!
IF THAT BY WHICH IT IS PUT IN MOTION BE ITSELF PUT IN MOTION, THEN THIS ALSO MUST NEEDS BE PUT IN MOTION BY ANOTHER, AND THAT BY ANOTHER AGAIN...
...BUT THIS CANNOT GO ON TO INFINITY, BECAUSE THEN THERE WOULD BE NO FIRST MOVER, AND, CONSEQUENTLY NO OTHER MOVER.
THEREFORE IT IS NECESSARY TO ARRIVE AT A FIRST MOVER, PUT IN MOTION BY NO OTHER...
...AND THIS EVERYONE UNDERSTANDS TO BE GOD!

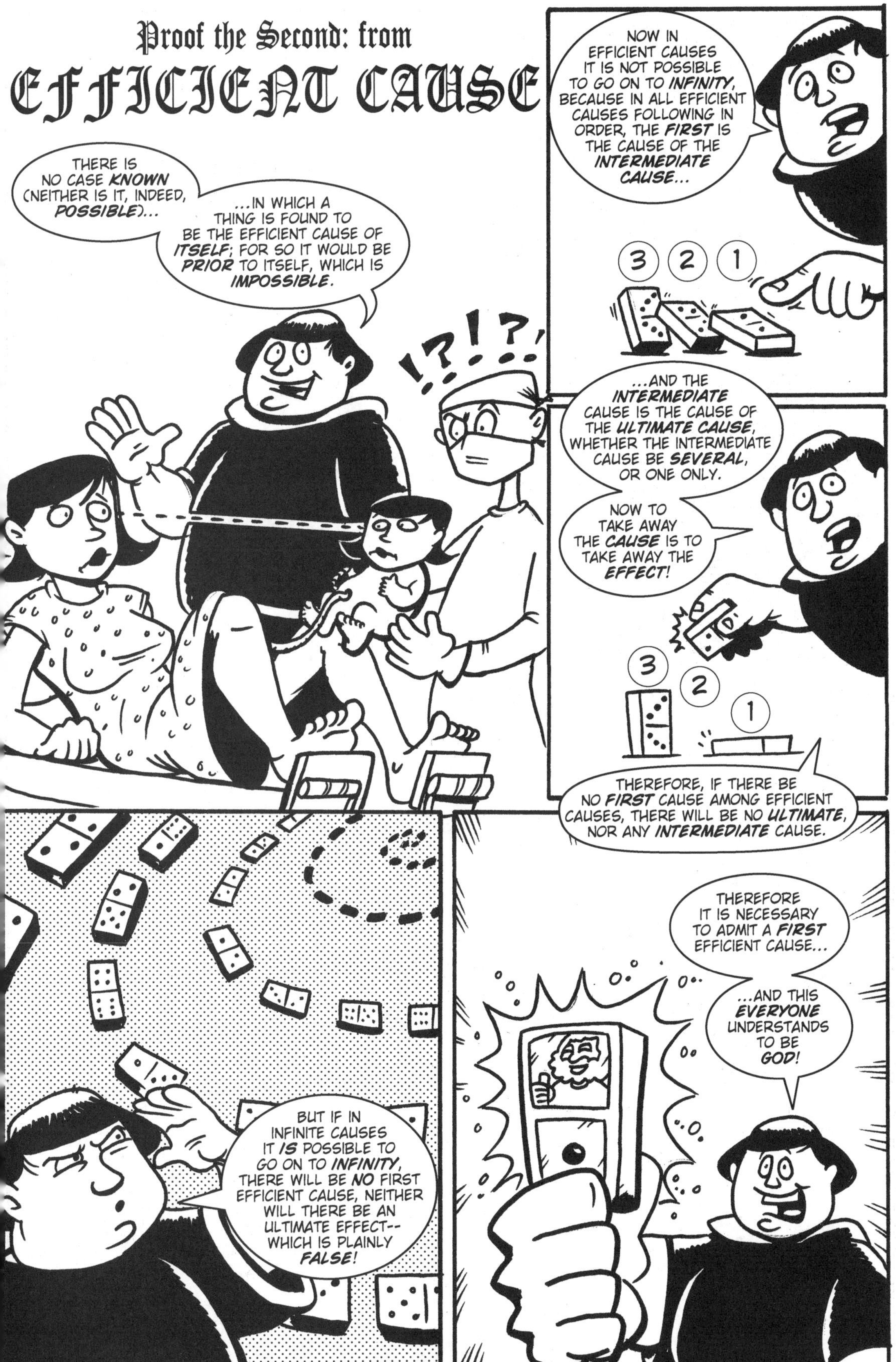
Proof the Second: from
EFFICIENT CAUSE
THERE IS NO CASE KNOWN (NEITHER IS IT, INDEED, POSSIBLE)...
...IN WHICH A THING IS FOUND TO BE THE EFFICIENT CAUSE OF ITSELF; FOR SO IT WOULD BE PRIOR TO ITSELF, WHICH IS IMPOSSIBLE.
!?!?!
NOW IN EFFICIENT CAUSES IT IS NOT POSSIBLE TO GO ON TO INFINITY, BECAUSE IN ALL EFFICIENT CAUSES FOLLOWING IN ORDER, THE FIRST IS THE CAUSE OF THE INTERMEDIATE CAUSE...
3 2 1
...AND THE INTERMEDIATE CAUSE IS THE CAUSE OF THE ULTIMATE CAUSE, WHETHER THE INTERMEDIATE CAUSE BE SEVERAL, OR ONE ONLY.
NOW TO TAKE AWAY THE CAUSE IS TO TAKE AWAY THE EFFECT!
3 2 1
THEREFORE, IF THERE BE NO FIRST CAUSE AMONG EFFICIENT CAUSES, THERE WILL BE NO ULTIMATE, NOR ANY INTERMEDIATE CAUSE.
BUT IF IN INFINITE CAUSES IT IS POSSIBLE TO GO ON TO INFINITY, THERE WILL BE NO FIRST EFFICIENT CAUSE, NEITHER WILL THERE BE AN ULTIMATE EFFECT-- WHICH IS PLAINLY FALSE!
THEREFORE IT IS NECESSARY TO ADMIT A FIRST EFFICIENT CAUSE...
...AND THIS EVERYONE UNDERSTANDS TO BE GOD!

Proof the Third: from NECESSARY vs. POSSIBLE BEING

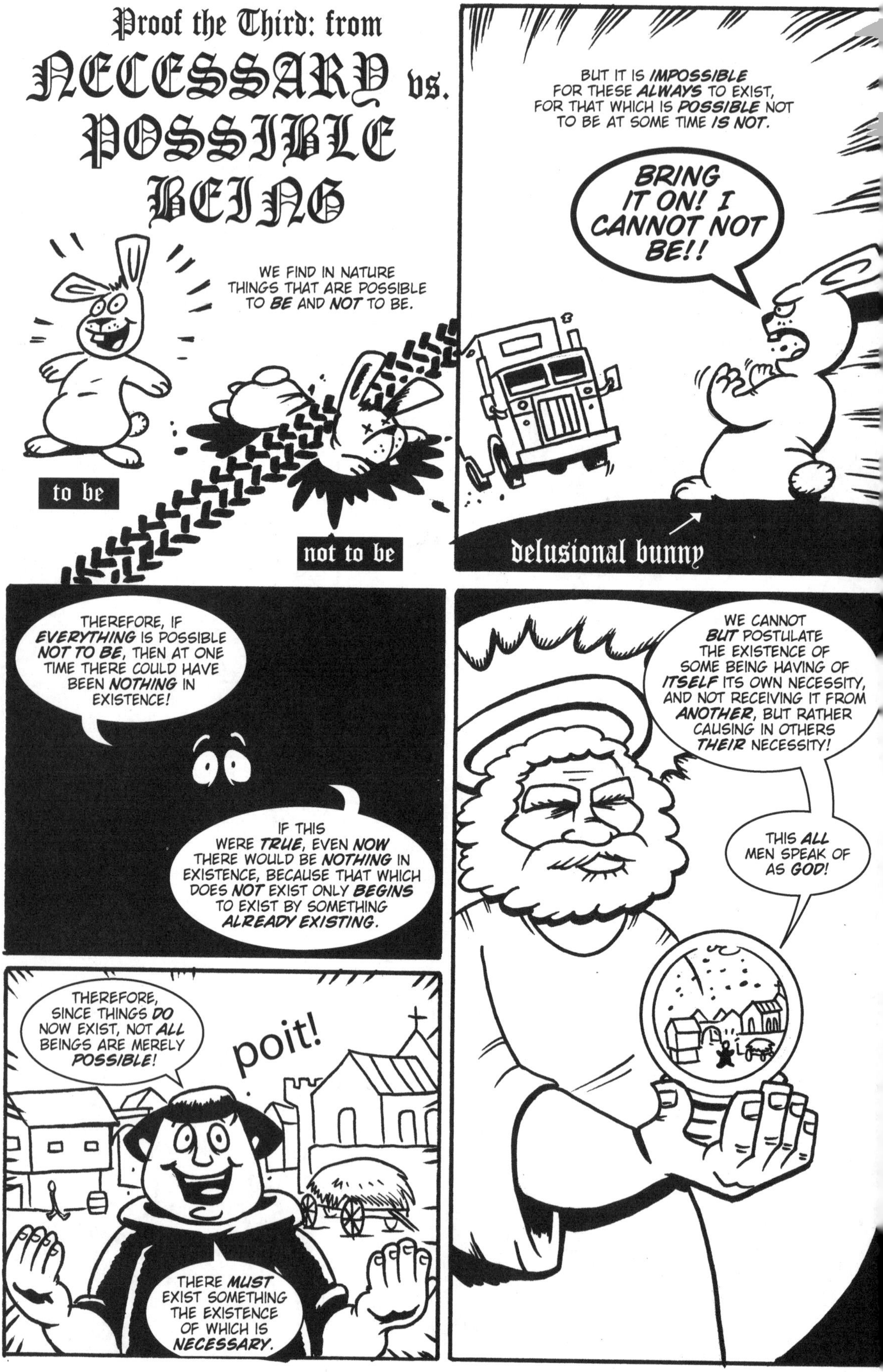

WE FIND IN NATURE THINGS THAT ARE POSSIBLE TO BE AND NOT TO BE.
to be
not to be
BUT IT IS IMPOSSIBLE FOR THESE ALWAYS TO EXIST, FOR THAT WHICH IS POSSIBLE NOT TO BE AT SOME TIME IS NOT.
BRING IT ON! I CANNOT NOT BE!!
delusional bunny
THEREFORE, IF EVERYTHING IS POSSIBLE NOT TO BE, THEN AT ONE TIME THERE COULD HAVE BEEN NOTHING IN EXISTENCE!
IF THIS WERE TRUE, EVEN NOW THERE WOULD BE NOTHING IN EXISTENCE, BECAUSE THAT WHICH DOES NOT EXIST ONLY BEGINS TO EXIST BY SOMETHING ALREADY EXISTING.
THEREFORE, SINCE THINGS DO NOW EXIST, NOT ALL BEINGS ARE MERELY POSSIBLE!
poit!
THERE MUST EXIST SOMETHING THE EXISTENCE OF WHICH IS NECESSARY.
WE CANNOT BUT POSTULATE THE EXISTENCE OF SOME BEING HAVING OF ITSELF ITS OWN NECESSITY, AND NOT RECEIVING IT FROM ANOTHER, BUT RATHER CAUSING IN OTHERS THEIR NECESSITY!
THIS ALL MEN SPEAK OF AS GOD!

Proof the Fourth: from the DEGREES OF PERFECTION

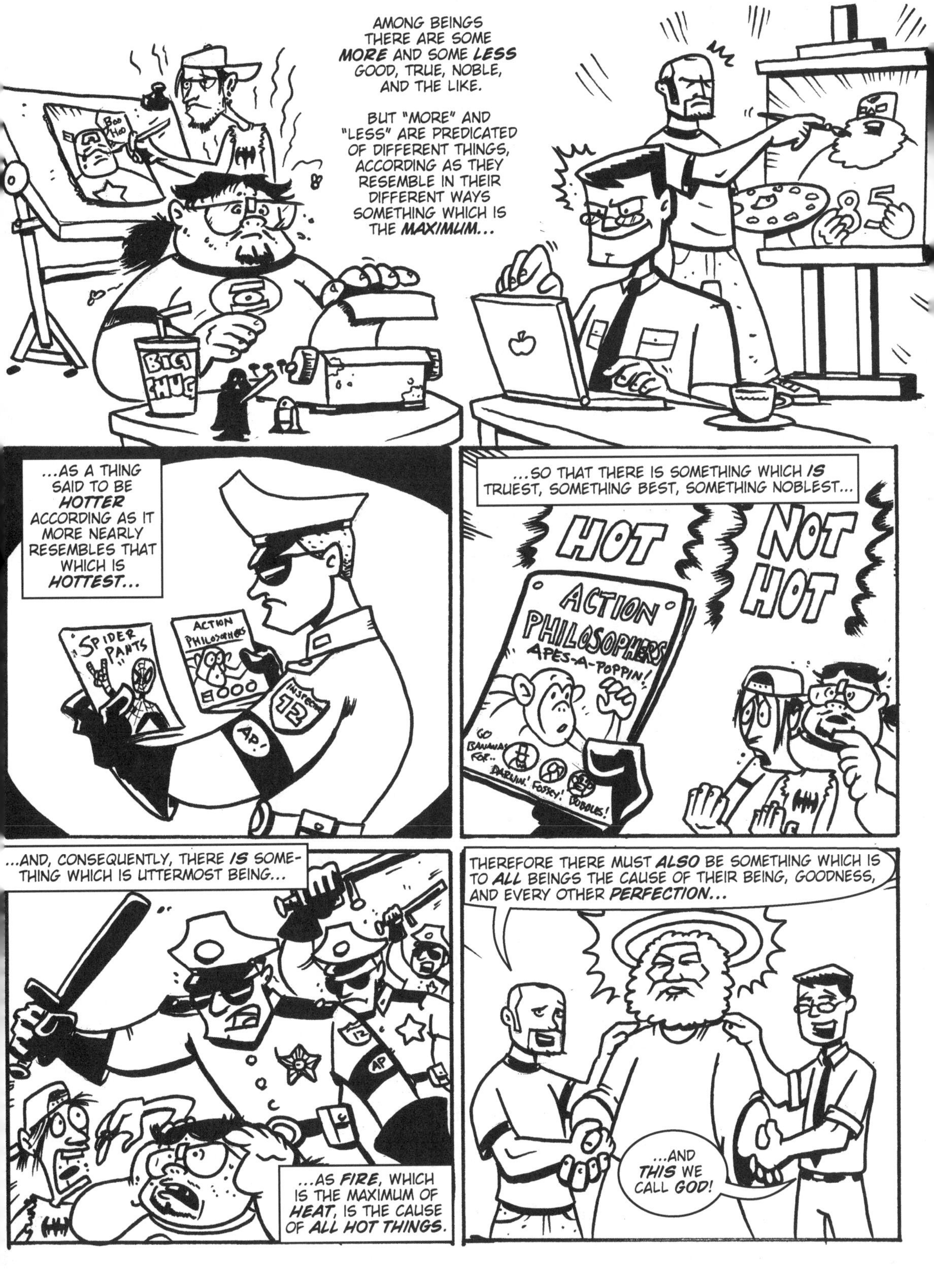

AMONG BEINGS THERE ARE SOME MORE AND SOME LESS GOOD, TRUE, NOBLE, AND THE LIKE.
BUT "MORE" AND "LESS" ARE PREDICATED OF DIFFERENT THINGS, ACCORDING AS THEY RESEMBLE IN THEIR DIFFERENT WAYS SOMETHING WHICH IS THE MAXIMUM...
BIG CHUG
...AS A THING SAID TO BE HOTTER ACCORDING AS IT MORE NEARLY RESEMBLES THAT WHICH IS HOTTEST...
SPIDER PANTS
ACTION PHILOSOPHERS
AP!
...SO THAT THERE IS SOMETHING WHICH IS TRUEST, SOMETHING BEST, SOMETHING NOBLEST...
HOT
NOT HOT
ACTION PHILOSOPHERS
APES-A-POPPIN!
GO BANANAS FOR..
DARWIN! FOSSEY! DUBOIS!
...AND, CONSEQUENTLY, THERE IS SOMETHING WHICH IS UTTERMOST BEING...
...AS FIRE, WHICH IS THE MAXIMUM OF HEAT, IS THE CAUSE OF ALL HOT THINGS.
THEREFORE THERE MUST ALSO BE SOMETHING WHICH IS TO ALL BEINGS THE CAUSE OF THEIR BEING, GOODNESS, AND EVERY OTHER PERFECTION...
...AND THIS WE CALL GOD!

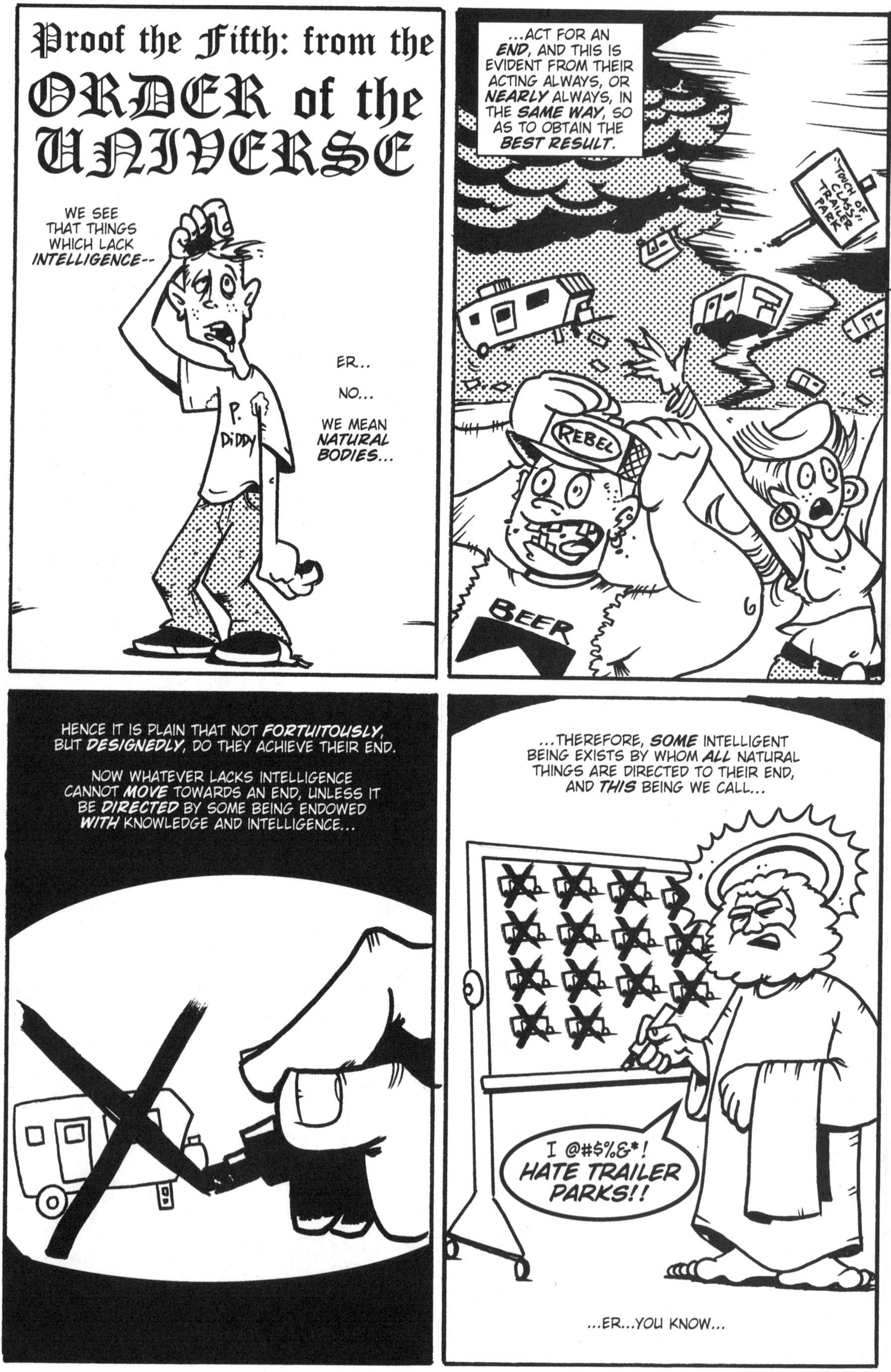
Proof the Fifth: from the ORDER of the UNIVERSE
WE SEE THAT THINGS WHICH LACK INTELLIGENCE--
P. DIDDY
ER...
NO...
WE MEAN NATURAL BODIES...
...ACT FOR AN END, AND THIS IS EVIDENT FROM THEIR ACTING ALWAYS, OR NEARLY ALWAYS, IN THE SAME WAY, SO AS TO OBTAIN THE BEST RESULT.
TOUCH OF CLASS TRAILER PARK
REBEL
BEER
HENCE IT IS PLAIN THAT NOT FORTUITOUSLY, BUT DESIGNEDLY, DO THEY ACHIEVE THEIR END.
NOW WHATEVER LACKS INTELLIGENCE CANNOT MOVE TOWARDS AN END, UNLESS IT BE DIRECTED BY SOME BEING ENDOWED WITH KNOWLEDGE AND INTELLIGENCE...
...THEREFORE, SOME INTELLIGENT BEING EXISTS BY WHOM ALL NATURAL THINGS ARE DIRECTED TO THEIR END, AND THIS BEING WE CALL...
I @#$%&*! HATE TRAILER PARKS!!
...ER...YOU KNOW...

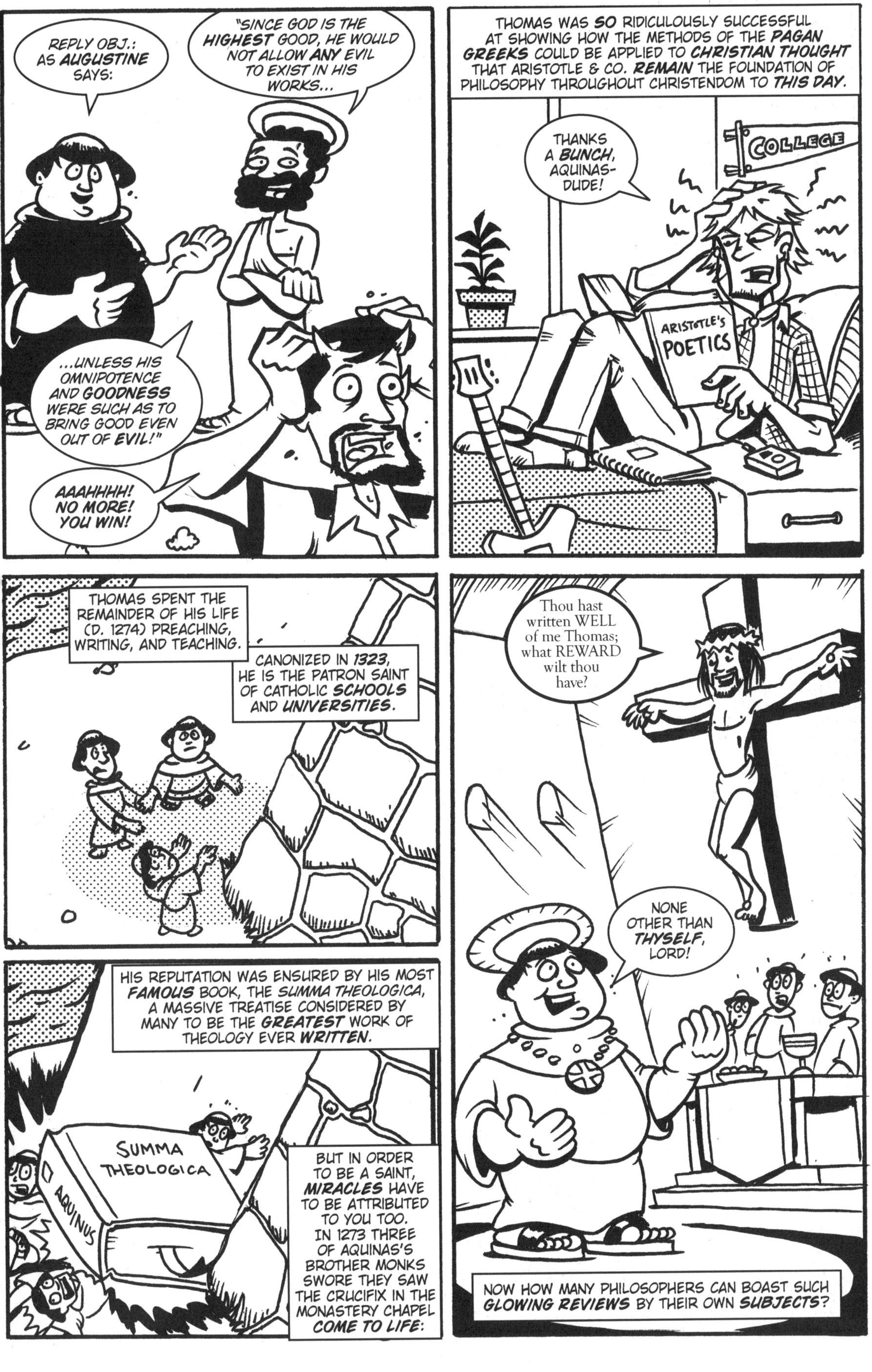
REPLY OBJ.: AS AUGUSTINE SAYS:
"SINCE GOD IS THE HIGHEST GOOD, HE WOULD NOT ALLOW ANY EVIL TO EXIST IN HIS WORKS...
...UNLESS HIS OMNIPOTENCE AND GOODNESS WERE SUCH AS TO BRING GOOD EVEN OUT OF EVIL!"
AAAHHHH! NO MORE! YOU WIN!
THOMAS WAS SO RIDICULOUSLY SUCCESSFUL AT SHOWING HOW THE METHODS OF THE PAGAN GREEKS COULD BE APPLIED TO CHRISTIAN THOUGHT THAT ARISTOTLE & CO. REMAIN THE FOUNDATION OF PHILOSOPHY THROUGHOUT CHRISTENDOM TO THIS DAY.
THANKS A BUNCH, AQUINAS-DUDE!
COLLEGE
ARISTOTLE'S POETICS
THOMAS SPENT THE REMAINDER OF HIS LIFE (D. 1274) PREACHING, WRITING, AND TEACHING.
CANONIZED IN 1323, HE IS THE PATRON SAINT OF CATHOLIC SCHOOLS AND UNIVERSITIES.
HIS REPUTATION WAS ENSURED BY HIS MOST FAMOUS BOOK, THE SUMMA THEOLOGICA, A MASSIVE TREATISE CONSIDERED BY MANY TO BE THE GREATEST WORK OF THEOLOGY EVER WRITTEN.
SUMMA THEOLOGICA
AQUINUS
BUT IN ORDER TO BE A SAINT, MIRACLES HAVE TO BE ATTRIBUTED TO YOU TOO. IN 1273 THREE OF AQUINAS'S BROTHER MONKS SWORE THEY SAW THE CRUCIFIX IN THE MONASTERY CHAPEL COME TO LIFE:
Thou hast written WELL of me Thomas; what REWARD wilt thou have?
NONE OTHER THAN THYSELF, LORD!
NOW HOW MANY PHILOSOPHERS CAN BOAST SUCH GLOWING REVIEWS BY THEIR OWN SUBJECTS?

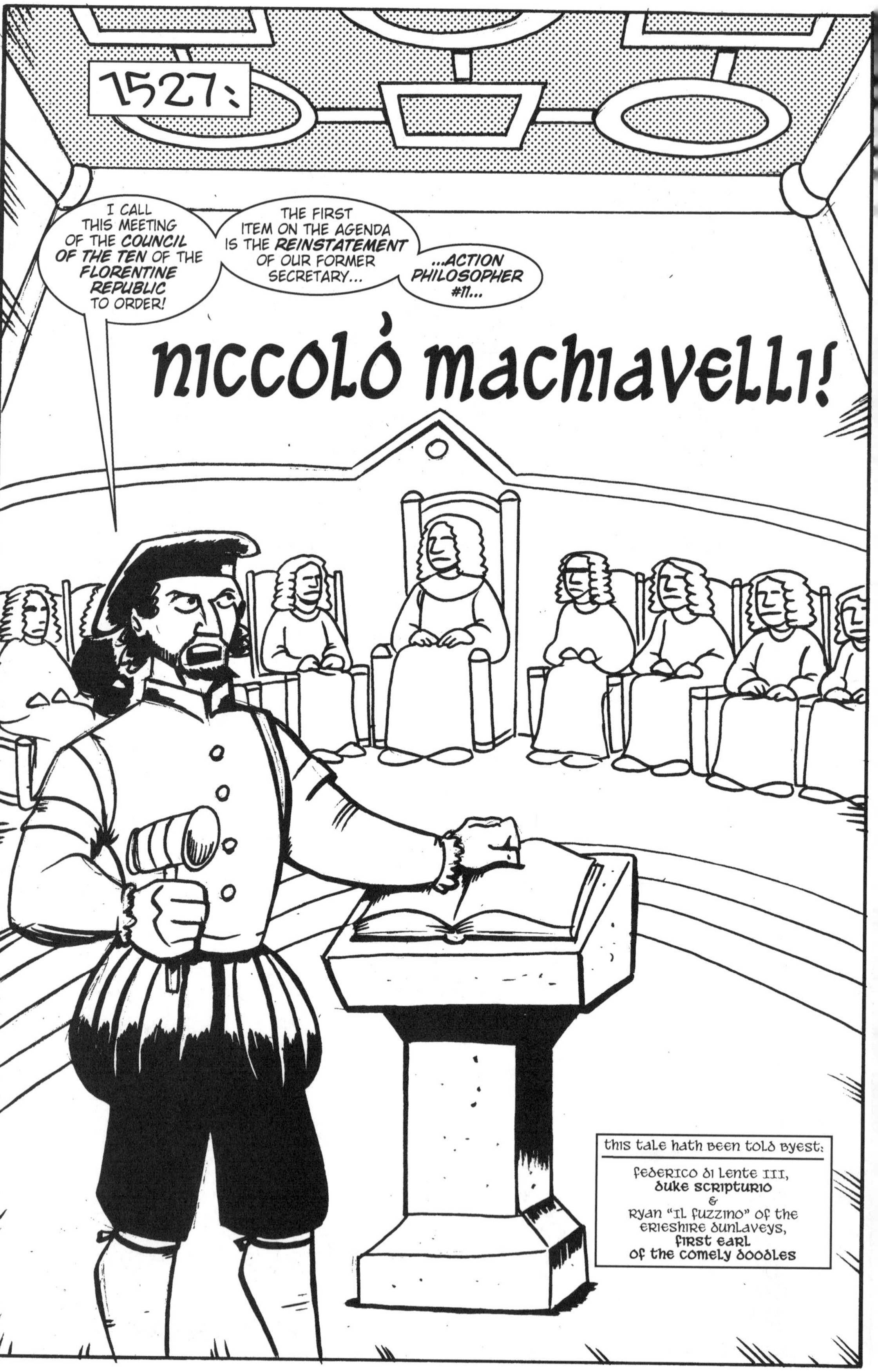

1527:
I CALL THIS MEETING OF THE COUNCIL OF THE TEN OF THE FLORENTINE REPUBLIC TO ORDER!
THE FIRST ITEM ON THE AGENDA IS THE REINSTATEMENT OF OUR FORMER SECRETARY...
...ACTION PHILOSOPHER #11...
NICCOLÒ MACHIAVELLI!
this tale hath been told byest:
Federico di Lente III, Duke Scripturio
&
Ryan "Il Fuzzino" of the Erieshire Dunlaveys, First Earl of the Comely Doodles

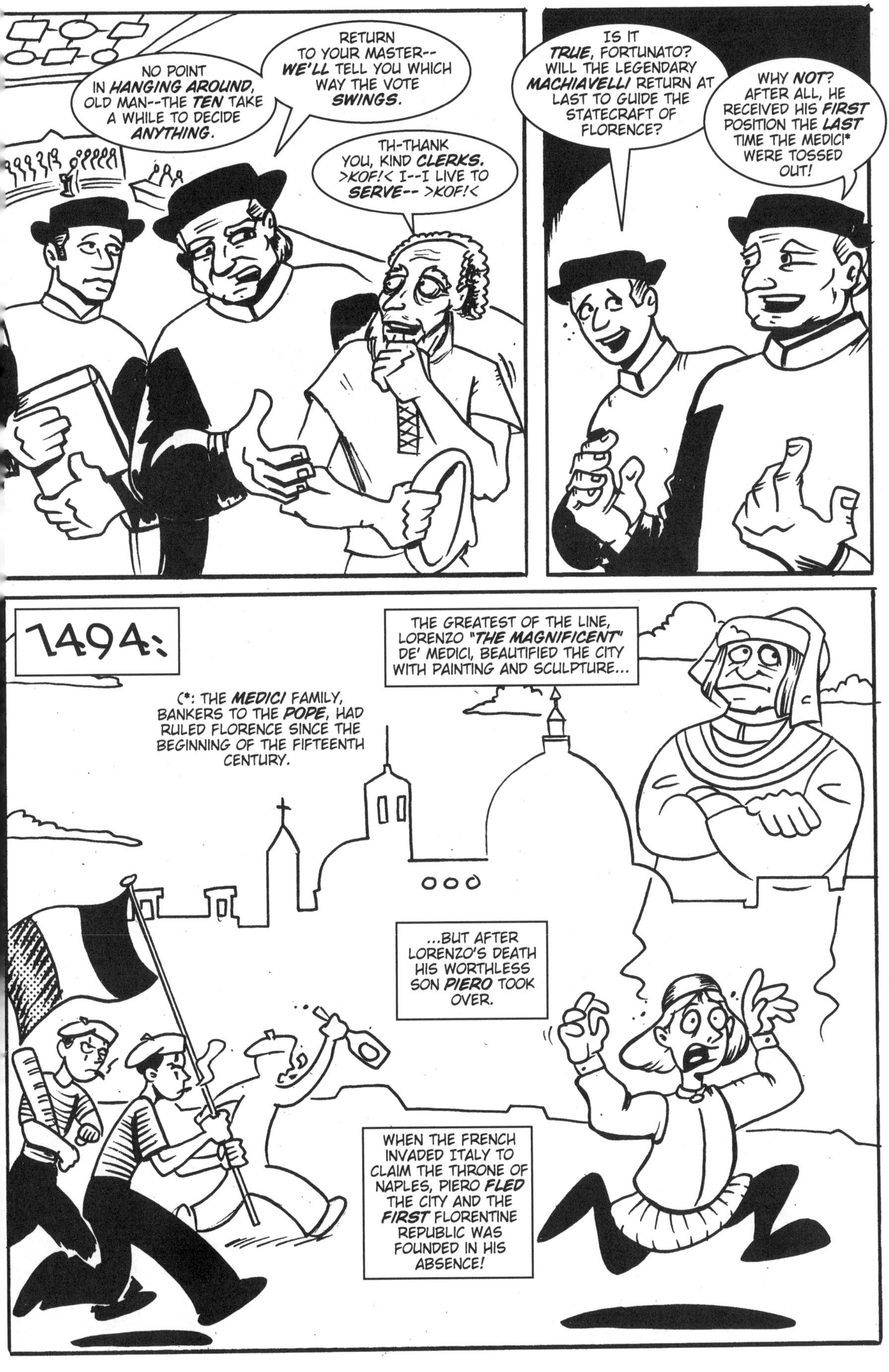
NO POINT IN HANGING AROUND, OLD MAN--THE TEN TAKE A WHILE TO DECIDE ANYTHING.
RETURN TO YOUR MASTER-- WE'LL TELL YOU WHICH WAY THE VOTE SWINGS.
TH-THANK YOU, KIND CLERKS. >KOF!< I--I LIVE TO SERVE-- >KOF!<
IS IT TRUE, FORTUNATO? WILL THE LEGENDARY MACHIAVELLI RETURN AT LAST TO GUIDE THE STATECRAFT OF FLORENCE?
WHY NOT? AFTER ALL, HE RECEIVED HIS FIRST POSITION THE LAST TIME THE MEDICI* WERE TOSSED OUT!
1494:
THE GREATEST OF THE LINE, LORENZO "THE MAGNIFICENT" DE' MEDICI, BEAUTIFIED THE CITY WITH PAINTING AND SCULPTURE...
(*: THE MEDICI FAMILY, BANKERS TO THE POPE, HAD RULED FLORENCE SINCE THE BEGINNING OF THE FIFTEENTH CENTURY.
...BUT AFTER LORENZO'S DEATH HIS WORTHLESS SON PIERO TOOK OVER.
WHEN THE FRENCH INVADED ITALY TO CLAIM THE THRONE OF NAPLES, PIERO FLED THE CITY AND THE FIRST FLORENTINE REPUBLIC WAS FOUNDED IN HIS ABSENCE!

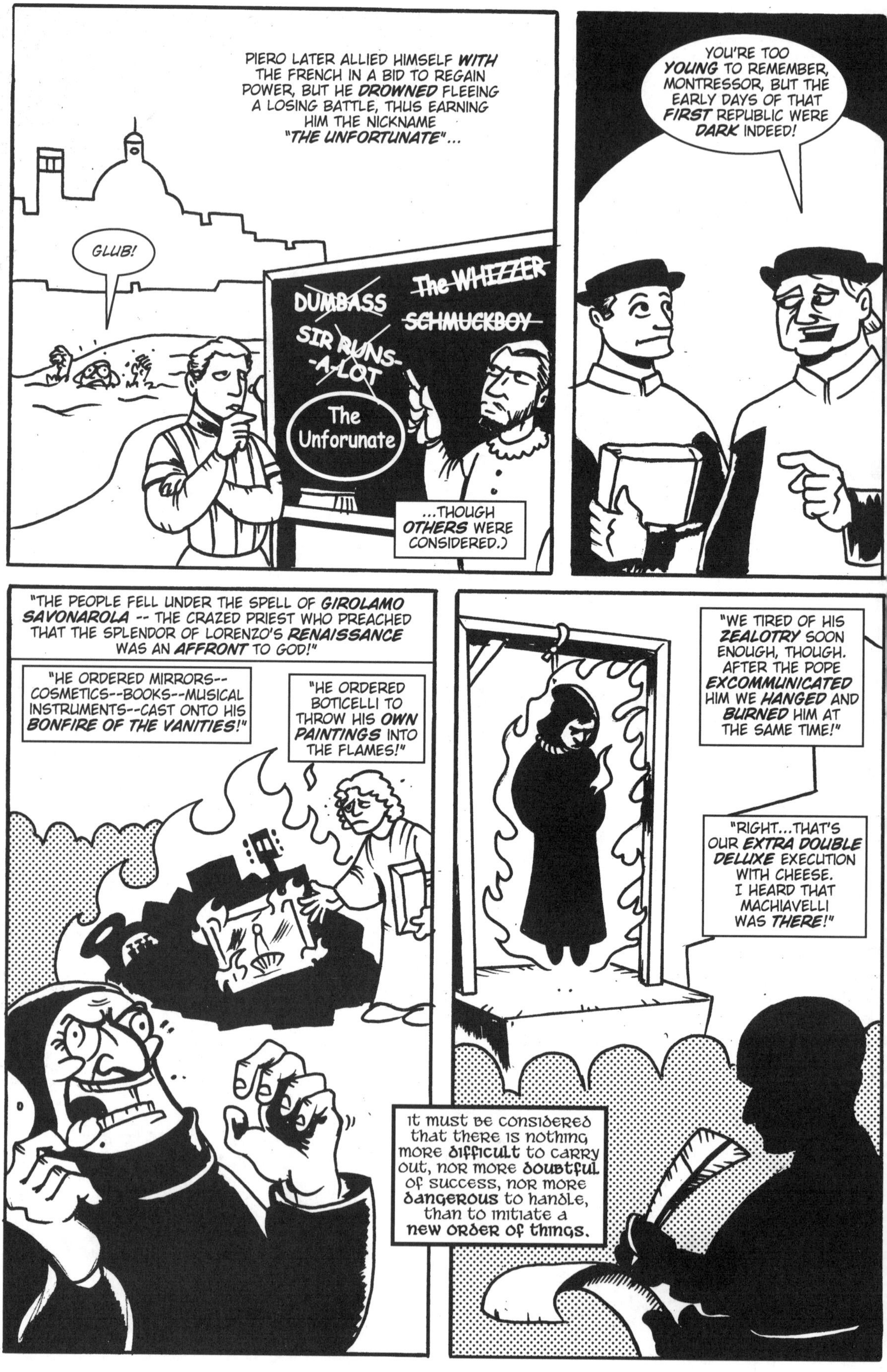
PIERO LATER ALLIED HIMSELF WITH THE FRENCH IN A BID TO REGAIN POWER, BUT HE DROWNED FLEEING A LOSING BATTLE, THUS EARNING HIM THE NICKNAME "THE UNFORTUNATE"...
GLUB!
DUMBASS
The WHIZZER
SCHMUCKBOY
SIR RUNS-A-LOT
The Unforunate
...THOUGH OTHERS WERE CONSIDERED.)
YOU'RE TOO YOUNG TO REMEMBER, MONTRESSOR, BUT THE EARLY DAYS OF THAT FIRST REPUBLIC WERE DARK INDEED!
"THE PEOPLE FELL UNDER THE SPELL OF GIROLAMO SAVONAROLA -- THE CRAZED PRIEST WHO PREACHED THAT THE SPLENDOR OF LORENZO'S RENAISSANCE WAS AN AFFRONT TO GOD!"
"HE ORDERED MIRRORS--COSMETICS--BOOKS--MUSICAL INSTRUMENTS--CAST ONTO HIS BONFIRE OF THE VANITIES!"
"HE ORDERED BOTICELLI TO THROW HIS OWN PAINTINGS INTO THE FLAMES!"
"WE TIRED OF HIS ZEALOTRY SOON ENOUGH, THOUGH. AFTER THE POPE EXCOMMUNICATED HIM WE HANGED AND BURNED HIM AT THE SAME TIME!"
"RIGHT...THAT'S OUR EXTRA DOUBLE DELUXE EXECUTION WITH CHEESE. I HEARD THAT MACHIAVELLI WAS THERE!"
It must be considered that there is nothing more difficult to carry out, nor more doubtful of success, nor more dangerous to handle, than to initiate a new order of things.

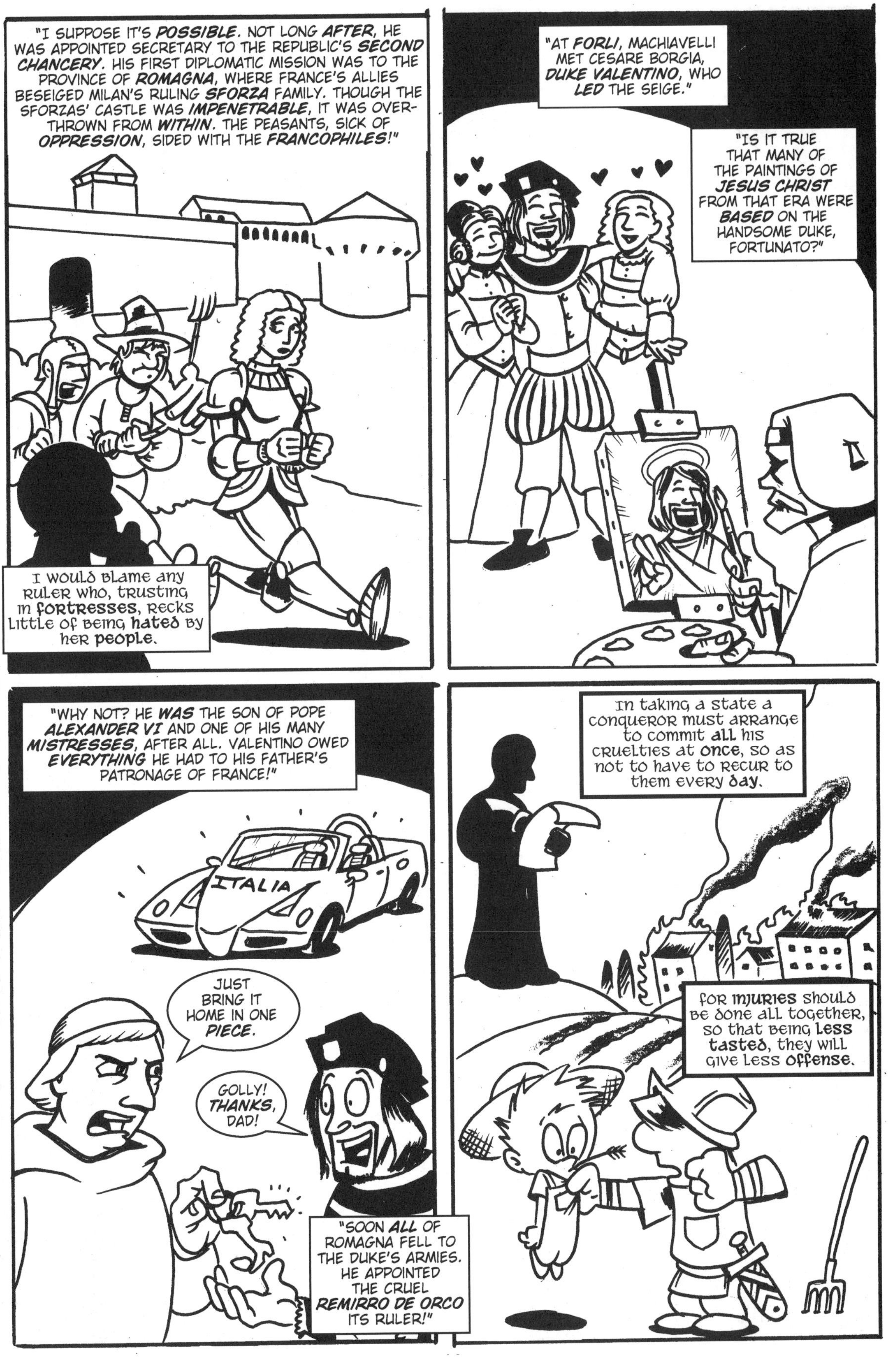
"I SUPPOSE IT'S POSSIBLE. NOT LONG AFTER, HE WAS APPOINTED SECRETARY TO THE REPUBLIC'S SECOND CHANCERY. HIS FIRST DIPLOMATIC MISSION WAS TO THE PROVINCE OF ROMAGNA, WHERE FRANCE'S ALLIES BESEIGED MILAN'S RULING SFORZA FAMILY. THOUGH THE SFORZAS' CASTLE WAS IMPENETRABLE, IT WAS OVERTHROWN FROM WITHIN. THE PEASANTS, SICK OF OPPRESSION, SIDED WITH THE FRANCOPHILES!"
I would blame any ruler who, trusting in fortresses, recks little of being hated by her people.
"AT FORLI, MACHIAVELLI MET CESARE BORGIA, DUKE VALENTINO, WHO LED THE SEIGE."
"IS IT TRUE THAT MANY OF THE PAINTINGS OF JESUS CHRIST FROM THAT ERA WERE BASED ON THE HANDSOME DUKE, FORTUNATO?"
"WHY NOT? HE WAS THE SON OF POPE ALEXANDER VI AND ONE OF HIS MANY MISTRESSES, AFTER ALL. VALENTINO OWED EVERYTHING HE HAD TO HIS FATHER'S PATRONAGE OF FRANCE!"
ITALIA
JUST BRING IT HOME IN ONE PIECE.
GOLLY! THANKS, DAD!
"SOON ALL OF ROMAGNA FELL TO THE DUKE'S ARMIES. HE APPOINTED THE CRUEL REMIRRO DE ORCO ITS RULER!"
In taking a state a conqueror must arrange to commit all his cruelties at once, so as not to have to recur to them every day.
For injuries should be done all together, so that being less tasted, they will give less offense.

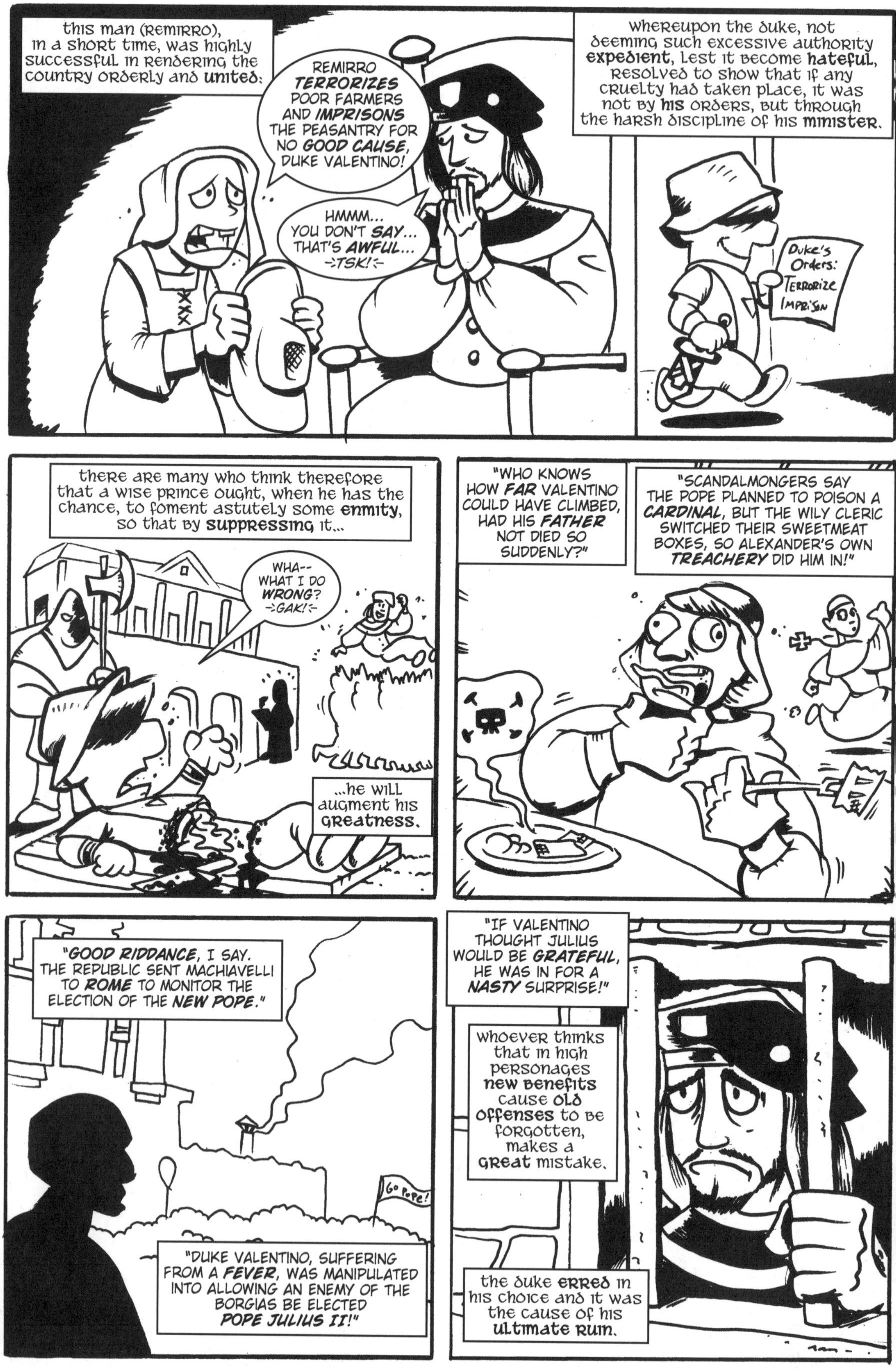
this man (Remirro), in a short time, was highly successful in rendering the country orderly and united:
REMIRRO TERRORIZES POOR FARMERS AND IMPRISONS THE PEASANTRY FOR NO GOOD CAUSE, DUKE VALENTINO!
HMMM... YOU DON'T SAY... THAT'S AWFUL... -TSK!-
whereupon the duke, not deeming such excessive authority expedient, lest it become hateful, resolved to show that if any cruelty had taken place, it was not by his orders, but through the harsh discipline of his minister.
Duke's Orders: Terrorize Imprison
there are many who think therefore that a wise prince ought, when he has the chance, to foment astutely some enmity, so that by suppressing it...
WHA-- WHAT I DO WRONG? -GAK!-
...he will augment his greatness.
"WHO KNOWS HOW FAR VALENTINO COULD HAVE CLIMBED, HAD HIS FATHER NOT DIED SO SUDDENLY?"
"SCANDALMONGERS SAY THE POPE PLANNED TO POISON A CARDINAL, BUT THE WILY CLERIC SWITCHED THEIR SWEETMEAT BOXES, SO ALEXANDER'S OWN TREACHERY DID HIM IN!"
"GOOD RIDDANCE, I SAY. THE REPUBLIC SENT MACHIAVELLI TO ROME TO MONITOR THE ELECTION OF THE NEW POPE."
Go Pope!
"DUKE VALENTINO, SUFFERING FROM A FEVER, WAS MANIPULATED INTO ALLOWING AN ENEMY OF THE BORGIAS BE ELECTED POPE JULIUS II!"
"IF VALENTINO THOUGHT JULIUS WOULD BE GRATEFUL, HE WAS IN FOR A NASTY SURPRISE!"
whoever thinks that in high personages new benefits cause old offenses to be forgotten, makes a great mistake.
the duke erred in his choice and it was the cause of his ultimate ruin.

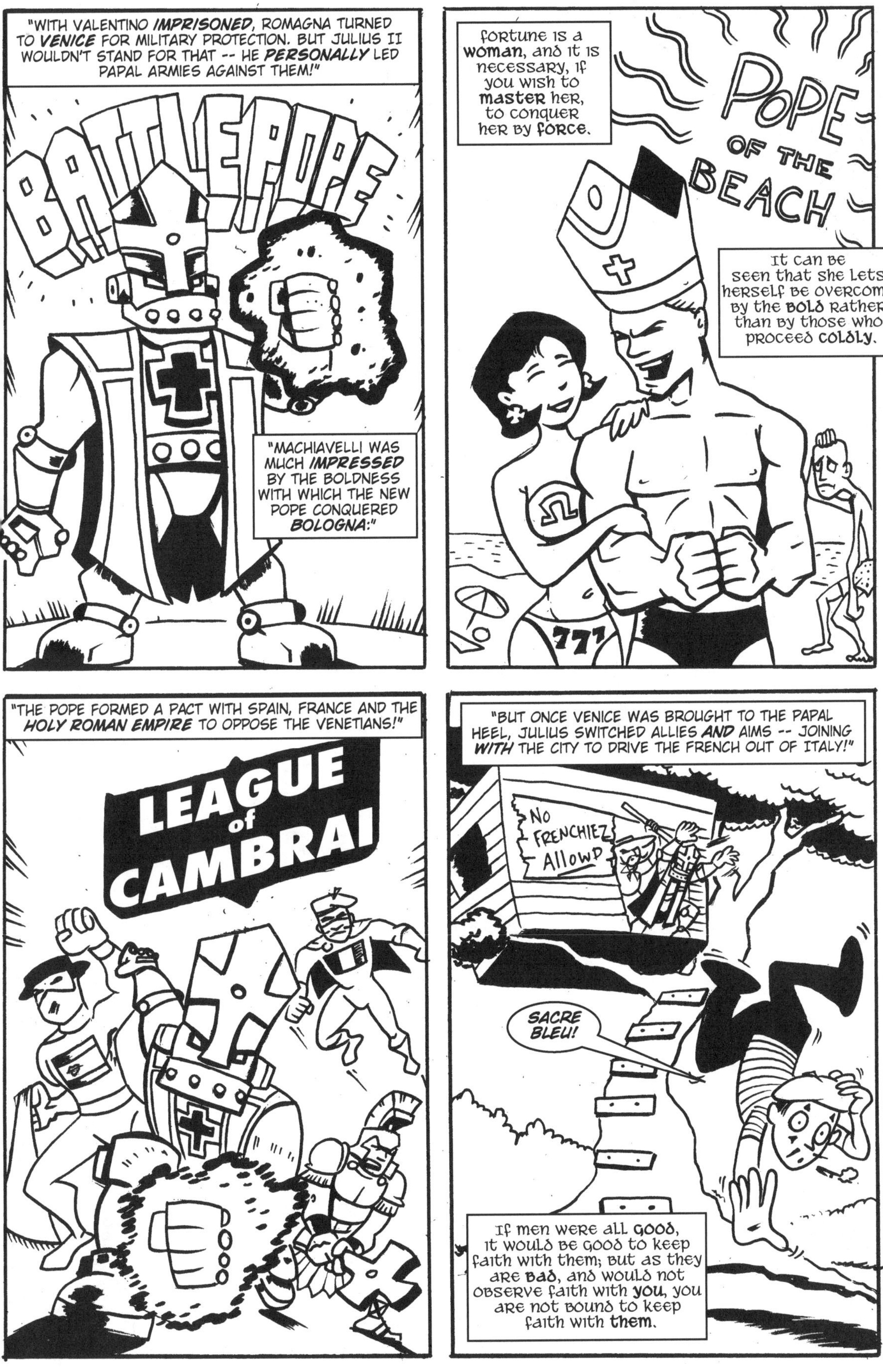

"WITH VALENTINO IMPRISONED, ROMAGNA TURNED TO VENICE FOR MILITARY PROTECTION. BUT JULIUS II WOULDN'T STAND FOR THAT -- HE PERSONALLY LED PAPAL ARMIES AGAINST THEM!"
BATTLEPOPE
"MACHIAVELLI WAS MUCH IMPRESSED BY THE BOLDNESS WITH WHICH THE NEW POPE CONQUERED BOLOGNA:"
fortune is a woman, and it is necessary, if you wish to master her, to conquer her by force.
POPE OF THE BEACH
It can be seen that she lets herself be overcome by the bold rather than by those who proceed coldly.
777
"THE POPE FORMED A PACT WITH SPAIN, FRANCE AND THE HOLY ROMAN EMPIRE TO OPPOSE THE VENETIANS!"
LEAGUE of CAMBRAI
"BUT ONCE VENICE WAS BROUGHT TO THE PAPAL HEEL, JULIUS SWITCHED ALLIES AND AIMS -- JOINING WITH THE CITY TO DRIVE THE FRENCH OUT OF ITALY!"
NO FRENCHIEZ ALLOWD
SACRE BLEU!
If men were all good, it would be good to keep faith with them; but as they are bad, and would not observe faith with you, you are not bound to keep faith with them.

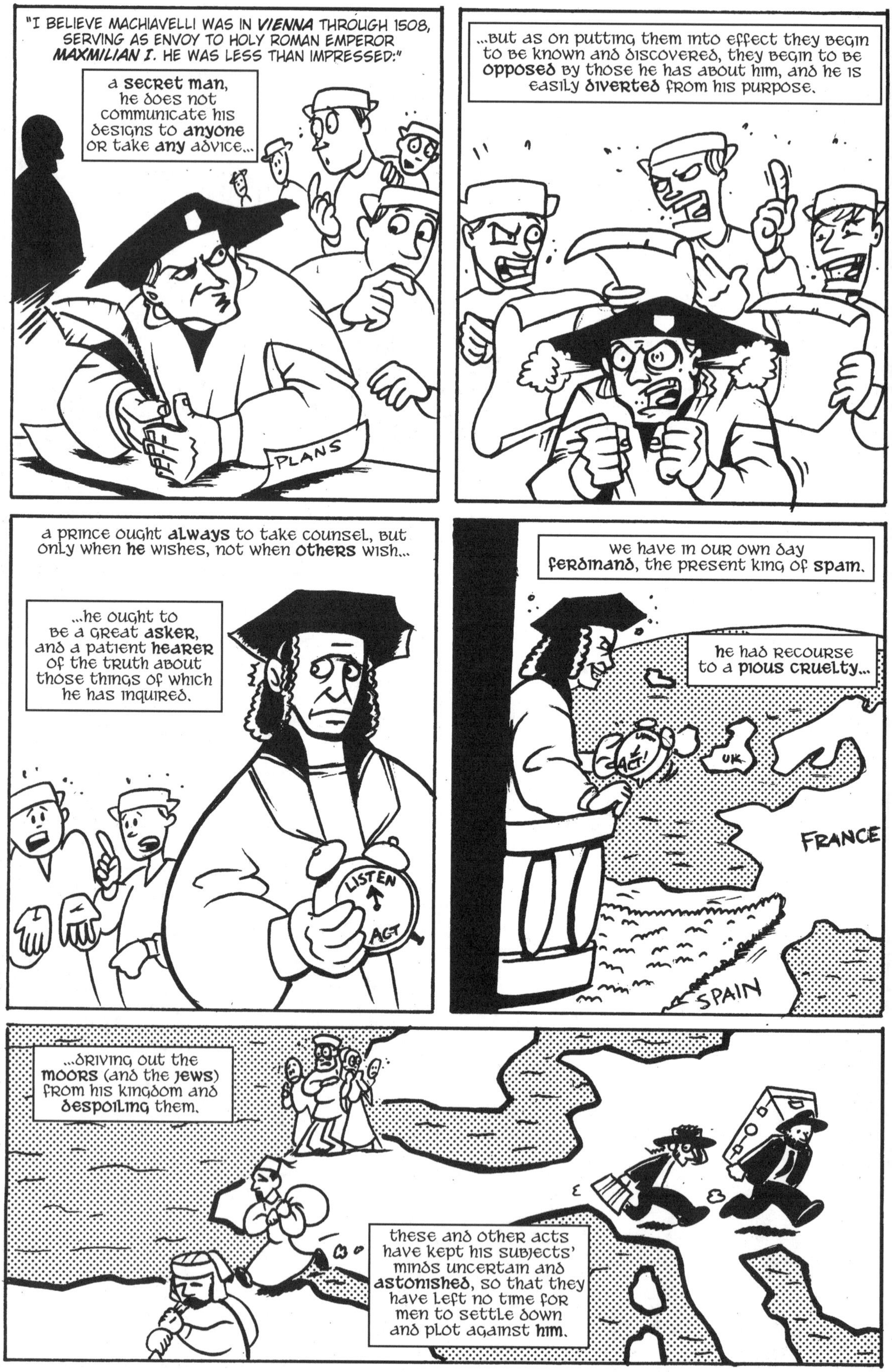

"I BELIEVE MACHIAVELLI WAS IN VIENNA THROUGH 1508, SERVING AS ENVOY TO HOLY ROMAN EMPEROR MAXMILIAN I. HE WAS LESS THAN IMPRESSED:"
a secret man, he does not communicate his designs to anyone or take any advice...
PLANS
...but as on putting them into effect they begin to be known and discovered, they begin to be opposed by those he has about him, and he is easily diverted from his purpose.
a prince ought always to take counsel, but only when he wishes, not when others wish...
...he ought to be a great asker, and a patient hearer of the truth about those things of which he has inquired.
LISTEN
ACT
we have in our own day ferdinand, the present king of spain.
he had recourse to a pious cruelty...
ACT!
UK
FRANCE
SPAIN
...driving out the moors (and the jews) from his kingdom and despoiling them.
these and other acts have kept his subjects' minds uncertain and astonished, so that they have left no time for men to settle down and plot against him.

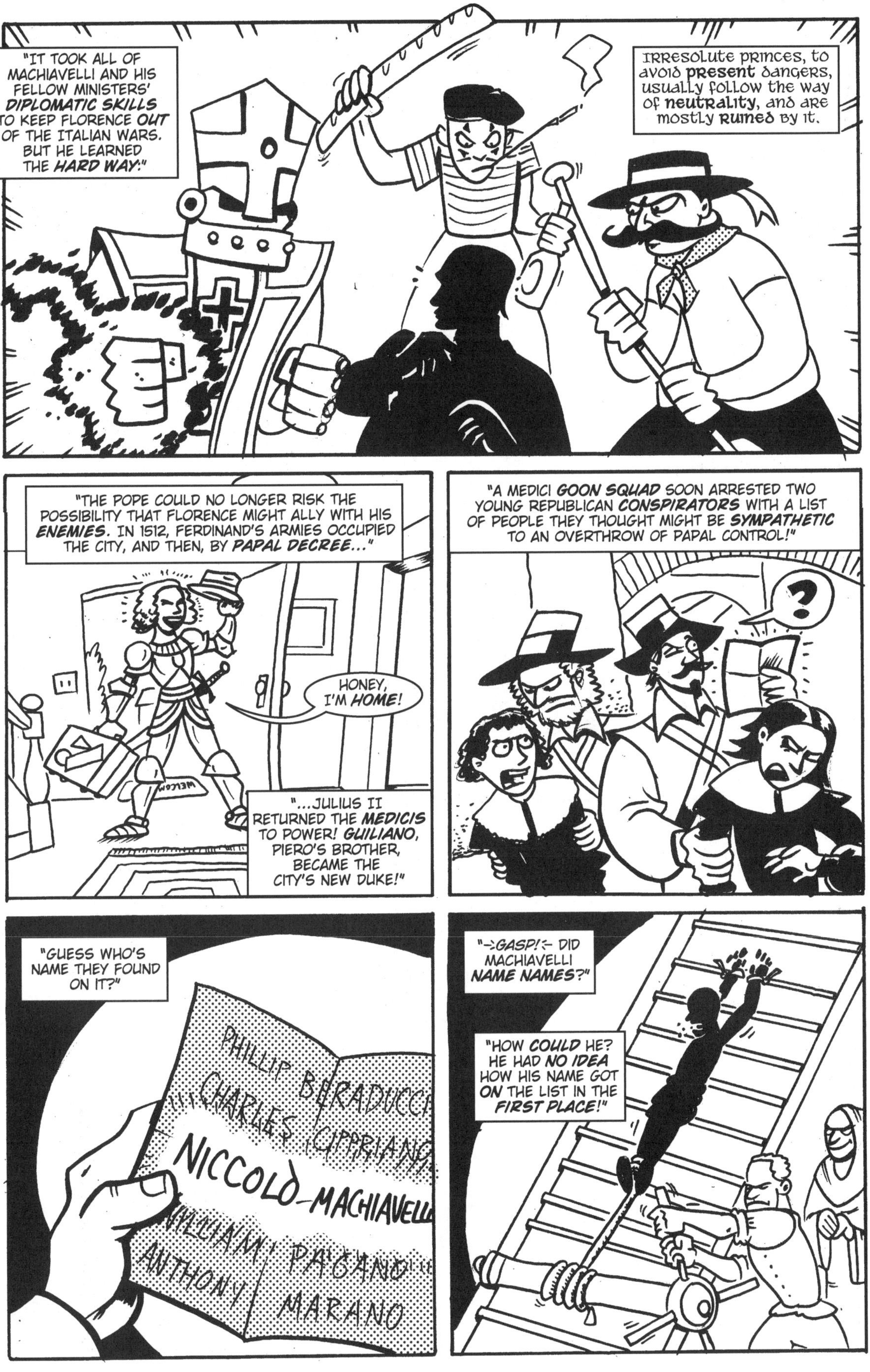

"IT TOOK ALL OF MACHIAVELLI AND HIS FELLOW MINISTERS' DIPLOMATIC SKILLS TO KEEP FLORENCE OUT OF THE ITALIAN WARS. BUT HE LEARNED THE HARD WAY:"
Irresolute princes, to avoid present dangers, usually follow the way of neutrality, and are mostly ruined by it.
"THE POPE COULD NO LONGER RISK THE POSSIBILITY THAT FLORENCE MIGHT ALLY WITH HIS ENEMIES. IN 1512, FERDINAND'S ARMIES OCCUPIED THE CITY, AND THEN, BY PAPAL DECREE..."
HONEY, I'M HOME!
"...JULIUS II RETURNED THE MEDICIS TO POWER! GUILIANO, PIERO'S BROTHER, BECAME THE CITY'S NEW DUKE!"
"A MEDICI GOON SQUAD SOON ARRESTED TWO YOUNG REPUBLICAN CONSPIRATORS WITH A LIST OF PEOPLE THEY THOUGHT MIGHT BE SYMPATHETIC TO AN OVERTHROW OF PAPAL CONTROL!"
?
"GUESS WHO'S NAME THEY FOUND ON IT?"
PHILLIP
CHARLES
NICCOLÒ MACHIAVELLI
WILLIAM
ANTHONY
PAGANO
MARANO
"→GASP!← DID MACHIAVELLI NAME NAMES?"
"HOW COULD HE? HE HAD NO IDEA HOW HIS NAME GOT ON THE LIST IN THE FIRST PLACE!"

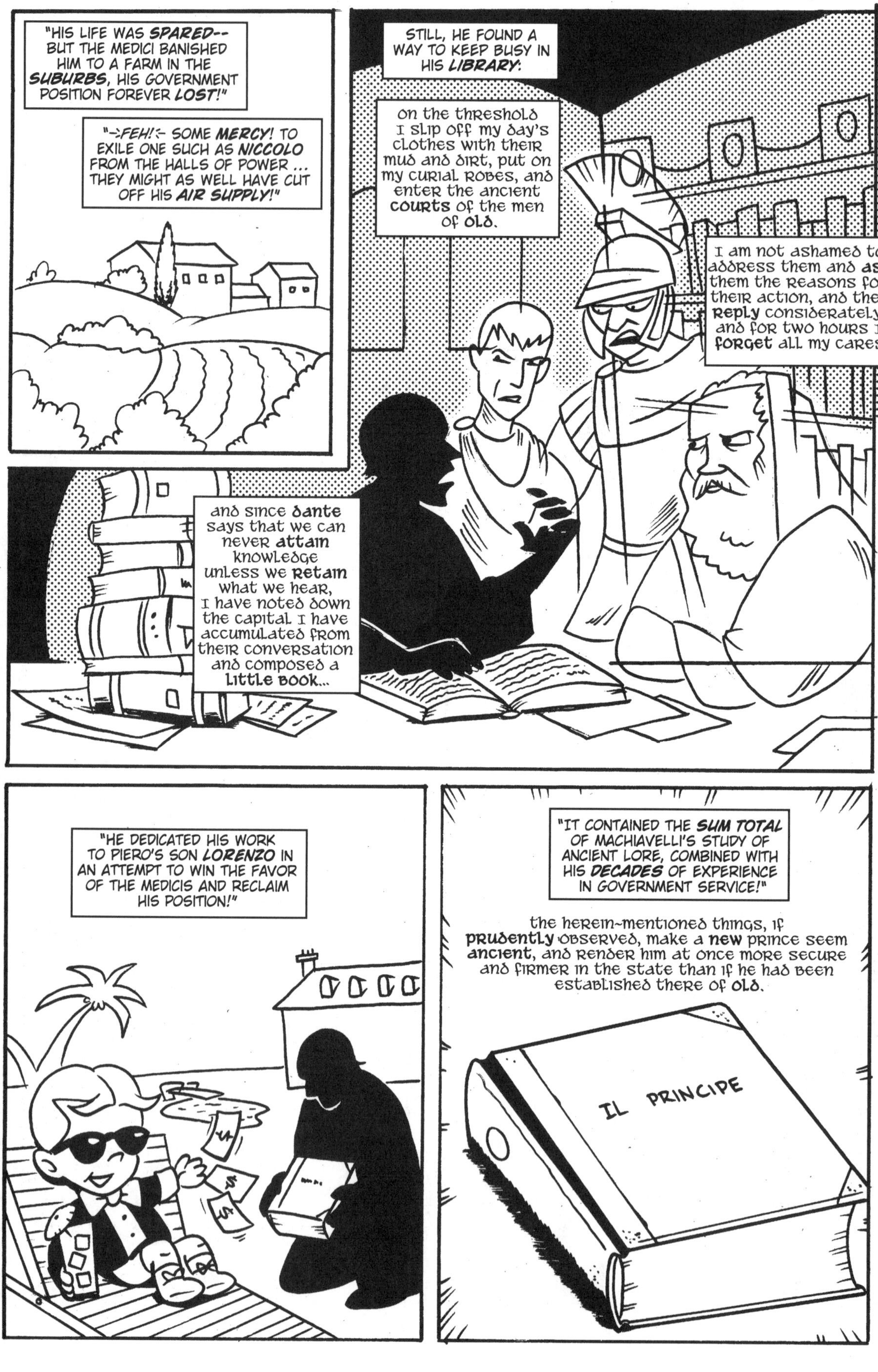
"HIS LIFE WAS SPARED-- BUT THE MEDICI BANISHED HIM TO A FARM IN THE SUBURBS, HIS GOVERNMENT POSITION FOREVER LOST!"
"FEH! SOME MERCY! TO EXILE ONE SUCH AS NICCOLO FROM THE HALLS OF POWER ... THEY MIGHT AS WELL HAVE CUT OFF HIS AIR SUPPLY!"
STILL, HE FOUND A WAY TO KEEP BUSY IN HIS LIBRARY:
On the threshold I slip off my day's clothes with their mud and dirt, put on my curial robes, and enter the ancient courts of the men of old.
I am not ashamed to address them and ask them the reasons for their action, and they reply considerately; and for two hours I forget all my cares.
and since dante says that we can never attain knowledge unless we retain what we hear, I have noted down the capital I have accumulated from their conversation and composed a little book...
"HE DEDICATED HIS WORK TO PIERO'S SON LORENZO IN AN ATTEMPT TO WIN THE FAVOR OF THE MEDICIS AND RECLAIM HIS POSITION!"
"IT CONTAINED THE SUM TOTAL OF MACHIAVELLI'S STUDY OF ANCIENT LORE, COMBINED WITH HIS DECADES OF EXPERIENCE IN GOVERNMENT SERVICE!"
the herein-mentioned things, if prudently observed, make a new prince seem ancient, and render him at once more secure and firmer in the state than if he had been established there of old.
IL PRINCIPE

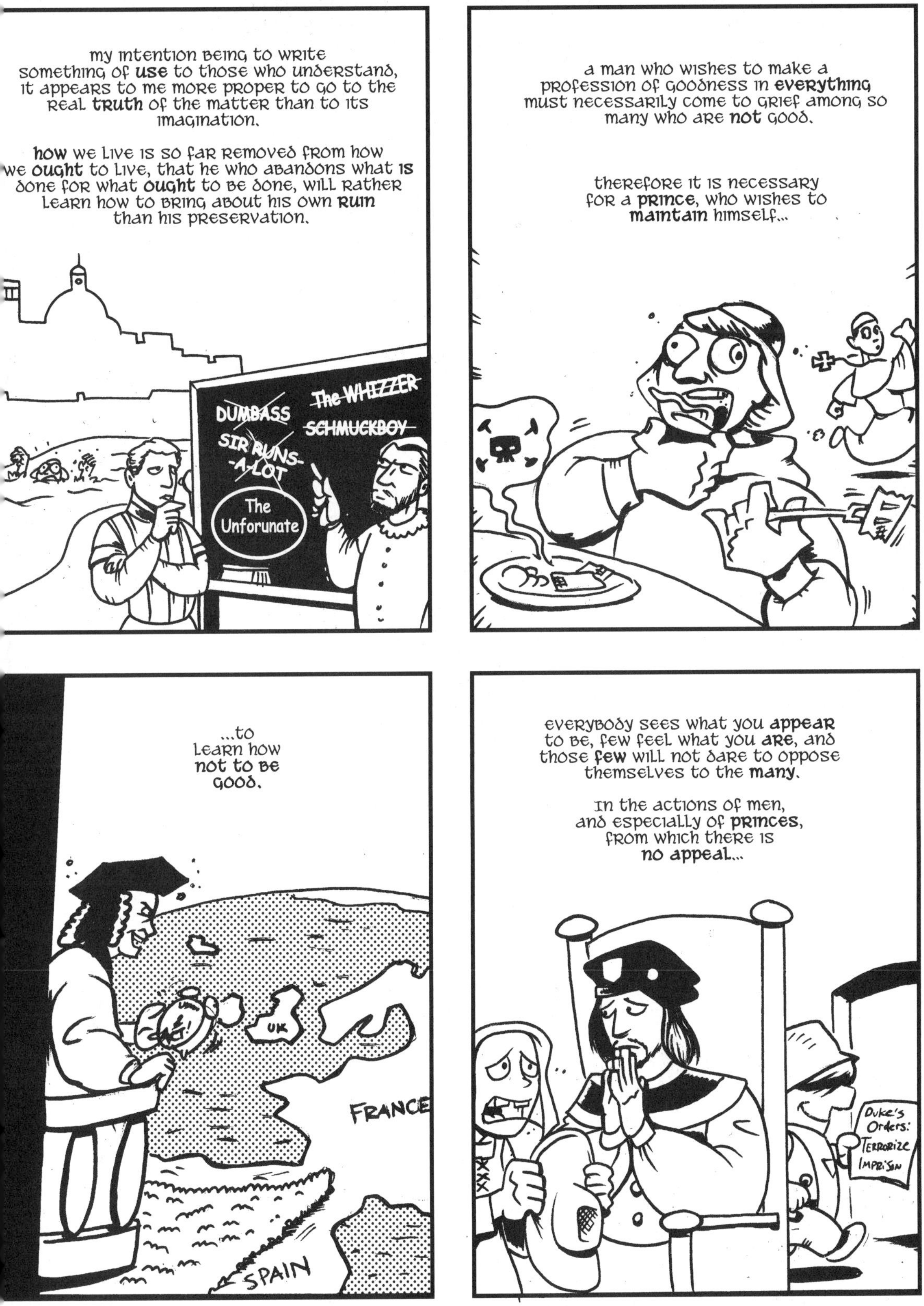
my intention being to write something of use to those who understand, it appears to me more proper to go to the real truth of the matter than to its imagination.
how we live is so far removed from how we ought to live, that he who abandons what is done for what ought to be done, will rather learn how to bring about his own ruin than his preservation.
DUMBASS
The WHIZZER
SCHMUCKBOY
SIR RUNS-A-LOT
The Unforunate
a man who wishes to make a profession of goodness in everything must necessarily come to grief among so many who are not good.
therefore it is necessary for a prince, who wishes to maintain himself...
...to learn how not to be good.
UK
FRANCE
SPAIN
everybody sees what you appear to be, few feel what you are, and those few will not dare to oppose themselves to the many.
in the actions of men, and especially of princes, from which there is no appeal...
Duke's Orders: Terrorize Imprison

...the end justifies the means.

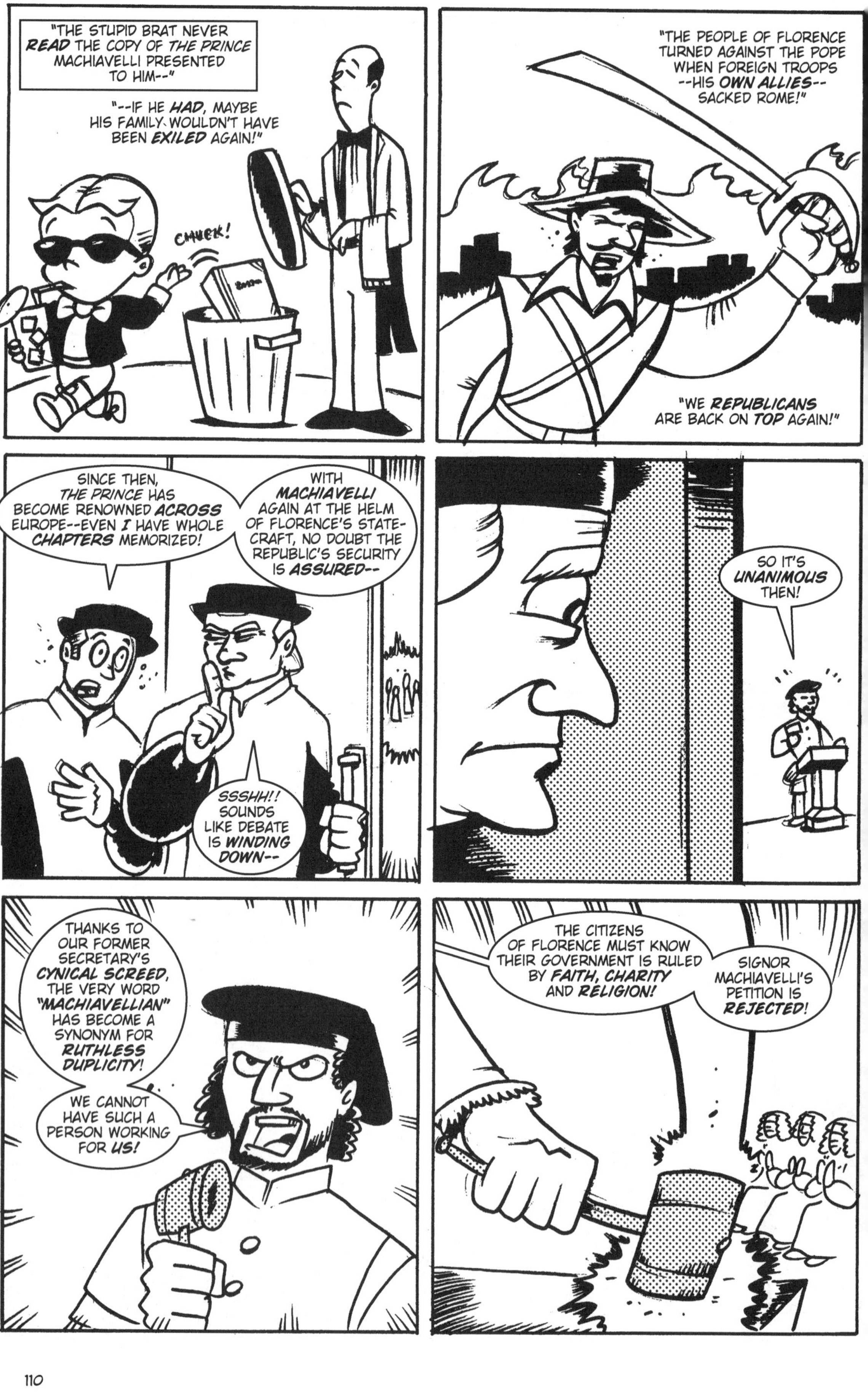
"THE STUPID BRAT NEVER READ THE COPY OF THE PRINCE MACHIAVELLI PRESENTED TO HIM--"
"--IF HE HAD, MAYBE HIS FAMILY WOULDN'T HAVE BEEN EXILED AGAIN!"
CHUCK!
"THE PEOPLE OF FLORENCE TURNED AGAINST THE POPE WHEN FOREIGN TROOPS --HIS OWN ALLIES-- SACKED ROME!"
"WE REPUBLICANS ARE BACK ON TOP AGAIN!"
SINCE THEN, THE PRINCE HAS BECOME RENOWNED ACROSS EUROPE--EVEN I HAVE WHOLE CHAPTERS MEMORIZED!
WITH MACHIAVELLI AGAIN AT THE HELM OF FLORENCE'S STATE-CRAFT, NO DOUBT THE REPUBLIC'S SECURITY IS ASSURED--
SSSHH!! SOUNDS LIKE DEBATE IS WINDING DOWN--
SO IT'S UNANIMOUS THEN!
THANKS TO OUR FORMER SECRETARY'S CYNICAL SCREED, THE VERY WORD "MACHIAVELLIAN" HAS BECOME A SYNONYM FOR RUTHLESS DUPLICITY!
WE CANNOT HAVE SUCH A PERSON WORKING FOR US!
THE CITIZENS OF FLORENCE MUST KNOW THEIR GOVERNMENT IS RULED BY FAITH, CHARITY AND RELIGION!
SIGNOR MACHIAVELLI'S PETITION IS REJECTED!

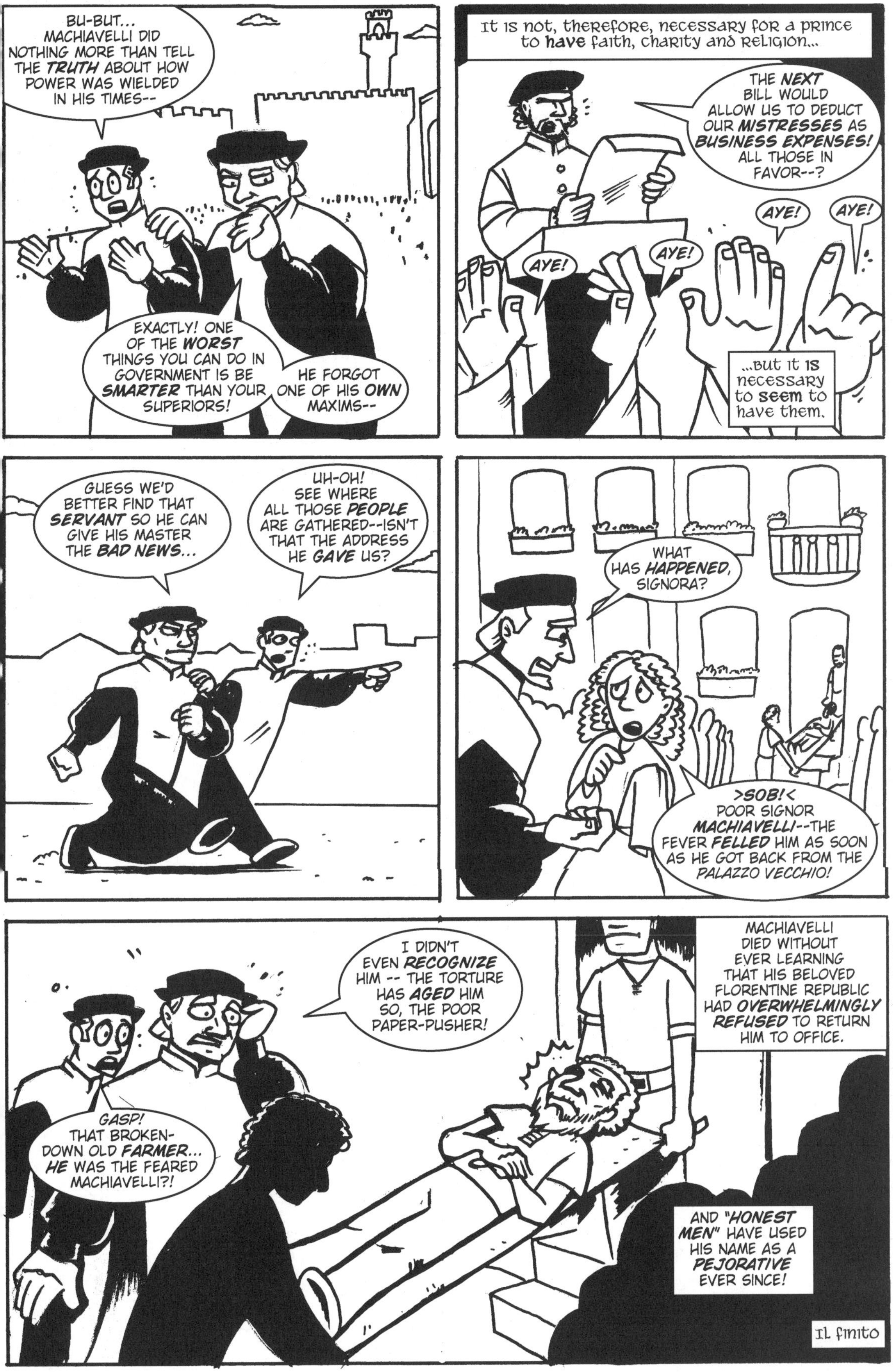
BU-BUT... MACHIAVELLI DID NOTHING MORE THAN TELL THE TRUTH ABOUT HOW POWER WAS WIELDED IN HIS TIMES--
EXACTLY! ONE OF THE WORST THINGS YOU CAN DO IN GOVERNMENT IS BE SMARTER THAN YOUR SUPERIORS!
HE FORGOT ONE OF HIS OWN MAXIMS--
It is not, therefore, necessary for a prince to have faith, charity and religion...
THE NEXT BILL WOULD ALLOW US TO DEDUCT OUR MISTRESSES AS BUSINESS EXPENSES! ALL THOSE IN FAVOR--?
AYE!
AYE!
AYE!
AYE!
...but it is necessary to seem to have them.
GUESS WE'D BETTER FIND THAT SERVANT SO HE CAN GIVE HIS MASTER THE BAD NEWS...
UH-OH! SEE WHERE ALL THOSE PEOPLE ARE GATHERED--ISN'T THAT THE ADDRESS HE GAVE US?
WHAT HAS HAPPENED, SIGNORA?
>SOB!< POOR SIGNOR MACHIAVELLI--THE FEVER FELLED HIM AS SOON AS HE GOT BACK FROM THE PALAZZO VECCHIO!
I DIDN'T EVEN RECOGNIZE HIM -- THE TORTURE HAS AGED HIM SO, THE POOR PAPER-PUSHER!
GASP! THAT BROKEN-DOWN OLD FARMER... HE WAS THE FEARED MACHIAVELLI?!
MACHIAVELLI DIED WITHOUT EVER LEARNING THAT HIS BELOVED FLORENTINE REPUBLIC HAD OVERWHELMINGLY REFUSED TO RETURN HIM TO OFFICE.
AND "HONEST MEN" HAVE USED HIS NAME AS A PEJORATIVE EVER SINCE!
IL FINITO

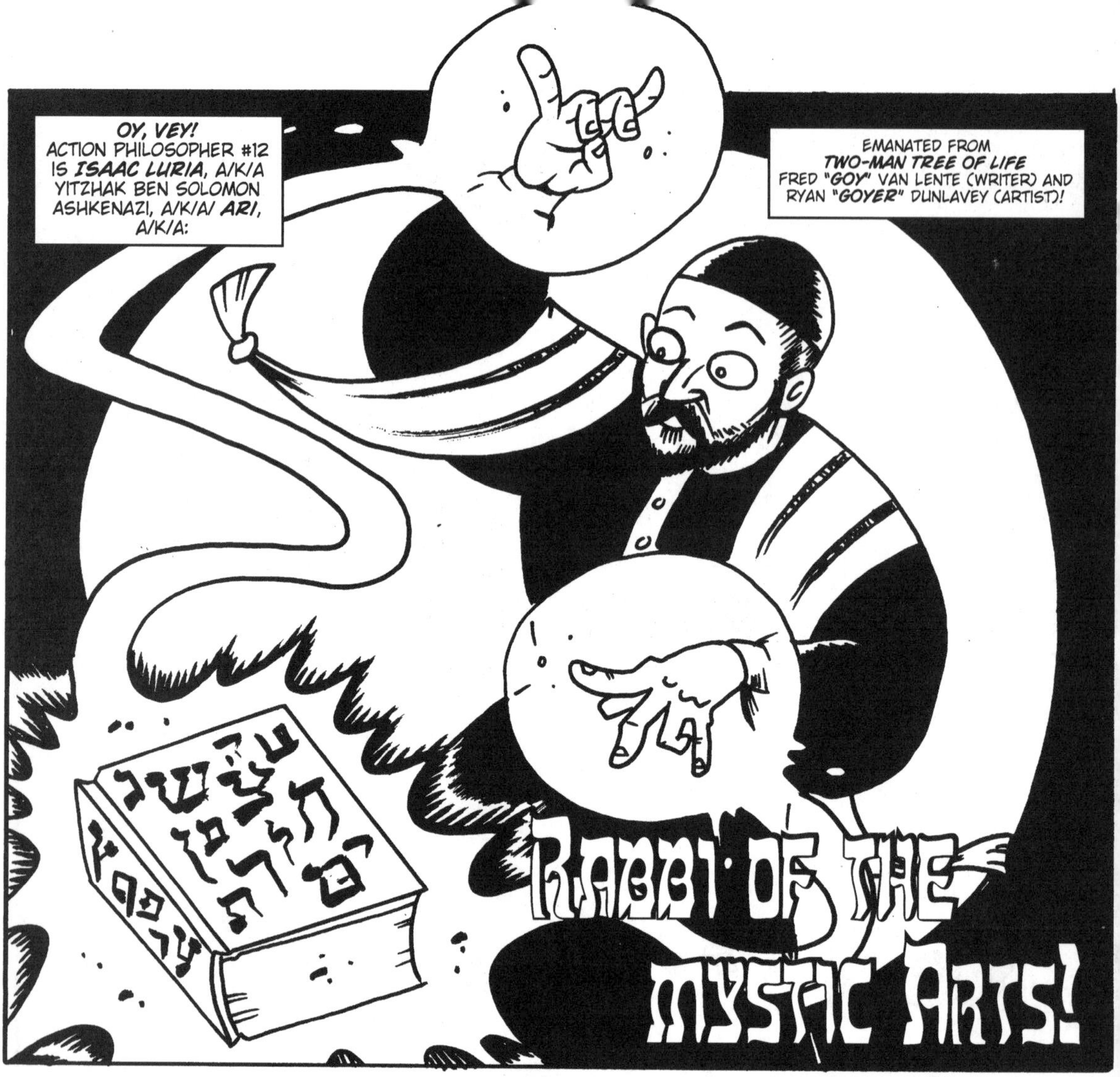
OY, VEY!
ACTION PHILOSOPHER #12 IS ***ISAAC LURIA***, A/K/A YITZHAK BEN SOLOMON ASHKENAZI, A/K/A/ ***ARI***, A/K/A:
EMANATED FROM ***TWO-MAN TREE OF LIFE***
FRED "***GOY***" VAN LENTE (WRITER) AND RYAN "***GOYER***" DUNLAVEY (ARTIST)!
RABBI OF THE MYSTIC ARTS!

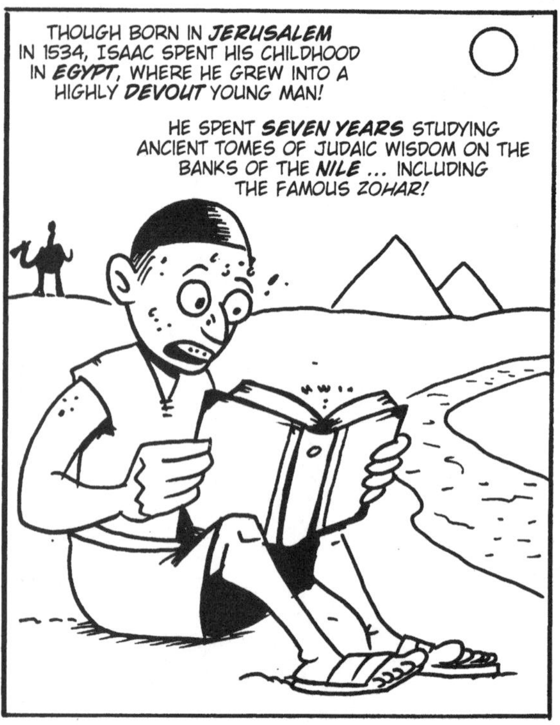
THOUGH BORN IN ***JERUSALEM*** IN 1534, ISAAC SPENT HIS CHILDHOOD IN ***EGYPT***, WHERE HE GREW INTO A HIGHLY ***DEVOUT*** YOUNG MAN!
HE SPENT ***SEVEN YEARS*** STUDYING ANCIENT TOMES OF JUDAIC WISDOM ON THE BANKS OF THE ***NILE*** ... INCLUDING THE FAMOUS *ZOHAR*!

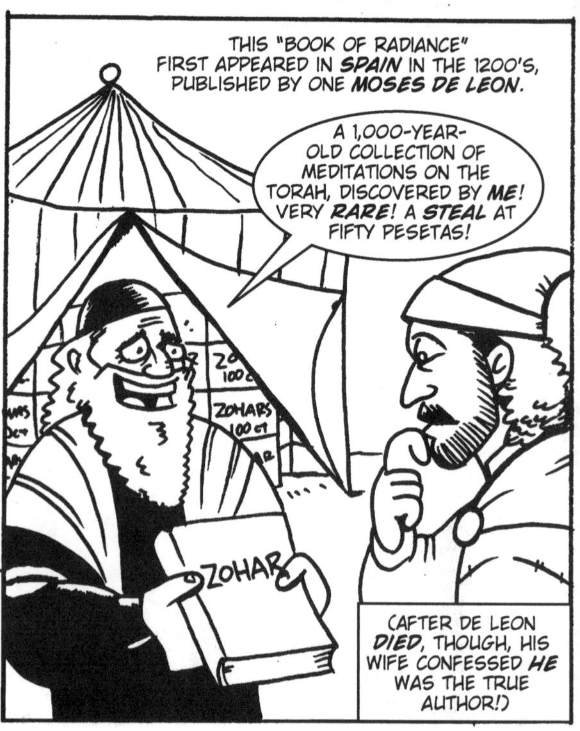
THIS "BOOK OF RADIANCE" FIRST APPEARED IN ***SPAIN*** IN THE 1200'S, PUBLISHED BY ONE ***MOSES DE LEON***.
A 1,000-YEAR-OLD COLLECTION OF MEDITATIONS ON THE TORAH, DISCOVERED BY ***ME***! VERY ***RARE***! A ***STEAL*** AT FIFTY PESETAS!
ZOHARS 100 ct
ZOHAR
(AFTER DE LEON ***DIED***, THOUGH, HIS WIFE CONFESSED ***HE*** WAS THE TRUE AUTHOR!)

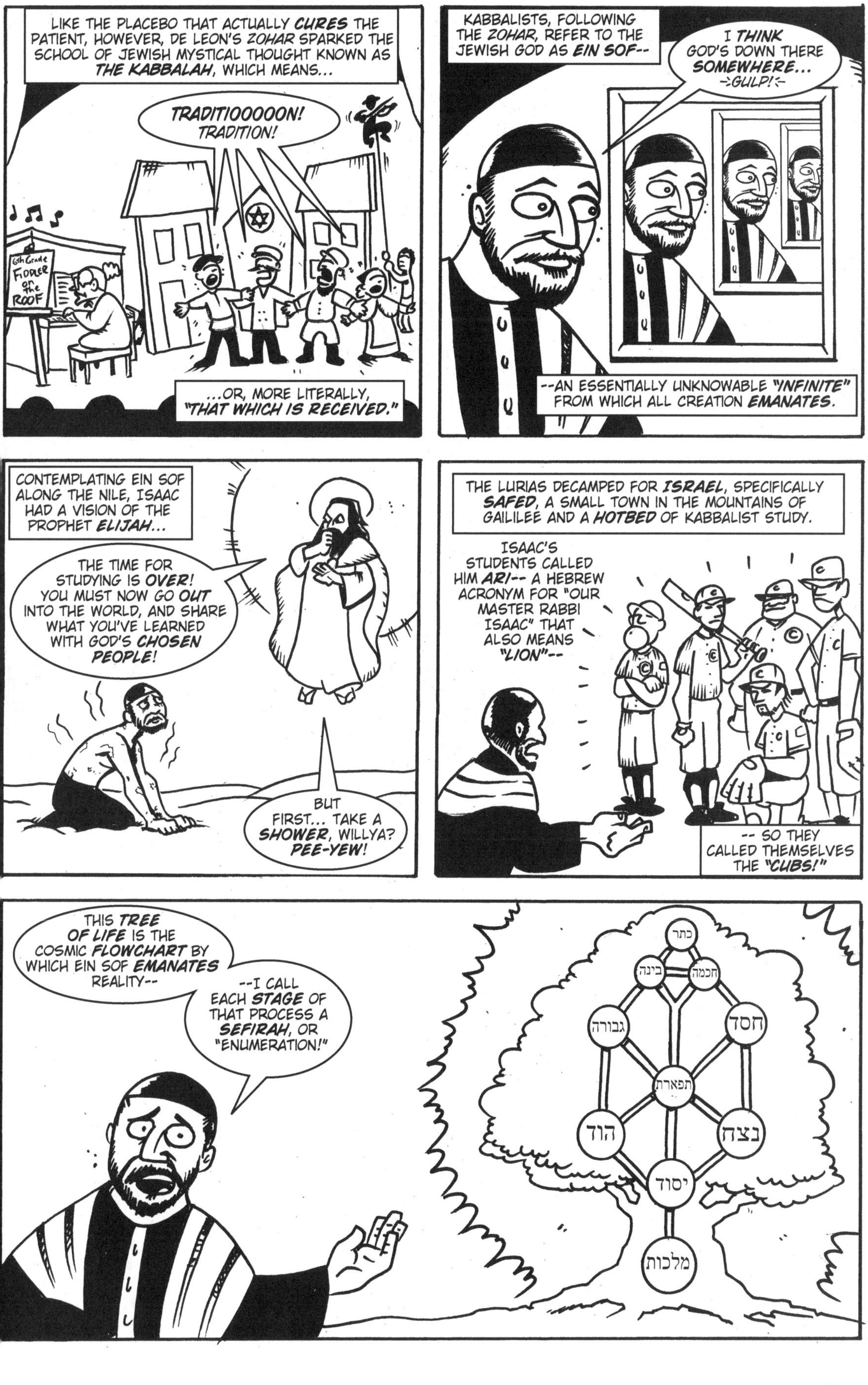
LIKE THE PLACEBO THAT ACTUALLY CURES THE PATIENT, HOWEVER, DE LEON'S ZOHAR SPARKED THE SCHOOL OF JEWISH MYSTICAL THOUGHT KNOWN AS THE KABBALAH, WHICH MEANS...
TRADITIOOOOON! TRADITION!
6th Grade FIDDLER on the ROOF
...OR, MORE LITERALLY, "THAT WHICH IS RECEIVED."
KABBALISTS, FOLLOWING THE ZOHAR, REFER TO THE JEWISH GOD AS EIN SOF--
I THINK GOD'S DOWN THERE SOMEWHERE... GULP!
--AN ESSENTIALLY UNKNOWABLE "INFINITE" FROM WHICH ALL CREATION EMANATES.
CONTEMPLATING EIN SOF ALONG THE NILE, ISAAC HAD A VISION OF THE PROPHET ELIJAH...
THE TIME FOR STUDYING IS OVER! YOU MUST NOW GO OUT INTO THE WORLD, AND SHARE WHAT YOU'VE LEARNED WITH GOD'S CHOSEN PEOPLE!
BUT FIRST... TAKE A SHOWER, WILLYA? PEE-YEW!
THE LURIAS DECAMPED FOR ISRAEL, SPECIFICALLY SAFED, A SMALL TOWN IN THE MOUNTAINS OF GAILILEE AND A HOTBED OF KABBALIST STUDY.
ISAAC'S STUDENTS CALLED HIM ARI-- A HEBREW ACRONYM FOR "OUR MASTER RABBI ISAAC" THAT ALSO MEANS "LION"--
-- SO THEY CALLED THEMSELVES THE "CUBS!"
THIS TREE OF LIFE IS THE COSMIC FLOWCHART BY WHICH EIN SOF EMANATES REALITY--
--I CALL EACH STAGE OF THAT PROCESS A SEFIRAH, OR "ENUMERATION!"
כתר
בינה
חכמה
גבורה
חסד
תפארת
הוד
נצח
יסוד
מלכות

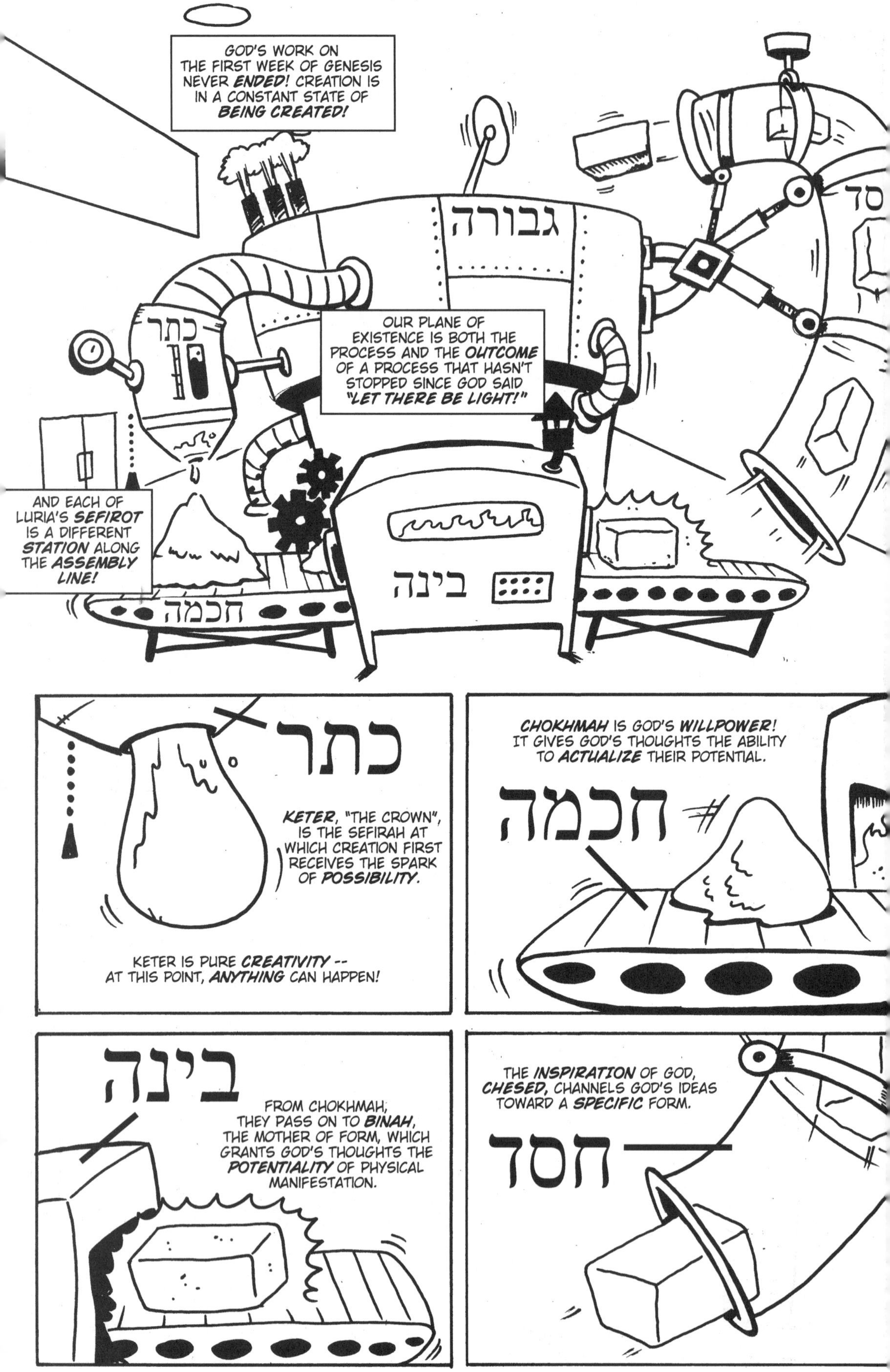
GOD'S WORK ON THE FIRST WEEK OF GENESIS NEVER ENDED! CREATION IS IN A CONSTANT STATE OF BEING CREATED!
גבורה
כתר
OUR PLANE OF EXISTENCE IS BOTH THE PROCESS AND THE OUTCOME OF A PROCESS THAT HASN'T STOPPED SINCE GOD SAID "LET THERE BE LIGHT!"
AND EACH OF LURIA'S SEFIROT IS A DIFFERENT STATION ALONG THE ASSEMBLY LINE!
חכמה
בינה
כתר
KETER, "THE CROWN", IS THE SEFIRAH AT WHICH CREATION FIRST RECEIVES THE SPARK OF POSSIBILITY.
KETER IS PURE CREATIVITY -- AT THIS POINT, ANYTHING CAN HAPPEN!
CHOKHMAH IS GOD'S WILLPOWER! IT GIVES GOD'S THOUGHTS THE ABILITY TO ACTUALIZE THEIR POTENTIAL.
חכמה
בינה
FROM CHOKHMAH, THEY PASS ON TO BINAH, THE MOTHER OF FORM, WHICH GRANTS GOD'S THOUGHTS THE POTENTIALITY OF PHYSICAL MANIFESTATION.
THE INSPIRATION OF GOD, CHESED, CHANNELS GOD'S IDEAS TOWARD A SPECIFIC FORM.
חסד

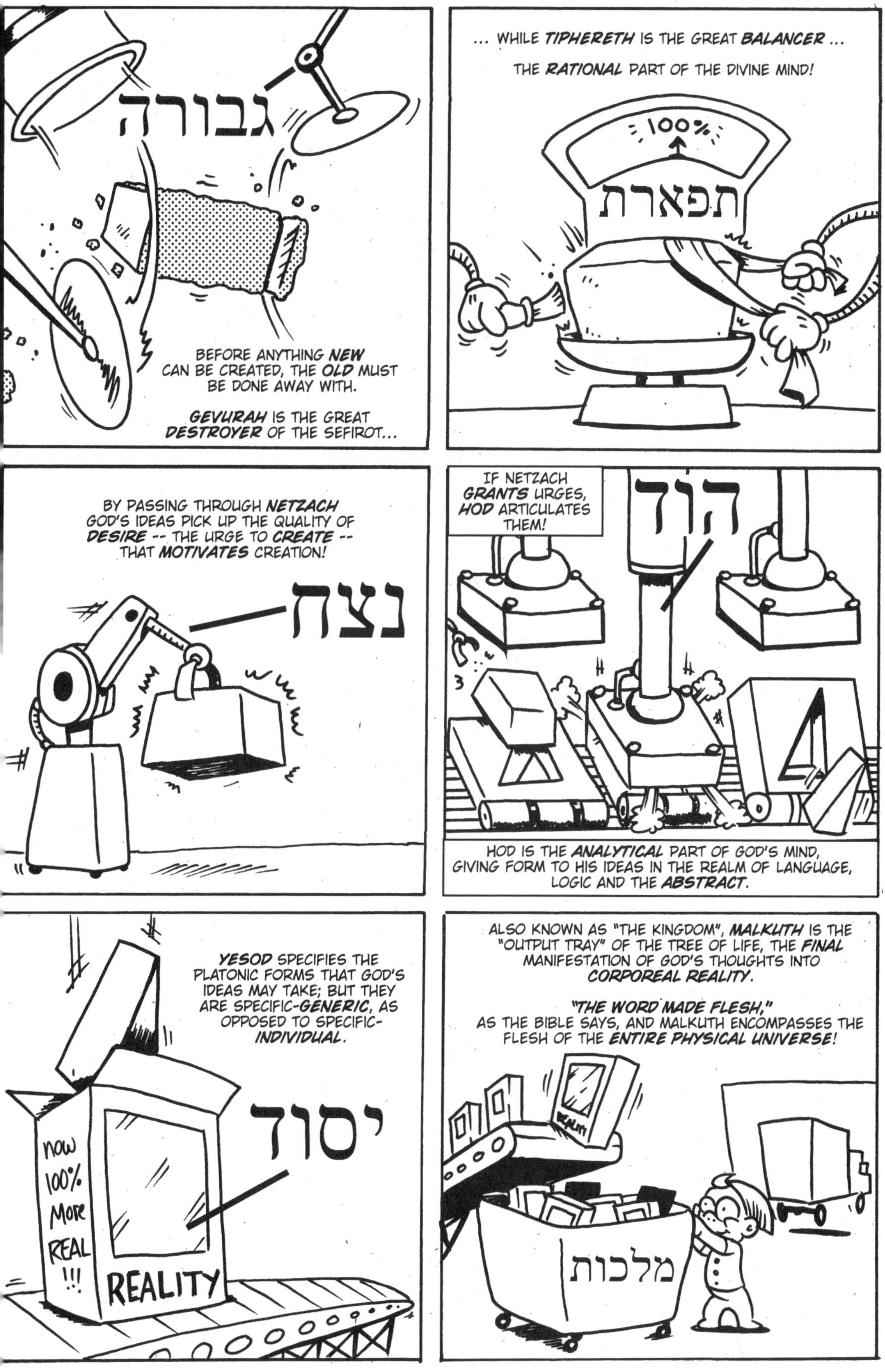
גבורה
BEFORE ANYTHING NEW CAN BE CREATED, THE OLD MUST BE DONE AWAY WITH.
GEVURAH IS THE GREAT DESTROYER OF THE SEFIROT...
... WHILE TIPHERETH IS THE GREAT BALANCER ...
THE RATIONAL PART OF THE DIVINE MIND!
100%
תפארת
BY PASSING THROUGH NETZACH GOD'S IDEAS PICK UP THE QUALITY OF DESIRE -- THE URGE TO CREATE -- THAT MOTIVATES CREATION!
נצח
IF NETZACH GRANTS URGES, HOD ARTICULATES THEM!
הוד
HOD IS THE ANALYTICAL PART OF GOD'S MIND, GIVING FORM TO HIS IDEAS IN THE REALM OF LANGUAGE, LOGIC AND THE ABSTRACT.
YESOD SPECIFIES THE PLATONIC FORMS THAT GOD'S IDEAS MAY TAKE; BUT THEY ARE SPECIFIC-GENERIC, AS OPPOSED TO SPECIFIC-INDIVIDUAL.
יסוד
now 100% More REAL !!!
REALITY
ALSO KNOWN AS "THE KINGDOM", MALKUTH IS THE "OUTPUT TRAY" OF THE TREE OF LIFE, THE FINAL MANIFESTATION OF GOD'S THOUGHTS INTO CORPOREAL REALITY.
"THE WORD MADE FLESH," AS THE BIBLE SAYS, AND MALKUTH ENCOMPASSES THE FLESH OF THE ENTIRE PHYSICAL UNIVERSE!
REALITY
מלכות

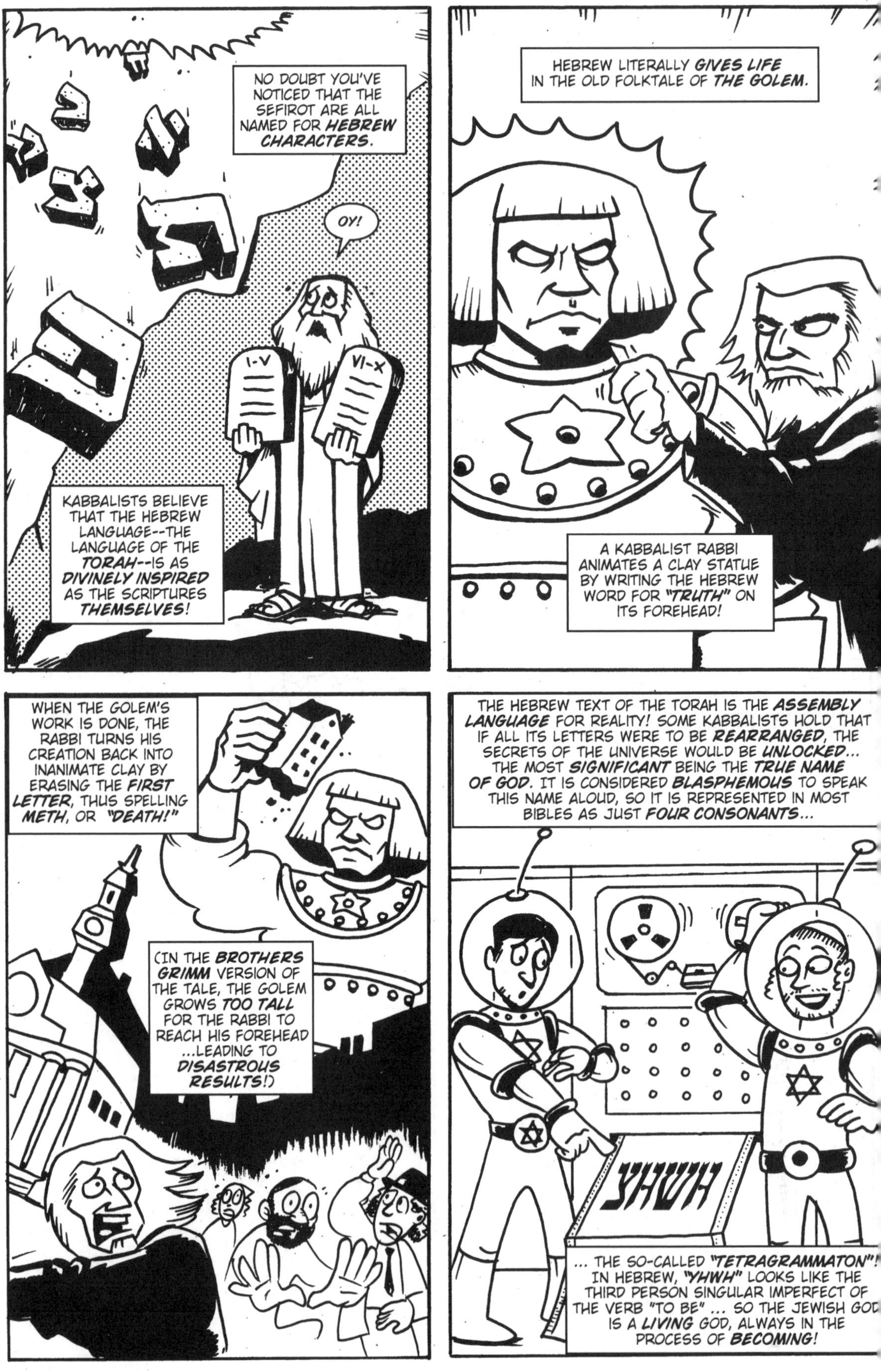
NO DOUBT YOU'VE NOTICED THAT THE SEFIROT ARE ALL NAMED FOR HEBREW CHARACTERS.
OY!
KABBALISTS BELIEVE THAT THE HEBREW LANGUAGE--THE LANGUAGE OF THE TORAH--IS AS DIVINELY INSPIRED AS THE SCRIPTURES THEMSELVES!
I-V
VI-X
HEBREW LITERALLY GIVES LIFE IN THE OLD FOLKTALE OF THE GOLEM.
A KABBALIST RABBI ANIMATES A CLAY STATUE BY WRITING THE HEBREW WORD FOR "TRUTH" ON ITS FOREHEAD!
WHEN THE GOLEM'S WORK IS DONE, THE RABBI TURNS HIS CREATION BACK INTO INANIMATE CLAY BY ERASING THE FIRST LETTER, THUS SPELLING METH, OR "DEATH!"
(IN THE BROTHERS GRIMM VERSION OF THE TALE, THE GOLEM GROWS TOO TALL FOR THE RABBI TO REACH HIS FOREHEAD ...LEADING TO DISASTROUS RESULTS!)
THE HEBREW TEXT OF THE TORAH IS THE ASSEMBLY LANGUAGE FOR REALITY! SOME KABBALISTS HOLD THAT IF ALL ITS LETTERS WERE TO BE REARRANGED, THE SECRETS OF THE UNIVERSE WOULD BE UNLOCKED... THE MOST SIGNIFICANT BEING THE TRUE NAME OF GOD. IT IS CONSIDERED BLASPHEMOUS TO SPEAK THIS NAME ALOUD, SO IT IS REPRESENTED IN MOST BIBLES AS JUST FOUR CONSONANTS...
YHWH
... THE SO-CALLED "TETRAGRAMMATON"! IN HEBREW, "YHWH" LOOKS LIKE THE THIRD PERSON SINGULAR IMPERFECT OF THE VERB "TO BE" ... SO THE JEWISH GOD IS A LIVING GOD, ALWAYS IN THE PROCESS OF BECOMING!

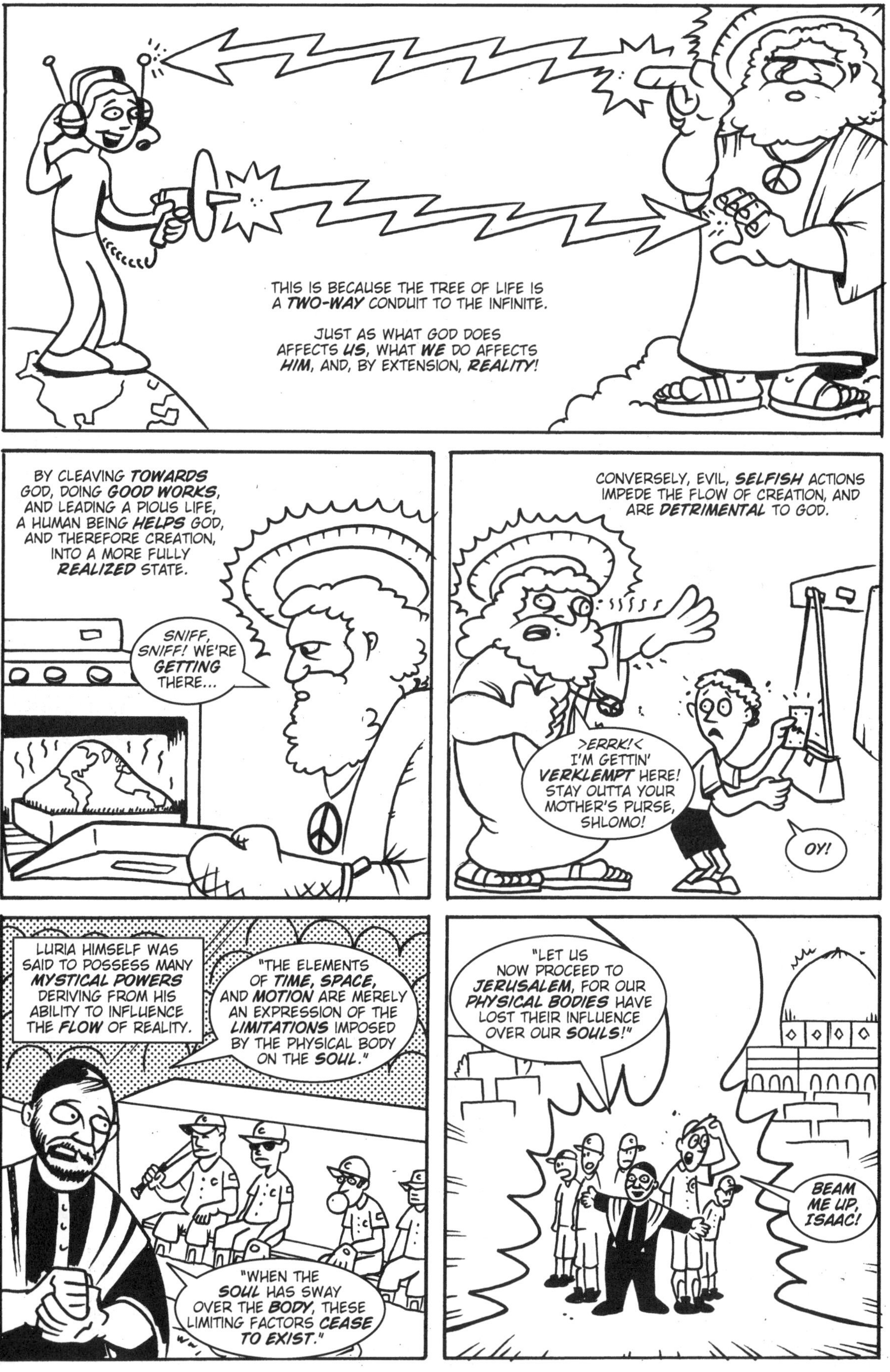

THIS IS BECAUSE THE TREE OF LIFE IS A TWO-WAY CONDUIT TO THE INFINITE.
JUST AS WHAT GOD DOES AFFECTS US, WHAT WE DO AFFECTS HIM, AND, BY EXTENSION, REALITY!
BY CLEAVING TOWARDS GOD, DOING GOOD WORKS, AND LEADING A PIOUS LIFE, A HUMAN BEING HELPS GOD, AND THEREFORE CREATION, INTO A MORE FULLY REALIZED STATE.
SNIFF, SNIFF! WE'RE GETTING THERE...
CONVERSELY, EVIL, SELFISH ACTIONS IMPEDE THE FLOW OF CREATION, AND ARE DETRIMENTAL TO GOD.
>ERRK!< I'M GETTIN' VERKLEMPT HERE! STAY OUTTA YOUR MOTHER'S PURSE, SHLOMO!
OY!
LURIA HIMSELF WAS SAID TO POSSESS MANY MYSTICAL POWERS DERIVING FROM HIS ABILITY TO INFLUENCE THE FLOW OF REALITY.
"THE ELEMENTS OF TIME, SPACE, AND MOTION ARE MERELY AN EXPRESSION OF THE LIMITATIONS IMPOSED BY THE PHYSICAL BODY ON THE SOUL."
"WHEN THE SOUL HAS SWAY OVER THE BODY, THESE LIMITING FACTORS CEASE TO EXIST."
"LET US NOW PROCEED TO JERUSALEM, FOR OUR PHYSICAL BODIES HAVE LOST THEIR INFLUENCE OVER OUR SOULS!"
BEAM ME UP, ISAAC!

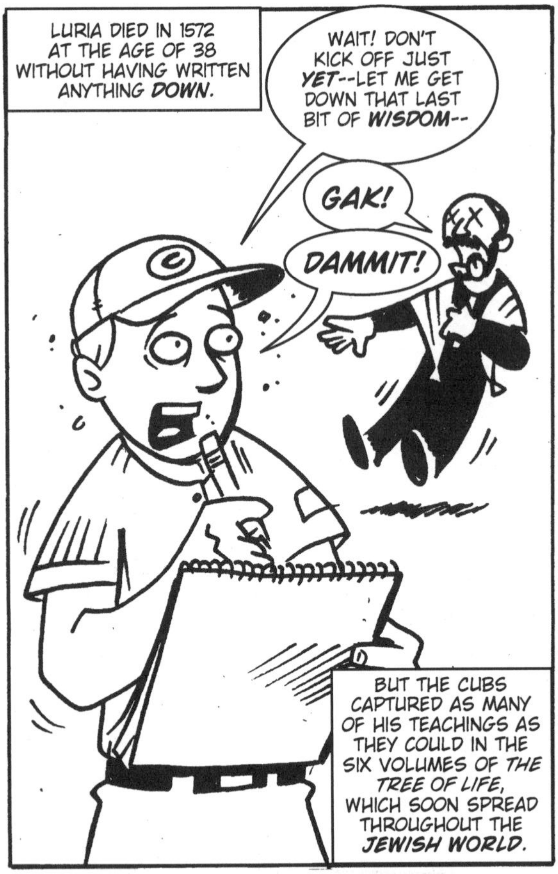

LURIA DIED IN 1572 AT THE AGE OF 38 WITHOUT HAVING WRITTEN ANYTHING DOWN.
WAIT! DON'T KICK OFF JUST YET--LET ME GET DOWN THAT LAST BIT OF WISDOM--
GAK!
DAMMIT!
BUT THE CUBS CAPTURED AS MANY OF HIS TEACHINGS AS THEY COULD IN THE SIX VOLUMES OF THE TREE OF LIFE, WHICH SOON SPREAD THROUGHOUT THE JEWISH WORLD.

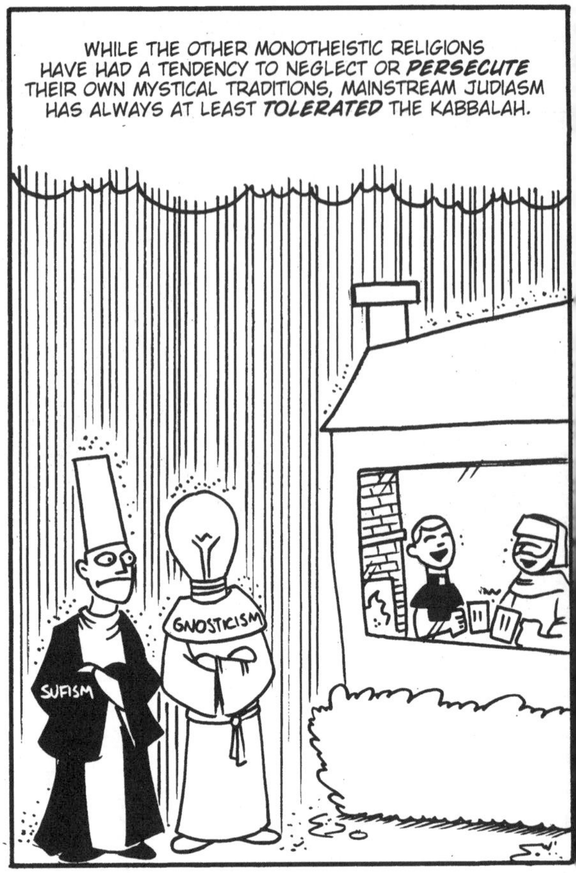

WHILE THE OTHER MONOTHEISTIC RELIGIONS HAVE HAD A TENDENCY TO NEGLECT OR PERSECUTE THEIR OWN MYSTICAL TRADITIONS, MAINSTREAM JUDIASM HAS ALWAYS AT LEAST TOLERATED THE KABBALAH.
SUFISM
GNOSTICISM

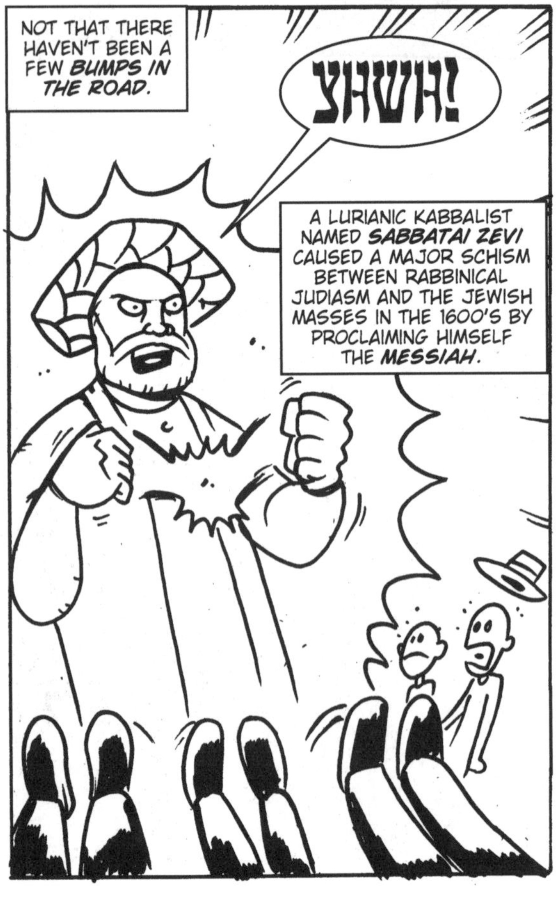

NOT THAT THERE HAVEN'T BEEN A FEW BUMPS IN THE ROAD.
YHWH!
A LURIANIC KABBALIST NAMED SABBATAI ZEVI CAUSED A MAJOR SCHISM BETWEEN RABBINICAL JUDIASM AND THE JEWISH MASSES IN THE 1600'S BY PROCLAIMING HIMSELF THE MESSIAH.

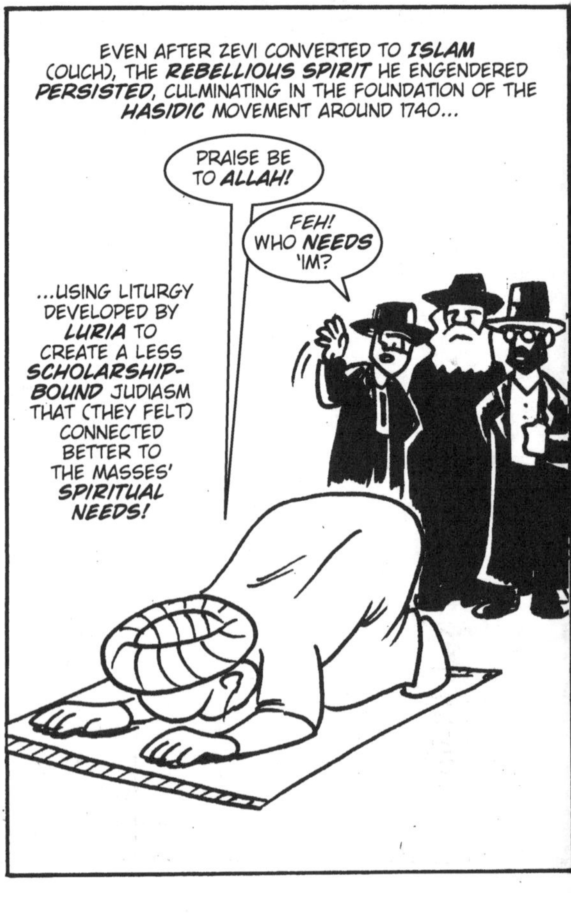

EVEN AFTER ZEVI CONVERTED TO ISLAM (OUCH), THE REBELLIOUS SPIRIT HE ENGENDERED PERSISTED, CULMINATING IN THE FOUNDATION OF THE HASIDIC MOVEMENT AROUND 1740...
PRAISE BE TO ALLAH!
FEH! WHO NEEDS 'IM?
...USING LITURGY DEVELOPED BY LURIA TO CREATE A LESS SCHOLARSHIP-BOUND JUDIASM THAT (THEY FELT) CONNECTED BETTER TO THE MASSES' SPIRITUAL NEEDS!

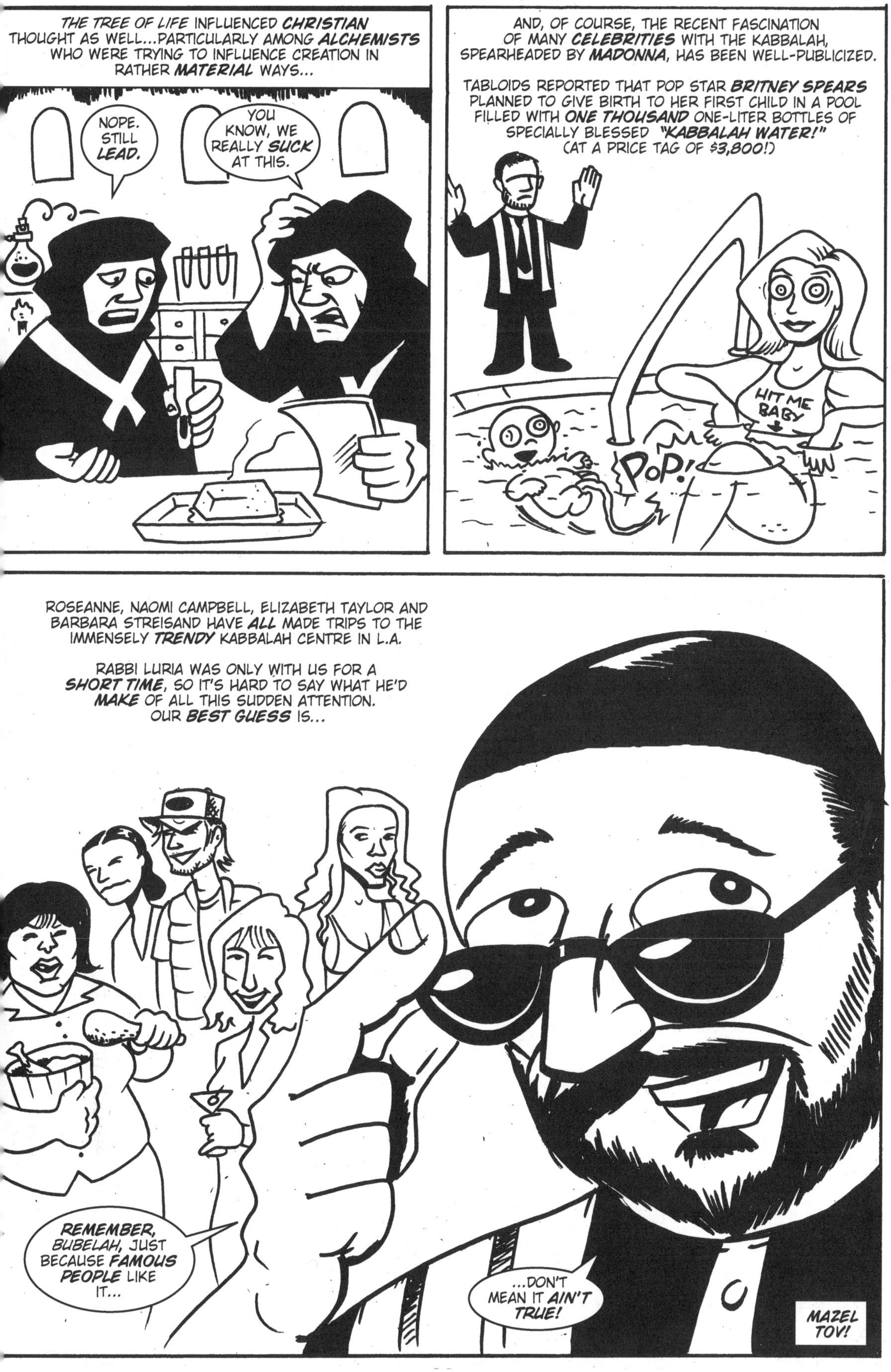
THE TREE OF LIFE INFLUENCED CHRISTIAN THOUGHT AS WELL...PARTICULARLY AMONG ALCHEMISTS WHO WERE TRYING TO INFLUENCE CREATION IN RATHER MATERIAL WAYS...
NOPE. STILL LEAD.
YOU KNOW, WE REALLY SUCK AT THIS.
AND, OF COURSE, THE RECENT FASCINATION OF MANY CELEBRITIES WITH THE KABBALAH, SPEARHEADED BY MADONNA, HAS BEEN WELL-PUBLICIZED.
TABLOIDS REPORTED THAT POP STAR BRITNEY SPEARS PLANNED TO GIVE BIRTH TO HER FIRST CHILD IN A POOL FILLED WITH ONE THOUSAND ONE-LITER BOTTLES OF SPECIALLY BLESSED "KABBALAH WATER!" (AT A PRICE TAG OF $3,800!)
HIT ME BABY
POP!
ROSEANNE, NAOMI CAMPBELL, ELIZABETH TAYLOR AND BARBARA STREISAND HAVE ALL MADE TRIPS TO THE IMMENSELY TRENDY KABBALAH CENTRE IN L.A.
RABBI LURIA WAS ONLY WITH US FOR A SHORT TIME, SO IT'S HARD TO SAY WHAT HE'D MAKE OF ALL THIS SUDDEN ATTENTION. OUR BEST GUESS IS...
REMEMBER, BUBELAH, JUST BECAUSE FAMOUS PEOPLE LIKE IT...
...DON'T MEAN IT AIN'T TRUE!
MAZEL TOV!

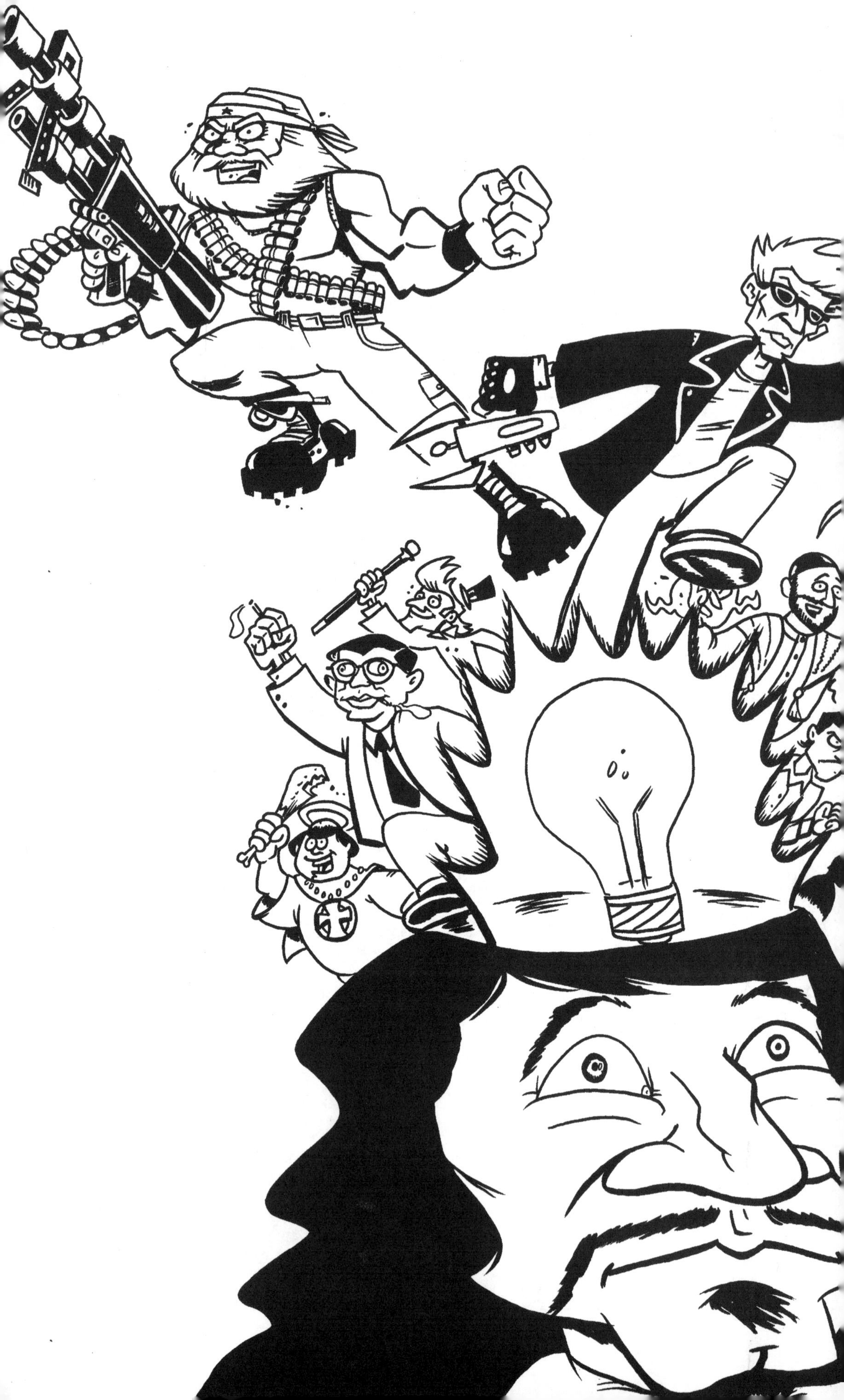

PART THREE:

BLINDED ME WITH *SCIENCE!*

(MODERN PHILOSOPHY)

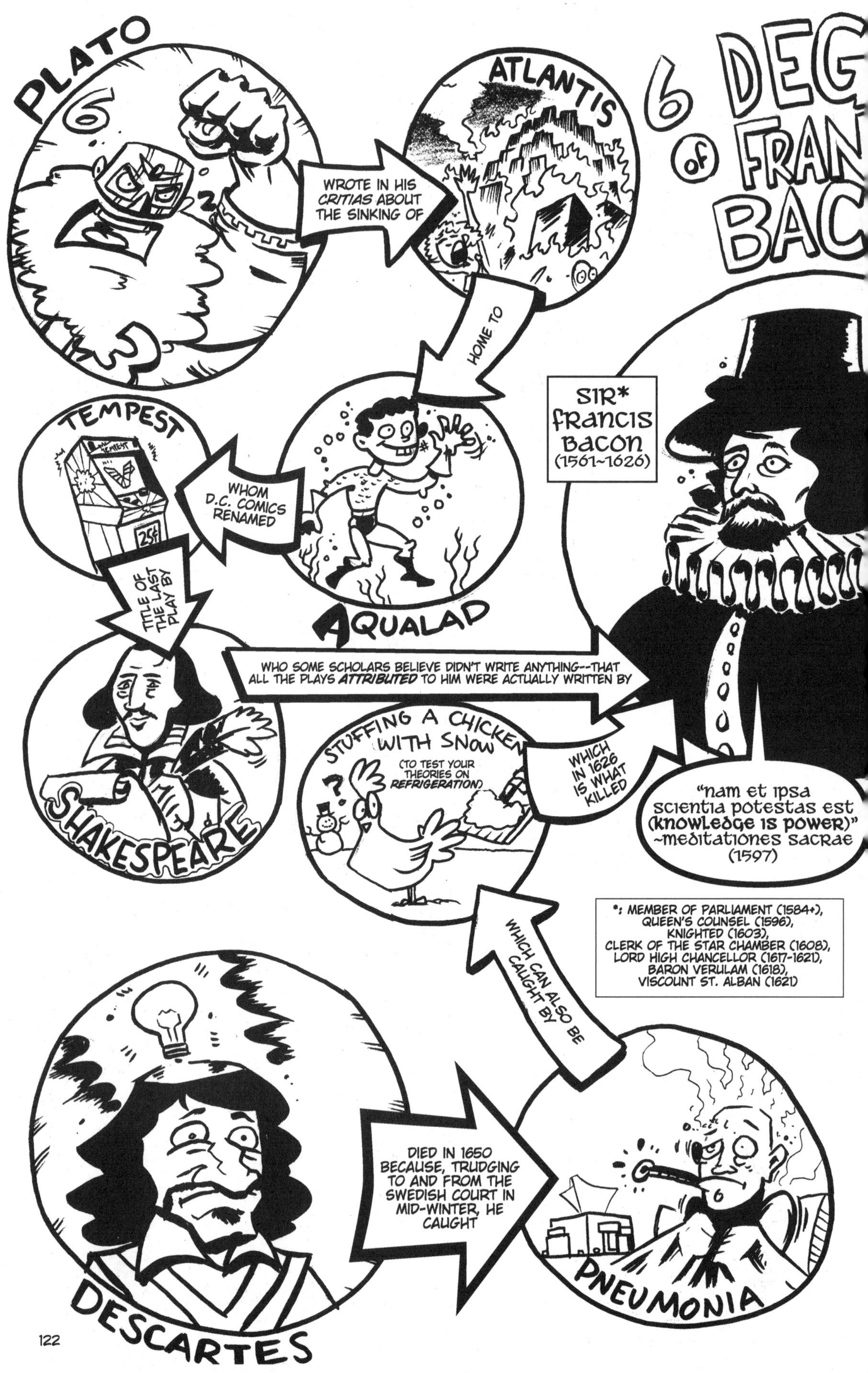
6 DEG
of FRAN
BAC
PLATO
WROTE IN HIS CRITIAS ABOUT THE SINKING OF
ATLANTIS
HOME TO
AQUALAD
WHOM D.C. COMICS RENAMED
TEMPEST
TEMPEST
25¢
TITLE OF THE LAST PLAY BY
SHAKESPEARE
WHO SOME SCHOLARS BELIEVE DIDN'T WRITE ANYTHING--THAT ALL THE PLAYS ATTRIBUTED TO HIM WERE ACTUALLY WRITTEN BY
SIR* FRANCIS BACON (1561~1626)
"nam et ipsa scientia potestas est (knowledge is power)" ~meditationes sacrae (1597)
*: MEMBER OF PARLIAMENT (1584+), QUEEN'S COUNSEL (1596), KNIGHTED (1603), CLERK OF THE STAR CHAMBER (1608), LORD HIGH CHANCELLOR (1617-1621), BARON VERULAM (1618), VISCOUNT ST. ALBAN (1621)
WHICH IN 1626 IS WHAT KILLED
STUFFING A CHICKEN WITH SNOW
(TO TEST YOUR THEORIES ON REFRIGERATION)
WHICH CAN ALSO BE CAUGHT BY
PNEUMONIA
DIED IN 1650 BECAUSE, TRUDGING TO AND FROM THE SWEDISH COURT IN MID-WINTER, HE CAUGHT
DESCARTES

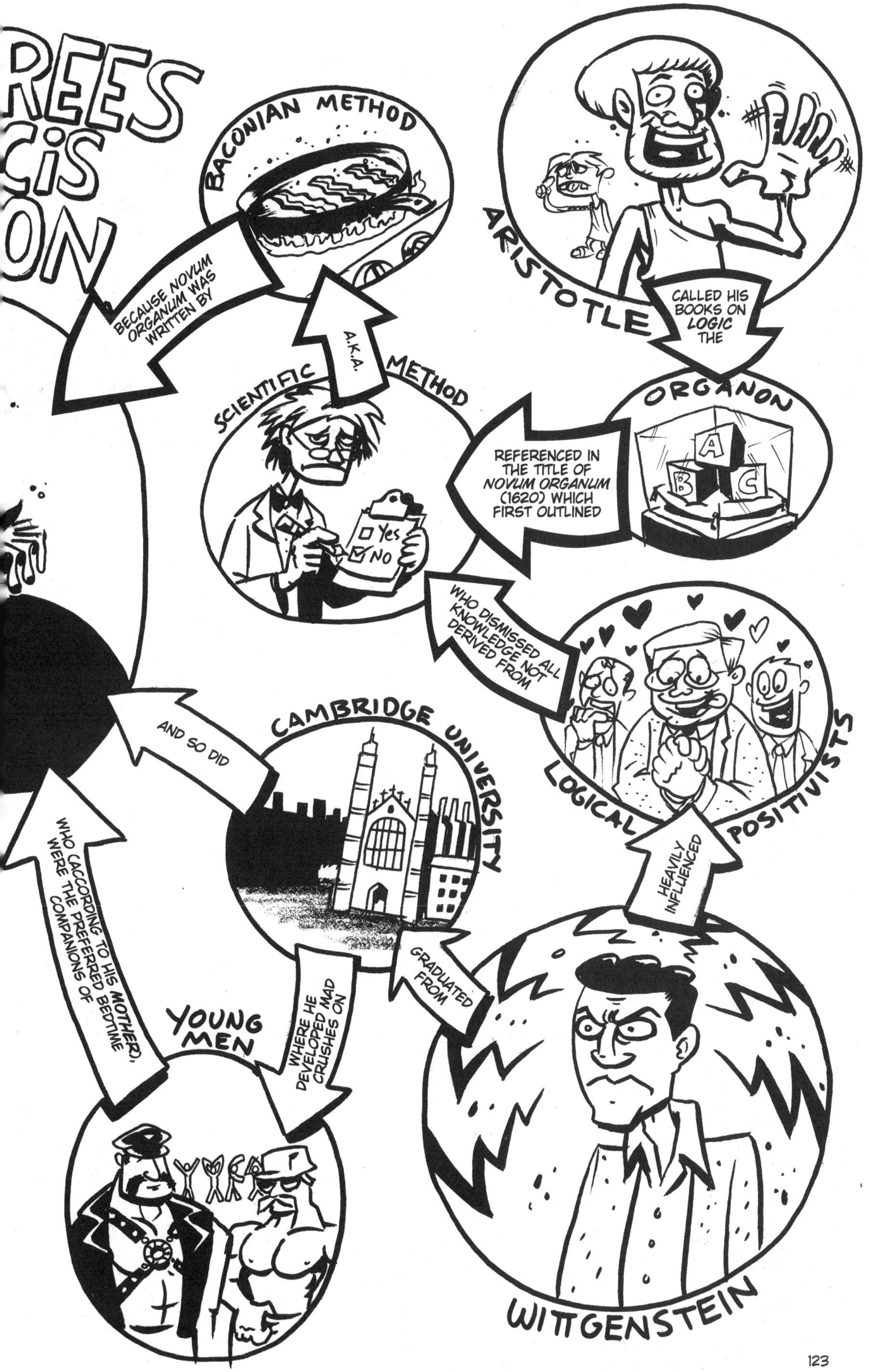
REES
CiS
ON
BACONIAN METHOD
BECAUSE NOVUM ORGANUM WAS WRITTEN BY
A.K.A.
ARISTOTLE
CALLED HIS BOOKS ON LOGIC THE
ORGANON
A B C
REFERENCED IN THE TITLE OF NOVUM ORGANUM (1620) WHICH FIRST OUTLINED
SCIENTIFIC METHOD
Yes
No
WHO DISMISSED ALL KNOWLEDGE NOT DERIVED FROM
LOGICAL POSITIVISTS
HEAVILY INFLUENCED
WITTGENSTEIN
GRADUATED FROM
CAMBRIDGE UNIVERSITY
AND SO DID
WHERE HE DEVELOPED MAD CRUSHES ON
YOUNG MEN
WHO (ACCORDING TO HIS MOTHER), WERE THE PREFERRED BEDTIME COMPANIONS OF

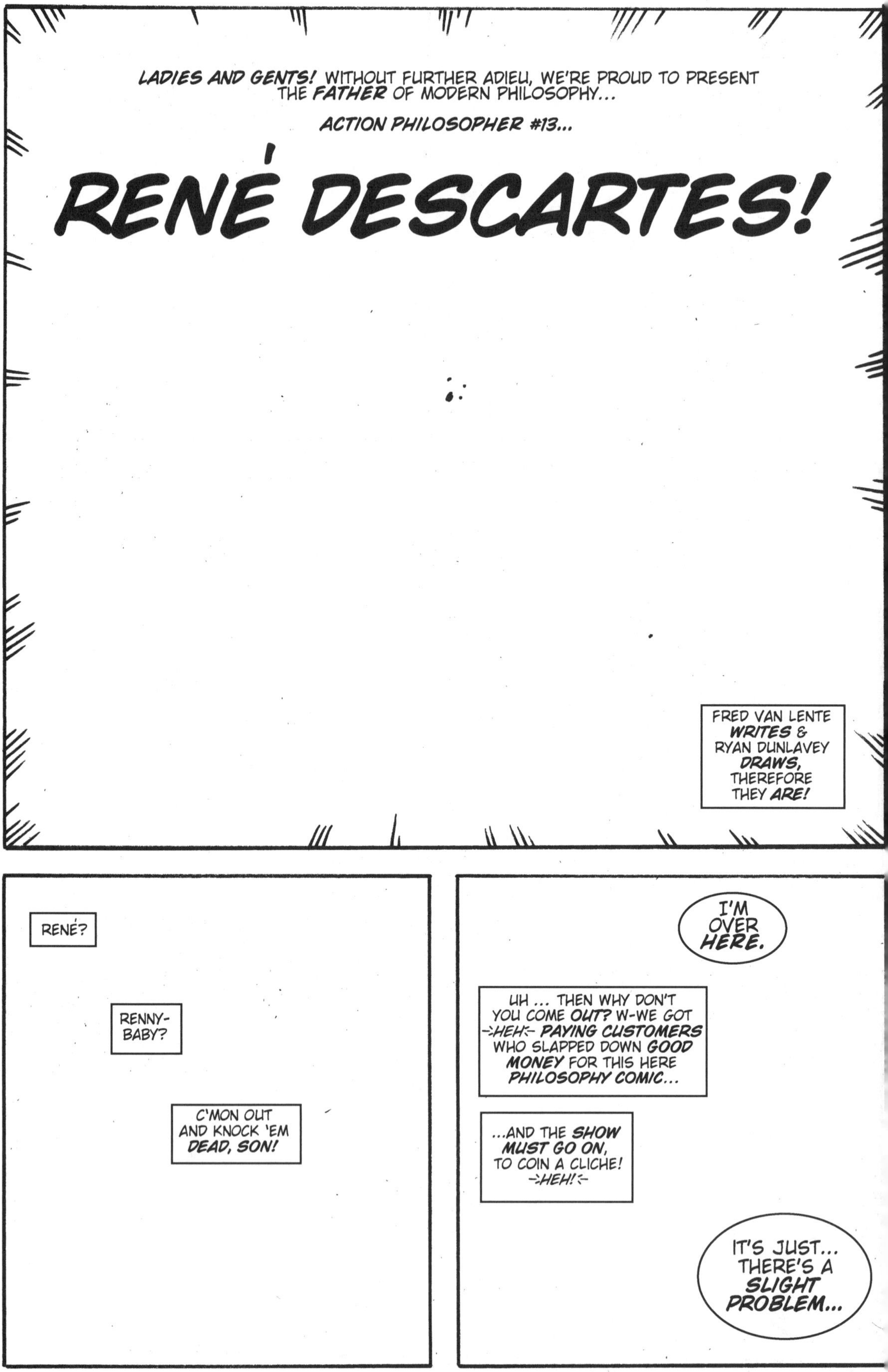
LADIES AND GENTS! WITHOUT FURTHER ADIEU, WE'RE PROUD TO PRESENT THE FATHER OF MODERN PHILOSOPHY...
ACTION PHILOSOPHER #13...
RENÉ DESCARTES!
FRED VAN LENTE WRITES & RYAN DUNLAVEY DRAWS, THEREFORE THEY ARE!
RENÉ?
RENNY-BABY?
C'MON OUT AND KNOCK 'EM DEAD, SON!
I'M OVER HERE.
UH ... THEN WHY DON'T YOU COME OUT? W-WE GOT -HEH- PAYING CUSTOMERS WHO SLAPPED DOWN GOOD MONEY FOR THIS HERE PHILOSOPHY COMIC...
...AND THE SHOW MUST GO ON, TO COIN A CLICHE! -HEH!-
IT'S JUST... THERE'S A SLIGHT PROBLEM...

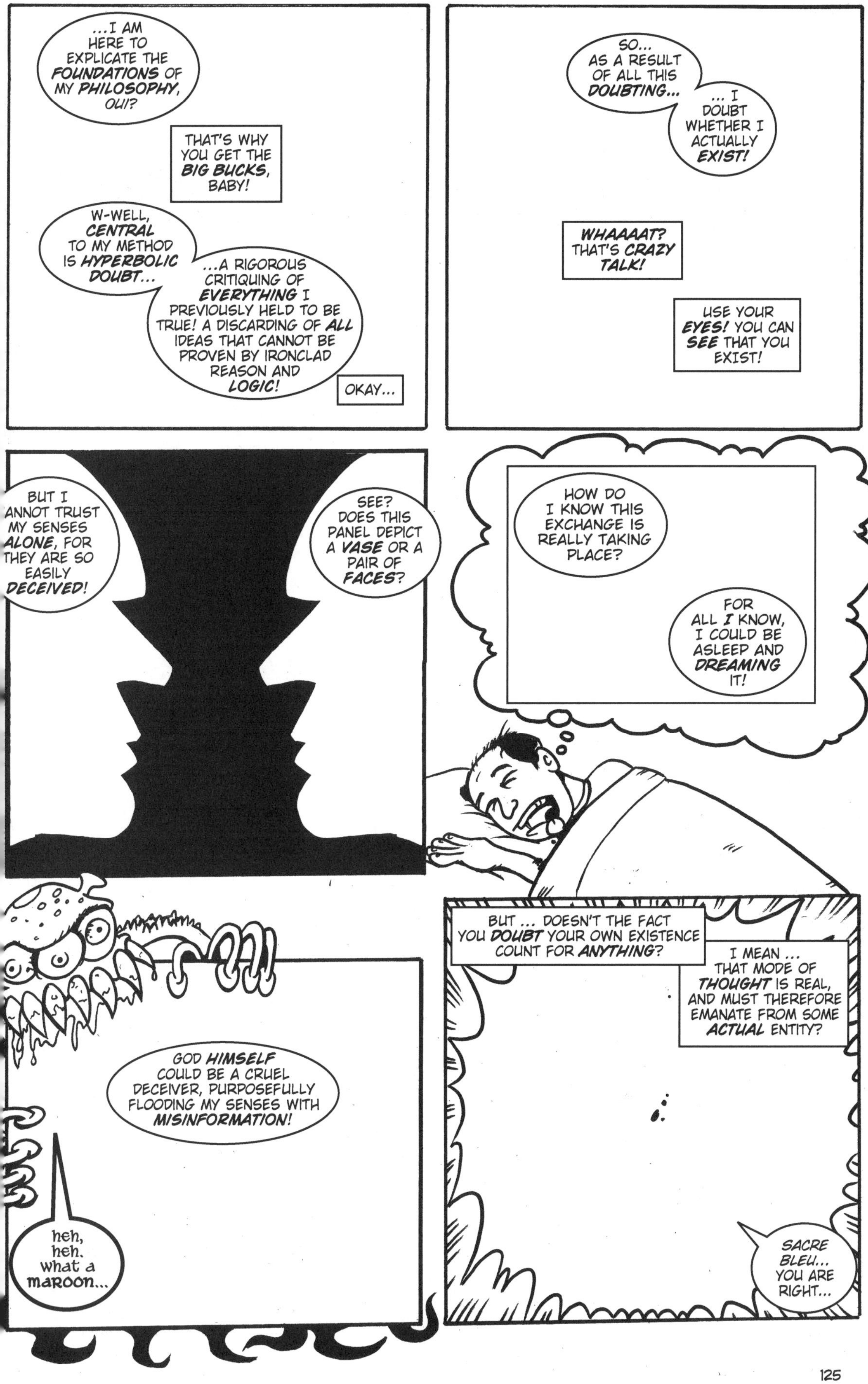

...I AM HERE TO EXPLICATE THE FOUNDATIONS OF MY PHILOSOPHY, OUI?
THAT'S WHY YOU GET THE BIG BUCKS, BABY!
W-WELL, CENTRAL TO MY METHOD IS HYPERBOLIC DOUBT...
...A RIGOROUS CRITIQUING OF EVERYTHING I PREVIOUSLY HELD TO BE TRUE! A DISCARDING OF ALL IDEAS THAT CANNOT BE PROVEN BY IRONCLAD REASON AND LOGIC!
OKAY...
SO... AS A RESULT OF ALL THIS DOUBTING...
... I DOUBT WHETHER I ACTUALLY EXIST!
WHAAAAT? THAT'S CRAZY TALK!
USE YOUR EYES! YOU CAN SEE THAT YOU EXIST!
BUT I ANNOT TRUST MY SENSES ALONE, FOR THEY ARE SO EASILY DECEIVED!
SEE? DOES THIS PANEL DEPICT A VASE OR A PAIR OF FACES?
HOW DO I KNOW THIS EXCHANGE IS REALLY TAKING PLACE?
FOR ALL I KNOW, I COULD BE ASLEEP AND DREAMING IT!
GOD HIMSELF COULD BE A CRUEL DECEIVER, PURPOSEFULLY FLOODING MY SENSES WITH MISINFORMATION!
heh, heh. what a maroon...
BUT ... DOESN'T THE FACT YOU DOUBT YOUR OWN EXISTENCE COUNT FOR ANYTHING?
I MEAN ... THAT MODE OF THOUGHT IS REAL, AND MUST THEREFORE EMANATE FROM SOME ACTUAL ENTITY?
SACRE BLEU... YOU ARE RIGHT...

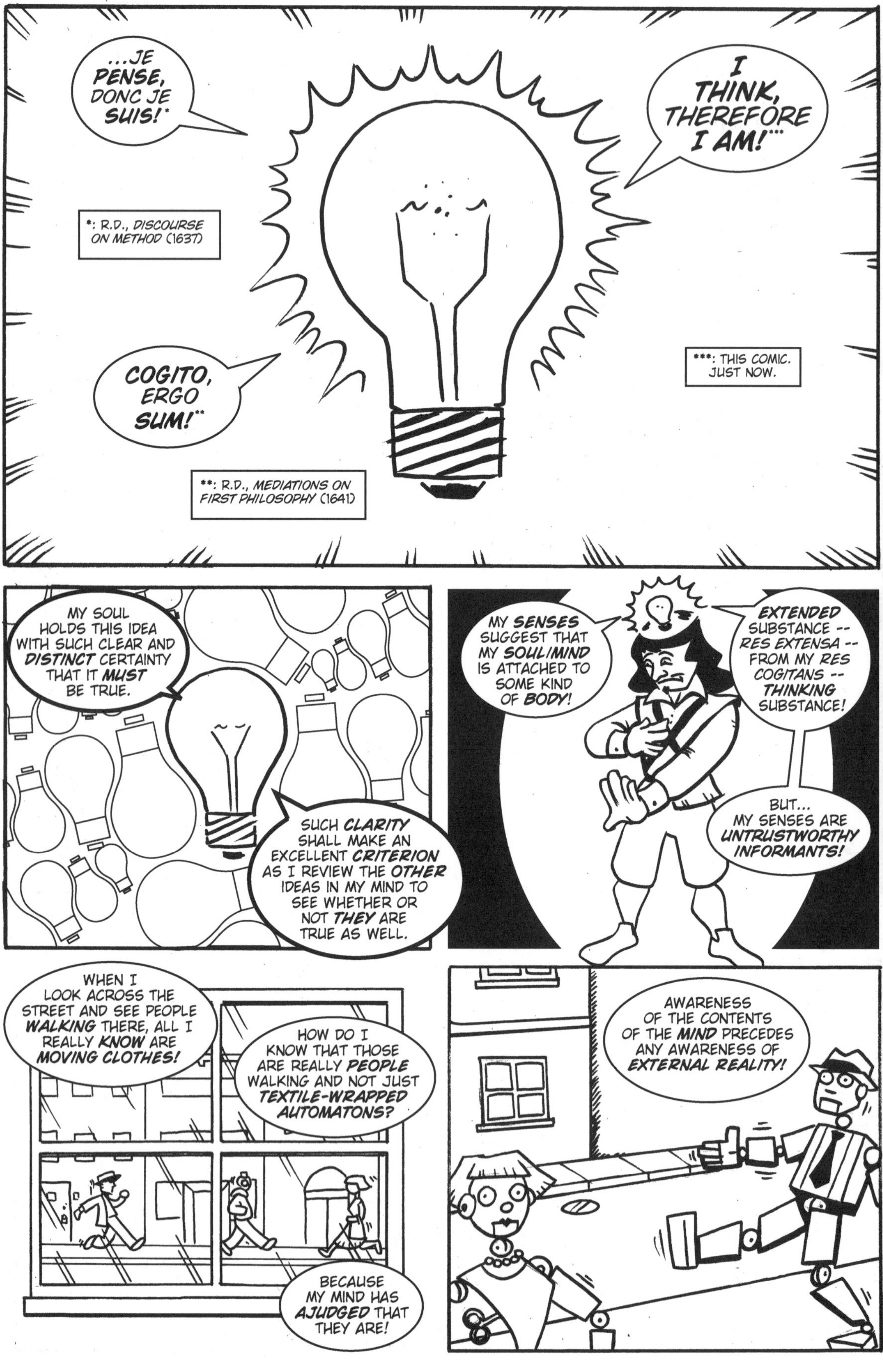
...JE PENSE, DONC JE SUIS!*
I THINK, THEREFORE I AM!***
*: R.D., DISCOURSE ON METHOD (1637)
COGITO, ERGO SUM!**
***: THIS COMIC. JUST NOW.
**: R.D., MEDIATIONS ON FIRST PHILOSOPHY (1641)
MY SOUL HOLDS THIS IDEA WITH SUCH CLEAR AND DISTINCT CERTAINTY THAT IT MUST BE TRUE.
SUCH CLARITY SHALL MAKE AN EXCELLENT CRITERION AS I REVIEW THE OTHER IDEAS IN MY MIND TO SEE WHETHER OR NOT THEY ARE TRUE AS WELL.
MY SENSES SUGGEST THAT MY SOUL/MIND IS ATTACHED TO SOME KIND OF BODY!
EXTENDED SUBSTANCE -- RES EXTENSA -- FROM MY RES COGITANS -- THINKING SUBSTANCE!
BUT... MY SENSES ARE UNTRUSTWORTHY INFORMANTS!
WHEN I LOOK ACROSS THE STREET AND SEE PEOPLE WALKING THERE, ALL I REALLY KNOW ARE MOVING CLOTHES!
HOW DO I KNOW THAT THOSE ARE REALLY PEOPLE WALKING AND NOT JUST TEXTILE-WRAPPED AUTOMATONS?
BECAUSE MY MIND HAS AJUDGED THAT THEY ARE!
AWARENESS OF THE CONTENTS OF THE MIND PRECEDES ANY AWARENESS OF EXTERNAL REALITY!

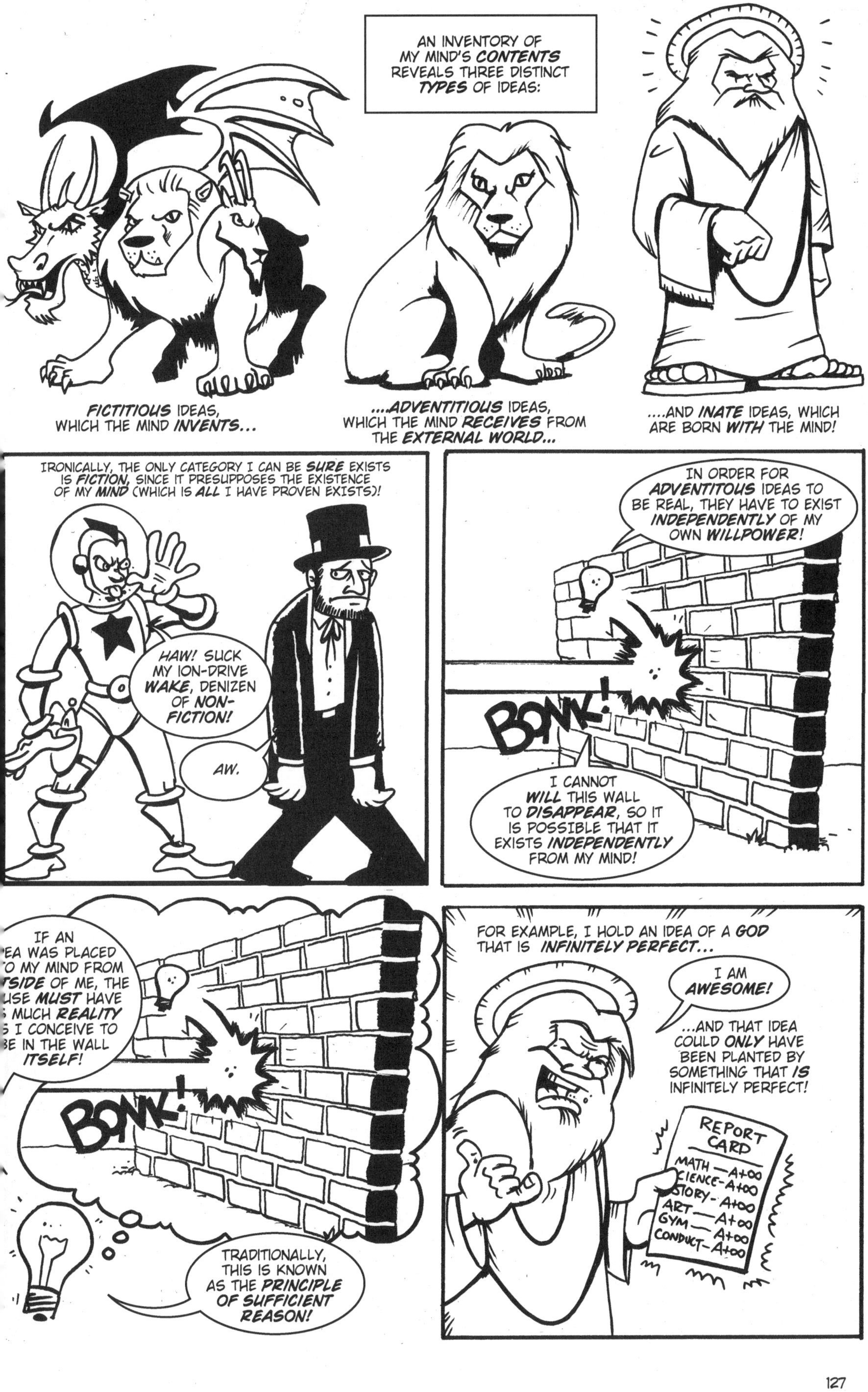

AN INVENTORY OF MY MIND'S CONTENTS REVEALS THREE DISTINCT TYPES OF IDEAS:
FICTITIOUS IDEAS, WHICH THE MIND INVENTS...
...ADVENTITIOUS IDEAS, WHICH THE MIND RECEIVES FROM THE EXTERNAL WORLD...
....AND INATE IDEAS, WHICH ARE BORN WITH THE MIND!
IRONICALLY, THE ONLY CATEGORY I CAN BE SURE EXISTS IS FICTION, SINCE IT PRESUPPOSES THE EXISTENCE OF MY MIND (WHICH IS ALL I HAVE PROVEN EXISTS)!
HAW! SUCK MY ION-DRIVE WAKE, DENIZEN OF NON-FICTION!
AW.
IN ORDER FOR ADVENTITOUS IDEAS TO BE REAL, THEY HAVE TO EXIST INDEPENDENTLY OF MY OWN WILLPOWER!
BONK!
I CANNOT WILL THIS WALL TO DISAPPEAR, SO IT IS POSSIBLE THAT IT EXISTS INDEPENDENTLY FROM MY MIND!
IF AN
EA WAS PLACED
O MY MIND FROM
TSIDE OF ME, THE
USE MUST HAVE
S MUCH REALITY
S I CONCEIVE TO
E IN THE WALL
ITSELF!
BONK!
TRADITIONALLY, THIS IS KNOWN AS THE PRINCIPLE OF SUFFICIENT REASON!
FOR EXAMPLE, I HOLD AN IDEA OF A GOD THAT IS INFINITELY PERFECT...
I AM AWESOME!
...AND THAT IDEA COULD ONLY HAVE BEEN PLANTED BY SOMETHING THAT IS INFINITELY PERFECT!
REPORT CARD
MATH — A+∞
CIENCE-A+∞
STORY- A+∞
ART — A+∞
GYM — A+∞
CONDUCT- A+∞

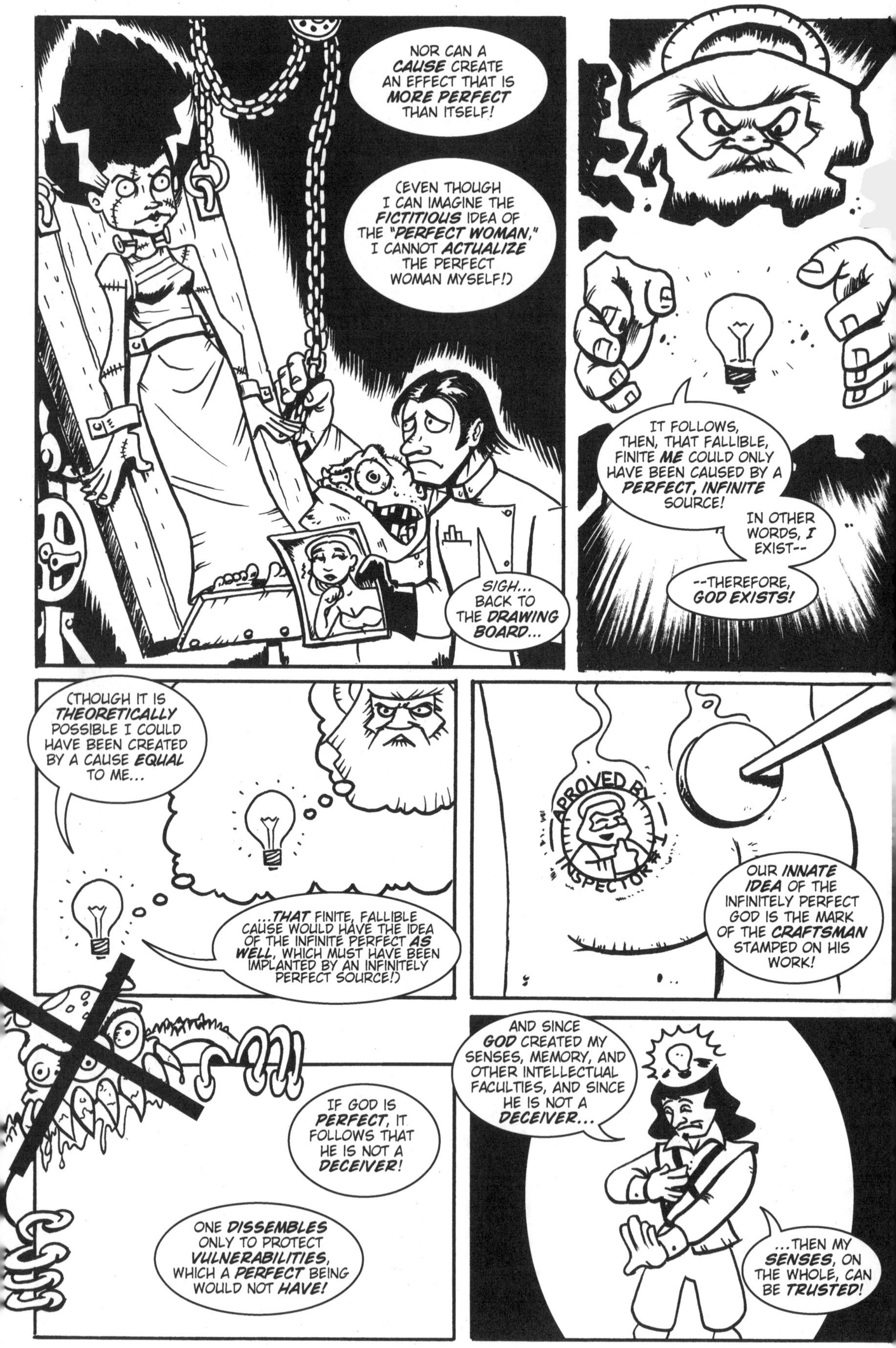
NOR CAN A CAUSE CREATE AN EFFECT THAT IS MORE PERFECT THAN ITSELF!
(EVEN THOUGH I CAN IMAGINE THE FICTITIOUS IDEA OF THE "PERFECT WOMAN," I CANNOT ACTUALIZE THE PERFECT WOMAN MYSELF!)
SIGH... BACK TO THE DRAWING BOARD...
IT FOLLOWS, THEN, THAT FALLIBLE, FINITE ME COULD ONLY HAVE BEEN CAUSED BY A PERFECT, INFINITE SOURCE!
IN OTHER WORDS, I EXIST--
--THEREFORE, GOD EXISTS!
(THOUGH IT IS THEORETICALLY POSSIBLE I COULD HAVE BEEN CREATED BY A CAUSE EQUAL TO ME...
...THAT FINITE, FALLIBLE CAUSE WOULD HAVE THE IDEA OF THE INFINITE PERFECT AS WELL, WHICH MUST HAVE BEEN IMPLANTED BY AN INFINITELY PERFECT SOURCE!)
APROVED BY INSPECTOR
OUR INNATE IDEA OF THE INFINITELY PERFECT GOD IS THE MARK OF THE CRAFTSMAN STAMPED ON HIS WORK!
IF GOD IS PERFECT, IT FOLLOWS THAT HE IS NOT A DECEIVER!
ONE DISSEMBLES ONLY TO PROTECT VULNERABILITIES, WHICH A PERFECT BEING WOULD NOT HAVE!
AND SINCE GOD CREATED MY SENSES, MEMORY, AND OTHER INTELLECTUAL FACULTIES, AND SINCE HE IS NOT A DECEIVER...
...THEN MY SENSES, ON THE WHOLE, CAN BE TRUSTED!

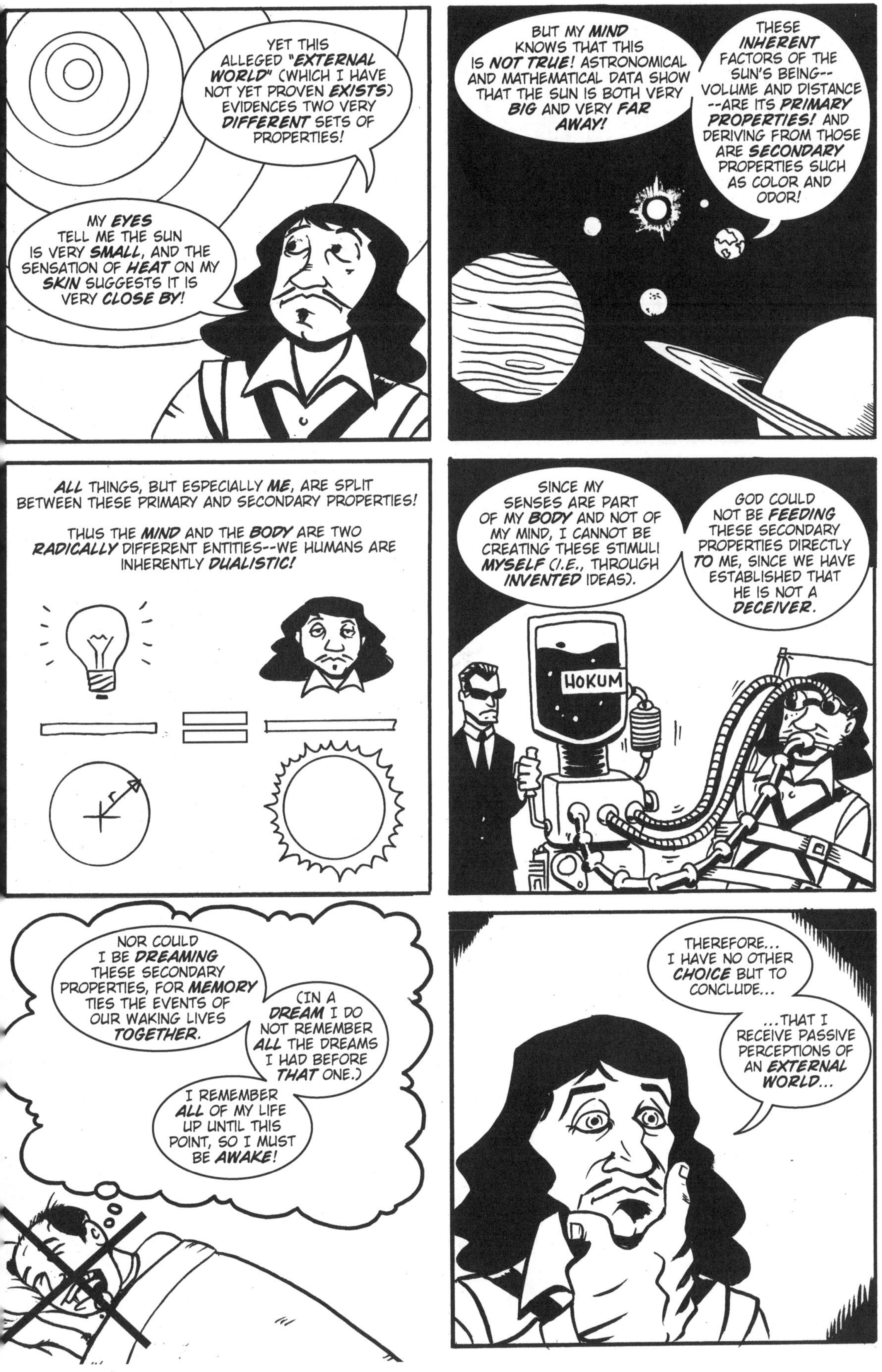
YET THIS ALLEGED "EXTERNAL WORLD" (WHICH I HAVE NOT YET PROVEN EXISTS) EVIDENCES TWO VERY DIFFERENT SETS OF PROPERTIES!
MY EYES TELL ME THE SUN IS VERY SMALL, AND THE SENSATION OF HEAT ON MY SKIN SUGGESTS IT IS VERY CLOSE BY!
BUT MY MIND KNOWS THAT THIS IS NOT TRUE! ASTRONOMICAL AND MATHEMATICAL DATA SHOW THAT THE SUN IS BOTH VERY BIG AND VERY FAR AWAY!
THESE INHERENT FACTORS OF THE SUN'S BEING--VOLUME AND DISTANCE--ARE ITS PRIMARY PROPERTIES! AND DERIVING FROM THOSE ARE SECONDARY PROPERTIES SUCH AS COLOR AND ODOR!
ALL THINGS, BUT ESPECIALLY ME, ARE SPLIT BETWEEN THESE PRIMARY AND SECONDARY PROPERTIES!
THUS THE MIND AND THE BODY ARE TWO RADICALLY DIFFERENT ENTITIES--WE HUMANS ARE INHERENTLY DUALISTIC!
r
SINCE MY SENSES ARE PART OF MY BODY AND NOT OF MY MIND, I CANNOT BE CREATING THESE STIMULI MYSELF (I.E., THROUGH INVENTED IDEAS).
GOD COULD NOT BE FEEDING THESE SECONDARY PROPERTIES DIRECTLY TO ME, SINCE WE HAVE ESTABLISHED THAT HE IS NOT A DECEIVER.
HOKUM
NOR COULD I BE DREAMING THESE SECONDARY PROPERTIES, FOR MEMORY TIES THE EVENTS OF OUR WAKING LIVES TOGETHER.
(IN A DREAM I DO NOT REMEMBER ALL THE DREAMS I HAD BEFORE THAT ONE.)
I REMEMBER ALL OF MY LIFE UP UNTIL THIS POINT, SO I MUST BE AWAKE!
THEREFORE... I HAVE NO OTHER CHOICE BUT TO CONCLUDE...
...THAT I RECEIVE PASSIVE PERCEPTIONS OF AN EXTERNAL WORLD...

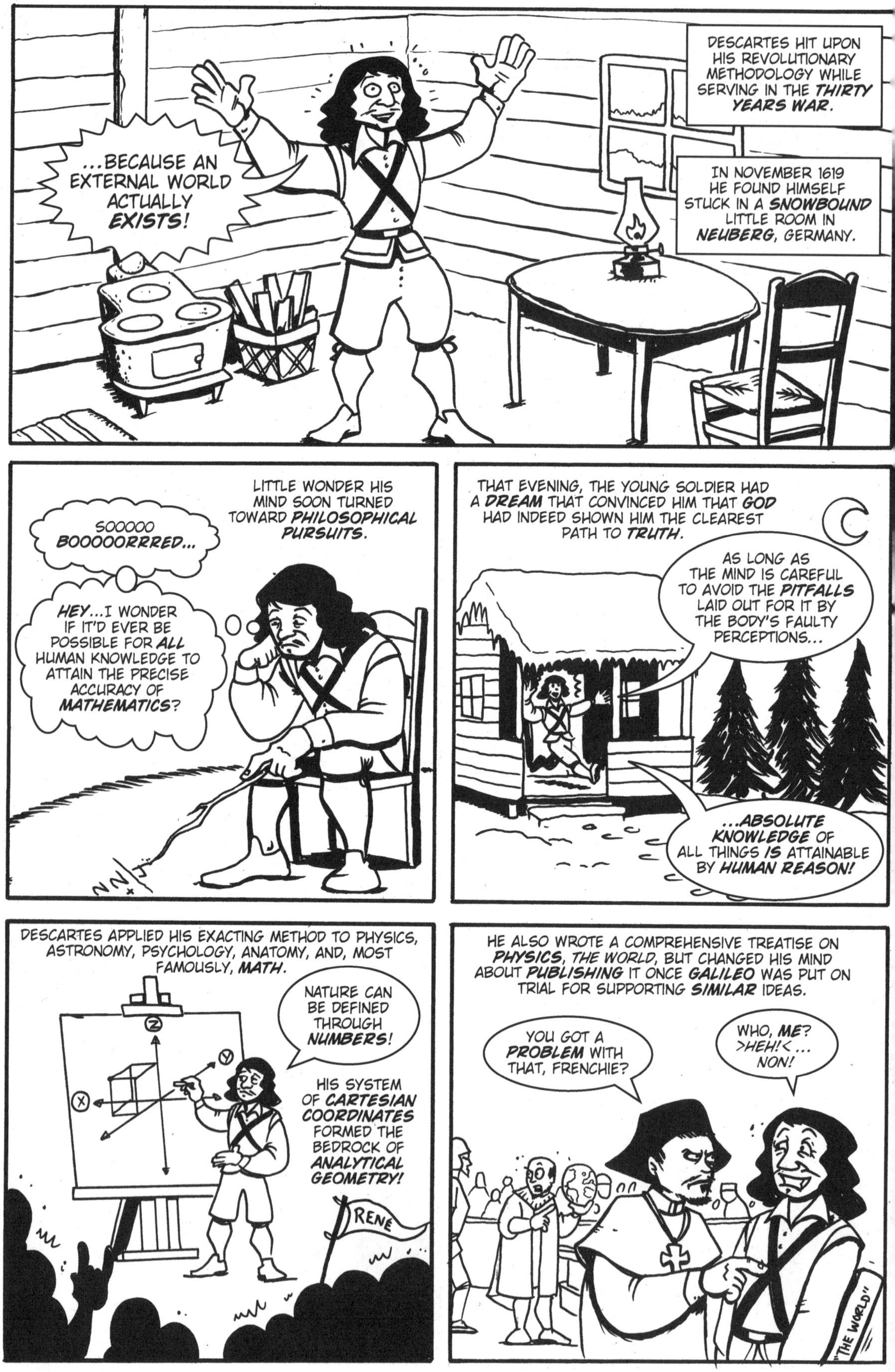
DESCARTES HIT UPON HIS REVOLUTIONARY METHODOLOGY WHILE SERVING IN THE THIRTY YEARS WAR.
IN NOVEMBER 1619 HE FOUND HIMSELF STUCK IN A SNOWBOUND LITTLE ROOM IN NEUBERG, GERMANY.
...BECAUSE AN EXTERNAL WORLD ACTUALLY EXISTS!
LITTLE WONDER HIS MIND SOON TURNED TOWARD PHILOSOPHICAL PURSUITS.
SOOOOO BOOOOORRRED...
HEY...I WONDER IF IT'D EVER BE POSSIBLE FOR ALL HUMAN KNOWLEDGE TO ATTAIN THE PRECISE ACCURACY OF MATHEMATICS?
THAT EVENING, THE YOUNG SOLDIER HAD A DREAM THAT CONVINCED HIM THAT GOD HAD INDEED SHOWN HIM THE CLEAREST PATH TO TRUTH.
AS LONG AS THE MIND IS CAREFUL TO AVOID THE PITFALLS LAID OUT FOR IT BY THE BODY'S FAULTY PERCEPTIONS...
...ABSOLUTE KNOWLEDGE OF ALL THINGS IS ATTAINABLE BY HUMAN REASON!
DESCARTES APPLIED HIS EXACTING METHOD TO PHYSICS, ASTRONOMY, PSYCHOLOGY, ANATOMY, AND, MOST FAMOUSLY, MATH.
NATURE CAN BE DEFINED THROUGH NUMBERS!
HIS SYSTEM OF CARTESIAN COORDINATES FORMED THE BEDROCK OF ANALYTICAL GEOMETRY!
Z
Y
X
RENÉ
HE ALSO WROTE A COMPREHENSIVE TREATISE ON PHYSICS, THE WORLD, BUT CHANGED HIS MIND ABOUT PUBLISHING IT ONCE GALILEO WAS PUT ON TRIAL FOR SUPPORTING SIMILAR IDEAS.
YOU GOT A PROBLEM WITH THAT, FRENCHIE?
WHO, ME? >HEH!<... NON!
"THE WORLD"

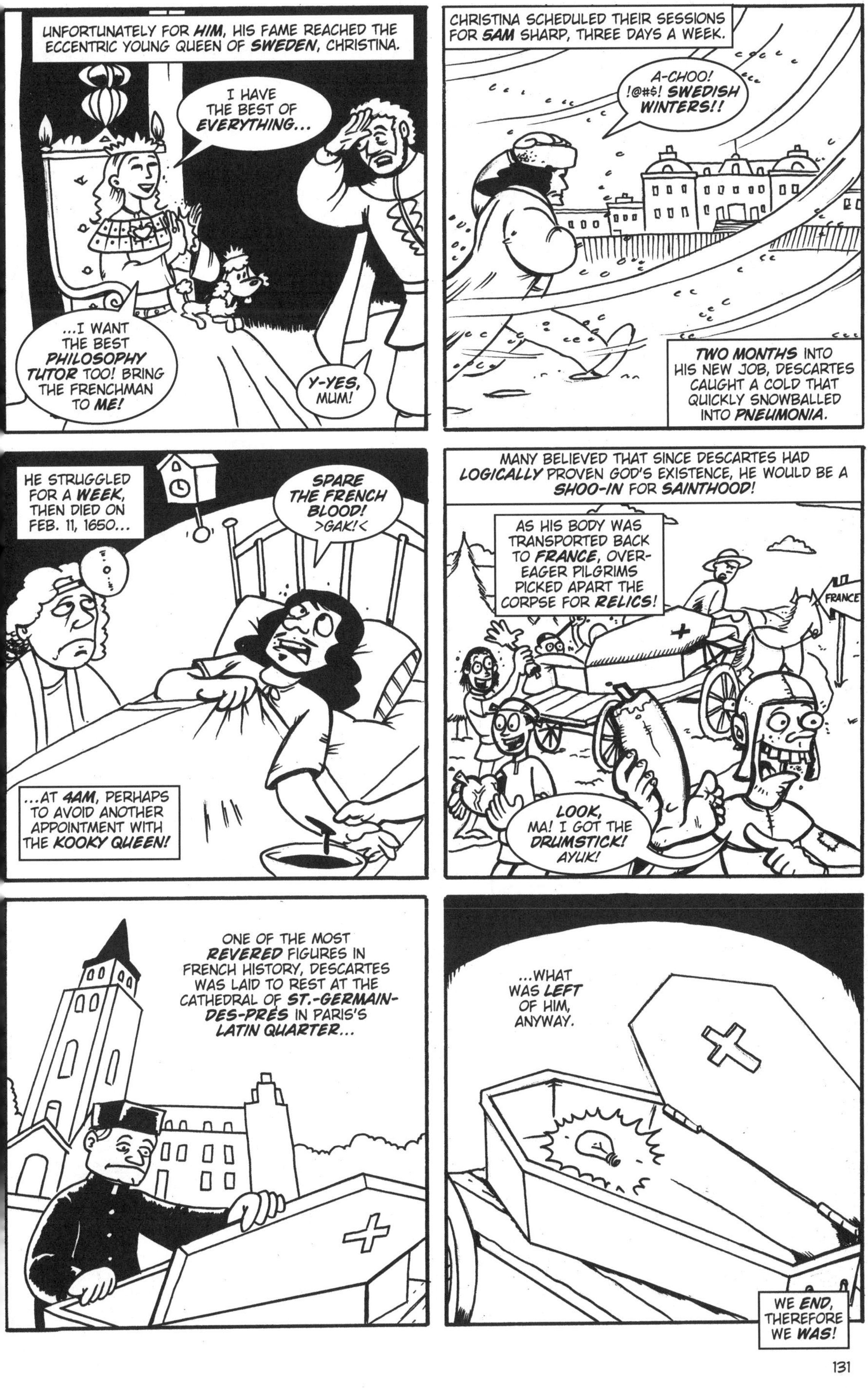
UNFORTUNATELY FOR HIM, HIS FAME REACHED THE ECCENTRIC YOUNG QUEEN OF SWEDEN, CHRISTINA.
I HAVE THE BEST OF EVERYTHING...
...I WANT THE BEST PHILOSOPHY TUTOR TOO! BRING THE FRENCHMAN TO ME!
Y-YES, MUM!
CHRISTINA SCHEDULED THEIR SESSIONS FOR 5AM SHARP, THREE DAYS A WEEK.
A-CHOO! !@#$! SWEDISH WINTERS!!
TWO MONTHS INTO HIS NEW JOB, DESCARTES CAUGHT A COLD THAT QUICKLY SNOWBALLED INTO PNEUMONIA.
HE STRUGGLED FOR A WEEK, THEN DIED ON FEB. 11, 1650...
SPARE THE FRENCH BLOOD! >GAK!<
...AT 4AM, PERHAPS TO AVOID ANOTHER APPOINTMENT WITH THE KOOKY QUEEN!
MANY BELIEVED THAT SINCE DESCARTES HAD LOGICALLY PROVEN GOD'S EXISTENCE, HE WOULD BE A SHOO-IN FOR SAINTHOOD!
AS HIS BODY WAS TRANSPORTED BACK TO FRANCE, OVER-EAGER PILGRIMS PICKED APART THE CORPSE FOR RELICS!
FRANCE
LOOK, MA! I GOT THE DRUMSTICK! AYUK!
ONE OF THE MOST REVERED FIGURES IN FRENCH HISTORY, DESCARTES WAS LAID TO REST AT THE CATHEDRAL OF ST.-GERMAIN-DES-PRÉS IN PARIS'S LATIN QUARTER...
...WHAT WAS LEFT OF HIM, ANYWAY.
WE END, THEREFORE WE WAS!

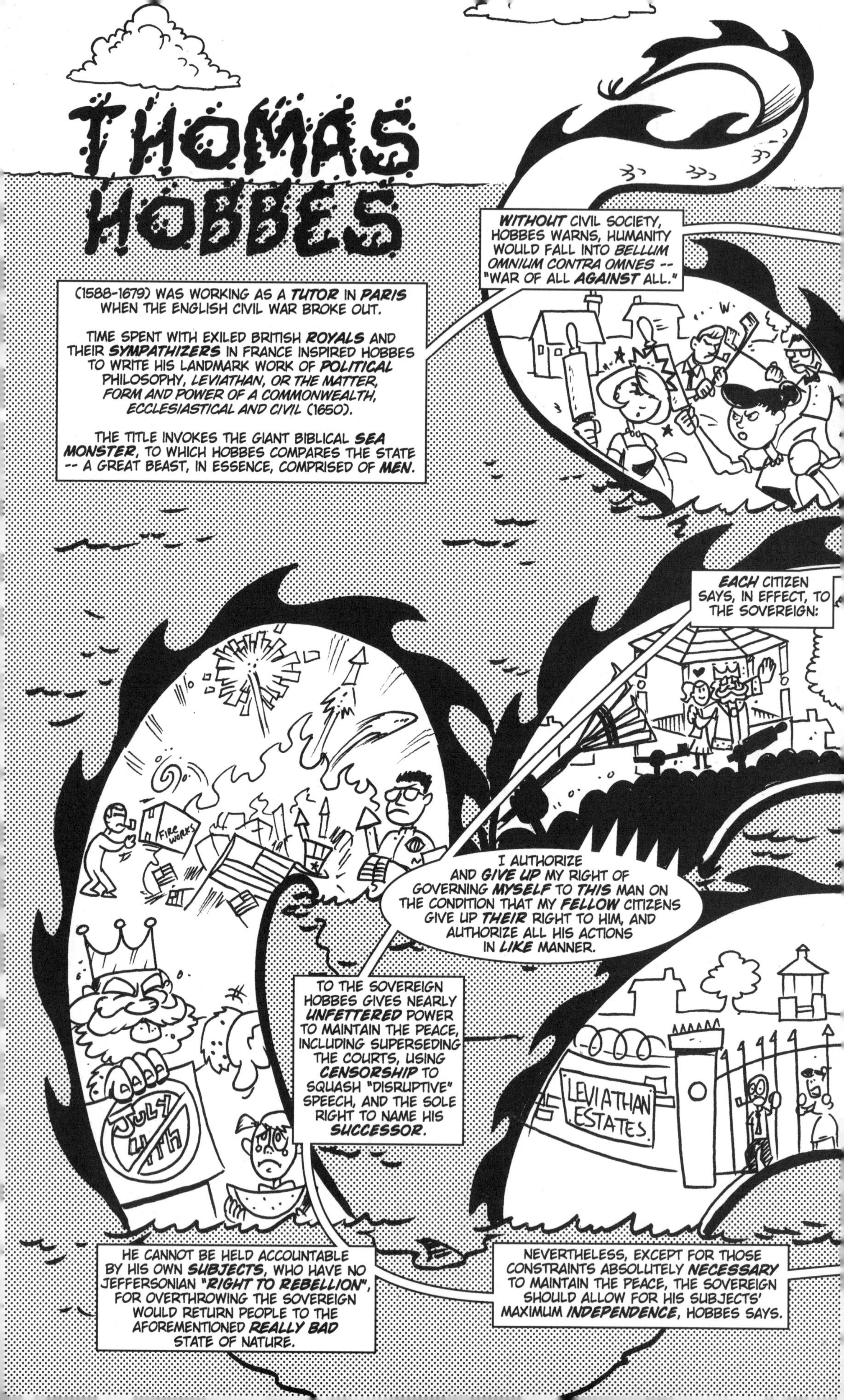
THOMAS HOBBES
(1588-1679) WAS WORKING AS A TUTOR IN PARIS WHEN THE ENGLISH CIVIL WAR BROKE OUT.
TIME SPENT WITH EXILED BRITISH ROYALS AND THEIR SYMPATHIZERS IN FRANCE INSPIRED HOBBES TO WRITE HIS LANDMARK WORK OF POLITICAL PHILOSOPHY, LEVIATHAN, OR THE MATTER, FORM AND POWER OF A COMMONWEALTH, ECCLESIASTICAL AND CIVIL (1650).
THE TITLE INVOKES THE GIANT BIBLICAL SEA MONSTER, TO WHICH HOBBES COMPARES THE STATE -- A GREAT BEAST, IN ESSENCE, COMPRISED OF MEN.
WITHOUT CIVIL SOCIETY, HOBBES WARNS, HUMANITY WOULD FALL INTO BELLUM OMNIUM CONTRA OMNES -- "WAR OF ALL AGAINST ALL."
EACH CITIZEN SAYS, IN EFFECT, TO THE SOVEREIGN:
I AUTHORIZE AND GIVE UP MY RIGHT OF GOVERNING MYSELF TO THIS MAN ON THE CONDITION THAT MY FELLOW CITIZENS GIVE UP THEIR RIGHT TO HIM, AND AUTHORIZE ALL HIS ACTIONS IN LIKE MANNER.
FIRE WORKS
JULY 4th
TO THE SOVEREIGN HOBBES GIVES NEARLY UNFETTERED POWER TO MAINTAIN THE PEACE, INCLUDING SUPERSEDING THE COURTS, USING CENSORSHIP TO SQUASH "DISRUPTIVE" SPEECH, AND THE SOLE RIGHT TO NAME HIS SUCCESSOR.
LEVIATHAN ESTATES
HE CANNOT BE HELD ACCOUNTABLE BY HIS OWN SUBJECTS, WHO HAVE NO JEFFERSONIAN "RIGHT TO REBELLION", FOR OVERTHROWING THE SOVEREIGN WOULD RETURN PEOPLE TO THE AFOREMENTIONED REALLY BAD STATE OF NATURE.
NEVERTHELESS, EXCEPT FOR THOSE CONSTRAINTS ABSOLUTELY NECESSARY TO MAINTAIN THE PEACE, THE SOVEREIGN SHOULD ALLOW FOR HIS SUBJECTS' MAXIMUM INDEPENDENCE, HOBBES SAYS.

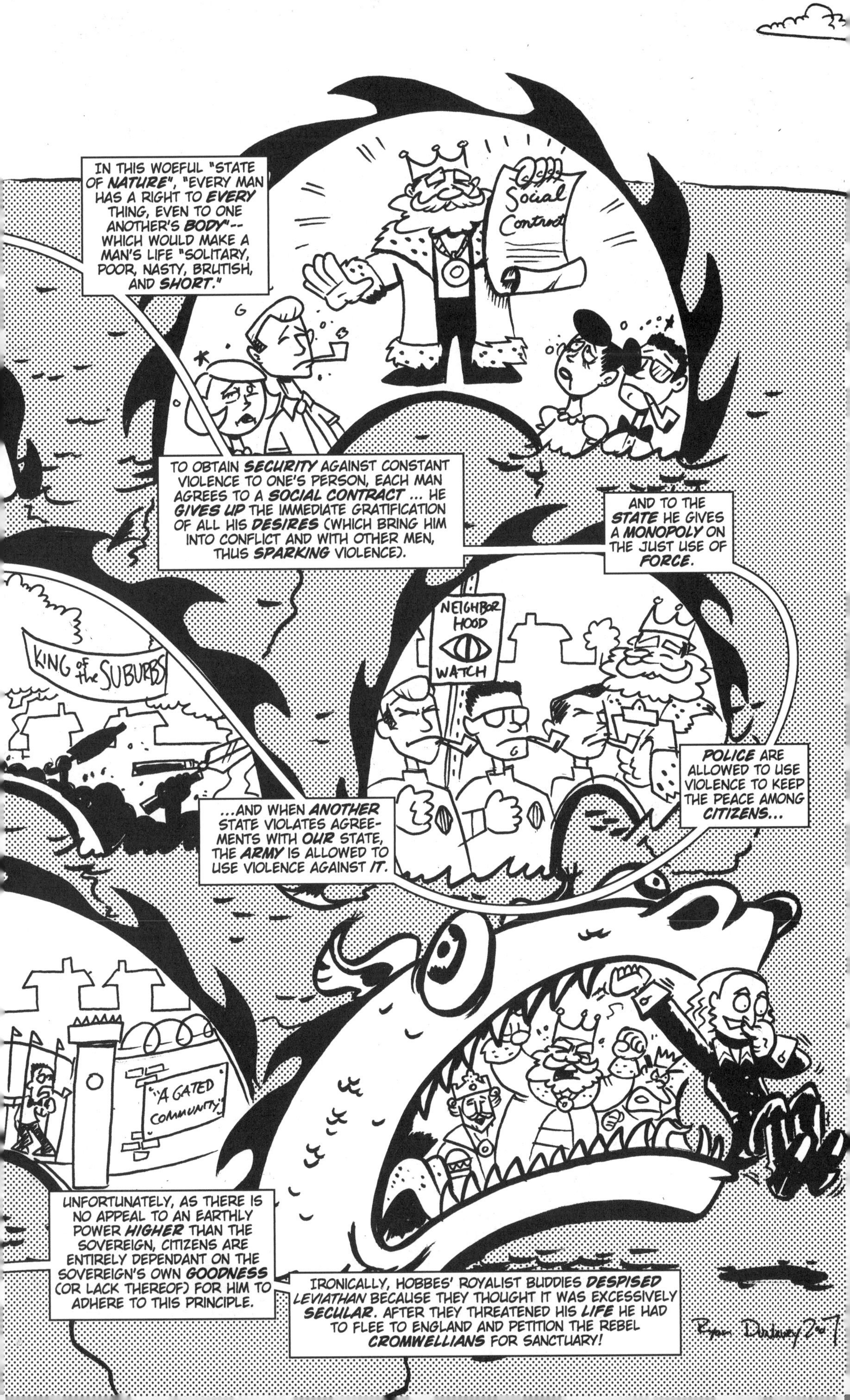

IN THIS WOEFUL "STATE OF NATURE", "EVERY MAN HAS A RIGHT TO EVERY THING, EVEN TO ONE ANOTHER'S BODY"-- WHICH WOULD MAKE A MAN'S LIFE "SOLITARY, POOR, NASTY, BRUTISH, AND SHORT."
Social Contract
TO OBTAIN SECURITY AGAINST CONSTANT VIOLENCE TO ONE'S PERSON, EACH MAN AGREES TO A SOCIAL CONTRACT ... HE GIVES UP THE IMMEDIATE GRATIFICATION OF ALL HIS DESIRES (WHICH BRING HIM INTO CONFLICT AND WITH OTHER MEN, THUS SPARKING VIOLENCE).
AND TO THE STATE HE GIVES A MONOPOLY ON THE JUST USE OF FORCE.
KING of the SUBURBS
NEIGHBOR HOOD WATCH
POLICE ARE ALLOWED TO USE VIOLENCE TO KEEP THE PEACE AMONG CITIZENS...
...AND WHEN ANOTHER STATE VIOLATES AGREEMENTS WITH OUR STATE, THE ARMY IS ALLOWED TO USE VIOLENCE AGAINST IT.
"A GATED COMMUNITY"
UNFORTUNATELY, AS THERE IS NO APPEAL TO AN EARTHLY POWER HIGHER THAN THE SOVEREIGN, CITIZENS ARE ENTIRELY DEPENDANT ON THE SOVEREIGN'S OWN GOODNESS (OR LACK THEREOF) FOR HIM TO ADHERE TO THIS PRINCIPLE.
IRONICALLY, HOBBES' ROYALIST BUDDIES DESPISED LEVIATHAN BECAUSE THEY THOUGHT IT WAS EXCESSIVELY SECULAR. AFTER THEY THREATENED HIS LIFE HE HAD TO FLEE TO ENGLAND AND PETITION THE REBEL CROMWELLIANS FOR SANCTUARY!
Ryan Dunlavey 2007

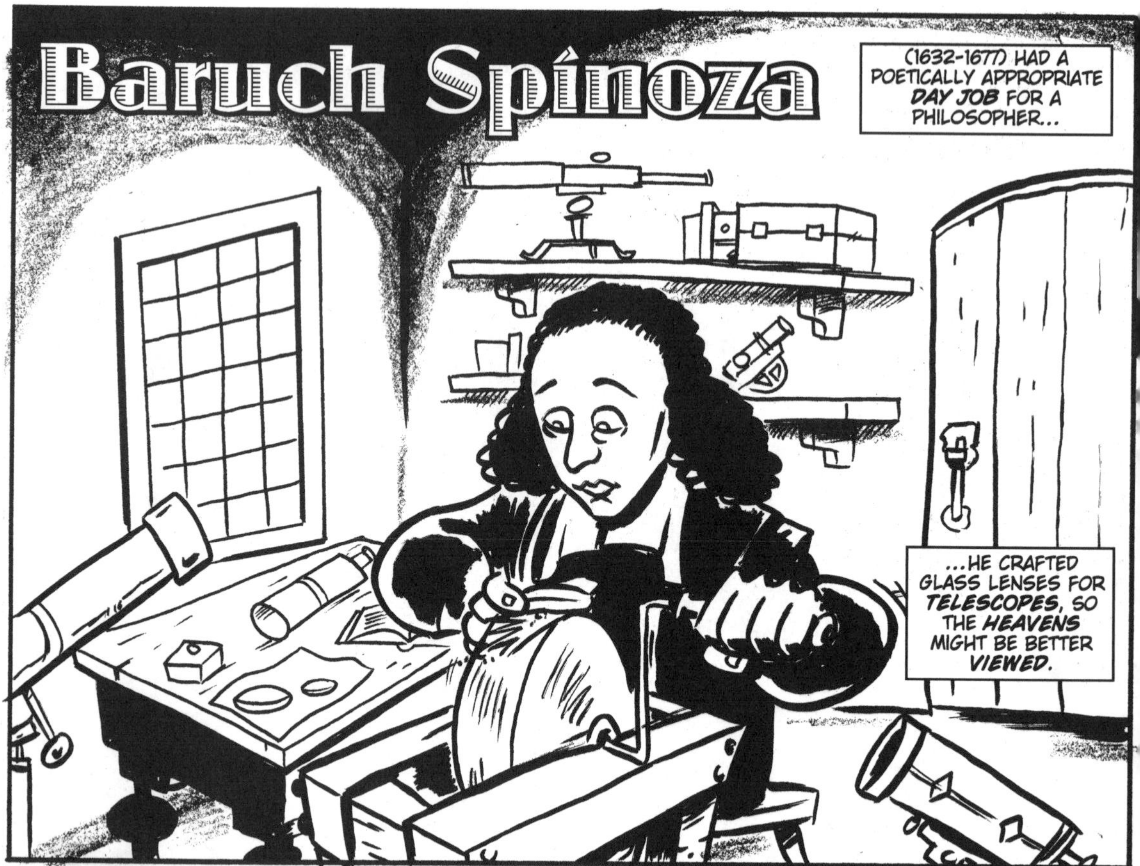
Baruch Spínoza
(1632-1677) HAD A POETICALLY APPROPRIATE DAY JOB FOR A PHILOSOPHER...
...HE CRAFTED GLASS LENSES FOR TELESCOPES, SO THE HEAVENS MIGHT BE BETTER VIEWED.

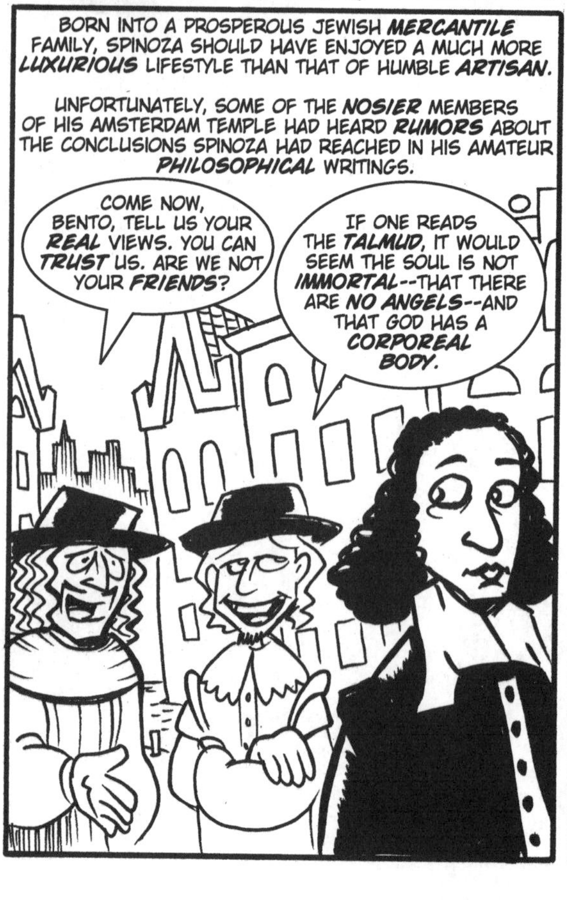
BORN INTO A PROSPEROUS JEWISH MERCANTILE FAMILY, SPINOZA SHOULD HAVE ENJOYED A MUCH MORE LUXURIOUS LIFESTYLE THAN THAT OF HUMBLE ARTISAN.
UNFORTUNATELY, SOME OF THE NOSIER MEMBERS OF HIS AMSTERDAM TEMPLE HAD HEARD RUMORS ABOUT THE CONCLUSIONS SPINOZA HAD REACHED IN HIS AMATEUR PHILOSOPHICAL WRITINGS.
COME NOW, BENTO, TELL US YOUR REAL VIEWS. YOU CAN TRUST US. ARE WE NOT YOUR FRIENDS?
IF ONE READS THE TALMUD, IT WOULD SEEM THE SOUL IS NOT IMMORTAL--THAT THERE ARE NO ANGELS--AND THAT GOD HAS A CORPOREAL BODY.

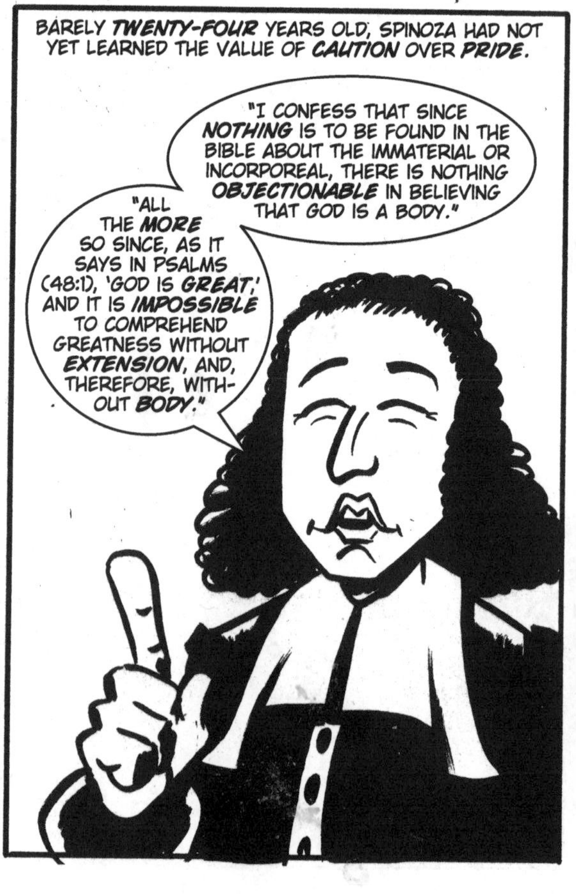
BARELY TWENTY-FOUR YEARS OLD, SPINOZA HAD NOT YET LEARNED THE VALUE OF CAUTION OVER PRIDE.
"I CONFESS THAT SINCE NOTHING IS TO BE FOUND IN THE BIBLE ABOUT THE IMMATERIAL OR INCORPOREAL, THERE IS NOTHING OBJECTIONABLE IN BELIEVING THAT GOD IS A BODY."
"ALL THE MORE SO SINCE, AS IT SAYS IN PSALMS (48:1), 'GOD IS GREAT,' AND IT IS IMPOSSIBLE TO COMPREHEND GREATNESS WITHOUT EXTENSION, AND, THEREFORE, WITHOUT BODY."

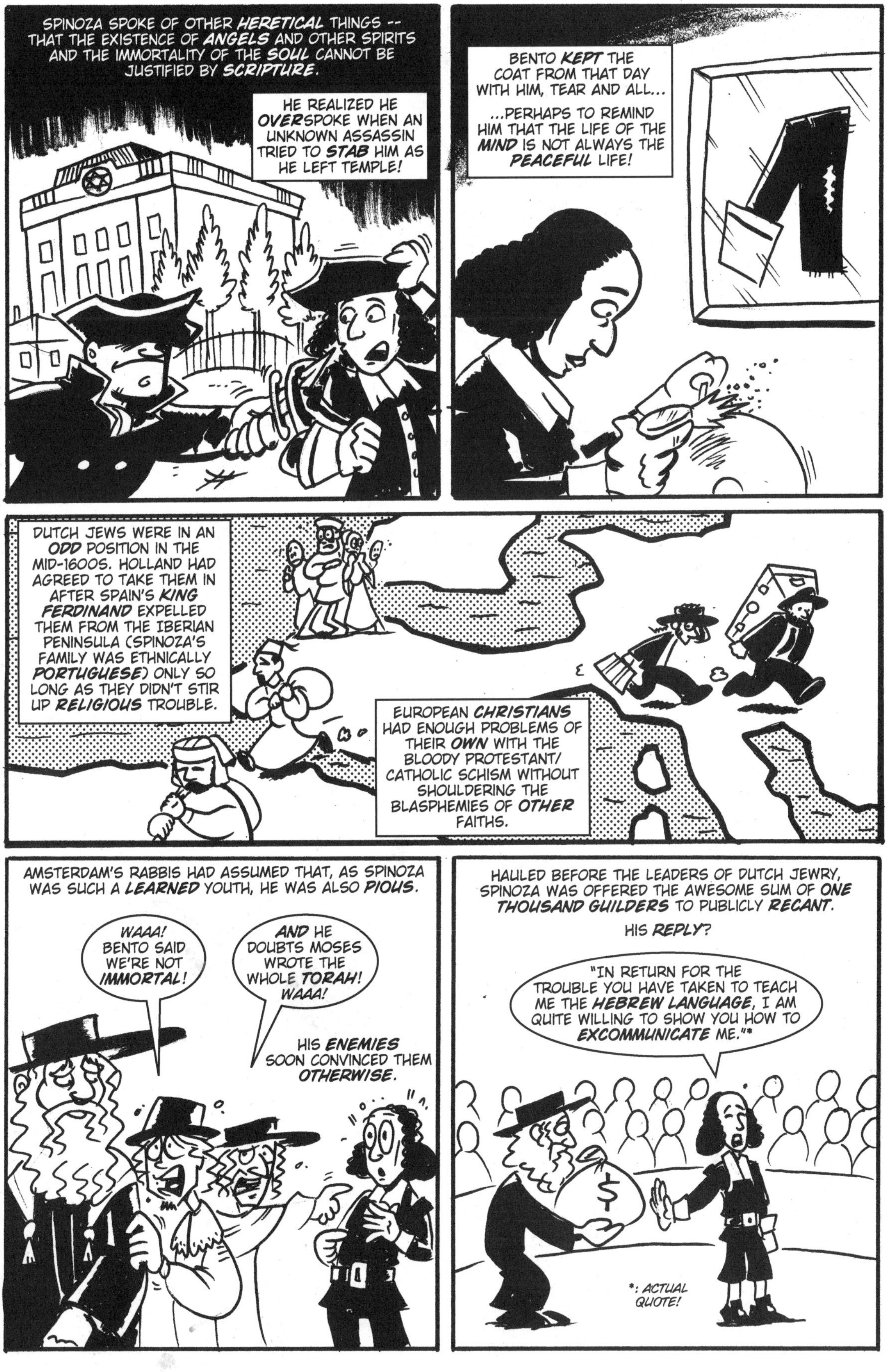
SPINOZA SPOKE OF OTHER HERETICAL THINGS -- THAT THE EXISTENCE OF ANGELS AND OTHER SPIRITS AND THE IMMORTALITY OF THE SOUL CANNOT BE JUSTIFIED BY SCRIPTURE.
HE REALIZED HE OVERSPOKE WHEN AN UNKNOWN ASSASSIN TRIED TO STAB HIM AS HE LEFT TEMPLE!
BENTO KEPT THE COAT FROM THAT DAY WITH HIM, TEAR AND ALL...
...PERHAPS TO REMIND HIM THAT THE LIFE OF THE MIND IS NOT ALWAYS THE PEACEFUL LIFE!
DUTCH JEWS WERE IN AN ODD POSITION IN THE MID-1600S. HOLLAND HAD AGREED TO TAKE THEM IN AFTER SPAIN'S KING FERDINAND EXPELLED THEM FROM THE IBERIAN PENINSULA (SPINOZA'S FAMILY WAS ETHNICALLY PORTUGUESE) ONLY SO LONG AS THEY DIDN'T STIR UP RELIGIOUS TROUBLE.
EUROPEAN CHRISTIANS HAD ENOUGH PROBLEMS OF THEIR OWN WITH THE BLOODY PROTESTANT/ CATHOLIC SCHISM WITHOUT SHOULDERING THE BLASPHEMIES OF OTHER FAITHS.
AMSTERDAM'S RABBIS HAD ASSUMED THAT, AS SPINOZA WAS SUCH A LEARNED YOUTH, HE WAS ALSO PIOUS.
WAAA! BENTO SAID WE'RE NOT IMMORTAL!
AND HE DOUBTS MOSES WROTE THE WHOLE TORAH! WAAA!
HIS ENEMIES SOON CONVINCED THEM OTHERWISE.
HAULED BEFORE THE LEADERS OF DUTCH JEWRY, SPINOZA WAS OFFERED THE AWESOME SUM OF ONE THOUSAND GUILDERS TO PUBLICLY RECANT.
HIS REPLY?
"IN RETURN FOR THE TROUBLE YOU HAVE TAKEN TO TEACH ME THE HEBREW LANGUAGE, I AM QUITE WILLING TO SHOW YOU HOW TO EXCOMMUNICATE ME."*
$
*: ACTUAL QUOTE!

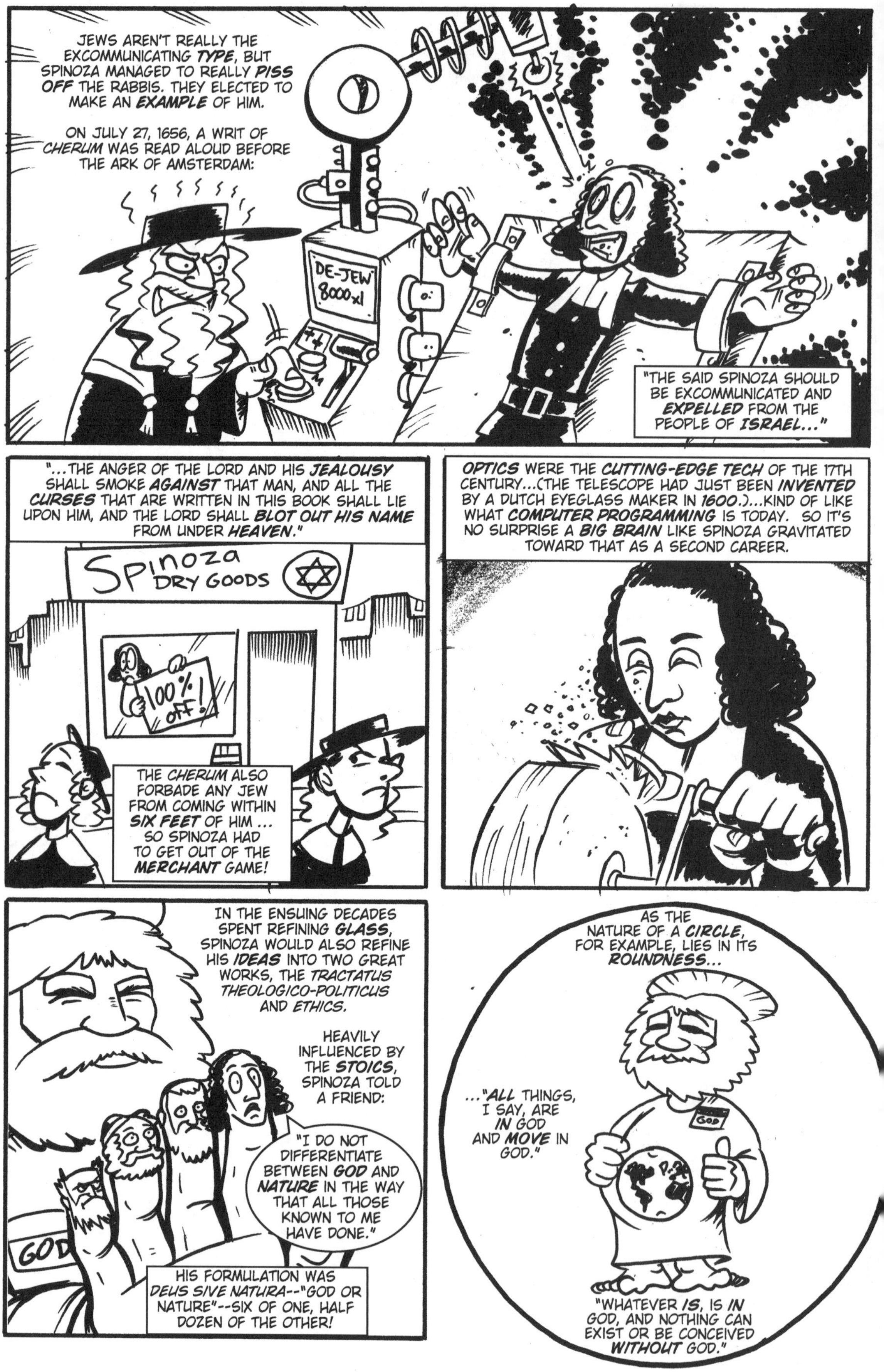
JEWS AREN'T REALLY THE EXCOMMUNICATING TYPE, BUT SPINOZA MANAGED TO REALLY PISS OFF THE RABBIS. THEY ELECTED TO MAKE AN EXAMPLE OF HIM.
ON JULY 27, 1656, A WRIT OF CHERUM WAS READ ALOUD BEFORE THE ARK OF AMSTERDAM:
DE-JEW 8000xl
"THE SAID SPINOZA SHOULD BE EXCOMMUNICATED AND EXPELLED FROM THE PEOPLE OF ISRAEL..."
"...THE ANGER OF THE LORD AND HIS JEALOUSY SHALL SMOKE AGAINST THAT MAN, AND ALL THE CURSES THAT ARE WRITTEN IN THIS BOOK SHALL LIE UPON HIM, AND THE LORD SHALL BLOT OUT HIS NAME FROM UNDER HEAVEN."
SPINOZA DRY GOODS
100% OFF!
THE CHERUM ALSO FORBADE ANY JEW FROM COMING WITHIN SIX FEET OF HIM ... SO SPINOZA HAD TO GET OUT OF THE MERCHANT GAME!
OPTICS WERE THE CUTTING-EDGE TECH OF THE 17TH CENTURY...(THE TELESCOPE HAD JUST BEEN INVENTED BY A DUTCH EYEGLASS MAKER IN 1600.)...KIND OF LIKE WHAT COMPUTER PROGRAMMING IS TODAY. SO IT'S NO SURPRISE A BIG BRAIN LIKE SPINOZA GRAVITATED TOWARD THAT AS A SECOND CAREER.
IN THE ENSUING DECADES SPENT REFINING GLASS, SPINOZA WOULD ALSO REFINE HIS IDEAS INTO TWO GREAT WORKS, THE TRACTATUS THEOLOGICO-POLITICUS AND ETHICS.
HEAVILY INFLUENCED BY THE STOICS, SPINOZA TOLD A FRIEND:
"I DO NOT DIFFERENTIATE BETWEEN GOD AND NATURE IN THE WAY THAT ALL THOSE KNOWN TO ME HAVE DONE."
GOD
HIS FORMULATION WAS DEUS SIVE NATURA--"GOD OR NATURE"--SIX OF ONE, HALF DOZEN OF THE OTHER!
AS THE NATURE OF A CIRCLE, FOR EXAMPLE, LIES IN ITS ROUNDNESS...
..."ALL THINGS, I SAY, ARE IN GOD AND MOVE IN GOD."
GOD
"WHATEVER IS, IS IN GOD, AND NOTHING CAN EXIST OR BE CONCEIVED WITHOUT GOD."

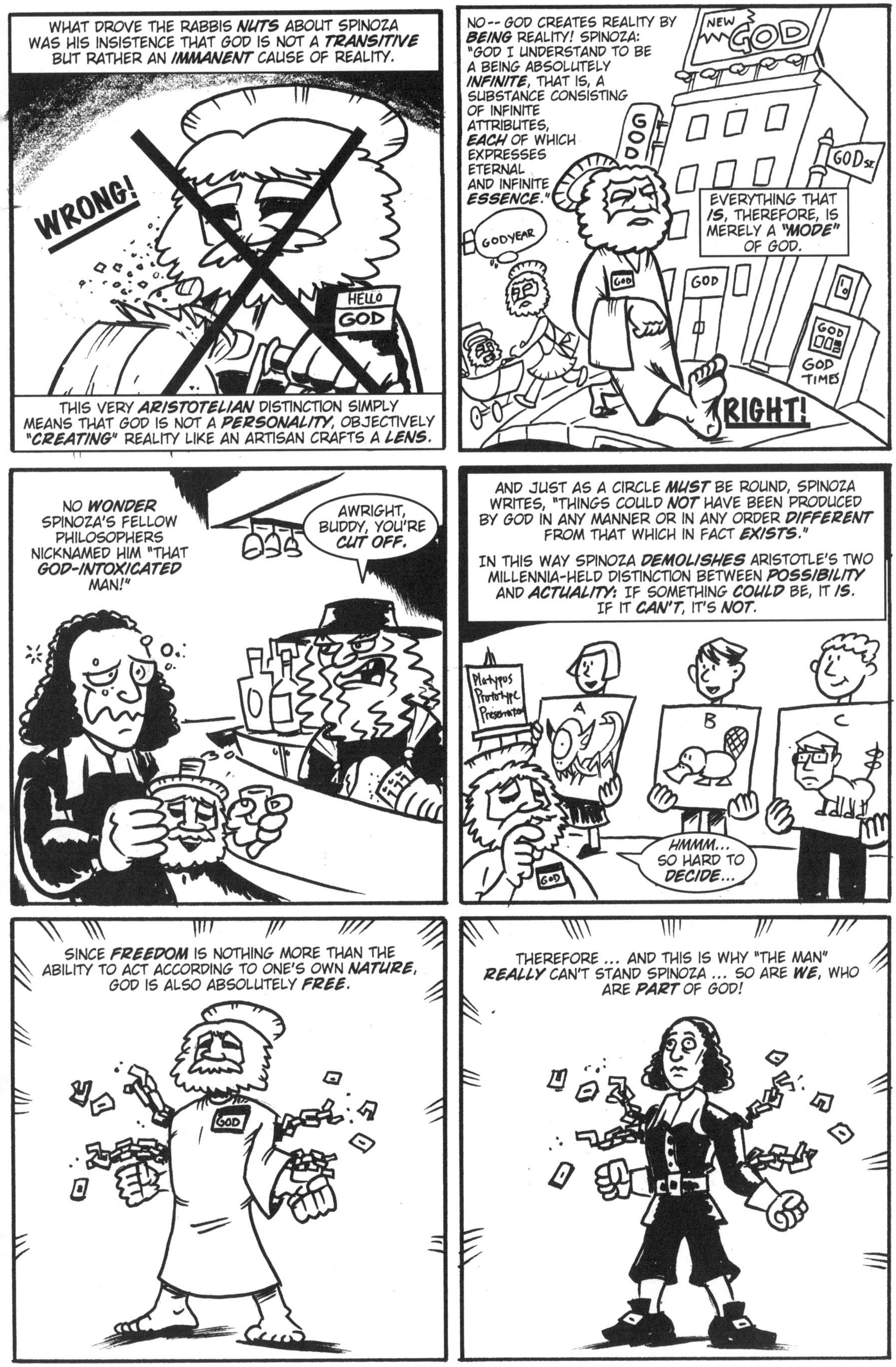
WHAT DROVE THE RABBIS NUTS ABOUT SPINOZA WAS HIS INSISTENCE THAT GOD IS NOT A TRANSITIVE BUT RATHER AN IMMANENT CAUSE OF REALITY.
WRONG!
HELLO
GOD
THIS VERY ARISTOTELIAN DISTINCTION SIMPLY MEANS THAT GOD IS NOT A PERSONALITY, OBJECTIVELY "CREATING" REALITY LIKE AN ARTISAN CRAFTS A LENS.
NO-- GOD CREATES REALITY BY BEING REALITY! SPINOZA: "GOD I UNDERSTAND TO BE A BEING ABSOLUTELY INFINITE, THAT IS, A SUBSTANCE CONSISTING OF INFINITE ATTRIBUTES, EACH OF WHICH EXPRESSES ETERNAL AND INFINITE ESSENCE."
NEW GOD
GOD
GOD ST.
EVERYTHING THAT IS, THEREFORE, IS MERELY A "MODE" OF GOD.
GODYEAR
GOD
GOD
GOD
GOD TIMES
RIGHT!
NO WONDER SPINOZA'S FELLOW PHILOSOPHERS NICKNAMED HIM "THAT GOD-INTOXICATED MAN!"
AWRIGHT, BUDDY, YOU'RE CUT OFF.
AND JUST AS A CIRCLE MUST BE ROUND, SPINOZA WRITES, "THINGS COULD NOT HAVE BEEN PRODUCED BY GOD IN ANY MANNER OR IN ANY ORDER DIFFERENT FROM THAT WHICH IN FACT EXISTS."
IN THIS WAY SPINOZA DEMOLISHES ARISTOTLE'S TWO MILLENNIA-HELD DISTINCTION BETWEEN POSSIBILITY AND ACTUALITY: IF SOMETHING COULD BE, IT IS. IF IT CAN'T, IT'S NOT.
Platypus Prototype Presentation
A
B
C
HMMM... SO HARD TO DECIDE...
GOD
SINCE FREEDOM IS NOTHING MORE THAN THE ABILITY TO ACT ACCORDING TO ONE'S OWN NATURE, GOD IS ALSO ABSOLUTELY FREE.
GOD
THEREFORE ... AND THIS IS WHY "THE MAN" REALLY CAN'T STAND SPINOZA ... SO ARE WE, WHO ARE PART OF GOD!

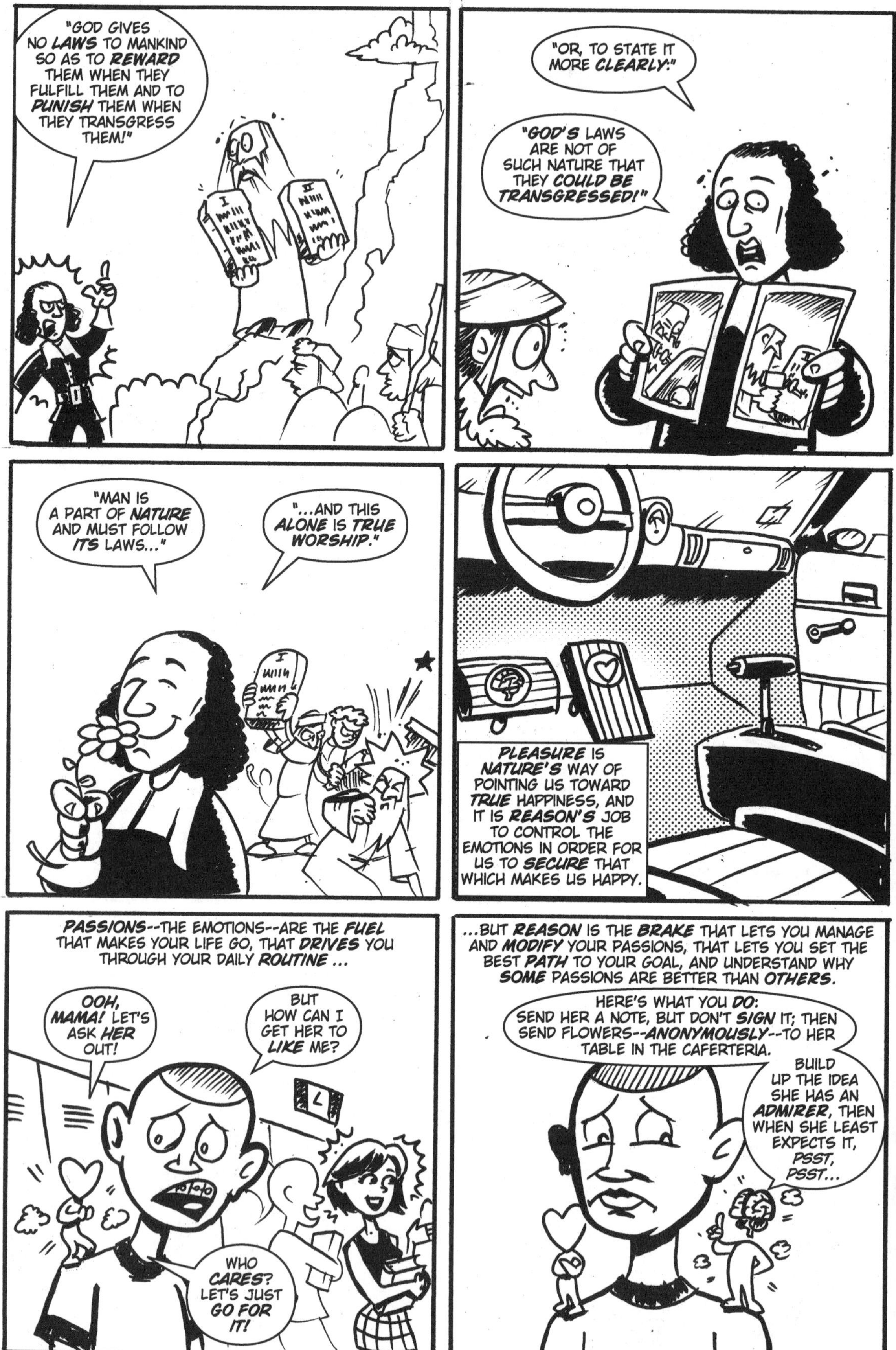
"GOD GIVES NO LAWS TO MANKIND SO AS TO REWARD THEM WHEN THEY FULFILL THEM AND TO PUNISH THEM WHEN THEY TRANSGRESS THEM!"
"OR, TO STATE IT MORE CLEARLY:"
"GOD'S LAWS ARE NOT OF SUCH NATURE THAT THEY COULD BE TRANSGRESSED!"
"MAN IS A PART OF NATURE AND MUST FOLLOW ITS LAWS..."
"...AND THIS ALONE IS TRUE WORSHIP."
PLEASURE IS NATURE'S WAY OF POINTING US TOWARD TRUE HAPPINESS, AND IT IS REASON'S JOB TO CONTROL THE EMOTIONS IN ORDER FOR US TO SECURE THAT WHICH MAKES US HAPPY.
PASSIONS--THE EMOTIONS--ARE THE FUEL THAT MAKES YOUR LIFE GO, THAT DRIVES YOU THROUGH YOUR DAILY ROUTINE ...
OOH, MAMA! LET'S ASK HER OUT!
BUT HOW CAN I GET HER TO LIKE ME?
WHO CARES? LET'S JUST GO FOR IT!
...BUT REASON IS THE BRAKE THAT LETS YOU MANAGE AND MODIFY YOUR PASSIONS, THAT LETS YOU SET THE BEST PATH TO YOUR GOAL, AND UNDERSTAND WHY SOME PASSIONS ARE BETTER THAN OTHERS.
HERE'S WHAT YOU DO: SEND HER A NOTE, BUT DON'T SIGN IT; THEN SEND FLOWERS--ANONYMOUSLY--TO HER TABLE IN THE CAFERTERIA.
BUILD UP THE IDEA SHE HAS AN ADMIRER, THEN WHEN SHE LEAST EXPECTS IT, PSST, PSST...

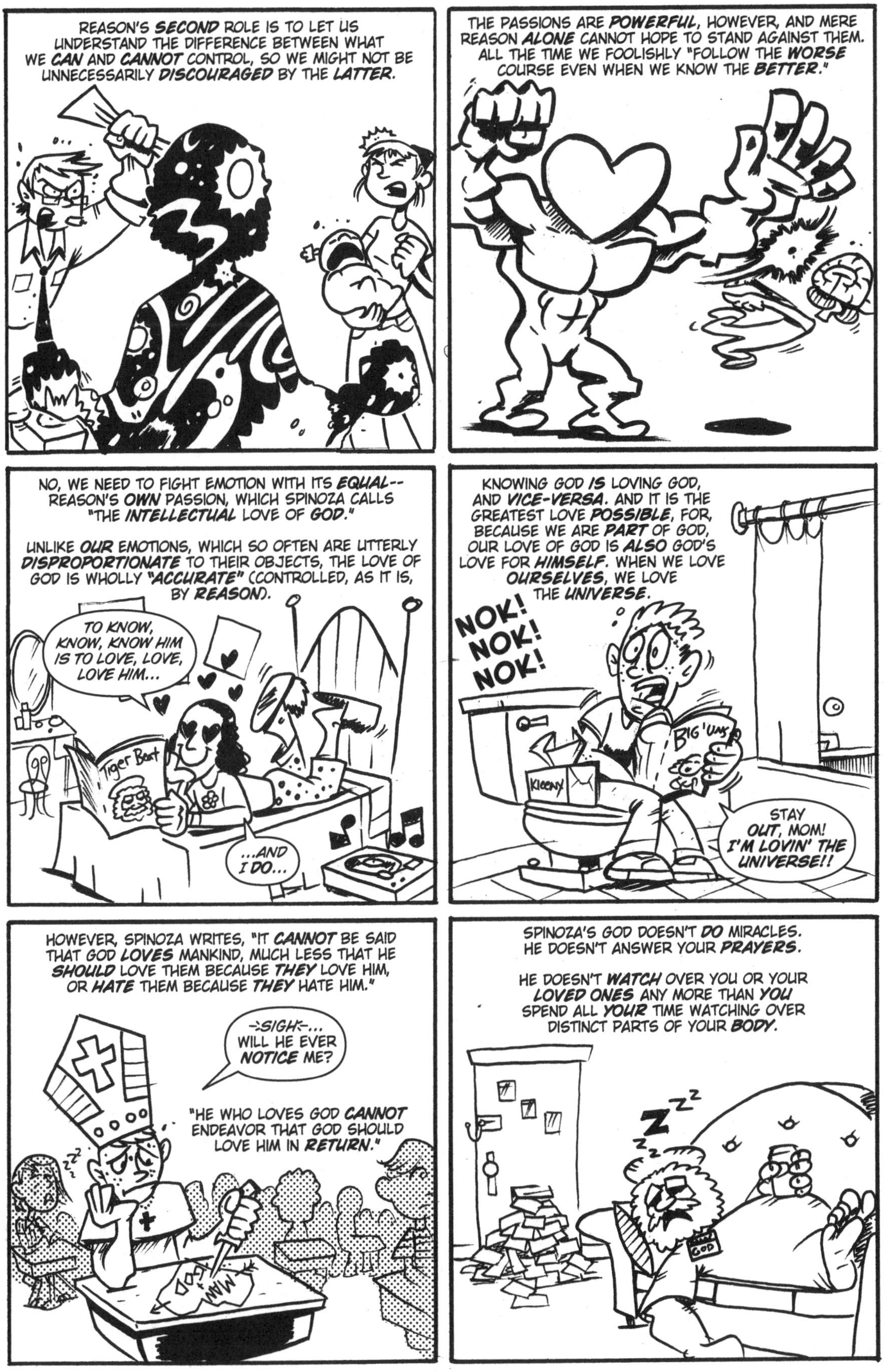
REASON'S SECOND ROLE IS TO LET US UNDERSTAND THE DIFFERENCE BETWEEN WHAT WE CAN AND CANNOT CONTROL, SO WE MIGHT NOT BE UNNECESSARILY DISCOURAGED BY THE LATTER.
THE PASSIONS ARE POWERFUL, HOWEVER, AND MERE REASON ALONE CANNOT HOPE TO STAND AGAINST THEM. ALL THE TIME WE FOOLISHLY "FOLLOW THE WORSE COURSE EVEN WHEN WE KNOW THE BETTER."
NO, WE NEED TO FIGHT EMOTION WITH ITS EQUAL-- REASON'S OWN PASSION, WHICH SPINOZA CALLS "THE INTELLECTUAL LOVE OF GOD."
UNLIKE OUR EMOTIONS, WHICH SO OFTEN ARE UTTERLY DISPROPORTIONATE TO THEIR OBJECTS, THE LOVE OF GOD IS WHOLLY "ACCURATE" (CONTROLLED, AS IT IS, BY REASON).
TO KNOW, KNOW, KNOW HIM IS TO LOVE, LOVE, LOVE HIM...
Tiger Beat
...AND I DO...
KNOWING GOD IS LOVING GOD, AND VICE-VERSA. AND IT IS THE GREATEST LOVE POSSIBLE, FOR, BECAUSE WE ARE PART OF GOD, OUR LOVE OF GOD IS ALSO GOD'S LOVE FOR HIMSELF. WHEN WE LOVE OURSELVES, WE LOVE THE UNIVERSE.
NOK! NOK! NOK!
BIG 'UNS
STAY OUT, MOM! I'M LOVIN' THE UNIVERSE!!
HOWEVER, SPINOZA WRITES, "IT CANNOT BE SAID THAT GOD LOVES MANKIND, MUCH LESS THAT HE SHOULD LOVE THEM BECAUSE THEY LOVE HIM, OR HATE THEM BECAUSE THEY HATE HIM."
-SIGH-... WILL HE EVER NOTICE ME?
"HE WHO LOVES GOD CANNOT ENDEAVOR THAT GOD SHOULD LOVE HIM IN RETURN."
SPINOZA'S GOD DOESN'T DO MIRACLES. HE DOESN'T ANSWER YOUR PRAYERS.
HE DOESN'T WATCH OVER YOU OR YOUR LOVED ONES ANY MORE THAN YOU SPEND ALL YOUR TIME WATCHING OVER DISTINCT PARTS OF YOUR BODY.
ZZZ
GOD

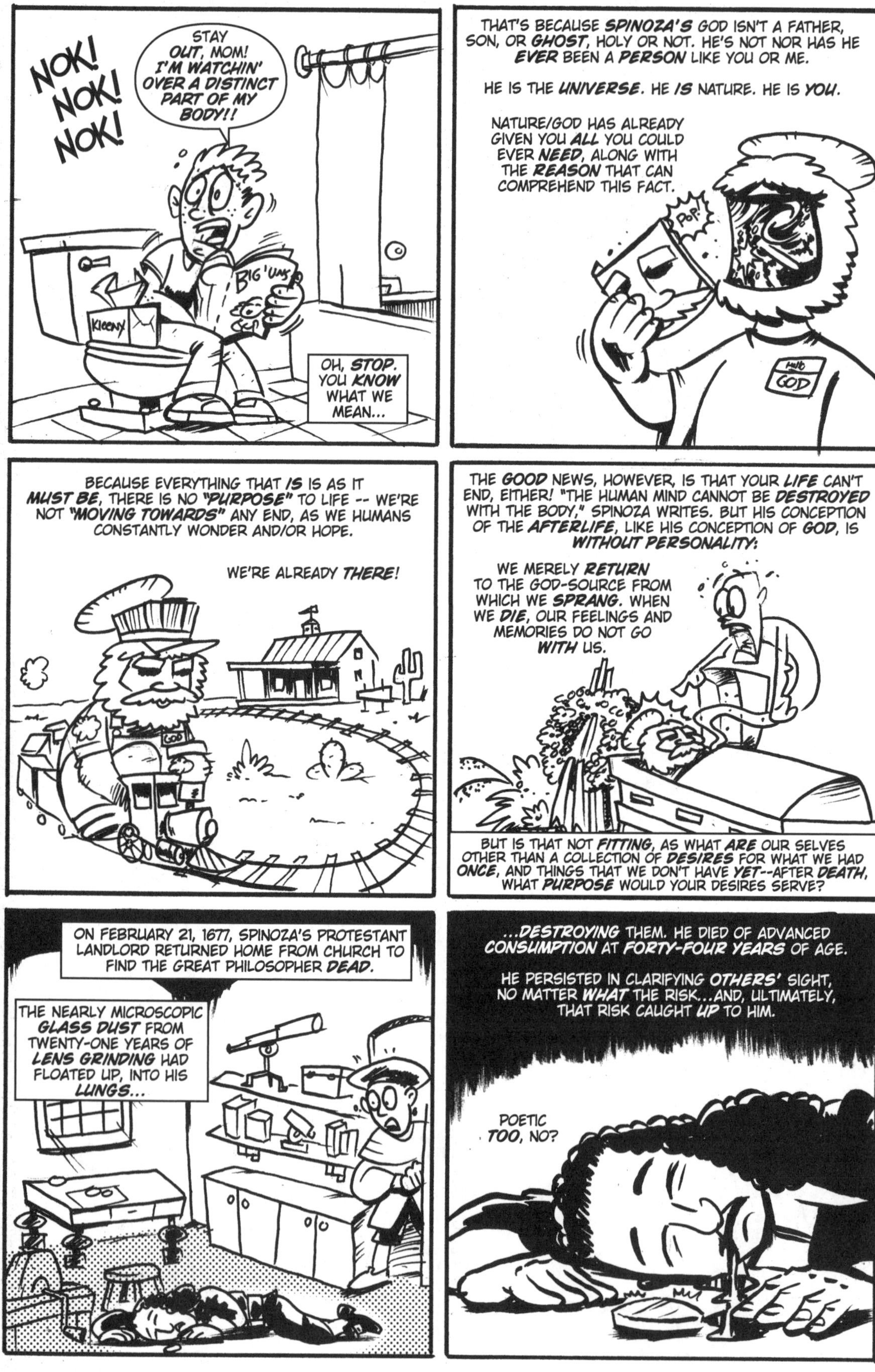

NOK! NOK! NOK!
STAY OUT, MOM! I'M WATCHIN' OVER A DISTINCT PART OF MY BODY!!
KLEENX
BIG 'UNS
OH, STOP. YOU KNOW WHAT WE MEAN...
THAT'S BECAUSE SPINOZA'S GOD ISN'T A FATHER, SON, OR GHOST, HOLY OR NOT. HE'S NOT NOR HAS HE EVER BEEN A PERSON LIKE YOU OR ME.
HE IS THE UNIVERSE. HE IS NATURE. HE IS YOU.
NATURE/GOD HAS ALREADY GIVEN YOU ALL YOU COULD EVER NEED, ALONG WITH THE REASON THAT CAN COMPREHEND THIS FACT.
POP!
GOD
BECAUSE EVERYTHING THAT IS IS AS IT MUST BE, THERE IS NO "PURPOSE" TO LIFE -- WE'RE NOT "MOVING TOWARDS" ANY END, AS WE HUMANS CONSTANTLY WONDER AND/OR HOPE.
WE'RE ALREADY THERE!
GOD
THE GOOD NEWS, HOWEVER, IS THAT YOUR LIFE CAN'T END, EITHER! "THE HUMAN MIND CANNOT BE DESTROYED WITH THE BODY," SPINOZA WRITES. BUT HIS CONCEPTION OF THE AFTERLIFE, LIKE HIS CONCEPTION OF GOD, IS WITHOUT PERSONALITY:
WE MERELY RETURN TO THE GOD-SOURCE FROM WHICH WE SPRANG. WHEN WE DIE, OUR FEELINGS AND MEMORIES DO NOT GO WITH US.
BUT IS THAT NOT FITTING, AS WHAT ARE OUR SELVES OTHER THAN A COLLECTION OF DESIRES FOR WHAT WE HAD ONCE, AND THINGS THAT WE DON'T HAVE YET--AFTER DEATH, WHAT PURPOSE WOULD YOUR DESIRES SERVE?
ON FEBRUARY 21, 1677, SPINOZA'S PROTESTANT LANDLORD RETURNED HOME FROM CHURCH TO FIND THE GREAT PHILOSOPHER DEAD.
THE NEARLY MICROSCOPIC GLASS DUST FROM TWENTY-ONE YEARS OF LENS GRINDING HAD FLOATED UP, INTO HIS LUNGS...
...DESTROYING THEM. HE DIED OF ADVANCED CONSUMPTION AT FORTY-FOUR YEARS OF AGE.
HE PERSISTED IN CLARIFYING OTHERS' SIGHT, NO MATTER WHAT THE RISK...AND, ULTIMATELY, THAT RISK CAUGHT UP TO HIM.
POETIC TOO, NO?

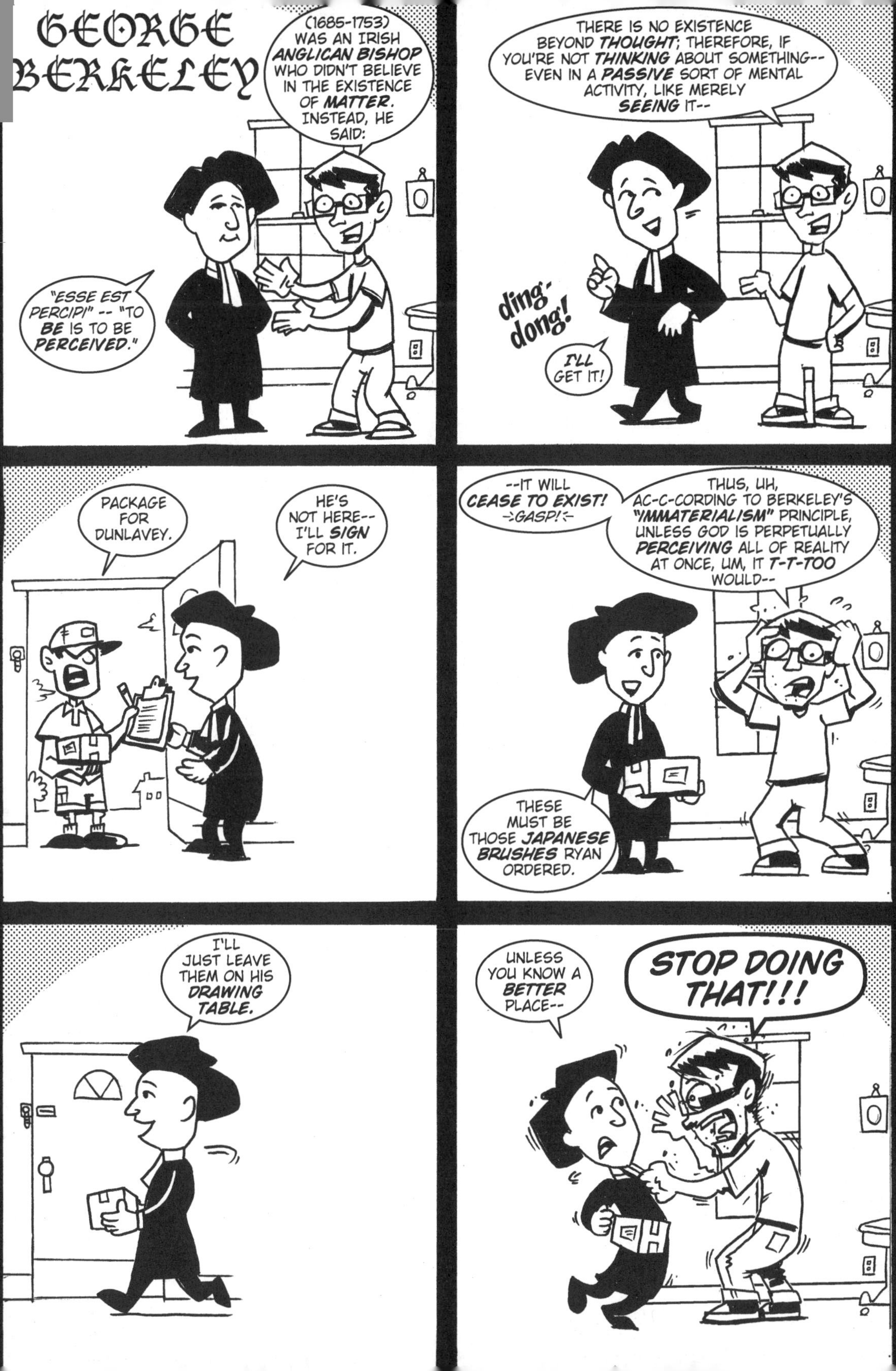
GEORGE BERKELEY
(1685-1753) WAS AN IRISH ANGLICAN BISHOP WHO DIDN'T BELIEVE IN THE EXISTENCE OF MATTER. INSTEAD, HE SAID:
"ESSE EST PERCIPI" -- "TO BE IS TO BE PERCEIVED."
THERE IS NO EXISTENCE BEYOND THOUGHT; THEREFORE, IF YOU'RE NOT THINKING ABOUT SOMETHING-- EVEN IN A PASSIVE SORT OF MENTAL ACTIVITY, LIKE MERELY SEEING IT--
ding-dong!
I'LL GET IT!
PACKAGE FOR DUNLAVEY.
HE'S NOT HERE-- I'LL SIGN FOR IT.
--IT WILL CEASE TO EXIST! ->GASP!<-
THUS, UH, AC-C-CORDING TO BERKELEY'S "IMMATERIALISM" PRINCIPLE, UNLESS GOD IS PERPETUALLY PERCEIVING ALL OF REALITY AT ONCE, UM, IT T-T-TOO WOULD--
THESE MUST BE THOSE JAPANESE BRUSHES RYAN ORDERED.
I'LL JUST LEAVE THEM ON HIS DRAWING TABLE.
UNLESS YOU KNOW A BETTER PLACE--
STOP DOING THAT!!!

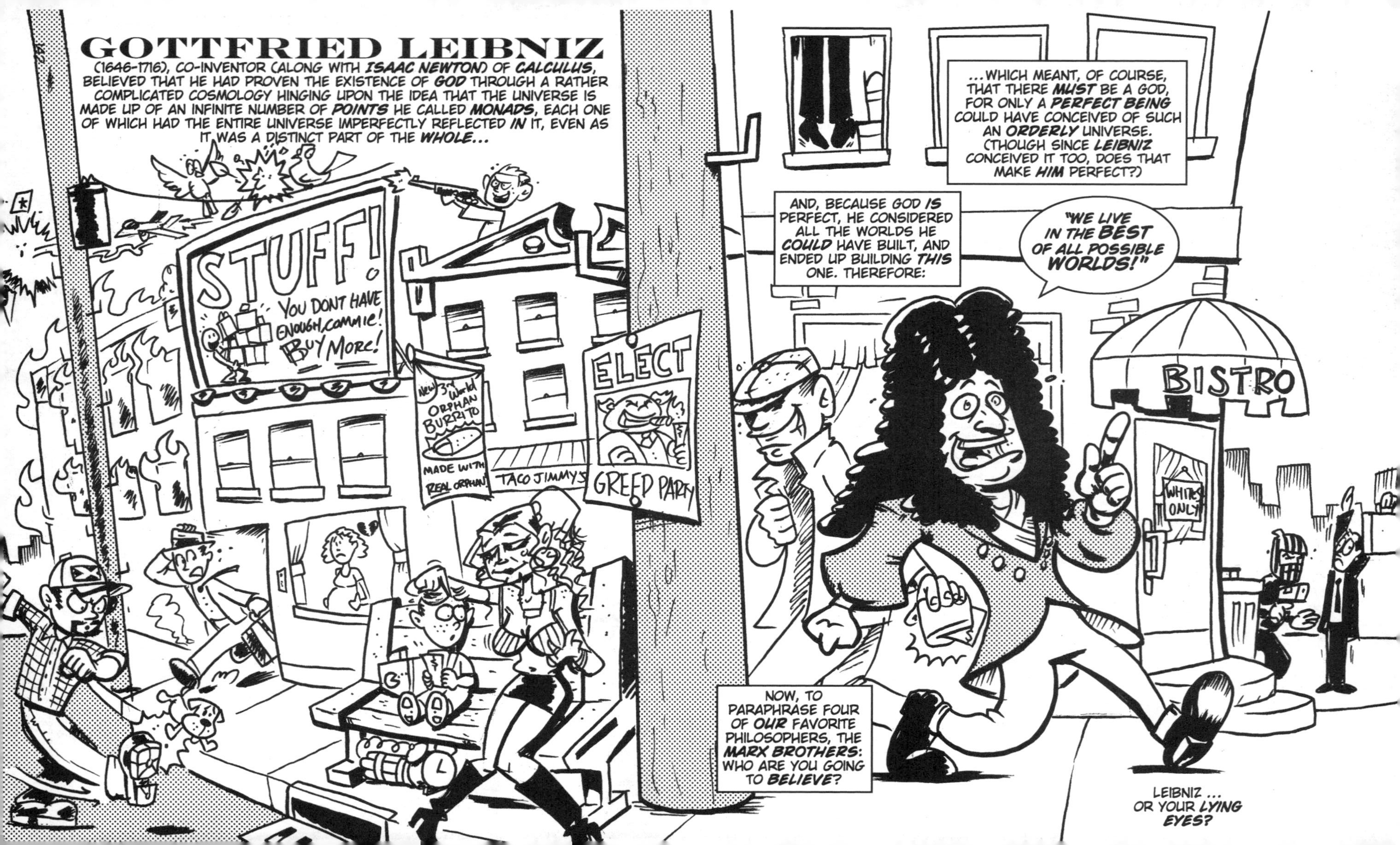
GOTTFRIED LEIBNIZ
(1646-1716), CO-INVENTOR (ALONG WITH ISAAC NEWTON) OF CALCULUS, BELIEVED THAT HE HAD PROVEN THE EXISTENCE OF GOD THROUGH A RATHER COMPLICATED COSMOLOGY HINGING UPON THE IDEA THAT THE UNIVERSE IS MADE UP OF AN INFINITE NUMBER OF POINTS HE CALLED MONADS, EACH ONE OF WHICH HAD THE ENTIRE UNIVERSE IMPERFECTLY REFLECTED IN IT, EVEN AS IT WAS A DISTINCT PART OF THE WHOLE...
STUFF!
YOU DONT HAVE ENOUGH, COMMIE! BUY MORE!
NEW 3rd World ORPHAN BURRITO
MADE WITH REAL ORPHAN!
TACO JIMMY'S
ELECT
GREED PARTY
...WHICH MEANT, OF COURSE, THAT THERE MUST BE A GOD, FOR ONLY A PERFECT BEING COULD HAVE CONCEIVED OF SUCH AN ORDERLY UNIVERSE. (THOUGH SINCE LEIBNIZ CONCEIVED IT TOO, DOES THAT MAKE HIM PERFECT?)
AND, BECAUSE GOD IS PERFECT, HE CONSIDERED ALL THE WORLDS HE COULD HAVE BUILT, AND ENDED UP BUILDING THIS ONE. THEREFORE:
"WE LIVE IN THE BEST OF ALL POSSIBLE WORLDS!"
BISTRO
WHITES ONLY
NOW, TO PARAPHRASE FOUR OF OUR FAVORITE PHILOSOPHERS, THE MARX BROTHERS: WHO ARE YOU GOING TO BELIEVE?
LEIBNIZ ... OR YOUR LYING EYES?

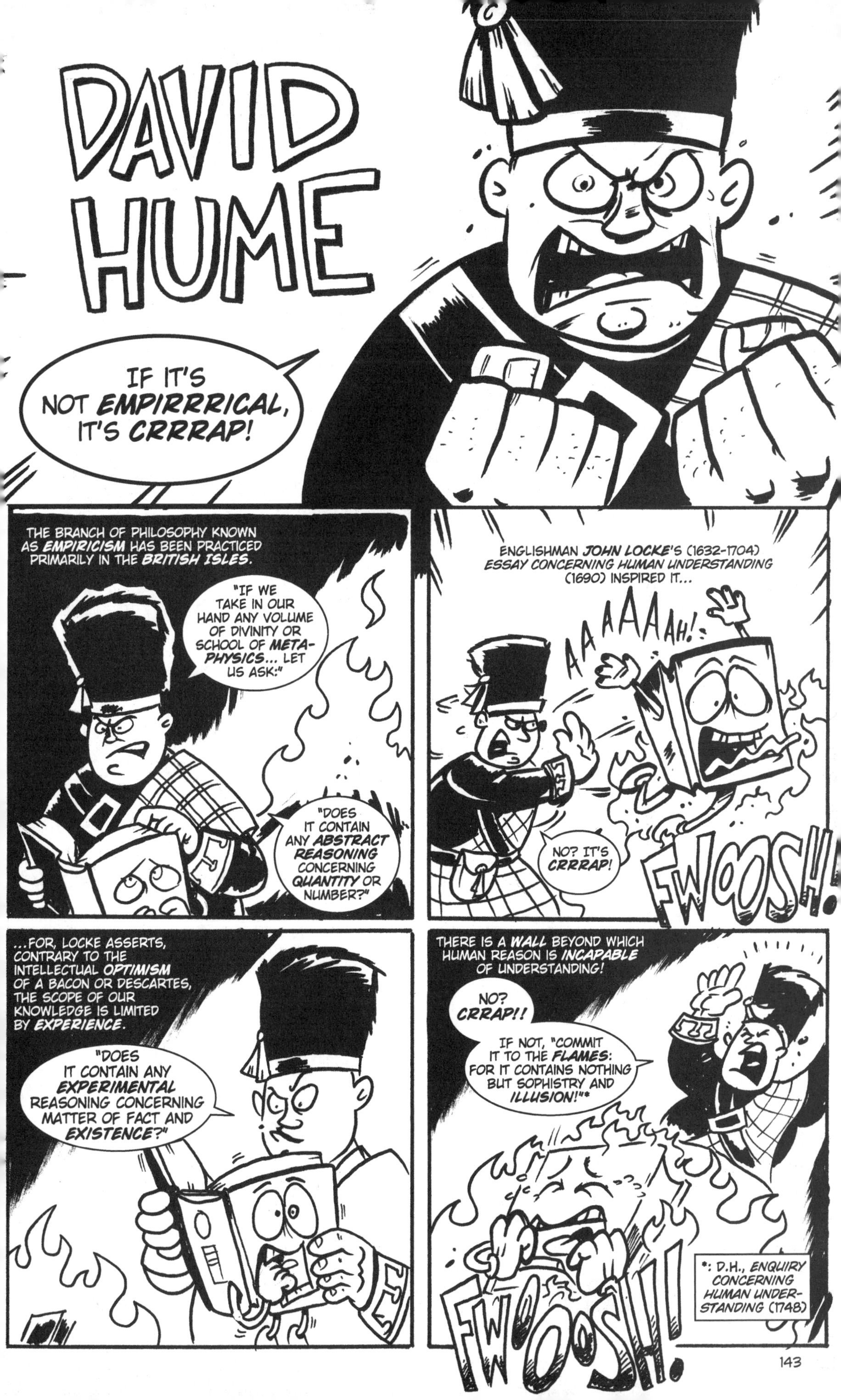
DAVID HUME
IF IT'S NOT EMPIRRRICAL, IT'S CRRRAP!
THE BRANCH OF PHILOSOPHY KNOWN AS EMPIRICISM HAS BEEN PRACTICED PRIMARILY IN THE BRITISH ISLES.
"IF WE TAKE IN OUR HAND ANY VOLUME OF DIVINITY OR SCHOOL OF META-PHYSICS... LET US ASK:"
"DOES IT CONTAIN ANY ABSTRACT REASONING CONCERNING QUANTITY OR NUMBER?"
ENGLISHMAN JOHN LOCKE'S (1632-1704) ESSAY CONCERNING HUMAN UNDERSTANDING (1690) INSPIRED IT...
AAAAAAH!
NO? IT'S CRRRAP!
FWOOSH!
...FOR, LOCKE ASSERTS, CONTRARY TO THE INTELLECTUAL OPTIMISM OF A BACON OR DESCARTES, THE SCOPE OF OUR KNOWLEDGE IS LIMITED BY EXPERIENCE.
"DOES IT CONTAIN ANY EXPERIMENTAL REASONING CONCERNING MATTER OF FACT AND EXISTENCE?"
THERE IS A WALL BEYOND WHICH HUMAN REASON IS INCAPABLE OF UNDERSTANDING!
NO? CRRAP!!
IF NOT, "COMMIT IT TO THE FLAMES: FOR IT CONTAINS NOTHING BUT SOPHISTRY AND ILLUSION!"*
FWOOSH!
*: D.H., ENQUIRY CONCERNING HUMAN UNDERSTANDING (1748)

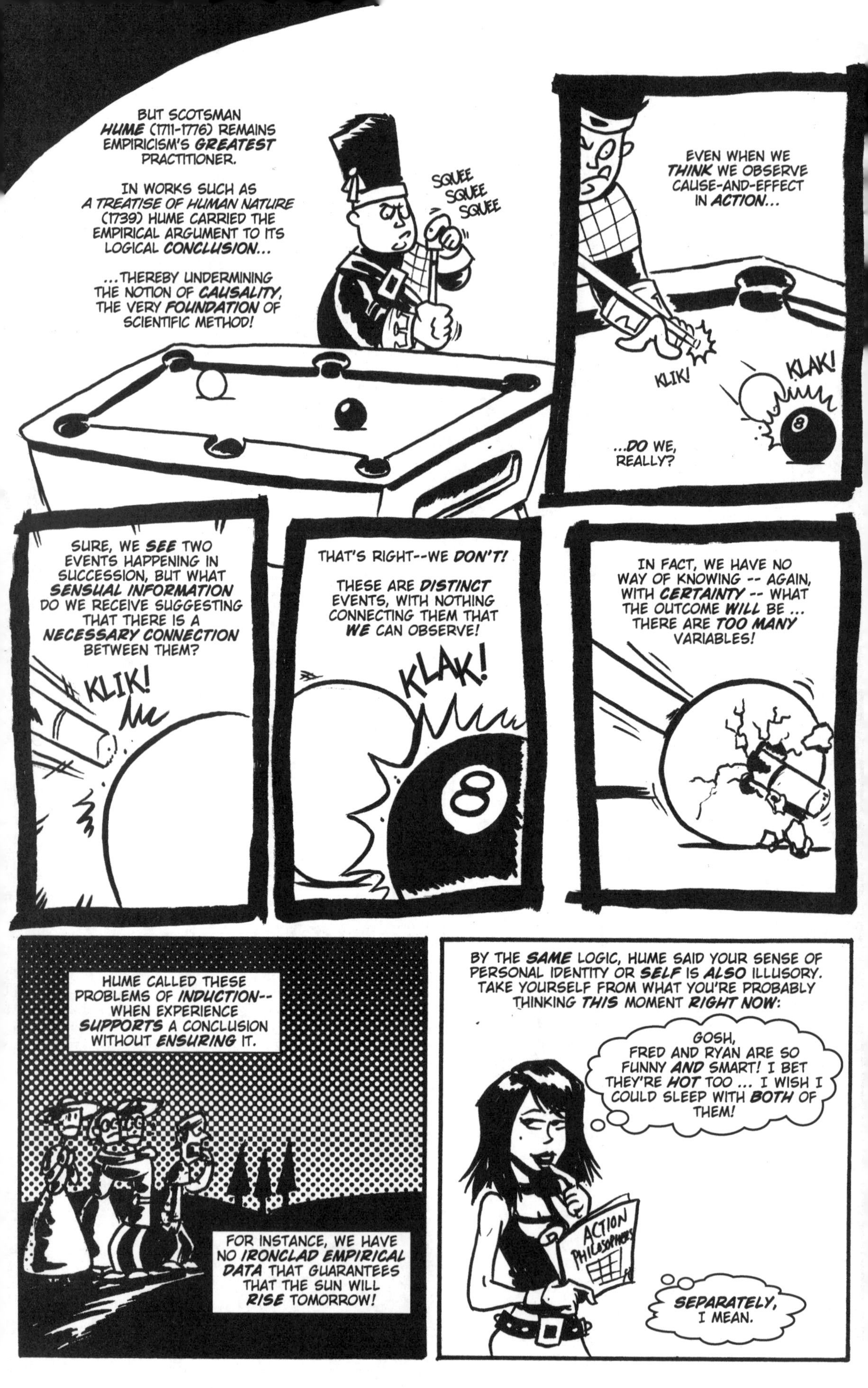
BUT SCOTSMAN HUME (1711-1776) REMAINS EMPIRICISM'S GREATEST PRACTITIONER.
IN WORKS SUCH AS A TREATISE OF HUMAN NATURE (1739) HUME CARRIED THE EMPIRICAL ARGUMENT TO ITS LOGICAL CONCLUSION...
...THEREBY UNDERMINING THE NOTION OF CAUSALITY, THE VERY FOUNDATION OF SCIENTIFIC METHOD!
SQUEE SQUEE SQUEE
EVEN WHEN WE THINK WE OBSERVE CAUSE-AND-EFFECT IN ACTION...
KLIK!
KLAK!
...DO WE, REALLY?
SURE, WE SEE TWO EVENTS HAPPENING IN SUCCESSION, BUT WHAT SENSUAL INFORMATION DO WE RECEIVE SUGGESTING THAT THERE IS A NECESSARY CONNECTION BETWEEN THEM?
KLIK!
THAT'S RIGHT--WE DON'T!
THESE ARE DISTINCT EVENTS, WITH NOTHING CONNECTING THEM THAT WE CAN OBSERVE!
KLAK!
8
IN FACT, WE HAVE NO WAY OF KNOWING -- AGAIN, WITH CERTAINTY -- WHAT THE OUTCOME WILL BE ... THERE ARE TOO MANY VARIABLES!
HUME CALLED THESE PROBLEMS OF INDUCTION-- WHEN EXPERIENCE SUPPORTS A CONCLUSION WITHOUT ENSURING IT.
FOR INSTANCE, WE HAVE NO IRONCLAD EMPIRICAL DATA THAT GUARANTEES THAT THE SUN WILL RISE TOMORROW!
BY THE SAME LOGIC, HUME SAID YOUR SENSE OF PERSONAL IDENTITY OR SELF IS ALSO ILLUSORY. TAKE YOURSELF FROM WHAT YOU'RE PROBABLY THINKING THIS MOMENT RIGHT NOW:
GOSH, FRED AND RYAN ARE SO FUNNY AND SMART! I BET THEY'RE HOT TOO ... I WISH I COULD SLEEP WITH BOTH OF THEM!
ACTION PHILOSOPHERS
SEPARATELY, I MEAN.

"WHEN I ENTER MOST ***INTIMATELY*** INTO WHAT I CALL ***MYSELF***," HUME WRITES, "I ALWAYS STUMBLE ON SOME PARTICULAR ***PERCEPTION*** OR OTHER, OF HEAT OR COLD, LOVE OR HATRED, PAIN OR PLEASURE. I NEVER CAN CATCH ***MYSELF*** AT ANY TIME ***WITHOUT*** A PERCEPTION AND NEVER CAN OBSERVE ANYTHING ***BUT*** THE PERCEPTION."

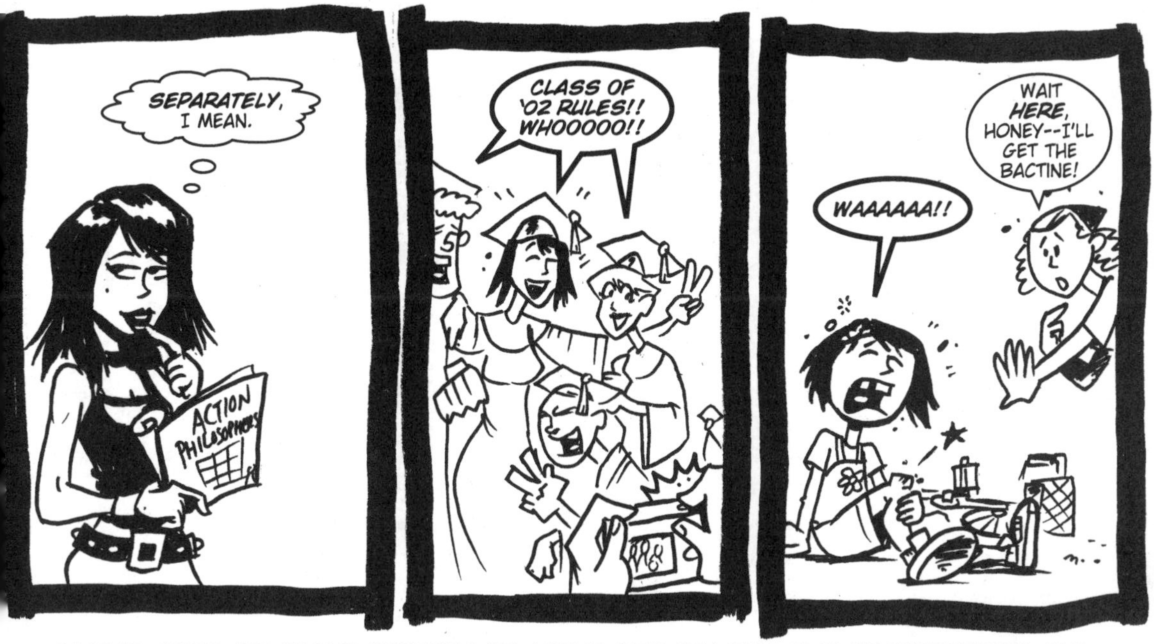
SEPARATELY, I MEAN.
ACTION PHILOSOPHERS
CLASS OF '02 RULES!! WHOOOOO!!
WAAAAAA!!
WAIT HERE, HONEY--I'LL GET THE BACTINE!

IN OTHER WORDS, OUR ALLEGED ***IDENTITIES*** ARE NOTHING MORE THAN THE SUM OF THE ***PERCEPTIONS*** WE'VE ACCUMULATED -- IT IS ONLY THAT "HABIT OF ***ASSOCIATION***" THAT CREATES CAUSE-AND-EFFECT THAT LEADS US TO BELIEVE WE HAVE ONE ***CONTINUOUS SELF*** -- THAT WE ARE THE ***SAME PERSON*** IN ***EACH*** OF THE MOMENTS OF OUR LIVES!

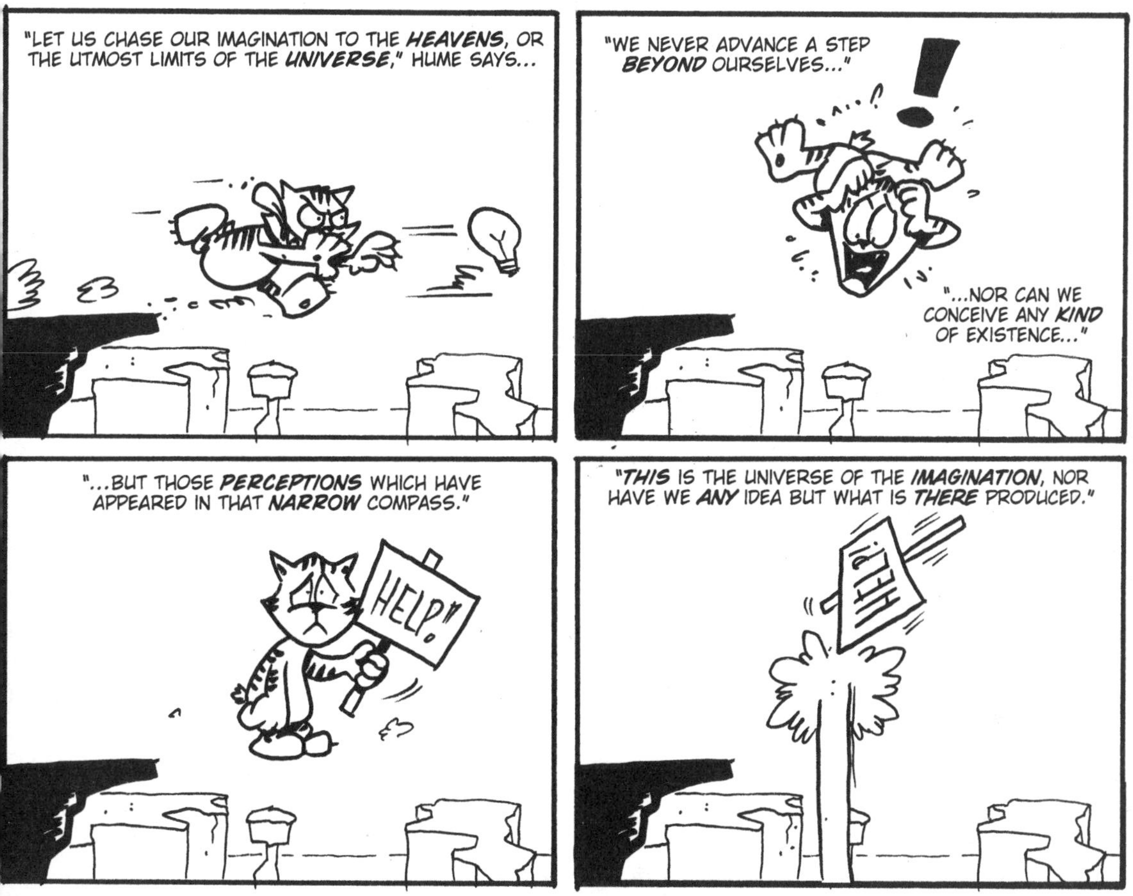
"LET US CHASE OUR IMAGINATION TO THE HEAVENS, OR THE UTMOST LIMITS OF THE UNIVERSE," HUME SAYS...
"WE NEVER ADVANCE A STEP BEYOND OURSELVES..."
"...NOR CAN WE CONCEIVE ANY KIND OF EXISTENCE..."
"...BUT THOSE PERCEPTIONS WHICH HAVE APPEARED IN THAT NARROW COMPASS."
HELP!
"THIS IS THE UNIVERSE OF THE IMAGINATION, NOR HAVE WE ANY IDEA BUT WHAT IS THERE PRODUCED."
HELP!

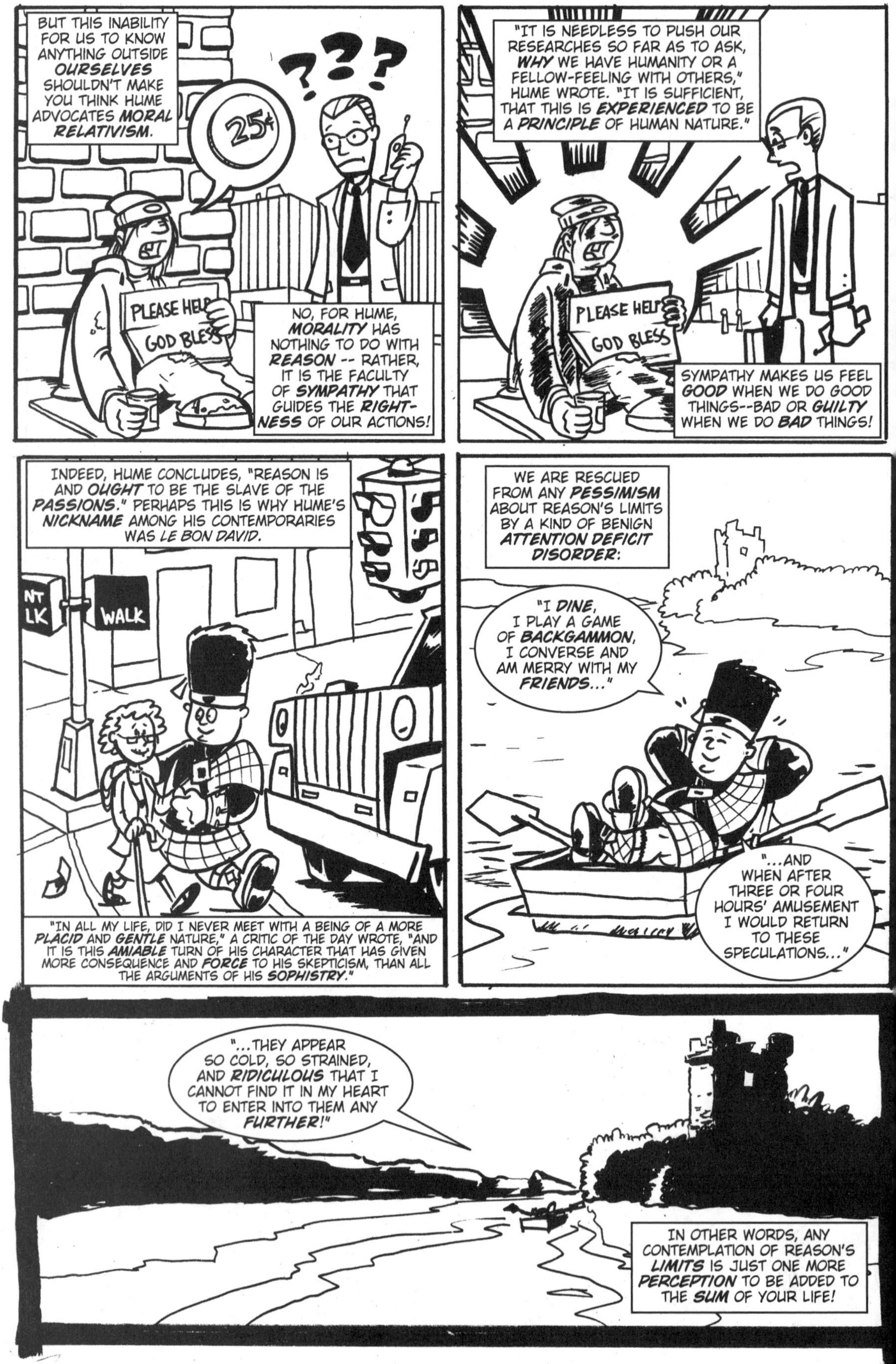
BUT THIS INABILITY FOR US TO KNOW ANYTHING OUTSIDE OURSELVES SHOULDN'T MAKE YOU THINK HUME ADVOCATES MORAL RELATIVISM.
25¢
???
PLEASE HELP
GOD BLESS
NO, FOR HUME, MORALITY HAS NOTHING TO DO WITH REASON -- RATHER, IT IS THE FACULTY OF SYMPATHY THAT GUIDES THE RIGHTNESS OF OUR ACTIONS!
"IT IS NEEDLESS TO PUSH OUR RESEARCHES SO FAR AS TO ASK, WHY WE HAVE HUMANITY OR A FELLOW-FEELING WITH OTHERS," HUME WROTE. "IT IS SUFFICIENT, THAT THIS IS EXPERIENCED TO BE A PRINCIPLE OF HUMAN NATURE."
PLEASE HELP
GOD BLESS
SYMPATHY MAKES US FEEL GOOD WHEN WE DO GOOD THINGS--BAD OR GUILTY WHEN WE DO BAD THINGS!
INDEED, HUME CONCLUDES, "REASON IS AND OUGHT TO BE THE SLAVE OF THE PASSIONS." PERHAPS THIS IS WHY HUME'S NICKNAME AMONG HIS CONTEMPORARIES WAS LE BON DAVID.
NT LK
WALK
"IN ALL MY LIFE, DID I NEVER MEET WITH A BEING OF A MORE PLACID AND GENTLE NATURE," A CRITIC OF THE DAY WROTE, "AND IT IS THIS AMIABLE TURN OF HIS CHARACTER THAT HAS GIVEN MORE CONSEQUENCE AND FORCE TO HIS SKEPTICISM, THAN ALL THE ARGUMENTS OF HIS SOPHISTRY."
WE ARE RESCUED FROM ANY PESSIMISM ABOUT REASON'S LIMITS BY A KIND OF BENIGN ATTENTION DEFICIT DISORDER:
"I DINE, I PLAY A GAME OF BACKGAMMON, I CONVERSE AND AM MERRY WITH MY FRIENDS..."
"...AND WHEN AFTER THREE OR FOUR HOURS' AMUSEMENT I WOULD RETURN TO THESE SPECULATIONS..."
"...THEY APPEAR SO COLD, SO STRAINED, AND RIDICULOUS THAT I CANNOT FIND IT IN MY HEART TO ENTER INTO THEM ANY FURTHER!"
IN OTHER WORDS, ANY CONTEMPLATION OF REASON'S LIMITS IS JUST ONE MORE PERCEPTION TO BE ADDED TO THE SUM OF YOUR LIFE!

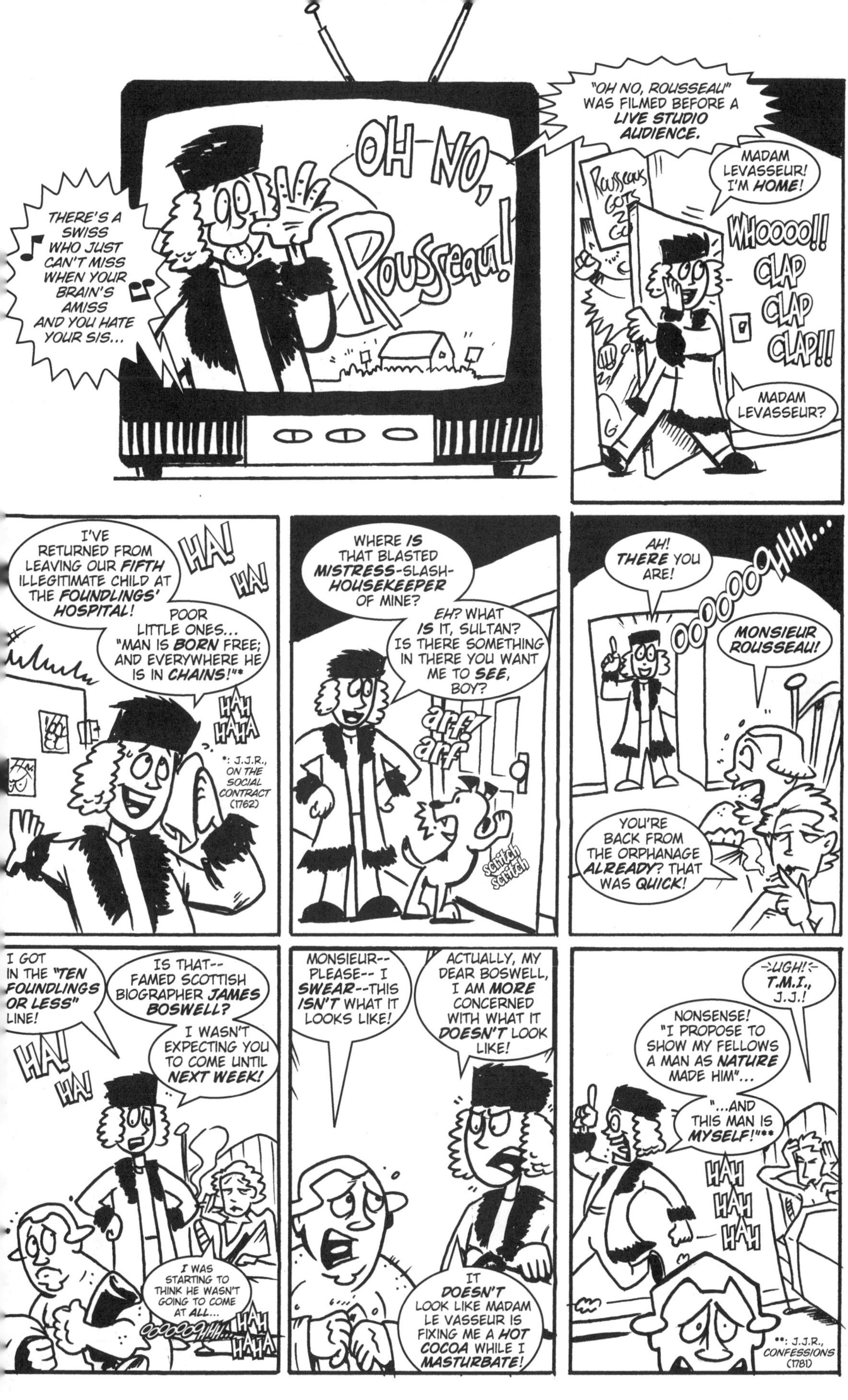
THERE'S A SWISS WHO JUST CAN'T MISS WHEN YOUR BRAIN'S AMISS AND YOU HATE YOUR SIS...
OH NO, ROUSSEAU!
"OH NO, ROUSSEAU" WAS FILMED BEFORE A LIVE STUDIO AUDIENCE.
MADAM LEVASSEUR! I'M HOME!
WHOOOO!!
CLAP CLAP CLAP!!
MADAM LEVASSEUR?
I'VE RETURNED FROM LEAVING OUR FIFTH ILLEGITIMATE CHILD AT THE FOUNDLINGS' HOSPITAL!
HA! HA!
POOR LITTLE ONES... "MAN IS BORN FREE; AND EVERYWHERE HE IS IN CHAINS!"*
HAH HAHA
*: J.J.R., ON THE SOCIAL CONTRACT (1762)
WHERE IS THAT BLASTED MISTRESS-SLASH-HOUSEKEEPER OF MINE?
EH? WHAT IS IT, SULTAN? IS THERE SOMETHING IN THERE YOU WANT ME TO SEE, BOY?
arf! arf!
scritch scritch
AH! THERE YOU ARE!
OOOOOOOHHH...
MONSIEUR ROUSSEAU!
YOU'RE BACK FROM THE ORPHANAGE ALREADY? THAT WAS QUICK!
I GOT IN THE "TEN FOUNDLINGS OR LESS" LINE!
HA! HA!
IS THAT-- FAMED SCOTTISH BIOGRAPHER JAMES BOSWELL?
I WASN'T EXPECTING YOU TO COME UNTIL NEXT WEEK!
I WAS STARTING TO THINK HE WASN'T GOING TO COME AT ALL...
OOOOOOHHH... HAH HAHA
MONSIEUR-- PLEASE-- I SWEAR--THIS ISN'T WHAT IT LOOKS LIKE!
ACTUALLY, MY DEAR BOSWELL, I AM MORE CONCERNED WITH WHAT IT DOESN'T LOOK LIKE!
IT DOESN'T LOOK LIKE MADAM LE VASSEUR IS FIXING ME A HOT COCOA WHILE I MASTURBATE!
UGH! T.M.I., J.J.!
NONSENSE! "I PROPOSE TO SHOW MY FELLOWS A MAN AS NATURE MADE HIM"...
"...AND THIS MAN IS MYSELF!"**
HAH HAH HAH
**: J.J.R., CONFESSIONS (1781)

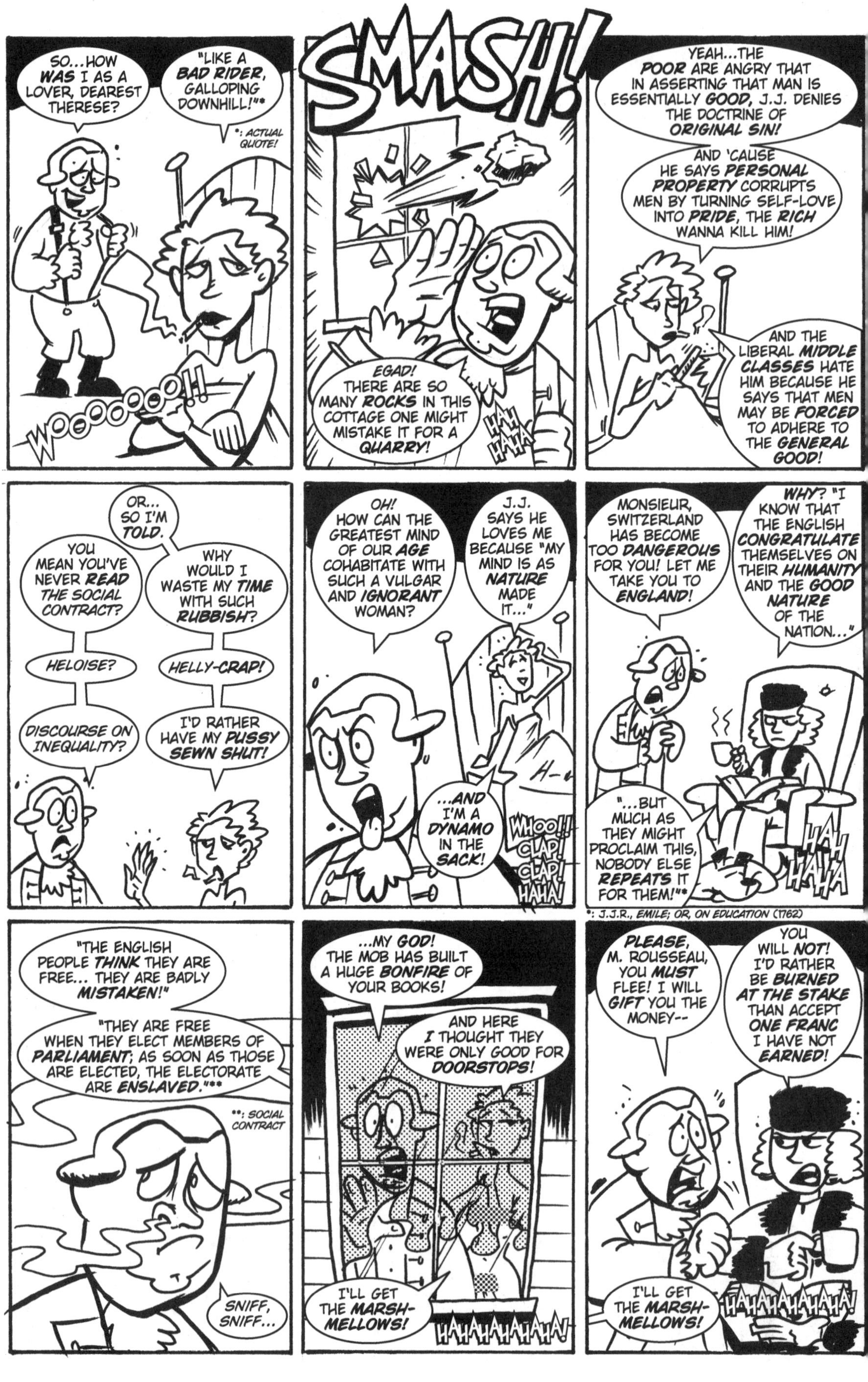
SO...HOW WAS I AS A LOVER, DEAREST THERESE?
"LIKE A BAD RIDER, GALLOPING DOWNHILL!"*
*: ACTUAL QUOTE!
WOOOOOOOOO!!
SMASH!
EGAD! THERE ARE SO MANY ROCKS IN THIS COTTAGE ONE MIGHT MISTAKE IT FOR A QUARRY!
HAH HAHA
YEAH...THE POOR ARE ANGRY THAT IN ASSERTING THAT MAN IS ESSENTIALLY GOOD, J.J. DENIES THE DOCTRINE OF ORIGINAL SIN!
AND 'CAUSE HE SAYS PERSONAL PROPERTY CORRUPTS MEN BY TURNING SELF-LOVE INTO PRIDE, THE RICH WANNA KILL HIM!
AND THE LIBERAL MIDDLE CLASSES HATE HIM BECAUSE HE SAYS THAT MEN MAY BE FORCED TO ADHERE TO THE GENERAL GOOD!
YOU MEAN YOU'VE NEVER READ THE SOCIAL CONTRACT?
OR... SO I'M TOLD.
WHY WOULD I WASTE MY TIME WITH SUCH RUBBISH?
HELOISE?
HELLY-CRAP!
DISCOURSE ON INEQUALITY?
I'D RATHER HAVE MY PUSSY SEWN SHUT!
OH! HOW CAN THE GREATEST MIND OF OUR AGE COHABITATE WITH SUCH A VULGAR AND IGNORANT WOMAN?
J.J. SAYS HE LOVES ME BECAUSE "MY MIND IS AS NATURE MADE IT..."
...AND I'M A DYNAMO IN THE SACK!
WHOO!! CLAP! CLAP! HAHA!
MONSIEUR, SWITZERLAND HAS BECOME TOO DANGEROUS FOR YOU! LET ME TAKE YOU TO ENGLAND!
WHY? "I KNOW THAT THE ENGLISH CONGRATULATE THEMSELVES ON THEIR HUMANITY AND THE GOOD NATURE OF THE NATION..."
"...BUT MUCH AS THEY MIGHT PROCLAIM THIS, NOBODY ELSE REPEATS IT FOR THEM!"*
HAH HAHA
*: J.J.R., EMILE; OR, ON EDUCATION (1762)
"THE ENGLISH PEOPLE THINK THEY ARE FREE... THEY ARE BADLY MISTAKEN!"
"THEY ARE FREE WHEN THEY ELECT MEMBERS OF PARLIAMENT; AS SOON AS THOSE ARE ELECTED, THE ELECTORATE ARE ENSLAVED."**
**: SOCIAL CONTRACT
SNIFF, SNIFF...
...MY GOD! THE MOB HAS BUILT A HUGE BONFIRE OF YOUR BOOKS!
AND HERE I THOUGHT THEY WERE ONLY GOOD FOR DOORSTOPS!
I'LL GET THE MARSH-MELLOWS!
HAHAHAHAHAHAHA!
PLEASE, M. ROUSSEAU, YOU MUST FLEE! I WILL GIFT YOU THE MONEY--
YOU WILL NOT! I'D RATHER BE BURNED AT THE STAKE THAN ACCEPT ONE FRANC I HAVE NOT EARNED!
I'LL GET THE MARSH-MELLOWS!
HAHAHAHAHAHAHA!

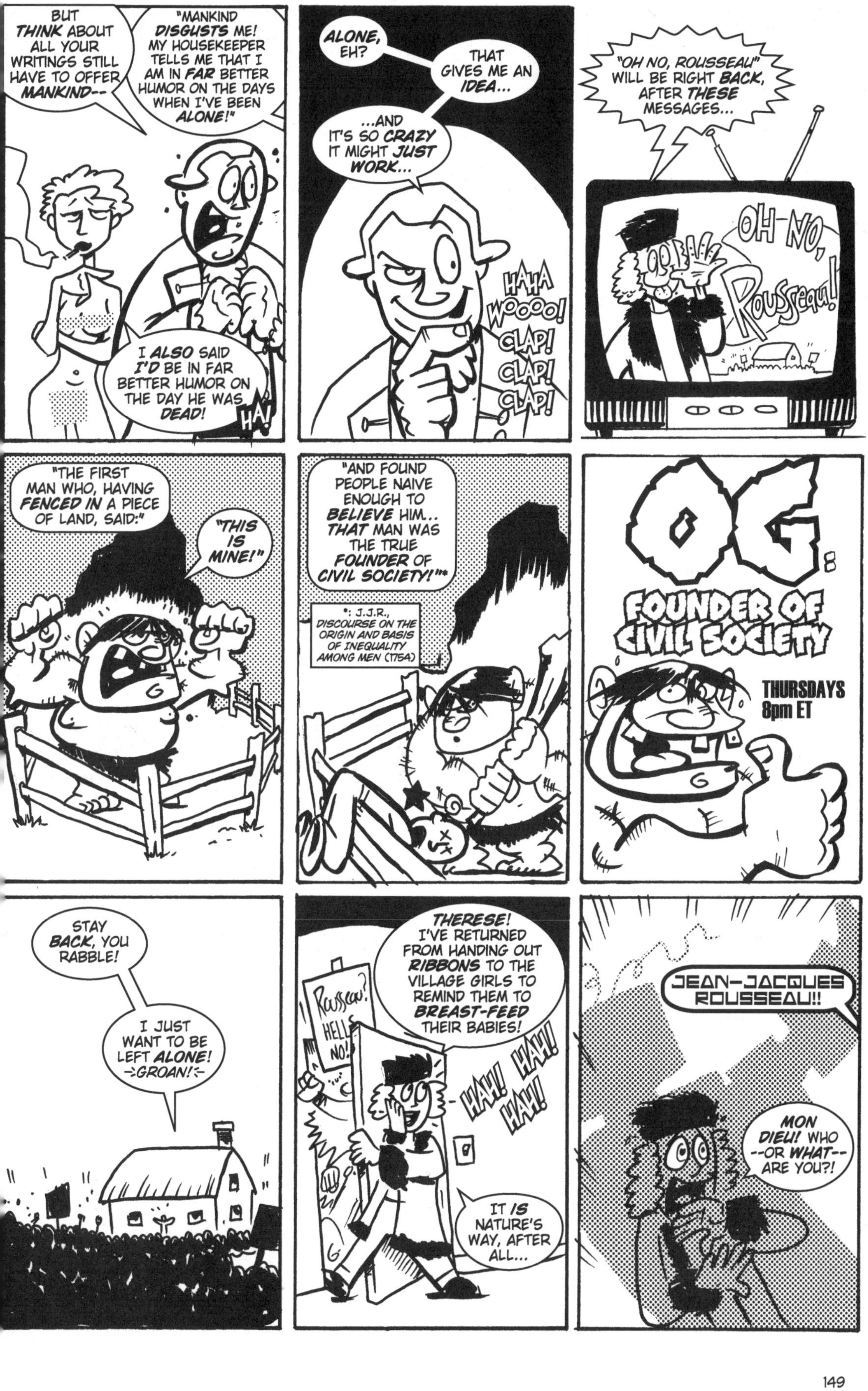
BUT THINK ABOUT ALL YOUR WRITINGS STILL HAVE TO OFFER MANKIND--
"MANKIND DISGUSTS ME! MY HOUSEKEEPER TELLS ME THAT I AM IN FAR BETTER HUMOR ON THE DAYS WHEN I'VE BEEN ALONE!"
I ALSO SAID I'D BE IN FAR BETTER HUMOR ON THE DAY HE WAS DEAD!
HA!
ALONE, EH?
THAT GIVES ME AN IDEA...
...AND IT'S SO CRAZY IT MIGHT JUST WORK...
HAHA
WOOOO!
CLAP!
CLAP!
CLAP!
"OH NO, ROUSSEAU" WILL BE RIGHT BACK, AFTER THESE MESSAGES...
OH NO, ROUSSEAU!
"THE FIRST MAN WHO, HAVING FENCED IN A PIECE OF LAND, SAID:"
"THIS IS MINE!"
"AND FOUND PEOPLE NAIVE ENOUGH TO BELIEVE HIM... THAT MAN WAS THE TRUE FOUNDER OF CIVIL SOCIETY!"*
*: J.J.R., DISCOURSE ON THE ORIGIN AND BASIS OF INEQUALITY AMONG MEN (1754)
OG:
FOUNDER OF CIVIL SOCIETY
THURSDAYS 8pm ET
STAY BACK, YOU RABBLE!
I JUST WANT TO BE LEFT ALONE! -GROAN!-
THERESE! I'VE RETURNED FROM HANDING OUT RIBBONS TO THE VILLAGE GIRLS TO REMIND THEM TO BREAST-FEED THEIR BABIES!
ROUSSEAU? HELL NO!
HAH! HAH! HAH!
IT IS NATURE'S WAY, AFTER ALL...
JEAN-JACQUES ROUSSEAU!!
MON DIEU! WHO --OR WHAT-- ARE YOU?!

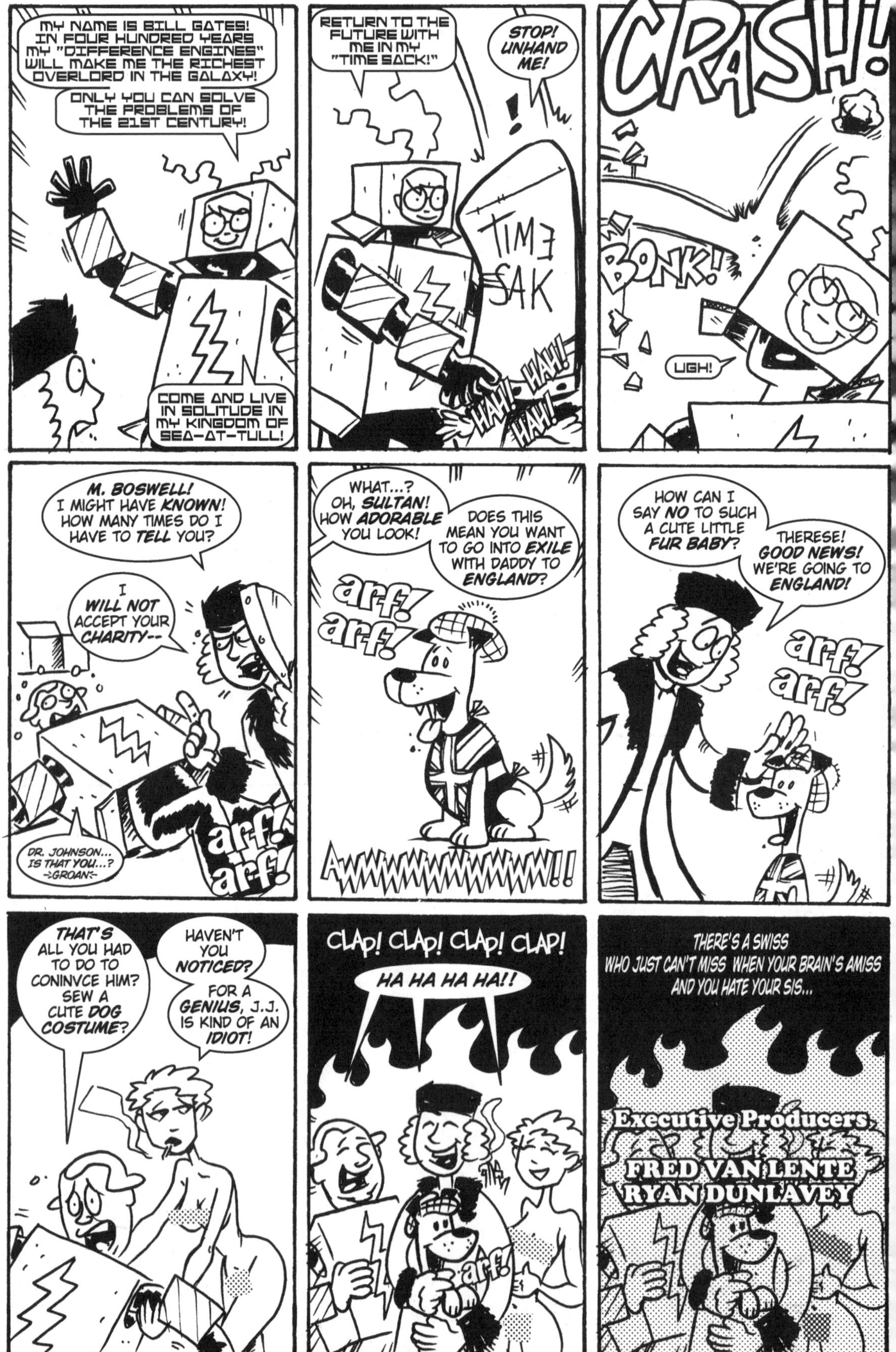
MY NAME IS BILL GATES! IN FOUR HUNDRED YEARS MY "DIFFERENCE ENGINES" WILL MAKE ME THE RICHEST OVERLORD IN THE GALAXY!
ONLY YOU CAN SOLVE THE PROBLEMS OF THE 21ST CENTURY!
COME AND LIVE IN SOLITUDE IN MY KINGDOM OF SEA-AT-TULL!
RETURN TO THE FUTURE WITH ME IN MY "TIME SACK!"
STOP! UNHAND ME!
!
TIME SAK
HAH! HAH! HAH! HAH!
CRASH!
BONK!
UGH!
M. BOSWELL! I MIGHT HAVE KNOWN! HOW MANY TIMES DO I HAVE TO TELL YOU?
I WILL NOT ACCEPT YOUR CHARITY--
DR. JOHNSON... IS THAT YOU...? -GROAN-
arf! arf!
WHAT...? OH, SULTAN! HOW ADORABLE YOU LOOK!
DOES THIS MEAN YOU WANT TO GO INTO EXILE WITH DADDY TO ENGLAND?
arf! arf!
AWWWWWWWWWWW!!
HOW CAN I SAY NO TO SUCH A CUTE LITTLE FUR BABY?
THERESE! GOOD NEWS! WE'RE GOING TO ENGLAND!
arf! arf!
THAT'S ALL YOU HAD TO DO TO CONINVCE HIM? SEW A CUTE DOG COSTUME?
HAVEN'T YOU NOTICED?
FOR A GENIUS, J.J. IS KIND OF AN IDIOT!
CLAP! CLAP! CLAP! CLAP!
HA HA HA HA!!
arf!
THERE'S A SWISS WHO JUST CAN'T MISS WHEN YOUR BRAIN'S AMISS AND YOU HATE YOUR SIS...
Executive Producers
FRED VAN LENTE
RYAN DUNLAVEY

IN JUNE, 1776, THE **CONTINENTAL CONGRESS** OF THE REBELLIOUS THIRTEEN AMERICAN COLONIES COULD AGREE ON ALMOST **NOTHING** -- EXCEPT THE NEED TO **ARTICULATE** THEIR GRIEVANCES WITH THE **BRITISH CROWN!**

THE MAN DRAFTED TO **DRAFT** THIS **DECLARATION** WAS THE **QUIETEST** DELEGATE IN CONGRESS--A MAN WHOSE OWN **SPEAKING VOICE** BARELY ROSE ABOVE A **WHISPER**--BUT WAS **UNANIMOUSLY AGREED** TO BE THE GREATEST **POLITICAL WRITER** IN THE COUNTRY...

...A MAN **WE** KNOW BETTER AS **ACTION PHILOSOPHER #4:**

Thomas Jefferson!

We mutually pledge to each other our lives, our fortunes and our sacred honor:
Frederick J. Van Lente (script)
Ryan/Michael Dunlavey (art)

JEFFERSON AUTHORED WHAT TURNED OUT TO BE **AMERICAN SCRIPTURE**, BUT IT WAS THE **CROWNING ACHIEVEMENT** OF **THE ENLIGHTENMENT**, ITSELF A **REVOLUTIONARY** SHIFT IN EUROPEAN PHILOSOPHY!

IN CONGRESS. JULY 4. 1776.

The unanimous Declaration of the thirteen united States of America.

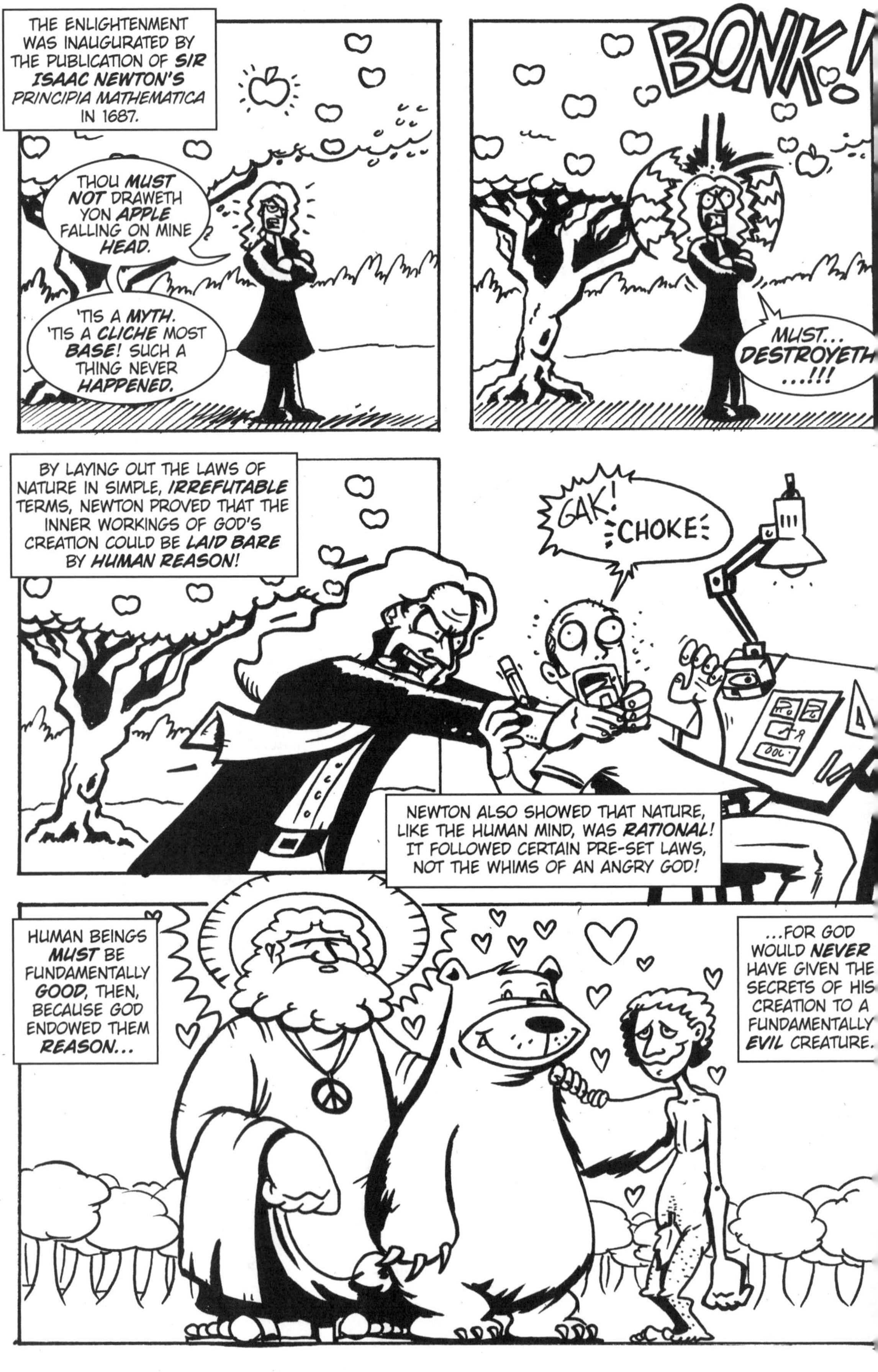

THE ENLIGHTENMENT WAS INAUGURATED BY THE PUBLICATION OF SIR ISAAC NEWTON'S PRINCIPIA MATHEMATICA IN 1687.
THOU MUST NOT DRAWETH YON APPLE FALLING ON MINE HEAD.
'TIS A MYTH. 'TIS A CLICHE MOST BASE! SUCH A THING NEVER HAPPENED.
BONK!
MUST... DESTROYETH ...!!!
BY LAYING OUT THE LAWS OF NATURE IN SIMPLE, IRREFUTABLE TERMS, NEWTON PROVED THAT THE INNER WORKINGS OF GOD'S CREATION COULD BE LAID BARE BY HUMAN REASON!
GAK! CHOKE
NEWTON ALSO SHOWED THAT NATURE, LIKE THE HUMAN MIND, WAS RATIONAL! IT FOLLOWED CERTAIN PRE-SET LAWS, NOT THE WHIMS OF AN ANGRY GOD!
HUMAN BEINGS MUST BE FUNDAMENTALLY GOOD, THEN, BECAUSE GOD ENDOWED THEM REASON...
...FOR GOD WOULD NEVER HAVE GIVEN THE SECRETS OF HIS CREATION TO A FUNDAMENTALLY EVIL CREATURE.

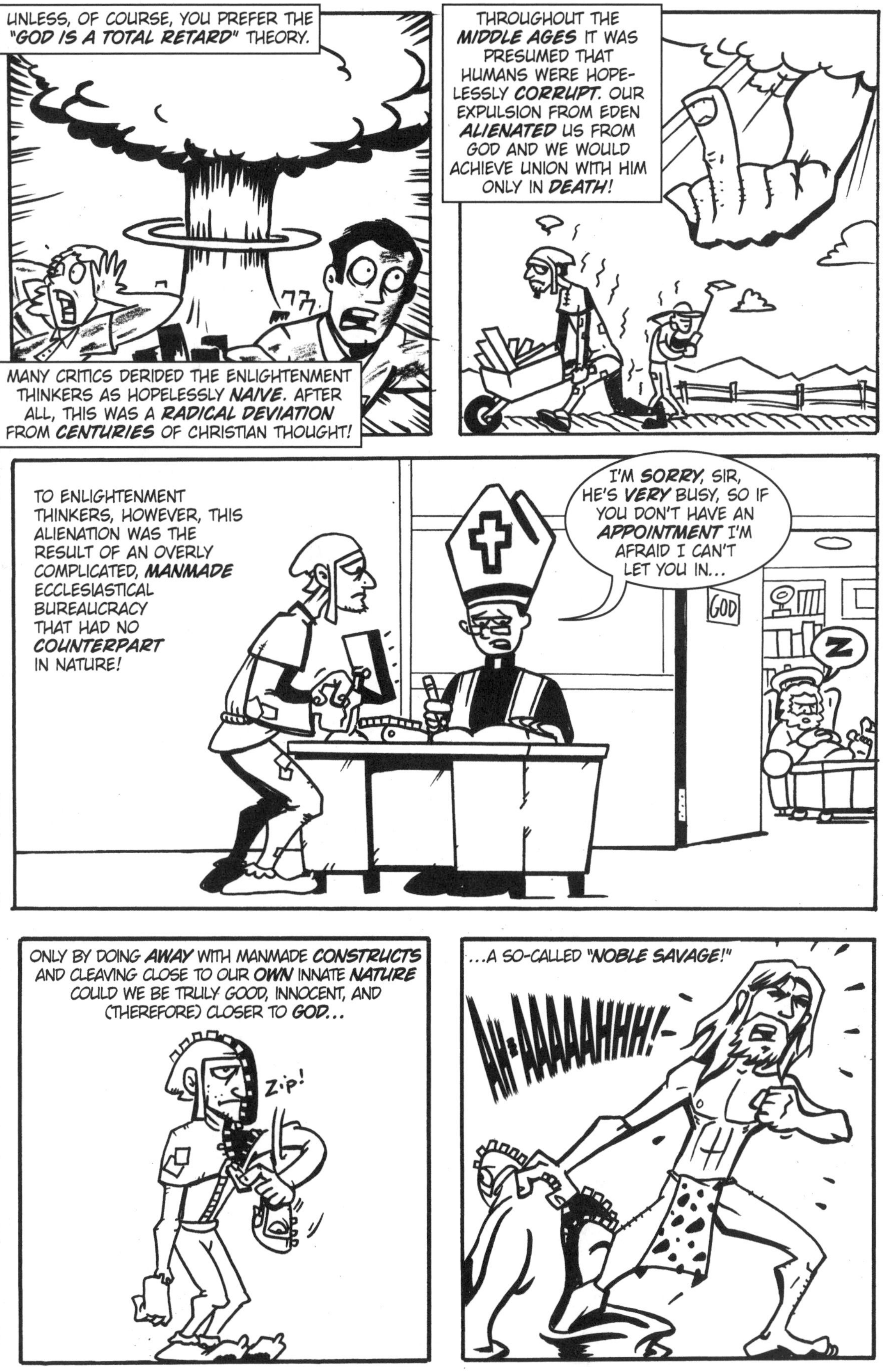
UNLESS, OF COURSE, YOU PREFER THE "GOD IS A TOTAL RETARD" THEORY.
MANY CRITICS DERIDED THE ENLIGHTENMENT THINKERS AS HOPELESSLY NAIVE. AFTER ALL, THIS WAS A RADICAL DEVIATION FROM CENTURIES OF CHRISTIAN THOUGHT!
THROUGHOUT THE MIDDLE AGES IT WAS PRESUMED THAT HUMANS WERE HOPELESSLY CORRUPT. OUR EXPULSION FROM EDEN ALIENATED US FROM GOD AND WE WOULD ACHIEVE UNION WITH HIM ONLY IN DEATH!
TO ENLIGHTENMENT THINKERS, HOWEVER, THIS ALIENATION WAS THE RESULT OF AN OVERLY COMPLICATED, MANMADE ECCLESIASTICAL BUREAUCRACY THAT HAD NO COUNTERPART IN NATURE!
I'M SORRY, SIR, HE'S VERY BUSY, SO IF YOU DON'T HAVE AN APPOINTMENT I'M AFRAID I CAN'T LET YOU IN...
GOD
Z
ONLY BY DOING AWAY WITH MANMADE CONSTRUCTS AND CLEAVING CLOSE TO OUR OWN INNATE NATURE COULD WE BE TRULY GOOD, INNOCENT, AND (THEREFORE) CLOSER TO GOD...
ZIP!
...A SO-CALLED "NOBLE SAVAGE!"
AH-AAAAAHHH!

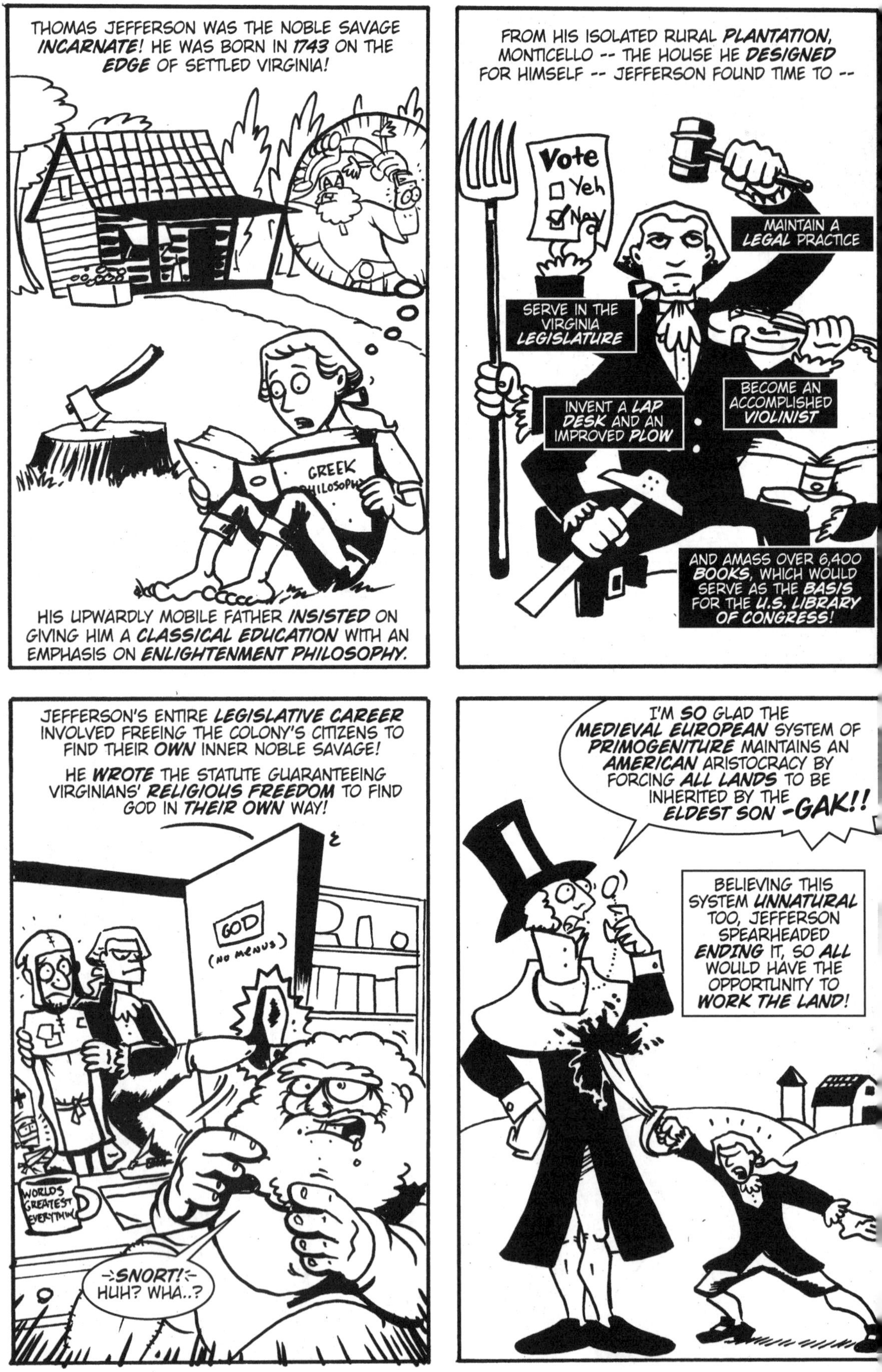
THOMAS JEFFERSON WAS THE NOBLE SAVAGE INCARNATE! HE WAS BORN IN 1743 ON THE EDGE OF SETTLED VIRGINIA!
GREEK PHILOSOPHY
HIS UPWARDLY MOBILE FATHER INSISTED ON GIVING HIM A CLASSICAL EDUCATION WITH AN EMPHASIS ON ENLIGHTENMENT PHILOSOPHY.
FROM HIS ISOLATED RURAL PLANTATION, MONTICELLO -- THE HOUSE HE DESIGNED FOR HIMSELF -- JEFFERSON FOUND TIME TO --
Vote
Yeh
Nay
MAINTAIN A LEGAL PRACTICE
SERVE IN THE VIRGINIA LEGISLATURE
INVENT A LAP DESK AND AN IMPROVED PLOW
BECOME AN ACCOMPLISHED VIOLINIST
AND AMASS OVER 6,400 BOOKS, WHICH WOULD SERVE AS THE BASIS FOR THE U.S. LIBRARY OF CONGRESS!
JEFFERSON'S ENTIRE LEGISLATIVE CAREER INVOLVED FREEING THE COLONY'S CITIZENS TO FIND THEIR OWN INNER NOBLE SAVAGE!
HE WROTE THE STATUTE GUARANTEEING VIRGINIANS' RELIGIOUS FREEDOM TO FIND GOD IN THEIR OWN WAY!
GOD
(NO MENUS)
WORLDS GREATEST EVERYTHING
-SNORT!- HUH? WHA..?
I'M SO GLAD THE MEDIEVAL EUROPEAN SYSTEM OF PRIMOGENITURE MAINTAINS AN AMERICAN ARISTOCRACY BY FORCING ALL LANDS TO BE INHERITED BY THE ELDEST SON -GAK!!
BELIEVING THIS SYSTEM UNNATURAL TOO, JEFFERSON SPEARHEADED ENDING IT, SO ALL WOULD HAVE THE OPPORTUNITY TO WORK THE LAND!

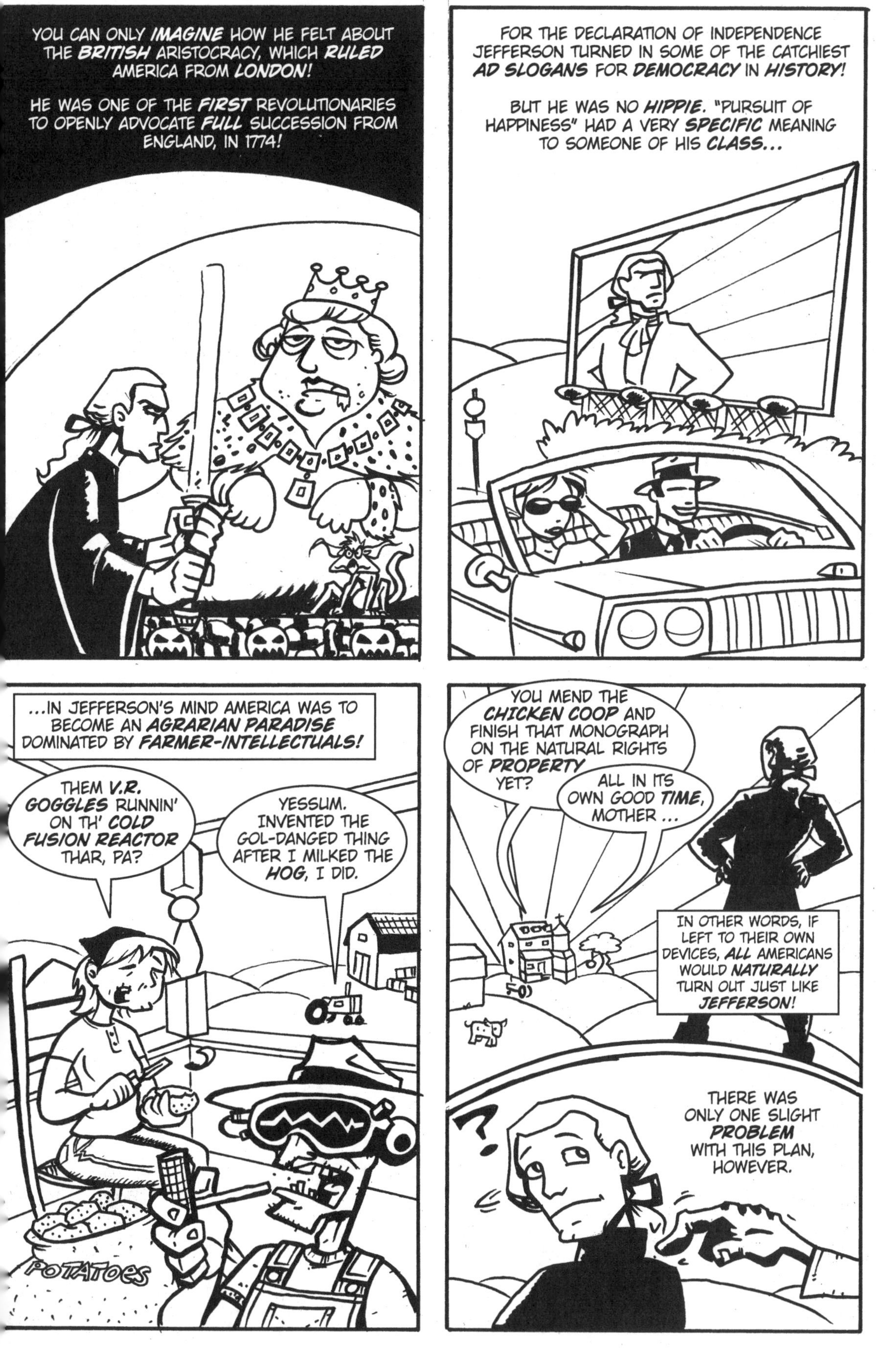
YOU CAN ONLY IMAGINE HOW HE FELT ABOUT THE BRITISH ARISTOCRACY, WHICH RULED AMERICA FROM LONDON!
HE WAS ONE OF THE FIRST REVOLUTIONARIES TO OPENLY ADVOCATE FULL SUCCESSION FROM ENGLAND, IN 1774!
FOR THE DECLARATION OF INDEPENDENCE JEFFERSON TURNED IN SOME OF THE CATCHIEST AD SLOGANS FOR DEMOCRACY IN HISTORY!
BUT HE WAS NO HIPPIE. "PURSUIT OF HAPPINESS" HAD A VERY SPECIFIC MEANING TO SOMEONE OF HIS CLASS...
...IN JEFFERSON'S MIND AMERICA WAS TO BECOME AN AGRARIAN PARADISE DOMINATED BY FARMER-INTELLECTUALS!
THEM V.R. GOGGLES RUNNIN' ON TH' COLD FUSION REACTOR THAR, PA?
YESSUM. INVENTED THE GOL-DANGED THING AFTER I MILKED THE HOG, I DID.
POTATOES
YOU MEND THE CHICKEN COOP AND FINISH THAT MONOGRAPH ON THE NATURAL RIGHTS OF PROPERTY YET?
ALL IN ITS OWN GOOD TIME, MOTHER ...
IN OTHER WORDS, IF LEFT TO THEIR OWN DEVICES, ALL AMERICANS WOULD NATURALLY TURN OUT JUST LIKE JEFFERSON!
THERE WAS ONLY ONE SLIGHT PROBLEM WITH THIS PLAN, HOWEVER.

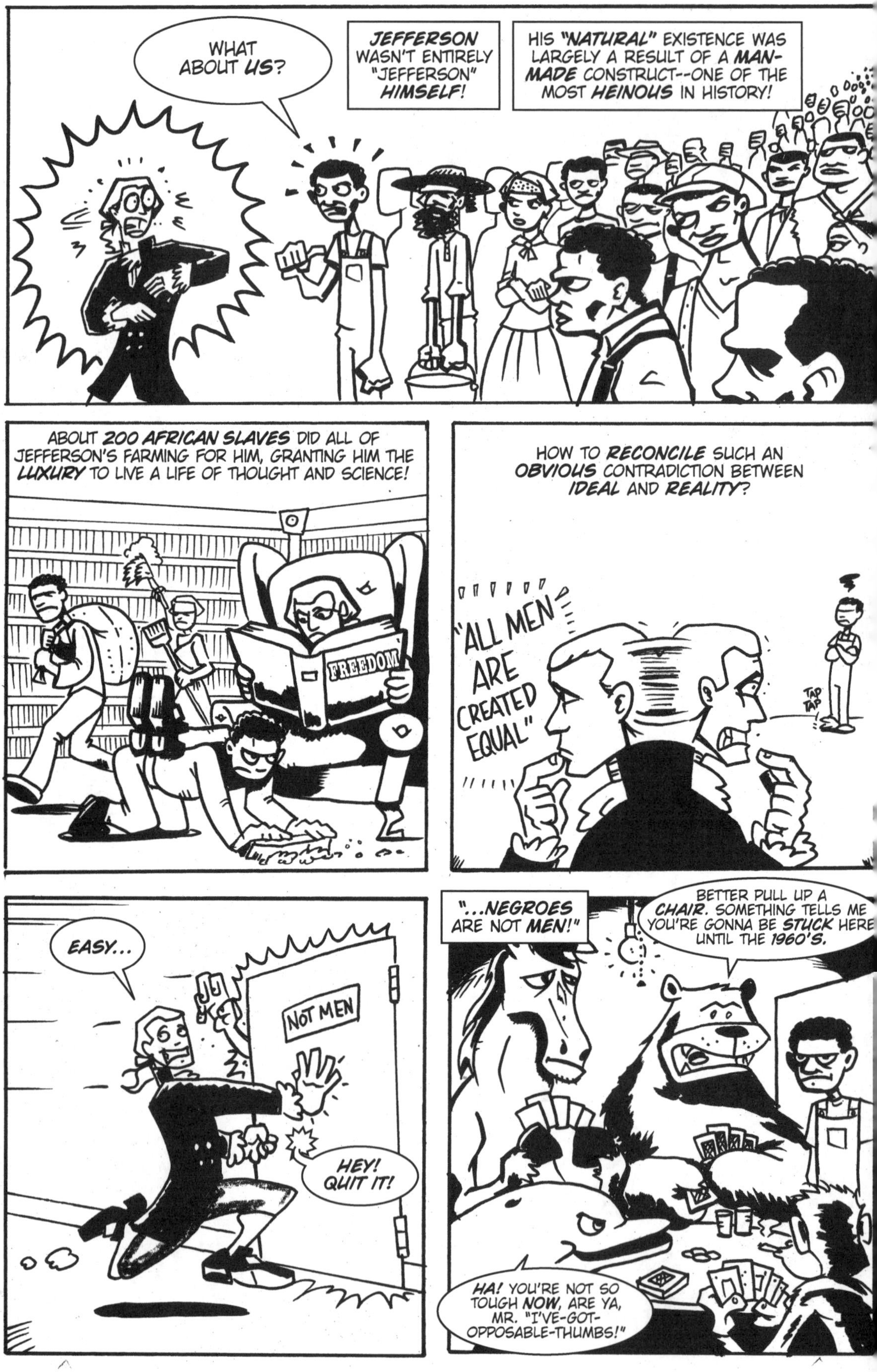
WHAT ABOUT US?
JEFFERSON WASN'T ENTIRELY "JEFFERSON" HIMSELF!
HIS "NATURAL" EXISTENCE WAS LARGELY A RESULT OF A MAN-MADE CONSTRUCT--ONE OF THE MOST HEINOUS IN HISTORY!
ABOUT 200 AFRICAN SLAVES DID ALL OF JEFFERSON'S FARMING FOR HIM, GRANTING HIM THE LUXURY TO LIVE A LIFE OF THOUGHT AND SCIENCE!
FREEDOM
HOW TO RECONCILE SUCH AN OBVIOUS CONTRADICTION BETWEEN IDEAL AND REALITY?
"ALL MEN ARE CREATED EQUAL"
TAP TAP
EASY...
NOT MEN
HEY! QUIT IT!
"...NEGROES ARE NOT MEN!"
BETTER PULL UP A CHAIR. SOMETHING TELLS ME YOU'RE GONNA BE STUCK HERE UNTIL THE 1960'S.
HA! YOU'RE NOT SO TOUGH NOW, ARE YA, MR. "I'VE-GOT-OPPOSABLE-THUMBS!"

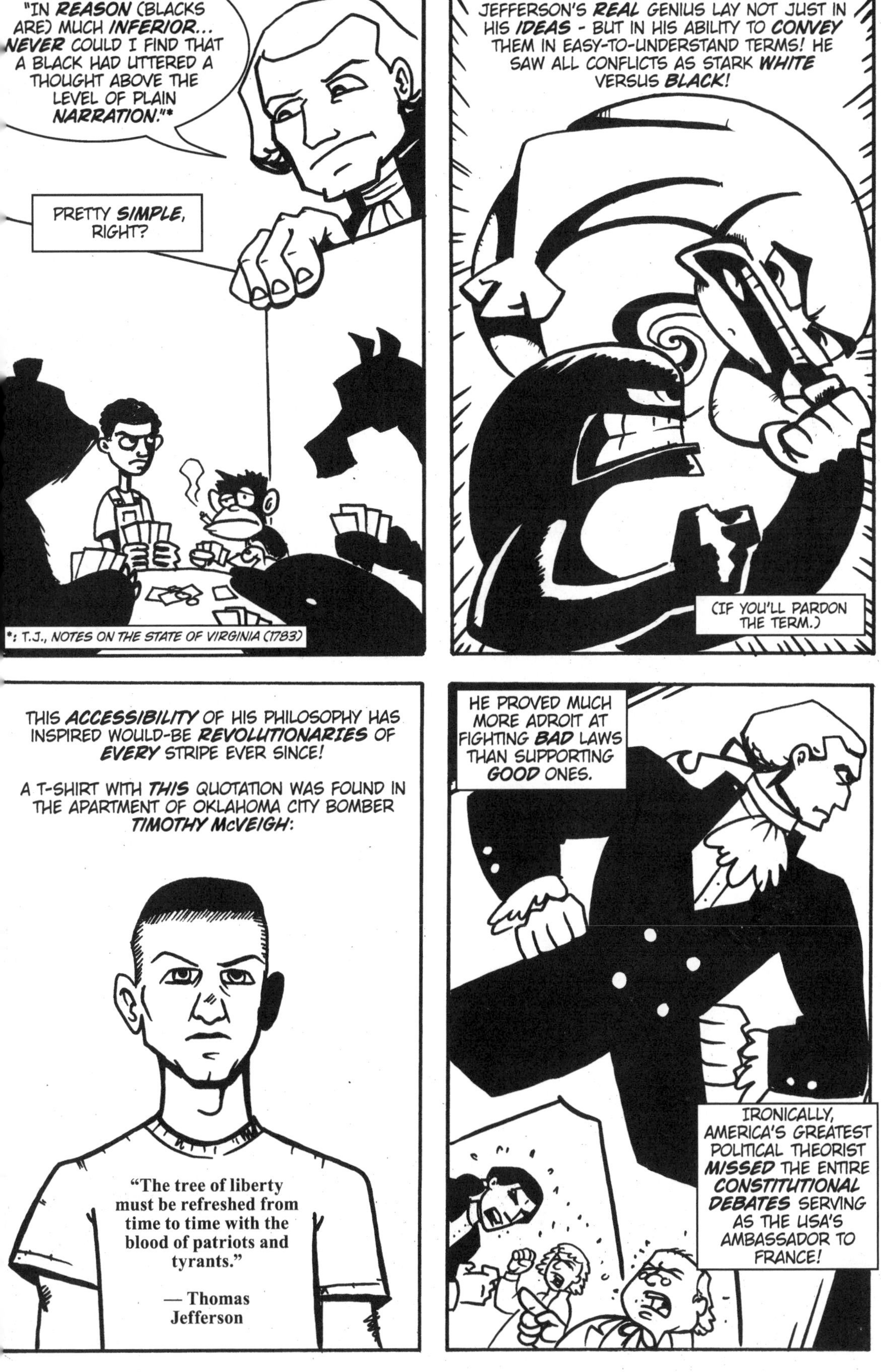
"IN REASON (BLACKS ARE) MUCH INFERIOR... NEVER COULD I FIND THAT A BLACK HAD UTTERED A THOUGHT ABOVE THE LEVEL OF PLAIN NARRATION."*
PRETTY SIMPLE, RIGHT?
*: T.J., NOTES ON THE STATE OF VIRGINIA (1783)
JEFFERSON'S REAL GENIUS LAY NOT JUST IN HIS IDEAS - BUT IN HIS ABILITY TO CONVEY THEM IN EASY-TO-UNDERSTAND TERMS! HE SAW ALL CONFLICTS AS STARK WHITE VERSUS BLACK!
(IF YOU'LL PARDON THE TERM.)
THIS ACCESSIBILITY OF HIS PHILOSOPHY HAS INSPIRED WOULD-BE REVOLUTIONARIES OF EVERY STRIPE EVER SINCE!
A T-SHIRT WITH THIS QUOTATION WAS FOUND IN THE APARTMENT OF OKLAHOMA CITY BOMBER TIMOTHY McVEIGH:
"The tree of liberty must be refreshed from time to time with the blood of patriots and tyrants."
— Thomas Jefferson
HE PROVED MUCH MORE ADROIT AT FIGHTING BAD LAWS THAN SUPPORTING GOOD ONES.
IRONICALLY, AMERICA'S GREATEST POLITICAL THEORIST MISSED THE ENTIRE CONSTITUTIONAL DEBATES SERVING AS THE USA'S AMBASSADOR TO FRANCE!

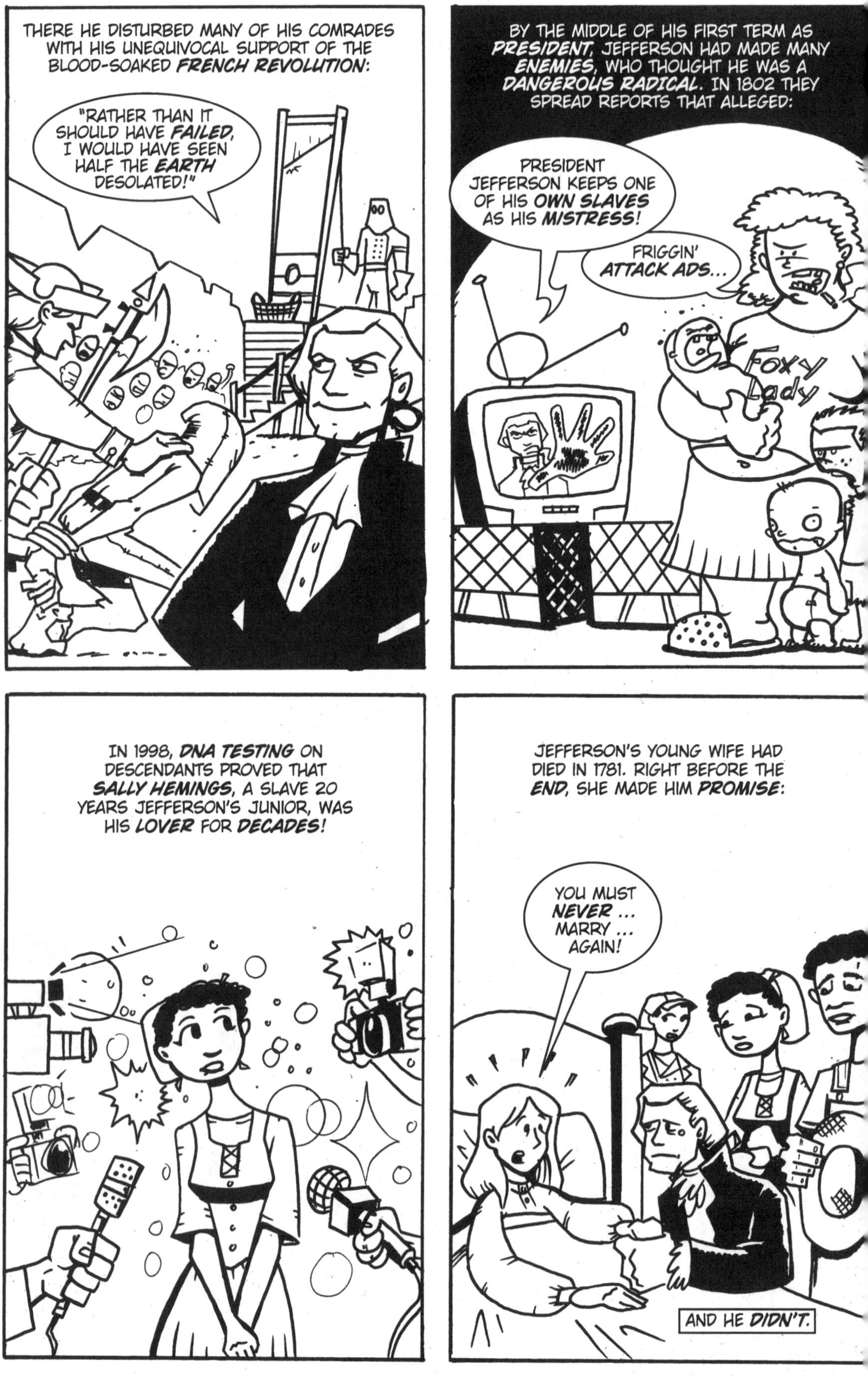
THERE HE DISTURBED MANY OF HIS COMRADES WITH HIS UNEQUIVOCAL SUPPORT OF THE BLOOD-SOAKED FRENCH REVOLUTION:
"RATHER THAN IT SHOULD HAVE FAILED, I WOULD HAVE SEEN HALF THE EARTH DESOLATED!"
BY THE MIDDLE OF HIS FIRST TERM AS PRESIDENT, JEFFERSON HAD MADE MANY ENEMIES, WHO THOUGHT HE WAS A DANGEROUS RADICAL. IN 1802 THEY SPREAD REPORTS THAT ALLEGED:
PRESIDENT JEFFERSON KEEPS ONE OF HIS OWN SLAVES AS HIS MISTRESS!
FRIGGIN' ATTACK ADS...
Foxy Lady
IN 1998, DNA TESTING ON DESCENDANTS PROVED THAT SALLY HEMINGS, A SLAVE 20 YEARS JEFFERSON'S JUNIOR, WAS HIS LOVER FOR DECADES!
JEFFERSON'S YOUNG WIFE HAD DIED IN 1781. RIGHT BEFORE THE END, SHE MADE HIM PROMISE:
YOU MUST NEVER ... MARRY ... AGAIN!
AND HE DIDN'T.

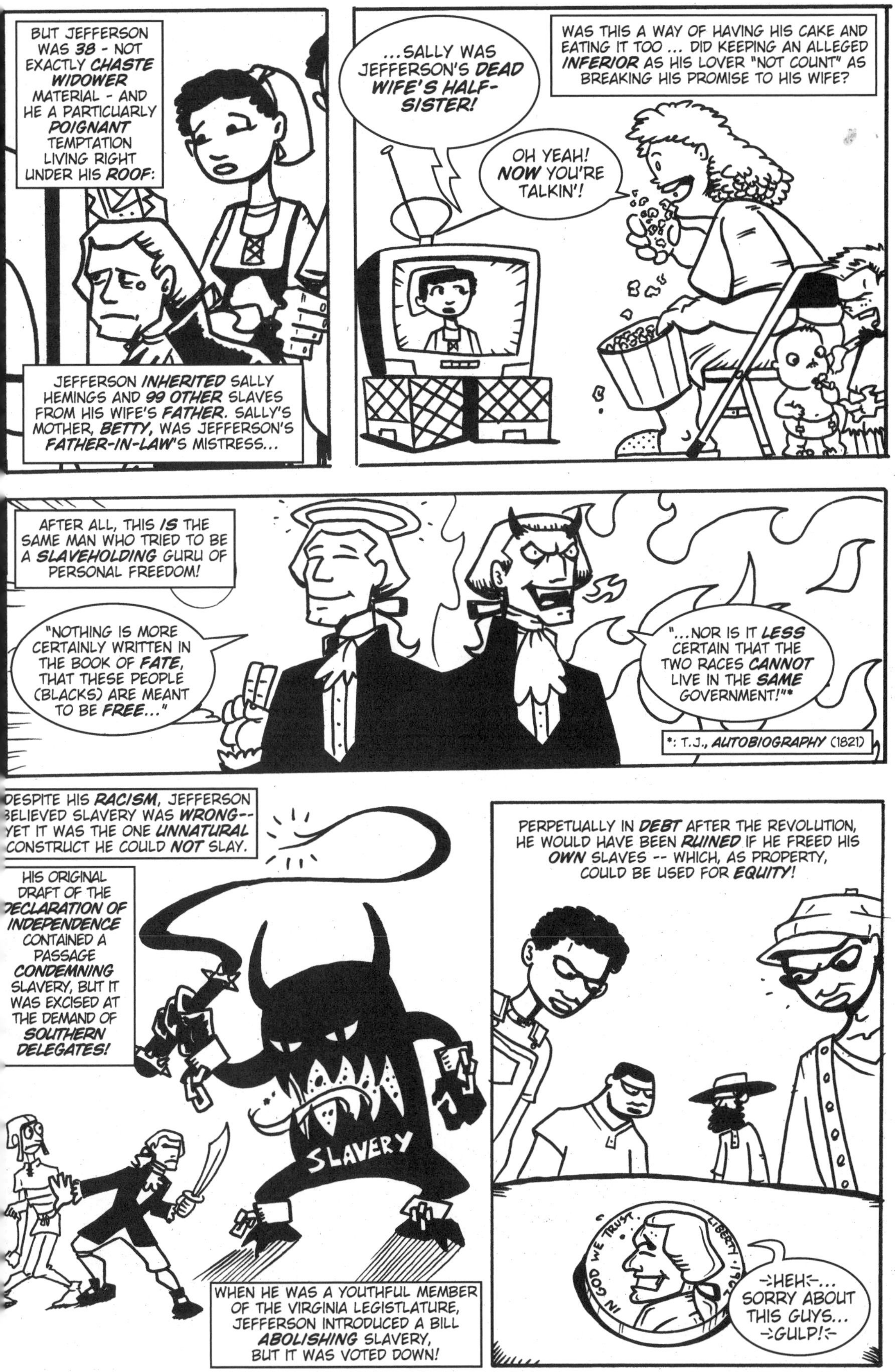

BUT JEFFERSON WAS 38 - NOT EXACTLY CHASTE WIDOWER MATERIAL - AND HE A PARTICUARLY POIGNANT TEMPTATION LIVING RIGHT UNDER HIS ROOF:
JEFFERSON INHERITED SALLY HEMINGS AND 99 OTHER SLAVES FROM HIS WIFE'S FATHER. SALLY'S MOTHER, BETTY, WAS JEFFERSON'S FATHER-IN-LAW'S MISTRESS...
...SALLY WAS JEFFERSON'S DEAD WIFE'S HALF-SISTER!
WAS THIS A WAY OF HAVING HIS CAKE AND EATING IT TOO ... DID KEEPING AN ALLEGED INFERIOR AS HIS LOVER "NOT COUNT" AS BREAKING HIS PROMISE TO HIS WIFE?
OH YEAH! NOW YOU'RE TALKIN'!
AFTER ALL, THIS IS THE SAME MAN WHO TRIED TO BE A SLAVEHOLDING GURU OF PERSONAL FREEDOM!
"NOTHING IS MORE CERTAINLY WRITTEN IN THE BOOK OF FATE, THAT THESE PEOPLE (BLACKS) ARE MEANT TO BE FREE..."
"...NOR IS IT LESS CERTAIN THAT THE TWO RACES CANNOT LIVE IN THE SAME GOVERNMENT!"*
*: T.J., AUTOBIOGRAPHY (1821)
DESPITE HIS RACISM, JEFFERSON BELIEVED SLAVERY WAS WRONG--YET IT WAS THE ONE UNNATURAL CONSTRUCT HE COULD NOT SLAY.
HIS ORIGINAL DRAFT OF THE DECLARATION OF INDEPENDENCE CONTAINED A PASSAGE CONDEMNING SLAVERY, BUT IT WAS EXCISED AT THE DEMAND OF SOUTHERN DELEGATES!
SLAVERY
WHEN HE WAS A YOUTHFUL MEMBER OF THE VIRGINIA LEGISTLATURE, JEFFERSON INTRODUCED A BILL ABOLISHING SLAVERY, BUT IT WAS VOTED DOWN!
PERPETUALLY IN DEBT AFTER THE REVOLUTION, HE WOULD HAVE BEEN RUINED IF HE FREED HIS OWN SLAVES -- WHICH, AS PROPERTY, COULD BE USED FOR EQUITY!
IN GOD WE TRUST
LIBERTY
-HEH-... SORRY ABOUT THIS GUYS... -GULP!-

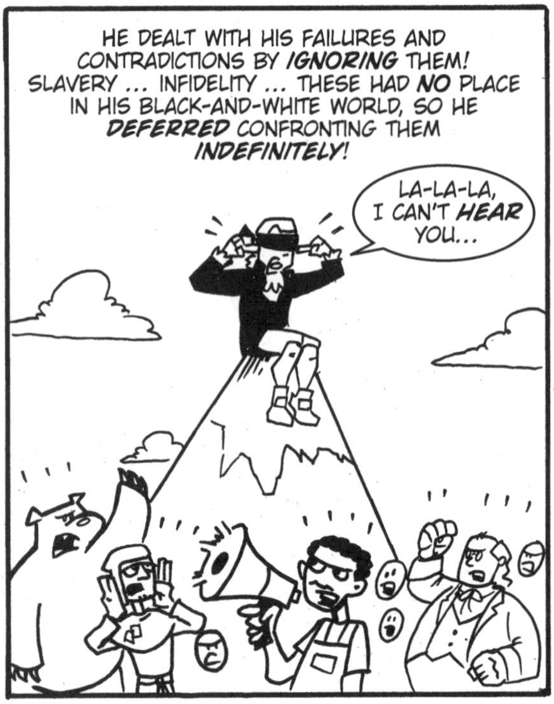
HE DEALT WITH HIS FAILURES AND CONTRADICTIONS BY *IGNORING* THEM! SLAVERY ... INFIDELITY ... THESE HAD *NO* PLACE IN HIS BLACK-AND-WHITE WORLD, SO HE *DEFERRED* CONFRONTING THEM *INDEFINITELY*!
LA-LA-LA, I CAN'T *HEAR* YOU...

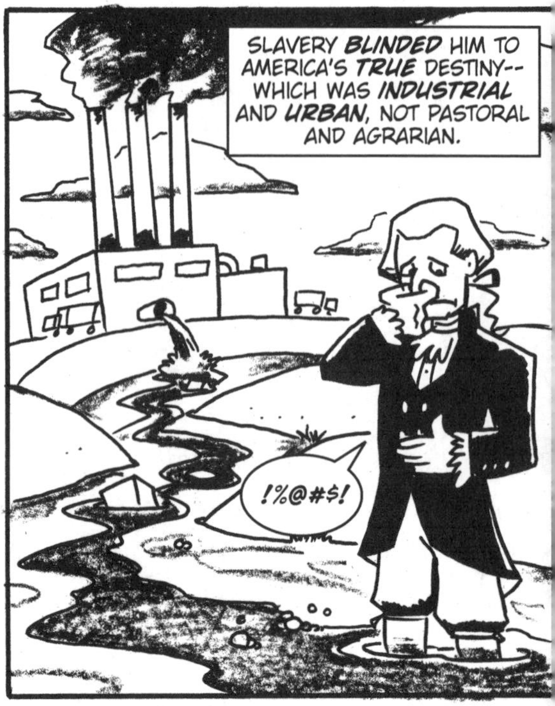
SLAVERY *BLINDED* HIM TO AMERICA'S *TRUE* DESTINY--WHICH WAS *INDUSTRIAL* AND *URBAN*, NOT PASTORAL AND AGRARIAN.
!%@#$!

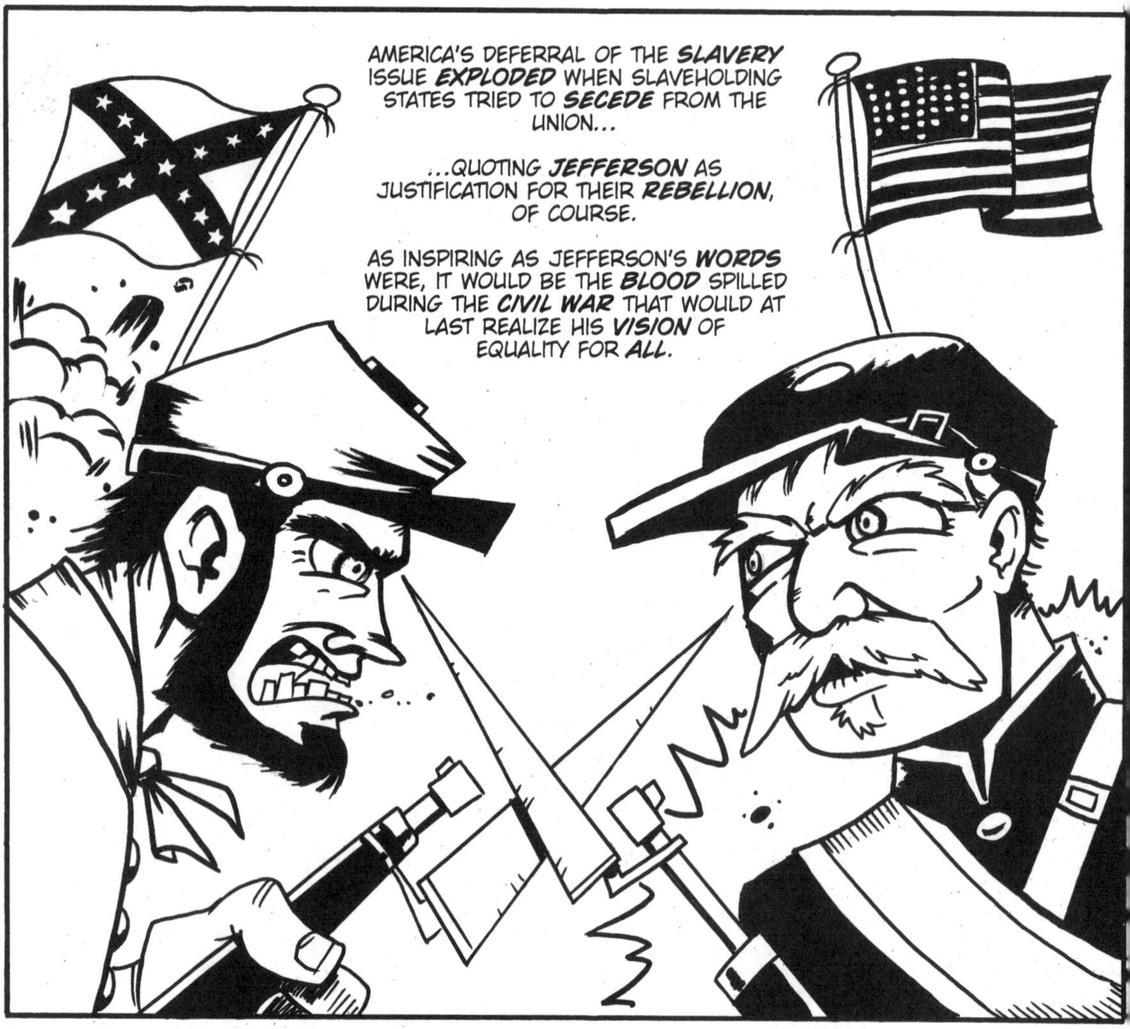
AMERICA'S DEFERRAL OF THE *SLAVERY* ISSUE *EXPLODED* WHEN SLAVEHOLDING STATES TRIED TO *SECEDE* FROM THE UNION...
...QUOTING *JEFFERSON* AS JUSTIFICATION FOR THEIR *REBELLION*, OF COURSE.
AS INSPIRING AS JEFFERSON'S *WORDS* WERE, IT WOULD BE THE *BLOOD* SPILLED DURING THE *CIVIL WAR* THAT WOULD AT LAST REALIZE HIS *VISION* OF EQUALITY FOR *ALL*.

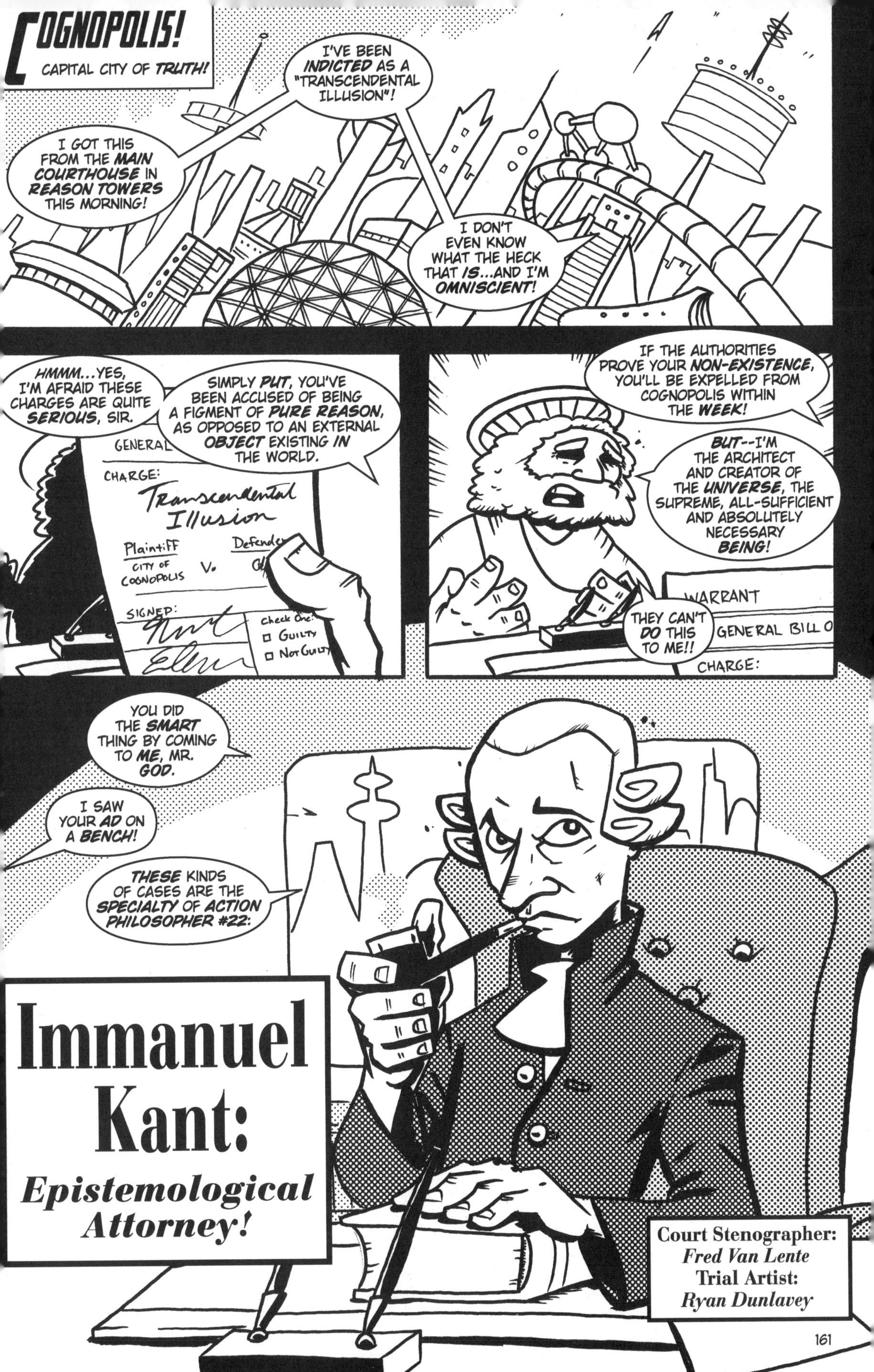
COGNOPOLIS!
CAPITAL CITY OF TRUTH!
I GOT THIS FROM THE MAIN COURTHOUSE IN REASON TOWERS THIS MORNING!
I'VE BEEN INDICTED AS A "TRANSCENDENTAL ILLUSION"!
I DON'T EVEN KNOW WHAT THE HECK THAT IS...AND I'M OMNISCIENT!
HMMM...YES, I'M AFRAID THESE CHARGES ARE QUITE SERIOUS, SIR.
SIMPLY PUT, YOU'VE BEEN ACCUSED OF BEING A FIGMENT OF PURE REASON, AS OPPOSED TO AN EXTERNAL OBJECT EXISTING IN THE WORLD.
GENERAL
CHARGE:
Transcendental Illusion
Plaintiff
Defende
CITY OF COGNOPOLIS
V.
SIGNED:
Check One:
GUILTY
NOT GUILTY
IF THE AUTHORITIES PROVE YOUR NON-EXISTENCE, YOU'LL BE EXPELLED FROM COGNOPOLIS WITHIN THE WEEK!
BUT--I'M THE ARCHITECT AND CREATOR OF THE UNIVERSE, THE SUPREME, ALL-SUFFICIENT AND ABSOLUTELY NECESSARY BEING!
THEY CAN'T DO THIS TO ME!!
WARRANT
GENERAL BILL O
CHARGE:
YOU DID THE SMART THING BY COMING TO ME, MR. GOD.
I SAW YOUR AD ON A BENCH!
THESE KINDS OF CASES ARE THE SPECIALTY OF ACTION PHILOSOPHER #22:
Immanuel Kant:
Epistemological Attorney!
Court Stenographer:
Fred Van Lente
Trial Artist:
Ryan Dunlavey

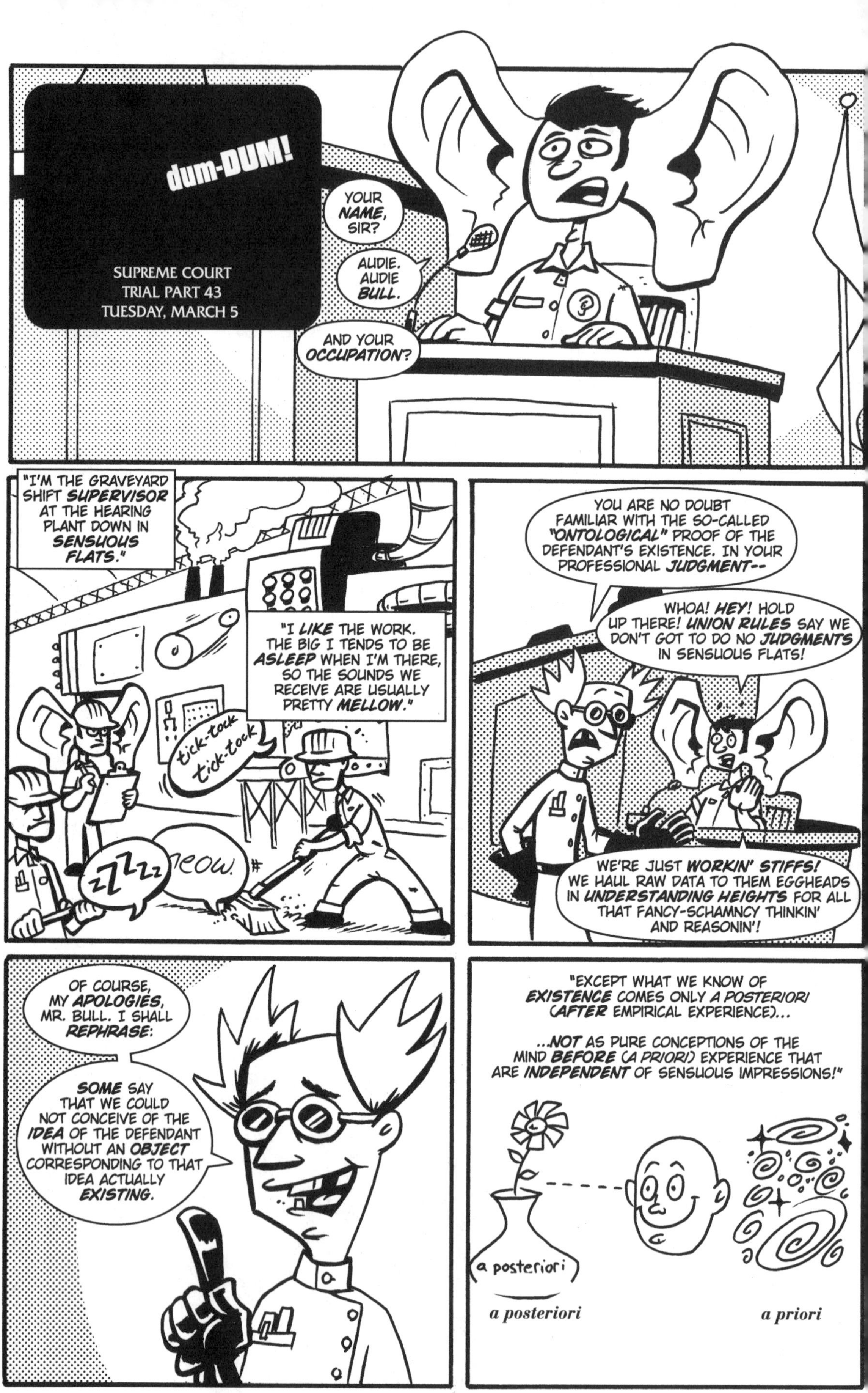
dum-DUM!
SUPREME COURT
TRIAL PART 43
TUESDAY, MARCH 5
YOUR NAME, SIR?
AUDIE. AUDIE BULL.
AND YOUR OCCUPATION?
"I'M THE GRAVEYARD SHIFT SUPERVISOR AT THE HEARING PLANT DOWN IN SENSUOUS FLATS."
"I LIKE THE WORK. THE BIG I TENDS TO BE ASLEEP WHEN I'M THERE, SO THE SOUNDS WE RECEIVE ARE USUALLY PRETTY MELLOW."
tick-tock tick-tock
zZZzz
meow
YOU ARE NO DOUBT FAMILIAR WITH THE SO-CALLED "ONTOLOGICAL" PROOF OF THE DEFENDANT'S EXISTENCE. IN YOUR PROFESSIONAL JUDGMENT--
WHOA! HEY! HOLD UP THERE! UNION RULES SAY WE DON'T GOT TO DO NO JUDGMENTS IN SENSUOUS FLATS!
WE'RE JUST WORKIN' STIFFS! WE HAUL RAW DATA TO THEM EGGHEADS IN UNDERSTANDING HEIGHTS FOR ALL THAT FANCY-SCHAMNCY THINKIN' AND REASONIN'!
OF COURSE, MY APOLOGIES, MR. BULL. I SHALL REPHRASE:
SOME SAY THAT WE COULD NOT CONCEIVE OF THE IDEA OF THE DEFENDANT WITHOUT AN OBJECT CORRESPONDING TO THAT IDEA ACTUALLY EXISTING.
"EXCEPT WHAT WE KNOW OF EXISTENCE COMES ONLY A POSTERIORI (AFTER EMPIRICAL EXPERIENCE)...
...NOT AS PURE CONCEPTIONS OF THE MIND BEFORE (A PRIORI) EXPERIENCE THAT ARE INDEPENDENT OF SENSUOUS IMPRESSIONS!"
a posteriori
a posteriori
a priori

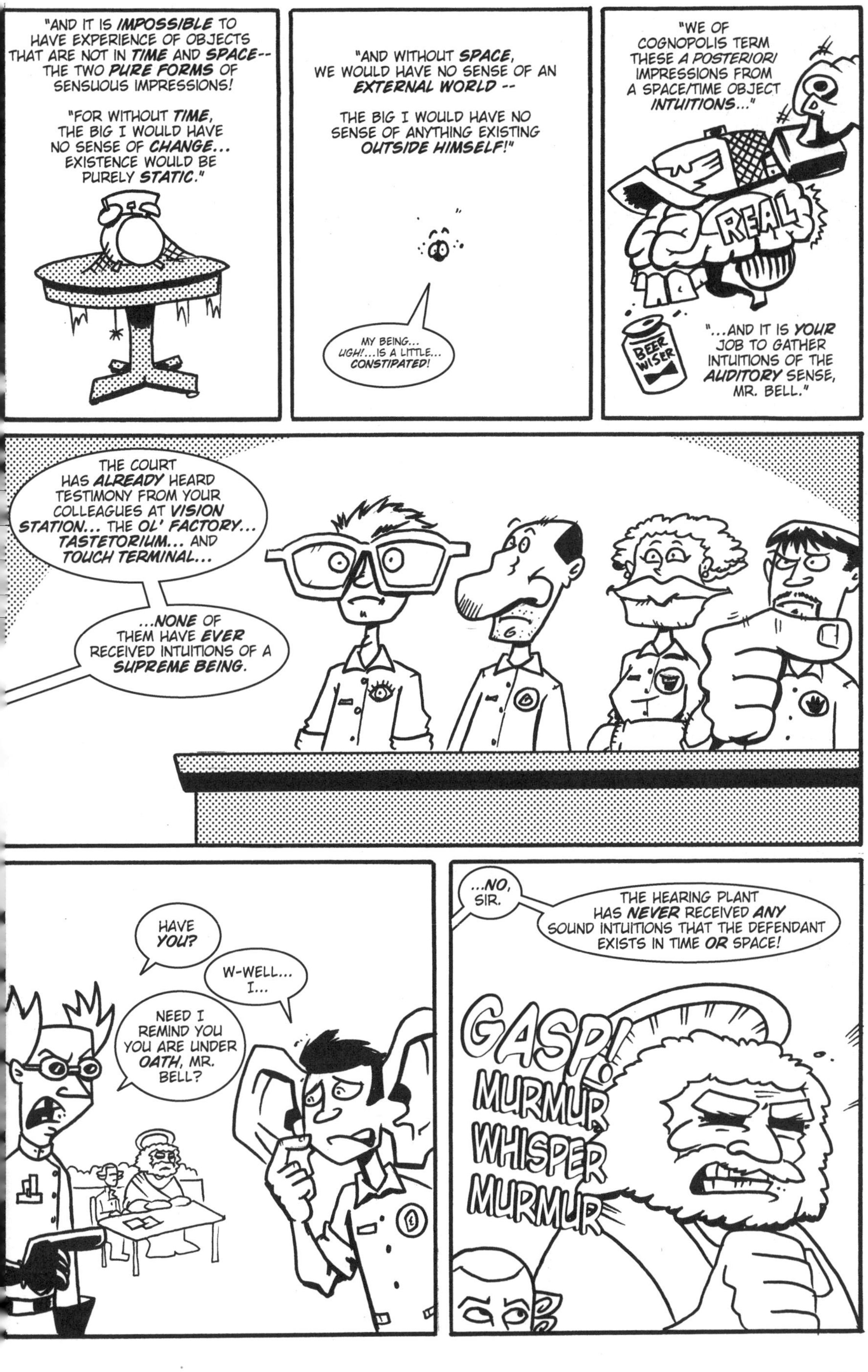
"AND IT IS IMPOSSIBLE TO HAVE EXPERIENCE OF OBJECTS THAT ARE NOT IN TIME AND SPACE-- THE TWO PURE FORMS OF SENSUOUS IMPRESSIONS!
"FOR WITHOUT TIME, THE BIG I WOULD HAVE NO SENSE OF CHANGE... EXISTENCE WOULD BE PURELY STATIC."
"AND WITHOUT SPACE, WE WOULD HAVE NO SENSE OF AN EXTERNAL WORLD --
THE BIG I WOULD HAVE NO SENSE OF ANYTHING EXISTING OUTSIDE HIMSELF!"
MY BEING... UGH!... IS A LITTLE... CONSTIPATED!
"WE OF COGNOPOLIS TERM THESE A POSTERIORI IMPRESSIONS FROM A SPACE/TIME OBJECT INTUITIONS..."
REAL
BEER WISER
"...AND IT IS YOUR JOB TO GATHER INTUITIONS OF THE AUDITORY SENSE, MR. BELL."
THE COURT HAS ALREADY HEARD TESTIMONY FROM YOUR COLLEAGUES AT VISION STATION... THE OL' FACTORY... TASTETORIUM... AND TOUCH TERMINAL...
...NONE OF THEM HAVE EVER RECEIVED INTUITIONS OF A SUPREME BEING.
HAVE YOU?
W-WELL... I...
NEED I REMIND YOU YOU ARE UNDER OATH, MR. BELL?
...NO, SIR.
THE HEARING PLANT HAS NEVER RECEIVED ANY SOUND INTUITIONS THAT THE DEFENDANT EXISTS IN TIME OR SPACE!
GASP!
MURMUR
WHISPER
MURMUR

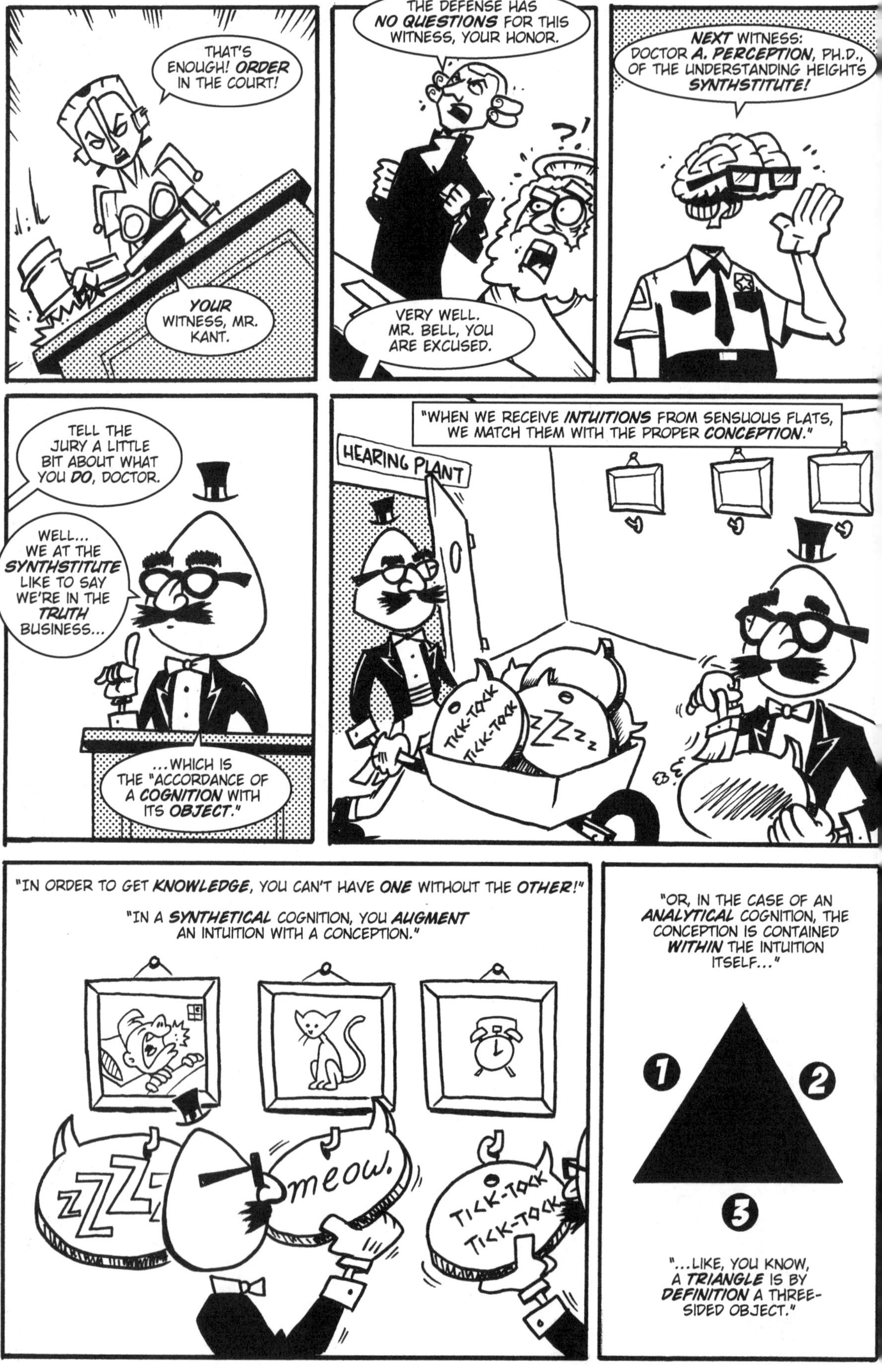
THAT'S ENOUGH! ORDER IN THE COURT!
YOUR WITNESS, MR. KANT.
THE DEFENSE HAS NO QUESTIONS FOR THIS WITNESS, YOUR HONOR.
?!
VERY WELL. MR. BELL, YOU ARE EXCUSED.
NEXT WITNESS: DOCTOR A. PERCEPTION, PH.D., OF THE UNDERSTANDING HEIGHTS SYNTHSTITUTE!
TELL THE JURY A LITTLE BIT ABOUT WHAT YOU DO, DOCTOR.
WELL... WE AT THE SYNTHSTITUTE LIKE TO SAY WE'RE IN THE TRUTH BUSINESS...
...WHICH IS THE "ACCORDANCE OF A COGNITION WITH ITS OBJECT."
"WHEN WE RECEIVE INTUITIONS FROM SENSUOUS FLATS, WE MATCH THEM WITH THE PROPER CONCEPTION."
HEARING PLANT
TICK-TOCK TICK-TOCK
ZZZzz
"IN ORDER TO GET KNOWLEDGE, YOU CAN'T HAVE ONE WITHOUT THE OTHER!"
"IN A SYNTHETICAL COGNITION, YOU AUGMENT AN INTUITION WITH A CONCEPTION."
ZZZ
meow.
TICK-TOCK TICK-TOCK
"OR, IN THE CASE OF AN ANALYTICAL COGNITION, THE CONCEPTION IS CONTAINED WITHIN THE INTUITION ITSELF..."
1
2
3
"...LIKE, YOU KNOW, A TRIANGLE IS BY DEFINITION A THREE-SIDED OBJECT."

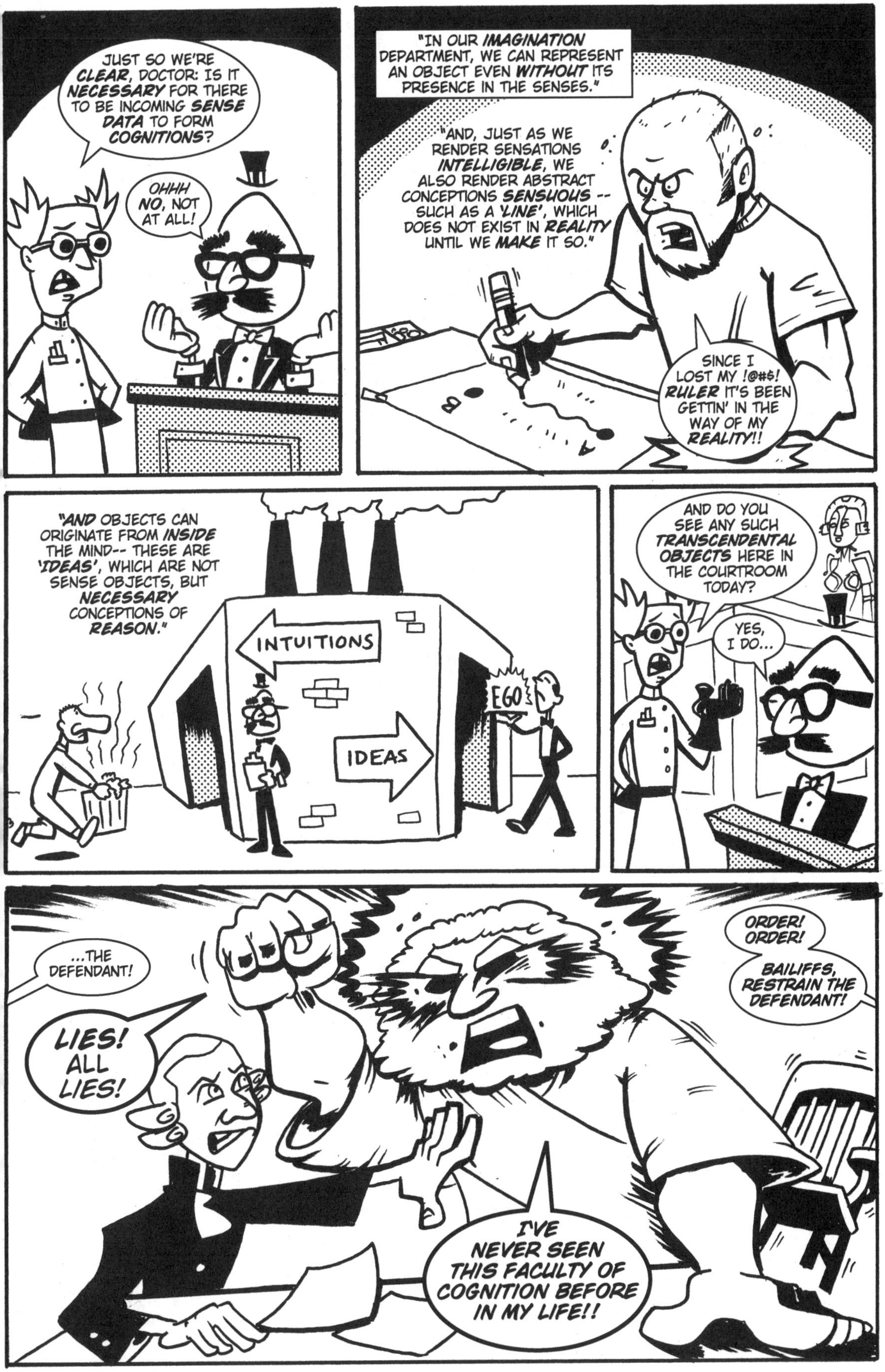
JUST SO WE'RE CLEAR, DOCTOR: IS IT NECESSARY FOR THERE TO BE INCOMING SENSE DATA TO FORM COGNITIONS?
OHHH NO, NOT AT ALL!
"IN OUR IMAGINATION DEPARTMENT, WE CAN REPRESENT AN OBJECT EVEN WITHOUT ITS PRESENCE IN THE SENSES."
"AND, JUST AS WE RENDER SENSATIONS INTELLIGIBLE, WE ALSO RENDER ABSTRACT CONCEPTIONS SENSUOUS -- SUCH AS A 'LINE', WHICH DOES NOT EXIST IN REALITY UNTIL WE MAKE IT SO."
SINCE I LOST MY !@#$! RULER IT'S BEEN GETTIN' IN THE WAY OF MY REALITY!!
"AND OBJECTS CAN ORIGINATE FROM INSIDE THE MIND-- THESE ARE 'IDEAS', WHICH ARE NOT SENSE OBJECTS, BUT NECESSARY CONCEPTIONS OF REASON."
INTUITIONS
EGO
IDEAS
AND DO YOU SEE ANY SUCH TRANSCENDENTAL OBJECTS HERE IN THE COURTROOM TODAY?
YES, I DO...
...THE DEFENDANT!
LIES! ALL LIES!
ORDER! ORDER!
BAILIFFS, RESTRAIN THE DEFENDANT!
I'VE NEVER SEEN THIS FACULTY OF COGNITION BEFORE IN MY LIFE!!

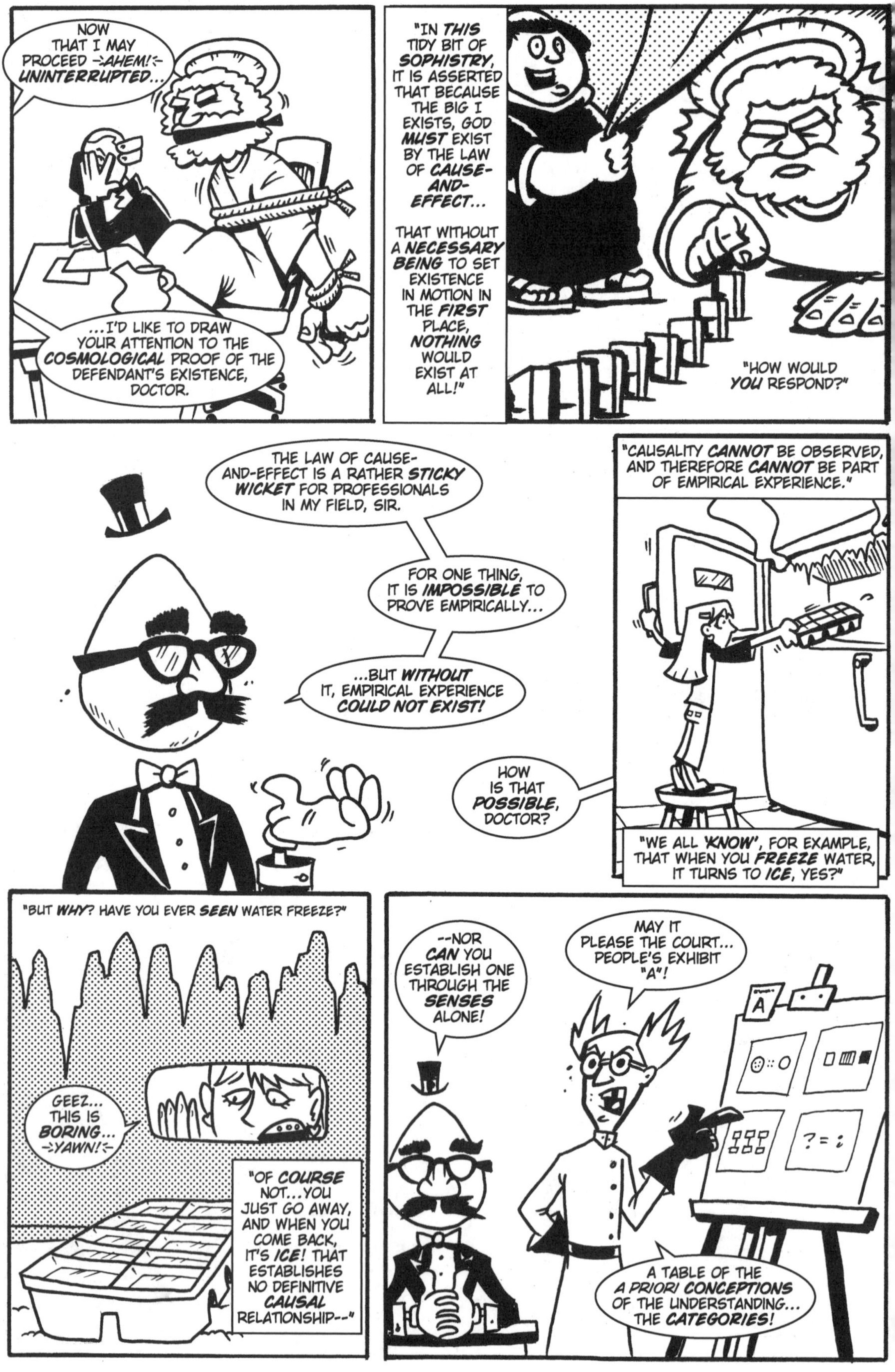
NOW THAT I MAY PROCEED -AHEM!- UNINTERRUPTED...
...I'D LIKE TO DRAW YOUR ATTENTION TO THE COSMOLOGICAL PROOF OF THE DEFENDANT'S EXISTENCE, DOCTOR.
"IN THIS TIDY BIT OF SOPHISTRY, IT IS ASSERTED THAT BECAUSE THE BIG I EXISTS, GOD MUST EXIST BY THE LAW OF CAUSE-AND-EFFECT...
THAT WITHOUT A NECESSARY BEING TO SET EXISTENCE IN MOTION IN THE FIRST PLACE, NOTHING WOULD EXIST AT ALL!"
"HOW WOULD YOU RESPOND?"
THE LAW OF CAUSE-AND-EFFECT IS A RATHER STICKY WICKET FOR PROFESSIONALS IN MY FIELD, SIR.
FOR ONE THING, IT IS IMPOSSIBLE TO PROVE EMPIRICALLY...
...BUT WITHOUT IT, EMPIRICAL EXPERIENCE COULD NOT EXIST!
HOW IS THAT POSSIBLE, DOCTOR?
"CAUSALITY CANNOT BE OBSERVED, AND THEREFORE CANNOT BE PART OF EMPIRICAL EXPERIENCE."
"WE ALL 'KNOW', FOR EXAMPLE, THAT WHEN YOU FREEZE WATER, IT TURNS TO ICE, YES?"
"BUT WHY? HAVE YOU EVER SEEN WATER FREEZE?"
GEEZ... THIS IS BORING... -YAWN!-
"OF COURSE NOT...YOU JUST GO AWAY, AND WHEN YOU COME BACK, IT'S ICE! THAT ESTABLISHES NO DEFINITIVE CAUSAL RELATIONSHIP--"
--NOR CAN YOU ESTABLISH ONE THROUGH THE SENSES ALONE!
MAY IT PLEASE THE COURT... PEOPLE'S EXHIBIT "A"!
A
A TABLE OF THE A PRIORI CONCEPTIONS OF THE UNDERSTANDING... THE CATEGORIES!

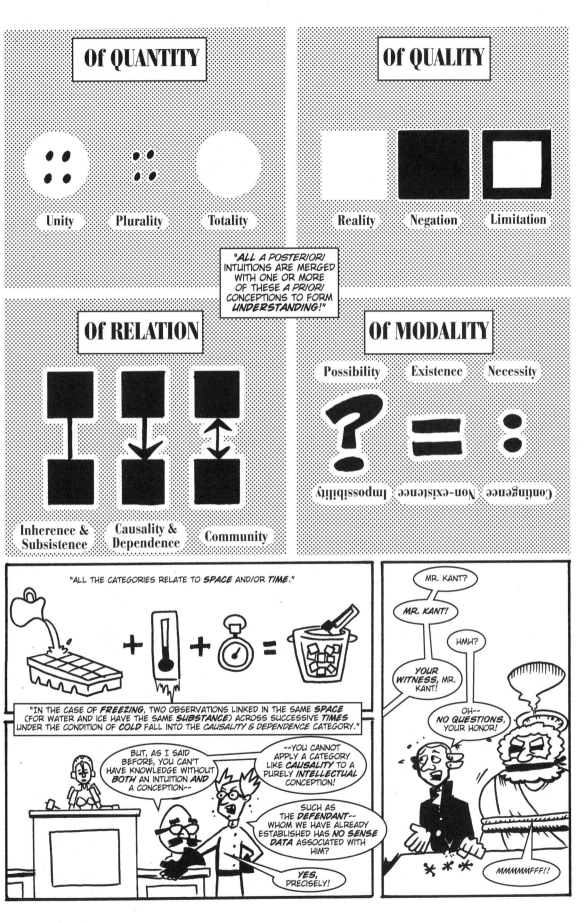

Of QUANTITY

Unity   Plurality   Totality

Of QUALITY

Reality   Negation   Limitation

"*ALL A POSTERIORI* INTUITIONS ARE MERGED WITH ONE OR MORE OF THESE *A PRIORI* CONCEPTIONS TO FORM *UNDERSTANDING!*"

Of RELATION

Inherence & Subsistence   Causality & Dependence   Community

Of MODALITY

Possibility   Existence   Necessity

Contingence   Non-existence   Impossibility

"ALL THE CATEGORIES RELATE TO *SPACE* AND/OR *TIME*."

"IN THE CASE OF *FREEZING*, TWO OBSERVATIONS LINKED IN THE SAME *SPACE* (FOR WATER AND ICE HAVE THE SAME *SUBSTANCE*) ACROSS SUCCESSIVE *TIMES* UNDER THE CONDITION OF *COLD* FALL INTO THE *CAUSALITY & DEPENDENCE* CATEGORY."

BUT, AS I SAID BEFORE, YOU CAN'T HAVE KNOWLEDGE WITHOUT *BOTH* AN INTUITION *AND* A CONCEPTION--

--YOU CANNOT APPLY A CATEGORY LIKE *CAUSALITY* TO A PURELY *INTELLECTUAL* CONCEPTION!

SUCH AS THE *DEFENDANT*-- WHOM WE HAVE ALREADY ESTABLISHED HAS *NO SENSE DATA* ASSOCIATED WITH HIM?

YES, PRECISELY!

MR. KANT?

MR. KANT!

HMH?

YOUR WITNESS, MR. KANT!

OH-- *NO QUESTIONS*, YOUR HONOR!

* * *

MMMMMFFF!!

167

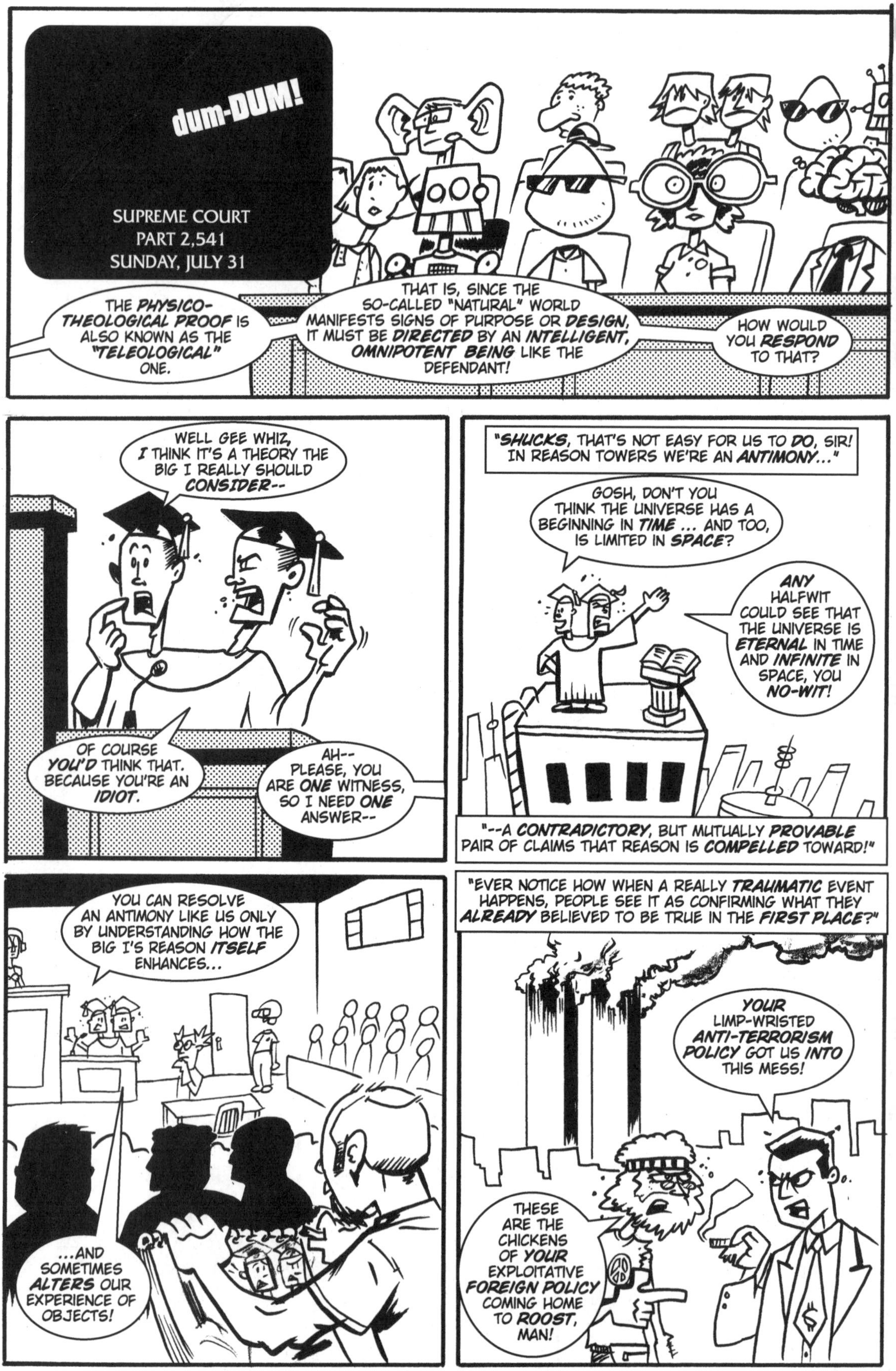

dum-DUM!
SUPREME COURT
PART 2,541
SUNDAY, JULY 31
THE PHYSICO-THEOLOGICAL PROOF IS ALSO KNOWN AS THE "TELEOLOGICAL" ONE.
THAT IS, SINCE THE SO-CALLED "NATURAL" WORLD MANIFESTS SIGNS OF PURPOSE OR DESIGN, IT MUST BE DIRECTED BY AN INTELLIGENT, OMNIPOTENT BEING LIKE THE DEFENDANT!
HOW WOULD YOU RESPOND TO THAT?
WELL GEE WHIZ, I THINK IT'S A THEORY THE BIG I REALLY SHOULD CONSIDER--
OF COURSE YOU'D THINK THAT. BECAUSE YOU'RE AN IDIOT.
AH-- PLEASE, YOU ARE ONE WITNESS, SO I NEED ONE ANSWER--
"SHUCKS, THAT'S NOT EASY FOR US TO DO, SIR! IN REASON TOWERS WE'RE AN ANTIMONY..."
GOSH, DON'T YOU THINK THE UNIVERSE HAS A BEGINNING IN TIME ... AND TOO, IS LIMITED IN SPACE?
ANY HALFWIT COULD SEE THAT THE UNIVERSE IS ETERNAL IN TIME AND INFINITE IN SPACE, YOU NO-WIT!
"--A CONTRADICTORY, BUT MUTUALLY PROVABLE PAIR OF CLAIMS THAT REASON IS COMPELLED TOWARD!"
YOU CAN RESOLVE AN ANTIMONY LIKE US ONLY BY UNDERSTANDING HOW THE BIG I'S REASON ITSELF ENHANCES...
...AND SOMETIMES ALTERS OUR EXPERIENCE OF OBJECTS!
"EVER NOTICE HOW WHEN A REALLY TRAUMATIC EVENT HAPPENS, PEOPLE SEE IT AS CONFIRMING WHAT THEY ALREADY BELIEVED TO BE TRUE IN THE FIRST PLACE?"
YOUR LIMP-WRISTED ANTI-TERRORISM POLICY GOT US INTO THIS MESS!
THESE ARE THE CHICKENS OF YOUR EXPLOITATIVE FOREIGN POLICY COMING HOME TO ROOST, MAN!

THAT'S BECAUSE, UNLESS WE'RE VIGILANT TO STOP IT, OUR REASON CAN IMPOSE ***ARTIFICIAL PATTERNS*** ON INCOMING DATA IN A MISGUIDED ATTEMPT TO RENDER THE ***EXTERNAL*** WORLD AS ORDERLY AS OUR ***INTERNAL*** ONE!

TAKE ***CONSPIRACY THEORY***, FOR INSTANCE. THE POPULAR ON-LINE DOCUMENTARY *LOOSE CHANGE* (*LOOSECHANGE911.COM*) CONTENDS THAT THESE ***SINISTER-SEEMING*** FACTS FORM A ***DAMNING PATTERN***:

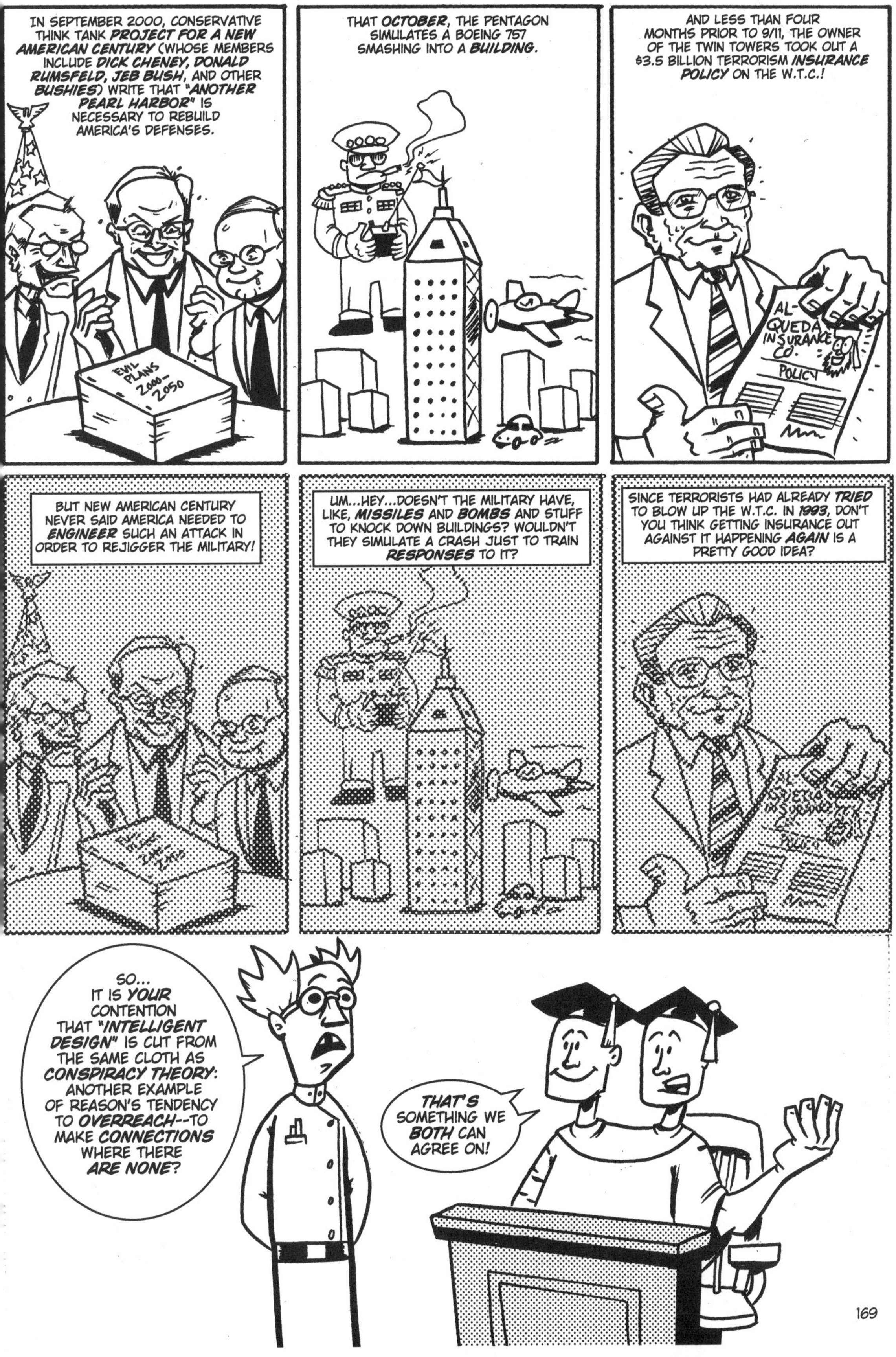
IN SEPTEMBER 2000, CONSERVATIVE THINK TANK PROJECT FOR A NEW AMERICAN CENTURY (WHOSE MEMBERS INCLUDE DICK CHENEY, DONALD RUMSFELD, JEB BUSH, AND OTHER BUSHIES) WRITE THAT "ANOTHER PEARL HARBOR" IS NECESSARY TO REBUILD AMERICA'S DEFENSES.
EVIL PLANS 2000–2050
THAT OCTOBER, THE PENTAGON SIMULATES A BOEING 757 SMASHING INTO A BUILDING.
AND LESS THAN FOUR MONTHS PRIOR TO 9/11, THE OWNER OF THE TWIN TOWERS TOOK OUT A $3.5 BILLION TERRORISM INSURANCE POLICY ON THE W.T.C.!
AL-QUEDA INSURANCE CO.
POLICY
BUT NEW AMERICAN CENTURY NEVER SAID AMERICA NEEDED TO ENGINEER SUCH AN ATTACK IN ORDER TO REJIGGER THE MILITARY!
UM...HEY...DOESN'T THE MILITARY HAVE, LIKE, MISSILES AND BOMBS AND STUFF TO KNOCK DOWN BUILDINGS? WOULDN'T THEY SIMULATE A CRASH JUST TO TRAIN RESPONSES TO IT?
SINCE TERRORISTS HAD ALREADY TRIED TO BLOW UP THE W.T.C. IN 1993, DON'T YOU THINK GETTING INSURANCE OUT AGAINST IT HAPPENING AGAIN IS A PRETTY GOOD IDEA?
SO... IT IS YOUR CONTENTION THAT "INTELLIGENT DESIGN" IS CUT FROM THE SAME CLOTH AS CONSPIRACY THEORY: ANOTHER EXAMPLE OF REASON'S TENDENCY TO OVERREACH--TO MAKE CONNECTIONS WHERE THERE ARE NONE?
THAT'S SOMETHING WE BOTH CAN AGREE ON!

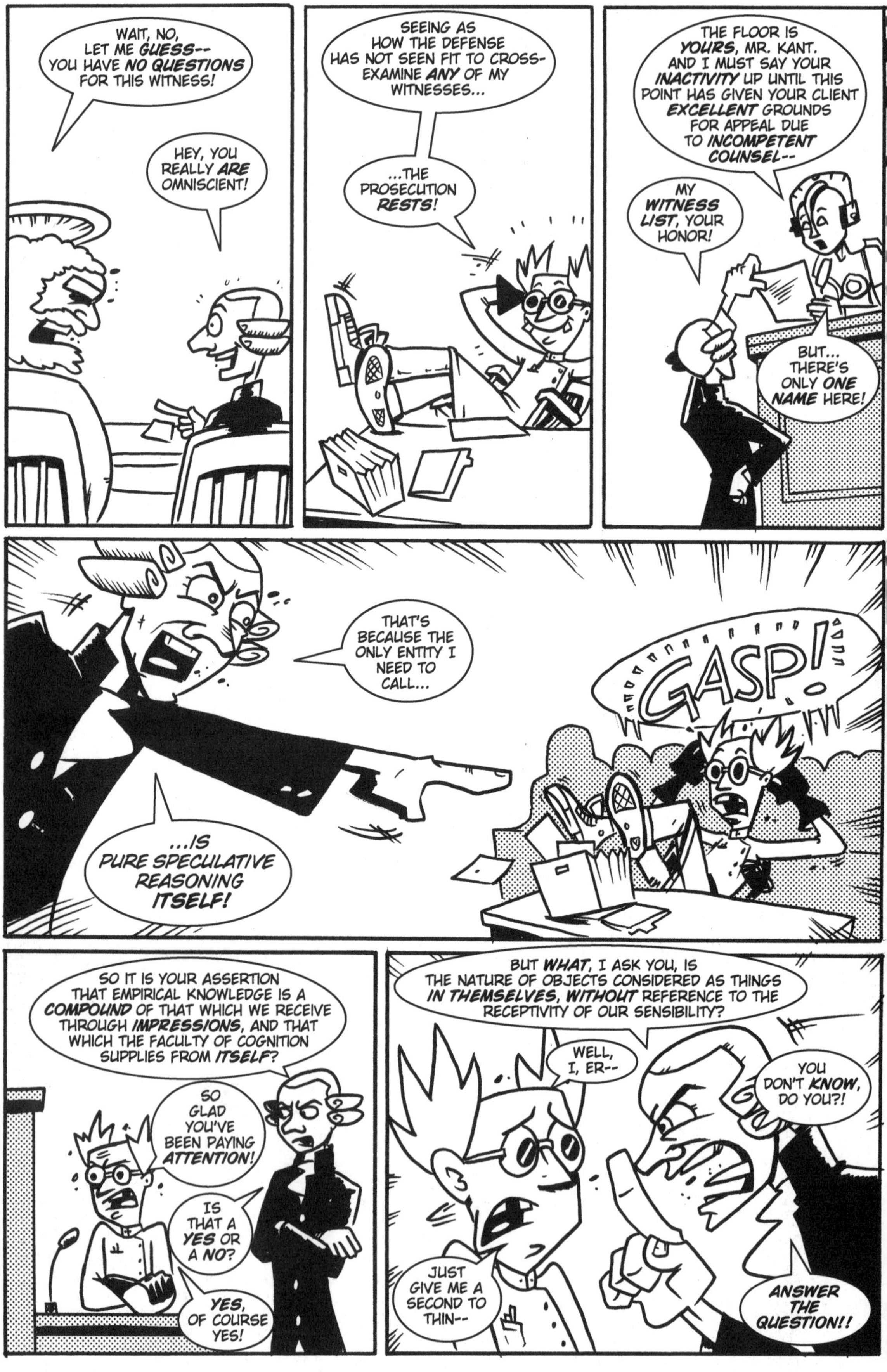
WAIT, NO, LET ME GUESS-- YOU HAVE NO QUESTIONS FOR THIS WITNESS!
HEY, YOU REALLY ARE OMNISCIENT!
SEEING AS HOW THE DEFENSE HAS NOT SEEN FIT TO CROSS-EXAMINE ANY OF MY WITNESSES...
...THE PROSECUTION RESTS!
THE FLOOR IS YOURS, MR. KANT. AND I MUST SAY YOUR INACTIVITY UP UNTIL THIS POINT HAS GIVEN YOUR CLIENT EXCELLENT GROUNDS FOR APPEAL DUE TO INCOMPETENT COUNSEL--
MY WITNESS LIST, YOUR HONOR!
BUT... THERE'S ONLY ONE NAME HERE!
THAT'S BECAUSE THE ONLY ENTITY I NEED TO CALL...
...IS PURE SPECULATIVE REASONING ITSELF!
GASP!
SO IT IS YOUR ASSERTION THAT EMPIRICAL KNOWLEDGE IS A COMPOUND OF THAT WHICH WE RECEIVE THROUGH IMPRESSIONS, AND THAT WHICH THE FACULTY OF COGNITION SUPPLIES FROM ITSELF?
SO GLAD YOU'VE BEEN PAYING ATTENTION!
IS THAT A YES OR A NO?
YES, OF COURSE YES!
BUT WHAT, I ASK YOU, IS THE NATURE OF OBJECTS CONSIDERED AS THINGS IN THEMSELVES, WITHOUT REFERENCE TO THE RECEPTIVITY OF OUR SENSIBILITY?
WELL, I, ER--
YOU DON'T KNOW, DO YOU?!
JUST GIVE ME A SECOND TO THIN--
ANSWER THE QUESTION!!

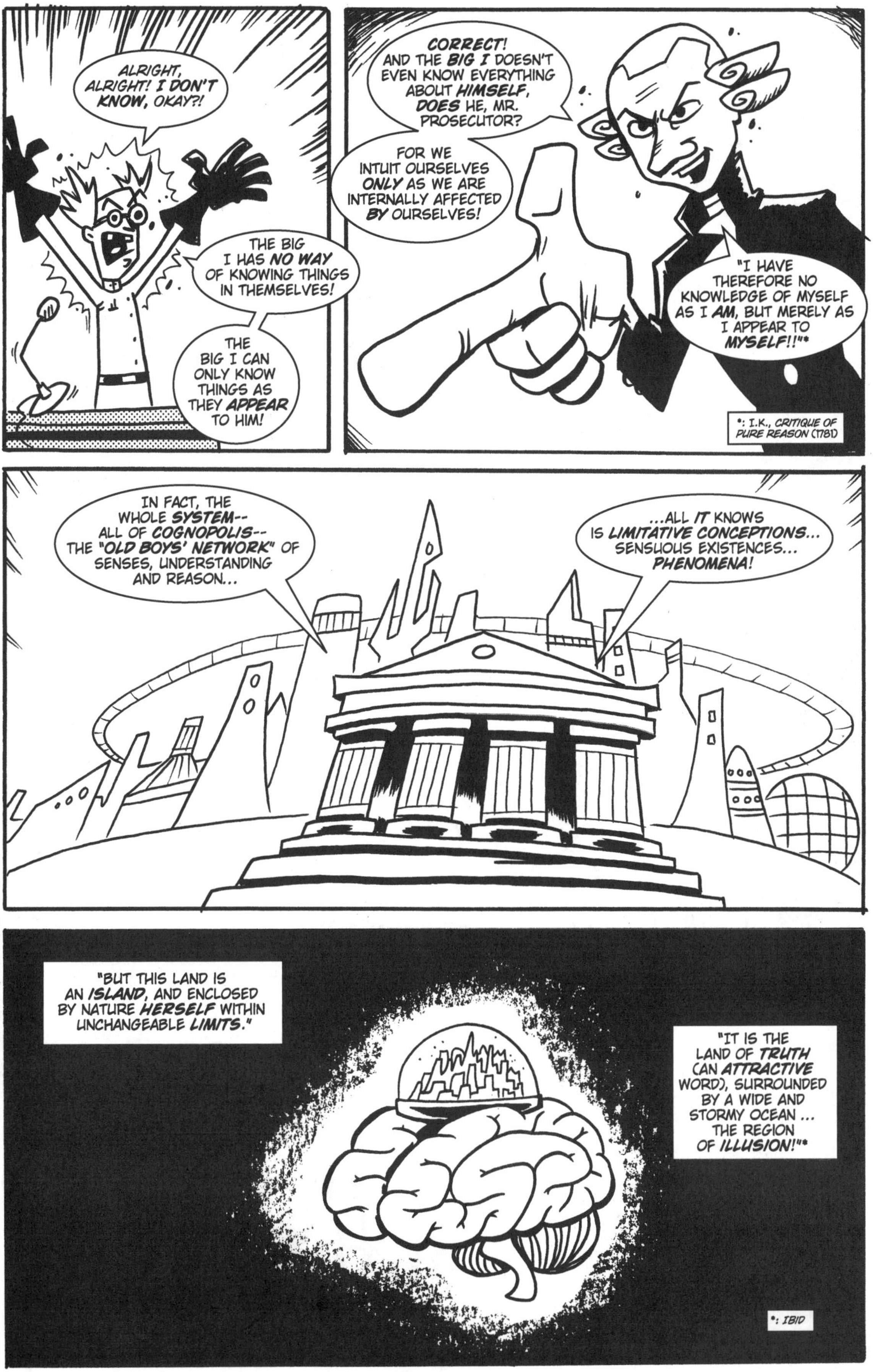

ALRIGHT, ALRIGHT! I DON'T KNOW, OKAY?!
THE BIG I HAS NO WAY OF KNOWING THINGS IN THEMSELVES!
THE BIG I CAN ONLY KNOW THINGS AS THEY APPEAR TO HIM!
CORRECT! AND THE BIG I DOESN'T EVEN KNOW EVERYTHING ABOUT HIMSELF, DOES HE, MR. PROSECUTOR?
FOR WE INTUIT OURSELVES ONLY AS WE ARE INTERNALLY AFFECTED BY OURSELVES!
"I HAVE THEREFORE NO KNOWLEDGE OF MYSELF AS I AM, BUT MERELY AS I APPEAR TO MYSELF!!"*
*: I.K., CRITIQUE OF PURE REASON (1781)
IN FACT, THE WHOLE SYSTEM-- ALL OF COGNOPOLIS-- THE "OLD BOYS' NETWORK" OF SENSES, UNDERSTANDING AND REASON...
...ALL IT KNOWS IS LIMITATIVE CONCEPTIONS... SENSUOUS EXISTENCES... PHENOMENA!
"BUT THIS LAND IS AN ISLAND, AND ENCLOSED BY NATURE HERSELF WITHIN UNCHANGEABLE LIMITS."
"IT IS THE LAND OF TRUTH (AN ATTRACTIVE WORD), SURROUNDED BY A WIDE AND STORMY OCEAN ... THE REGION OF ILLUSION!"*
*: IBID

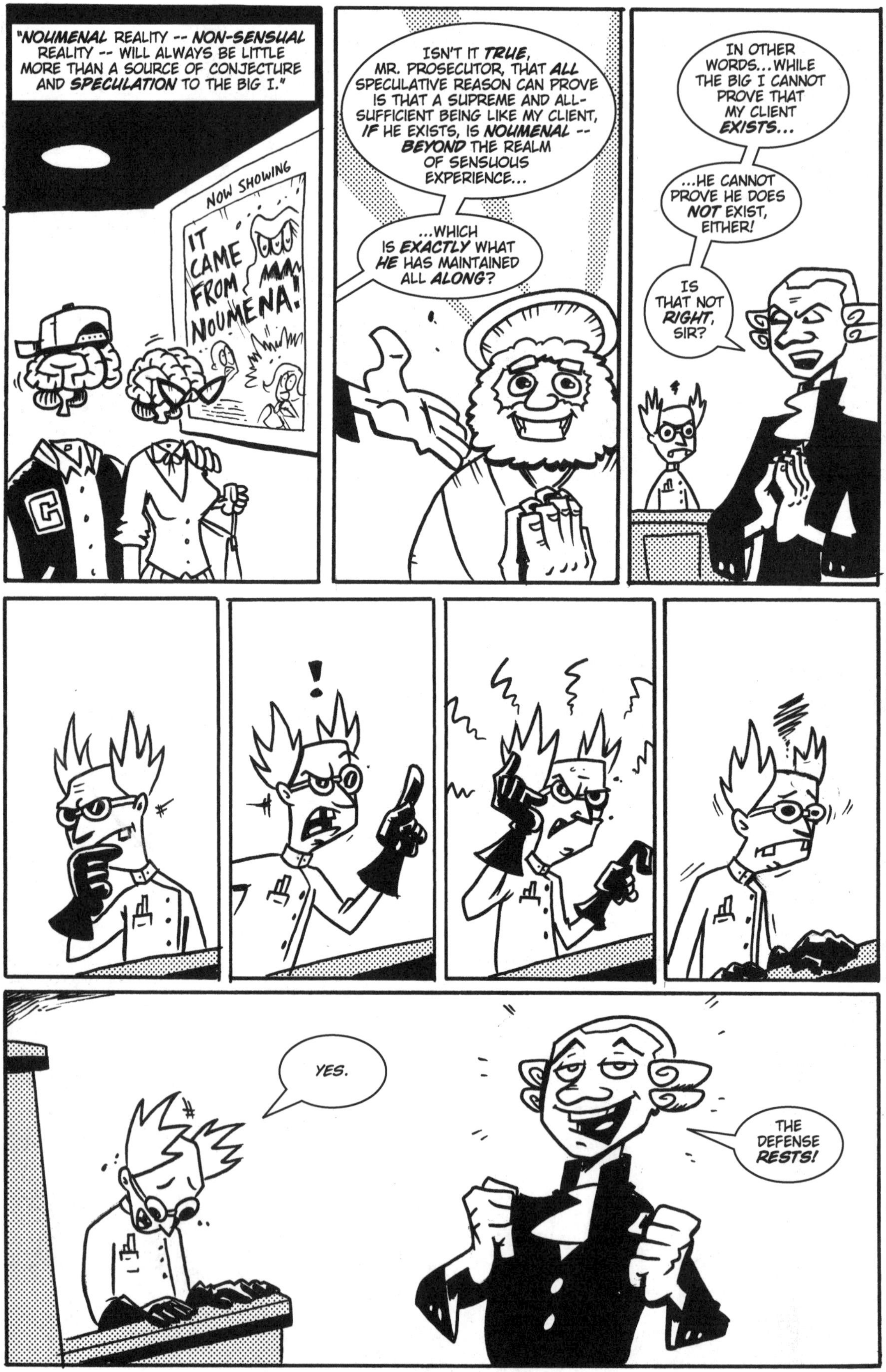

"NOUMENAL REALITY -- NON-SENSUAL REALITY -- WILL ALWAYS BE LITTLE MORE THAN A SOURCE OF CONJECTURE AND SPECULATION TO THE BIG I."
NOW SHOWING
IT CAME FROM NOUMENA!
ISN'T IT TRUE, MR. PROSECUTOR, THAT ALL SPECULATIVE REASON CAN PROVE IS THAT A SUPREME AND ALL-SUFFICIENT BEING LIKE MY CLIENT, IF HE EXISTS, IS NOUMENAL -- BEYOND THE REALM OF SENSUOUS EXPERIENCE...
...WHICH IS EXACTLY WHAT HE HAS MAINTAINED ALL ALONG?
IN OTHER WORDS...WHILE THE BIG I CANNOT PROVE THAT MY CLIENT EXISTS...
...HE CANNOT PROVE HE DOES NOT EXIST, EITHER!
IS THAT NOT RIGHT, SIR?
YES.
THE DEFENSE RESTS!

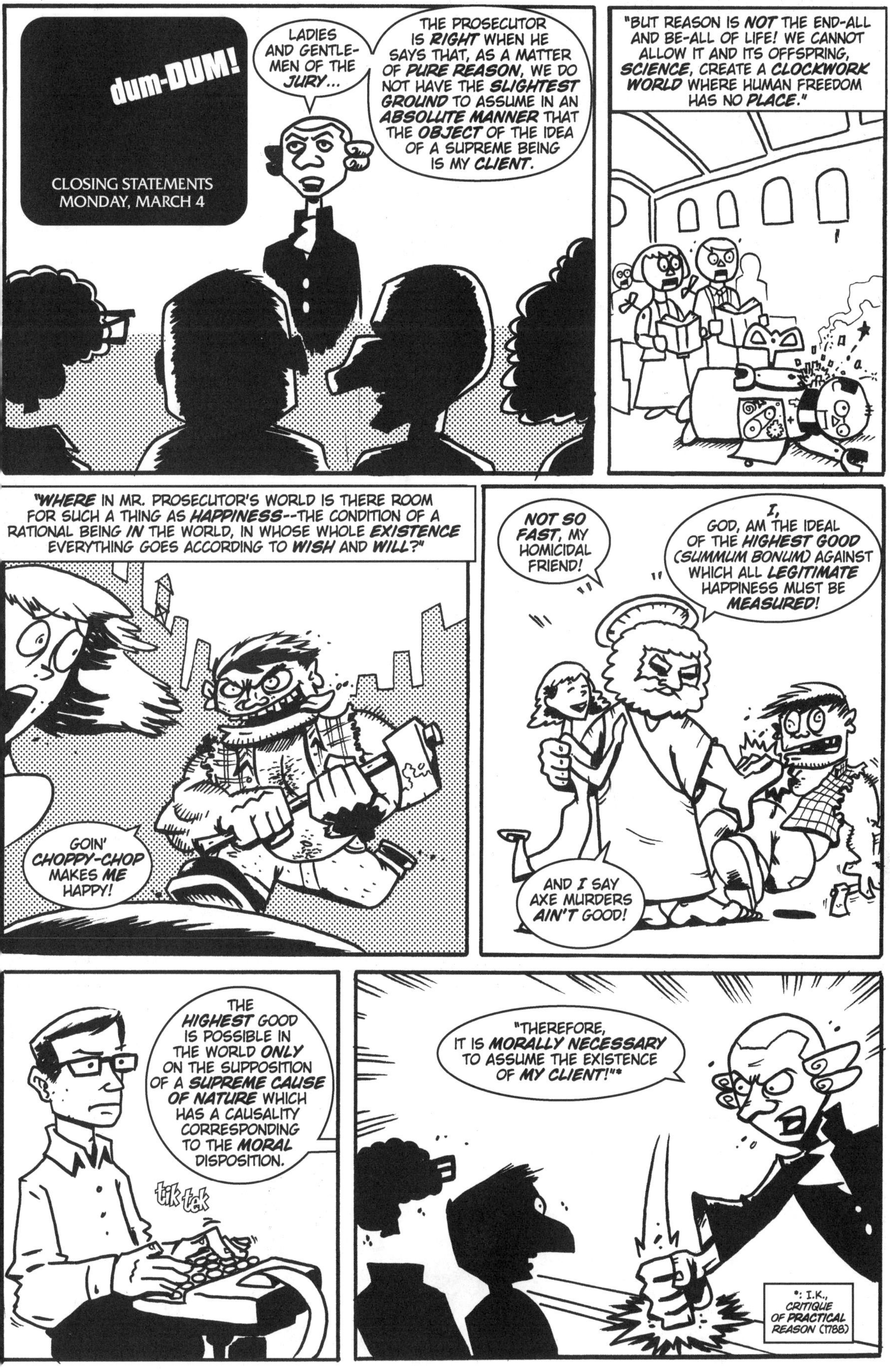
dum-DUM!
CLOSING STATEMENTS
MONDAY, MARCH 4
LADIES AND GENTLEMEN OF THE JURY...
THE PROSECUTOR IS RIGHT WHEN HE SAYS THAT, AS A MATTER OF PURE REASON, WE DO NOT HAVE THE SLIGHTEST GROUND TO ASSUME IN AN ABSOLUTE MANNER THAT THE OBJECT OF THE IDEA OF A SUPREME BEING IS MY CLIENT.
"BUT REASON IS NOT THE END-ALL AND BE-ALL OF LIFE! WE CANNOT ALLOW IT AND ITS OFFSPRING, SCIENCE, CREATE A CLOCKWORK WORLD WHERE HUMAN FREEDOM HAS NO PLACE."
"WHERE IN MR. PROSECUTOR'S WORLD IS THERE ROOM FOR SUCH A THING AS HAPPINESS--THE CONDITION OF A RATIONAL BEING IN THE WORLD, IN WHOSE WHOLE EXISTENCE EVERYTHING GOES ACCORDING TO WISH AND WILL?"
GOIN' CHOPPY-CHOP MAKES ME HAPPY!
NOT SO FAST, MY HOMICIDAL FRIEND!
I, GOD, AM THE IDEAL OF THE HIGHEST GOOD (SUMMUM BONUM) AGAINST WHICH ALL LEGITIMATE HAPPINESS MUST BE MEASURED!
AND I SAY AXE MURDERS AIN'T GOOD!
THE HIGHEST GOOD IS POSSIBLE IN THE WORLD ONLY ON THE SUPPOSITION OF A SUPREME CAUSE OF NATURE WHICH HAS A CAUSALITY CORRESPONDING TO THE MORAL DISPOSITION.
tik tek
"THEREFORE, IT IS MORALLY NECESSARY TO ASSUME THE EXISTENCE OF MY CLIENT!"*
*: I.K., CRITIQUE OF PRACTICAL REASON (1788)

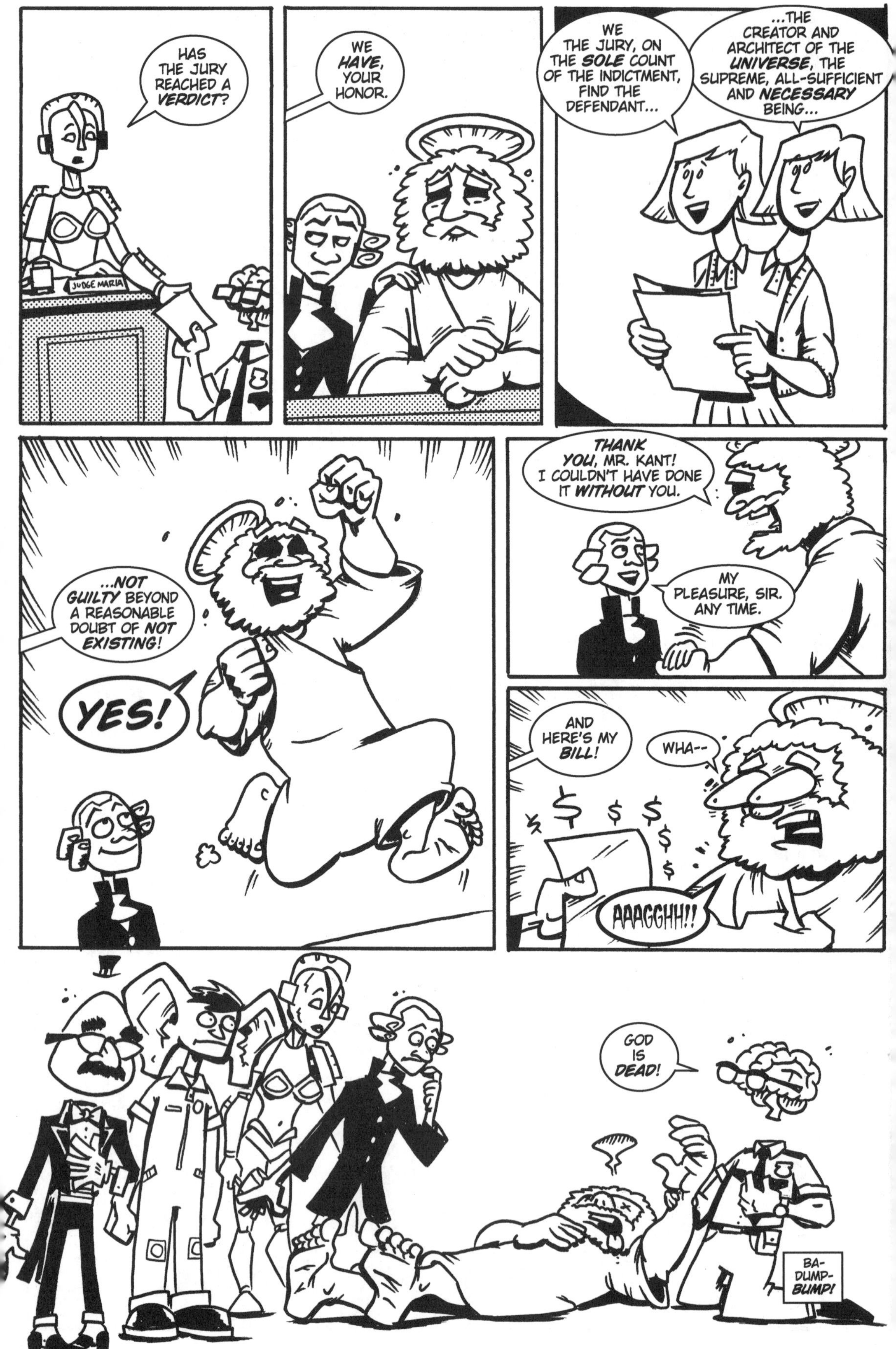

HAS THE JURY REACHED A VERDICT?
JUDGE MARIA
WE HAVE, YOUR HONOR.
WE THE JURY, ON THE SOLE COUNT OF THE INDICTMENT, FIND THE DEFENDANT...
...THE CREATOR AND ARCHITECT OF THE UNIVERSE, THE SUPREME, ALL-SUFFICIENT AND NECESSARY BEING...
...NOT GUILTY BEYOND A REASONABLE DOUBT OF NOT EXISTING!
YES!
THANK YOU, MR. KANT! I COULDN'T HAVE DONE IT WITHOUT YOU.
MY PLEASURE, SIR. ANY TIME.
AND HERE'S MY BILL!
WHA--
AAAGGHH!!
GOD IS DEAD!
BA-DUMP-BUMP!

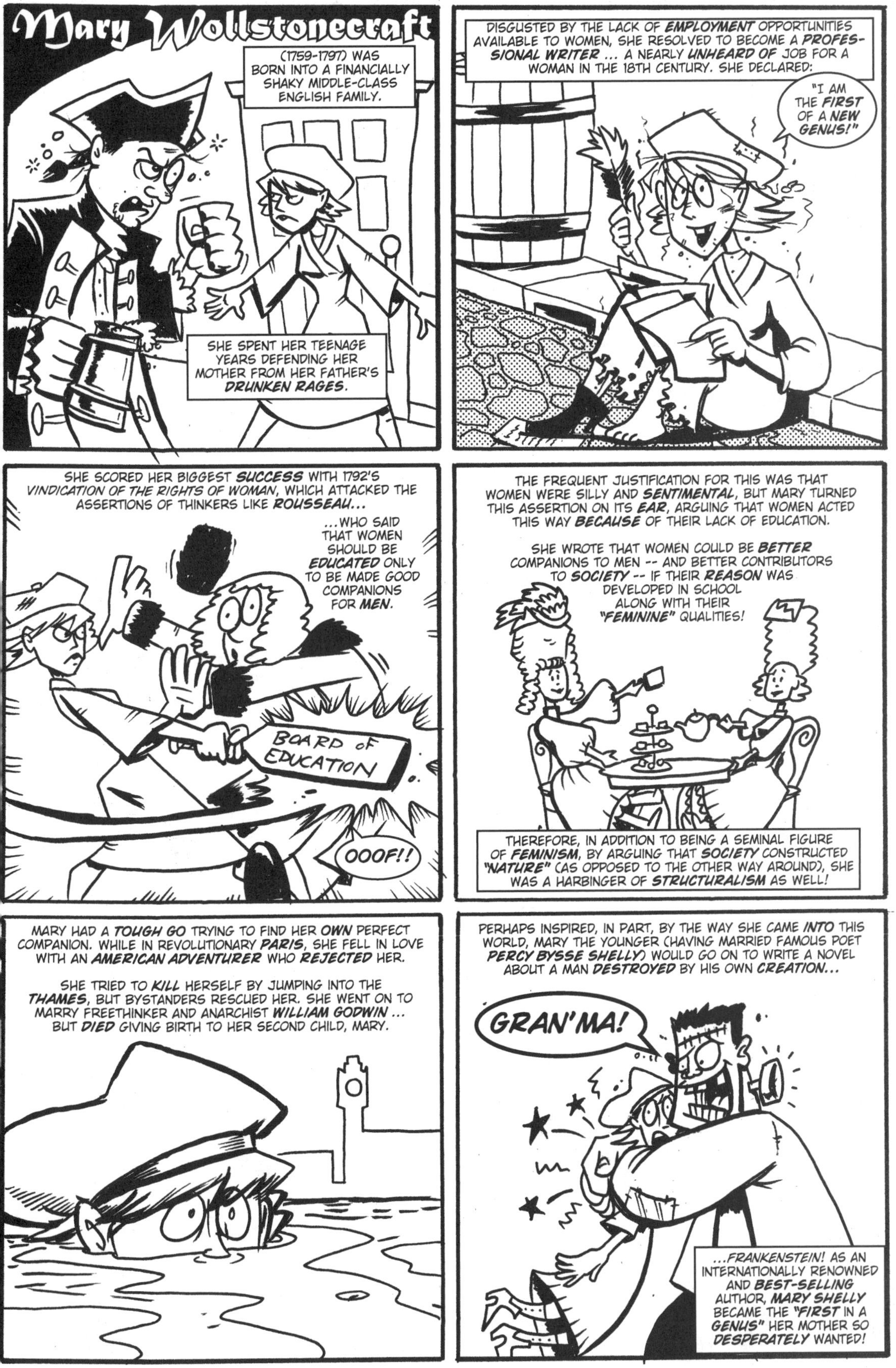

Mary Wollstonecraft
(1759-1797) WAS BORN INTO A FINANCIALLY SHAKY MIDDLE-CLASS ENGLISH FAMILY.
SHE SPENT HER TEENAGE YEARS DEFENDING HER MOTHER FROM HER FATHER'S DRUNKEN RAGES.
DISGUSTED BY THE LACK OF EMPLOYMENT OPPORTUNITIES AVAILABLE TO WOMEN, SHE RESOLVED TO BECOME A PROFESSIONAL WRITER ... A NEARLY UNHEARD OF JOB FOR A WOMAN IN THE 18TH CENTURY. SHE DECLARED:
"I AM THE FIRST OF A NEW GENUS!"
SHE SCORED HER BIGGEST SUCCESS WITH 1792'S VINDICATION OF THE RIGHTS OF WOMAN, WHICH ATTACKED THE ASSERTIONS OF THINKERS LIKE ROUSSEAU...
...WHO SAID THAT WOMEN SHOULD BE EDUCATED ONLY TO BE MADE GOOD COMPANIONS FOR MEN.
BOARD OF EDUCATION
OOOF!!
THE FREQUENT JUSTIFICATION FOR THIS WAS THAT WOMEN WERE SILLY AND SENTIMENTAL, BUT MARY TURNED THIS ASSERTION ON ITS EAR, ARGUING THAT WOMEN ACTED THIS WAY BECAUSE OF THEIR LACK OF EDUCATION.
SHE WROTE THAT WOMEN COULD BE BETTER COMPANIONS TO MEN -- AND BETTER CONTRIBUTORS TO SOCIETY -- IF THEIR REASON WAS DEVELOPED IN SCHOOL ALONG WITH THEIR "FEMININE" QUALITIES!
THEREFORE, IN ADDITION TO BEING A SEMINAL FIGURE OF FEMINISM, BY ARGUING THAT SOCIETY CONSTRUCTED "NATURE" (AS OPPOSED TO THE OTHER WAY AROUND), SHE WAS A HARBINGER OF STRUCTURALISM AS WELL!
MARY HAD A TOUGH GO TRYING TO FIND HER OWN PERFECT COMPANION. WHILE IN REVOLUTIONARY PARIS, SHE FELL IN LOVE WITH AN AMERICAN ADVENTURER WHO REJECTED HER.
SHE TRIED TO KILL HERSELF BY JUMPING INTO THE THAMES, BUT BYSTANDERS RESCUED HER. SHE WENT ON TO MARRY FREETHINKER AND ANARCHIST WILLIAM GODWIN ... BUT DIED GIVING BIRTH TO HER SECOND CHILD, MARY.
PERHAPS INSPIRED, IN PART, BY THE WAY SHE CAME INTO THIS WORLD, MARY THE YOUNGER (HAVING MARRIED FAMOUS POET PERCY BYSSE SHELLY) WOULD GO ON TO WRITE A NOVEL ABOUT A MAN DESTROYED BY HIS OWN CREATION...
GRAN'MA!
...FRANKENSTEIN! AS AN INTERNATIONALLY RENOWNED AND BEST-SELLING AUTHOR, MARY SHELLY BECAME THE "FIRST IN A GENUS" HER MOTHER SO DESPERATELY WANTED!

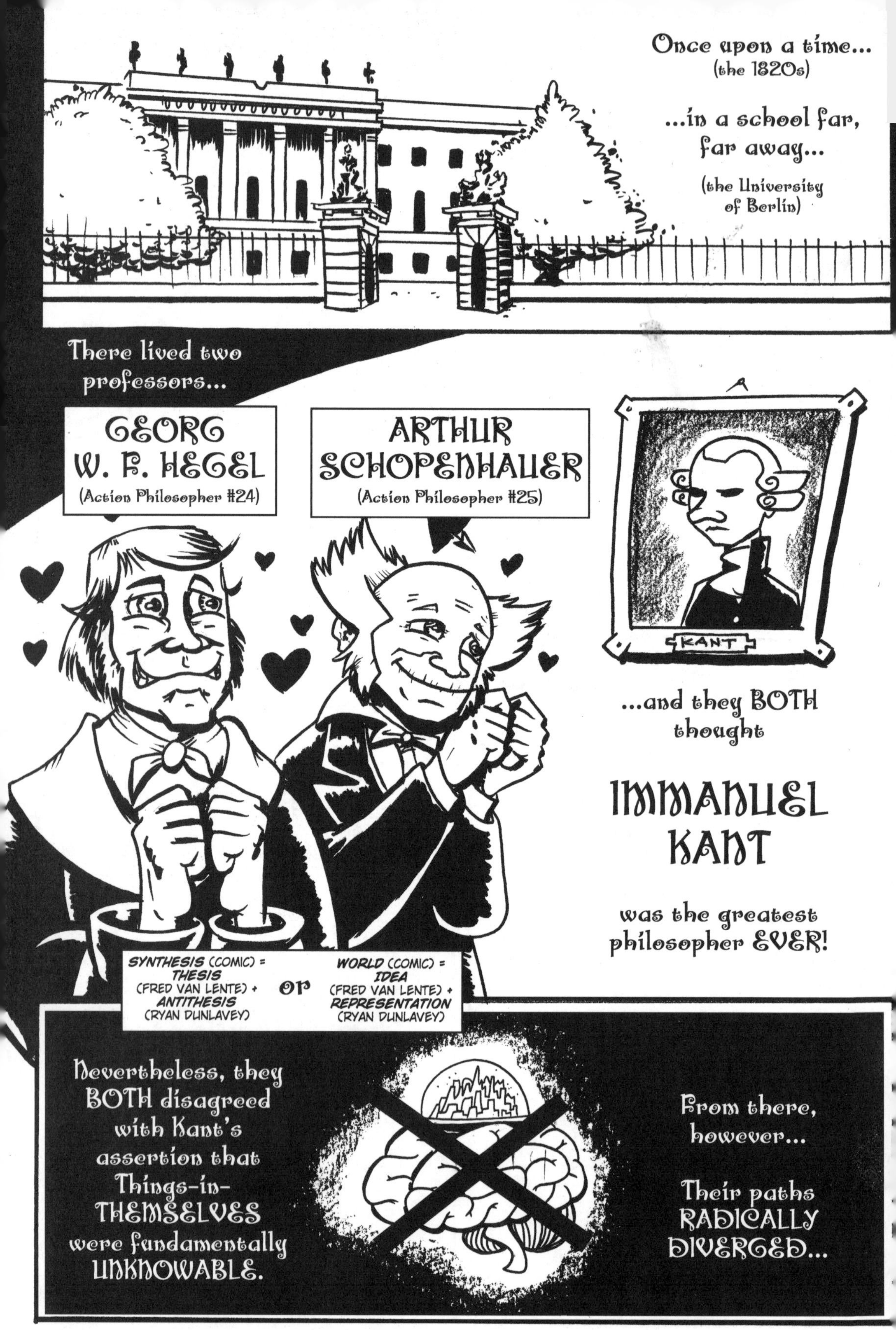

Once upon a time...
(the 1820s)
...in a school far, far away...
(the University of Berlin)
There lived two professors...
GEORG W. F. HEGEL
(Action Philosopher #24)
ARTHUR SCHOPENHAUER
(Action Philosopher #25)
KANT
...and they BOTH thought
IMMANUEL KANT
was the greatest philosopher EVER!
SYNTHESIS (COMIC) = THESIS (FRED VAN LENTE) + ANTITHESIS (RYAN DUNLAVEY)
or
WORLD (COMIC) = IDEA (FRED VAN LENTE) + REPRESENTATION (RYAN DUNLAVEY)
Nevertheless, they BOTH disagreed with Kant's assertion that Things-in-THEMSELVES were fundamentally UNKNOWABLE.
From there, however...
Their paths RADICALLY DIVERGED...

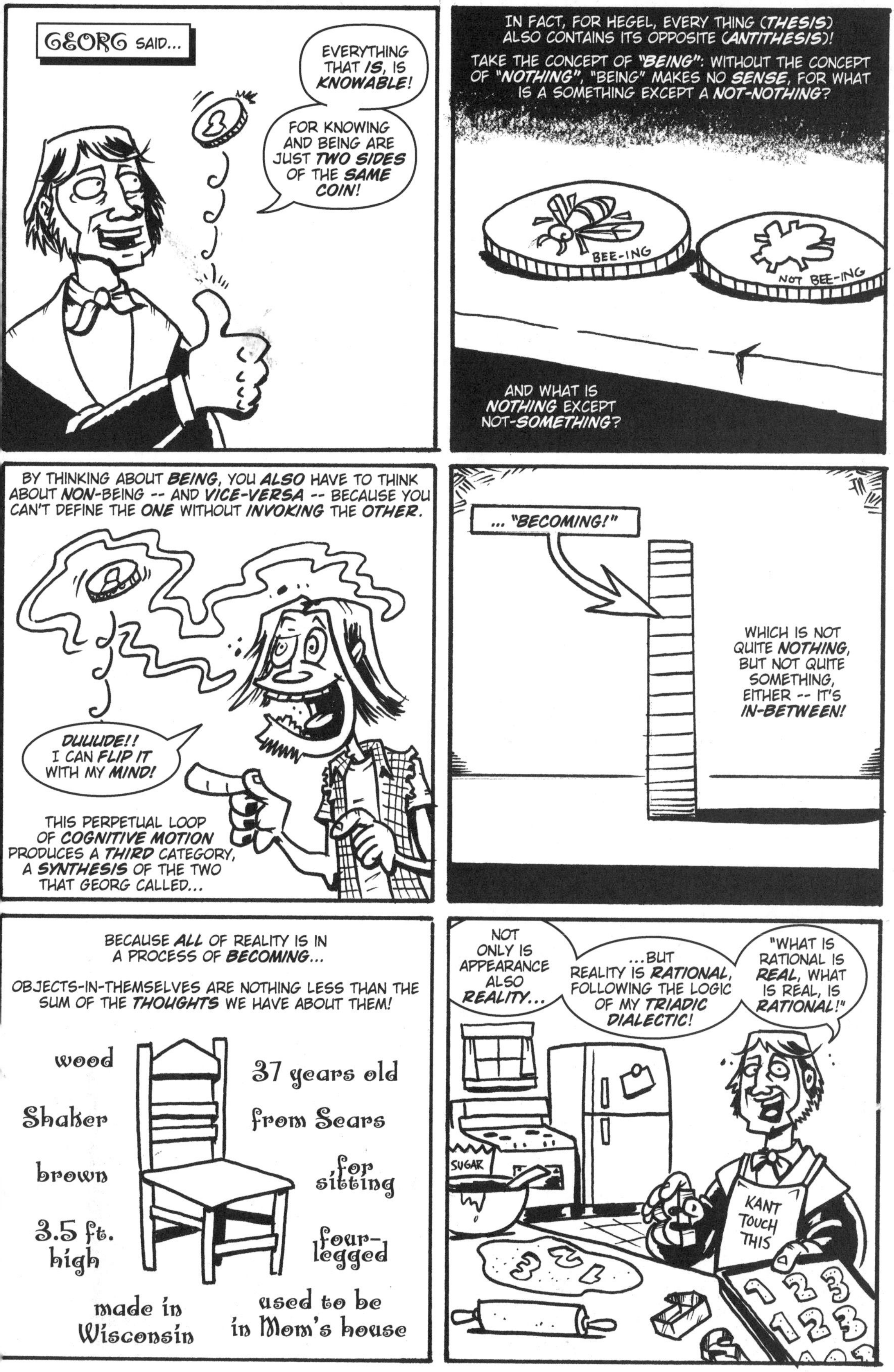
GEORG SAID...
EVERYTHING THAT IS, IS KNOWABLE!
FOR KNOWING AND BEING ARE JUST TWO SIDES OF THE SAME COIN!
IN FACT, FOR HEGEL, EVERY THING (THESIS) ALSO CONTAINS ITS OPPOSITE (ANTITHESIS)!
TAKE THE CONCEPT OF "BEING": WITHOUT THE CONCEPT OF "NOTHING", "BEING" MAKES NO SENSE, FOR WHAT IS A SOMETHING EXCEPT A NOT-NOTHING?
BEE-ING
NOT BEE-ING
AND WHAT IS NOTHING EXCEPT NOT-SOMETHING?
BY THINKING ABOUT BEING, YOU ALSO HAVE TO THINK ABOUT NON-BEING -- AND VICE-VERSA -- BECAUSE YOU CAN'T DEFINE THE ONE WITHOUT INVOKING THE OTHER.
DUUUDE!! I CAN FLIP IT WITH MY MIND!
THIS PERPETUAL LOOP OF COGNITIVE MOTION PRODUCES A THIRD CATEGORY, A SYNTHESIS OF THE TWO THAT GEORG CALLED...
... "BECOMING!"
WHICH IS NOT QUITE NOTHING, BUT NOT QUITE SOMETHING, EITHER -- IT'S IN-BETWEEN!
BECAUSE ALL OF REALITY IS IN A PROCESS OF BECOMING...
OBJECTS-IN-THEMSELVES ARE NOTHING LESS THAN THE SUM OF THE THOUGHTS WE HAVE ABOUT THEM!
wood
37 years old
Shaker
from Sears
brown
for sitting
3.5 ft. high
four-legged
made in Wisconsin
used to be in Mom's house
NOT ONLY IS APPEARANCE ALSO REALITY...
...BUT REALITY IS RATIONAL, FOLLOWING THE LOGIC OF MY TRIADIC DIALECTIC!
"WHAT IS RATIONAL IS REAL, WHAT IS REAL, IS RATIONAL!"
SUGAR
KANT TOUCH THIS

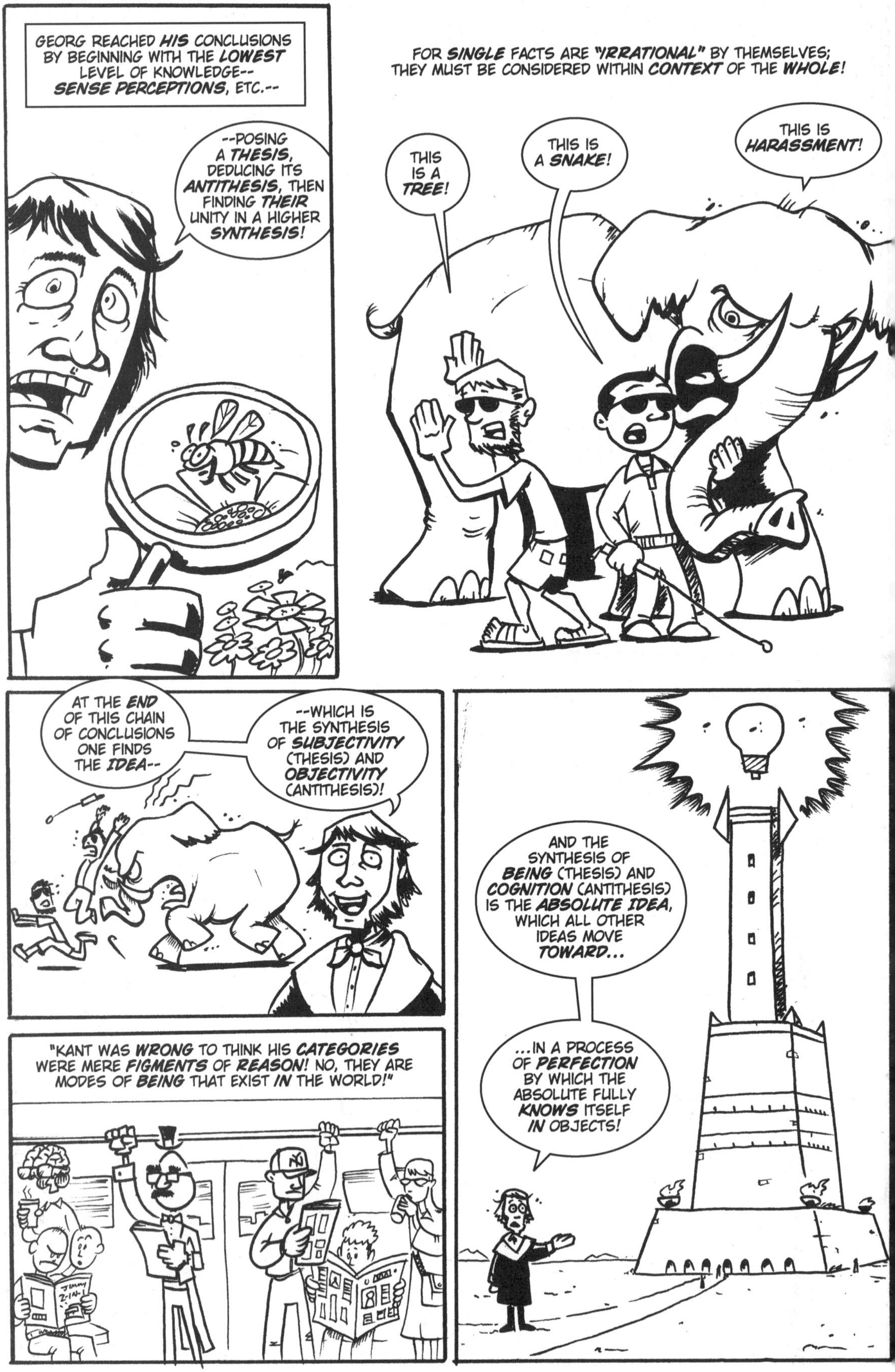
GEORG REACHED HIS CONCLUSIONS BY BEGINNING WITH THE LOWEST LEVEL OF KNOWLEDGE-- SENSE PERCEPTIONS, ETC.--
--POSING A THESIS, DEDUCING ITS ANTITHESIS, THEN FINDING THEIR UNITY IN A HIGHER SYNTHESIS!
FOR SINGLE FACTS ARE "IRRATIONAL" BY THEMSELVES; THEY MUST BE CONSIDERED WITHIN CONTEXT OF THE WHOLE!
THIS IS A TREE!
THIS IS A SNAKE!
THIS IS HARASSMENT!
AT THE END OF THIS CHAIN OF CONCLUSIONS ONE FINDS THE IDEA--
--WHICH IS THE SYNTHESIS OF SUBJECTIVITY (THESIS) AND OBJECTIVITY (ANTITHESIS)!
"KANT WAS WRONG TO THINK HIS CATEGORIES WERE MERE FIGMENTS OF REASON! NO, THEY ARE MODES OF BEING THAT EXIST IN THE WORLD!"
AND THE SYNTHESIS OF BEING (THESIS) AND COGNITION (ANTITHESIS) IS THE ABSOLUTE IDEA, WHICH ALL OTHER IDEAS MOVE TOWARD...
...IN A PROCESS OF PERFECTION BY WHICH THE ABSOLUTE FULLY KNOWS ITSELF IN OBJECTS!

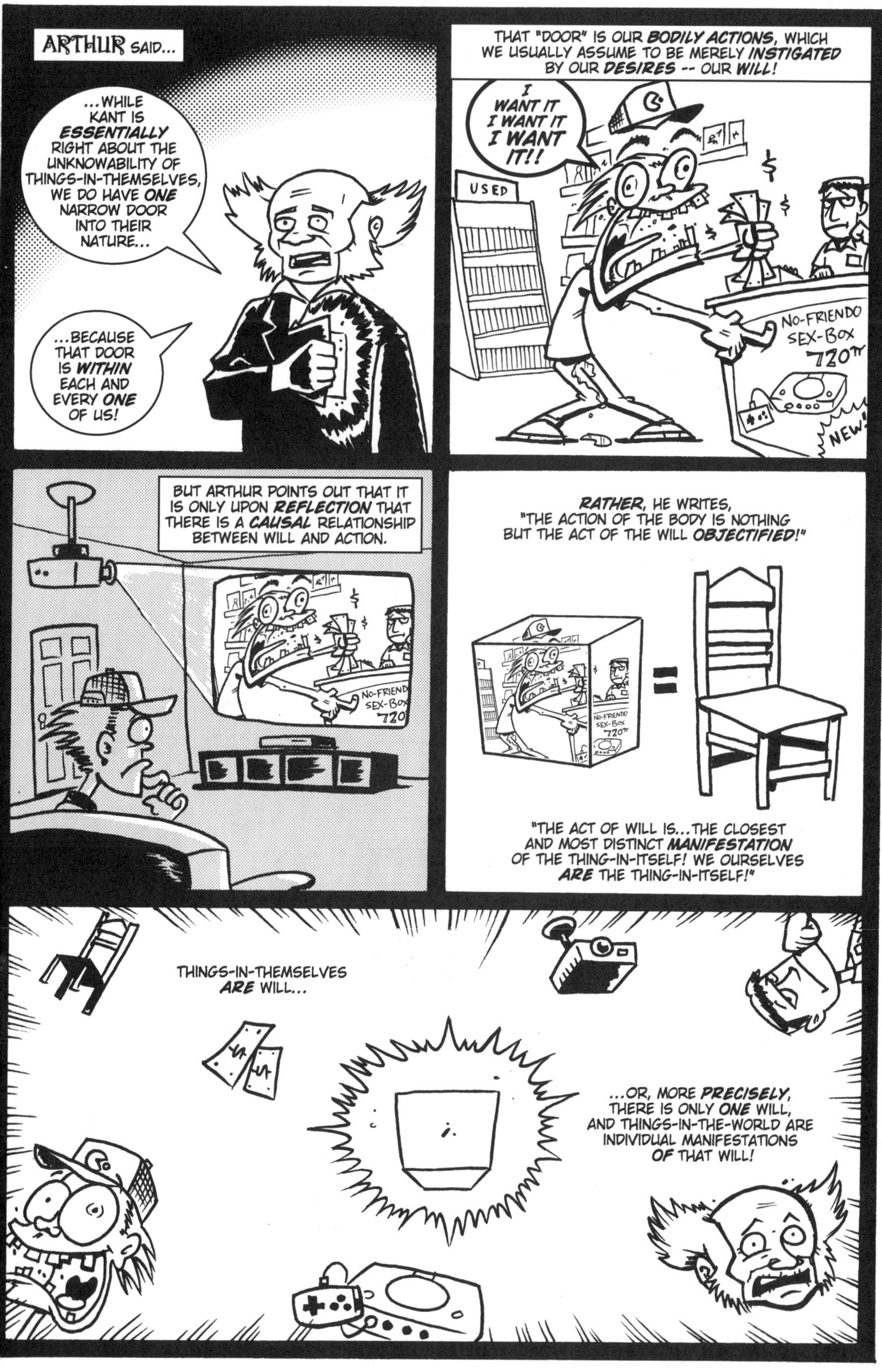

ARTHUR SAID...
...WHILE KANT IS ESSENTIALLY RIGHT ABOUT THE UNKNOWABILITY OF THINGS-IN-THEMSELVES, WE DO HAVE ONE NARROW DOOR INTO THEIR NATURE...
...BECAUSE THAT DOOR IS WITHIN EACH AND EVERY ONE OF US!
THAT "DOOR" IS OUR BODILY ACTIONS, WHICH WE USUALLY ASSUME TO BE MERELY INSTIGATED BY OUR DESIRES -- OUR WILL!
I WANT IT I WANT IT I WANT IT!!
USED
NO-FRIENDO SEX-BOX 720
NEW!
BUT ARTHUR POINTS OUT THAT IT IS ONLY UPON REFLECTION THAT THERE IS A CAUSAL RELATIONSHIP BETWEEN WILL AND ACTION.
RATHER, HE WRITES, "THE ACTION OF THE BODY IS NOTHING BUT THE ACT OF THE WILL OBJECTIFIED!"
"THE ACT OF WILL IS...THE CLOSEST AND MOST DISTINCT MANIFESTATION OF THE THING-IN-ITSELF! WE OURSELVES ARE THE THING-IN-ITSELF!"
THINGS-IN-THEMSELVES ARE WILL...
...OR, MORE PRECISELY, THERE IS ONLY ONE WILL, AND THINGS-IN-THE-WORLD ARE INDIVIDUAL MANIFESTATIONS OF THAT WILL!

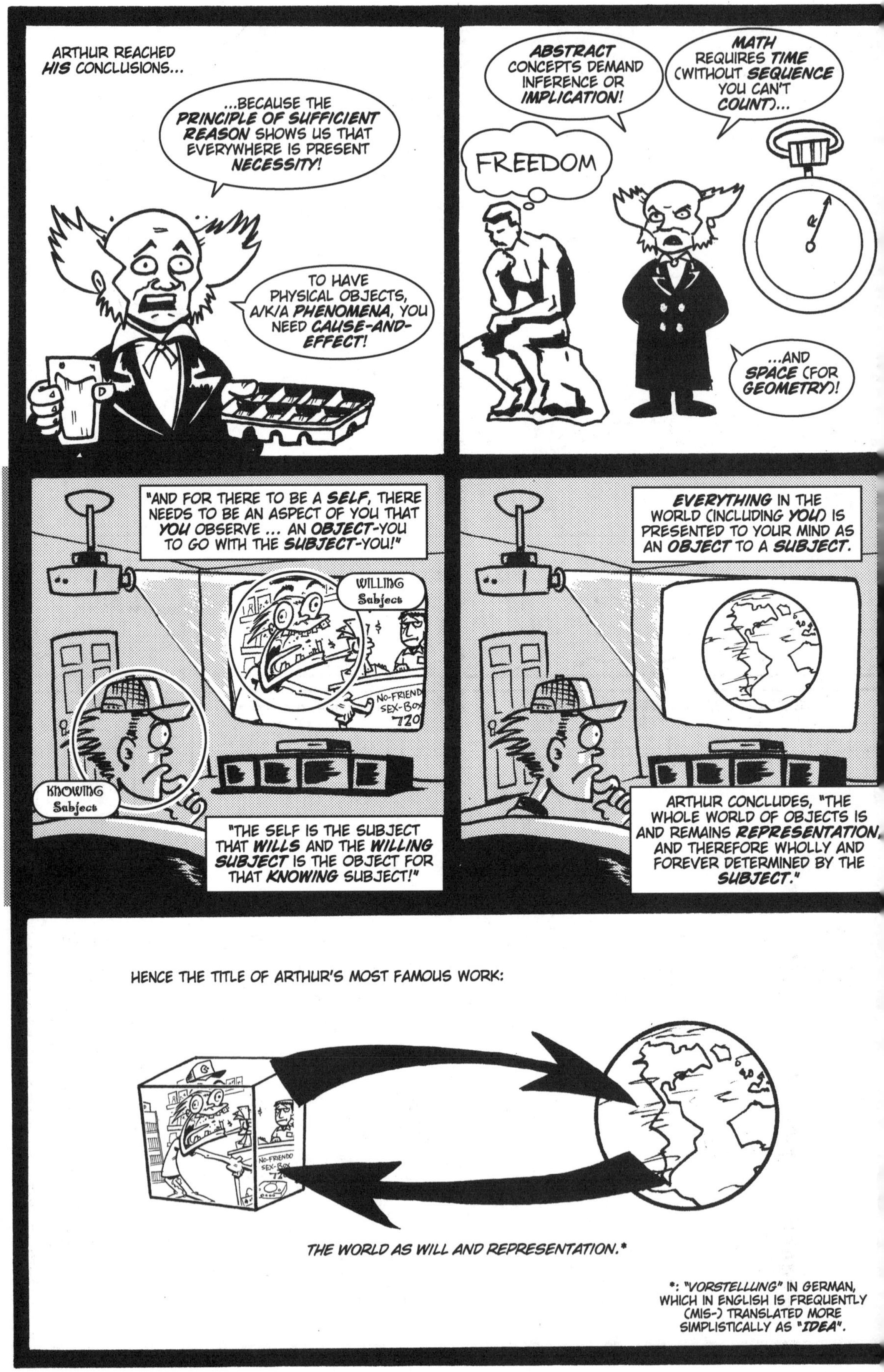

ARTHUR REACHED HIS CONCLUSIONS...
...BECAUSE THE PRINCIPLE OF SUFFICIENT REASON SHOWS US THAT EVERYWHERE IS PRESENT NECESSITY!
TO HAVE PHYSICAL OBJECTS, A/K/A PHENOMENA, YOU NEED CAUSE-AND-EFFECT!
ABSTRACT CONCEPTS DEMAND INFERENCE OR IMPLICATION!
FREEDOM
MATH REQUIRES TIME (WITHOUT SEQUENCE YOU CAN'T COUNT)...
...AND SPACE (FOR GEOMETRY)!
"AND FOR THERE TO BE A SELF, THERE NEEDS TO BE AN ASPECT OF YOU THAT YOU OBSERVE ... AN OBJECT-YOU TO GO WITH THE SUBJECT-YOU!"
WILLING Subject
No-Friend Sex-Box 720
KNOWING Subject
"THE SELF IS THE SUBJECT THAT WILLS AND THE WILLING SUBJECT IS THE OBJECT FOR THAT KNOWING SUBJECT!"
EVERYTHING IN THE WORLD (INCLUDING YOU) IS PRESENTED TO YOUR MIND AS AN OBJECT TO A SUBJECT.
ARTHUR CONCLUDES, "THE WHOLE WORLD OF OBJECTS IS AND REMAINS REPRESENTATION, AND THEREFORE WHOLLY AND FOREVER DETERMINED BY THE SUBJECT."
HENCE THE TITLE OF ARTHUR'S MOST FAMOUS WORK:
No-Friendo Sex-Box 720
THE WORLD AS WILL AND REPRESENTATION.*
*: "VORSTELLUNG" IN GERMAN, WHICH IN ENGLISH IS FREQUENTLY (MIS-) TRANSLATED MORE SIMPLISTICALLY AS "IDEA".

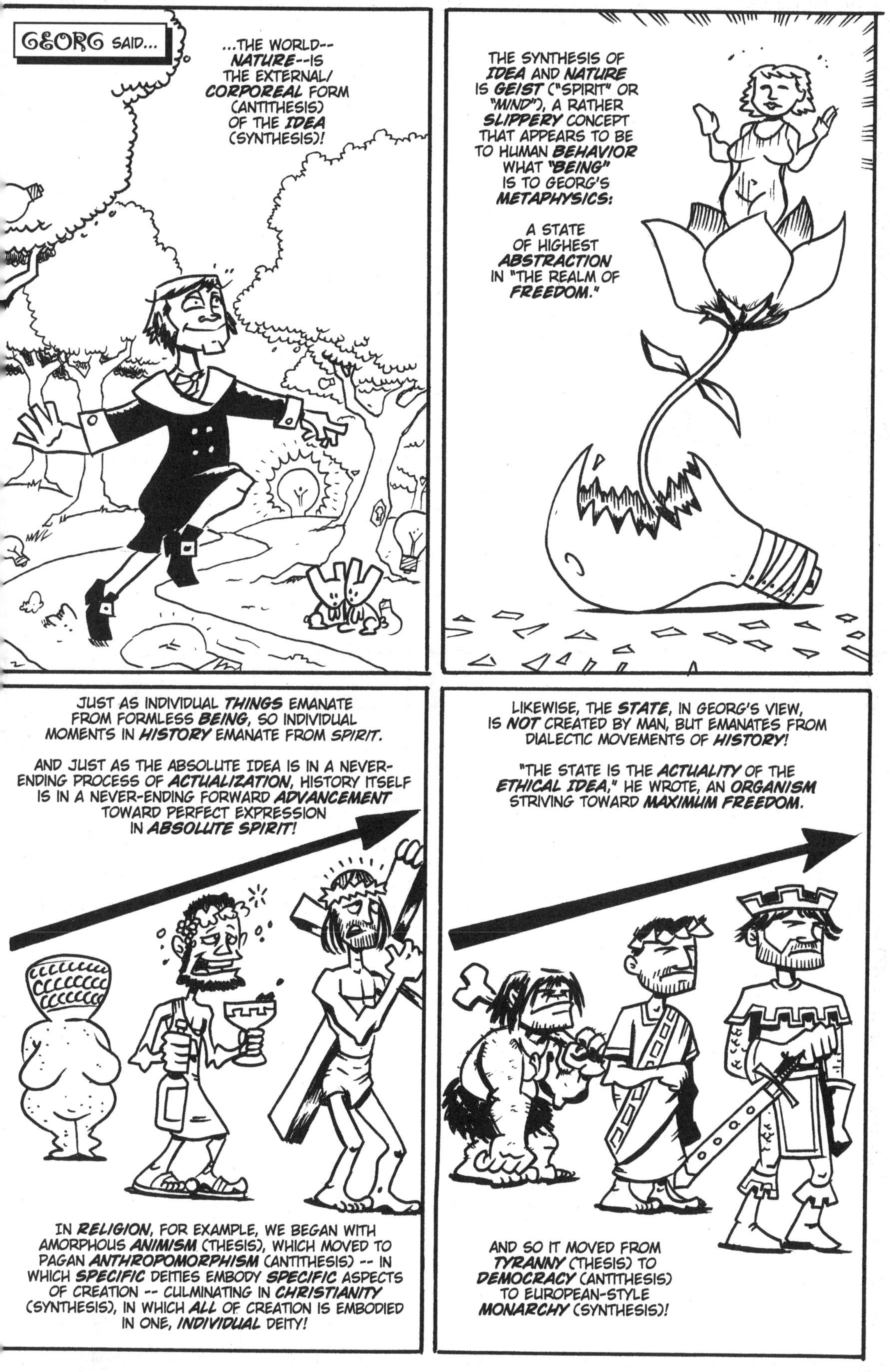
GEORG SAID...
...THE WORLD--NATURE--IS THE EXTERNAL/CORPOREAL FORM (ANTITHESIS) OF THE IDEA (SYNTHESIS)!
THE SYNTHESIS OF IDEA AND NATURE IS GEIST ("SPIRIT" OR "MIND"), A RATHER SLIPPERY CONCEPT THAT APPEARS TO BE TO HUMAN BEHAVIOR WHAT "BEING" IS TO GEORG'S METAPHYSICS:
A STATE OF HIGHEST ABSTRACTION IN "THE REALM OF FREEDOM."
JUST AS INDIVIDUAL THINGS EMANATE FROM FORMLESS BEING, SO INDIVIDUAL MOMENTS IN HISTORY EMANATE FROM SPIRIT.
AND JUST AS THE ABSOLUTE IDEA IS IN A NEVER-ENDING PROCESS OF ACTUALIZATION, HISTORY ITSELF IS IN A NEVER-ENDING FORWARD ADVANCEMENT TOWARD PERFECT EXPRESSION IN ABSOLUTE SPIRIT!
IN RELIGION, FOR EXAMPLE, WE BEGAN WITH AMORPHOUS ANIMISM (THESIS), WHICH MOVED TO PAGAN ANTHROPOMORPHISM (ANTITHESIS) -- IN WHICH SPECIFIC DEITIES EMBODY SPECIFIC ASPECTS OF CREATION -- CULMINATING IN CHRISTIANITY (SYNTHESIS), IN WHICH ALL OF CREATION IS EMBODIED IN ONE, INDIVIDUAL DEITY!
LIKEWISE, THE STATE, IN GEORG'S VIEW, IS NOT CREATED BY MAN, BUT EMANATES FROM DIALECTIC MOVEMENTS OF HISTORY!
"THE STATE IS THE ACTUALITY OF THE ETHICAL IDEA," HE WROTE, AN ORGANISM STRIVING TOWARD MAXIMUM FREEDOM.
AND SO IT MOVED FROM TYRANNY (THESIS) TO DEMOCRACY (ANTITHESIS) TO EUROPEAN-STYLE MONARCHY (SYNTHESIS)!

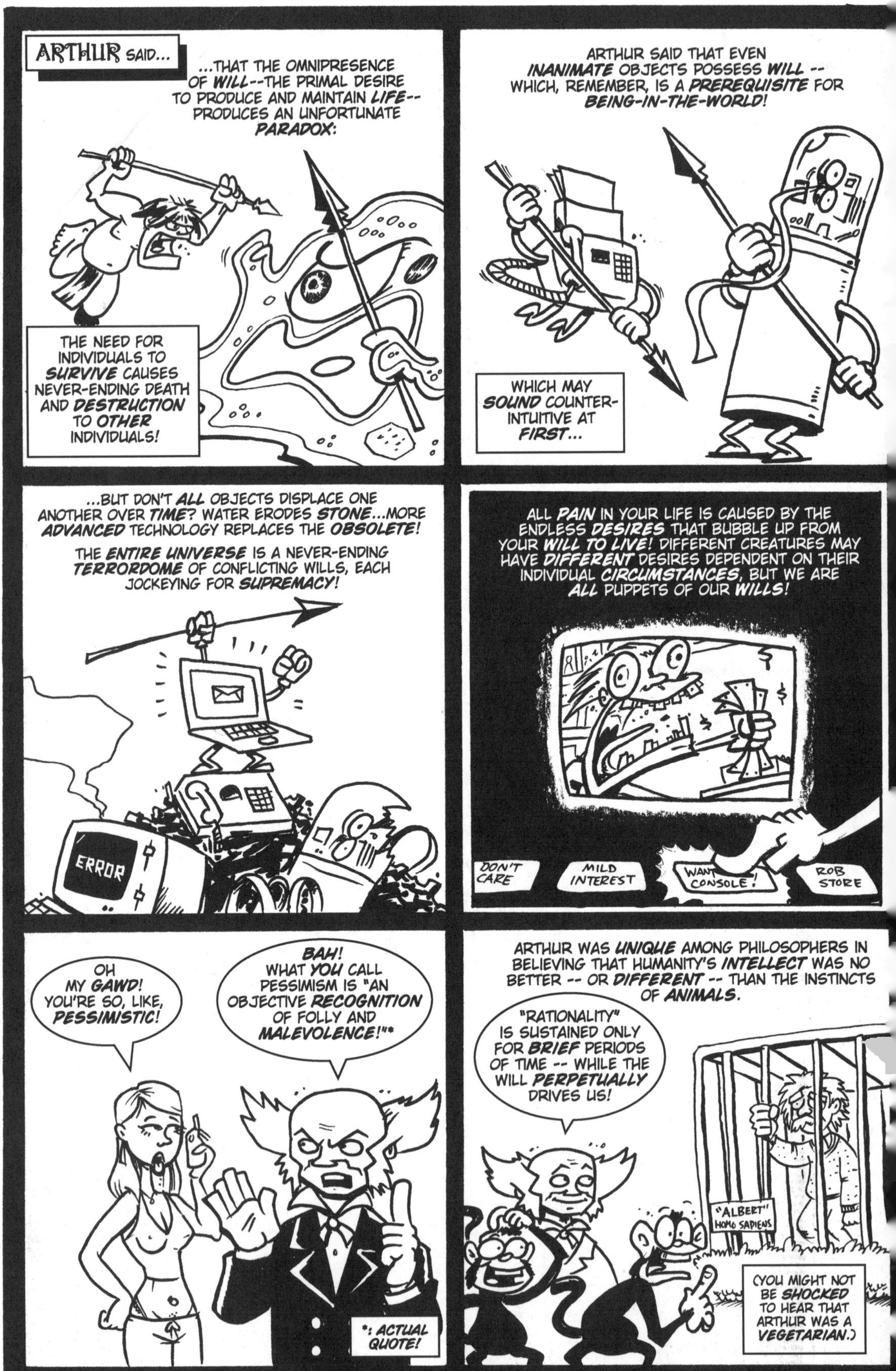
ARTHUR SAID...
...THAT THE OMNIPRESENCE OF WILL--THE PRIMAL DESIRE TO PRODUCE AND MAINTAIN LIFE--PRODUCES AN UNFORTUNATE PARADOX:
THE NEED FOR INDIVIDUALS TO SURVIVE CAUSES NEVER-ENDING DEATH AND DESTRUCTION TO OTHER INDIVIDUALS!
ARTHUR SAID THAT EVEN INANIMATE OBJECTS POSSESS WILL -- WHICH, REMEMBER, IS A PREREQUISITE FOR BEING-IN-THE-WORLD!
WHICH MAY SOUND COUNTER-INTUITIVE AT FIRST...
...BUT DON'T ALL OBJECTS DISPLACE ONE ANOTHER OVER TIME? WATER ERODES STONE...MORE ADVANCED TECHNOLOGY REPLACES THE OBSOLETE!
THE ENTIRE UNIVERSE IS A NEVER-ENDING TERRORDOME OF CONFLICTING WILLS, EACH JOCKEYING FOR SUPREMACY!
ERROR
ALL PAIN IN YOUR LIFE IS CAUSED BY THE ENDLESS DESIRES THAT BUBBLE UP FROM YOUR WILL TO LIVE! DIFFERENT CREATURES MAY HAVE DIFFERENT DESIRES DEPENDENT ON THEIR INDIVIDUAL CIRCUMSTANCES, BUT WE ARE ALL PUPPETS OF OUR WILLS!
DON'T CARE
MILD INTEREST
WANT CONSOLE!
ROB STORE
OH MY GAWD! YOU'RE SO, LIKE, PESSIMISTIC!
BAH! WHAT YOU CALL PESSIMISM IS "AN OBJECTIVE RECOGNITION OF FOLLY AND MALEVOLENCE!"*
*: ACTUAL QUOTE!
ARTHUR WAS UNIQUE AMONG PHILOSOPHERS IN BELIEVING THAT HUMANITY'S INTELLECT WAS NO BETTER -- OR DIFFERENT -- THAN THE INSTINCTS OF ANIMALS.
"RATIONALITY" IS SUSTAINED ONLY FOR BRIEF PERIODS OF TIME -- WHILE THE WILL PERPETUALLY DRIVES US!
"ALBERT" HOMO SAPIENS
(YOU MIGHT NOT BE SHOCKED TO HEAR THAT ARTHUR WAS A VEGETARIAN.)

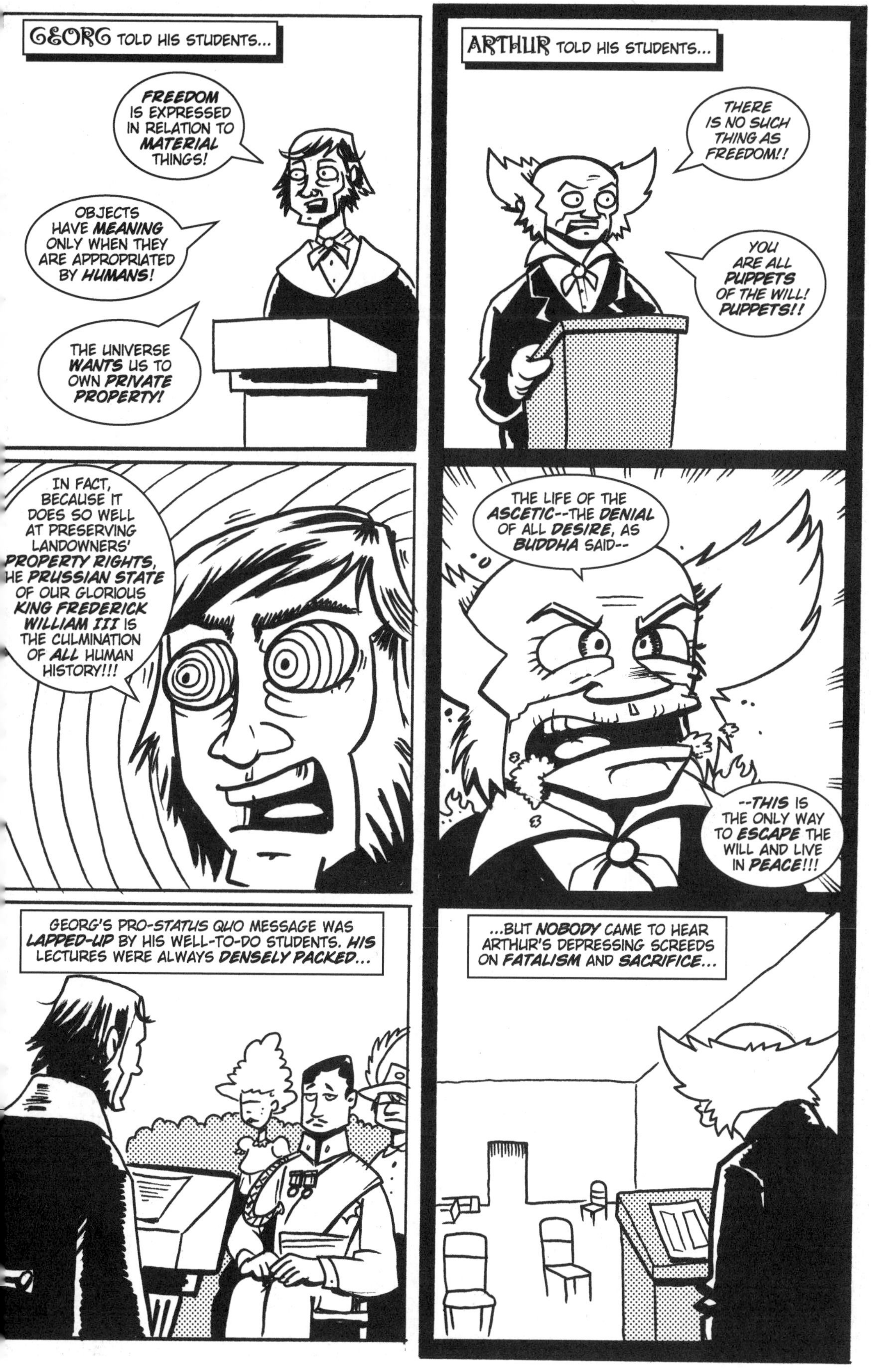
GEORG TOLD HIS STUDENTS...
FREEDOM IS EXPRESSED IN RELATION TO MATERIAL THINGS!
OBJECTS HAVE MEANING ONLY WHEN THEY ARE APPROPRIATED BY HUMANS!
THE UNIVERSE WANTS US TO OWN PRIVATE PROPERTY!
ARTHUR TOLD HIS STUDENTS...
THERE IS NO SUCH THING AS FREEDOM!!
YOU ARE ALL PUPPETS OF THE WILL! PUPPETS!!
IN FACT, BECAUSE IT DOES SO WELL AT PRESERVING LANDOWNERS' PROPERTY RIGHTS, THE PRUSSIAN STATE OF OUR GLORIOUS KING FREDERICK WILLIAM III IS THE CULMINATION OF ALL HUMAN HISTORY!!!
THE LIFE OF THE ASCETIC--THE DENIAL OF ALL DESIRE, AS BUDDHA SAID--
--THIS IS THE ONLY WAY TO ESCAPE THE WILL AND LIVE IN PEACE!!!
GEORG'S PRO-STATUS QUO MESSAGE WAS LAPPED-UP BY HIS WELL-TO-DO STUDENTS. HIS LECTURES WERE ALWAYS DENSELY PACKED...
...BUT NOBODY CAME TO HEAR ARTHUR'S DEPRESSING SCREEDS ON FATALISM AND SACRIFICE...

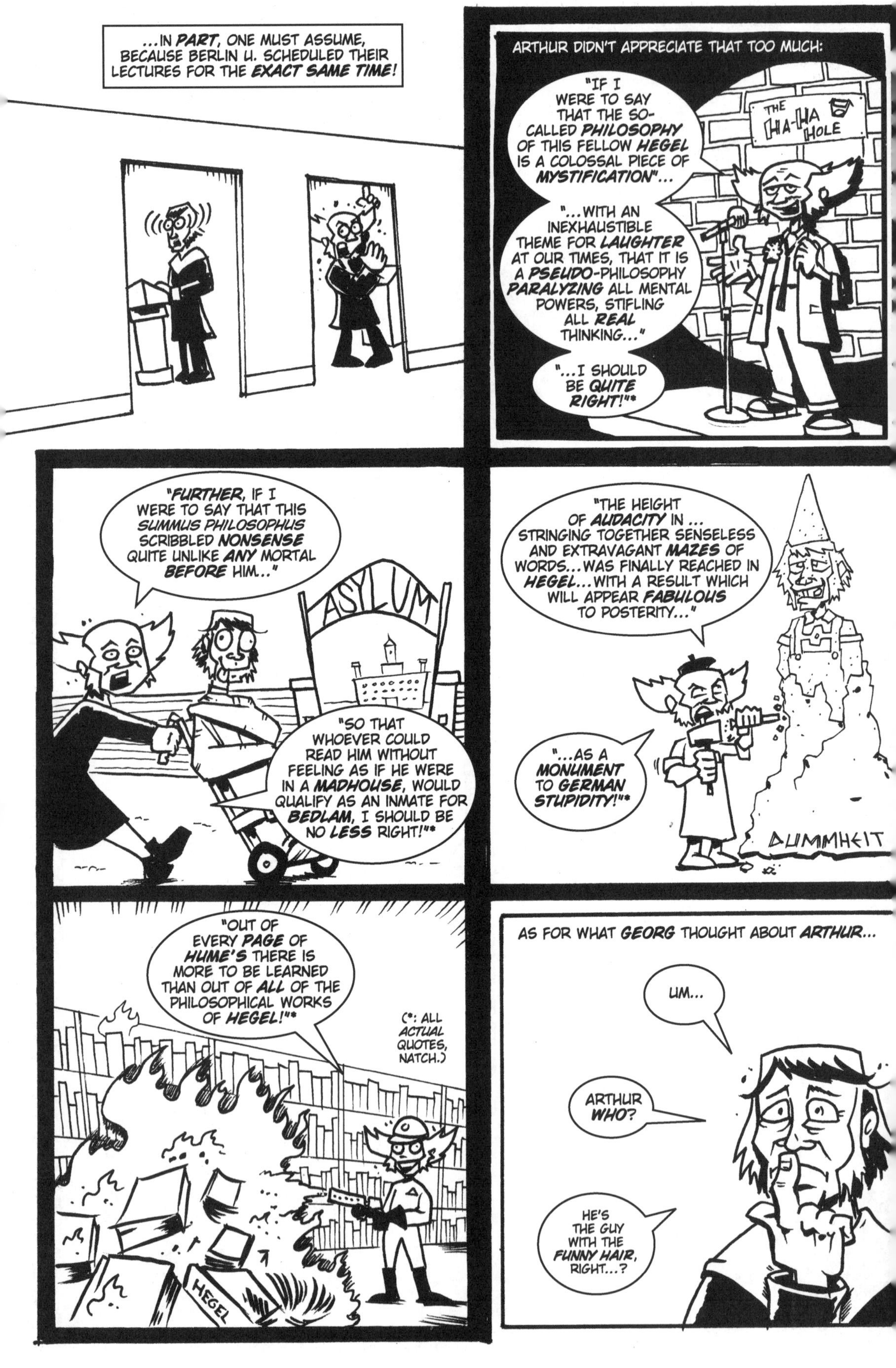

...IN PART, ONE MUST ASSUME, BECAUSE BERLIN U. SCHEDULED THEIR LECTURES FOR THE EXACT SAME TIME!
ARTHUR DIDN'T APPRECIATE THAT TOO MUCH:
"IF I WERE TO SAY THAT THE SO-CALLED PHILOSOPHY OF THIS FELLOW HEGEL IS A COLOSSAL PIECE OF MYSTIFICATION"...
"...WITH AN INEXHAUSTIBLE THEME FOR LAUGHTER AT OUR TIMES, THAT IT IS A PSEUDO-PHILOSOPHY PARALYZING ALL MENTAL POWERS, STIFLING ALL REAL THINKING..."
"...I SHOULD BE QUITE RIGHT!"*
THE HA-HA HOLE
"FURTHER, IF I WERE TO SAY THAT THIS SUMMUS PHILOSOPHUS SCRIBBLED NONSENSE QUITE UNLIKE ANY MORTAL BEFORE HIM..."
ASYLUM
"SO THAT WHOEVER COULD READ HIM WITHOUT FEELING AS IF HE WERE IN A MADHOUSE, WOULD QUALIFY AS AN INMATE FOR BEDLAM, I SHOULD BE NO LESS RIGHT!"*
"THE HEIGHT OF AUDACITY IN ... STRINGING TOGETHER SENSELESS AND EXTRAVAGANT MAZES OF WORDS...WAS FINALLY REACHED IN HEGEL...WITH A RESULT WHICH WILL APPEAR FABULOUS TO POSTERITY..."
"...AS A MONUMENT TO GERMAN STUPIDITY!"*
DUMMHEIT
"OUT OF EVERY PAGE OF HUME'S THERE IS MORE TO BE LEARNED THAN OUT OF ALL OF THE PHILOSOPHICAL WORKS OF HEGEL!"*
(*: ALL ACTUAL QUOTES, NATCH.)
HEGEL
AS FOR WHAT GEORG THOUGHT ABOUT ARTHUR...
UM...
ARTHUR WHO?
HE'S THE GUY WITH THE FUNNY HAIR, RIGHT...?

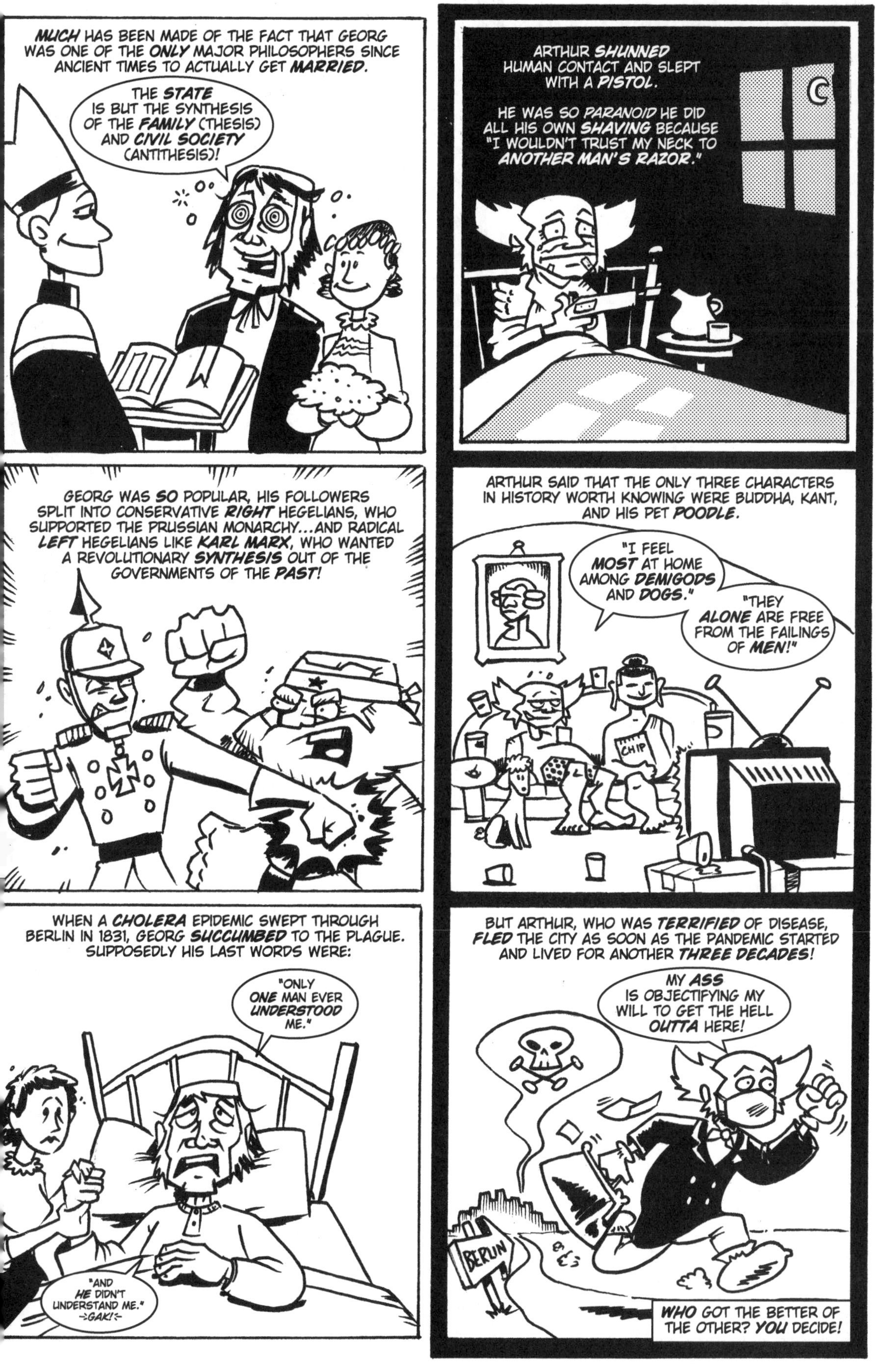
MUCH HAS BEEN MADE OF THE FACT THAT GEORG WAS ONE OF THE ONLY MAJOR PHILOSOPHERS SINCE ANCIENT TIMES TO ACTUALLY GET MARRIED.
THE STATE IS BUT THE SYNTHESIS OF THE FAMILY (THESIS) AND CIVIL SOCIETY (ANTITHESIS)!
ARTHUR SHUNNED HUMAN CONTACT AND SLEPT WITH A PISTOL.
HE WAS SO PARANOID HE DID ALL HIS OWN SHAVING BECAUSE "I WOULDN'T TRUST MY NECK TO ANOTHER MAN'S RAZOR."
GEORG WAS SO POPULAR, HIS FOLLOWERS SPLIT INTO CONSERVATIVE RIGHT HEGELIANS, WHO SUPPORTED THE PRUSSIAN MONARCHY...AND RADICAL LEFT HEGELIANS LIKE KARL MARX, WHO WANTED A REVOLUTIONARY SYNTHESIS OUT OF THE GOVERNMENTS OF THE PAST!
ARTHUR SAID THAT THE ONLY THREE CHARACTERS IN HISTORY WORTH KNOWING WERE BUDDHA, KANT, AND HIS PET POODLE.
"I FEEL MOST AT HOME AMONG DEMIGODS AND DOGS."
"THEY ALONE ARE FREE FROM THE FAILINGS OF MEN!"
CHIP
WHEN A CHOLERA EPIDEMIC SWEPT THROUGH BERLIN IN 1831, GEORG SUCCUMBED TO THE PLAGUE. SUPPOSEDLY HIS LAST WORDS WERE:
"ONLY ONE MAN EVER UNDERSTOOD ME."
"AND HE DIDN'T UNDERSTAND ME." -GAK!-
BUT ARTHUR, WHO WAS TERRIFIED OF DISEASE, FLED THE CITY AS SOON AS THE PANDEMIC STARTED AND LIVED FOR ANOTHER THREE DECADES!
MY ASS IS OBJECTIFYING MY WILL TO GET THE HELL OUTTA HERE!
BERLIN
WHO GOT THE BETTER OF THE OTHER? YOU DECIDE!

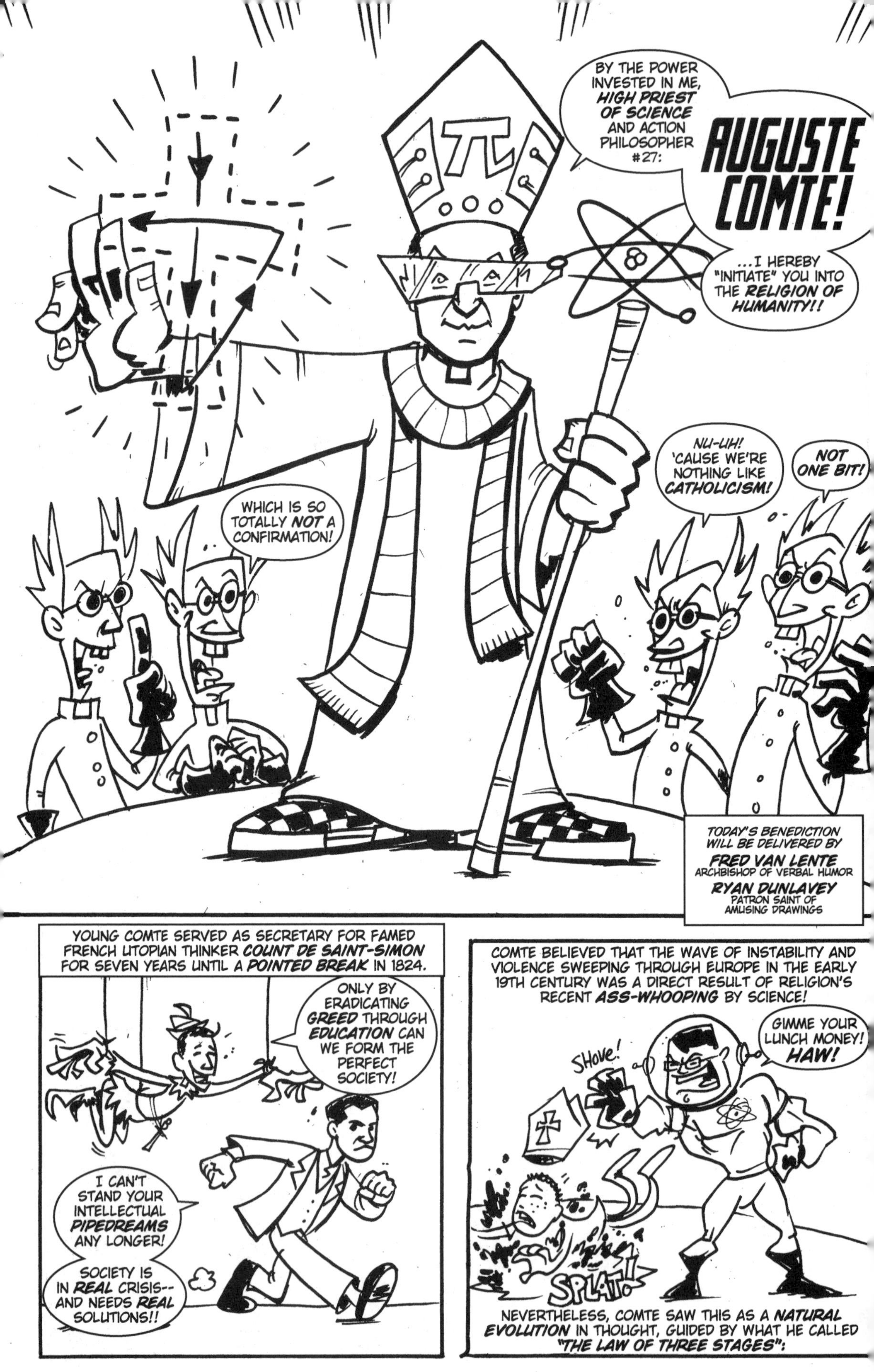
BY THE POWER INVESTED IN ME, HIGH PRIEST OF SCIENCE AND ACTION PHILOSOPHER #27:
AUGUSTE COMTE!
...I HEREBY "INITIATE" YOU INTO THE RELIGION OF HUMANITY!!
WHICH IS SO TOTALLY NOT A CONFIRMATION!
NU-UH! 'CAUSE WE'RE NOTHING LIKE CATHOLICISM!
NOT ONE BIT!
TODAY'S BENEDICTION WILL BE DELIVERED BY
FRED VAN LENTE
ARCHBISHOP OF VERBAL HUMOR
RYAN DUNLAVEY
PATRON SAINT OF AMUSING DRAWINGS
YOUNG COMTE SERVED AS SECRETARY FOR FAMED FRENCH UTOPIAN THINKER COUNT DE SAINT-SIMON FOR SEVEN YEARS UNTIL A POINTED BREAK IN 1824.
ONLY BY ERADICATING GREED THROUGH EDUCATION CAN WE FORM THE PERFECT SOCIETY!
I CAN'T STAND YOUR INTELLECTUAL PIPEDREAMS ANY LONGER!
SOCIETY IS IN REAL CRISIS-- AND NEEDS REAL SOLUTIONS!!
COMTE BELIEVED THAT THE WAVE OF INSTABILITY AND VIOLENCE SWEEPING THROUGH EUROPE IN THE EARLY 19TH CENTURY WAS A DIRECT RESULT OF RELIGION'S RECENT ASS-WHOOPING BY SCIENCE!
GIMME YOUR LUNCH MONEY! HAW!
SHOVE!
SPLAT!
NEVERTHELESS, COMTE SAW THIS AS A NATURAL EVOLUTION IN THOUGHT, GUIDED BY WHAT HE CALLED "THE LAW OF THREE STAGES":

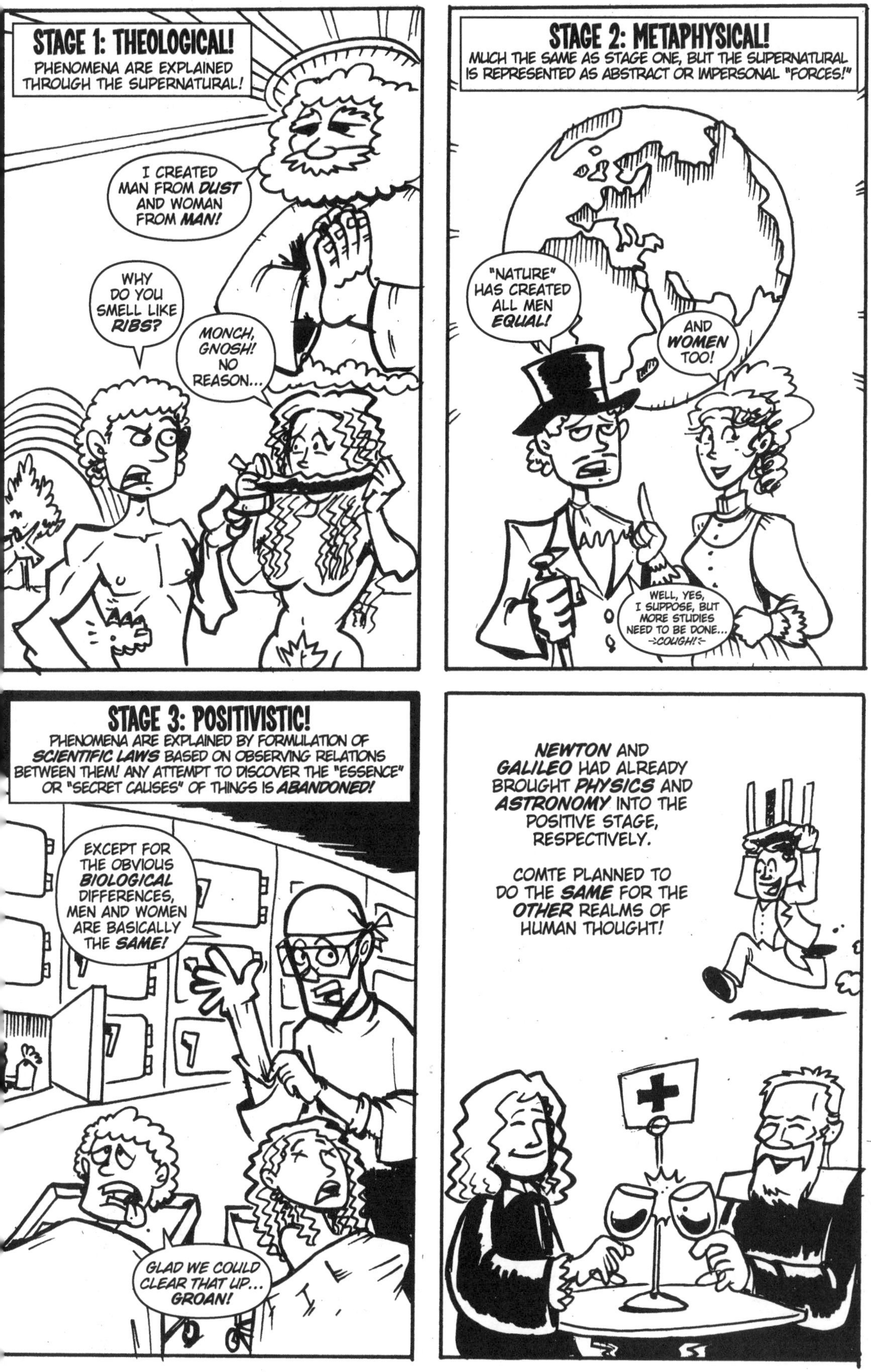
STAGE 1: THEOLOGICAL!
PHENOMENA ARE EXPLAINED THROUGH THE SUPERNATURAL!
I CREATED MAN FROM DUST AND WOMAN FROM MAN!
WHY DO YOU SMELL LIKE RIBS?
MONCH, GNOSH! NO REASON...
STAGE 2: METAPHYSICAL!
MUCH THE SAME AS STAGE ONE, BUT THE SUPERNATURAL IS REPRESENTED AS ABSTRACT OR IMPERSONAL "FORCES!"
"NATURE" HAS CREATED ALL MEN EQUAL!
AND WOMEN TOO!
WELL, YES, I SUPPOSE, BUT MORE STUDIES NEED TO BE DONE... ->COUGH!<-
STAGE 3: POSITIVISTIC!
PHENOMENA ARE EXPLAINED BY FORMULATION OF SCIENTIFIC LAWS BASED ON OBSERVING RELATIONS BETWEEN THEM! ANY ATTEMPT TO DISCOVER THE "ESSENCE" OR "SECRET CAUSES" OF THINGS IS ABANDONED!
EXCEPT FOR THE OBVIOUS BIOLOGICAL DIFFERENCES, MEN AND WOMEN ARE BASICALLY THE SAME!
GLAD WE COULD CLEAR THAT UP... GROAN!
NEWTON AND GALILEO HAD ALREADY BROUGHT PHYSICS AND ASTRONOMY INTO THE POSITIVE STAGE, RESPECTIVELY.
COMTE PLANNED TO DO THE SAME FOR THE OTHER REALMS OF HUMAN THOUGHT!

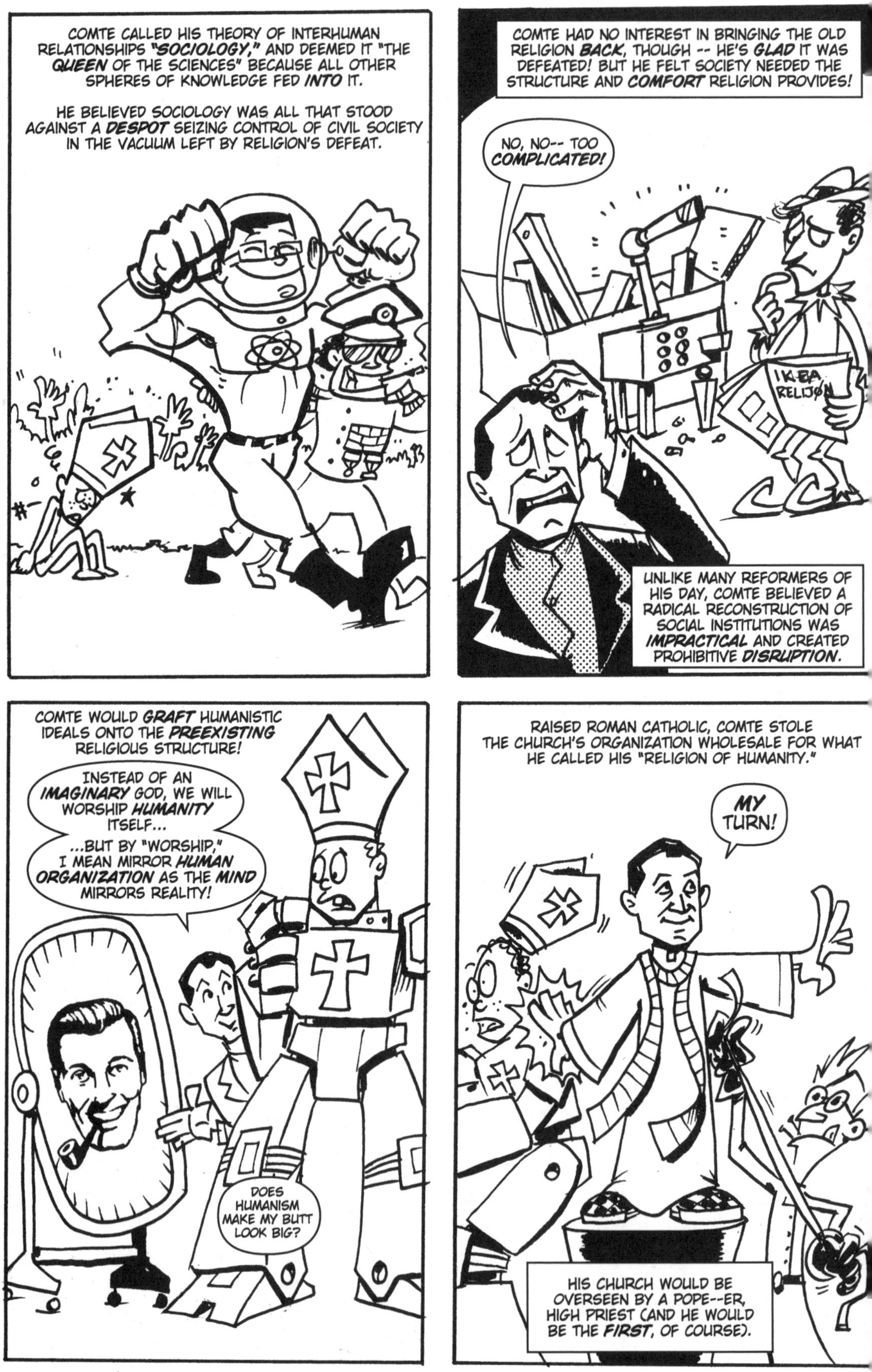
COMTE CALLED HIS THEORY OF INTERHUMAN RELATIONSHIPS "SOCIOLOGY," AND DEEMED IT "THE QUEEN OF THE SCIENCES" BECAUSE ALL OTHER SPHERES OF KNOWLEDGE FED INTO IT.
HE BELIEVED SOCIOLOGY WAS ALL THAT STOOD AGAINST A DESPOT SEIZING CONTROL OF CIVIL SOCIETY IN THE VACUUM LEFT BY RELIGION'S DEFEAT.
COMTE HAD NO INTEREST IN BRINGING THE OLD RELIGION BACK, THOUGH -- HE'S GLAD IT WAS DEFEATED! BUT HE FELT SOCIETY NEEDED THE STRUCTURE AND COMFORT RELIGION PROVIDES!
NO, NO-- TOO COMPLICATED!
IKEA RELIJØN
UNLIKE MANY REFORMERS OF HIS DAY, COMTE BELIEVED A RADICAL RECONSTRUCTION OF SOCIAL INSTITUTIONS WAS IMPRACTICAL AND CREATED PROHIBITIVE DISRUPTION.
COMTE WOULD GRAFT HUMANISTIC IDEALS ONTO THE PREEXISTING RELIGIOUS STRUCTURE!
INSTEAD OF AN IMAGINARY GOD, WE WILL WORSHIP HUMANITY ITSELF...
...BUT BY "WORSHIP," I MEAN MIRROR HUMAN ORGANIZATION AS THE MIND MIRRORS REALITY!
DOES HUMANISM MAKE MY BUTT LOOK BIG?
RAISED ROMAN CATHOLIC, COMTE STOLE THE CHURCH'S ORGANIZATION WHOLESALE FOR WHAT HE CALLED HIS "RELIGION OF HUMANITY."
MY TURN!
HIS CHURCH WOULD BE OVERSEEN BY A POPE--ER, HIGH PRIEST (AND HE WOULD BE THE FIRST, OF COURSE).

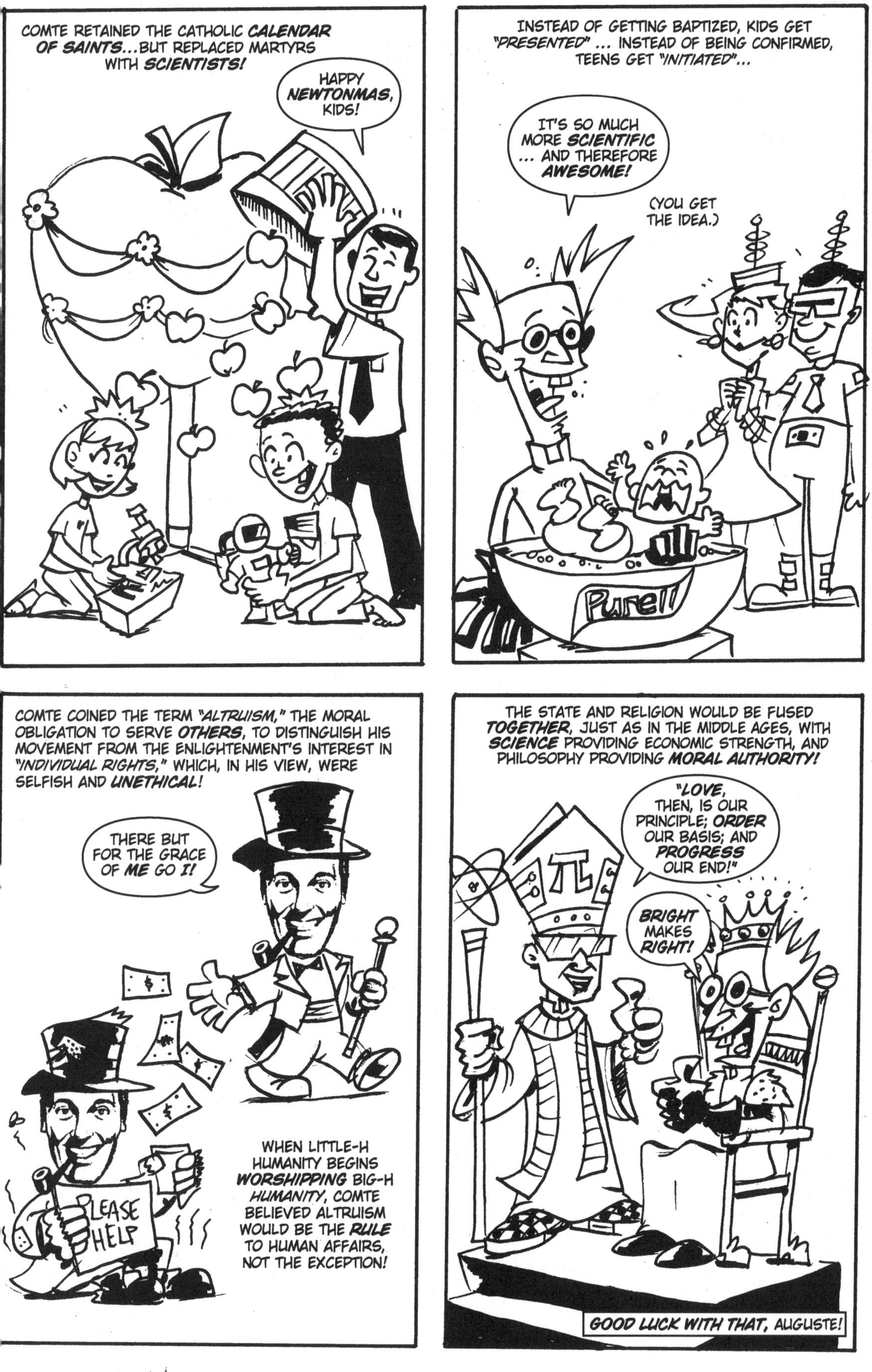
COMTE RETAINED THE CATHOLIC CALENDAR OF SAINTS...BUT REPLACED MARTYRS WITH SCIENTISTS!
HAPPY NEWTONMAS, KIDS!
INSTEAD OF GETTING BAPTIZED, KIDS GET "PRESENTED" ... INSTEAD OF BEING CONFIRMED, TEENS GET "INITIATED"...
IT'S SO MUCH MORE SCIENTIFIC ... AND THEREFORE AWESOME!
(YOU GET THE IDEA.)
Purell
COMTE COINED THE TERM "ALTRUISM," THE MORAL OBLIGATION TO SERVE OTHERS, TO DISTINGUISH HIS MOVEMENT FROM THE ENLIGHTENMENT'S INTEREST IN "INDIVIDUAL RIGHTS," WHICH, IN HIS VIEW, WERE SELFISH AND UNETHICAL!
THERE BUT FOR THE GRACE OF ME GO I!
PLEASE HELP
WHEN LITTLE-H HUMANITY BEGINS WORSHIPPING BIG-H HUMANITY, COMTE BELIEVED ALTRUISM WOULD BE THE RULE TO HUMAN AFFAIRS, NOT THE EXCEPTION!
THE STATE AND RELIGION WOULD BE FUSED TOGETHER, JUST AS IN THE MIDDLE AGES, WITH SCIENCE PROVIDING ECONOMIC STRENGTH, AND PHILOSOPHY PROVIDING MORAL AUTHORITY!
"LOVE, THEN, IS OUR PRINCIPLE; ORDER OUR BASIS; AND PROGRESS OUR END!"
BRIGHT MAKES RIGHT!
GOOD LUCK WITH THAT, AUGUSTE!

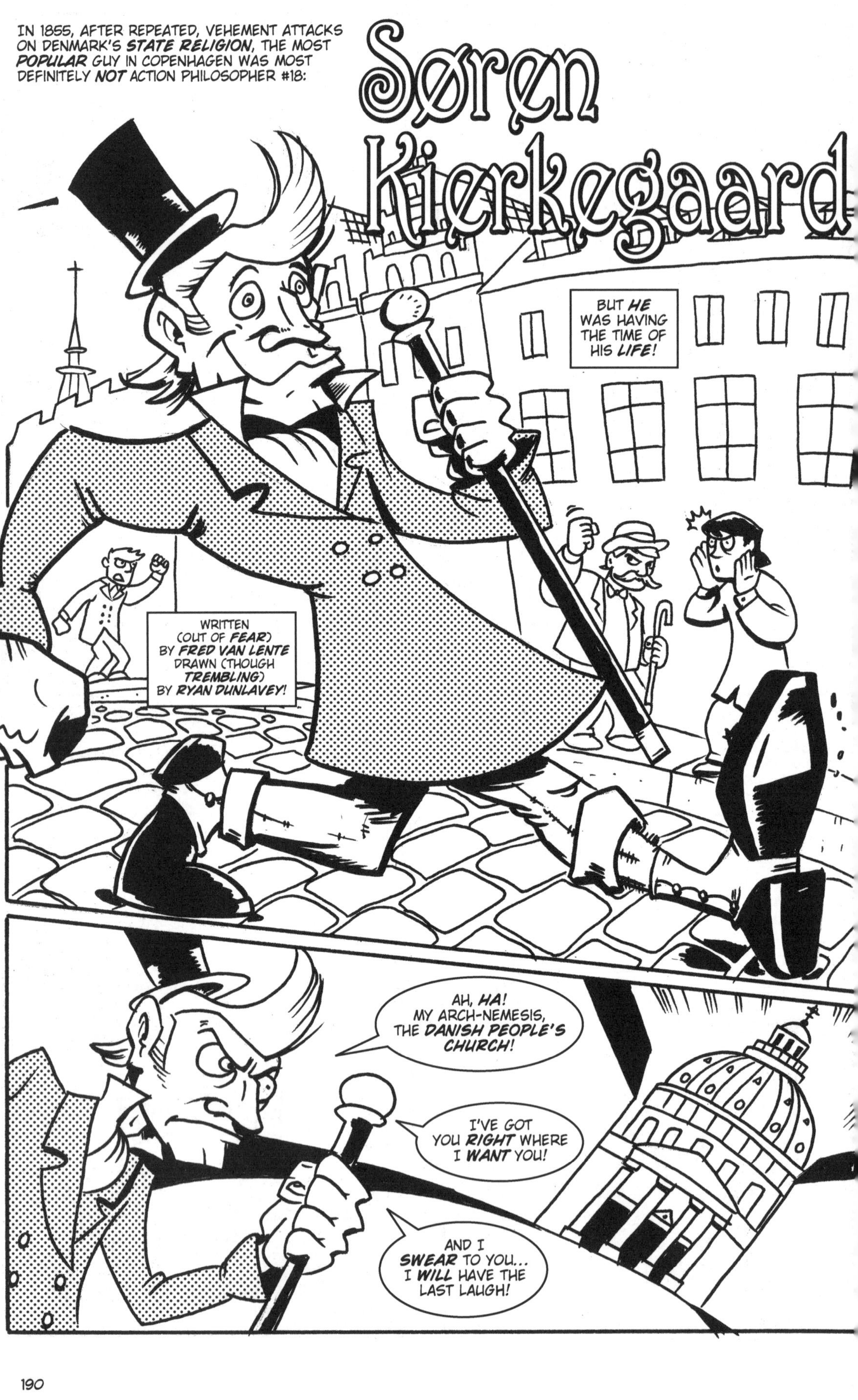
IN 1855, AFTER REPEATED, VEHEMENT ATTACKS ON DENMARK'S STATE RELIGION, THE MOST POPULAR GUY IN COPENHAGEN WAS MOST DEFINITELY NOT ACTION PHILOSOPHER #18:
Søren Kierkegaard
BUT HE WAS HAVING THE TIME OF HIS LIFE!
WRITTEN (OUT OF FEAR) BY FRED VAN LENTE DRAWN (THOUGH TREMBLING) BY RYAN DUNLAVEY!
AH, HA! MY ARCH-NEMESIS, THE DANISH PEOPLE'S CHURCH!
I'VE GOT YOU RIGHT WHERE I WANT YOU!
AND I SWEAR TO YOU... I WILL HAVE THE LAST LAUGH!

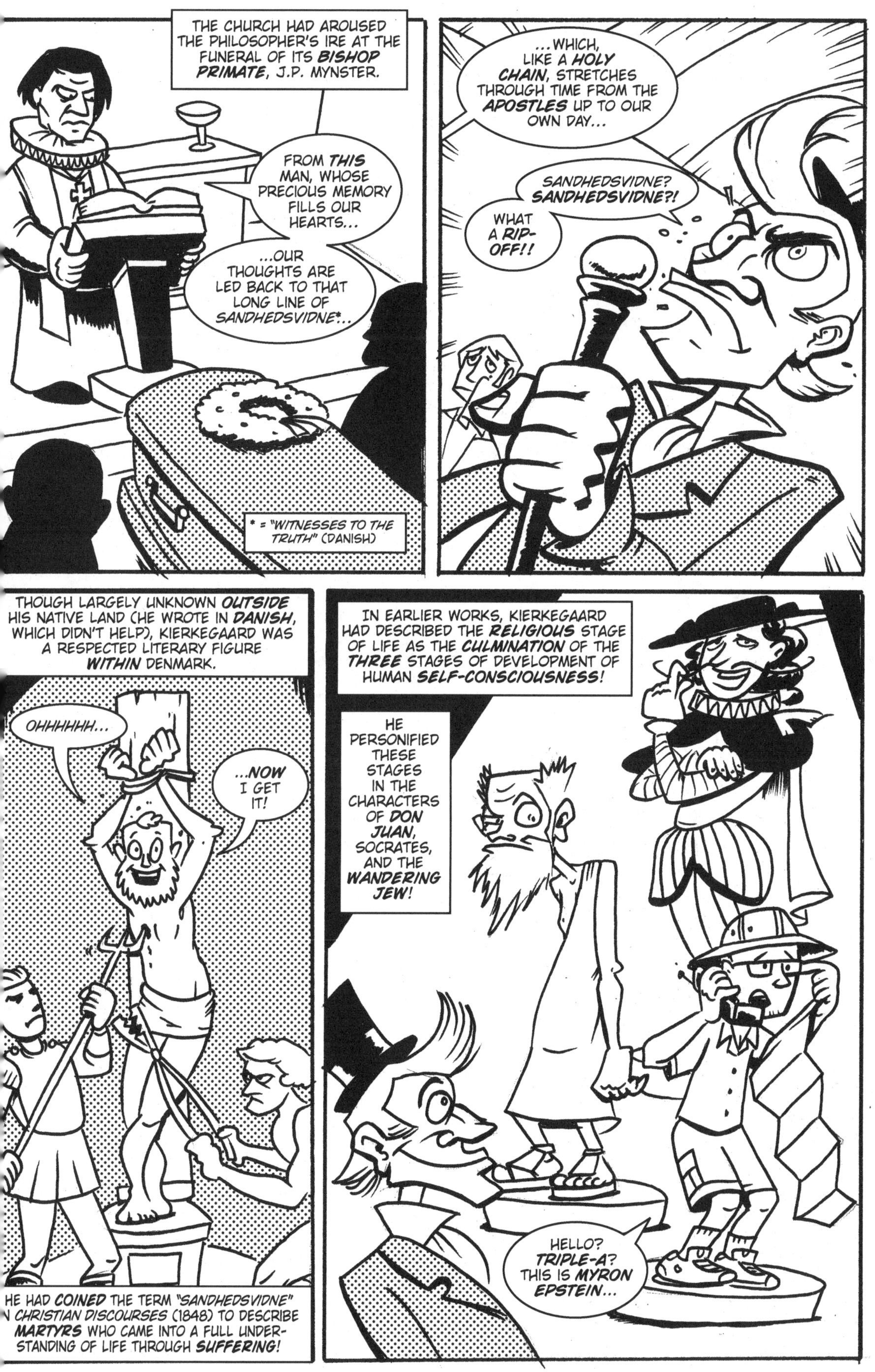
THE CHURCH HAD AROUSED THE PHILOSOPHER'S IRE AT THE FUNERAL OF ITS BISHOP PRIMATE, J.P. MYNSTER.
FROM THIS MAN, WHOSE PRECIOUS MEMORY FILLS OUR HEARTS...
...OUR THOUGHTS ARE LED BACK TO THAT LONG LINE OF SANDHEDSVIDNE*...
* = "WITNESSES TO THE TRUTH" (DANISH)
...WHICH, LIKE A HOLY CHAIN, STRETCHES THROUGH TIME FROM THE APOSTLES UP TO OUR OWN DAY...
SANDHEDSVIDNE? SANDHEDSVIDNE?!
WHAT A RIP-OFF!!
THOUGH LARGELY UNKNOWN OUTSIDE HIS NATIVE LAND (HE WROTE IN DANISH, WHICH DIDN'T HELP), KIERKEGAARD WAS A RESPECTED LITERARY FIGURE WITHIN DENMARK.
OHHHHHH...
...NOW I GET IT!
HE HAD COINED THE TERM "SANDHEDSVIDNE" IN CHRISTIAN DISCOURSES (1848) TO DESCRIBE MARTYRS WHO CAME INTO A FULL UNDERSTANDING OF LIFE THROUGH SUFFERING!
IN EARLIER WORKS, KIERKEGAARD HAD DESCRIBED THE RELIGIOUS STAGE OF LIFE AS THE CULMINATION OF THE THREE STAGES OF DEVELOPMENT OF HUMAN SELF-CONSCIOUSNESS!
HE PERSONIFIED THESE STAGES IN THE CHARACTERS OF DON JUAN, SOCRATES, AND THE WANDERING JEW!
HELLO? TRIPLE-A? THIS IS MYRON EPSTEIN...

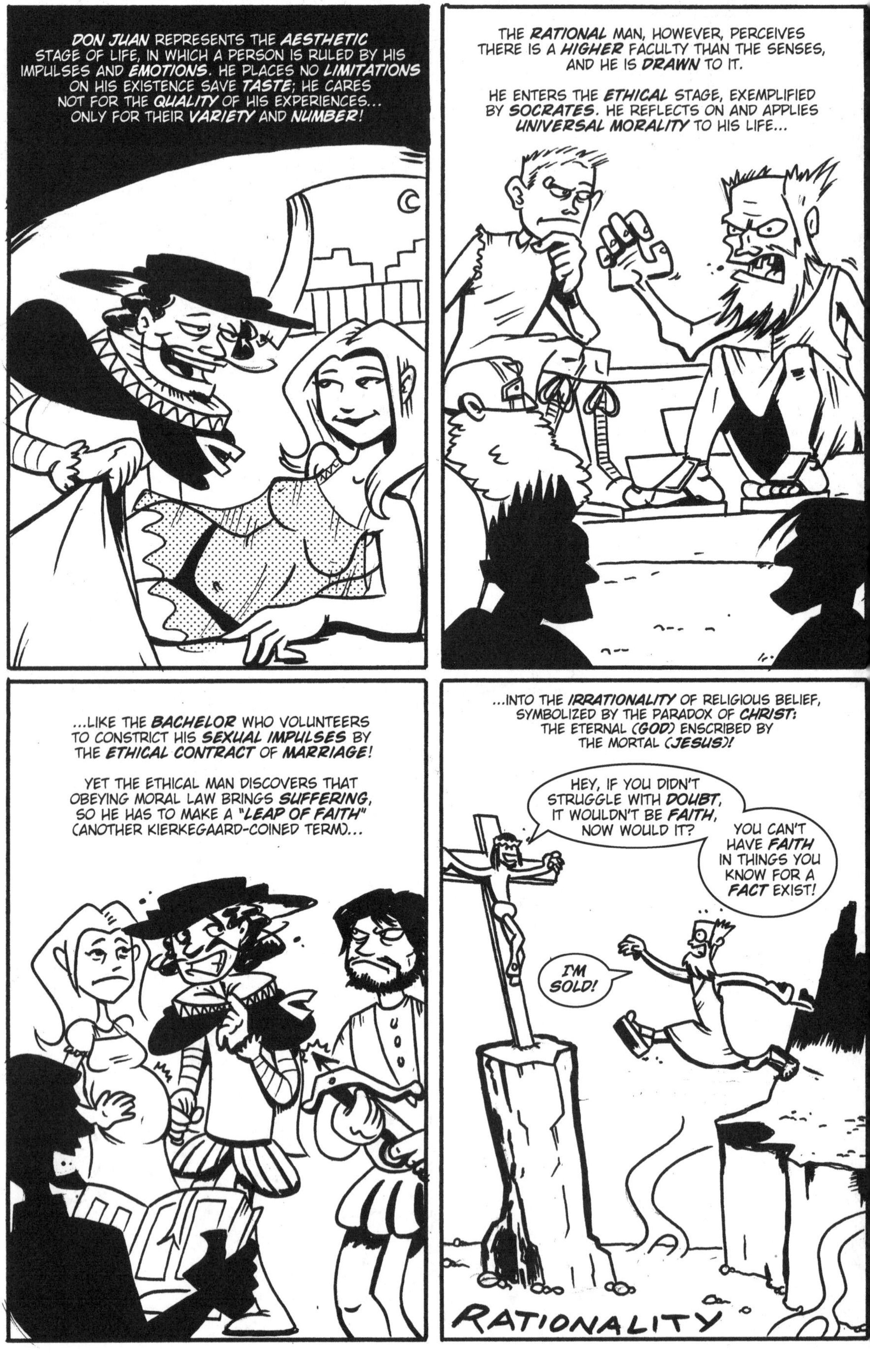
DON JUAN REPRESENTS THE AESTHETIC STAGE OF LIFE, IN WHICH A PERSON IS RULED BY HIS IMPULSES AND EMOTIONS. HE PLACES NO LIMITATIONS ON HIS EXISTENCE SAVE TASTE; HE CARES NOT FOR THE QUALITY OF HIS EXPERIENCES... ONLY FOR THEIR VARIETY AND NUMBER!
THE RATIONAL MAN, HOWEVER, PERCEIVES THERE IS A HIGHER FACULTY THAN THE SENSES, AND HE IS DRAWN TO IT.
HE ENTERS THE ETHICAL STAGE, EXEMPLIFIED BY SOCRATES. HE REFLECTS ON AND APPLIES UNIVERSAL MORALITY TO HIS LIFE...
...LIKE THE BACHELOR WHO VOLUNTEERS TO CONSTRICT HIS SEXUAL IMPULSES BY THE ETHICAL CONTRACT OF MARRIAGE!
YET THE ETHICAL MAN DISCOVERS THAT OBEYING MORAL LAW BRINGS SUFFERING, SO HE HAS TO MAKE A "LEAP OF FAITH" (ANOTHER KIERKEGAARD-COINED TERM)...
...INTO THE IRRATIONALITY OF RELIGIOUS BELIEF, SYMBOLIZED BY THE PARADOX OF CHRIST: THE ETERNAL (GOD) ENSCRIBED BY THE MORTAL (JESUS)!
HEY, IF YOU DIDN'T STRUGGLE WITH DOUBT, IT WOULDN'T BE FAITH, NOW WOULD IT?
YOU CAN'T HAVE FAITH IN THINGS YOU KNOW FOR A FACT EXIST!
I'M SOLD!
RATIONALITY

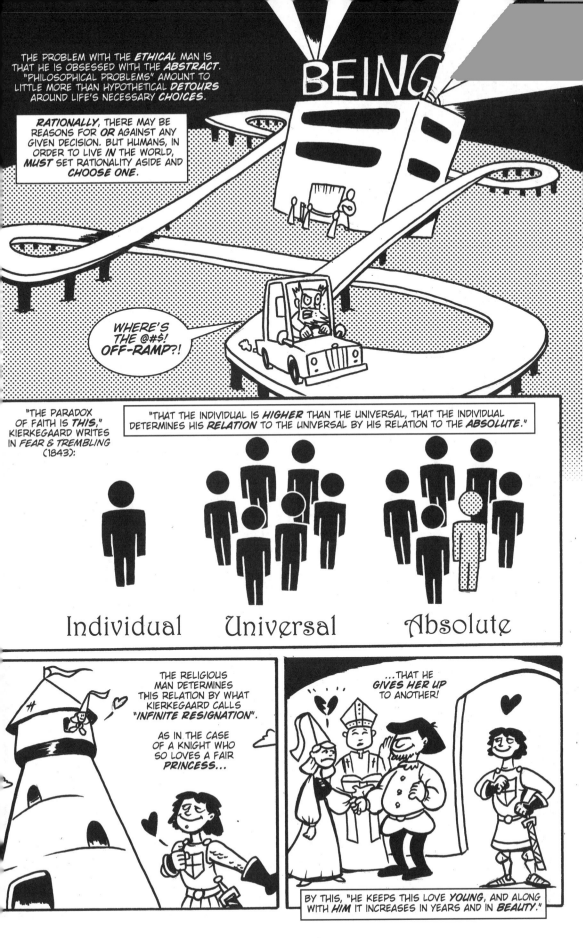

THE PROBLEM WITH THE *ETHICAL* MAN IS THAT HE IS OBSESSED WITH THE *ABSTRACT*. "PHILOSOPHICAL PROBLEMS" AMOUNT TO LITTLE MORE THAN HYPOTHETICAL *DETOURS* AROUND LIFE'S NECESSARY *CHOICES*.

RATIONALLY, THERE MAY BE REASONS FOR *OR* AGAINST ANY GIVEN DECISION. BUT HUMANS, IN ORDER TO LIVE *IN* THE WORLD, *MUST* SET RATIONALITY ASIDE AND *CHOOSE ONE*.

BEING

WHERE'S THE @#$! OFF-RAMP?!

"THE PARADOX OF FAITH IS *THIS*," KIERKEGAARD WRITES IN *FEAR & TREMBLING* (1843):

"THAT THE INDIVIDUAL IS *HIGHER* THAN THE UNIVERSAL, THAT THE INDIVIDUAL DETERMINES HIS *RELATION* TO THE UNIVERSAL BY HIS RELATION TO THE *ABSOLUTE*."

Individual   Universal   Absolute

THE RELIGIOUS MAN DETERMINES THIS RELATION BY WHAT KIERKEGAARD CALLS "*INFINITE RESIGNATION*".

AS IN THE CASE OF A KNIGHT WHO SO LOVES A FAIR *PRINCESS*...

...THAT HE *GIVES HER UP* TO ANOTHER!

BY THIS, "HE KEEPS THIS LOVE *YOUNG*, AND ALONG WITH *HIM* IT INCREASES IN YEARS AND IN *BEAUTY*."

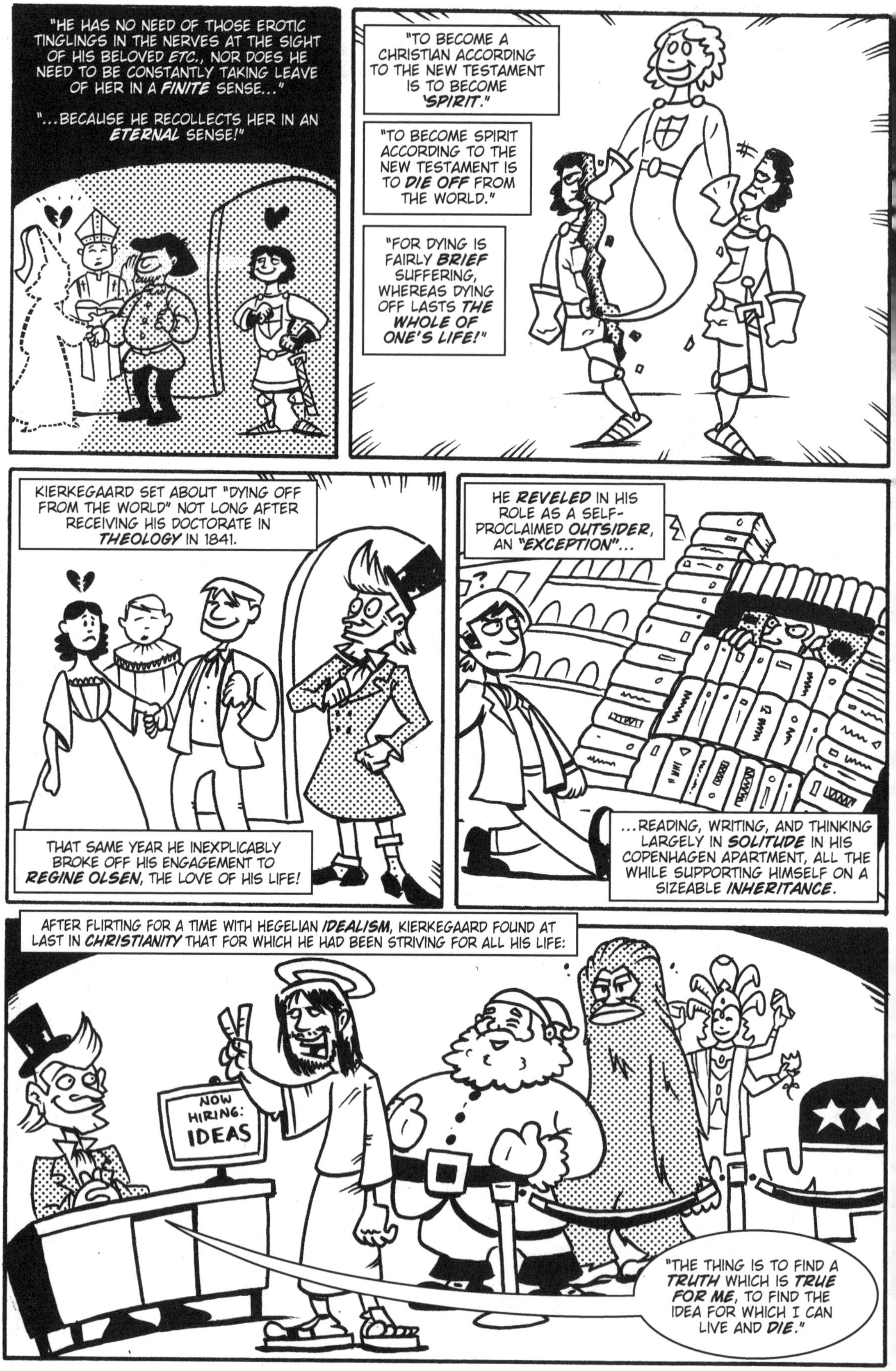
"HE HAS NO NEED OF THOSE EROTIC TINGLINGS IN THE NERVES AT THE SIGHT OF HIS BELOVED ETC., NOR DOES HE NEED TO BE CONSTANTLY TAKING LEAVE OF HER IN A FINITE SENSE..."
"...BECAUSE HE RECOLLECTS HER IN AN ETERNAL SENSE!"
"TO BECOME A CHRISTIAN ACCORDING TO THE NEW TESTAMENT IS TO BECOME 'SPIRIT."
"TO BECOME SPIRIT ACCORDING TO THE NEW TESTAMENT IS TO DIE OFF FROM THE WORLD."
"FOR DYING IS FAIRLY BRIEF SUFFERING, WHEREAS DYING OFF LASTS THE WHOLE OF ONE'S LIFE!"
KIERKEGAARD SET ABOUT "DYING OFF FROM THE WORLD" NOT LONG AFTER RECEIVING HIS DOCTORATE IN THEOLOGY IN 1841.
THAT SAME YEAR HE INEXPLICABLY BROKE OFF HIS ENGAGEMENT TO REGINE OLSEN, THE LOVE OF HIS LIFE!
HE REVELED IN HIS ROLE AS A SELF-PROCLAIMED OUTSIDER, AN "EXCEPTION"...
?
...READING, WRITING, AND THINKING LARGELY IN SOLITUDE IN HIS COPENHAGEN APARTMENT, ALL THE WHILE SUPPORTING HIMSELF ON A SIZEABLE INHERITANCE.
AFTER FLIRTING FOR A TIME WITH HEGELIAN IDEALISM, KIERKEGAARD FOUND AT LAST IN CHRISTIANITY THAT FOR WHICH HE HAD BEEN STRIVING FOR ALL HIS LIFE:
NOW HIRING: IDEAS
"THE THING IS TO FIND A TRUTH WHICH IS TRUE FOR ME, TO FIND THE IDEA FOR WHICH I CAN LIVE AND DIE."

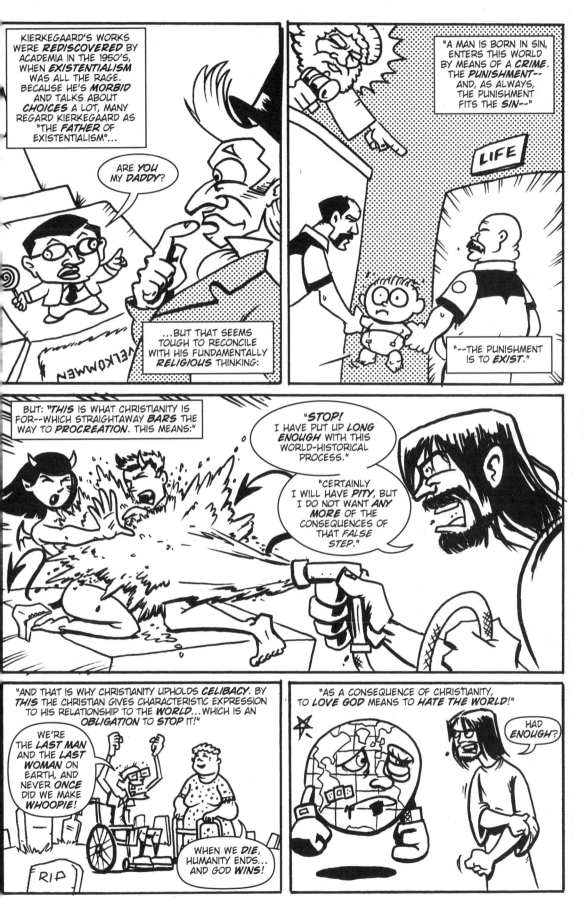

KIERKEGAARD'S WORKS WERE *REDISCOVERED* BY ACADEMIA IN THE 1950'S, WHEN *EXISTENTIALISM* WAS ALL THE RAGE. BECAUSE HE'S *MORBID* AND TALKS ABOUT *CHOICES* A LOT, MANY REGARD KIERKEGAARD AS "THE *FATHER* OF EXISTENTIALISM"...

ARE *YOU* MY *DADDY*?

...BUT THAT SEEMS TOUGH TO RECONCILE WITH HIS FUNDAMENTALLY *RELIGIOUS* THINKING:

VELKOMMEN

"A MAN IS BORN IN SIN, ENTERS THIS WORLD BY MEANS OF A *CRIME*. THE *PUNISHMENT*-- AND, AS ALWAYS, THE PUNISHMENT FITS THE *SIN*--"

LIFE

"--THE PUNISHMENT IS TO *EXIST*."

BUT: "*THIS* IS WHAT CHRISTIANITY IS FOR--WHICH STRAIGHTAWAY *BARS* THE WAY TO *PROCREATION*. THIS MEANS:"

"*STOP!* I HAVE PUT UP *LONG ENOUGH* WITH THIS WORLD-HISTORICAL PROCESS."

"*CERTAINLY* I WILL HAVE *PITY*, BUT I DO NOT WANT *ANY MORE* OF THE CONSEQUENCES OF THAT *FALSE STEP*."

"AND THAT IS WHY CHRISTIANITY UPHOLDS *CELIBACY*. BY *THIS* THE CHRISTIAN GIVES CHARACTERISTIC EXPRESSION TO HIS RELATIONSHIP TO THE *WORLD*...WHICH IS AN *OBLIGATION* TO *STOP* IT!"

WE'RE THE *LAST MAN* AND THE *LAST WOMAN* ON EARTH, AND NEVER *ONCE* DID WE MAKE *WHOOPIE*!

WHEN WE *DIE*, HUMANITY ENDS... AND GOD *WINS*!

RIP

"AS A CONSEQUENCE OF CHRISTIANITY, TO *LOVE GOD* MEANS TO *HATE THE WORLD*!"

HAD *ENOUGH*?

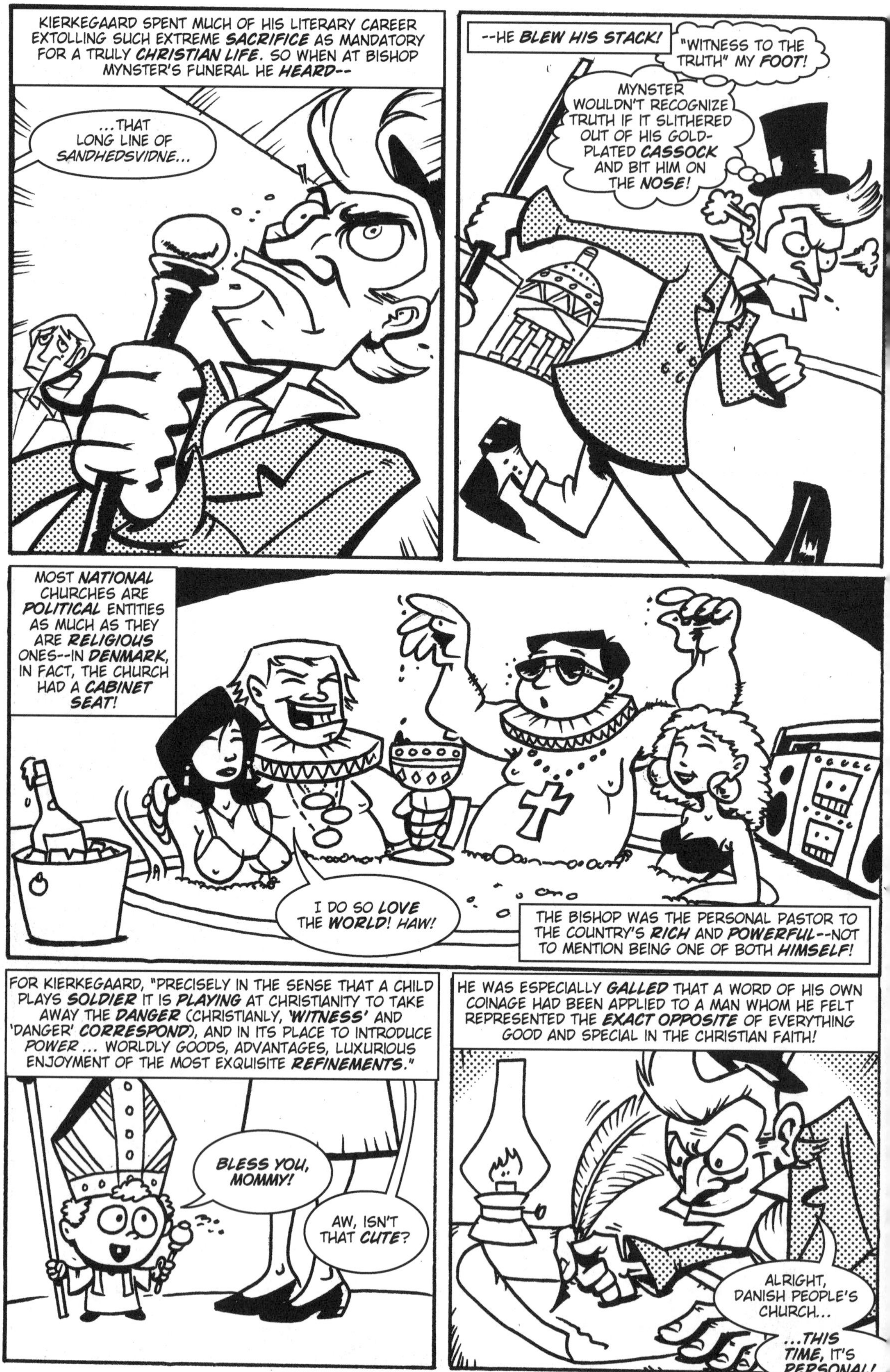
KIERKEGAARD SPENT MUCH OF HIS LITERARY CAREER EXTOLLING SUCH EXTREME SACRIFICE AS MANDATORY FOR A TRULY CHRISTIAN LIFE. SO WHEN AT BISHOP MYNSTER'S FUNERAL HE HEARD--
...THAT LONG LINE OF SANDHEDSVIDNE...
--HE BLEW HIS STACK!
"WITNESS TO THE TRUTH" MY FOOT!
MYNSTER WOULDN'T RECOGNIZE TRUTH IF IT SLITHERED OUT OF HIS GOLD-PLATED CASSOCK AND BIT HIM ON THE NOSE!
MOST NATIONAL CHURCHES ARE POLITICAL ENTITIES AS MUCH AS THEY ARE RELIGIOUS ONES--IN DENMARK, IN FACT, THE CHURCH HAD A CABINET SEAT!
I DO SO LOVE THE WORLD! HAW!
THE BISHOP WAS THE PERSONAL PASTOR TO THE COUNTRY'S RICH AND POWERFUL--NOT TO MENTION BEING ONE OF BOTH HIMSELF!
FOR KIERKEGAARD, "PRECISELY IN THE SENSE THAT A CHILD PLAYS SOLDIER IT IS PLAYING AT CHRISTIANITY TO TAKE AWAY THE DANGER (CHRISTIANLY, 'WITNESS' AND 'DANGER' CORRESPOND), AND IN ITS PLACE TO INTRODUCE POWER ... WORLDLY GOODS, ADVANTAGES, LUXURIOUS ENJOYMENT OF THE MOST EXQUISITE REFINEMENTS."
BLESS YOU, MOMMY!
AW, ISN'T THAT CUTE?
HE WAS ESPECIALLY GALLED THAT A WORD OF HIS OWN COINAGE HAD BEEN APPLIED TO A MAN WHOM HE FELT REPRESENTED THE EXACT OPPOSITE OF EVERYTHING GOOD AND SPECIAL IN THE CHRISTIAN FAITH!
ALRIGHT, DANISH PEOPLE'S CHURCH...
...THIS TIME, IT'S PERSONAL!

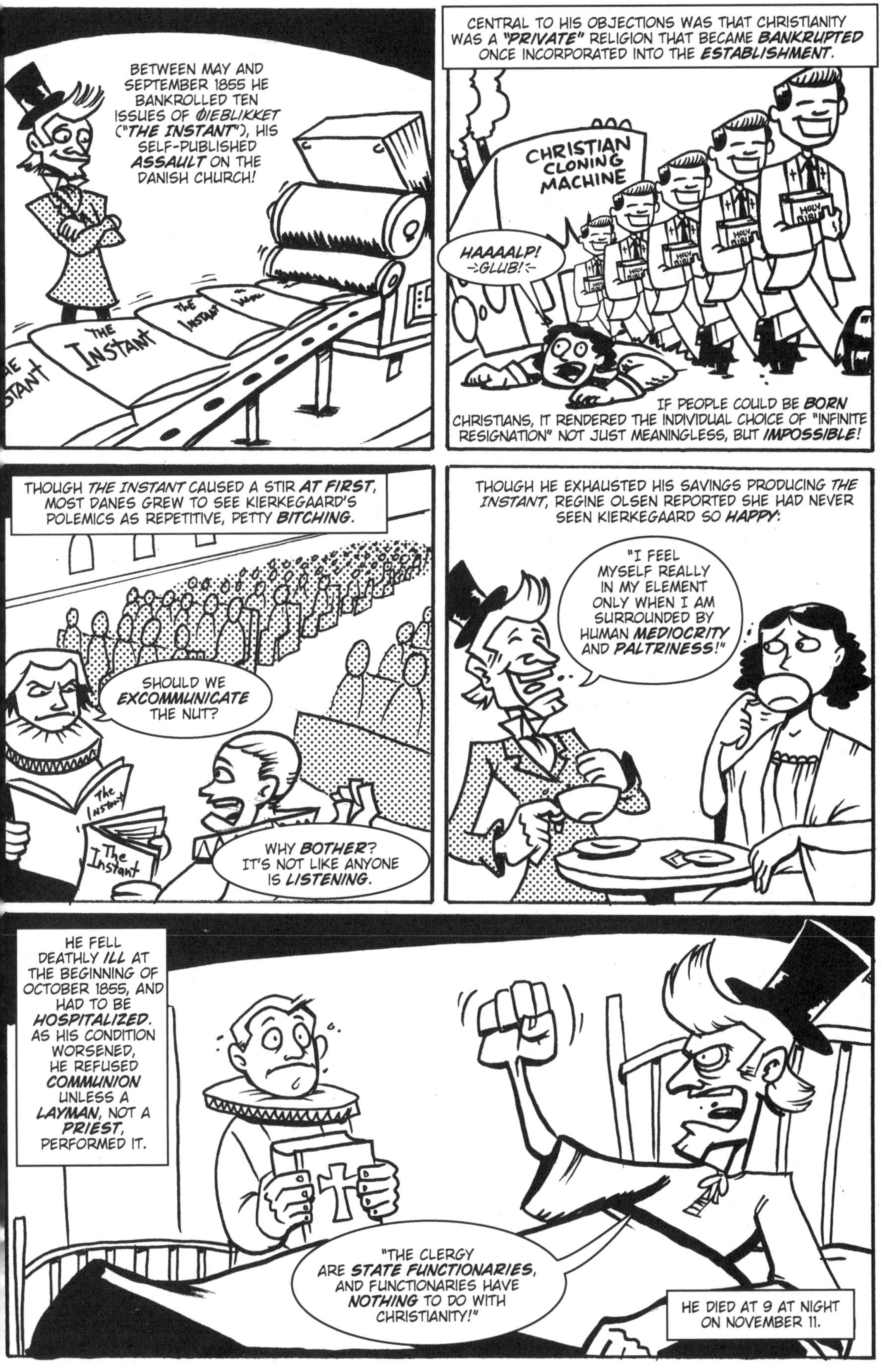
BETWEEN MAY AND SEPTEMBER 1855 HE BANKROLLED TEN ISSUES OF ØIEBLIKKET ("THE INSTANT"), HIS SELF-PUBLISHED ASSAULT ON THE DANISH CHURCH!
THE INSTANT
THE INSTANT
CENTRAL TO HIS OBJECTIONS WAS THAT CHRISTIANITY WAS A "PRIVATE" RELIGION THAT BECAME BANKRUPTED ONCE INCORPORATED INTO THE ESTABLISHMENT.
CHRISTIAN CLONING MACHINE
HAAAALP! GLUB!
HOLY BIBLE
IF PEOPLE COULD BE BORN CHRISTIANS, IT RENDERED THE INDIVIDUAL CHOICE OF "INFINITE RESIGNATION" NOT JUST MEANINGLESS, BUT IMPOSSIBLE!
THOUGH THE INSTANT CAUSED A STIR AT FIRST, MOST DANES GREW TO SEE KIERKEGAARD'S POLEMICS AS REPETITIVE, PETTY BITCHING.
SHOULD WE EXCOMMUNICATE THE NUT?
The Instant
The Instant
WHY BOTHER? IT'S NOT LIKE ANYONE IS LISTENING.
THOUGH HE EXHAUSTED HIS SAVINGS PRODUCING THE INSTANT, REGINE OLSEN REPORTED SHE HAD NEVER SEEN KIERKEGAARD SO HAPPY:
"I FEEL MYSELF REALLY IN MY ELEMENT ONLY WHEN I AM SURROUNDED BY HUMAN MEDIOCRITY AND PALTRINESS!"
HE FELL DEATHLY ILL AT THE BEGINNING OF OCTOBER 1855, AND HAD TO BE HOSPITALIZED. AS HIS CONDITION WORSENED, HE REFUSED COMMUNION UNLESS A LAYMAN, NOT A PRIEST, PERFORMED IT.
"THE CLERGY ARE STATE FUNCTIONARIES, AND FUNCTIONARIES HAVE NOTHING TO DO WITH CHRISTIANITY!"
HE DIED AT 9 AT NIGHT ON NOVEMBER 11.

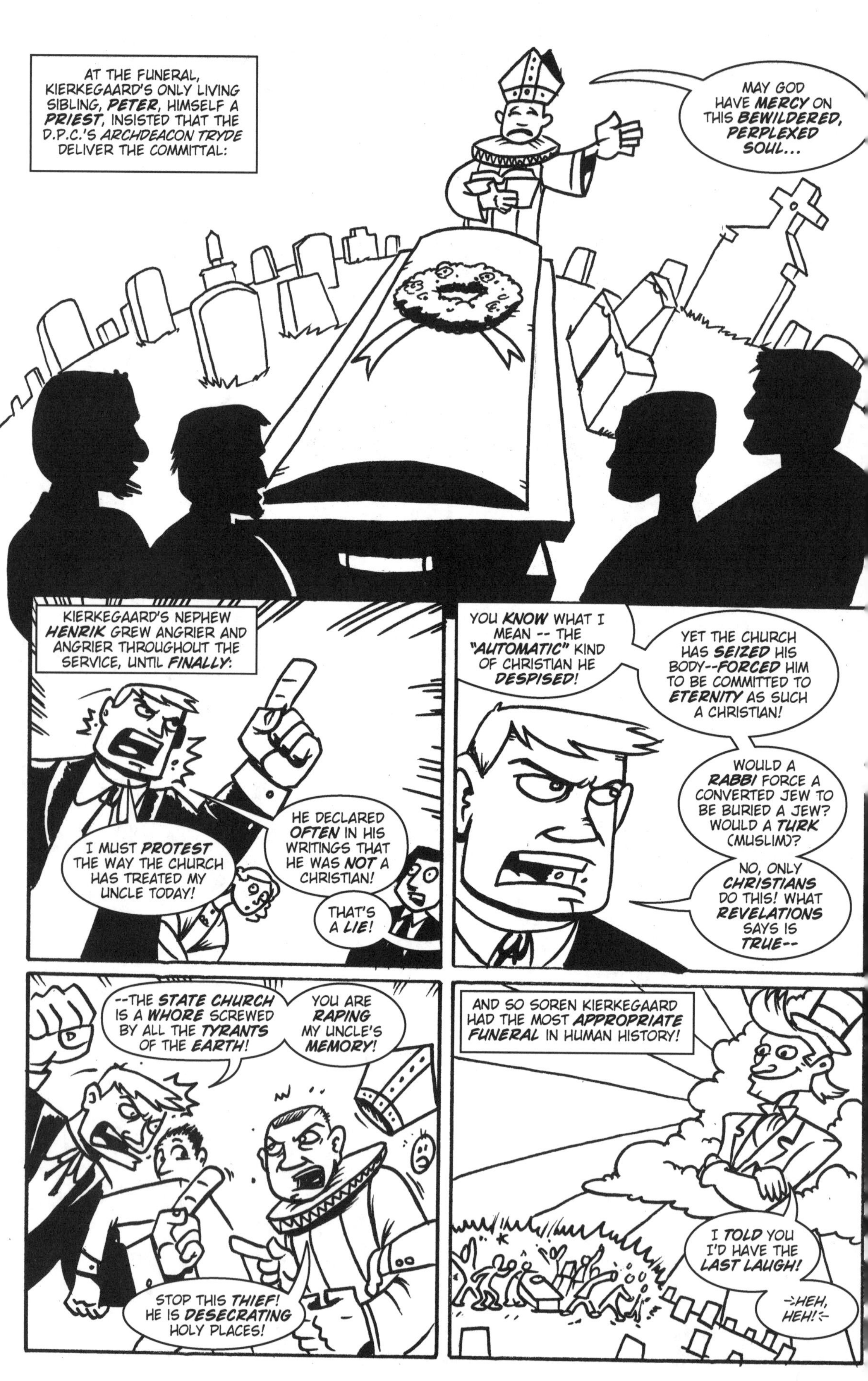
AT THE FUNERAL, KIERKEGAARD'S ONLY LIVING SIBLING, PETER, HIMSELF A PRIEST, INSISTED THAT THE D.P.C.'S ARCHDEACON TRYDE DELIVER THE COMMITTAL:
MAY GOD HAVE MERCY ON THIS BEWILDERED, PERPLEXED SOUL...
KIERKEGAARD'S NEPHEW HENRIK GREW ANGRIER AND ANGRIER THROUGHOUT THE SERVICE, UNTIL FINALLY:
I MUST PROTEST THE WAY THE CHURCH HAS TREATED MY UNCLE TODAY!
HE DECLARED OFTEN IN HIS WRITINGS THAT HE WAS NOT A CHRISTIAN!
THAT'S A LIE!
YOU KNOW WHAT I MEAN -- THE "AUTOMATIC" KIND OF CHRISTIAN HE DESPISED!
YET THE CHURCH HAS SEIZED HIS BODY--FORCED HIM TO BE COMMITTED TO ETERNITY AS SUCH A CHRISTIAN!
WOULD A RABBI FORCE A CONVERTED JEW TO BE BURIED A JEW? WOULD A TURK (MUSLIM)?
NO, ONLY CHRISTIANS DO THIS! WHAT REVELATIONS SAYS IS TRUE--
--THE STATE CHURCH IS A WHORE SCREWED BY ALL THE TYRANTS OF THE EARTH!
YOU ARE RAPING MY UNCLE'S MEMORY!
STOP THIS THIEF! HE IS DESECRATING HOLY PLACES!
AND SO SOREN KIERKEGAARD HAD THE MOST APPROPRIATE FUNERAL IN HUMAN HISTORY!
I TOLD YOU I'D HAVE THE LAST LAUGH!
HEH, HEH!

PART FOUR:

OUR STUPID AGE OF "ISMs"

(CONTEMPORARY PHILOSOPHY)

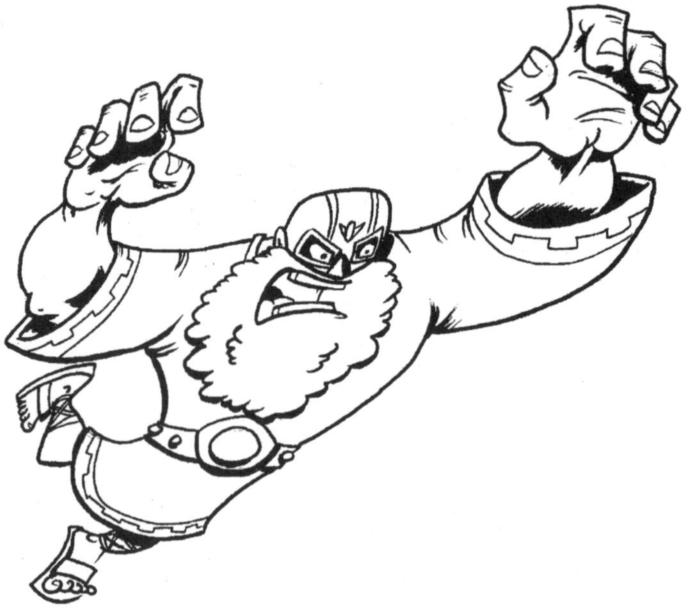

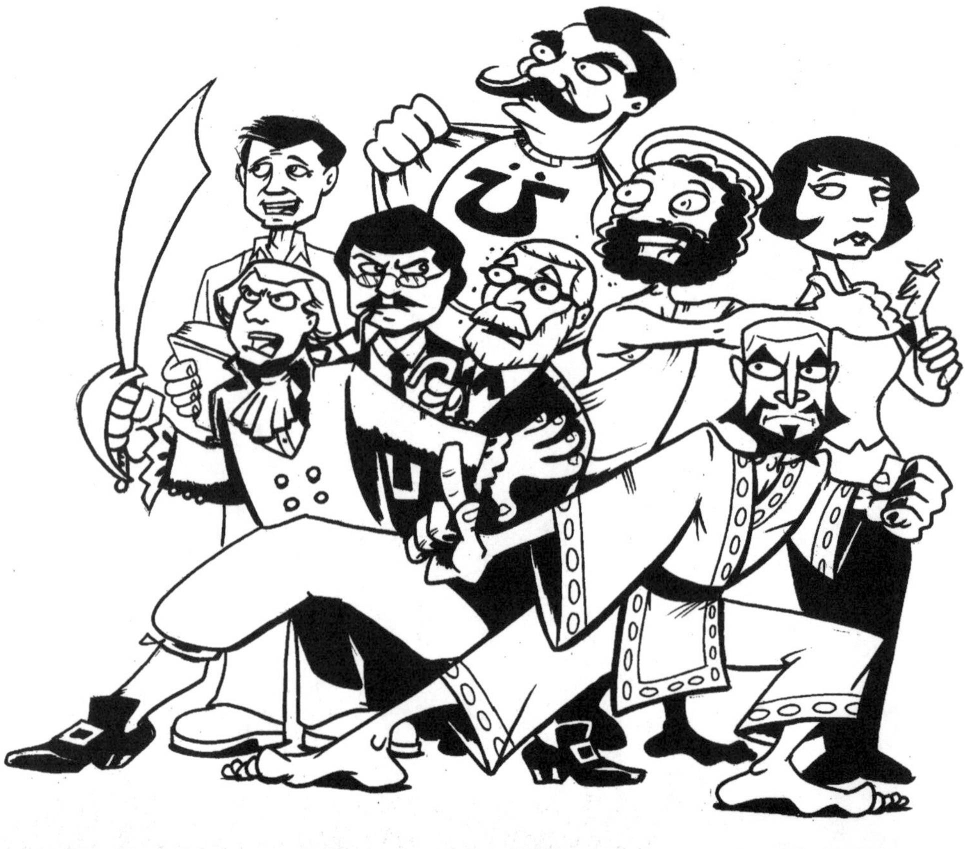

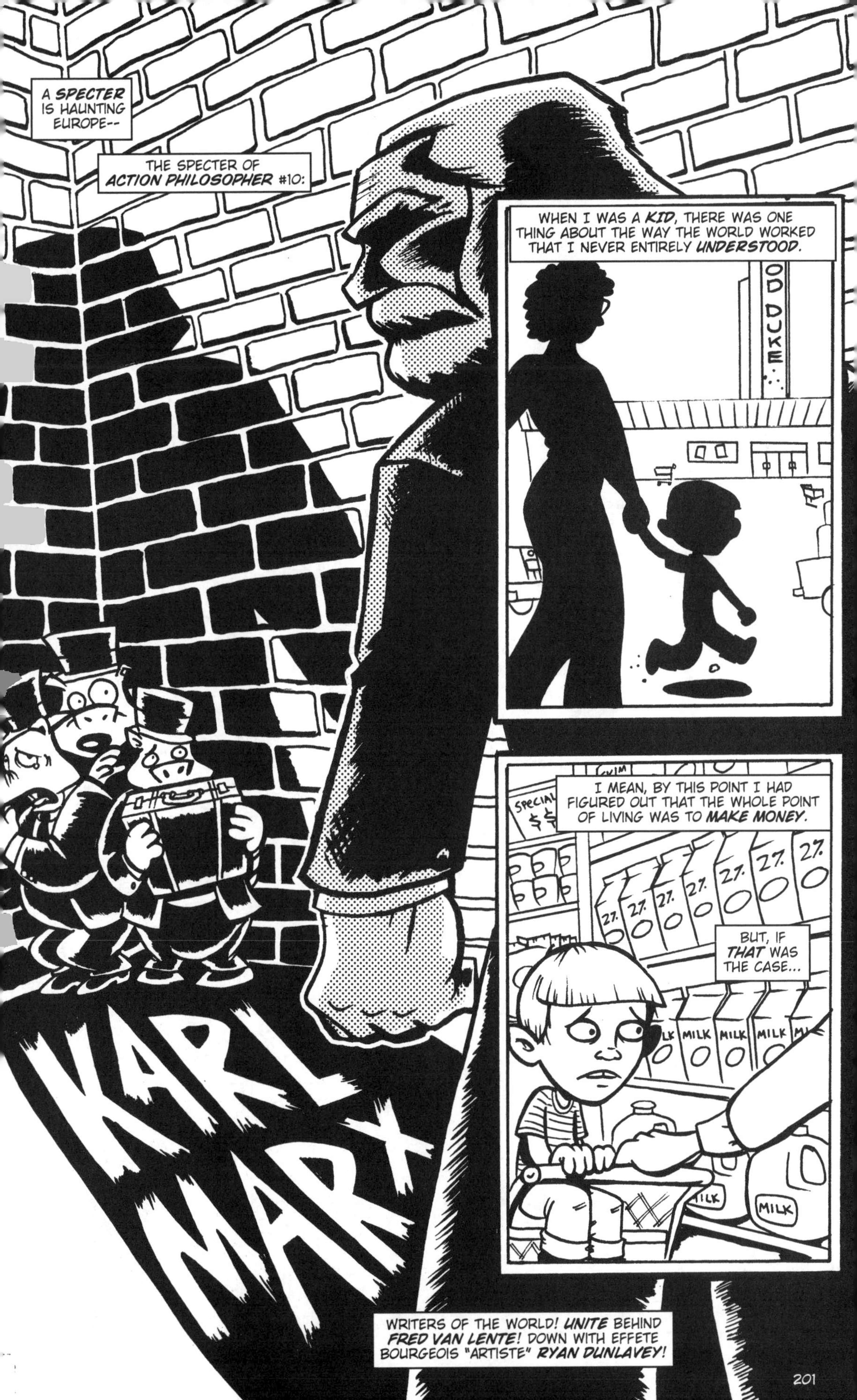
A SPECTER IS HAUNTING EUROPE--
THE SPECTER OF ACTION PHILOSOPHER #10:
KARL MARX
WHEN I WAS A KID, THERE WAS ONE THING ABOUT THE WAY THE WORLD WORKED THAT I NEVER ENTIRELY UNDERSTOOD.
OD DUKE
I MEAN, BY THIS POINT I HAD FIGURED OUT THAT THE WHOLE POINT OF LIVING WAS TO MAKE MONEY.
SPECIAL
BUT, IF THAT WAS THE CASE...
MILK
WRITERS OF THE WORLD! UNITE BEHIND FRED VAN LENTE! DOWN WITH EFFETE BOURGEOIS "ARTISTE" RYAN DUNLAVEY!

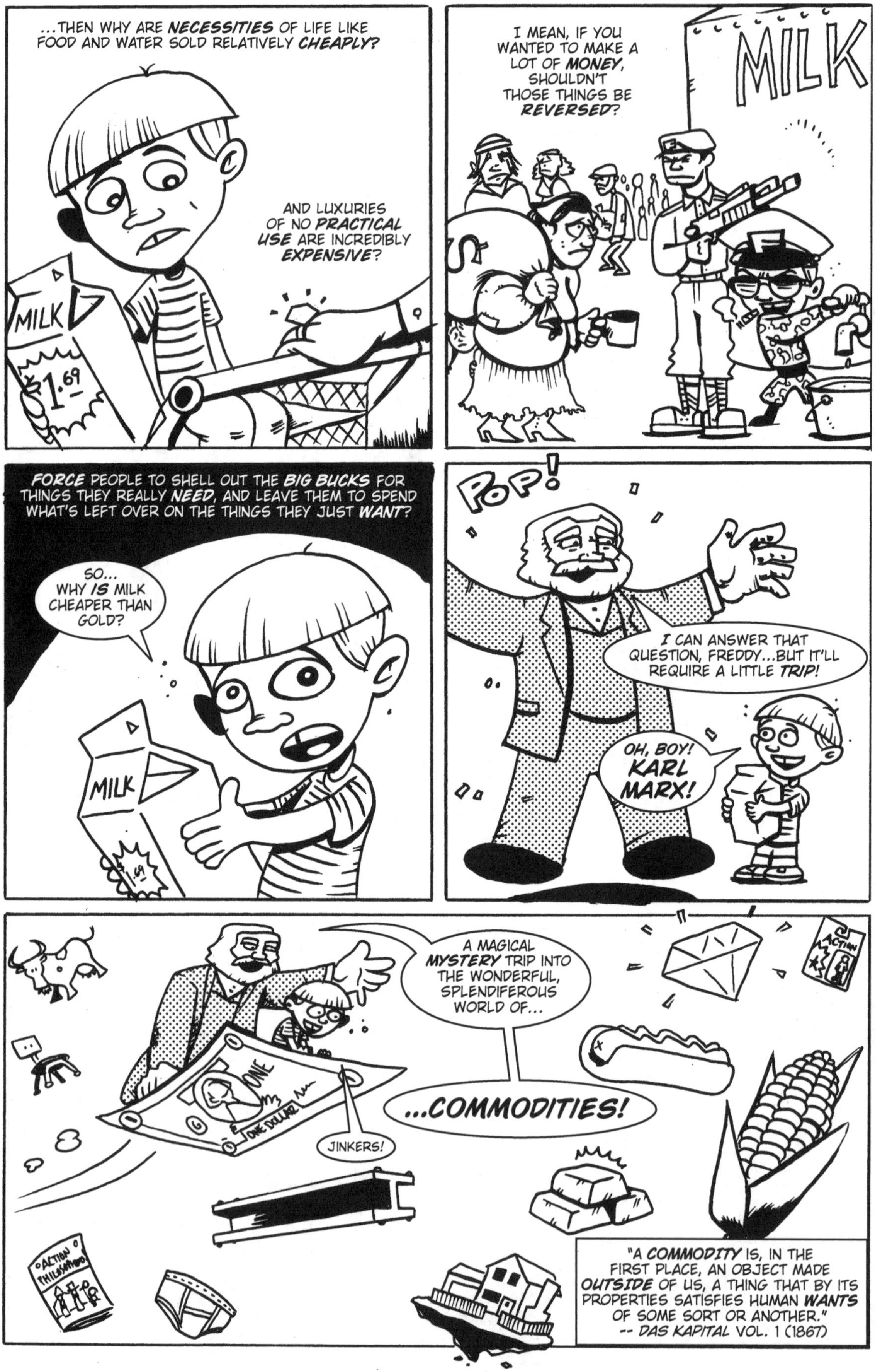

...THEN WHY ARE NECESSITIES OF LIFE LIKE FOOD AND WATER SOLD RELATIVELY CHEAPLY?
AND LUXURIES OF NO PRACTICAL USE ARE INCREDIBLY EXPENSIVE?
MILK
$1.69
I MEAN, IF YOU WANTED TO MAKE A LOT OF MONEY, SHOULDN'T THOSE THINGS BE REVERSED?
MILK
FORCE PEOPLE TO SHELL OUT THE BIG BUCKS FOR THINGS THEY REALLY NEED, AND LEAVE THEM TO SPEND WHAT'S LEFT OVER ON THE THINGS THEY JUST WANT?
SO... WHY IS MILK CHEAPER THAN GOLD?
MILK
POP!
I CAN ANSWER THAT QUESTION, FREDDY...BUT IT'LL REQUIRE A LITTLE TRIP!
OH, BOY! KARL MARX!
A MAGICAL MYSTERY TRIP INTO THE WONDERFUL, SPLENDIFEROUS WORLD OF...
...COMMODITIES!
JINKERS!
ONE
ONE DOLLAR
ACTION
ACTION PHILOSOPHERS
"A COMMODITY IS, IN THE FIRST PLACE, AN OBJECT MADE OUTSIDE OF US, A THING THAT BY ITS PROPERTIES SATISFIES HUMAN WANTS OF SOME SORT OR ANOTHER."
-- DAS KAPITAL VOL. 1 (1867)

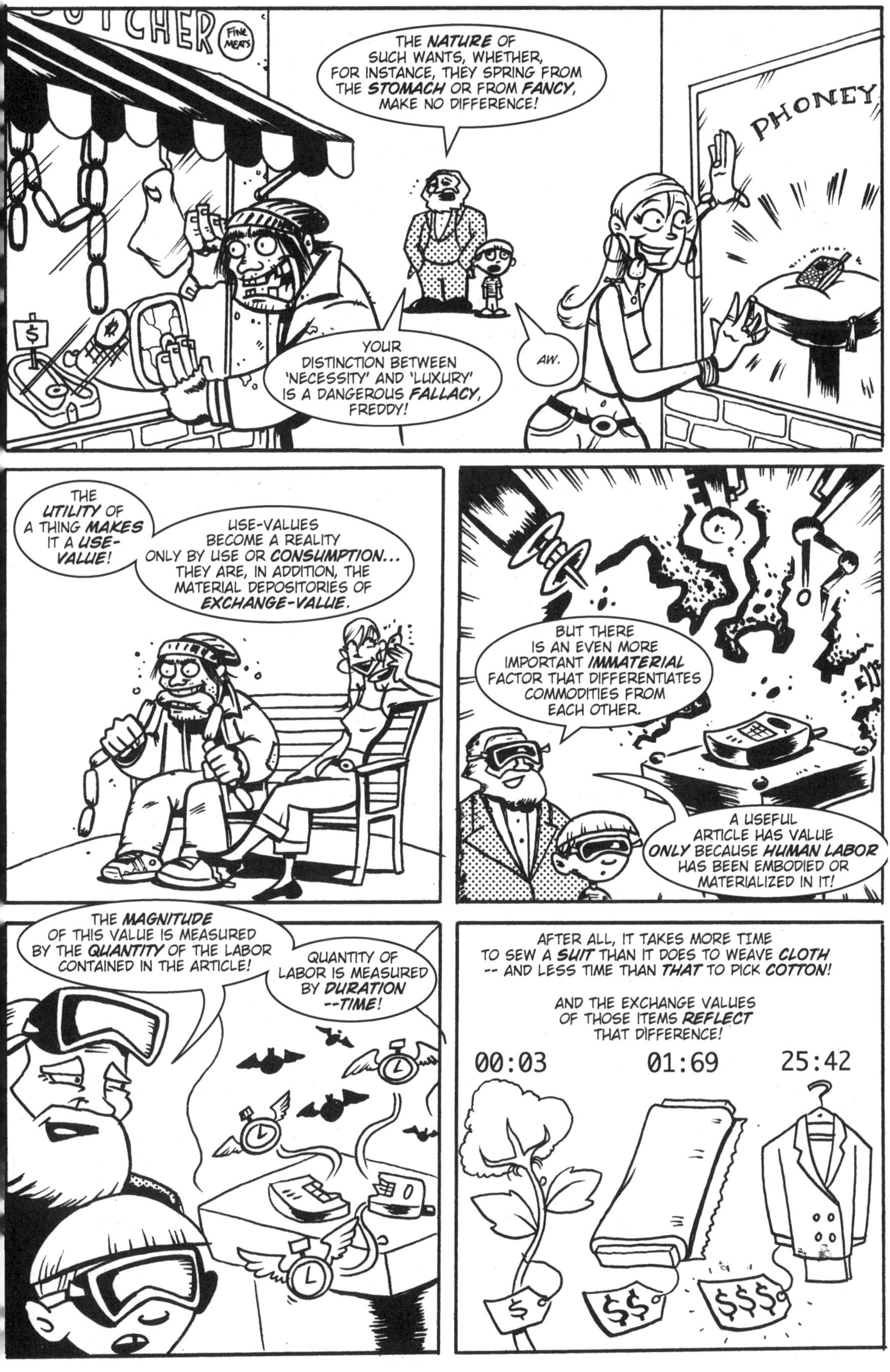

BUTCHER
FINE MEATS
THE NATURE OF SUCH WANTS, WHETHER, FOR INSTANCE, THEY SPRING FROM THE STOMACH OR FROM FANCY, MAKE NO DIFFERENCE!
PHONEY
YOUR DISTINCTION BETWEEN 'NECESSITY' AND 'LUXURY' IS A DANGEROUS FALLACY, FREDDY!
AW.
THE UTILITY OF A THING MAKES IT A USE-VALUE!
USE-VALUES BECOME A REALITY ONLY BY USE OR CONSUMPTION... THEY ARE, IN ADDITION, THE MATERIAL DEPOSITORIES OF EXCHANGE-VALUE.
BUT THERE IS AN EVEN MORE IMPORTANT IMMATERIAL FACTOR THAT DIFFERENTIATES COMMODITIES FROM EACH OTHER.
A USEFUL ARTICLE HAS VALUE ONLY BECAUSE HUMAN LABOR HAS BEEN EMBODIED OR MATERIALIZED IN IT!
THE MAGNITUDE OF THIS VALUE IS MEASURED BY THE QUANTITY OF THE LABOR CONTAINED IN THE ARTICLE!
QUANTITY OF LABOR IS MEASURED BY DURATION --TIME!
AFTER ALL, IT TAKES MORE TIME TO SEW A SUIT THAN IT DOES TO WEAVE CLOTH -- AND LESS TIME THAN THAT TO PICK COTTON!
AND THE EXCHANGE VALUES OF THOSE ITEMS REFLECT THAT DIFFERENCE!
00:03
01:69
25:42
$
$$
$$$

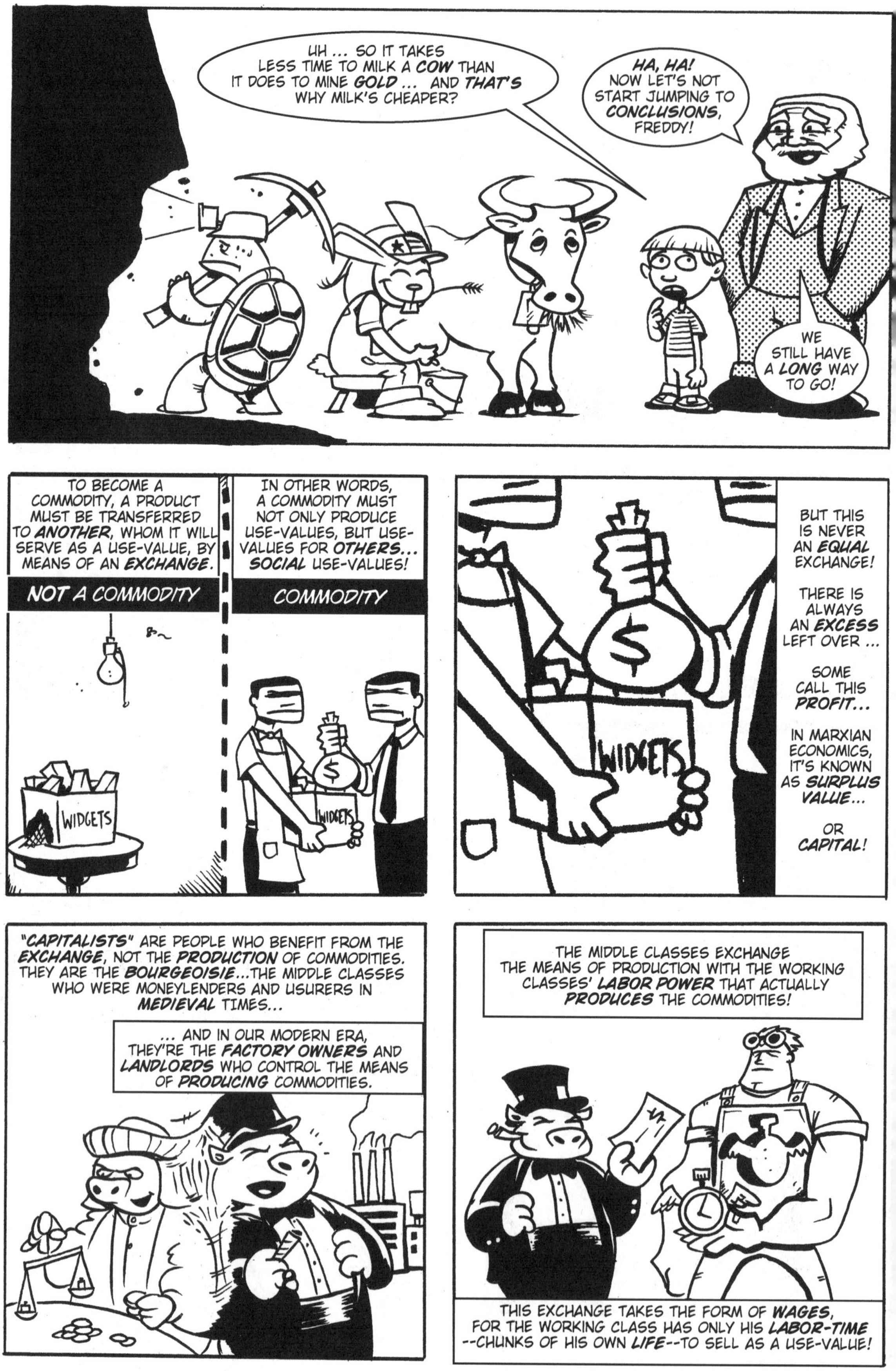
UH ... SO IT TAKES LESS TIME TO MILK A COW THAN IT DOES TO MINE GOLD ... AND THAT'S WHY MILK'S CHEAPER?
HA, HA! NOW LET'S NOT START JUMPING TO CONCLUSIONS, FREDDY!
WE STILL HAVE A LONG WAY TO GO!
TO BECOME A COMMODITY, A PRODUCT MUST BE TRANSFERRED TO ANOTHER, WHOM IT WILL SERVE AS A USE-VALUE, BY MEANS OF AN EXCHANGE.
NOT A COMMODITY
WIDGETS
IN OTHER WORDS, A COMMODITY MUST NOT ONLY PRODUCE USE-VALUES, BUT USE-VALUES FOR OTHERS... SOCIAL USE-VALUES!
COMMODITY
WIDGETS
WIDGETS
BUT THIS IS NEVER AN EQUAL EXCHANGE!
THERE IS ALWAYS AN EXCESS LEFT OVER ...
SOME CALL THIS PROFIT...
IN MARXIAN ECONOMICS, IT'S KNOWN AS SURPLUS VALUE...
OR CAPITAL!
"CAPITALISTS" ARE PEOPLE WHO BENEFIT FROM THE EXCHANGE, NOT THE PRODUCTION OF COMMODITIES. THEY ARE THE BOURGEOISIE...THE MIDDLE CLASSES WHO WERE MONEYLENDERS AND USURERS IN MEDIEVAL TIMES...
... AND IN OUR MODERN ERA, THEY'RE THE FACTORY OWNERS AND LANDLORDS WHO CONTROL THE MEANS OF PRODUCING COMMODITIES.
THE MIDDLE CLASSES EXCHANGE THE MEANS OF PRODUCTION WITH THE WORKING CLASSES' LABOR POWER THAT ACTUALLY PRODUCES THE COMMODITIES!
THIS EXCHANGE TAKES THE FORM OF WAGES, FOR THE WORKING CLASS HAS ONLY HIS LABOR-TIME --CHUNKS OF HIS OWN LIFE--TO SELL AS A USE-VALUE!

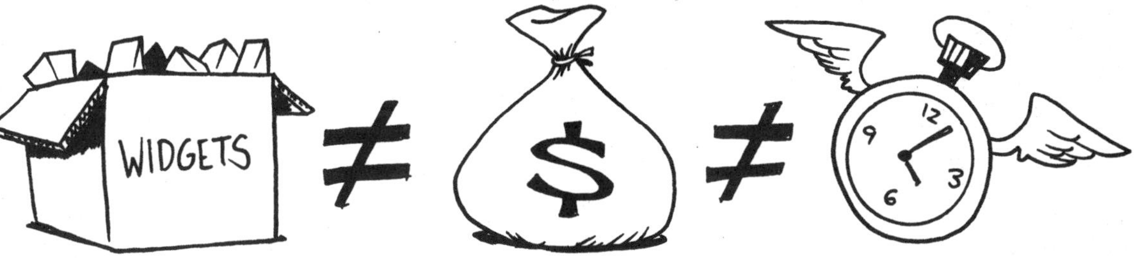
WIDGETS
≠
$
≠

THE KEY TO CREATING SURPLUS VALUE IS TO MAKE SURE THAT WAGES REMAIN ***LESS*** THAN THE EXCHANGE VALUE OF THE COMMODITIES THAT THE WORKERS PRODUCE.

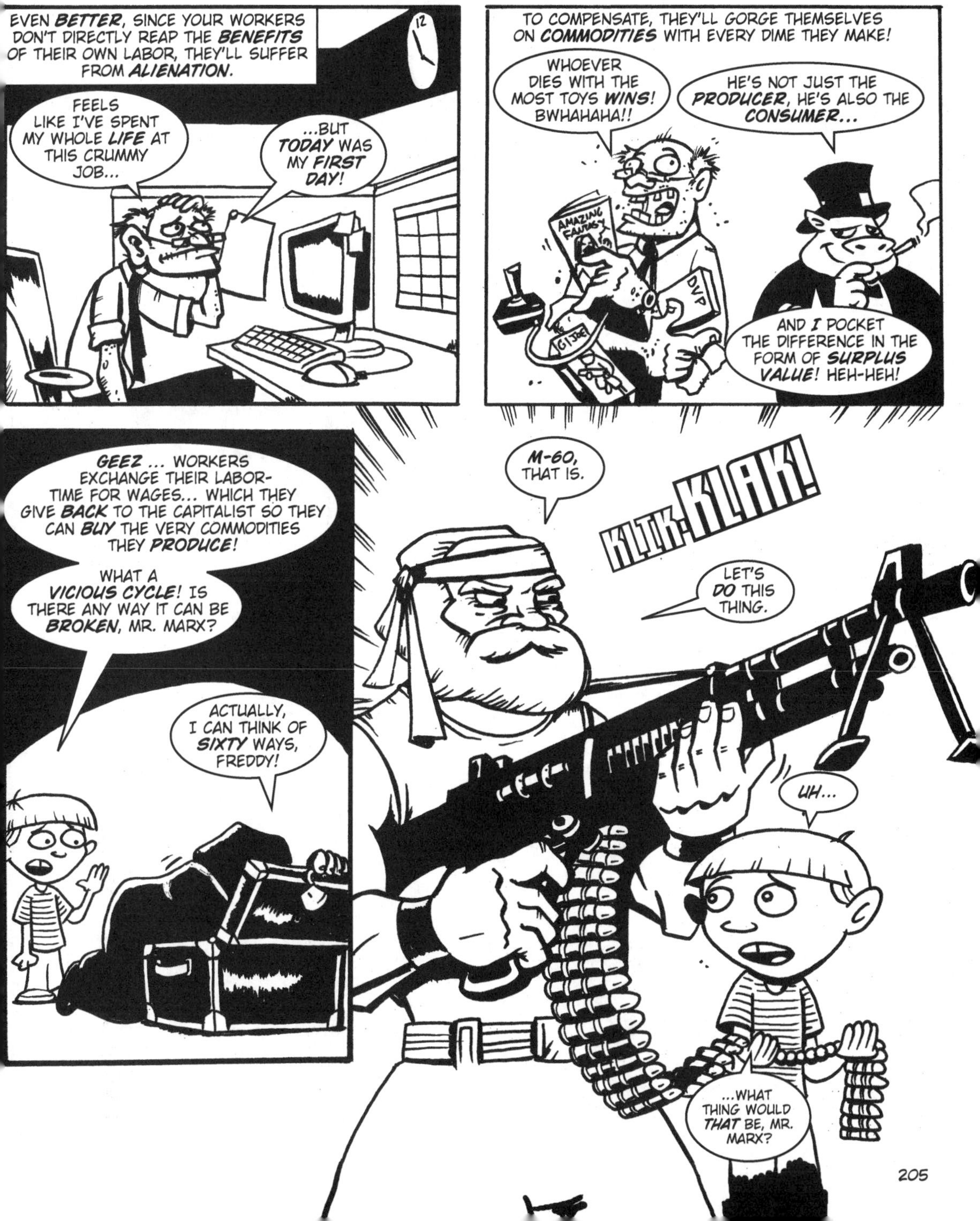
EVEN BETTER, SINCE YOUR WORKERS DON'T DIRECTLY REAP THE BENEFITS OF THEIR OWN LABOR, THEY'LL SUFFER FROM ALIENATION.
FEELS LIKE I'VE SPENT MY WHOLE LIFE AT THIS CRUMMY JOB...
...BUT TODAY WAS MY FIRST DAY!
TO COMPENSATE, THEY'LL GORGE THEMSELVES ON COMMODITIES WITH EVERY DIME THEY MAKE!
WHOEVER DIES WITH THE MOST TOYS WINS! BWHAHAHA!!
HE'S NOT JUST THE PRODUCER, HE'S ALSO THE CONSUMER...
AMAZING FANTASY
DVD
GI JOE
AND I POCKET THE DIFFERENCE IN THE FORM OF SURPLUS VALUE! HEH-HEH!
GEEZ ... WORKERS EXCHANGE THEIR LABOR-TIME FOR WAGES... WHICH THEY GIVE BACK TO THE CAPITALIST SO THEY CAN BUY THE VERY COMMODITIES THEY PRODUCE!
WHAT A VICIOUS CYCLE! IS THERE ANY WAY IT CAN BE BROKEN, MR. MARX?
ACTUALLY, I CAN THINK OF SIXTY WAYS, FREDDY!
M-60, THAT IS.
KLIK-KLAK!
LET'S DO THIS THING.
UH...
...WHAT THING WOULD THAT BE, MR. MARX?

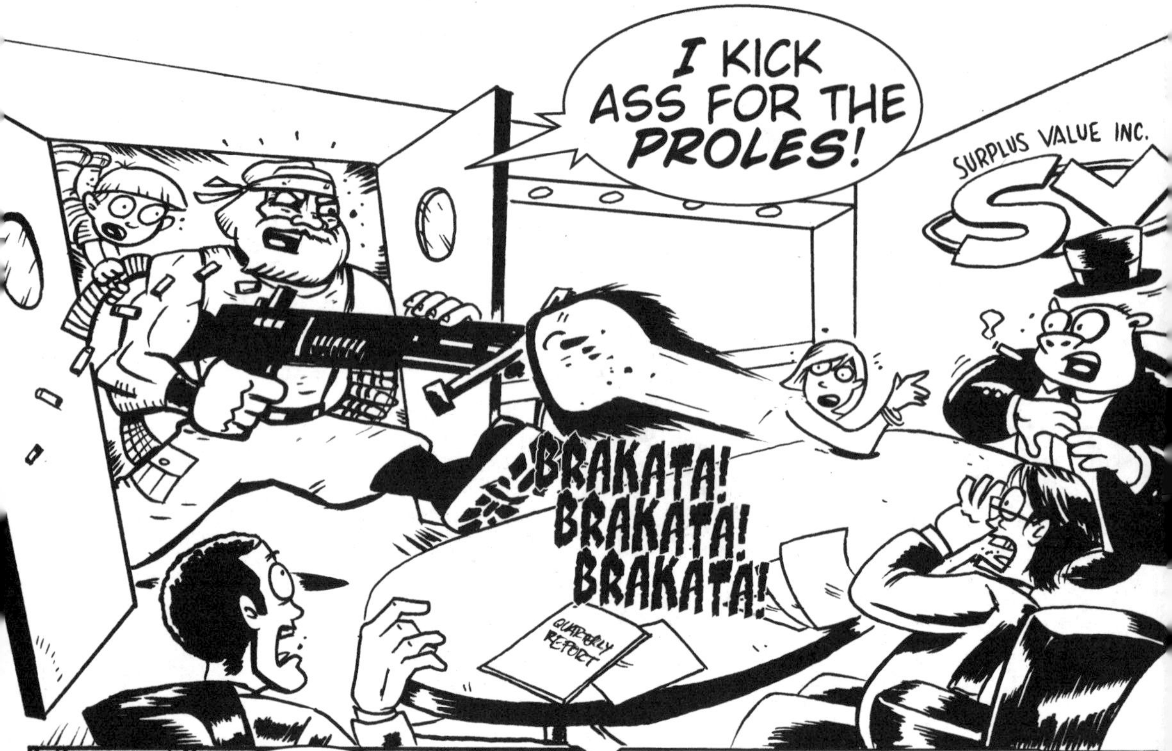
I KICK ASS FOR THE PROLES!
SURPLUS VALUE INC.
BRAKATA! BRAKATA! BRAKATA!
QUARTERLY REPORT

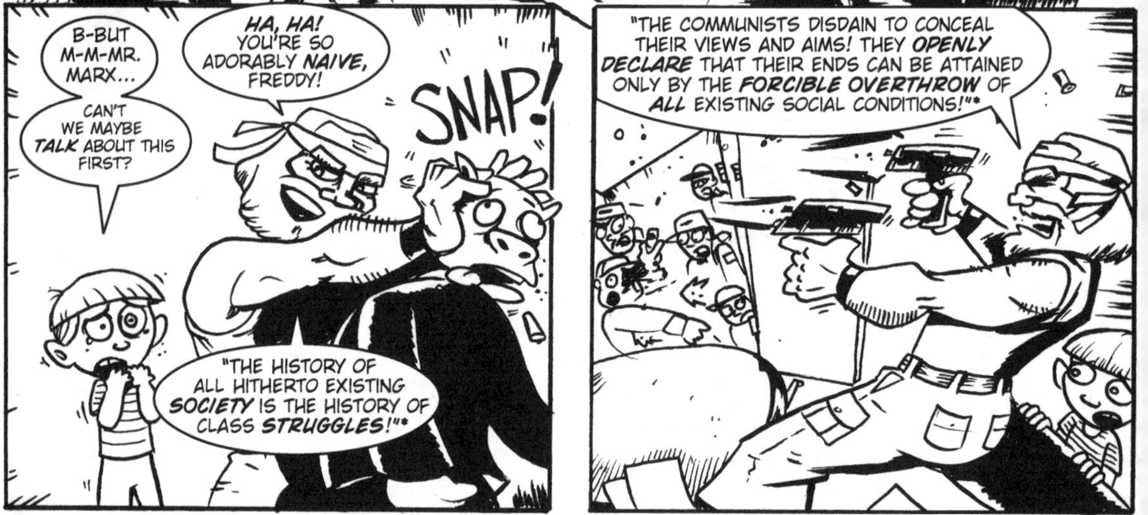
B-BUT M-M-MR. MARX...
CAN'T WE MAYBE TALK ABOUT THIS FIRST?
HA, HA! YOU'RE SO ADORABLY NAIVE, FREDDY!
SNAP!
"THE HISTORY OF ALL HITHERTO EXISTING SOCIETY IS THE HISTORY OF CLASS STRUGGLES!"*
"THE COMMUNISTS DISDAIN TO CONCEAL THEIR VIEWS AND AIMS! THEY OPENLY DECLARE THAT THEIR ENDS CAN BE ATTAINED ONLY BY THE FORCIBLE OVERTHROW OF ALL EXISTING SOCIAL CONDITIONS!"*

*: K.M. & F. ENGELS, *MANIFESTO OF THE COMMUNIST PARTY* (1847)

*: DITTO

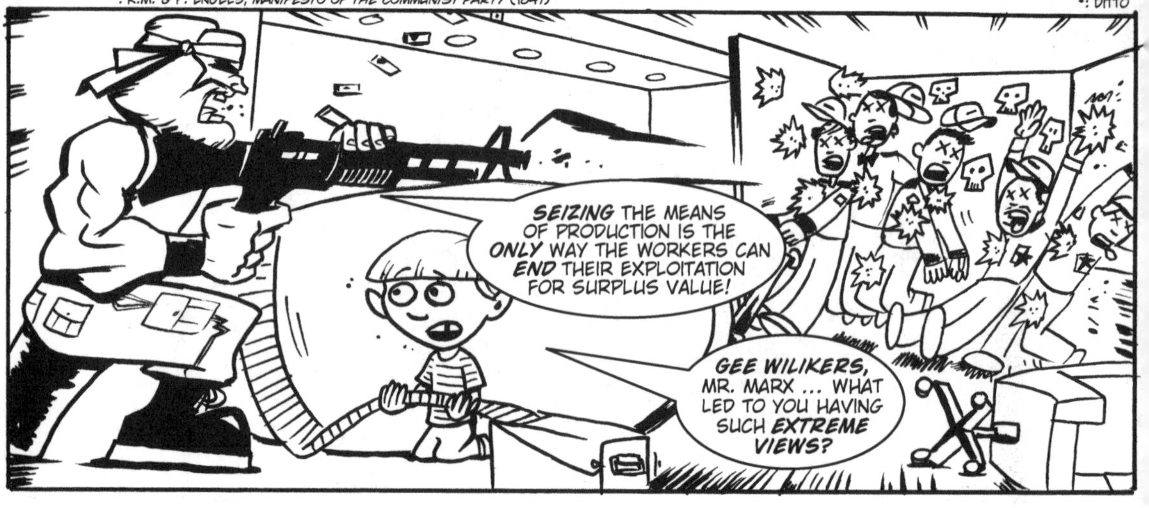
SEIZING THE MEANS OF PRODUCTION IS THE ONLY WAY THE WORKERS CAN END THEIR EXPLOITATION FOR SURPLUS VALUE!
GEE WILIKERS, MR. MARX ... WHAT LED TO YOU HAVING SUCH EXTREME VIEWS?

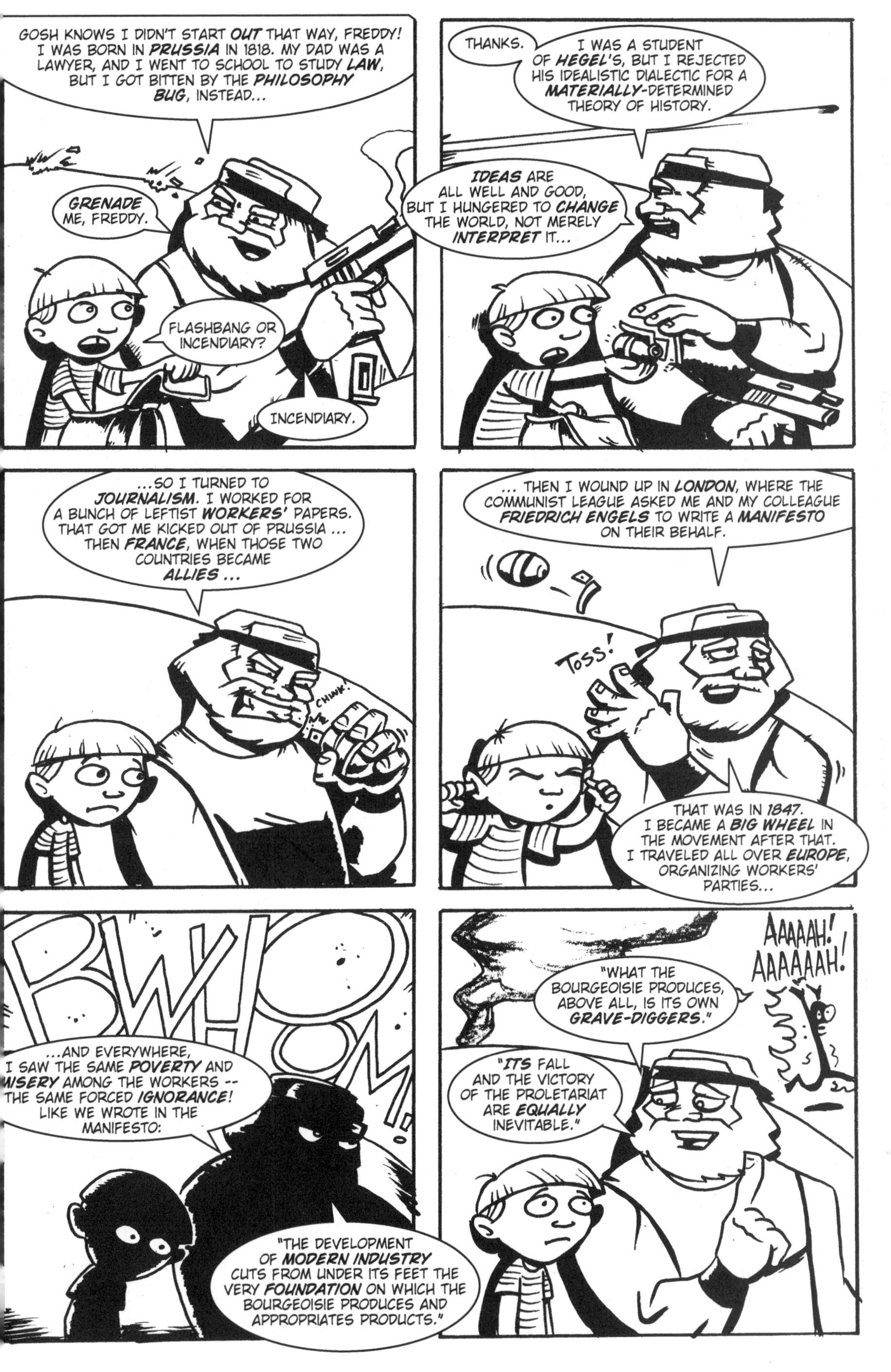

GOSH KNOWS I DIDN'T START OUT THAT WAY, FREDDY! I WAS BORN IN PRUSSIA IN 1818. MY DAD WAS A LAWYER, AND I WENT TO SCHOOL TO STUDY LAW, BUT I GOT BITTEN BY THE PHILOSOPHY BUG, INSTEAD...
GRENADE ME, FREDDY.
FLASHBANG OR INCENDIARY?
INCENDIARY.
THANKS.
I WAS A STUDENT OF HEGEL'S, BUT I REJECTED HIS IDEALISTIC DIALECTIC FOR A MATERIALLY-DETERMINED THEORY OF HISTORY.
IDEAS ARE ALL WELL AND GOOD, BUT I HUNGERED TO CHANGE THE WORLD, NOT MERELY INTERPRET IT...
...SO I TURNED TO JOURNALISM. I WORKED FOR A BUNCH OF LEFTIST WORKERS' PAPERS. THAT GOT ME KICKED OUT OF PRUSSIA ... THEN FRANCE, WHEN THOSE TWO COUNTRIES BECAME ALLIES ...
CHINK!
... THEN I WOUND UP IN LONDON, WHERE THE COMMUNIST LEAGUE ASKED ME AND MY COLLEAGUE FRIEDRICH ENGELS TO WRITE A MANIFESTO ON THEIR BEHALF.
TOSS!
THAT WAS IN 1847. I BECAME A BIG WHEEL IN THE MOVEMENT AFTER THAT. I TRAVELED ALL OVER EUROPE, ORGANIZING WORKERS' PARTIES...
BWHOOM!
...AND EVERYWHERE, I SAW THE SAME POVERTY AND MISERY AMONG THE WORKERS -- THE SAME FORCED IGNORANCE! LIKE WE WROTE IN THE MANIFESTO:
"THE DEVELOPMENT OF MODERN INDUSTRY CUTS FROM UNDER ITS FEET THE VERY FOUNDATION ON WHICH THE BOURGEOISIE PRODUCES AND APPROPRIATES PRODUCTS."
AAAAAH! AAAAAAH!
"WHAT THE BOURGEOISIE PRODUCES, ABOVE ALL, IS ITS OWN GRAVE-DIGGERS."
"ITS FALL AND THE VICTORY OF THE PROLETARIAT ARE EQUALLY INEVITABLE."

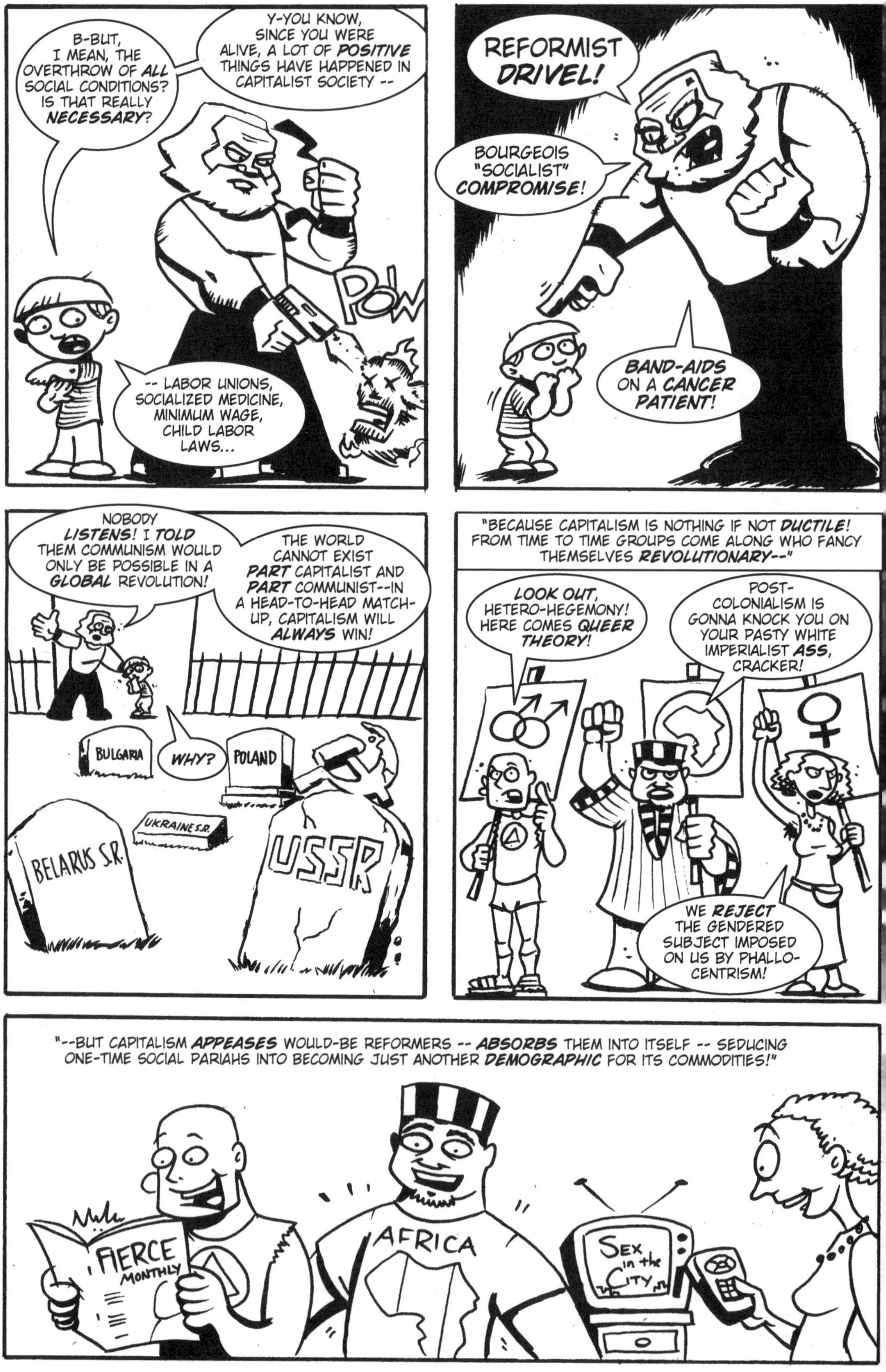
B-BUT, I MEAN, THE OVERTHROW OF ALL SOCIAL CONDITIONS? IS THAT REALLY NECESSARY?
Y-YOU KNOW, SINCE YOU WERE ALIVE, A LOT OF POSITIVE THINGS HAVE HAPPENED IN CAPITALIST SOCIETY --
POW
-- LABOR UNIONS, SOCIALIZED MEDICINE, MINIMUM WAGE, CHILD LABOR LAWS...
REFORMIST DRIVEL!
BOURGEOIS "SOCIALIST" COMPROMISE!
BAND-AIDS ON A CANCER PATIENT!
NOBODY LISTENS! I TOLD THEM COMMUNISM WOULD ONLY BE POSSIBLE IN A GLOBAL REVOLUTION!
THE WORLD CANNOT EXIST PART CAPITALIST AND PART COMMUNIST--IN A HEAD-TO-HEAD MATCH-UP, CAPITALISM WILL ALWAYS WIN!
BULGARIA
WHY?
POLAND
UKRAINE S.R.
BELARUS S.R.
USSR
"BECAUSE CAPITALISM IS NOTHING IF NOT DUCTILE! FROM TIME TO TIME GROUPS COME ALONG WHO FANCY THEMSELVES REVOLUTIONARY--"
LOOK OUT, HETERO-HEGEMONY! HERE COMES QUEER THEORY!
POST-COLONIALISM IS GONNA KNOCK YOU ON YOUR PASTY WHITE IMPERIALIST ASS, CRACKER!
WE REJECT THE GENDERED SUBJECT IMPOSED ON US BY PHALLO-CENTRISM!
"--BUT CAPITALISM APPEASES WOULD-BE REFORMERS -- ABSORBS THEM INTO ITSELF -- SEDUCING ONE-TIME SOCIAL PARIAHS INTO BECOMING JUST ANOTHER DEMOGRAPHIC FOR ITS COMMODITIES!"
FIERCE MONTHLY
AFRICA
SEX in the CITY

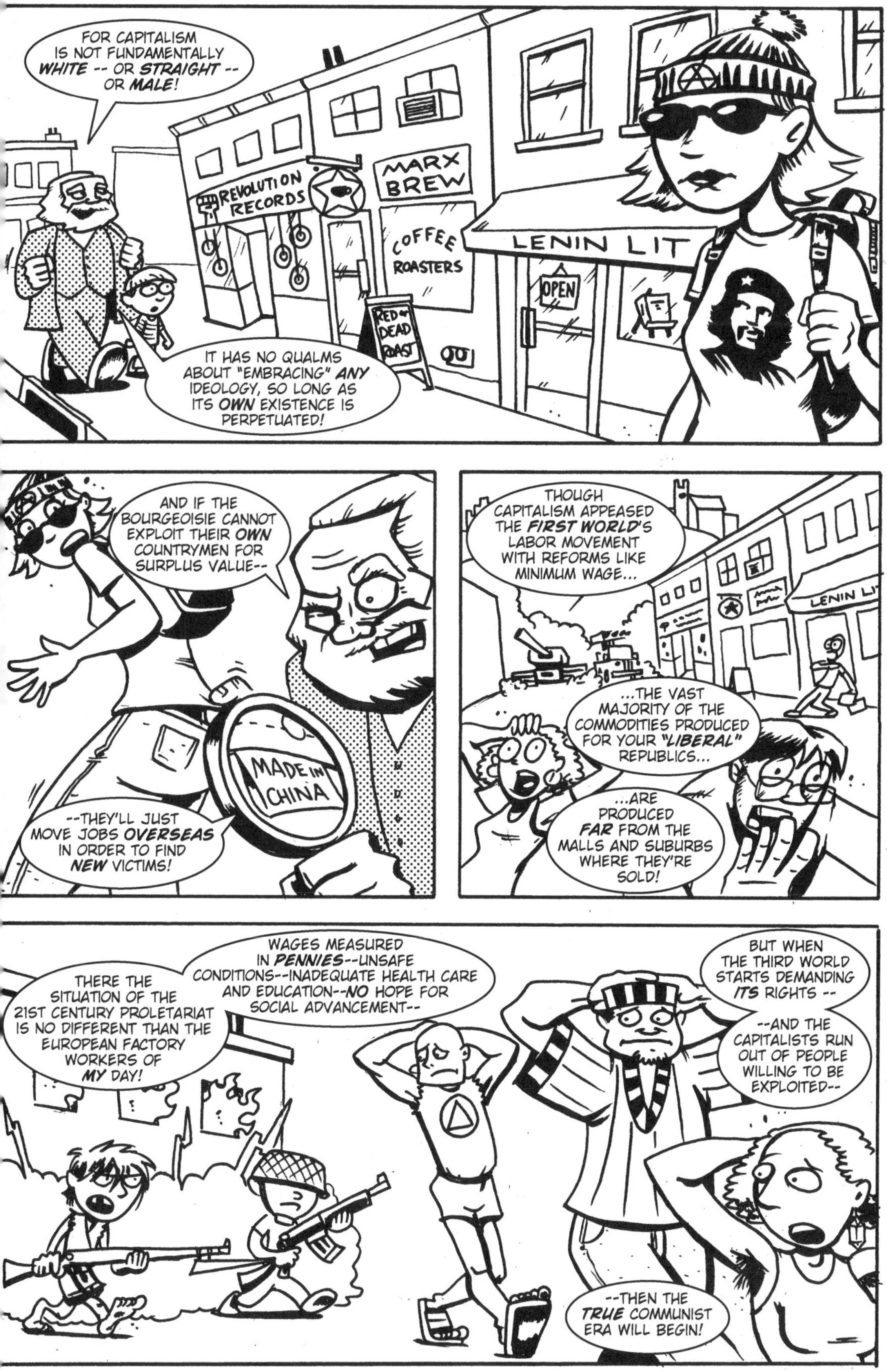
FOR CAPITALISM IS NOT FUNDAMENTALLY *WHITE* -- OR *STRAIGHT* -- OR *MALE*!
REVOLUTION RECORDS
MARX BREW
COFFEE ROASTERS
LENIN LIT
OPEN
RED DEAD ROAST
IT HAS NO QUALMS ABOUT "EMBRACING" *ANY* IDEOLOGY, SO LONG AS ITS *OWN* EXISTENCE IS PERPETUATED!
AND IF THE BOURGEOISIE CANNOT EXPLOIT THEIR *OWN* COUNTRYMEN FOR SURPLUS VALUE--
MADE IN CHINA
--THEY'LL JUST MOVE JOBS *OVERSEAS* IN ORDER TO FIND *NEW* VICTIMS!
THOUGH CAPITALISM APPEASED THE *FIRST WORLD*'S LABOR MOVEMENT WITH REFORMS LIKE MINIMUM WAGE...
LENIN LIT
...THE VAST MAJORITY OF THE COMMODITIES PRODUCED FOR YOUR *"LIBERAL"* REPUBLICS...
...ARE PRODUCED *FAR* FROM THE MALLS AND SUBURBS WHERE THEY'RE SOLD!
THERE THE SITUATION OF THE 21ST CENTURY PROLETARIAT IS NO DIFFERENT THAN THE EUROPEAN FACTORY WORKERS OF *MY* DAY!
WAGES MEASURED IN *PENNIES*--UNSAFE CONDITIONS--INADEQUATE HEALTH CARE AND EDUCATION--*NO* HOPE FOR SOCIAL ADVANCEMENT--
BUT WHEN THE THIRD WORLD STARTS DEMANDING *ITS* RIGHTS --
--AND THE CAPITALISTS RUN OUT OF PEOPLE WILLING TO BE EXPLOITED--
--THEN THE *TRUE* COMMUNIST ERA WILL BEGIN!

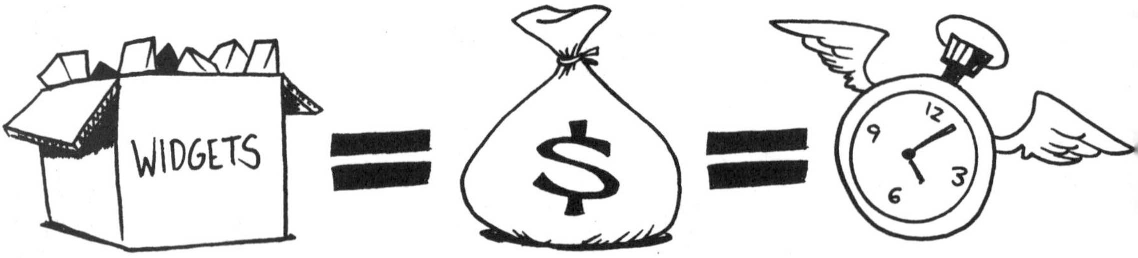
WIDGETS
$

"ONCE THE WORKERS SEIZE THE MEANS OF PRODUCTION, SURPLUS VALUE WILL BE *ELIMINATED!*
THE BASIS OF THE *COMMUNIST* ECONOMY IS:"

"From each according to his abilities, to each according to his needs."

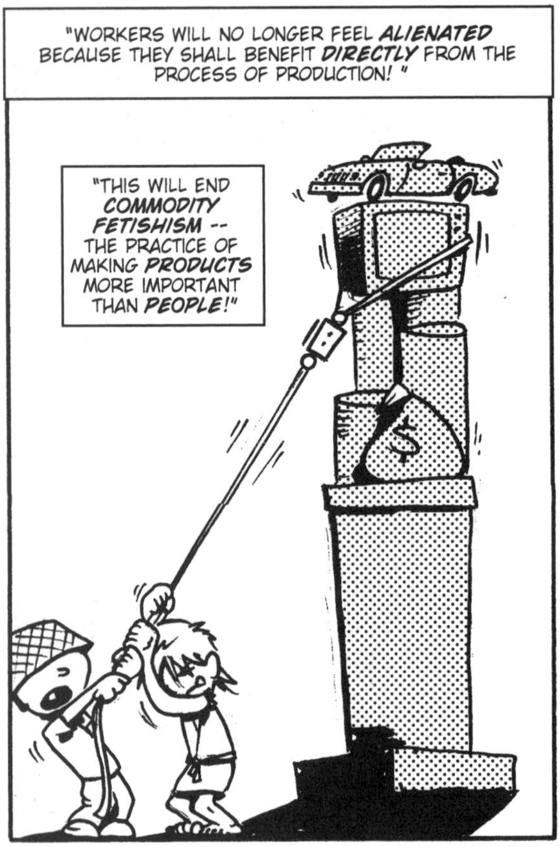
"WORKERS WILL NO LONGER FEEL *ALIENATED* BECAUSE THEY SHALL BENEFIT *DIRECTLY* FROM THE PROCESS OF PRODUCTION! "
"THIS WILL END *COMMODITY FETISHISM* -- THE PRACTICE OF MAKING *PRODUCTS* MORE IMPORTANT THAN *PEOPLE!*"

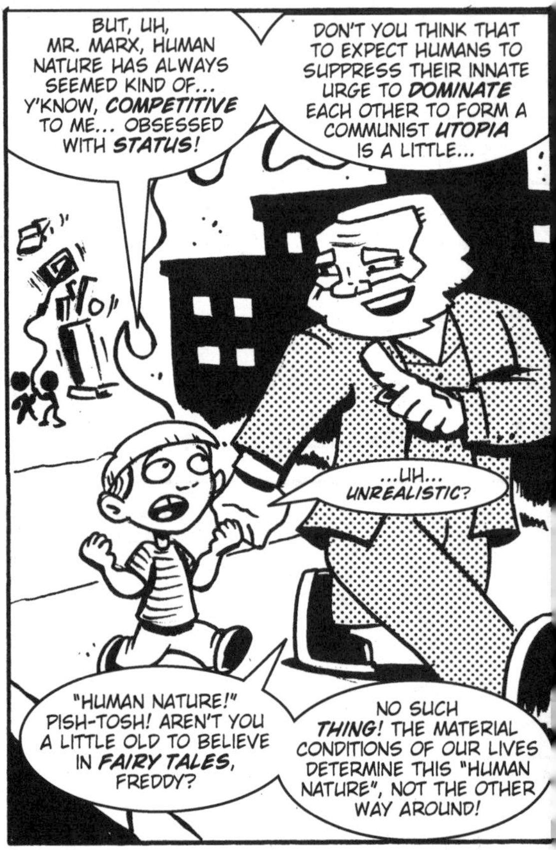
BUT, UH, MR. MARX, HUMAN NATURE HAS ALWAYS SEEMED KIND OF... Y'KNOW, *COMPETITIVE* TO ME... OBSESSED WITH *STATUS!*
DON'T YOU THINK THAT TO EXPECT HUMANS TO SUPPRESS THEIR INNATE URGE TO *DOMINATE* EACH OTHER TO FORM A COMMUNIST *UTOPIA* IS A LITTLE...
...UH... *UNREALISTIC?*
"HUMAN NATURE!" PISH-TOSH! AREN'T YOU A LITTLE OLD TO BELIEVE IN *FAIRY TALES*, FREDDY?
NO SUCH *THING!* THE MATERIAL CONDITIONS OF OUR LIVES DETERMINE THIS "HUMAN NATURE", NOT THE OTHER WAY AROUND!

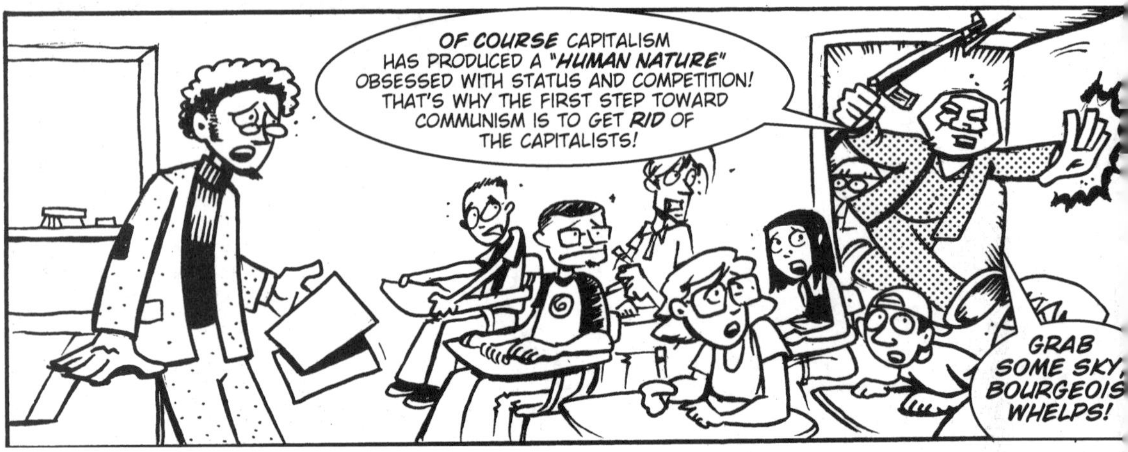
OF COURSE CAPITALISM HAS PRODUCED A *"HUMAN NATURE"* OBSESSED WITH STATUS AND COMPETITION! THAT'S WHY THE FIRST STEP TOWARD COMMUNISM IS TO GET *RID* OF THE CAPITALISTS!
GRAB SOME SKY, BOURGEOIS WHELPS!

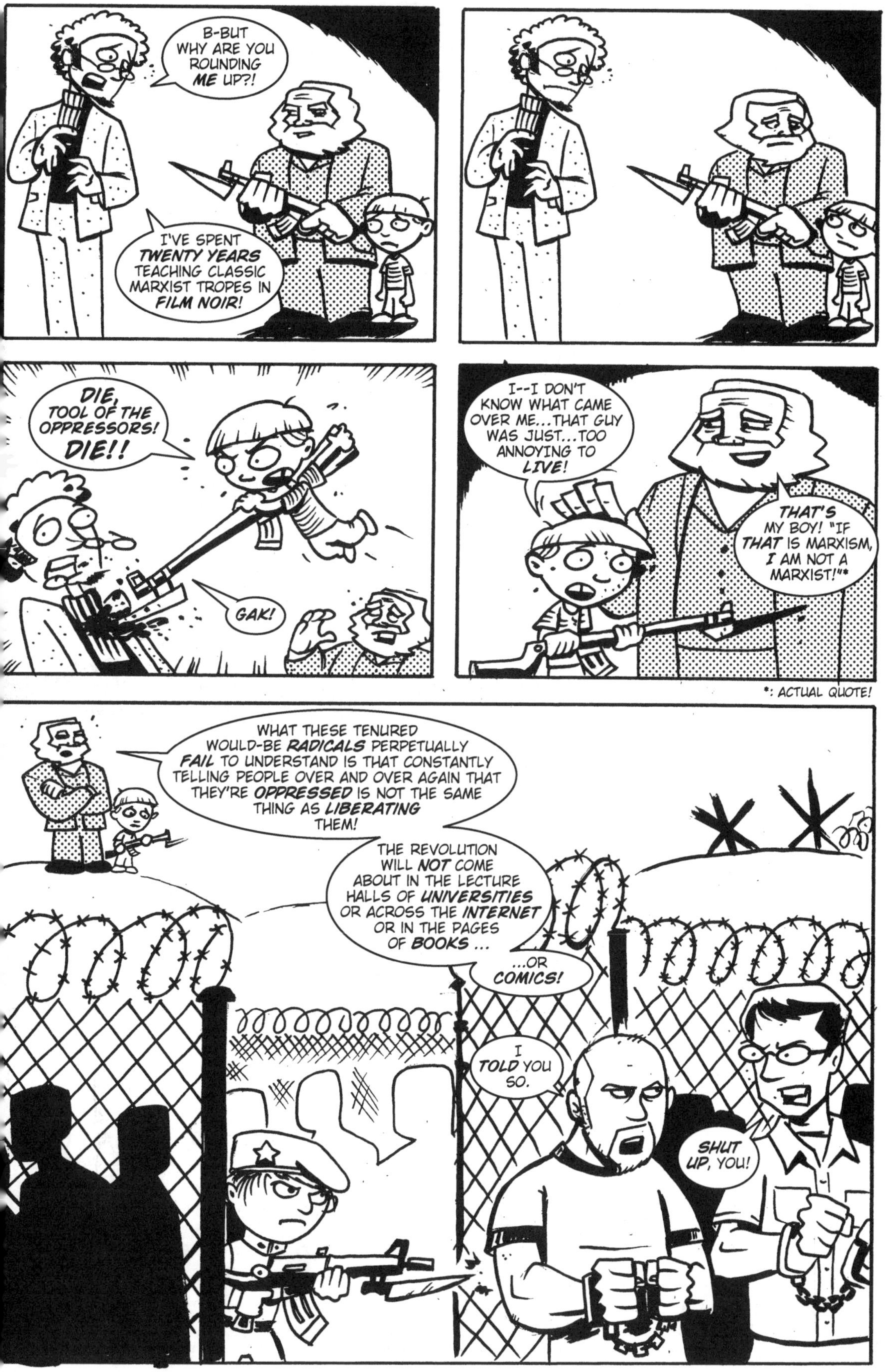

B-BUT WHY ARE YOU ROUNDING ME UP?!
I'VE SPENT TWENTY YEARS TEACHING CLASSIC MARXIST TROPES IN FILM NOIR!
DIE, TOOL OF THE OPPRESSORS! DIE!!
GAK!
I--I DON'T KNOW WHAT CAME OVER ME...THAT GUY WAS JUST...TOO ANNOYING TO LIVE!
THAT'S MY BOY! "IF THAT IS MARXISM, I AM NOT A MARXIST!"*
*: ACTUAL QUOTE!
WHAT THESE TENURED WOULD-BE RADICALS PERPETUALLY FAIL TO UNDERSTAND IS THAT CONSTANTLY TELLING PEOPLE OVER AND OVER AGAIN THAT THEY'RE OPPRESSED IS NOT THE SAME THING AS LIBERATING THEM!
THE REVOLUTION WILL NOT COME ABOUT IN THE LECTURE HALLS OF UNIVERSITIES OR ACROSS THE INTERNET OR IN THE PAGES OF BOOKS ...
...OR COMICS!
I TOLD YOU SO.
SHUT UP, YOU!

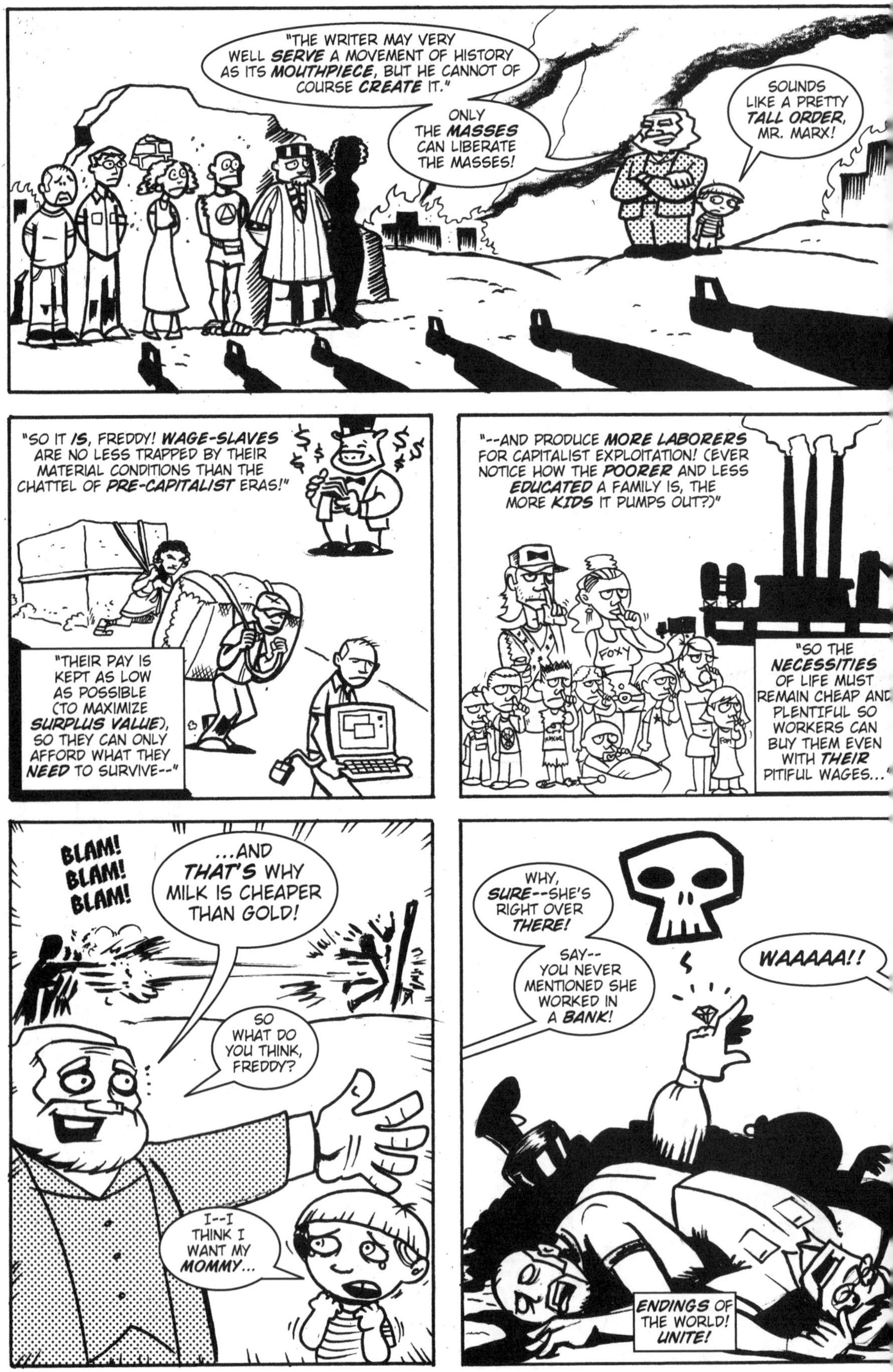
"THE WRITER MAY VERY WELL SERVE A MOVEMENT OF HISTORY AS ITS MOUTHPIECE, BUT HE CANNOT OF COURSE CREATE IT."
ONLY THE MASSES CAN LIBERATE THE MASSES!
SOUNDS LIKE A PRETTY TALL ORDER, MR. MARX!
"SO IT IS, FREDDY! WAGE-SLAVES ARE NO LESS TRAPPED BY THEIR MATERIAL CONDITIONS THAN THE CHATTEL OF PRE-CAPITALIST ERAS!"
"THEIR PAY IS KEPT AS LOW AS POSSIBLE (TO MAXIMIZE SURPLUS VALUE), SO THEY CAN ONLY AFFORD WHAT THEY NEED TO SURVIVE--"
"--AND PRODUCE MORE LABORERS FOR CAPITALIST EXPLOITATION! (EVER NOTICE HOW THE POORER AND LESS EDUCATED A FAMILY IS, THE MORE KIDS IT PUMPS OUT?)"
FOXY
"SO THE NECESSITIES OF LIFE MUST REMAIN CHEAP AND PLENTIFUL SO WORKERS CAN BUY THEM EVEN WITH THEIR PITIFUL WAGES..."
BLAM! BLAM! BLAM!
...AND THAT'S WHY MILK IS CHEAPER THAN GOLD!
SO WHAT DO YOU THINK, FREDDY?
I--I THINK I WANT MY MOMMY...
WHY, SURE--SHE'S RIGHT OVER THERE!
SAY-- YOU NEVER MENTIONED SHE WORKED IN A BANK!
WAAAAA!!
ENDINGS OF THE WORLD! UNITE!

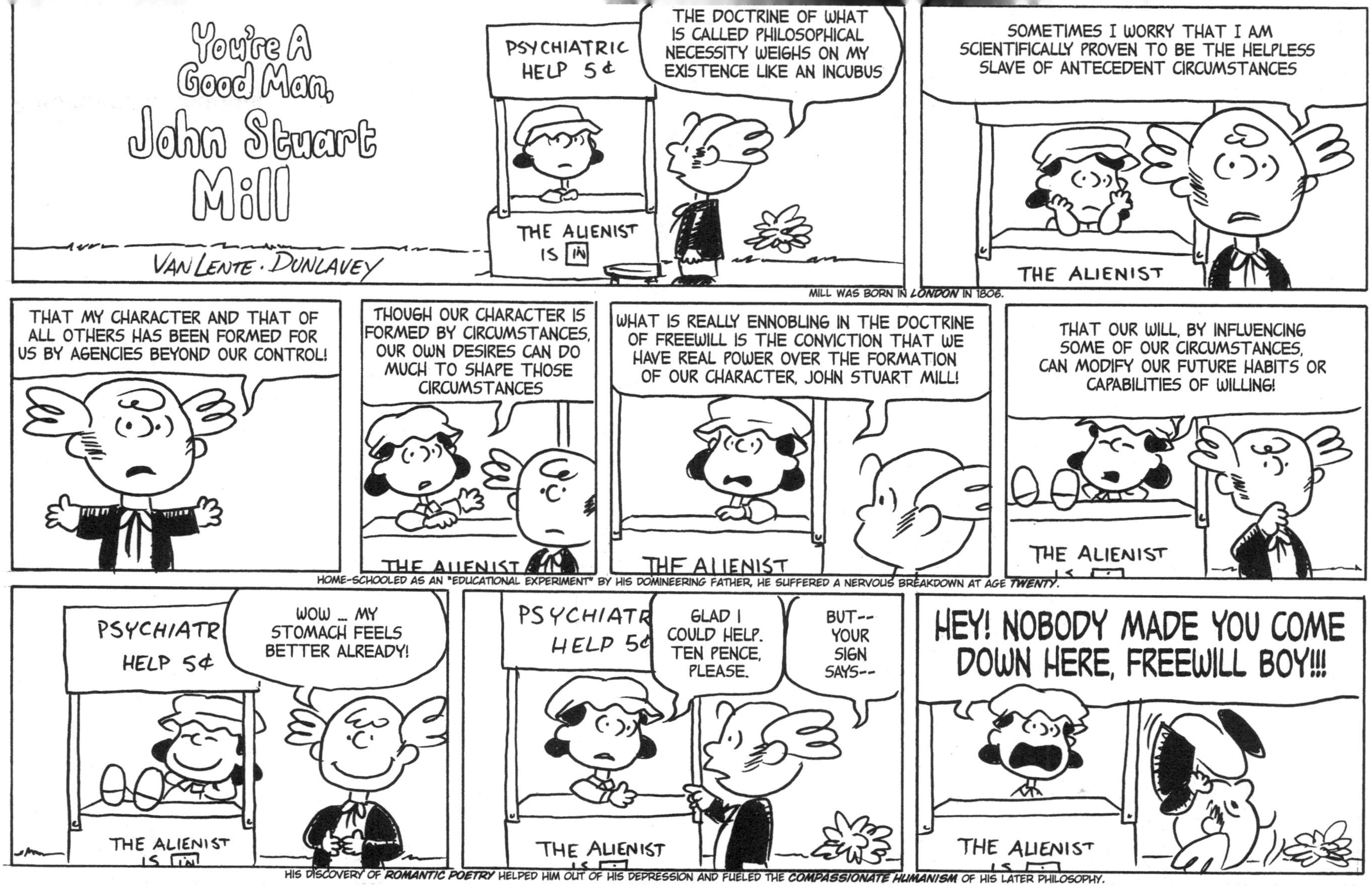
You're A Good Man, John Stuart Mill
VAN LENTE · DUNLAVEY
PSYCHIATRIC HELP 5¢
THE ALIENIST IS IN
THE DOCTRINE OF WHAT IS CALLED PHILOSOPHICAL NECESSITY WEIGHS ON MY EXISTENCE LIKE AN INCUBUS
SOMETIMES I WORRY THAT I AM SCIENTIFICALLY PROVEN TO BE THE HELPLESS SLAVE OF ANTECEDENT CIRCUMSTANCES
THE ALIENIST
MILL WAS BORN IN LONDON IN 1806.
THAT MY CHARACTER AND THAT OF ALL OTHERS HAS BEEN FORMED FOR US BY AGENCIES BEYOND OUR CONTROL!
THOUGH OUR CHARACTER IS FORMED BY CIRCUMSTANCES, OUR OWN DESIRES CAN DO MUCH TO SHAPE THOSE CIRCUMSTANCES
WHAT IS REALLY ENNOBLING IN THE DOCTRINE OF FREEWILL IS THE CONVICTION THAT WE HAVE REAL POWER OVER THE FORMATION OF OUR CHARACTER, JOHN STUART MILL!
THAT OUR WILL, BY INFLUENCING SOME OF OUR CIRCUMSTANCES, CAN MODIFY OUR FUTURE HABITS OR CAPABILITIES OF WILLING!
THE ALIENIST
HOME-SCHOOLED AS AN "EDUCATIONAL EXPERIMENT" BY HIS DOMINEERING FATHER, HE SUFFERED A NERVOUS BREAKDOWN AT AGE TWENTY.
PSYCHIATR HELP 5¢
WOW ... MY STOMACH FEELS BETTER ALREADY!
THE ALIENIST IS IN
PSYCHIATR HELP 5¢
GLAD I COULD HELP. TEN PENCE, PLEASE.
BUT-- YOUR SIGN SAYS--
THE ALIENIST
HEY! NOBODY MADE YOU COME DOWN HERE, FREEWILL BOY!!!
THE ALIENIST
HIS DISCOVERY OF ROMANTIC POETRY HELPED HIM OUT OF HIS DEPRESSION AND FUELED THE COMPASSIONATE HUMANISM OF HIS LATER PHILOSOPHY.

The Greatest Happiness Principle is...

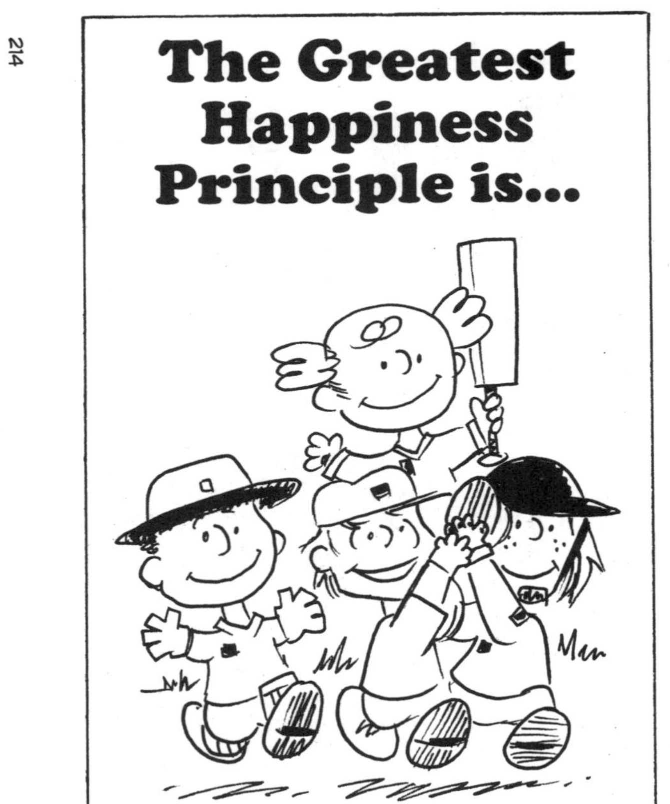

..."actions are right in proportion as they tend to promote happiness, wrong as they tend to produce the reverse of happiness."

Happiness is...

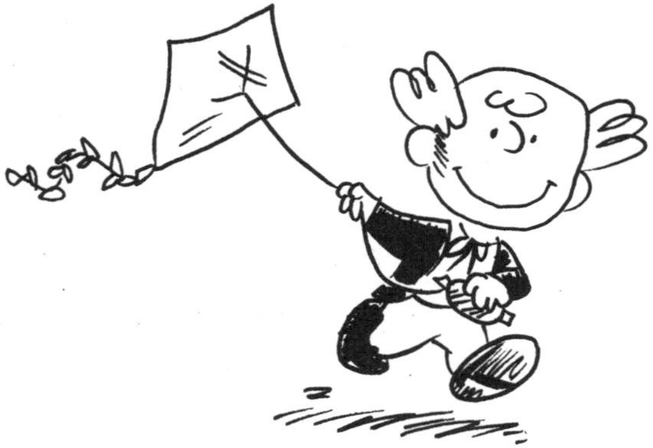

..."intended pleasure, and the absence of pain."

Unhappiness is...

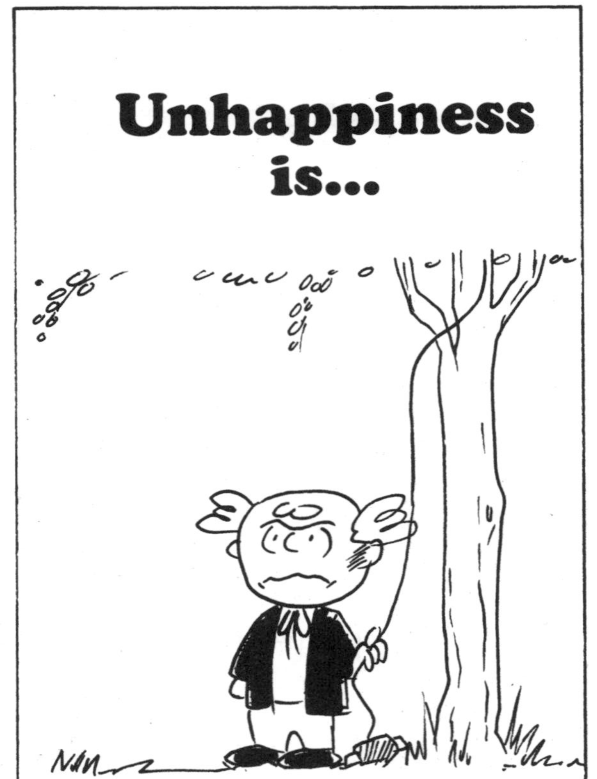

..."pain, and the privation of pleasure."

—John Stuart Mill, "Utilitarianism" (1863)

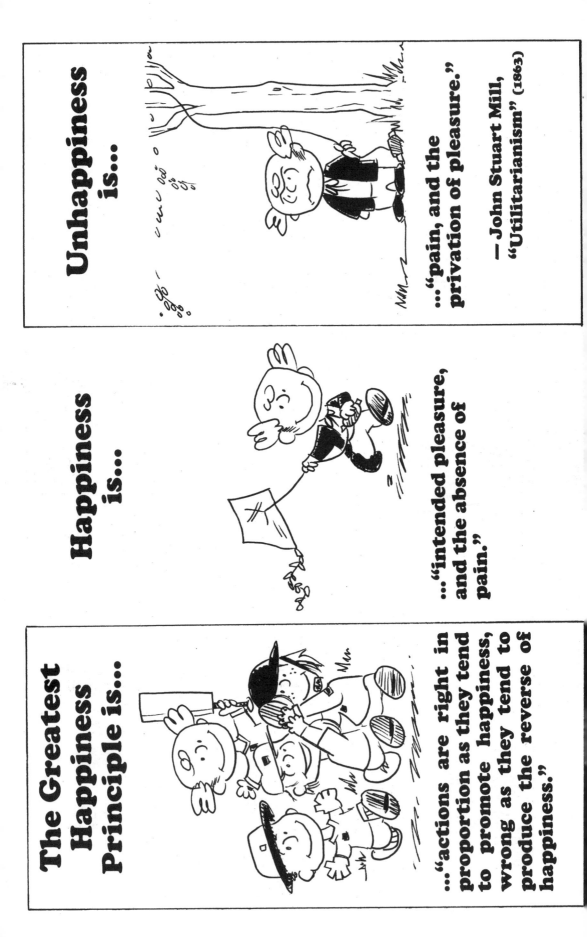

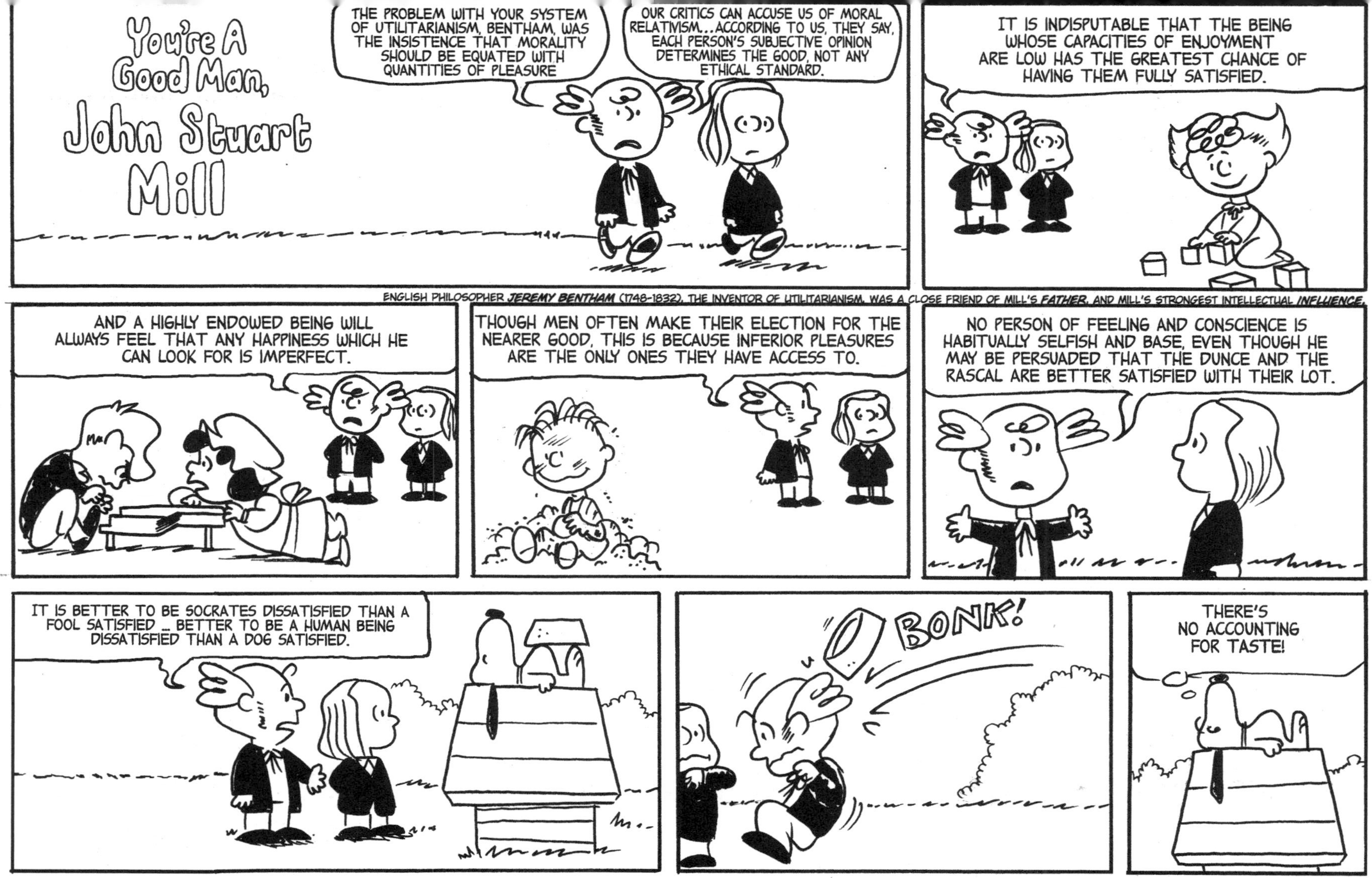
You're A Good Man, John Stuart Mill
THE PROBLEM WITH YOUR SYSTEM OF UTILITARIANISM, BENTHAM, WAS THE INSISTENCE THAT MORALITY SHOULD BE EQUATED WITH QUANTITIES OF PLEASURE
OUR CRITICS CAN ACCUSE US OF MORAL RELATIVISM...ACCORDING TO US, THEY SAY, EACH PERSON'S SUBJECTIVE OPINION DETERMINES THE GOOD, NOT ANY ETHICAL STANDARD.
IT IS INDISPUTABLE THAT THE BEING WHOSE CAPACITIES OF ENJOYMENT ARE LOW HAS THE GREATEST CHANCE OF HAVING THEM FULLY SATISFIED.
ENGLISH PHILOSOPHER JEREMY BENTHAM (1748-1832), THE INVENTOR OF UTILITARIANISM, WAS A CLOSE FRIEND OF MILL'S FATHER, AND MILL'S STRONGEST INTELLECTUAL INFLUENCE.
AND A HIGHLY ENDOWED BEING WILL ALWAYS FEEL THAT ANY HAPPINESS WHICH HE CAN LOOK FOR IS IMPERFECT.
THOUGH MEN OFTEN MAKE THEIR ELECTION FOR THE NEARER GOOD, THIS IS BECAUSE INFERIOR PLEASURES ARE THE ONLY ONES THEY HAVE ACCESS TO.
NO PERSON OF FEELING AND CONSCIENCE IS HABITUALLY SELFISH AND BASE, EVEN THOUGH HE MAY BE PERSUADED THAT THE DUNCE AND THE RASCAL ARE BETTER SATISFIED WITH THEIR LOT.
IT IS BETTER TO BE SOCRATES DISSATISFIED THAN A FOOL SATISFIED ... BETTER TO BE A HUMAN BEING DISSATISFIED THAN A DOG SATISFIED.
BONK!
THERE'S NO ACCOUNTING FOR TASTE!

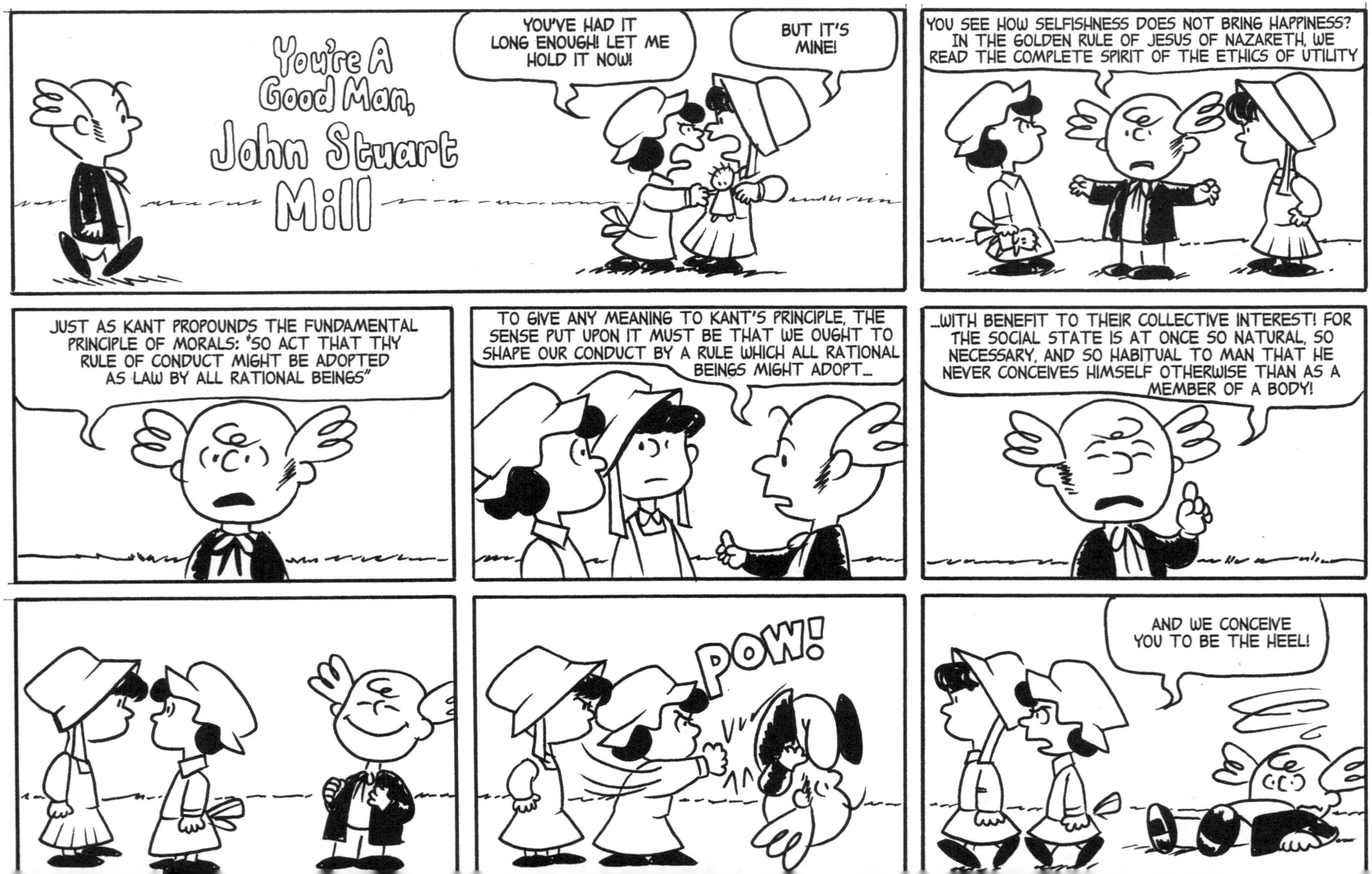
You're A Good Man, John Stuart Mill
YOU'VE HAD IT LONG ENOUGH! LET ME HOLD IT NOW!
BUT IT'S MINE!
YOU SEE HOW SELFISHNESS DOES NOT BRING HAPPINESS? IN THE GOLDEN RULE OF JESUS OF NAZARETH, WE READ THE COMPLETE SPIRIT OF THE ETHICS OF UTILITY
JUST AS KANT PROPOUNDS THE FUNDAMENTAL PRINCIPLE OF MORALS: "SO ACT THAT THY RULE OF CONDUCT MIGHT BE ADOPTED AS LAW BY ALL RATIONAL BEINGS"
TO GIVE ANY MEANING TO KANT'S PRINCIPLE, THE SENSE PUT UPON IT MUST BE THAT WE OUGHT TO SHAPE OUR CONDUCT BY A RULE WHICH ALL RATIONAL BEINGS MIGHT ADOPT...
...WITH BENEFIT TO THEIR COLLECTIVE INTEREST! FOR THE SOCIAL STATE IS AT ONCE SO NATURAL, SO NECESSARY, AND SO HABITUAL TO MAN THAT HE NEVER CONCEIVES HIMSELF OTHERWISE THAN AS A MEMBER OF A BODY!
POW!
AND WE CONCEIVE YOU TO BE THE HEEL!

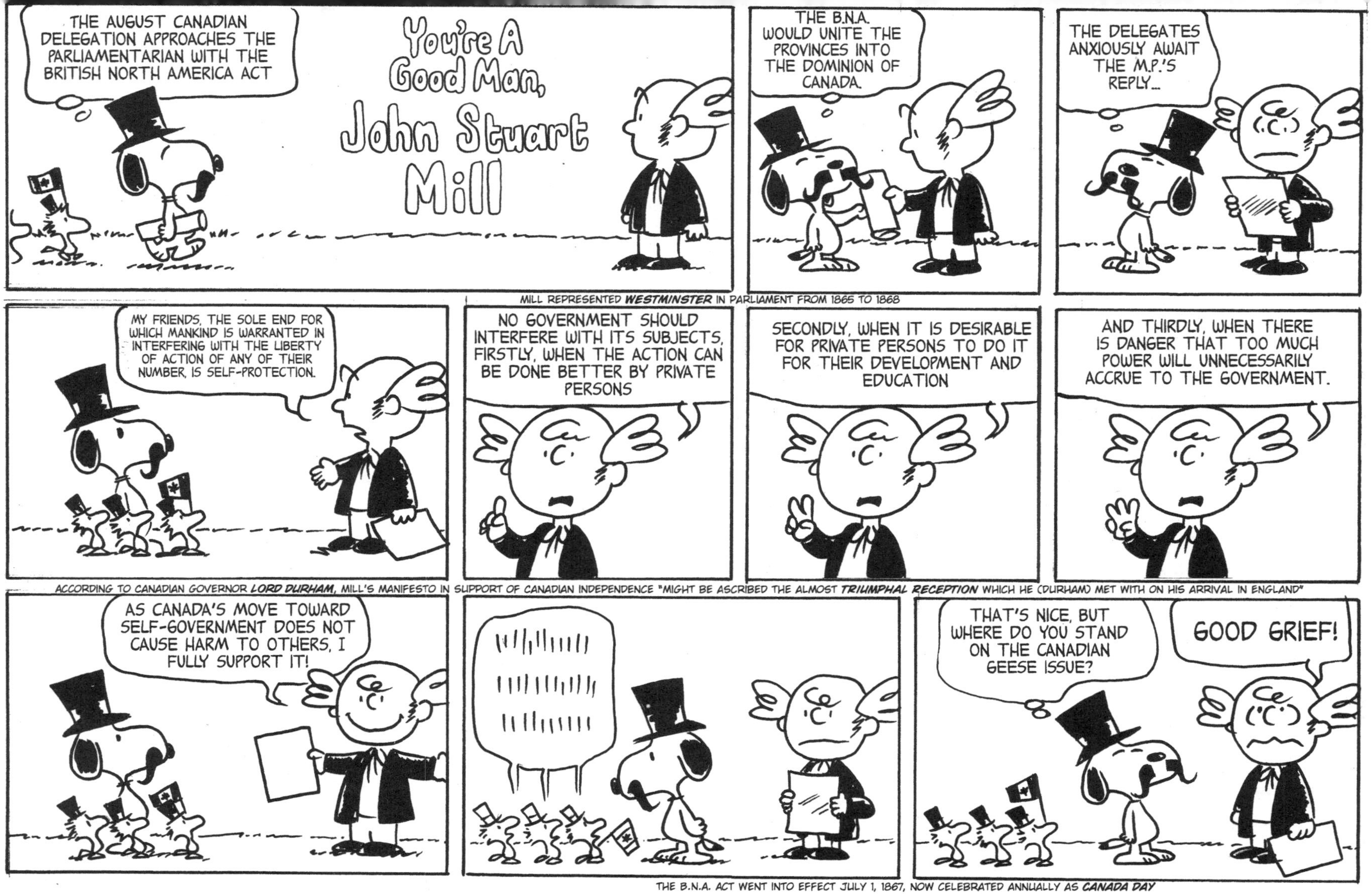
THE AUGUST CANADIAN DELEGATION APPROACHES THE PARLIAMENTARIAN WITH THE BRITISH NORTH AMERICA ACT
You're A Good Man, John Stuart Mill
THE B.N.A. WOULD UNITE THE PROVINCES INTO THE DOMINION OF CANADA.
THE DELEGATES ANXIOUSLY AWAIT THE M.P.'S REPLY...
MILL REPRESENTED **WESTMINSTER** IN PARLIAMENT FROM 1865 TO 1868
MY FRIENDS, THE SOLE END FOR WHICH MANKIND IS WARRANTED IN INTERFERING WITH THE LIBERTY OF ACTION OF ANY OF THEIR NUMBER, IS SELF-PROTECTION.
NO GOVERNMENT SHOULD INTERFERE WITH ITS SUBJECTS, FIRSTLY, WHEN THE ACTION CAN BE DONE BETTER BY PRIVATE PERSONS
SECONDLY, WHEN IT IS DESIRABLE FOR PRIVATE PERSONS TO DO IT FOR THEIR DEVELOPMENT AND EDUCATION
AND THIRDLY, WHEN THERE IS DANGER THAT TOO MUCH POWER WILL UNNECESSARILY ACCRUE TO THE GOVERNMENT.
ACCORDING TO CANADIAN GOVERNOR **LORD DURHAM**, MILL'S MANIFESTO IN SUPPORT OF CANADIAN INDEPENDENCE "MIGHT BE ASCRIBED THE ALMOST **TRIUMPHAL RECEPTION** WHICH HE (DURHAM) MET WITH ON HIS ARRIVAL IN ENGLAND"
AS CANADA'S MOVE TOWARD SELF-GOVERNMENT DOES NOT CAUSE HARM TO OTHERS, I FULLY SUPPORT IT!
THAT'S NICE, BUT WHERE DO YOU STAND ON THE CANADIAN GEESE ISSUE?
GOOD GRIEF!
THE B.N.A. ACT WENT INTO EFFECT JULY 1, 1867, NOW CELEBRATED ANNUALLY AS **CANADA DAY**

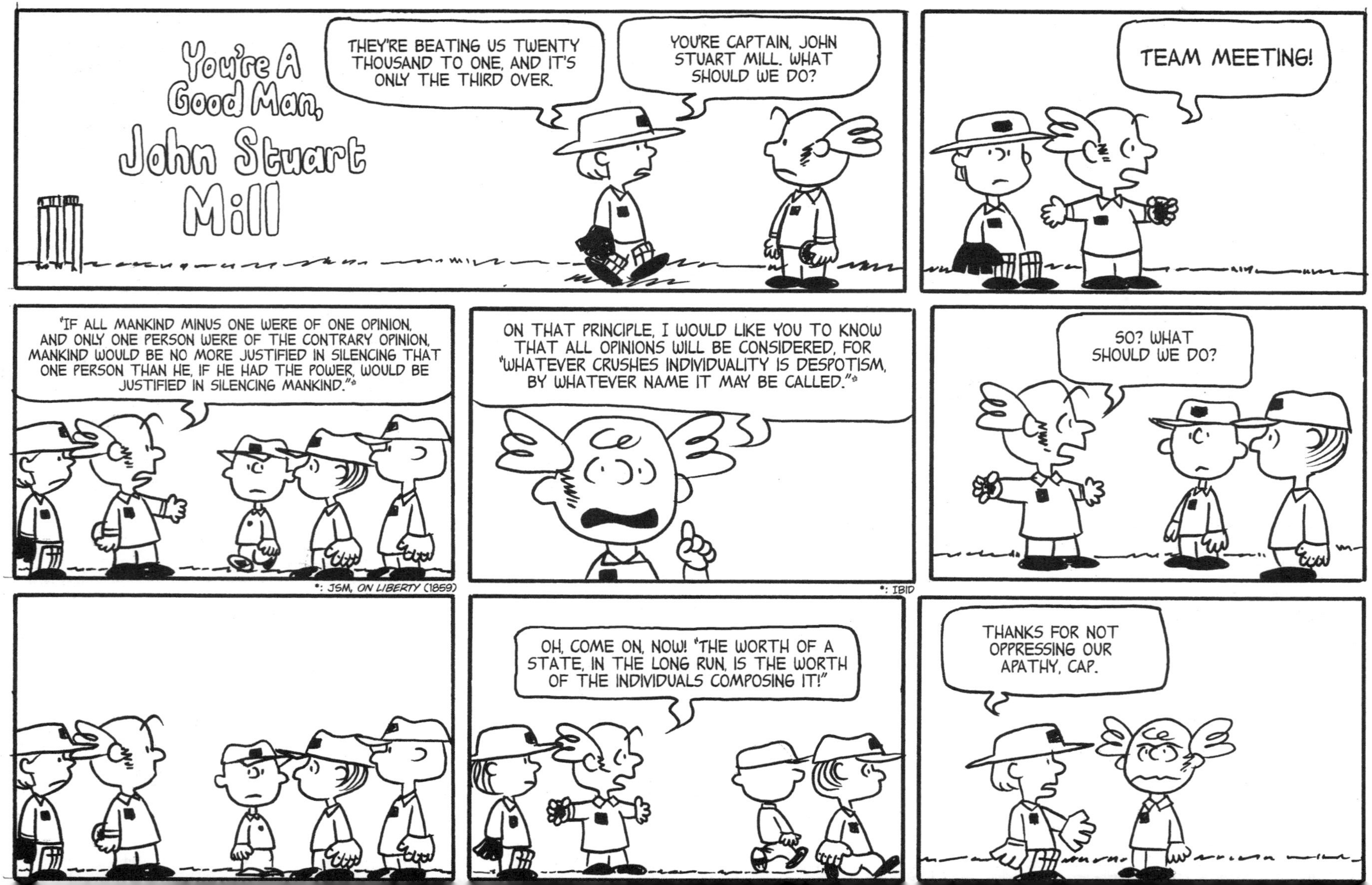
You're A Good Man, John Stuart Mill
THEY'RE BEATING US TWENTY THOUSAND TO ONE, AND IT'S ONLY THE THIRD OVER.
YOU'RE CAPTAIN, JOHN STUART MILL. WHAT SHOULD WE DO?
TEAM MEETING!
"IF ALL MANKIND MINUS ONE WERE OF ONE OPINION, AND ONLY ONE PERSON WERE OF THE CONTRARY OPINION, MANKIND WOULD BE NO MORE JUSTIFIED IN SILENCING THAT ONE PERSON THAN HE, IF HE HAD THE POWER, WOULD BE JUSTIFIED IN SILENCING MANKIND."*
*: JSM, ON LIBERTY (1859)
ON THAT PRINCIPLE, I WOULD LIKE YOU TO KNOW THAT ALL OPINIONS WILL BE CONSIDERED, FOR "WHATEVER CRUSHES INDIVIDUALITY IS DESPOTISM, BY WHATEVER NAME IT MAY BE CALLED."*
*: IBID
SO? WHAT SHOULD WE DO?
OH, COME ON, NOW! "THE WORTH OF A STATE, IN THE LONG RUN, IS THE WORTH OF THE INDIVIDUALS COMPOSING IT!"
THANKS FOR NOT OPPRESSING OUR APATHY, CAP.

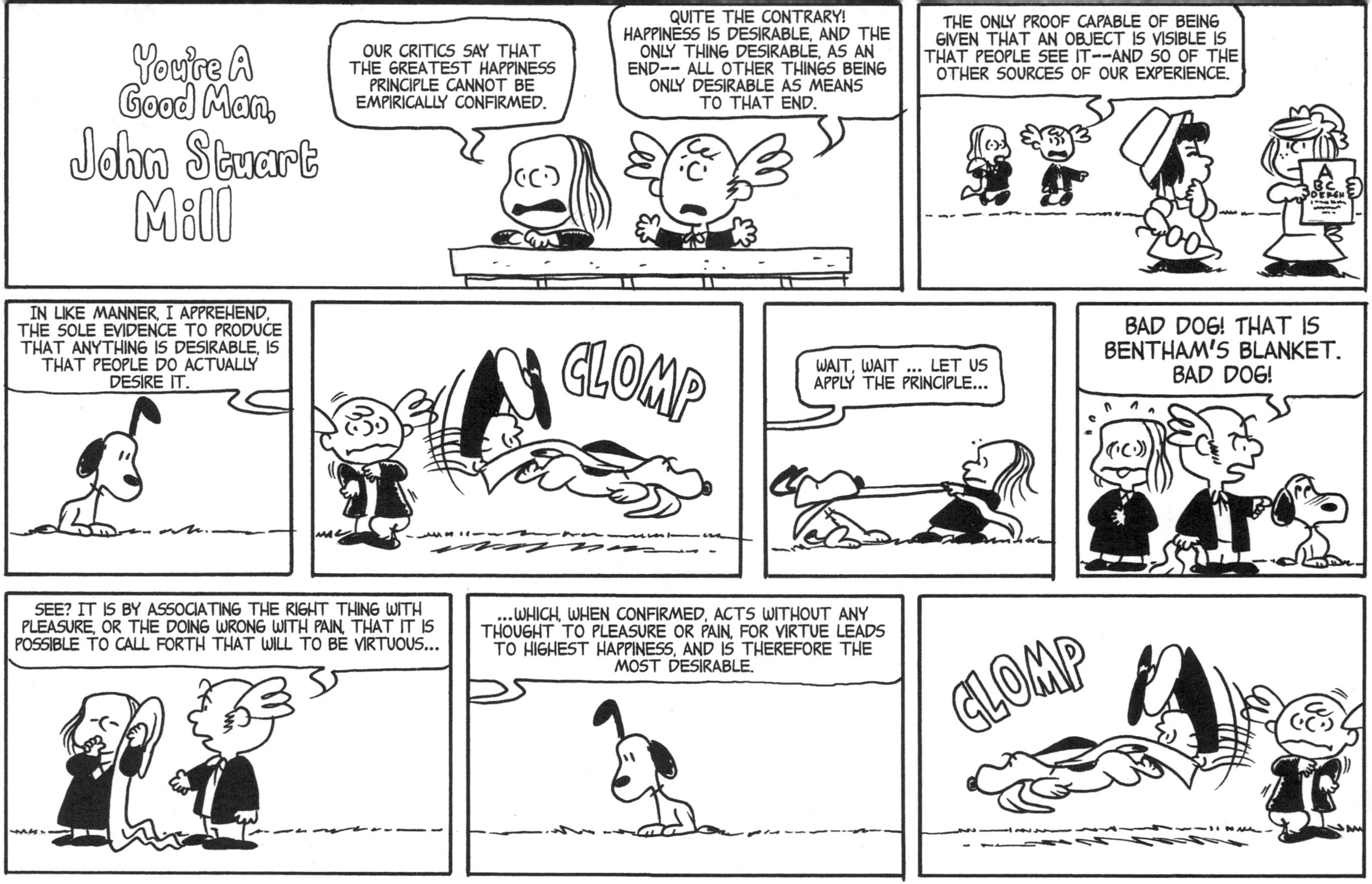
You're A Good Man, John Stuart Mill
OUR CRITICS SAY THAT THE GREATEST HAPPINESS PRINCIPLE CANNOT BE EMPIRICALLY CONFIRMED.
QUITE THE CONTRARY! HAPPINESS IS DESIRABLE, AND THE ONLY THING DESIRABLE, AS AN END-- ALL OTHER THINGS BEING ONLY DESIRABLE AS MEANS TO THAT END.
THE ONLY PROOF CAPABLE OF BEING GIVEN THAT AN OBJECT IS VISIBLE IS THAT PEOPLE SEE IT--AND SO OF THE OTHER SOURCES OF OUR EXPERIENCE.
IN LIKE MANNER, I APPREHEND, THE SOLE EVIDENCE TO PRODUCE THAT ANYTHING IS DESIRABLE, IS THAT PEOPLE DO ACTUALLY DESIRE IT.
CLOMP
WAIT, WAIT ... LET US APPLY THE PRINCIPLE...
BAD DOG! THAT IS BENTHAM'S BLANKET. BAD DOG!
SEE? IT IS BY ASSOCIATING THE RIGHT THING WITH PLEASURE, OR THE DOING WRONG WITH PAIN, THAT IT IS POSSIBLE TO CALL FORTH THAT WILL TO BE VIRTUOUS...
...WHICH, WHEN CONFIRMED, ACTS WITHOUT ANY THOUGHT TO PLEASURE OR PAIN, FOR VIRTUE LEADS TO HIGHEST HAPPINESS, AND IS THEREFORE THE MOST DESIRABLE.
CLOMP

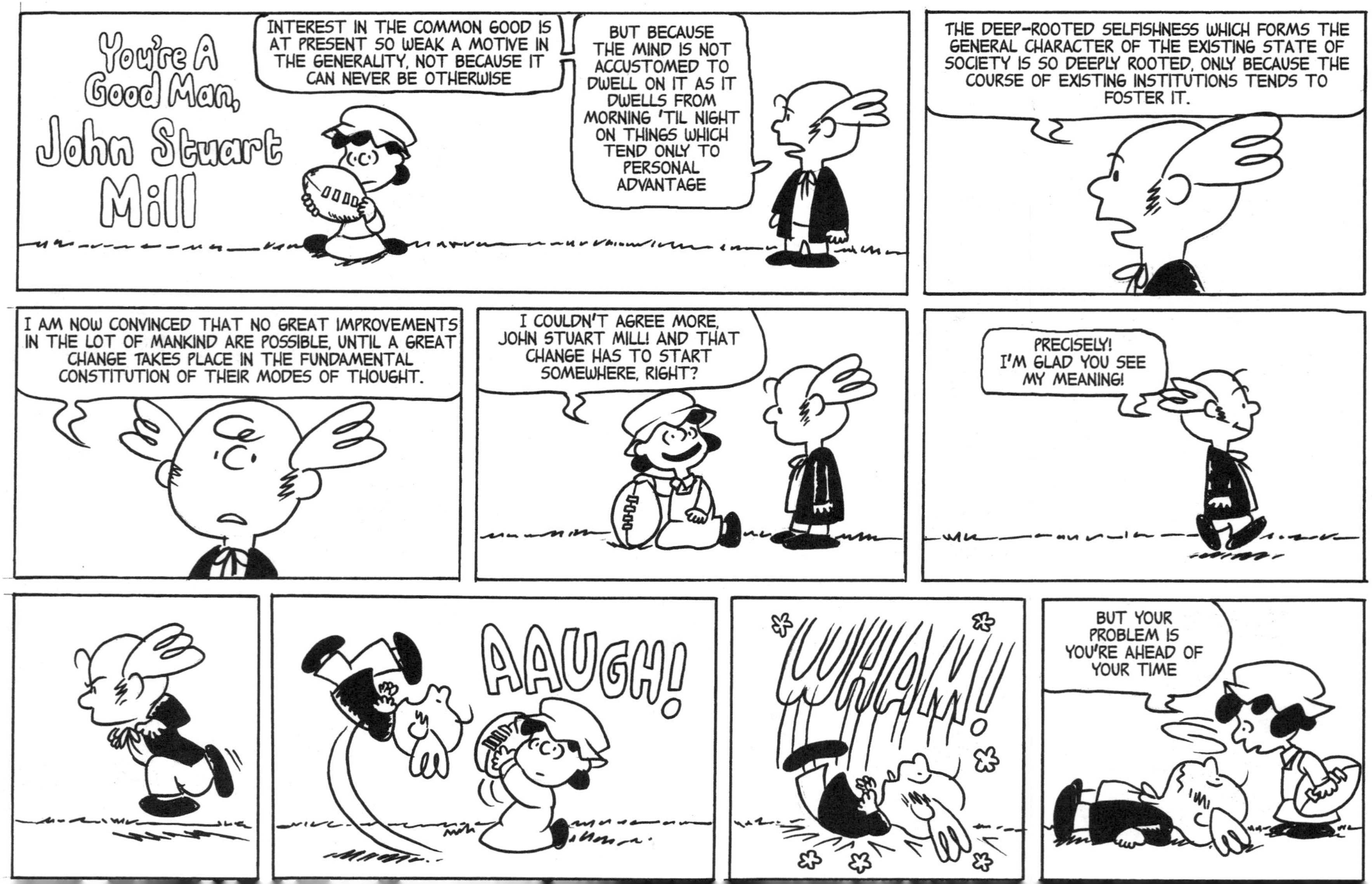
You're A Good Man, John Stuart Mill
INTEREST IN THE COMMON GOOD IS AT PRESENT SO WEAK A MOTIVE IN THE GENERALITY, NOT BECAUSE IT CAN NEVER BE OTHERWISE
BUT BECAUSE THE MIND IS NOT ACCUSTOMED TO DWELL ON IT AS IT DWELLS FROM MORNING 'TIL NIGHT ON THINGS WHICH TEND ONLY TO PERSONAL ADVANTAGE
THE DEEP-ROOTED SELFISHNESS WHICH FORMS THE GENERAL CHARACTER OF THE EXISTING STATE OF SOCIETY IS SO DEEPLY ROOTED, ONLY BECAUSE THE COURSE OF EXISTING INSTITUTIONS TENDS TO FOSTER IT.
I AM NOW CONVINCED THAT NO GREAT IMPROVEMENTS IN THE LOT OF MANKIND ARE POSSIBLE, UNTIL A GREAT CHANGE TAKES PLACE IN THE FUNDAMENTAL CONSTITUTION OF THEIR MODES OF THOUGHT.
I COULDN'T AGREE MORE, JOHN STUART MILL! AND THAT CHANGE HAS TO START SOMEWHERE, RIGHT?
PRECISELY! I'M GLAD YOU SEE MY MEANING!
AAUGH!
WHAM!
BUT YOUR PROBLEM IS YOU'RE AHEAD OF YOUR TIME

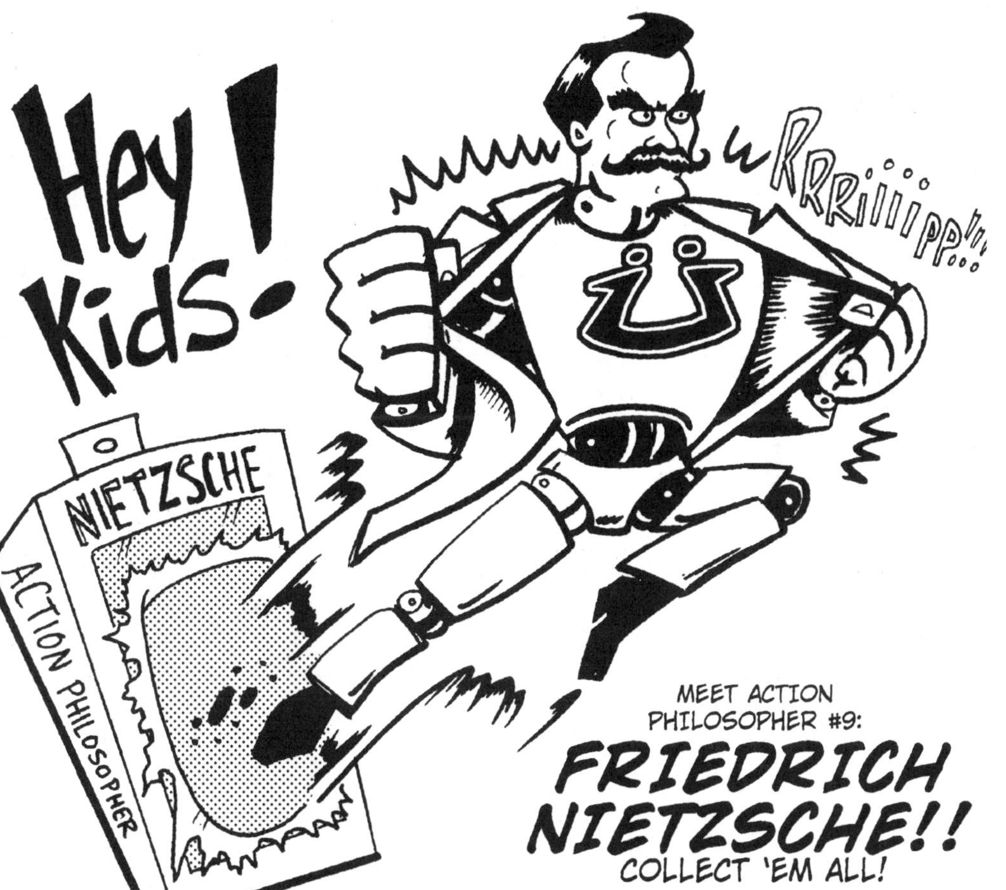
Hey Kids!
wRRRiiiiipp!!
NIETZSCHE
ACTION PHILOSOPHER
MEET ACTION PHILOSOPHER #9:
FRIEDRICH NIETZSCHE!!
COLLECT 'EM ALL!

WRITTEN BY FRED VAN LENTE • ILLUSTRATED BY RYAN DUNLAVEY

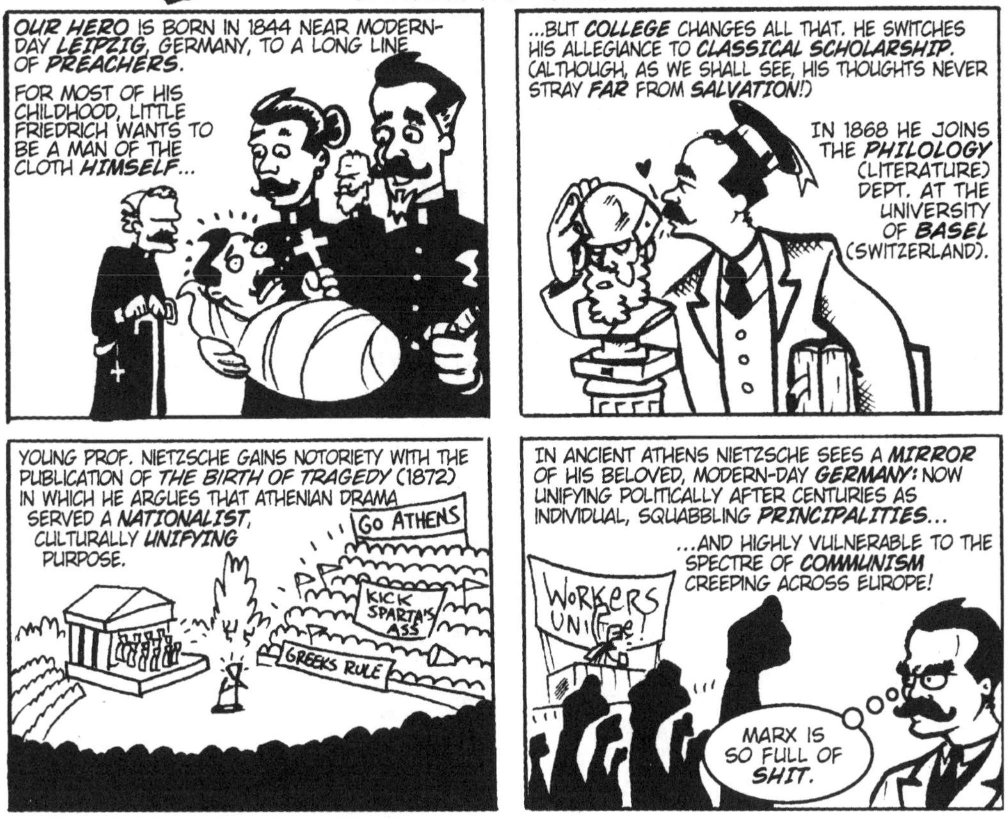
OUR HERO IS BORN IN 1844 NEAR MODERN-DAY LEIPZIG, GERMANY, TO A LONG LINE OF PREACHERS.
FOR MOST OF HIS CHILDHOOD, LITTLE FRIEDRICH WANTS TO BE A MAN OF THE CLOTH HIMSELF...
...BUT COLLEGE CHANGES ALL THAT. HE SWITCHES HIS ALLEGIANCE TO CLASSICAL SCHOLARSHIP. (ALTHOUGH, AS WE SHALL SEE, HIS THOUGHTS NEVER STRAY FAR FROM SALVATION!)
IN 1868 HE JOINS THE PHILOLOGY (LITERATURE) DEPT. AT THE UNIVERSITY OF BASEL (SWITZERLAND).
YOUNG PROF. NIETZSCHE GAINS NOTORIETY WITH THE PUBLICATION OF THE BIRTH OF TRAGEDY (1872) IN WHICH HE ARGUES THAT ATHENIAN DRAMA SERVED A NATIONALIST, CULTURALLY UNIFYING PURPOSE.
GO ATHENS
KICK SPARTA'S ASS
GREEKS RULE
IN ANCIENT ATHENS NIETZSCHE SEES A MIRROR OF HIS BELOVED, MODERN-DAY GERMANY: NOW UNIFYING POLITICALLY AFTER CENTURIES AS INDIVIDUAL, SQUABBLING PRINCIPALITIES...
...AND HIGHLY VULNERABLE TO THE SPECTRE OF COMMUNISM CREEPING ACROSS EUROPE!
WORKERS UNITE!
MARX IS SO FULL OF SHIT.

NIETZSCHE'S POOR HEALTH FORCES HIM TO PREMATURELY ***RETIRE*** FROM TEACHING IN 1878, AND NOW HE HAS TIME TO ***DEVELOP*** THIS ANTI-SOCIALIST IDEAS MORE ***THOROUGHLY...*** AND HE ENDS UP CRITIQUING ***ALL*** OF WESTERN SOCIETY!

SAID CRITIQUE CAN PERHAPS BE MOST EASILY SUMMED-UP WITH THE STATEMENT:

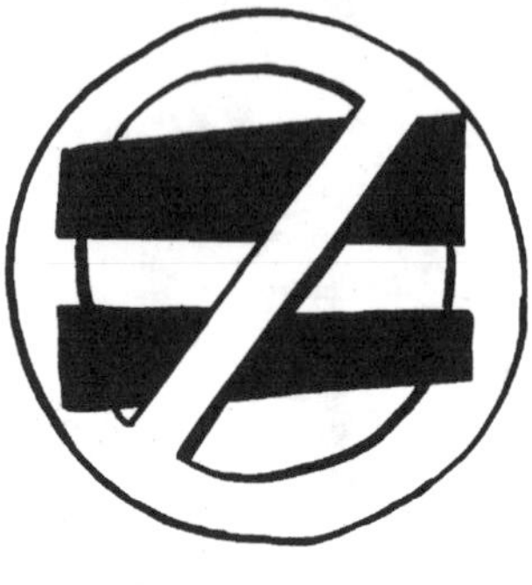

"***EQUALITY*** IS A HUMAN-CREATED CONCEPT, ***BOGUS*** AND ULTIMATELY ***CORRUPTING.***"

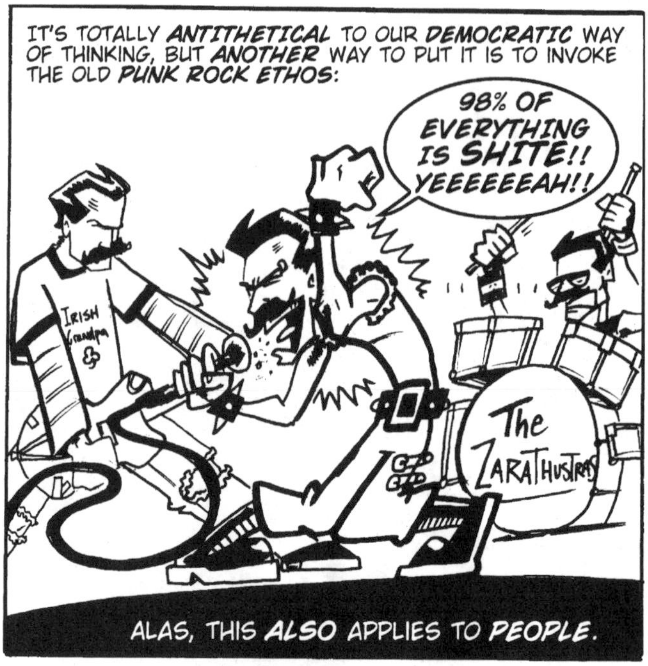
IT'S TOTALLY ANTITHETICAL TO OUR DEMOCRATIC WAY OF THINKING, BUT ANOTHER WAY TO PUT IT IS TO INVOKE THE OLD PUNK ROCK ETHOS:
98% OF EVERYTHING IS SHITE!! YEEEEEEAH!!
IRISH Grandpa
The ZARATHUSTRAS
ALAS, THIS ALSO APPLIES TO PEOPLE.

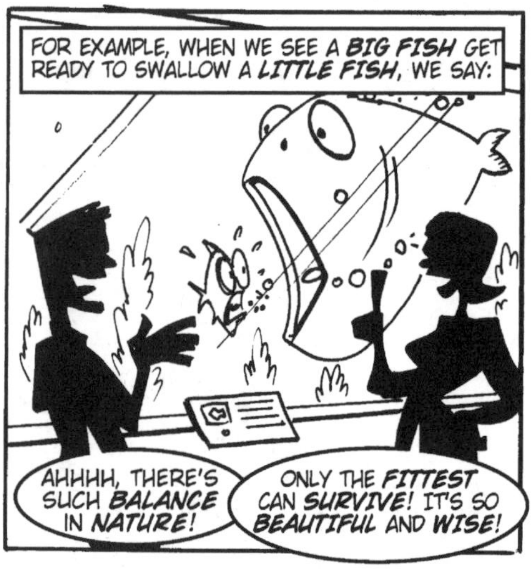
FOR EXAMPLE, WHEN WE SEE A BIG FISH GET READY TO SWALLOW A LITTLE FISH, WE SAY:
AHHHH, THERE'S SUCH BALANCE IN NATURE!
ONLY THE FITTEST CAN SURVIVE! IT'S SO BEAUTIFUL AND WISE!

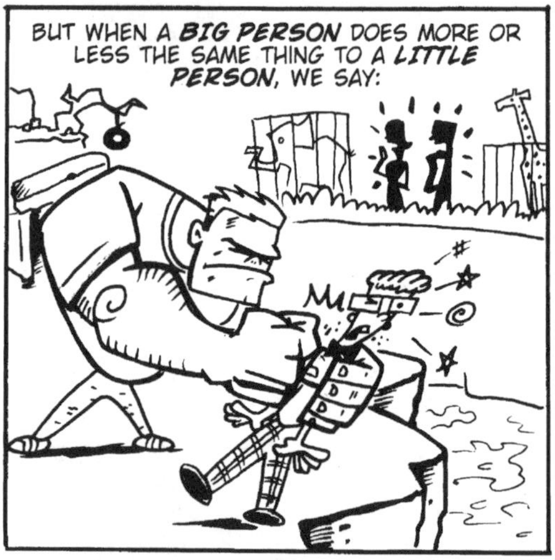
BUT WHEN A BIG PERSON DOES MORE OR LESS THE SAME THING TO A LITTLE PERSON, WE SAY:

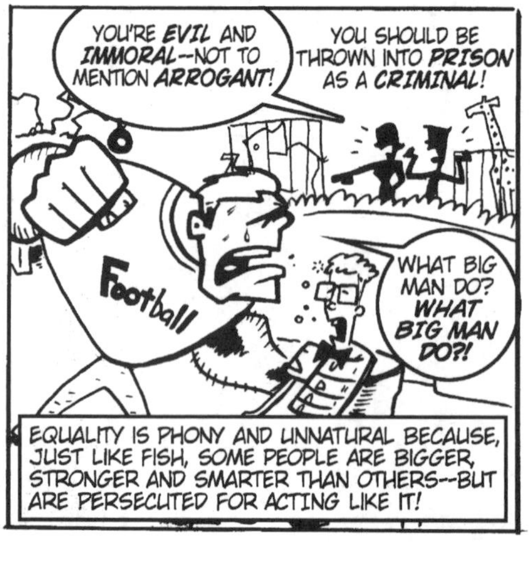
YOU'RE EVIL AND IMMORAL--NOT TO MENTION ARROGANT!
YOU SHOULD BE THROWN INTO PRISON AS A CRIMINAL!
Football
WHAT BIG MAN DO? WHAT BIG MAN DO?!
EQUALITY IS PHONY AND UNNATURAL BECAUSE, JUST LIKE FISH, SOME PEOPLE ARE BIGGER, STRONGER AND SMARTER THAN OTHERS--BUT ARE PERSECUTED FOR ACTING LIKE IT!

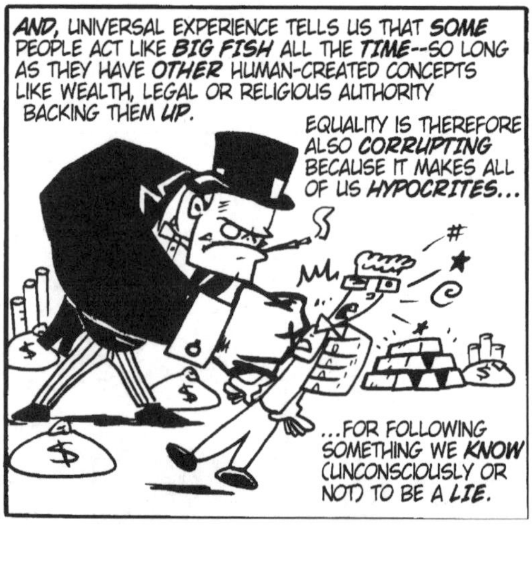
AND, UNIVERSAL EXPERIENCE TELLS US THAT SOME PEOPLE ACT LIKE BIG FISH ALL THE TIME--SO LONG AS THEY HAVE OTHER HUMAN-CREATED CONCEPTS LIKE WEALTH, LEGAL OR RELIGIOUS AUTHORITY BACKING THEM UP.
EQUALITY IS THEREFORE ALSO CORRUPTING BECAUSE IT MAKES ALL OF US HYPOCRITES...
...FOR FOLLOWING SOMETHING WE KNOW (UNCONSCIOUSLY OR NOT) TO BE A LIE.

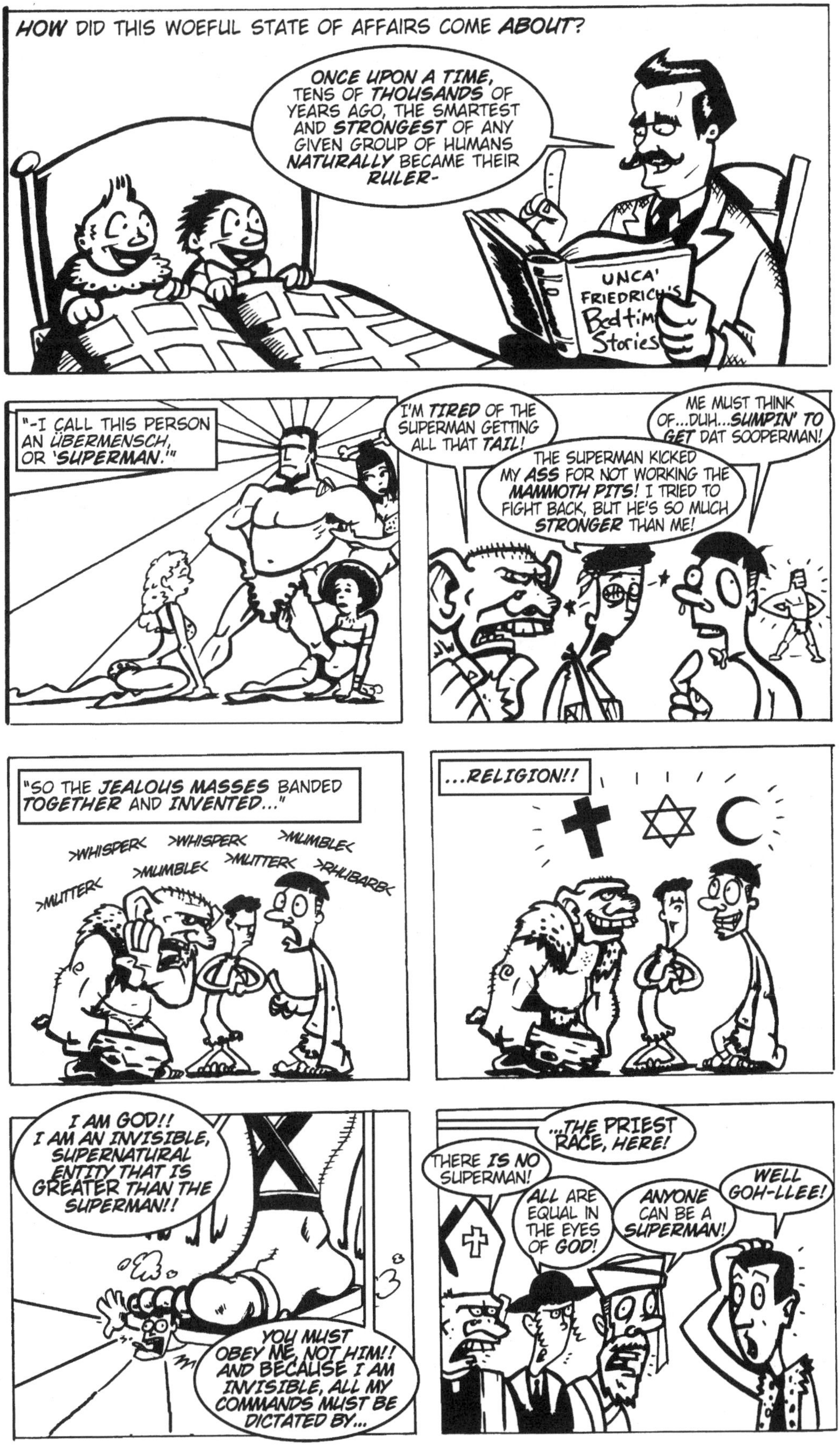
HOW DID THIS WOEFUL STATE OF AFFAIRS COME ABOUT?
ONCE UPON A TIME, TENS OF THOUSANDS OF YEARS AGO, THE SMARTEST AND STRONGEST OF ANY GIVEN GROUP OF HUMANS NATURALLY BECAME THEIR RULER-
UNCA' FRIEDRICH'S Bedtim Stories
"-I CALL THIS PERSON AN ÜBERMENSCH, OR 'SUPERMAN.'"
I'M TIRED OF THE SUPERMAN GETTING ALL THAT TAIL!
ME MUST THINK OF...DUH...SUMPIN' TO GET DAT SOOPERMAN!
THE SUPERMAN KICKED MY ASS FOR NOT WORKING THE MAMMOTH PITS! I TRIED TO FIGHT BACK, BUT HE'S SO MUCH STRONGER THAN ME!
"SO THE JEALOUS MASSES BANDED TOGETHER AND INVENTED..."
>WHISPER< >WHISPER< >MUMBLE<
>MUMBLE< >MUTTER< >RHUBARB<
>MUTTER<
...RELIGION!!
I AM GOD!! I AM AN INVISIBLE, SUPERNATURAL ENTITY THAT IS GREATER THAN THE SUPERMAN!!
YOU MUST OBEY ME, NOT HIM!! AND BECAUSE I AM INVISIBLE, ALL MY COMMANDS MUST BE DICTATED BY...
...THE PRIEST RACE, HERE!
THERE IS NO SUPERMAN!
ALL ARE EQUAL IN THE EYES OF GOD!
ANYONE CAN BE A SUPERMAN!
WELL GOH-LLEE!

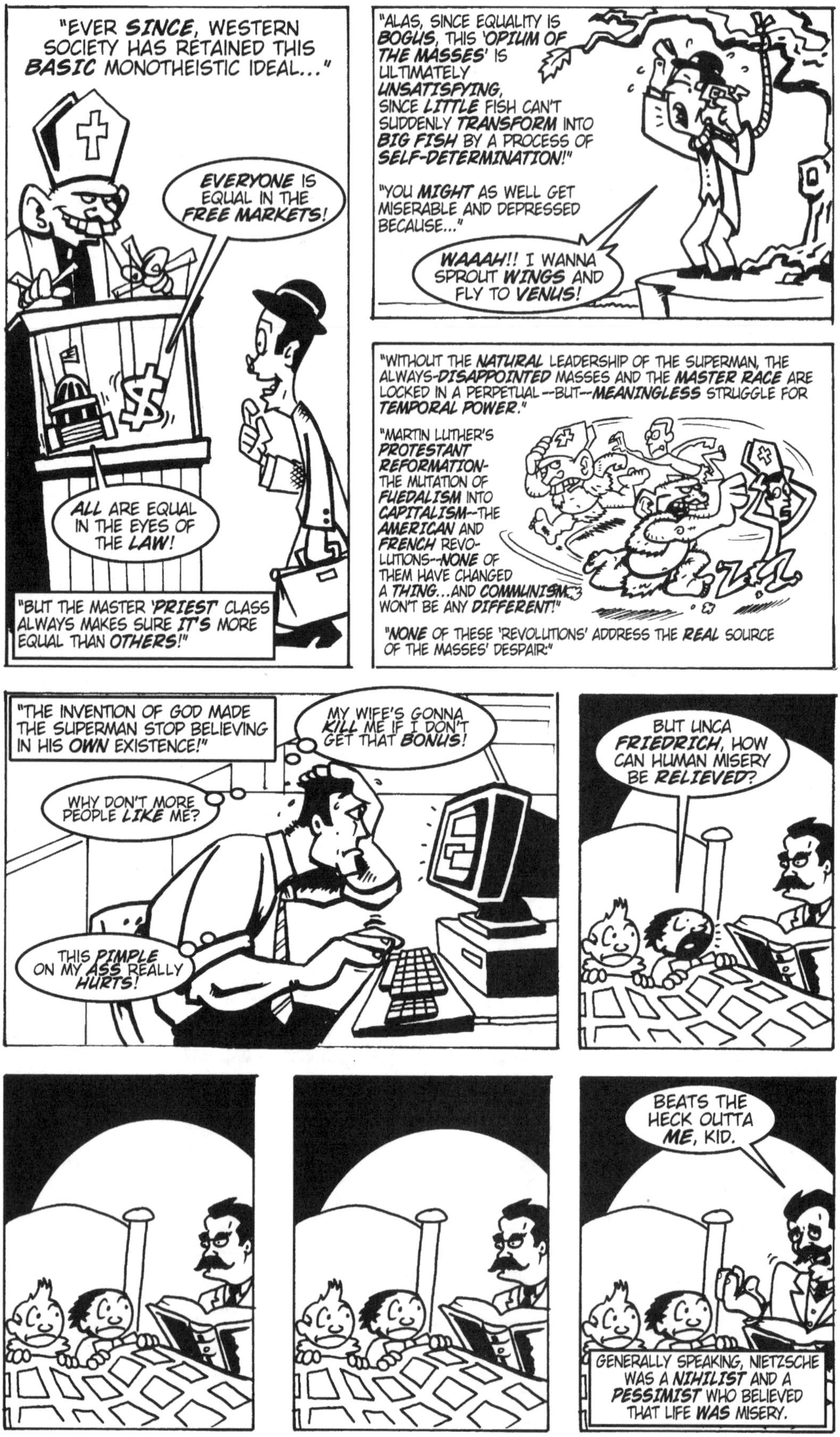
"EVER SINCE, WESTERN SOCIETY HAS RETAINED THIS BASIC MONOTHEISTIC IDEAL..."
EVERYONE IS EQUAL IN THE FREE MARKETS!
ALL ARE EQUAL IN THE EYES OF THE LAW!
"BUT THE MASTER 'PRIEST' CLASS ALWAYS MAKES SURE IT'S MORE EQUAL THAN OTHERS!"
"ALAS, SINCE EQUALITY IS BOGUS, THIS 'OPIUM OF THE MASSES' IS ULTIMATELY UNSATISFYING, SINCE LITTLE FISH CAN'T SUDDENLY TRANSFORM INTO BIG FISH BY A PROCESS OF SELF-DETERMINATION!"
"YOU MIGHT AS WELL GET MISERABLE AND DEPRESSED BECAUSE..."
WAAAH!! I WANNA SPROUT WINGS AND FLY TO VENUS!
"WITHOUT THE NATURAL LEADERSHIP OF THE SUPERMAN, THE ALWAYS-DISAPPOINTED MASSES AND THE MASTER RACE ARE LOCKED IN A PERPETUAL --BUT-- MEANINGLESS STRUGGLE FOR TEMPORAL POWER."
"MARTIN LUTHER'S PROTESTANT REFORMATION- THE MUTATION OF FUEDALISM INTO CAPITALISM--THE AMERICAN AND FRENCH REVOLUTIONS--NONE OF THEM HAVE CHANGED A THING...AND COMMUNISM WON'T BE ANY DIFFERENT!"
"NONE OF THESE 'REVOLUTIONS' ADDRESS THE REAL SOURCE OF THE MASSES' DESPAIR:"
"THE INVENTION OF GOD MADE THE SUPERMAN STOP BELIEVING IN HIS OWN EXISTENCE!"
MY WIFE'S GONNA KILL ME IF I DON'T GET THAT BONUS!
WHY DON'T MORE PEOPLE LIKE ME?
THIS PIMPLE ON MY ASS REALLY HURTS!
BUT UNCA FRIEDRICH, HOW CAN HUMAN MISERY BE RELIEVED?
BEATS THE HECK OUTTA ME, KID.
GENERALLY SPEAKING, NIETZSCHE WAS A NIHILIST AND A PESSIMIST WHO BELIEVED THAT LIFE WAS MISERY.

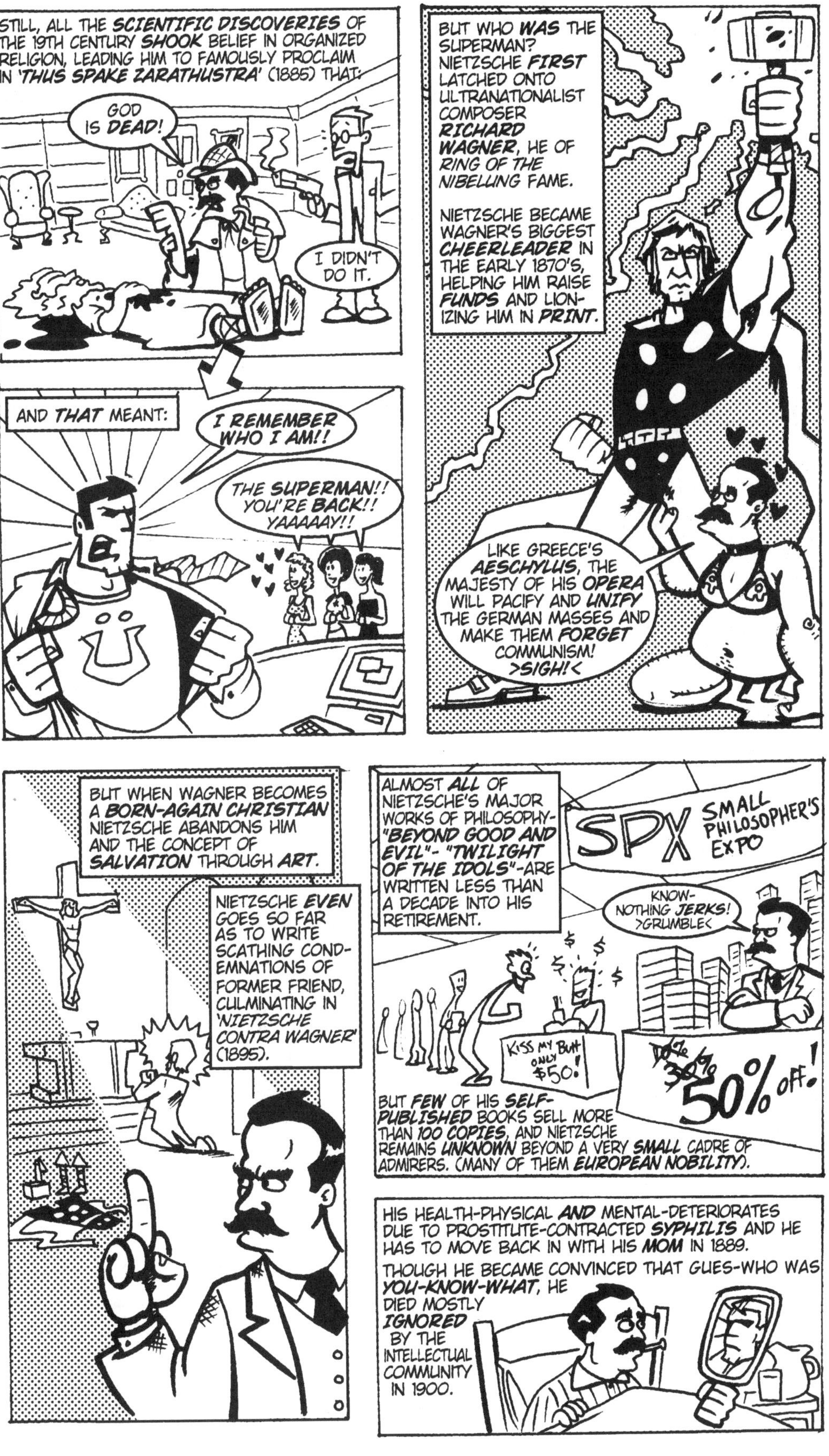
STILL, ALL THE SCIENTIFIC DISCOVERIES OF THE 19TH CENTURY SHOOK BELIEF IN ORGANIZED RELIGION, LEADING HIM TO FAMOUSLY PROCLAIM IN 'THUS SPAKE ZARATHUSTRA' (1885) THAT:
GOD IS DEAD!
I DIDN'T DO IT.
AND THAT MEANT:
I REMEMBER WHO I AM!!
THE SUPERMAN!! YOU'RE BACK!! YAAAAAY!!
BUT WHO WAS THE SUPERMAN? NIETZSCHE FIRST LATCHED ONTO ULTRANATIONALIST COMPOSER RICHARD WAGNER, HE OF RING OF THE NIBELUNG FAME.
NIETZSCHE BECAME WAGNER'S BIGGEST CHEERLEADER IN THE EARLY 1870'S, HELPING HIM RAISE FUNDS AND LIONIZING HIM IN PRINT.
LIKE GREECE'S AESCHYLUS, THE MAJESTY OF HIS OPERA WILL PACIFY AND UNIFY THE GERMAN MASSES AND MAKE THEM FORGET COMMUNISM! >SIGH!<
BUT WHEN WAGNER BECOMES A BORN-AGAIN CHRISTIAN NIETZSCHE ABANDONS HIM AND THE CONCEPT OF SALVATION THROUGH ART.
NIETZSCHE EVEN GOES SO FAR AS TO WRITE SCATHING CONDEMNATIONS OF FORMER FRIEND, CULMINATING IN 'NIETZSCHE CONTRA WAGNER' (1895).
ALMOST ALL OF NIETZSCHE'S MAJOR WORKS OF PHILOSOPHY- "BEYOND GOOD AND EVIL"- "TWILIGHT OF THE IDOLS"-ARE WRITTEN LESS THAN A DECADE INTO HIS RETIREMENT.
SPX SMALL PHILOSOPHER'S EXPO
KNOW-NOTHING JERKS! >GRUMBLE<
KISS MY BUTT ONLY $50!
30% 50% OFF!
BUT FEW OF HIS SELF-PUBLISHED BOOKS SELL MORE THAN 100 COPIES, AND NIETZSCHE REMAINS UNKNOWN BEYOND A VERY SMALL CADRE OF ADMIRERS. (MANY OF THEM EUROPEAN NOBILITY).
HIS HEALTH-PHYSICAL AND MENTAL-DETERIORATES DUE TO PROSTITUTE-CONTRACTED SYPHILIS AND HE HAS TO MOVE BACK IN WITH HIS MOM IN 1889.
THOUGH HE BECAME CONVINCED THAT GUES-WHO WAS YOU-KNOW-WHAT, HE DIED MOSTLY IGNORED BY THE INTELLECTUAL COMMUNITY IN 1900.

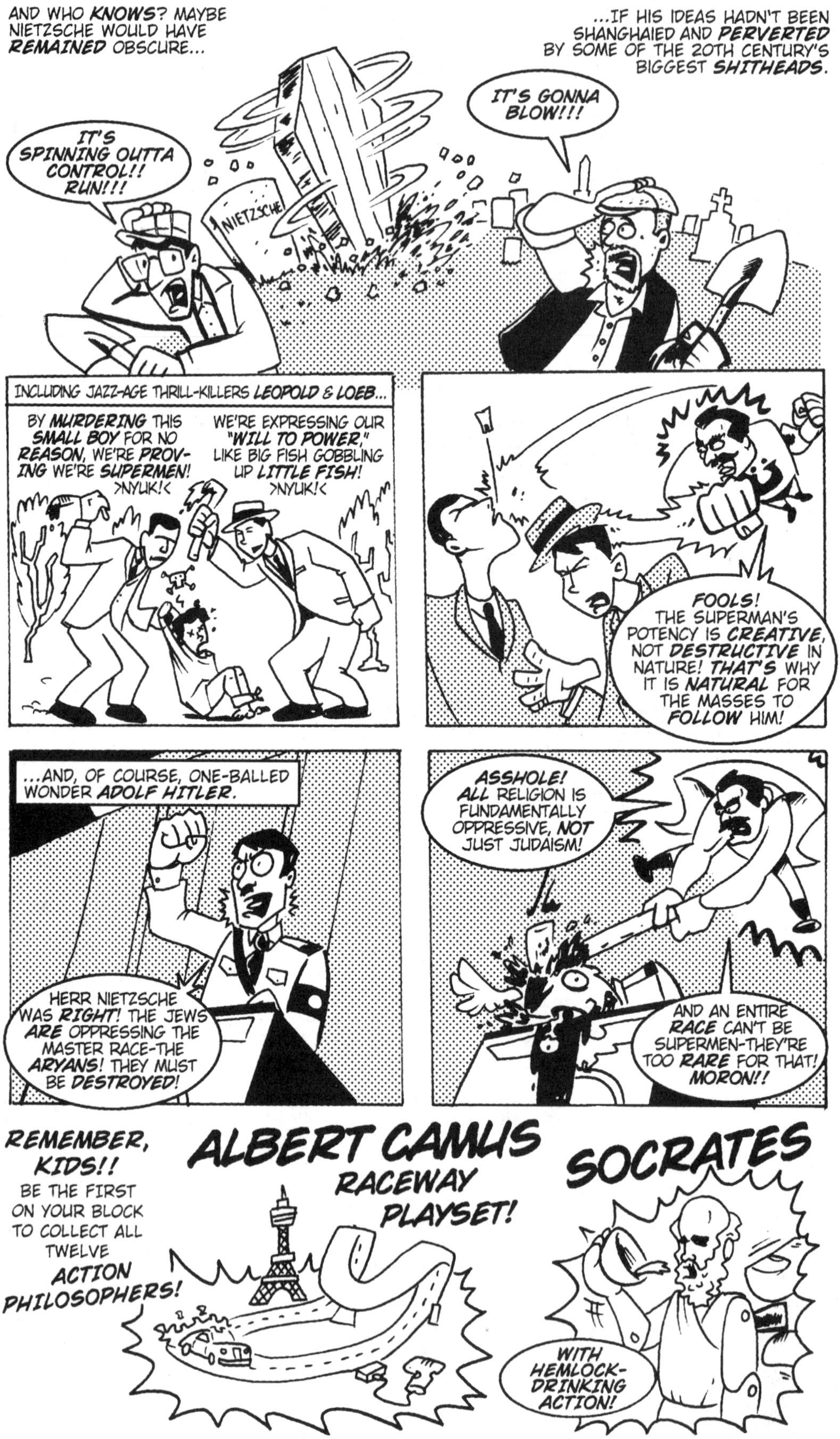
AND WHO KNOWS? MAYBE NIETZSCHE WOULD HAVE REMAINED OBSCURE...
...IF HIS IDEAS HADN'T BEEN SHANGHAIED AND PERVERTED BY SOME OF THE 20TH CENTURY'S BIGGEST SHITHEADS.
IT'S SPINNING OUTTA CONTROL!! RUN!!!
NIETZSCHE
IT'S GONNA BLOW!!!
INCLUDING JAZZ-AGE THRILL-KILLERS LEOPOLD & LOEB...
BY MURDERING THIS SMALL BOY FOR NO REASON, WE'RE PROVING WE'RE SUPERMEN! >NYUK!<
WE'RE EXPRESSING OUR "WILL TO POWER," LIKE BIG FISH GOBBLING UP LITTLE FISH! >NYUK!<
FOOLS! THE SUPERMAN'S POTENCY IS CREATIVE, NOT DESTRUCTIVE IN NATURE! THAT'S WHY IT IS NATURAL FOR THE MASSES TO FOLLOW HIM!
...AND, OF COURSE, ONE-BALLED WONDER ADOLF HITLER.
HERR NIETZSCHE WAS RIGHT! THE JEWS ARE OPPRESSING THE MASTER RACE-THE ARYANS! THEY MUST BE DESTROYED!
ASSHOLE! ALL RELIGION IS FUNDAMENTALLY OPPRESSIVE, NOT JUST JUDAISM!
AND AN ENTIRE RACE CAN'T BE SUPERMEN-THEY'RE TOO RARE FOR THAT! MORON!!
REMEMBER, KIDS!! BE THE FIRST ON YOUR BLOCK TO COLLECT ALL TWELVE ACTION PHILOSOPHERS!
ALBERT CAMUS RACEWAY PLAYSET!
SOCRATES
WITH HEMLOCK-DRINKING ACTION!

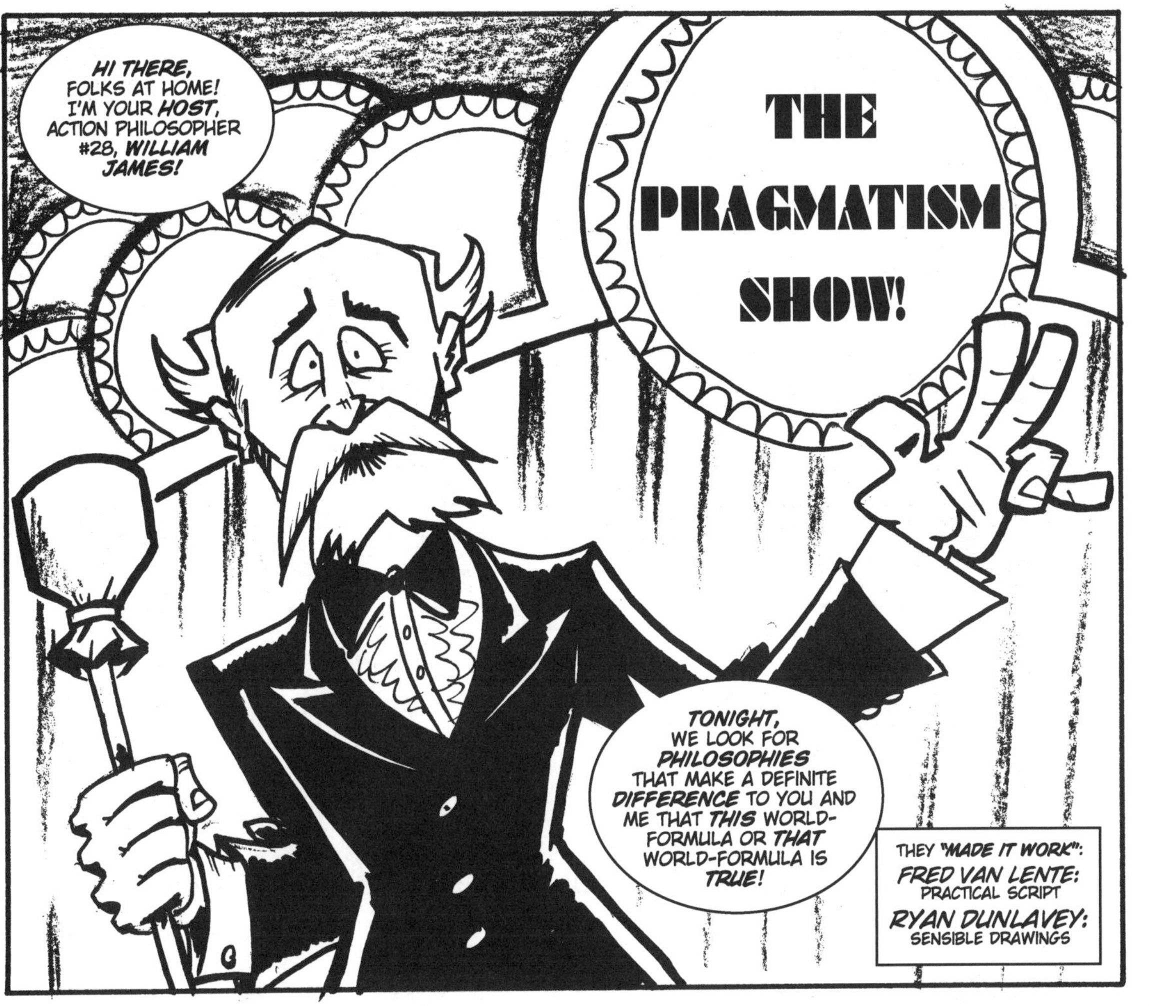
HI THERE, FOLKS AT HOME! I'M YOUR HOST, ACTION PHILOSOPHER #28, WILLIAM JAMES!
THE PRAGMATISM SHOW!
TONIGHT, WE LOOK FOR PHILOSOPHIES THAT MAKE A DEFINITE DIFFERENCE TO YOU AND ME THAT THIS WORLD-FORMULA OR THAT WORLD-FORMULA IS TRUE!
THEY "MADE IT WORK": FRED VAN LENTE: PRACTICAL SCRIPT RYAN DUNLAVEY: SENSIBLE DRAWINGS

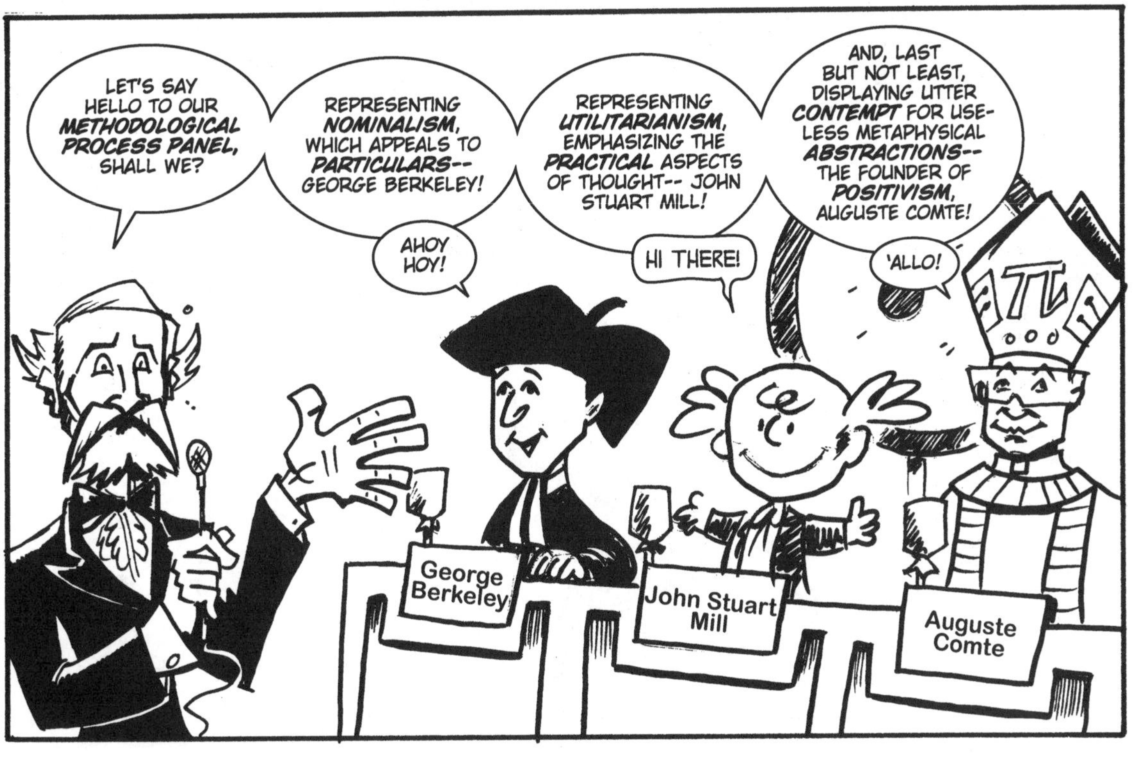
LET'S SAY HELLO TO OUR METHODOLOGICAL PROCESS PANEL, SHALL WE?
REPRESENTING NOMINALISM, WHICH APPEALS TO PARTICULARS-- GEORGE BERKELEY!
REPRESENTING UTILITARIANISM, EMPHASIZING THE PRACTICAL ASPECTS OF THOUGHT-- JOHN STUART MILL!
AND, LAST BUT NOT LEAST, DISPLAYING UTTER CONTEMPT FOR USE-LESS METAPHYSICAL ABSTRACTIONS-- THE FOUNDER OF POSITIVISM, AUGUSTE COMTE!
AHOY HOY!
HI THERE!
'ALLO!
George Berkeley
John Stuart Mill
Auguste Comte

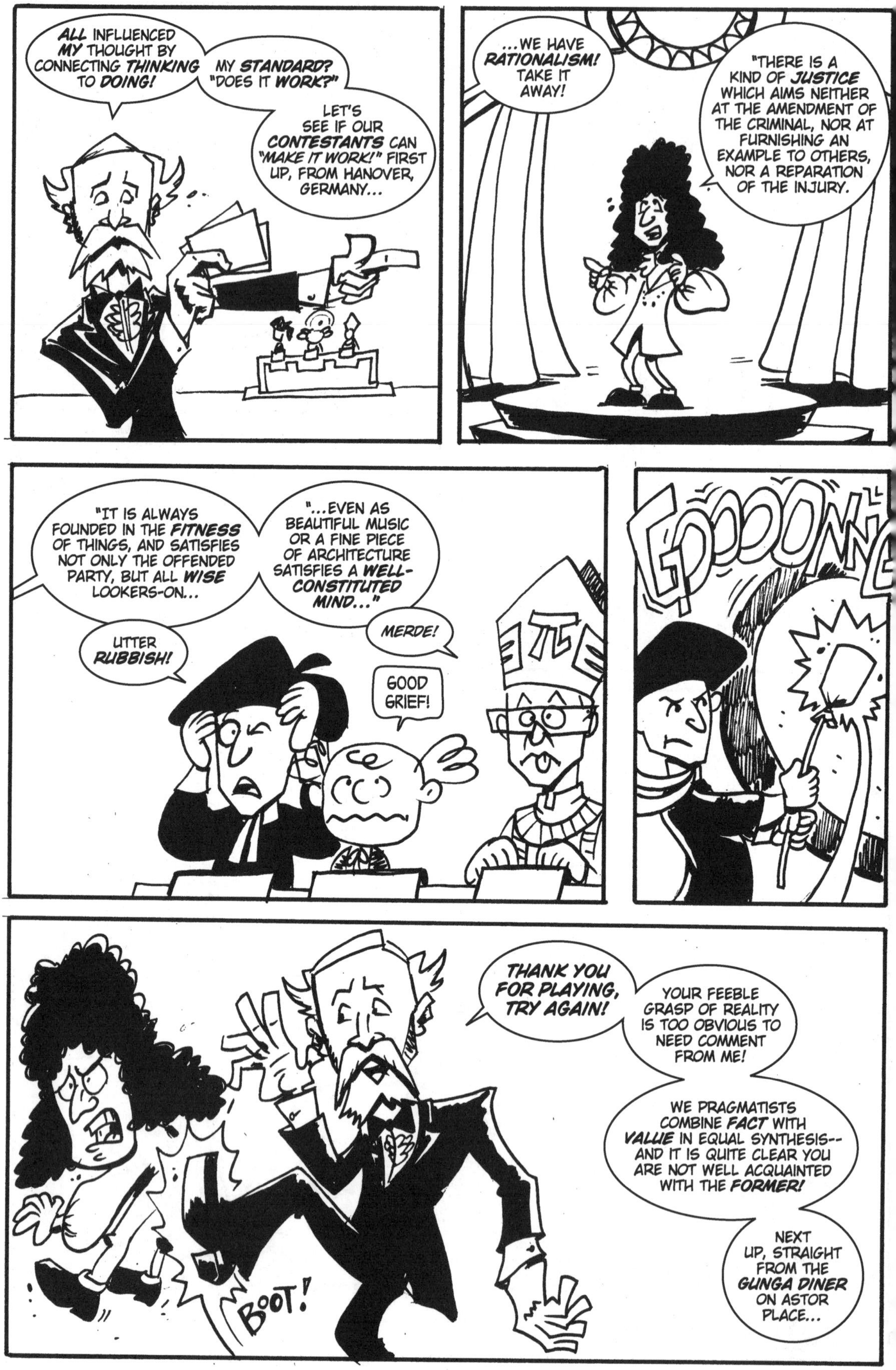
ALL INFLUENCED MY THOUGHT BY CONNECTING THINKING TO DOING!
MY STANDARD? "DOES IT WORK?"
LET'S SEE IF OUR CONTESTANTS CAN "MAKE IT WORK!" FIRST UP, FROM HANOVER, GERMANY...
...WE HAVE RATIONALISM! TAKE IT AWAY!
"THERE IS A KIND OF JUSTICE WHICH AIMS NEITHER AT THE AMENDMENT OF THE CRIMINAL, NOR AT FURNISHING AN EXAMPLE TO OTHERS, NOR A REPARATION OF THE INJURY.
"IT IS ALWAYS FOUNDED IN THE FITNESS OF THINGS, AND SATISFIES NOT ONLY THE OFFENDED PARTY, BUT ALL WISE LOOKERS-ON...
"...EVEN AS BEAUTIFUL MUSIC OR A FINE PIECE OF ARCHITECTURE SATISFIES A WELL-CONSTITUTED MIND..."
UTTER RUBBISH!
MERDE!
GOOD GRIEF!
GOOOONNG
THANK YOU FOR PLAYING, TRY AGAIN!
YOUR FEEBLE GRASP OF REALITY IS TOO OBVIOUS TO NEED COMMENT FROM ME!
WE PRAGMATISTS COMBINE FACT WITH VALUE IN EQUAL SYNTHESIS-- AND IT IS QUITE CLEAR YOU ARE NOT WELL ACQUAINTED WITH THE FORMER!
NEXT UP, STRAIGHT FROM THE GUNGA DINER ON ASTOR PLACE...
BOOT!

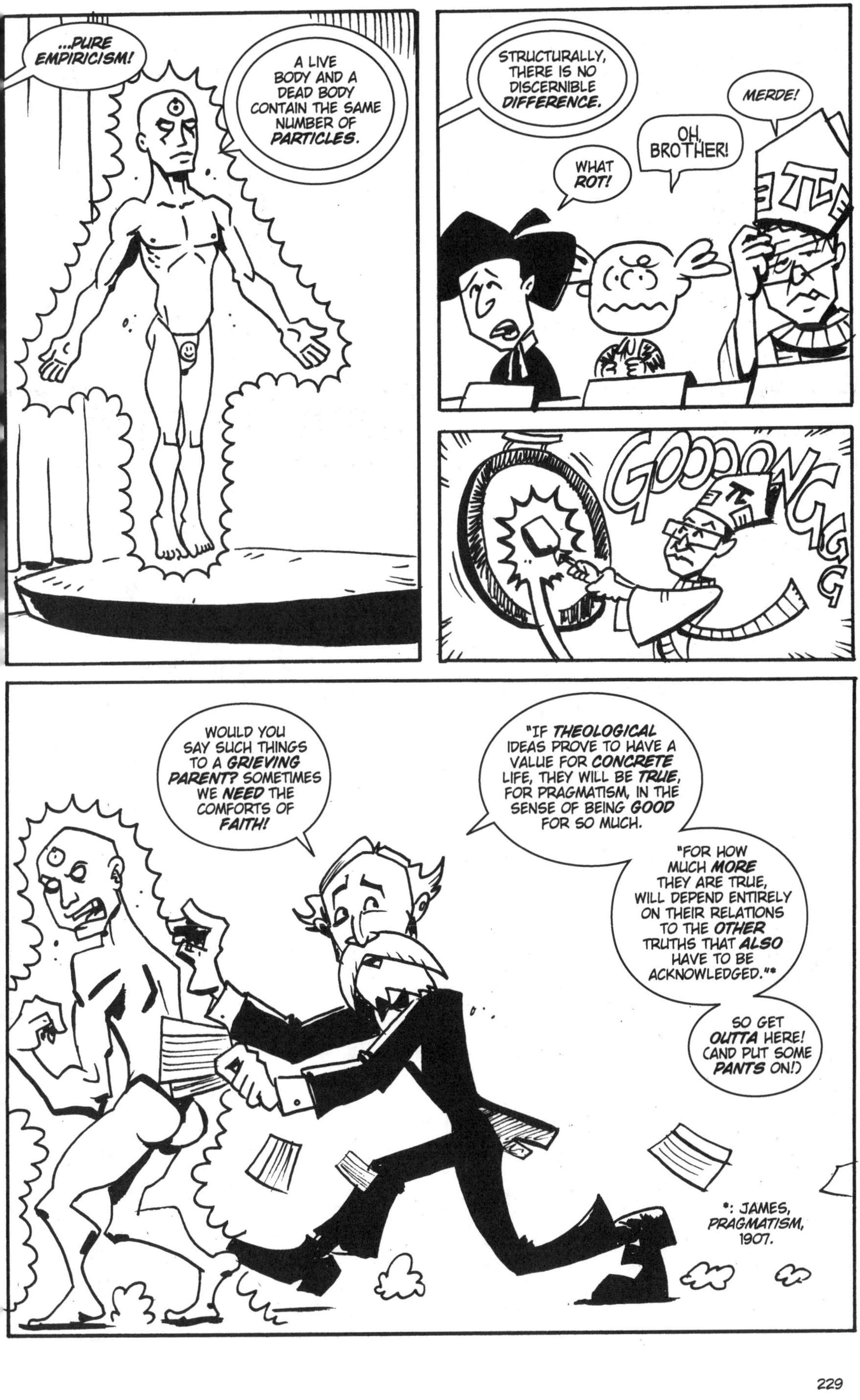
...PURE EMPIRICISM!
A LIVE BODY AND A DEAD BODY CONTAIN THE SAME NUMBER OF PARTICLES.
STRUCTURALLY, THERE IS NO DISCERNIBLE DIFFERENCE.
MERDE!
OH, BROTHER!
WHAT ROT!
GOOOONGGG
WOULD YOU SAY SUCH THINGS TO A GRIEVING PARENT? SOMETIMES WE NEED THE COMFORTS OF FAITH!
"IF THEOLOGICAL IDEAS PROVE TO HAVE A VALUE FOR CONCRETE LIFE, THEY WILL BE TRUE, FOR PRAGMATISM, IN THE SENSE OF BEING GOOD FOR SO MUCH.
"FOR HOW MUCH MORE THEY ARE TRUE, WILL DEPEND ENTIRELY ON THEIR RELATIONS TO THE OTHER TRUTHS THAT ALSO HAVE TO BE ACKNOWLEDGED."*
SO GET OUTTA HERE! (AND PUT SOME PANTS ON!)
*: JAMES, PRAGMATISM, 1907.

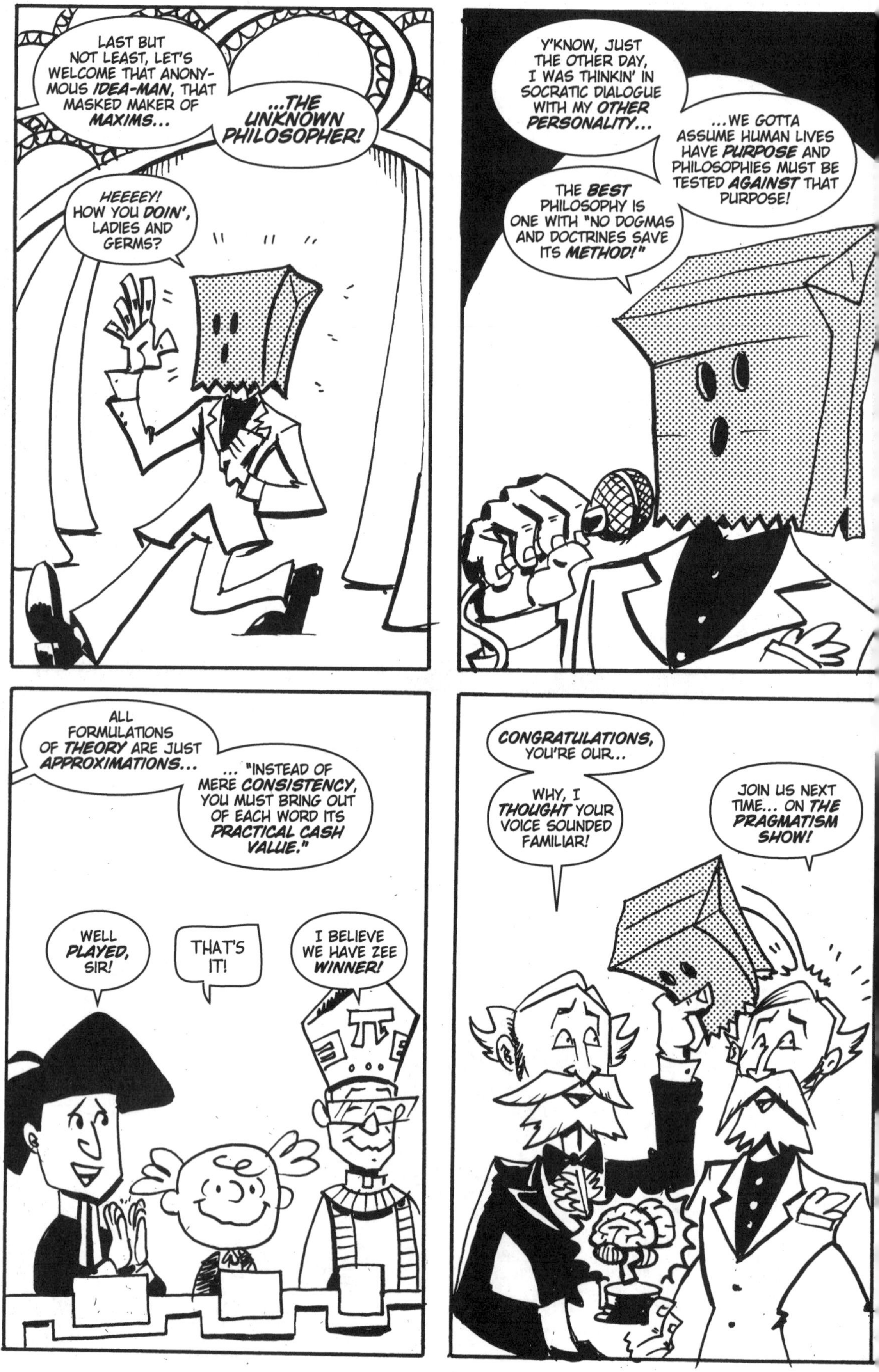

LAST BUT NOT LEAST, LET'S WELCOME THAT ANONY-MOUS IDEA-MAN, THAT MASKED MAKER OF MAXIMS...
...THE UNKNOWN PHILOSOPHER!
HEEEEY! HOW YOU DOIN', LADIES AND GERMS?
Y'KNOW, JUST THE OTHER DAY, I WAS THINKIN' IN SOCRATIC DIALOGUE WITH MY OTHER PERSONALITY...
...WE GOTTA ASSUME HUMAN LIVES HAVE PURPOSE AND PHILOSOPHIES MUST BE TESTED AGAINST THAT PURPOSE!
THE BEST PHILOSOPHY IS ONE WITH "NO DOGMAS AND DOCTRINES SAVE ITS METHOD!"
ALL FORMULATIONS OF THEORY ARE JUST APPROXIMATIONS...
... "INSTEAD OF MERE CONSISTENCY, YOU MUST BRING OUT OF EACH WORD ITS PRACTICAL CASH VALUE."
WELL PLAYED, SIR!
THAT'S IT!
I BELIEVE WE HAVE ZEE WINNER!
CONGRATULATIONS, YOU'RE OUR...
WHY, I THOUGHT YOUR VOICE SOUNDED FAMILIAR!
JOIN US NEXT TIME... ON THE PRAGMATISM SHOW!

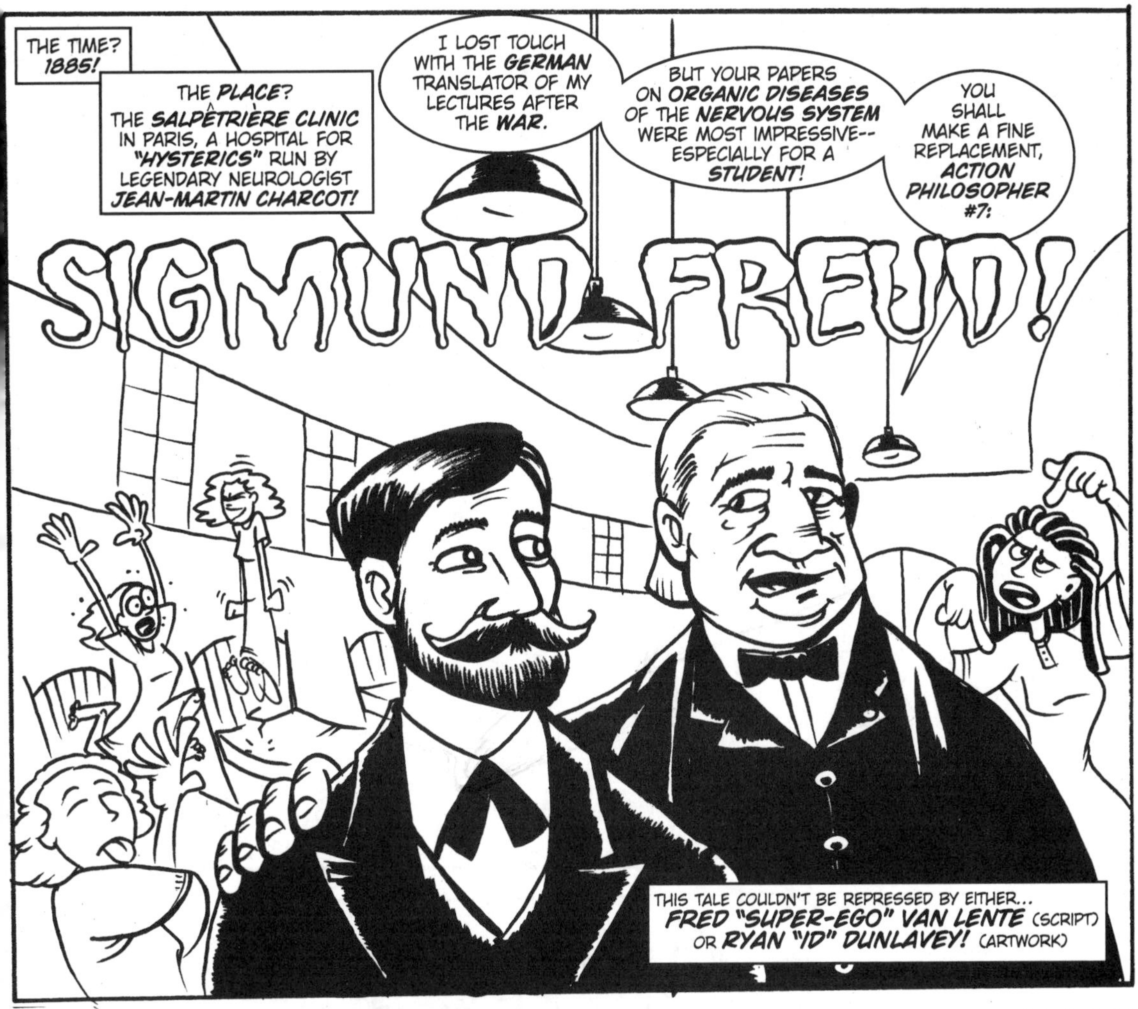
THE TIME? 1885!
THE PLACE? THE SALPÊTRIÈRE CLINIC IN PARIS, A HOSPITAL FOR "HYSTERICS" RUN BY LEGENDARY NEUROLOGIST JEAN-MARTIN CHARCOT!
I LOST TOUCH WITH THE GERMAN TRANSLATOR OF MY LECTURES AFTER THE WAR.
BUT YOUR PAPERS ON ORGANIC DISEASES OF THE NERVOUS SYSTEM WERE MOST IMPRESSIVE-- ESPECIALLY FOR A STUDENT!
YOU SHALL MAKE A FINE REPLACEMENT, ACTION PHILOSOPHER #7:
SIGMUND FREUD!
THIS TALE COULDN'T BE REPRESSED BY EITHER... FRED "SUPER-EGO" VAN LENTE (SCRIPT) OR RYAN "ID" DUNLAVEY! (ARTWORK)

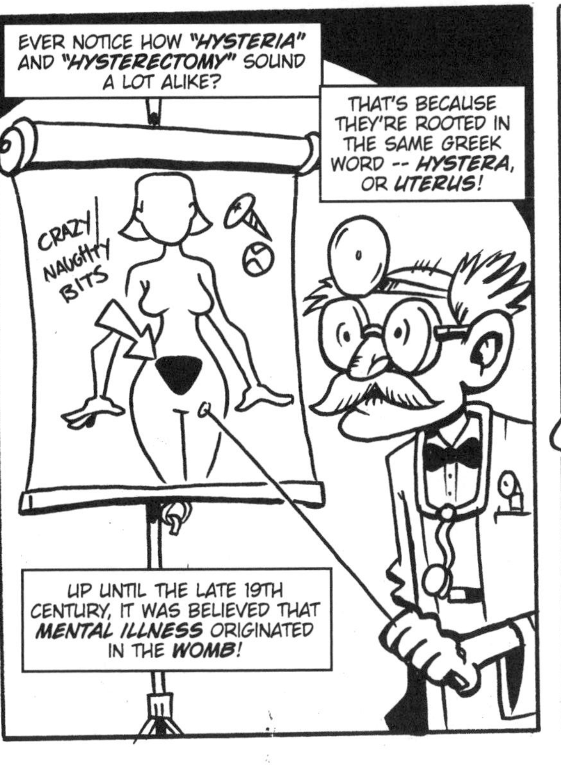
EVER NOTICE HOW "HYSTERIA" AND "HYSTERECTOMY" SOUND A LOT ALIKE?
THAT'S BECAUSE THEY'RE ROOTED IN THE SAME GREEK WORD -- HYSTERA, OR UTERUS!
CRAZY NAUGHTY BITS
UP UNTIL THE LATE 19TH CENTURY, IT WAS BELIEVED THAT MENTAL ILLNESS ORIGINATED IN THE WOMB!

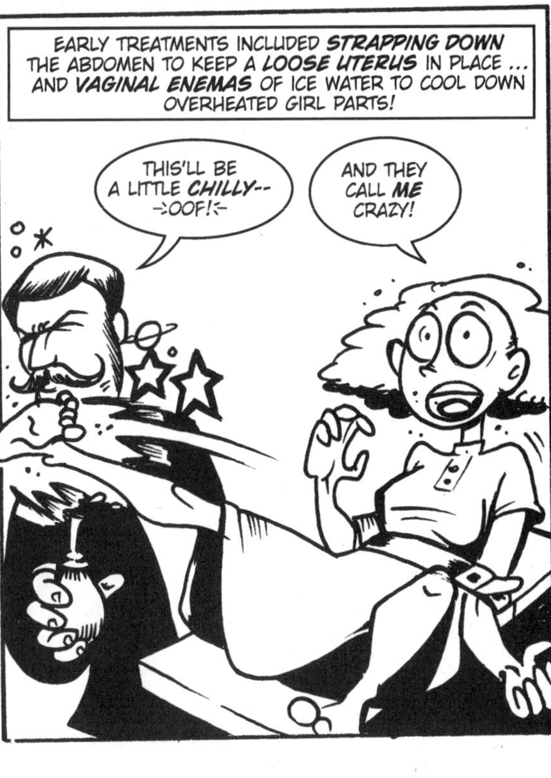
EARLY TREATMENTS INCLUDED STRAPPING DOWN THE ABDOMEN TO KEEP A LOOSE UTERUS IN PLACE ... AND VAGINAL ENEMAS OF ICE WATER TO COOL DOWN OVERHEATED GIRL PARTS!
THIS'LL BE A LITTLE CHILLY-- -OOF!-
AND THEY CALL ME CRAZY!

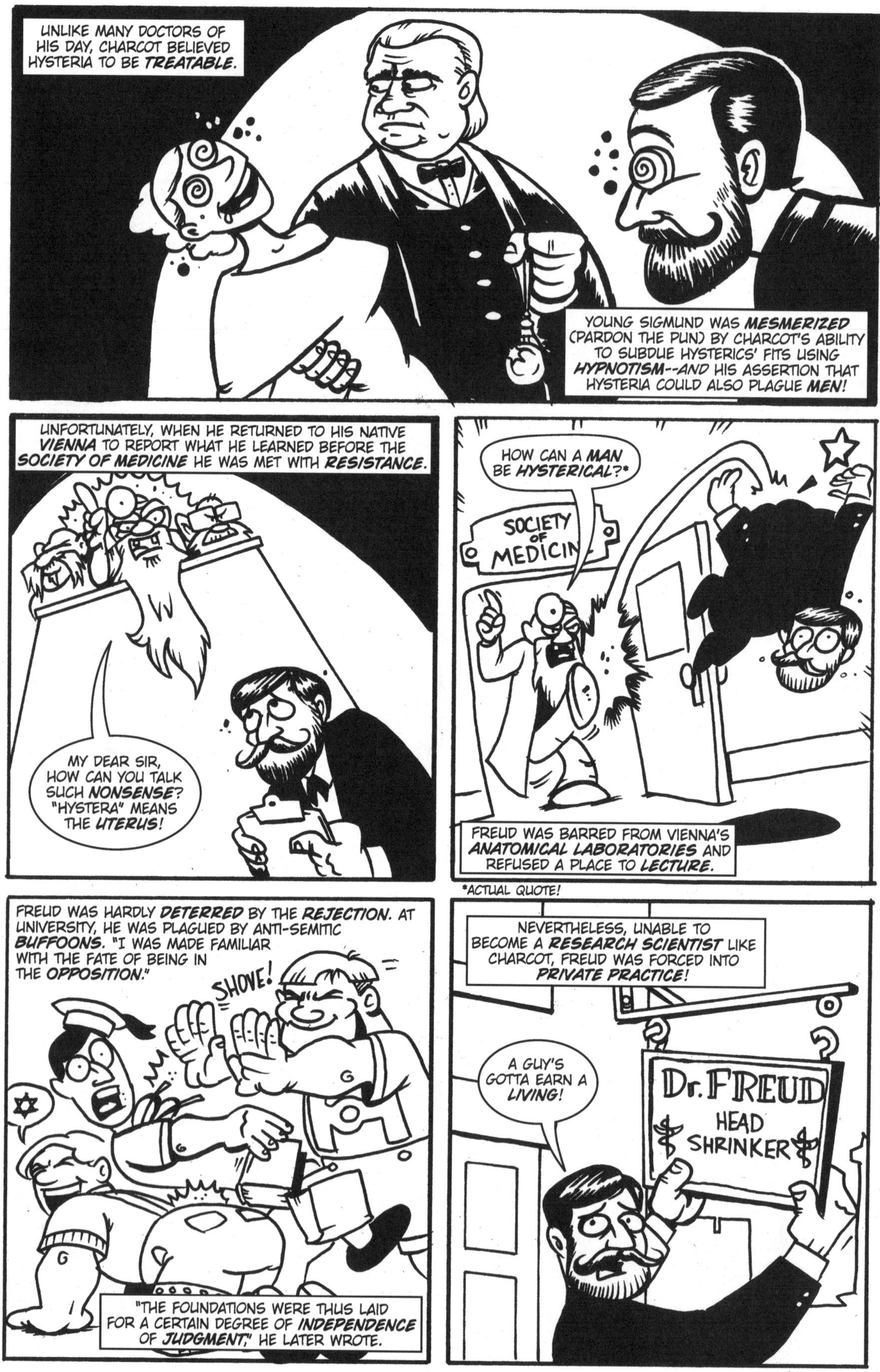
UNLIKE MANY DOCTORS OF HIS DAY, CHARCOT BELIEVED HYSTERIA TO BE TREATABLE.
YOUNG SIGMUND WAS MESMERIZED (PARDON THE PUN) BY CHARCOT'S ABILITY TO SUBDUE HYSTERICS' FITS USING HYPNOTISM--AND HIS ASSERTION THAT HYSTERIA COULD ALSO PLAGUE MEN!
UNFORTUNATELY, WHEN HE RETURNED TO HIS NATIVE VIENNA TO REPORT WHAT HE LEARNED BEFORE THE SOCIETY OF MEDICINE HE WAS MET WITH RESISTANCE.
MY DEAR SIR, HOW CAN YOU TALK SUCH NONSENSE? "HYSTERA" MEANS THE UTERUS!
HOW CAN A MAN BE HYSTERICAL?*
SOCIETY OF MEDICIN
FREUD WAS BARRED FROM VIENNA'S ANATOMICAL LABORATORIES AND REFUSED A PLACE TO LECTURE.
*ACTUAL QUOTE!
FREUD WAS HARDLY DETERRED BY THE REJECTION. AT UNIVERSITY, HE WAS PLAGUED BY ANTI-SEMITIC BUFFOONS. "I WAS MADE FAMILIAR WITH THE FATE OF BEING IN THE OPPOSITION."
SHOVE!
"THE FOUNDATIONS WERE THUS LAID FOR A CERTAIN DEGREE OF INDEPENDENCE OF JUDGMENT," HE LATER WROTE.
NEVERTHELESS, UNABLE TO BECOME A RESEARCH SCIENTIST LIKE CHARCOT, FREUD WAS FORCED INTO PRIVATE PRACTICE!
A GUY'S GOTTA EARN A LIVING!
Dr. FREUD
HEAD SHRINKER

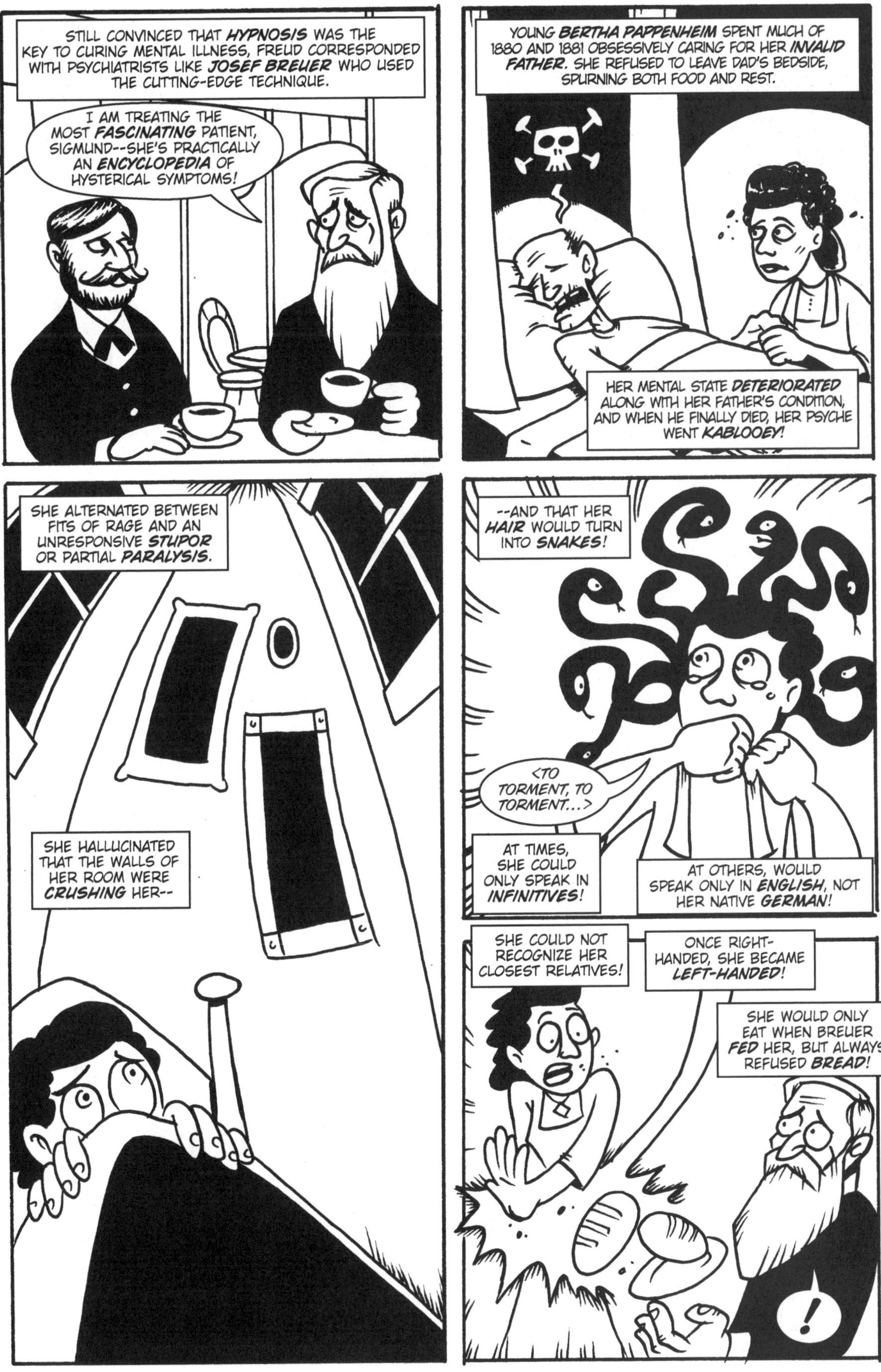
STILL CONVINCED THAT HYPNOSIS WAS THE KEY TO CURING MENTAL ILLNESS, FREUD CORRESPONDED WITH PSYCHIATRISTS LIKE JOSEF BREUER WHO USED THE CUTTING-EDGE TECHNIQUE.
I AM TREATING THE MOST FASCINATING PATIENT, SIGMUND--SHE'S PRACTICALLY AN ENCYCLOPEDIA OF HYSTERICAL SYMPTOMS!
YOUNG BERTHA PAPPENHEIM SPENT MUCH OF 1880 AND 1881 OBSESSIVELY CARING FOR HER INVALID FATHER. SHE REFUSED TO LEAVE DAD'S BEDSIDE, SPURNING BOTH FOOD AND REST.
HER MENTAL STATE DETERIORATED ALONG WITH HER FATHER'S CONDITION, AND WHEN HE FINALLY DIED, HER PSYCHE WENT KABLOOEY!
SHE ALTERNATED BETWEEN FITS OF RAGE AND AN UNRESPONSIVE STUPOR OR PARTIAL PARALYSIS.
SHE HALLUCINATED THAT THE WALLS OF HER ROOM WERE CRUSHING HER--
--AND THAT HER HAIR WOULD TURN INTO SNAKES!
<TO TORMENT, TO TORMENT...>
AT TIMES, SHE COULD ONLY SPEAK IN INFINITIVES!
AT OTHERS, WOULD SPEAK ONLY IN ENGLISH, NOT HER NATIVE GERMAN!
SHE COULD NOT RECOGNIZE HER CLOSEST RELATIVES!
ONCE RIGHT-HANDED, SHE BECAME LEFT-HANDED!
SHE WOULD ONLY EAT WHEN BREUER FED HER, BUT ALWAYS REFUSED BREAD!
!

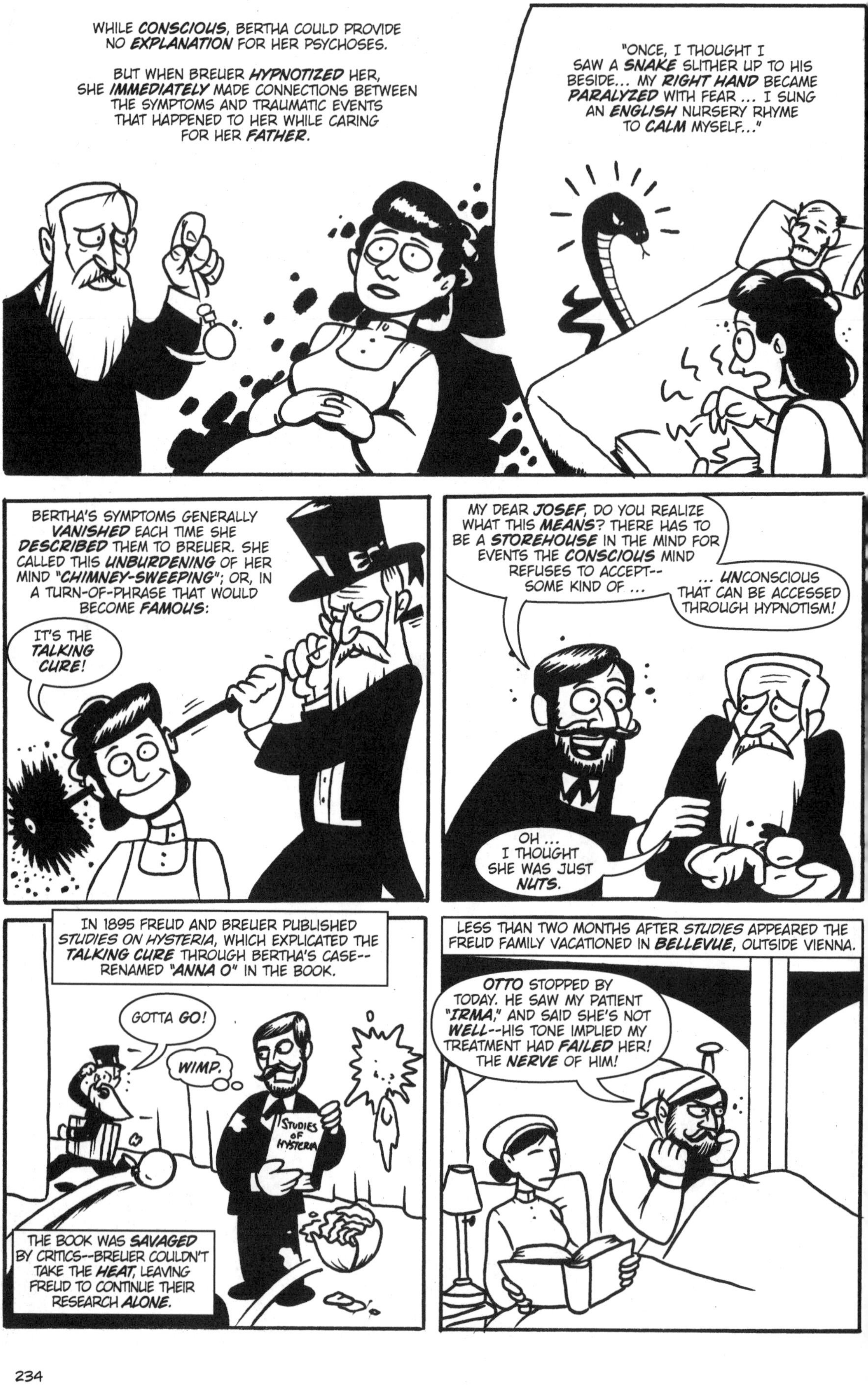
WHILE CONSCIOUS, BERTHA COULD PROVIDE NO EXPLANATION FOR HER PSYCHOSES.
BUT WHEN BREUER HYPNOTIZED HER, SHE IMMEDIATELY MADE CONNECTIONS BETWEEN THE SYMPTOMS AND TRAUMATIC EVENTS THAT HAPPENED TO HER WHILE CARING FOR HER FATHER.
"ONCE, I THOUGHT I SAW A SNAKE SLITHER UP TO HIS BESIDE... MY RIGHT HAND BECAME PARALYZED WITH FEAR ... I SUNG AN ENGLISH NURSERY RHYME TO CALM MYSELF..."
BERTHA'S SYMPTOMS GENERALLY VANISHED EACH TIME SHE DESCRIBED THEM TO BREUER. SHE CALLED THIS UNBURDENING OF HER MIND "CHIMNEY-SWEEPING"; OR, IN A TURN-OF-PHRASE THAT WOULD BECOME FAMOUS:
IT'S THE TALKING CURE!
MY DEAR JOSEF, DO YOU REALIZE WHAT THIS MEANS? THERE HAS TO BE A STOREHOUSE IN THE MIND FOR EVENTS THE CONSCIOUS MIND REFUSES TO ACCEPT-- SOME KIND OF ...
... UNCONSCIOUS THAT CAN BE ACCESSED THROUGH HYPNOTISM!
OH ... I THOUGHT SHE WAS JUST NUTS.
IN 1895 FREUD AND BREUER PUBLISHED STUDIES ON HYSTERIA, WHICH EXPLICATED THE TALKING CURE THROUGH BERTHA'S CASE-- RENAMED "ANNA O" IN THE BOOK.
GOTTA GO!
WIMP.
STUDIES OF HYSTERIA
THE BOOK WAS SAVAGED BY CRITICS--BREUER COULDN'T TAKE THE HEAT, LEAVING FREUD TO CONTINUE THEIR RESEARCH ALONE.
LESS THAN TWO MONTHS AFTER STUDIES APPEARED THE FREUD FAMILY VACATIONED IN BELLEVUE, OUTSIDE VIENNA.
OTTO STOPPED BY TODAY. HE SAW MY PATIENT "IRMA," AND SAID SHE'S NOT WELL--HIS TONE IMPLIED MY TREATMENT HAD FAILED HER! THE NERVE OF HIM!

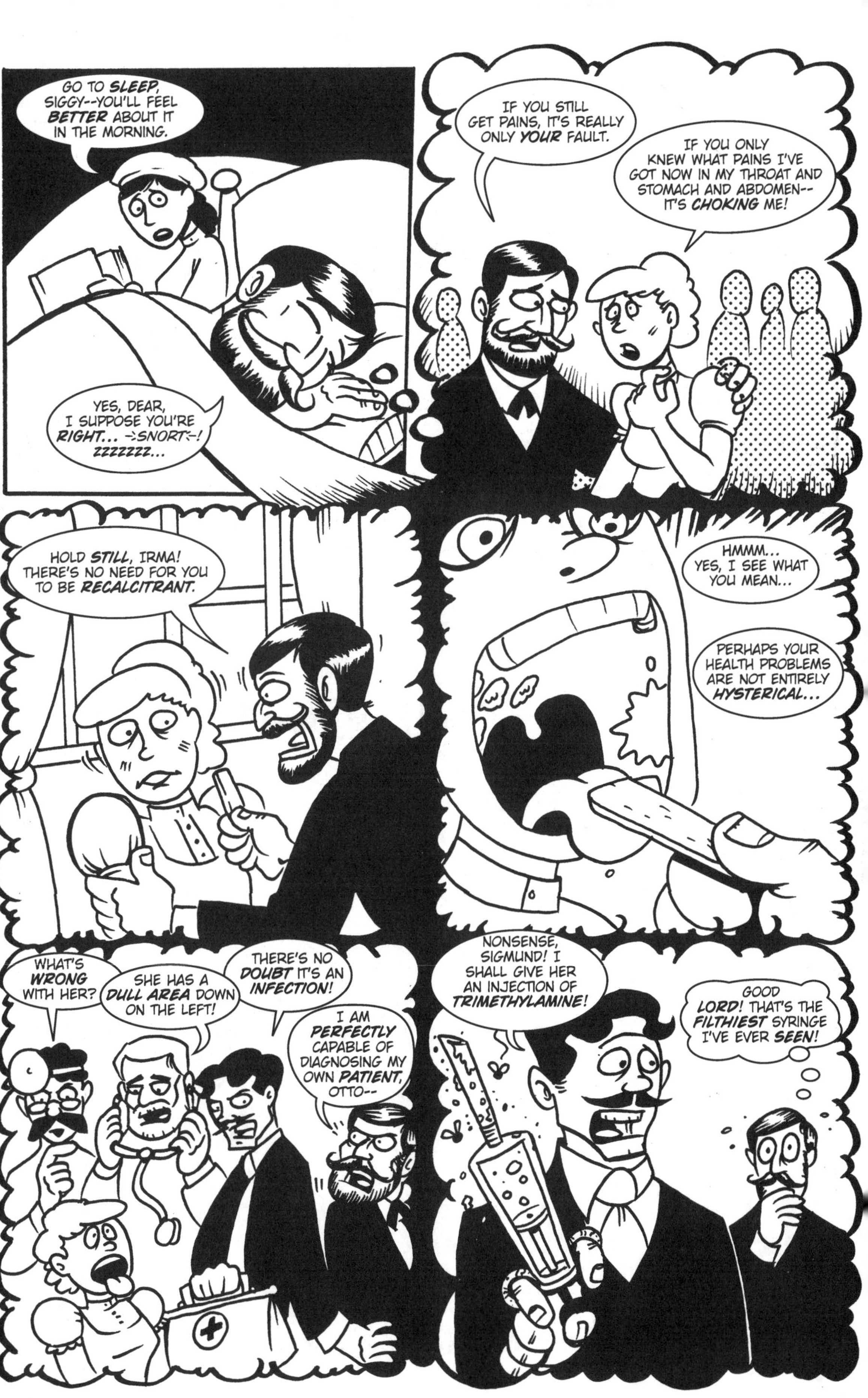
GO TO SLEEP, SIGGY--YOU'LL FEEL BETTER ABOUT IT IN THE MORNING.
YES, DEAR, I SUPPOSE YOU'RE RIGHT... -SNORT-! ZZZZZZZ...
IF YOU STILL GET PAINS, IT'S REALLY ONLY YOUR FAULT.
IF YOU ONLY KNEW WHAT PAINS I'VE GOT NOW IN MY THROAT AND STOMACH AND ABDOMEN-- IT'S CHOKING ME!
HOLD STILL, IRMA! THERE'S NO NEED FOR YOU TO BE RECALCITRANT.
HMMM... YES, I SEE WHAT YOU MEAN...
PERHAPS YOUR HEALTH PROBLEMS ARE NOT ENTIRELY HYSTERICAL...
WHAT'S WRONG WITH HER?
SHE HAS A DULL AREA DOWN ON THE LEFT!
THERE'S NO DOUBT IT'S AN INFECTION!
I AM PERFECTLY CAPABLE OF DIAGNOSING MY OWN PATIENT, OTTO--
NONSENSE, SIGMUND! I SHALL GIVE HER AN INJECTION OF TRIMETHYLAMINE!
GOOD LORD! THAT'S THE FILTHIEST SYRINGE I'VE EVER SEEN!

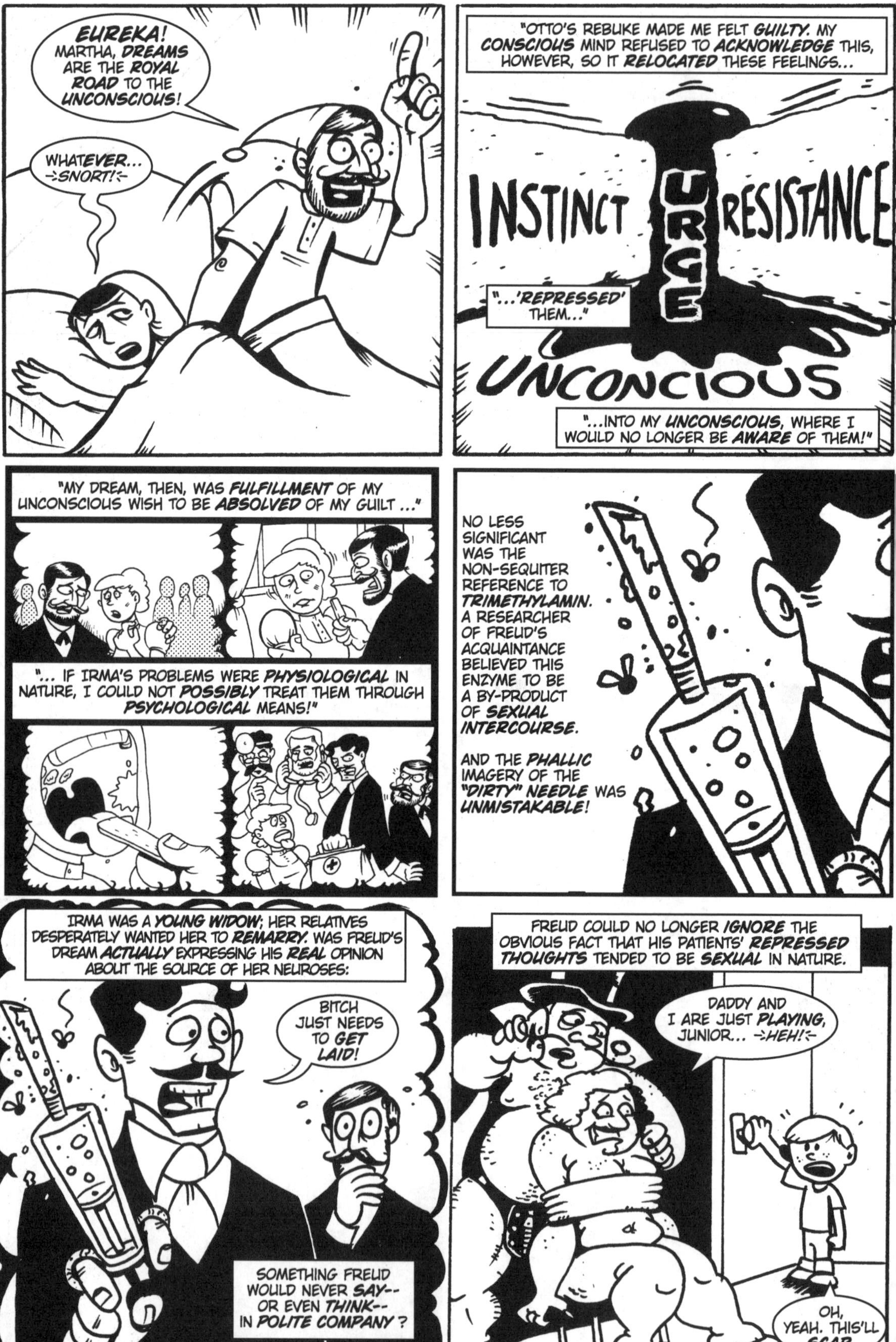
EUREKA! MARTHA, DREAMS ARE THE ROYAL ROAD TO THE UNCONSCIOUS!
WHATEVER... ->SNORT!<-
"OTTO'S REBUKE MADE ME FELT GUILTY. MY CONSCIOUS MIND REFUSED TO ACKNOWLEDGE THIS, HOWEVER, SO IT RELOCATED THESE FEELINGS...
INSTINCT
URGE
RESISTANCE
"...'REPRESSED' THEM..."
UNCONCIOUS
"...INTO MY UNCONSCIOUS, WHERE I WOULD NO LONGER BE AWARE OF THEM!"
"MY DREAM, THEN, WAS FULFILLMENT OF MY UNCONSCIOUS WISH TO BE ABSOLVED OF MY GUILT ..."
"... IF IRMA'S PROBLEMS WERE PHYSIOLOGICAL IN NATURE, I COULD NOT POSSIBLY TREAT THEM THROUGH PSYCHOLOGICAL MEANS!"
NO LESS SIGNIFICANT WAS THE NON-SEQUITER REFERENCE TO TRIMETHYLAMIN. A RESEARCHER OF FREUD'S ACQUAINTANCE BELIEVED THIS ENZYME TO BE A BY-PRODUCT OF SEXUAL INTERCOURSE.
AND THE PHALLIC IMAGERY OF THE "DIRTY" NEEDLE WAS UNMISTAKABLE!
IRMA WAS A YOUNG WIDOW; HER RELATIVES DESPERATELY WANTED HER TO REMARRY. WAS FREUD'S DREAM ACTUALLY EXPRESSING HIS REAL OPINION ABOUT THE SOURCE OF HER NEUROSES:
BITCH JUST NEEDS TO GET LAID!
SOMETHING FREUD WOULD NEVER SAY-- OR EVEN THINK-- IN POLITE COMPANY ?
FREUD COULD NO LONGER IGNORE THE OBVIOUS FACT THAT HIS PATIENTS' REPRESSED THOUGHTS TENDED TO BE SEXUAL IN NATURE.
DADDY AND I ARE JUST PLAYING, JUNIOR... ->HEH!<-
OH, YEAH. THIS'LL SCAR.

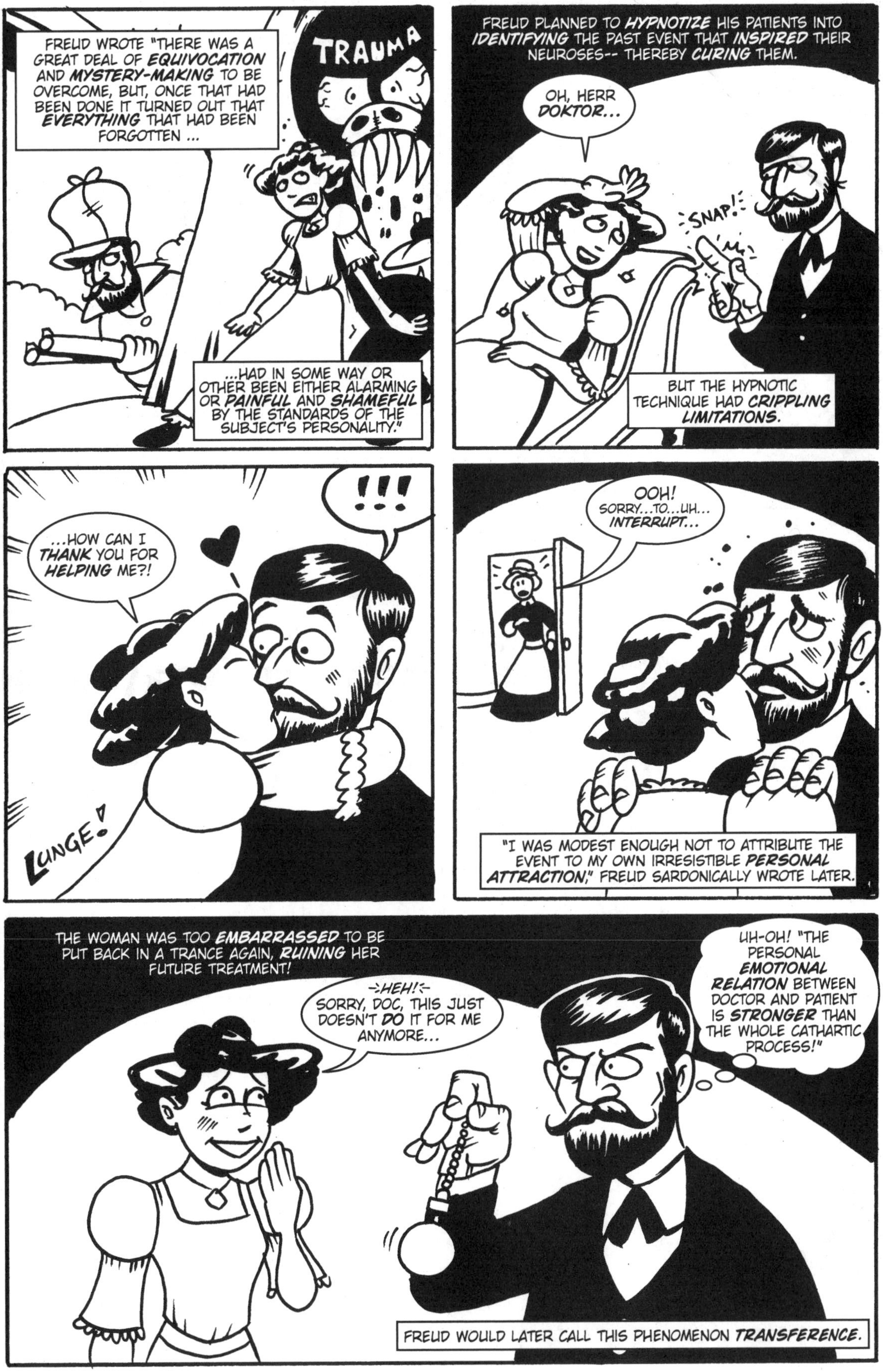
FREUD WROTE "THERE WAS A GREAT DEAL OF EQUIVOCATION AND MYSTERY-MAKING TO BE OVERCOME, BUT, ONCE THAT HAD BEEN DONE IT TURNED OUT THAT EVERYTHING THAT HAD BEEN FORGOTTEN ...
TRAUMA
...HAD IN SOME WAY OR OTHER BEEN EITHER ALARMING OR PAINFUL AND SHAMEFUL BY THE STANDARDS OF THE SUBJECT'S PERSONALITY."
FREUD PLANNED TO HYPNOTIZE HIS PATIENTS INTO IDENTIFYING THE PAST EVENT THAT INSPIRED THEIR NEUROSES-- THEREBY CURING THEM.
OH, HERR DOKTOR...
SNAP!
BUT THE HYPNOTIC TECHNIQUE HAD CRIPPLING LIMITATIONS.
...HOW CAN I THANK YOU FOR HELPING ME?!
!!!
LUNGE!
OOH! SORRY...TO...UH... INTERRUPT...
"I WAS MODEST ENOUGH NOT TO ATTRIBUTE THE EVENT TO MY OWN IRRESISTIBLE PERSONAL ATTRACTION," FREUD SARDONICALLY WROTE LATER.
THE WOMAN WAS TOO EMBARRASSED TO BE PUT BACK IN A TRANCE AGAIN, RUINING HER FUTURE TREATMENT!
HEH! SORRY, DOC, THIS JUST DOESN'T DO IT FOR ME ANYMORE...
UH-OH! "THE PERSONAL EMOTIONAL RELATION BETWEEN DOCTOR AND PATIENT IS STRONGER THAN THE WHOLE CATHARTIC PROCESS!"
FREUD WOULD LATER CALL THIS PHENOMENON TRANSFERENCE.

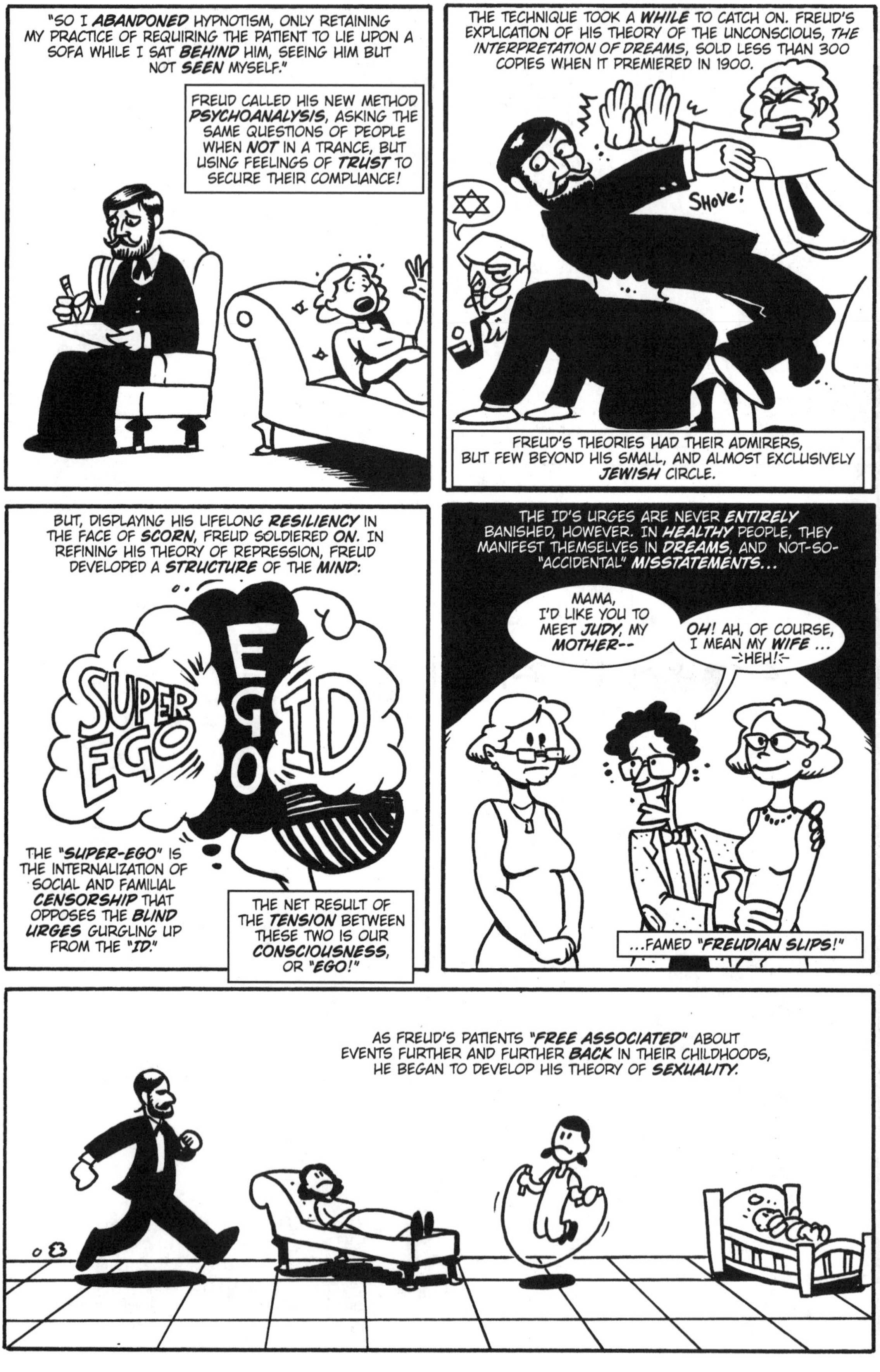
"SO I ABANDONED HYPNOTISM, ONLY RETAINING MY PRACTICE OF REQUIRING THE PATIENT TO LIE UPON A SOFA WHILE I SAT BEHIND HIM, SEEING HIM BUT NOT SEEN MYSELF."
FREUD CALLED HIS NEW METHOD PSYCHOANALYSIS, ASKING THE SAME QUESTIONS OF PEOPLE WHEN NOT IN A TRANCE, BUT USING FEELINGS OF TRUST TO SECURE THEIR COMPLIANCE!
THE TECHNIQUE TOOK A WHILE TO CATCH ON. FREUD'S EXPLICATION OF HIS THEORY OF THE UNCONSCIOUS, THE INTERPRETATION OF DREAMS, SOLD LESS THAN 300 COPIES WHEN IT PREMIERED IN 1900.
SHOVE!
FREUD'S THEORIES HAD THEIR ADMIRERS, BUT FEW BEYOND HIS SMALL, AND ALMOST EXCLUSIVELY JEWISH CIRCLE.
BUT, DISPLAYING HIS LIFELONG RESILIENCY IN THE FACE OF SCORN, FREUD SOLDIERED ON. IN REFINING HIS THEORY OF REPRESSION, FREUD DEVELOPED A STRUCTURE OF THE MIND:
SUPER EGO
EGO
ID
THE "SUPER-EGO" IS THE INTERNALIZATION OF SOCIAL AND FAMILIAL CENSORSHIP THAT OPPOSES THE BLIND URGES GURGLING UP FROM THE "ID."
THE NET RESULT OF THE TENSION BETWEEN THESE TWO IS OUR CONSCIOUSNESS, OR "EGO!"
THE ID'S URGES ARE NEVER ENTIRELY BANISHED, HOWEVER. IN HEALTHY PEOPLE, THEY MANIFEST THEMSELVES IN DREAMS, AND NOT-SO-"ACCIDENTAL" MISSTATEMENTS...
MAMA, I'D LIKE YOU TO MEET JUDY, MY MOTHER--
OH! AH, OF COURSE, I MEAN MY WIFE ... HEH!
...FAMED "FREUDIAN SLIPS!"
AS FREUD'S PATIENTS "FREE ASSOCIATED" ABOUT EVENTS FURTHER AND FURTHER BACK IN THEIR CHILDHOODS, HE BEGAN TO DEVELOP HIS THEORY OF SEXUALITY.

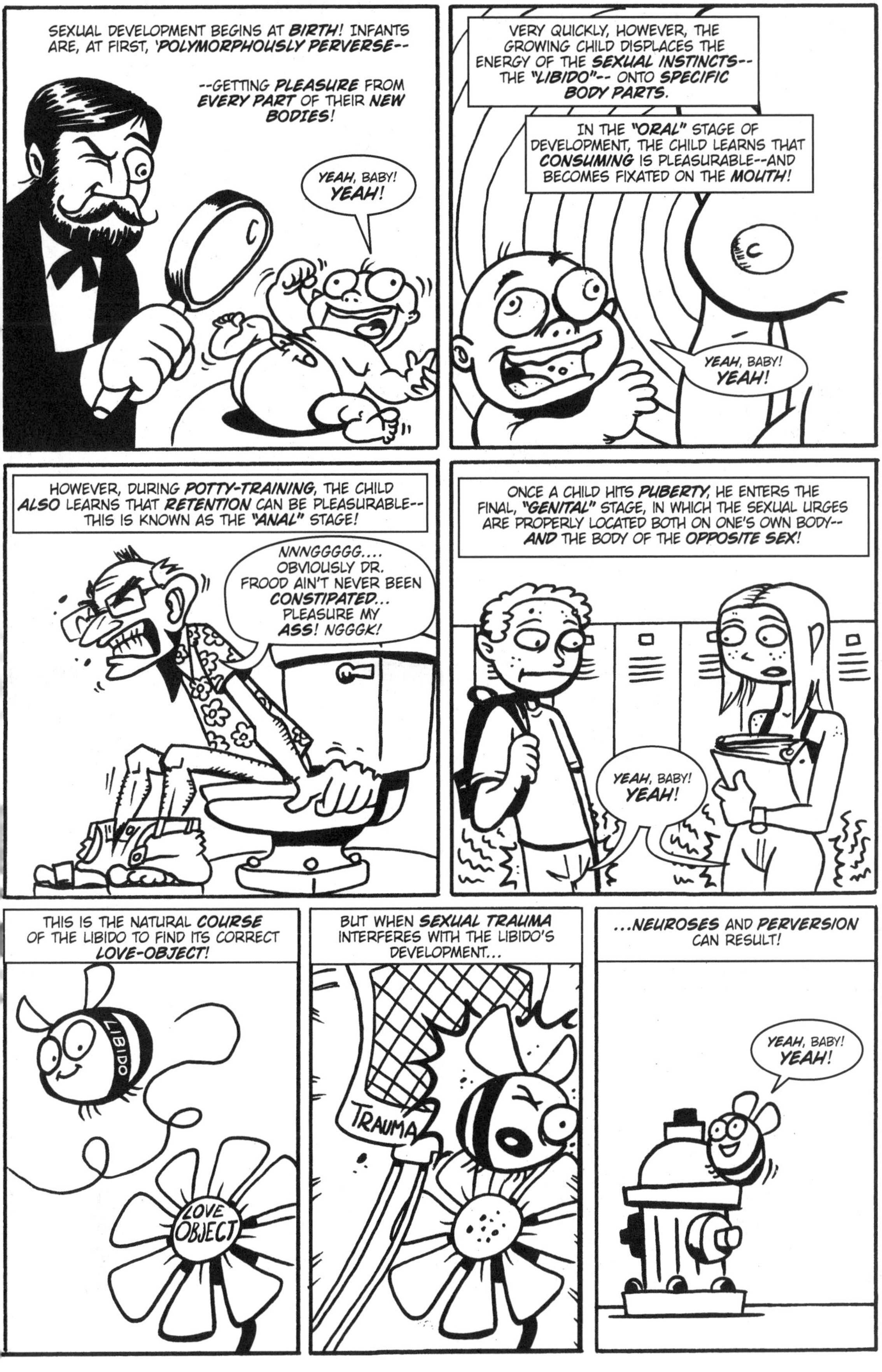
SEXUAL DEVELOPMENT BEGINS AT BIRTH! INFANTS ARE, AT FIRST, 'POLYMORPHOUSLY PERVERSE--
--GETTING PLEASURE FROM EVERY PART OF THEIR NEW BODIES!
YEAH, BABY! YEAH!
VERY QUICKLY, HOWEVER, THE GROWING CHILD DISPLACES THE ENERGY OF THE SEXUAL INSTINCTS-- THE "LIBIDO"-- ONTO SPECIFIC BODY PARTS.
IN THE "ORAL" STAGE OF DEVELOPMENT, THE CHILD LEARNS THAT CONSUMING IS PLEASURABLE--AND BECOMES FIXATED ON THE MOUTH!
YEAH, BABY! YEAH!
HOWEVER, DURING POTTY-TRAINING, THE CHILD ALSO LEARNS THAT RETENTION CAN BE PLEASURABLE-- THIS IS KNOWN AS THE "ANAL" STAGE!
NNNGGGGG.... OBVIOUSLY DR. FROOD AIN'T NEVER BEEN CONSTIPATED... PLEASURE MY ASS! NGGGK!
ONCE A CHILD HITS PUBERTY, HE ENTERS THE FINAL, "GENITAL" STAGE, IN WHICH THE SEXUAL URGES ARE PROPERLY LOCATED BOTH ON ONE'S OWN BODY-- AND THE BODY OF THE OPPOSITE SEX!
YEAH, BABY! YEAH!
THIS IS THE NATURAL COURSE OF THE LIBIDO TO FIND ITS CORRECT LOVE-OBJECT!
LIBIDO
LOVE OBJECT
BUT WHEN SEXUAL TRAUMA INTERFERES WITH THE LIBIDO'S DEVELOPMENT...
TRAUMA
...NEUROSES AND PERVERSION CAN RESULT!
YEAH, BABY! YEAH!

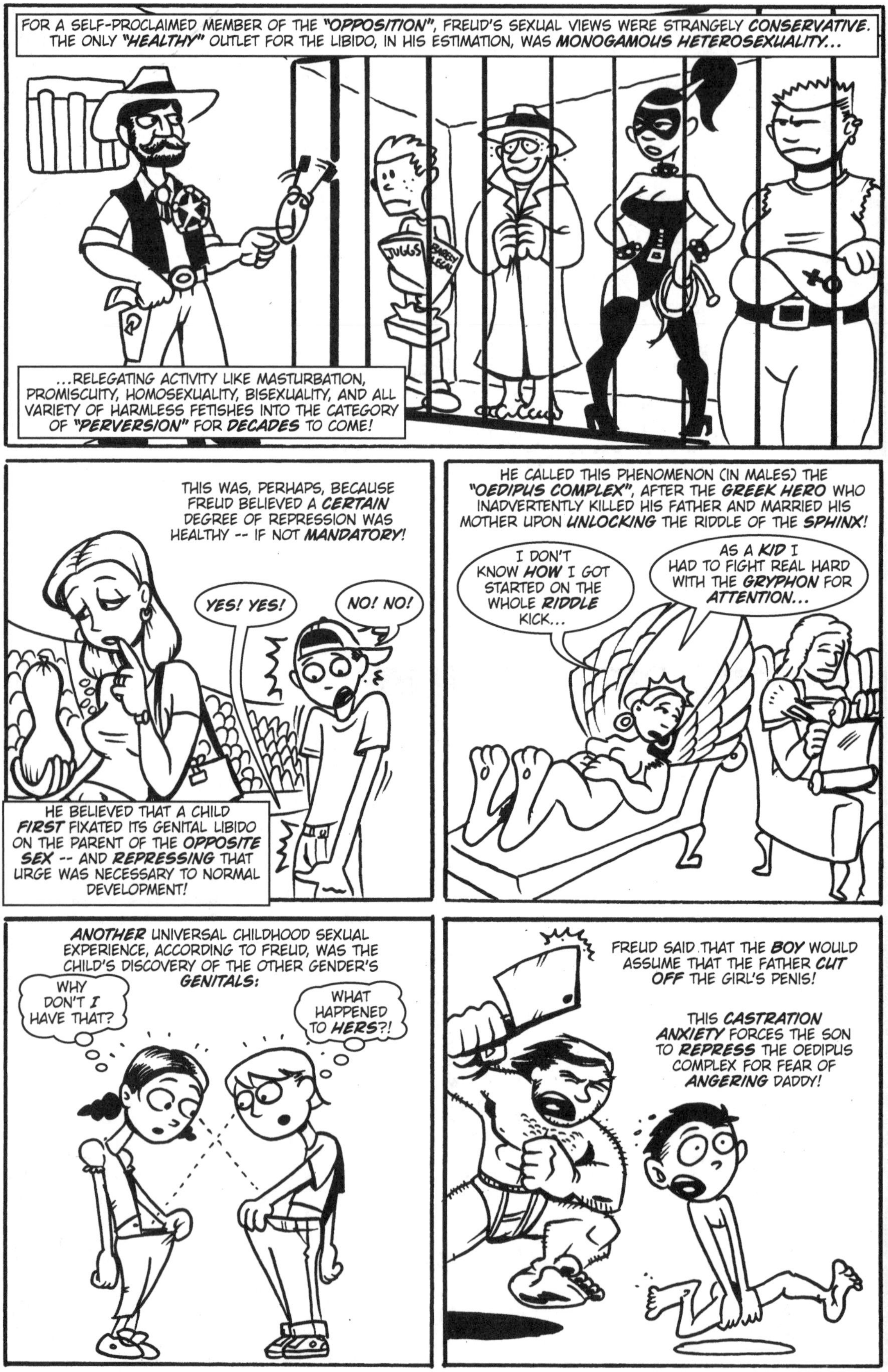

FOR A SELF-PROCLAIMED MEMBER OF THE "OPPOSITION", FREUD'S SEXUAL VIEWS WERE STRANGELY CONSERVATIVE. THE ONLY "HEALTHY" OUTLET FOR THE LIBIDO, IN HIS ESTIMATION, WAS MONOGAMOUS HETEROSEXUALITY...
JUGGS
BARELY LEGAL
...RELEGATING ACTIVITY LIKE MASTURBATION, PROMISCUITY, HOMOSEXUALITY, BISEXUALITY, AND ALL VARIETY OF HARMLESS FETISHES INTO THE CATEGORY OF "PERVERSION" FOR DECADES TO COME!
THIS WAS, PERHAPS, BECAUSE FREUD BELIEVED A CERTAIN DEGREE OF REPRESSION WAS HEALTHY -- IF NOT MANDATORY!
YES! YES!
NO! NO!
HE BELIEVED THAT A CHILD FIRST FIXATED ITS GENITAL LIBIDO ON THE PARENT OF THE OPPOSITE SEX -- AND REPRESSING THAT URGE WAS NECESSARY TO NORMAL DEVELOPMENT!
HE CALLED THIS PHENOMENON (IN MALES) THE "OEDIPUS COMPLEX", AFTER THE GREEK HERO WHO INADVERTENTLY KILLED HIS FATHER AND MARRIED HIS MOTHER UPON UNLOCKING THE RIDDLE OF THE SPHINX!
I DON'T KNOW HOW I GOT STARTED ON THE WHOLE RIDDLE KICK...
AS A KID I HAD TO FIGHT REAL HARD WITH THE GRYPHON FOR ATTENTION...
ANOTHER UNIVERSAL CHILDHOOD SEXUAL EXPERIENCE, ACCORDING TO FREUD, WAS THE CHILD'S DISCOVERY OF THE OTHER GENDER'S GENITALS:
WHY DON'T I HAVE THAT?
WHAT HAPPENED TO HERS?!
FREUD SAID THAT THE BOY WOULD ASSUME THAT THE FATHER CUT OFF THE GIRL'S PENIS!
THIS CASTRATION ANXIETY FORCES THE SON TO REPRESS THE OEDIPUS COMPLEX FOR FEAR OF ANGERING DADDY!

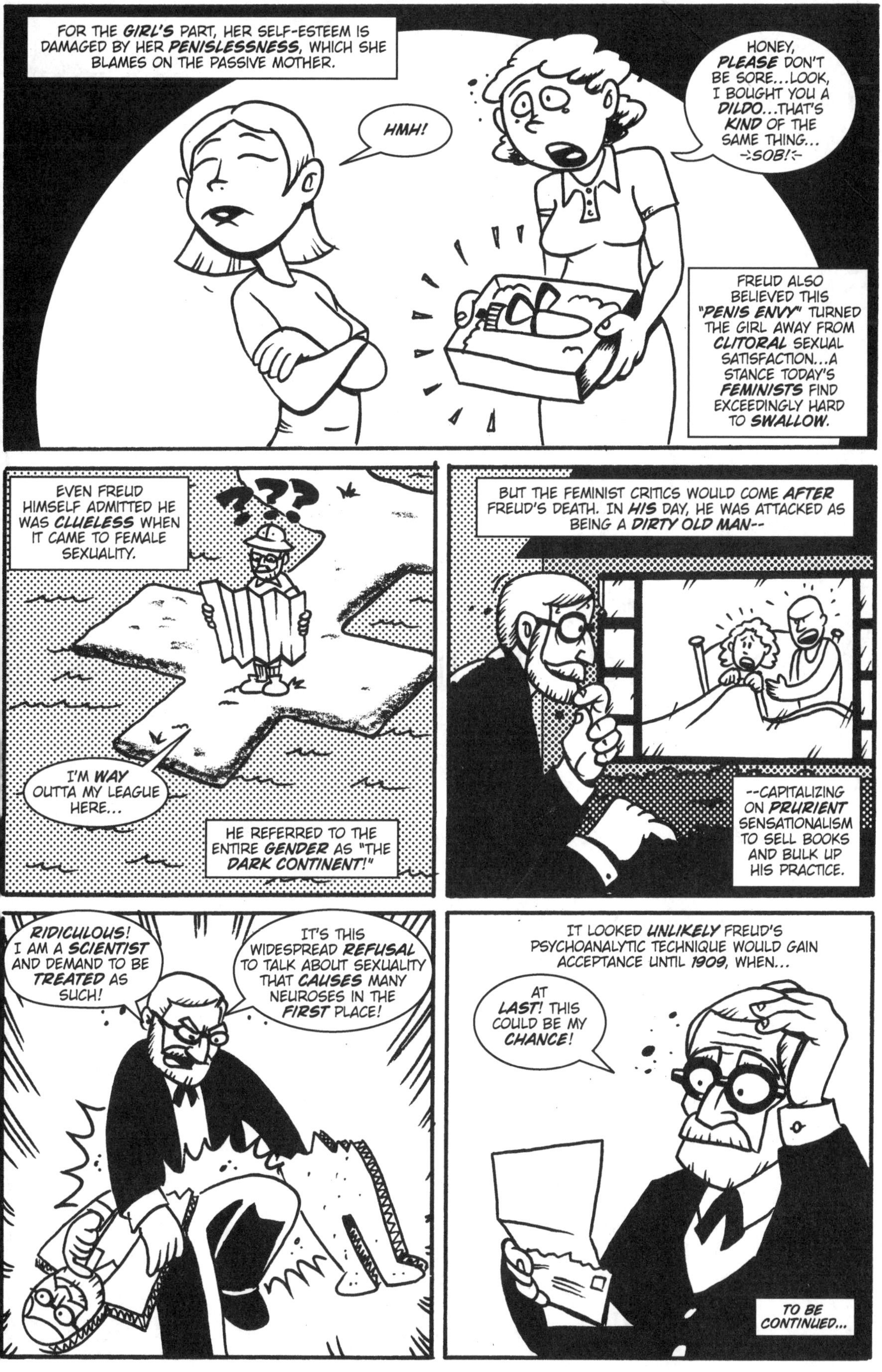
FOR THE GIRL'S PART, HER SELF-ESTEEM IS DAMAGED BY HER PENISLESSNESS, WHICH SHE BLAMES ON THE PASSIVE MOTHER.
HMH!
HONEY, PLEASE DON'T BE SORE...LOOK, I BOUGHT YOU A DILDO...THAT'S KIND OF THE SAME THING... -SOB!-
FREUD ALSO BELIEVED THIS "PENIS ENVY" TURNED THE GIRL AWAY FROM CLITORAL SEXUAL SATISFACTION...A STANCE TODAY'S FEMINISTS FIND EXCEEDINGLY HARD TO SWALLOW.
EVEN FREUD HIMSELF ADMITTED HE WAS CLUELESS WHEN IT CAME TO FEMALE SEXUALITY.
I'M WAY OUTTA MY LEAGUE HERE...
HE REFERRED TO THE ENTIRE GENDER AS "THE DARK CONTINENT!"
BUT THE FEMINIST CRITICS WOULD COME AFTER FREUD'S DEATH. IN HIS DAY, HE WAS ATTACKED AS BEING A DIRTY OLD MAN--
--CAPITALIZING ON PRURIENT SENSATIONALISM TO SELL BOOKS AND BULK UP HIS PRACTICE.
RIDICULOUS! I AM A SCIENTIST AND DEMAND TO BE TREATED AS SUCH!
IT'S THIS WIDESPREAD REFUSAL TO TALK ABOUT SEXUALITY THAT CAUSES MANY NEUROSES IN THE FIRST PLACE!
IT LOOKED UNLIKELY FREUD'S PSYCHOANALYTIC TECHNIQUE WOULD GAIN ACCEPTANCE UNTIL 1909, WHEN...
AT LAST! THIS COULD BE MY CHANCE!
TO BE CONTINUED...

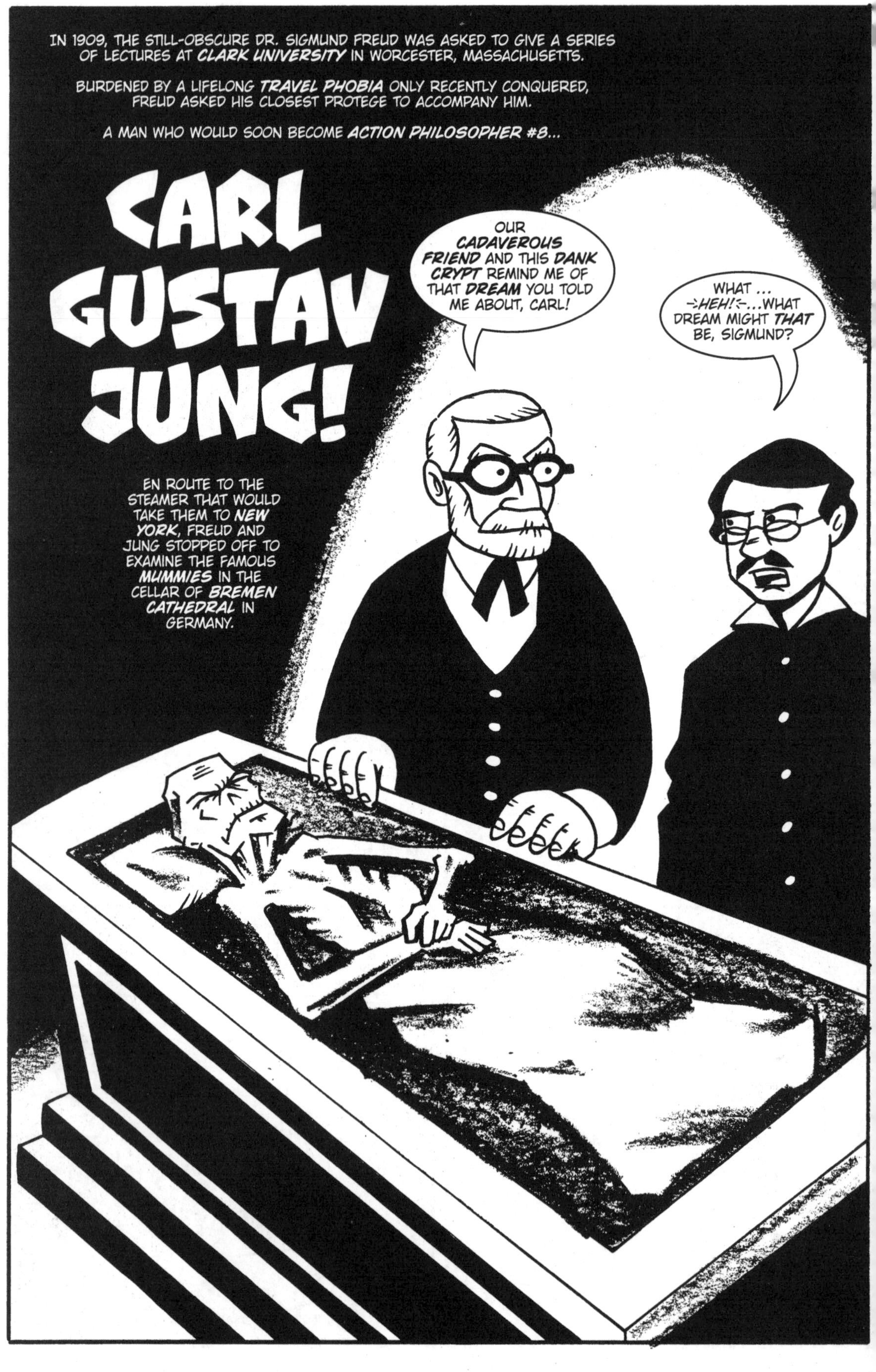
IN 1909, THE STILL-OBSCURE DR. SIGMUND FREUD WAS ASKED TO GIVE A SERIES OF LECTURES AT CLARK UNIVERSITY IN WORCESTER, MASSACHUSETTS.
BURDENED BY A LIFELONG TRAVEL PHOBIA ONLY RECENTLY CONQUERED, FREUD ASKED HIS CLOSEST PROTEGE TO ACCOMPANY HIM.
A MAN WHO WOULD SOON BECOME ACTION PHILOSOPHER #8...
CARL GUSTAV JUNG!
EN ROUTE TO THE STEAMER THAT WOULD TAKE THEM TO NEW YORK, FREUD AND JUNG STOPPED OFF TO EXAMINE THE FAMOUS MUMMIES IN THE CELLAR OF BREMEN CATHEDRAL IN GERMANY.
OUR CADAVEROUS FRIEND AND THIS DANK CRYPT REMIND ME OF THAT DREAM YOU TOLD ME ABOUT, CARL!
WHAT ... HEH! ...WHAT DREAM MIGHT THAT BE, SIGMUND?

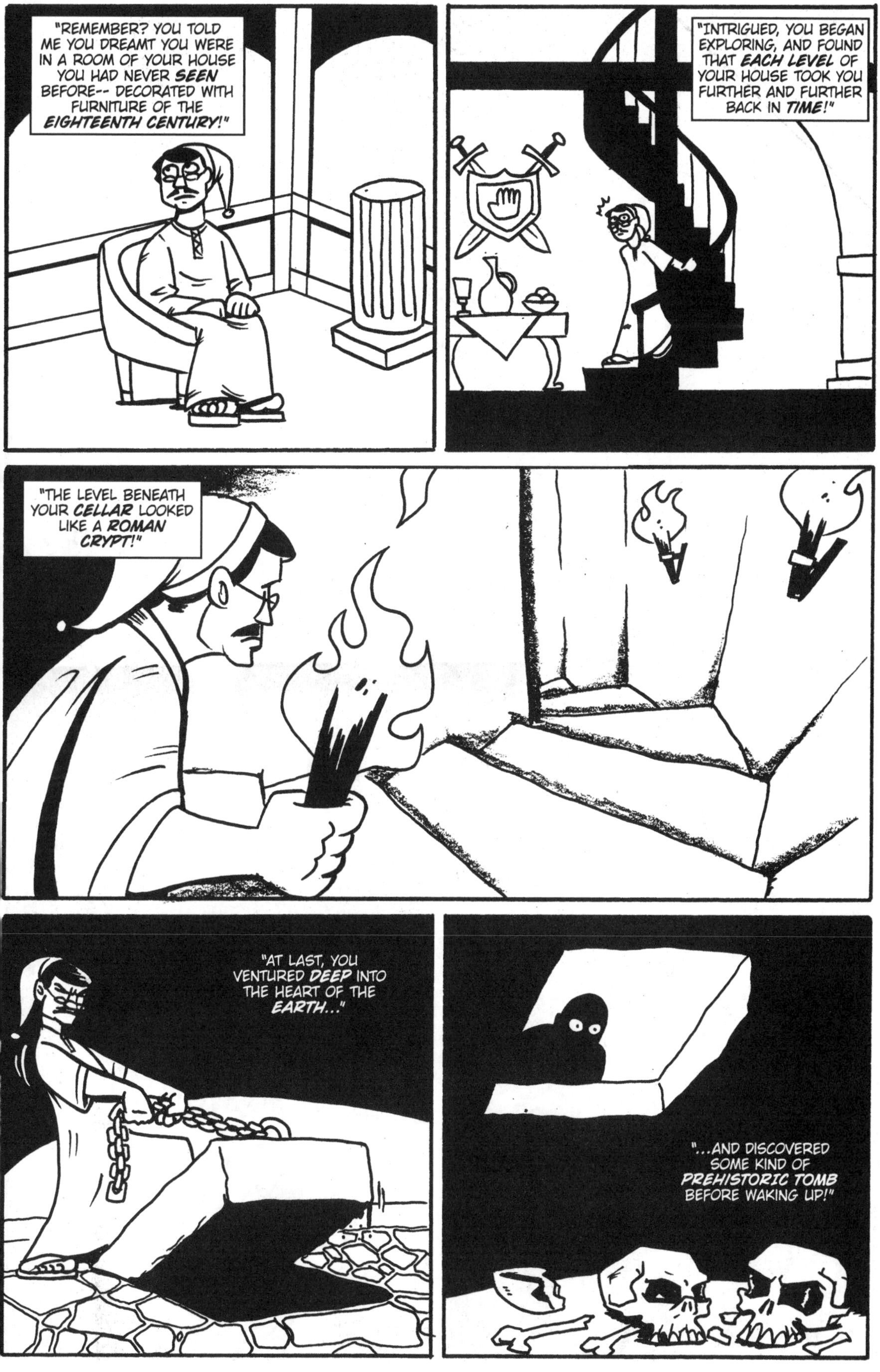
"REMEMBER? YOU TOLD ME YOU DREAMT YOU WERE IN A ROOM OF YOUR HOUSE YOU HAD NEVER SEEN BEFORE-- DECORATED WITH FURNITURE OF THE EIGHTEENTH CENTURY!"
"INTRIGUED, YOU BEGAN EXPLORING, AND FOUND THAT EACH LEVEL OF YOUR HOUSE TOOK YOU FURTHER AND FURTHER BACK IN TIME!"
"THE LEVEL BENEATH YOUR CELLAR LOOKED LIKE A ROMAN CRYPT!"
"AT LAST, YOU VENTURED DEEP INTO THE HEART OF THE EARTH..."
"...AND DISCOVERED SOME KIND OF PREHISTORIC TOMB BEFORE WAKING UP!"

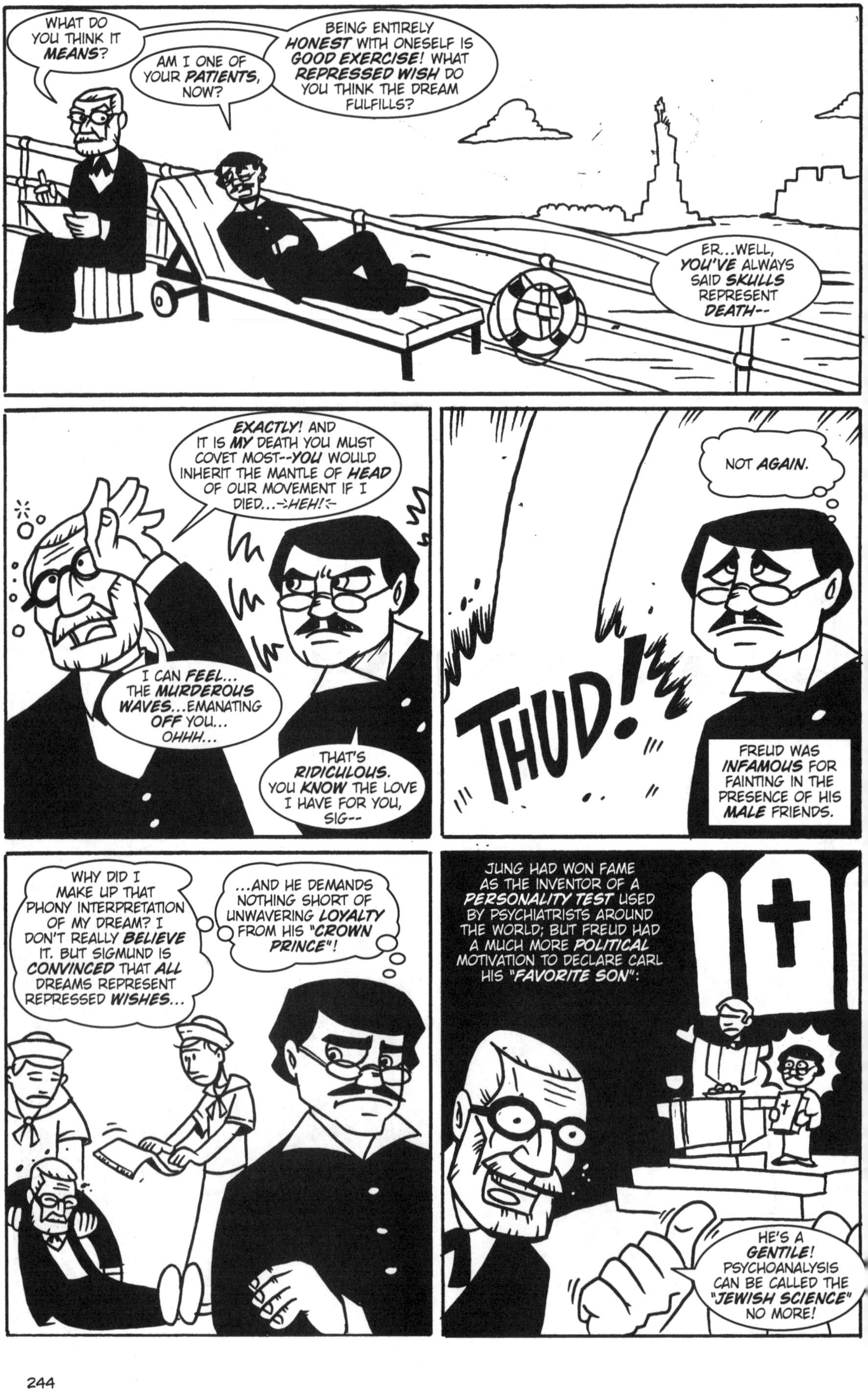

WHAT DO YOU THINK IT MEANS?
AM I ONE OF YOUR PATIENTS, NOW?
BEING ENTIRELY HONEST WITH ONESELF IS GOOD EXERCISE! WHAT REPRESSED WISH DO YOU THINK THE DREAM FULFILLS?
ER...WELL, YOU'VE ALWAYS SAID SKULLS REPRESENT DEATH--
EXACTLY! AND IT IS MY DEATH YOU MUST COVET MOST--YOU WOULD INHERIT THE MANTLE OF HEAD OF OUR MOVEMENT IF I DIED... HEH!
I CAN FEEL... THE MURDEROUS WAVES...EMANATING OFF YOU... OHHH...
THAT'S RIDICULOUS. YOU KNOW THE LOVE I HAVE FOR YOU, SIG--
NOT AGAIN.
THUD!
FREUD WAS INFAMOUS FOR FAINTING IN THE PRESENCE OF HIS MALE FRIENDS.
WHY DID I MAKE UP THAT PHONY INTERPRETATION OF MY DREAM? I DON'T REALLY BELIEVE IT. BUT SIGMUND IS CONVINCED THAT ALL DREAMS REPRESENT REPRESSED WISHES...
...AND HE DEMANDS NOTHING SHORT OF UNWAVERING LOYALTY FROM HIS "CROWN PRINCE"!
JUNG HAD WON FAME AS THE INVENTOR OF A PERSONALITY TEST USED BY PSYCHIATRISTS AROUND THE WORLD; BUT FREUD HAD A MUCH MORE POLITICAL MOTIVATION TO DECLARE CARL HIS "FAVORITE SON":
HE'S A GENTILE! PSYCHOANALYSIS CAN BE CALLED THE "JEWISH SCIENCE" NO MORE!

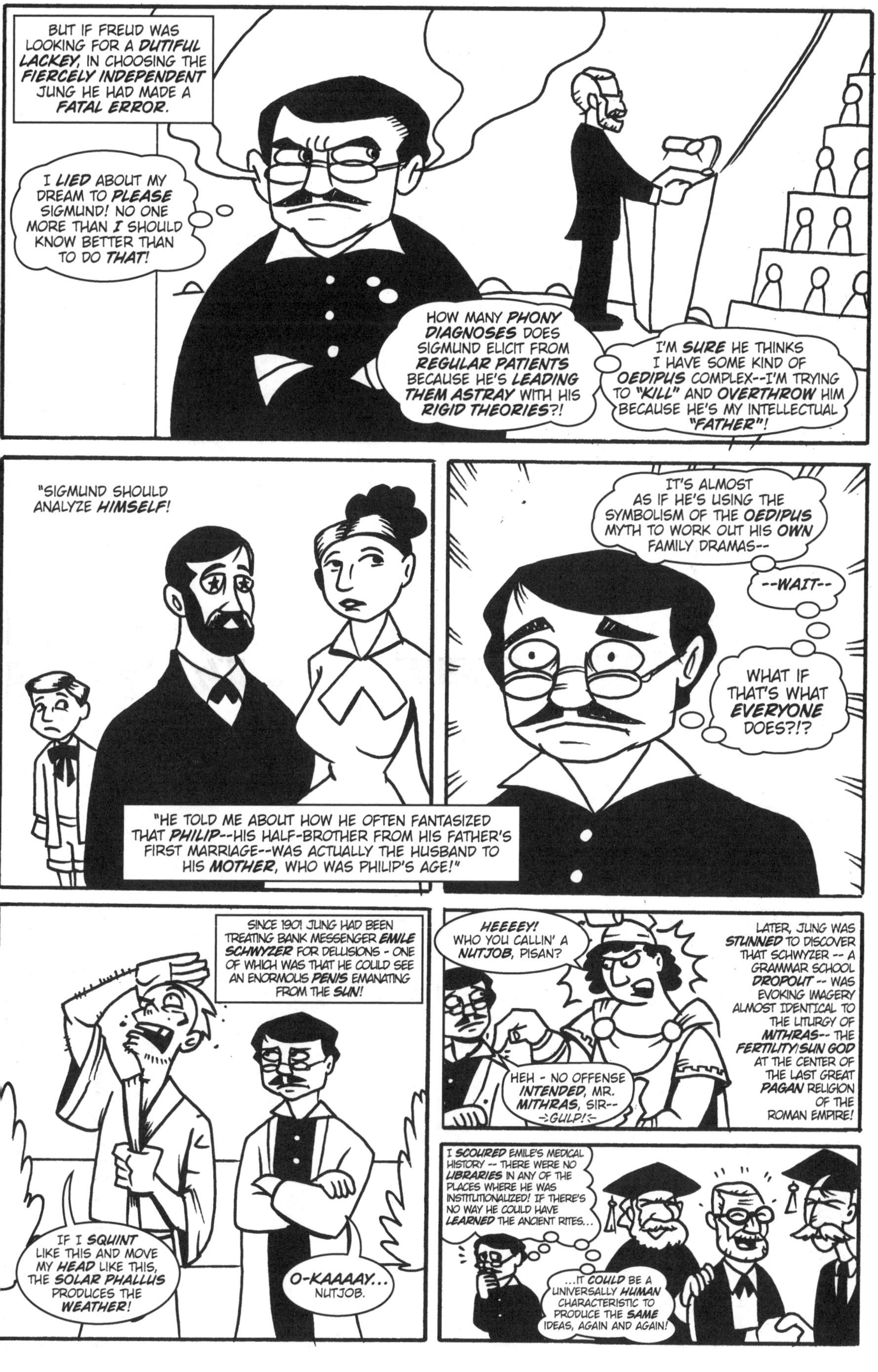
BUT IF FREUD WAS LOOKING FOR A DUTIFUL LACKEY, IN CHOOSING THE FIERCELY INDEPENDENT JUNG HE HAD MADE A FATAL ERROR.
I LIED ABOUT MY DREAM TO PLEASE SIGMUND! NO ONE MORE THAN I SHOULD KNOW BETTER THAN TO DO THAT!
HOW MANY PHONY DIAGNOSES DOES SIGMUND ELICIT FROM REGULAR PATIENTS BECAUSE HE'S LEADING THEM ASTRAY WITH HIS RIGID THEORIES?!
I'M SURE HE THINKS I HAVE SOME KIND OF OEDIPUS COMPLEX--I'M TRYING TO "KILL" AND OVERTHROW HIM BECAUSE HE'S MY INTELLECTUAL "FATHER"!
"SIGMUND SHOULD ANALYZE HIMSELF!
"HE TOLD ME ABOUT HOW HE OFTEN FANTASIZED THAT PHILIP--HIS HALF-BROTHER FROM HIS FATHER'S FIRST MARRIAGE--WAS ACTUALLY THE HUSBAND TO HIS MOTHER, WHO WAS PHILIP'S AGE!"
IT'S ALMOST AS IF HE'S USING THE SYMBOLISM OF THE OEDIPUS MYTH TO WORK OUT HIS OWN FAMILY DRAMAS--
--WAIT--
WHAT IF THAT'S WHAT EVERYONE DOES?!?
SINCE 1901 JUNG HAD BEEN TREATING BANK MESSENGER EMILE SCHWYZER FOR DELUSIONS - ONE OF WHICH WAS THAT HE COULD SEE AN ENORMOUS PENIS EMANATING FROM THE SUN!
IF I SQUINT LIKE THIS AND MOVE MY HEAD LIKE THIS, THE SOLAR PHALLUS PRODUCES THE WEATHER!
O-KAAAAY... NUTJOB.
HEEEEY! WHO YOU CALLIN' A NUTJOB, PISAN?
HEH - NO OFFENSE INTENDED, MR. MITHRAS, SIR--
GULP!
LATER, JUNG WAS STUNNED TO DISCOVER THAT SCHWYZER -- A GRAMMAR SCHOOL DROPOUT -- WAS EVOKING IMAGERY ALMOST IDENTICAL TO THE LITURGY OF MITHRAS-- THE FERTILITY/SUN GOD AT THE CENTER OF THE LAST GREAT PAGAN RELIGION OF THE ROMAN EMPIRE!
I SCOURED EMILE'S MEDICAL HISTORY -- THERE WERE NO LIBRARIES IN ANY OF THE PLACES WHERE HE WAS INSTITUTIONALIZED! IF THERE'S NO WAY HE COULD HAVE LEARNED THE ANCIENT RITES...
...IT COULD BE A UNIVERSALLY HUMAN CHARACTERISTIC TO PRODUCE THE SAME IDEAS, AGAIN AND AGAIN!

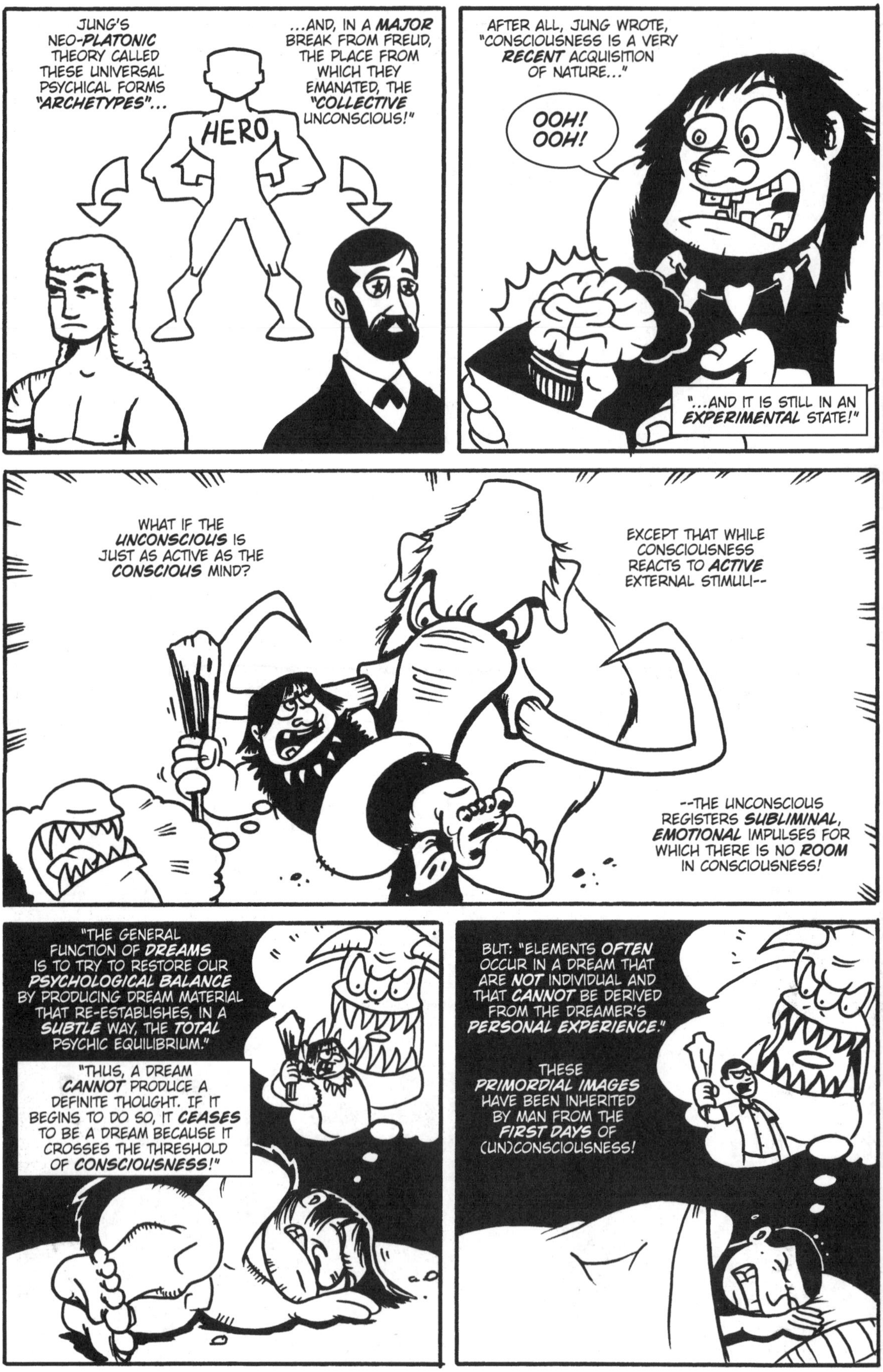
JUNG'S NEO-PLATONIC THEORY CALLED THESE UNIVERSAL PSYCHICAL FORMS "ARCHETYPES"...
...AND, IN A MAJOR BREAK FROM FREUD, THE PLACE FROM WHICH THEY EMANATED, THE "COLLECTIVE UNCONSCIOUS!"
HERO
AFTER ALL, JUNG WROTE, "CONSCIOUSNESS IS A VERY RECENT ACQUISITION OF NATURE..."
OOH! OOH!
"...AND IT IS STILL IN AN EXPERIMENTAL STATE!"
WHAT IF THE UNCONSCIOUS IS JUST AS ACTIVE AS THE CONSCIOUS MIND?
EXCEPT THAT WHILE CONSCIOUSNESS REACTS TO ACTIVE EXTERNAL STIMULI--
--THE UNCONSCIOUS REGISTERS SUBLIMINAL, EMOTIONAL IMPULSES FOR WHICH THERE IS NO ROOM IN CONSCIOUSNESS!
"THE GENERAL FUNCTION OF DREAMS IS TO TRY TO RESTORE OUR PSYCHOLOGICAL BALANCE BY PRODUCING DREAM MATERIAL THAT RE-ESTABLISHES, IN A SUBTLE WAY, THE TOTAL PSYCHIC EQUILIBRIUM."
"THUS, A DREAM CANNOT PRODUCE A DEFINITE THOUGHT. IF IT BEGINS TO DO SO, IT CEASES TO BE A DREAM BECAUSE IT CROSSES THE THRESHOLD OF CONSCIOUSNESS!"
BUT: "ELEMENTS OFTEN OCCUR IN A DREAM THAT ARE NOT INDIVIDUAL AND THAT CANNOT BE DERIVED FROM THE DREAMER'S PERSONAL EXPERIENCE."
THESE PRIMORDIAL IMAGES HAVE BEEN INHERITED BY MAN FROM THE FIRST DAYS OF (UN)CONSCIOUSNESS!

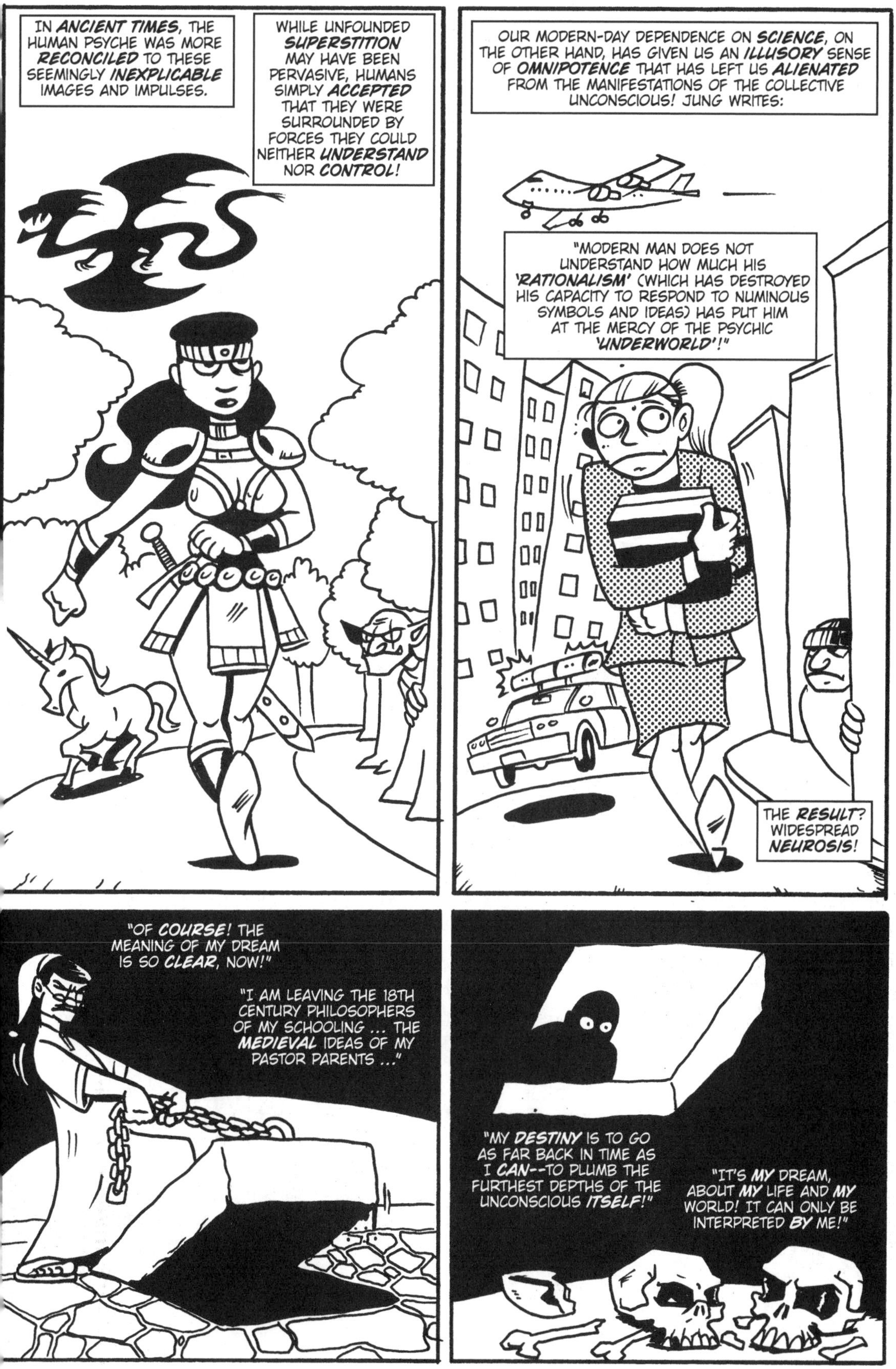
IN ANCIENT TIMES, THE HUMAN PSYCHE WAS MORE RECONCILED TO THESE SEEMINGLY INEXPLICABLE IMAGES AND IMPULSES.
WHILE UNFOUNDED SUPERSTITION MAY HAVE BEEN PERVASIVE, HUMANS SIMPLY ACCEPTED THAT THEY WERE SURROUNDED BY FORCES THEY COULD NEITHER UNDERSTAND NOR CONTROL!
OUR MODERN-DAY DEPENDENCE ON SCIENCE, ON THE OTHER HAND, HAS GIVEN US AN ILLUSORY SENSE OF OMNIPOTENCE THAT HAS LEFT US ALIENATED FROM THE MANIFESTATIONS OF THE COLLECTIVE UNCONSCIOUS! JUNG WRITES:
"MODERN MAN DOES NOT UNDERSTAND HOW MUCH HIS 'RATIONALISM' (WHICH HAS DESTROYED HIS CAPACITY TO RESPOND TO NUMINOUS SYMBOLS AND IDEAS) HAS PUT HIM AT THE MERCY OF THE PSYCHIC 'UNDERWORLD'!"
THE RESULT? WIDESPREAD NEUROSIS!
"OF COURSE! THE MEANING OF MY DREAM IS SO CLEAR, NOW!"
"I AM LEAVING THE 18TH CENTURY PHILOSOPHERS OF MY SCHOOLING ... THE MEDIEVAL IDEAS OF MY PASTOR PARENTS ..."
"MY DESTINY IS TO GO AS FAR BACK IN TIME AS I CAN--TO PLUMB THE FURTHEST DEPTHS OF THE UNCONSCIOUS ITSELF!"
"IT'S MY DREAM, ABOUT MY LIFE AND MY WORLD! IT CAN ONLY BE INTERPRETED BY ME!"

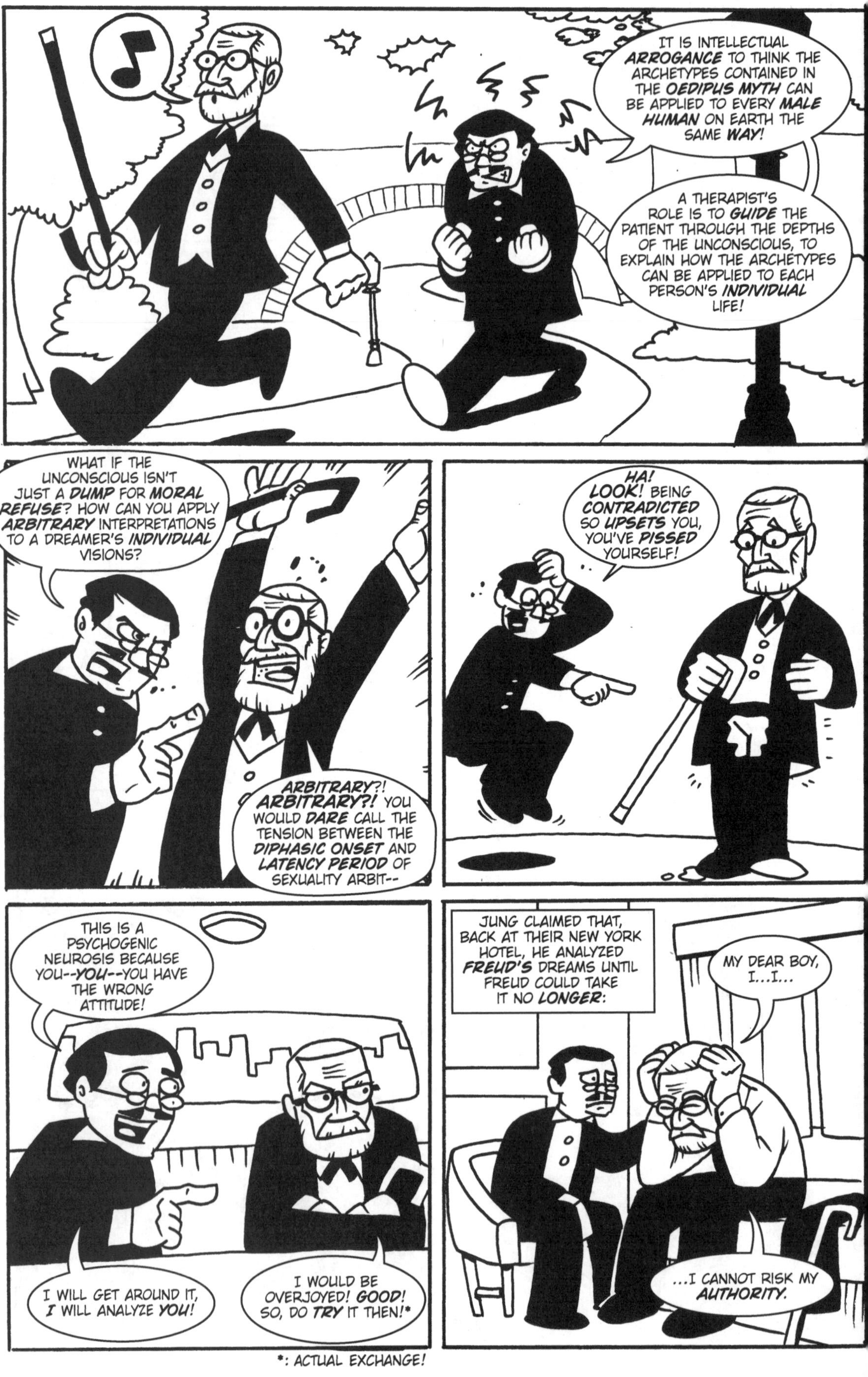
IT IS INTELLECTUAL ARROGANCE TO THINK THE ARCHETYPES CONTAINED IN THE OEDIPUS MYTH CAN BE APPLIED TO EVERY MALE HUMAN ON EARTH THE SAME WAY!
A THERAPIST'S ROLE IS TO GUIDE THE PATIENT THROUGH THE DEPTHS OF THE UNCONSCIOUS, TO EXPLAIN HOW THE ARCHETYPES CAN BE APPLIED TO EACH PERSON'S INDIVIDUAL LIFE!
WHAT IF THE UNCONSCIOUS ISN'T JUST A DUMP FOR MORAL REFUSE? HOW CAN YOU APPLY ARBITRARY INTERPRETATIONS TO A DREAMER'S INDIVIDUAL VISIONS?
ARBITRARY?! ARBITRARY?! YOU WOULD DARE CALL THE TENSION BETWEEN THE DIPHASIC ONSET AND LATENCY PERIOD OF SEXUALITY ARBIT--
HA! LOOK! BEING CONTRADICTED SO UPSETS YOU, YOU'VE PISSED YOURSELF!
THIS IS A PSYCHOGENIC NEUROSIS BECAUSE YOU--YOU--YOU HAVE THE WRONG ATTITUDE!
I WILL GET AROUND IT, I WILL ANALYZE YOU!
I WOULD BE OVERJOYED! GOOD! SO, DO TRY IT THEN!*
JUNG CLAIMED THAT, BACK AT THEIR NEW YORK HOTEL, HE ANALYZED FREUD'S DREAMS UNTIL FREUD COULD TAKE IT NO LONGER:
MY DEAR BOY, I...I...
...I CANNOT RISK MY AUTHORITY.

*: ACTUAL EXCHANGE!

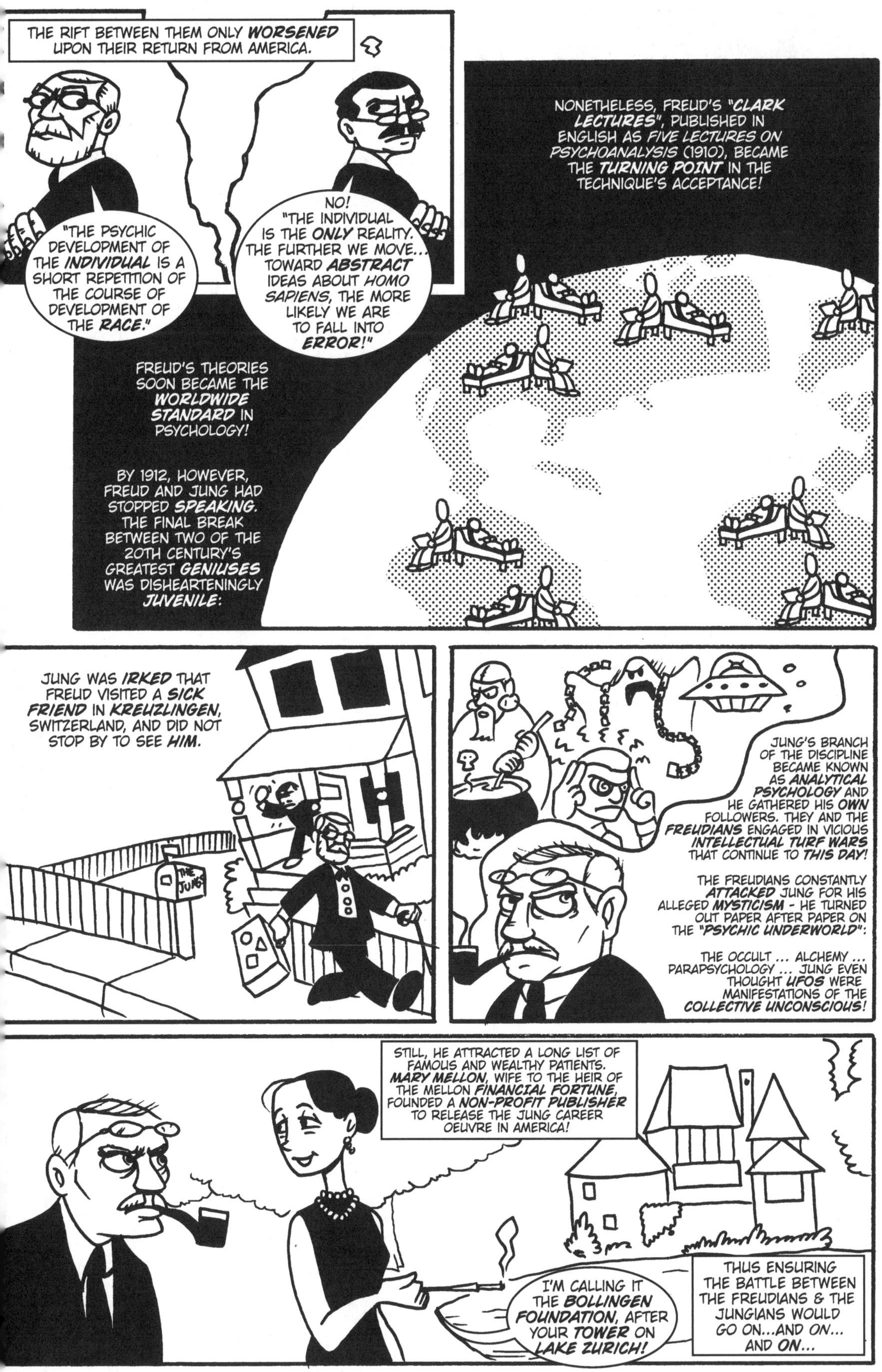
THE RIFT BETWEEN THEM ONLY WORSENED UPON THEIR RETURN FROM AMERICA.
"THE PSYCHIC DEVELOPMENT OF THE INDIVIDUAL IS A SHORT REPETITION OF THE COURSE OF DEVELOPMENT OF THE RACE."
NO! "THE INDIVIDUAL IS THE ONLY REALITY. THE FURTHER WE MOVE... TOWARD ABSTRACT IDEAS ABOUT HOMO SAPIENS, THE MORE LIKELY WE ARE TO FALL INTO ERROR!"
NONETHELESS, FREUD'S "CLARK LECTURES", PUBLISHED IN ENGLISH AS FIVE LECTURES ON PSYCHOANALYSIS (1910), BECAME THE TURNING POINT IN THE TECHNIQUE'S ACCEPTANCE!
FREUD'S THEORIES SOON BECAME THE WORLDWIDE STANDARD IN PSYCHOLOGY!
BY 1912, HOWEVER, FREUD AND JUNG HAD STOPPED SPEAKING. THE FINAL BREAK BETWEEN TWO OF THE 20TH CENTURY'S GREATEST GENIUSES WAS DISHEARTENINGLY JUVENILE:
JUNG WAS IRKED THAT FREUD VISITED A SICK FRIEND IN KREUZLINGEN, SWITZERLAND, AND DID NOT STOP BY TO SEE HIM.
THE JUNGS
JUNG'S BRANCH OF THE DISCIPLINE BECAME KNOWN AS ANALYTICAL PSYCHOLOGY AND HE GATHERED HIS OWN FOLLOWERS. THEY AND THE FREUDIANS ENGAGED IN VICIOUS INTELLECTUAL TURF WARS THAT CONTINUE TO THIS DAY!
THE FREUDIANS CONSTANTLY ATTACKED JUNG FOR HIS ALLEGED MYSTICISM - HE TURNED OUT PAPER AFTER PAPER ON THE "PSYCHIC UNDERWORLD":
THE OCCULT ... ALCHEMY ... PARAPSYCHOLOGY ... JUNG EVEN THOUGHT UFOS WERE MANIFESTATIONS OF THE COLLECTIVE UNCONSCIOUS!
STILL, HE ATTRACTED A LONG LIST OF FAMOUS AND WEALTHY PATIENTS. MARY MELLON, WIFE TO THE HEIR OF THE MELLON FINANCIAL FORTUNE, FOUNDED A NON-PROFIT PUBLISHER TO RELEASE THE JUNG CAREER OEUVRE IN AMERICA!
I'M CALLING IT THE BOLLINGEN FOUNDATION, AFTER YOUR TOWER ON LAKE ZURICH!
THUS ENSURING THE BATTLE BETWEEN THE FREUDIANS & THE JUNGIANS WOULD GO ON...AND ON... AND ON...

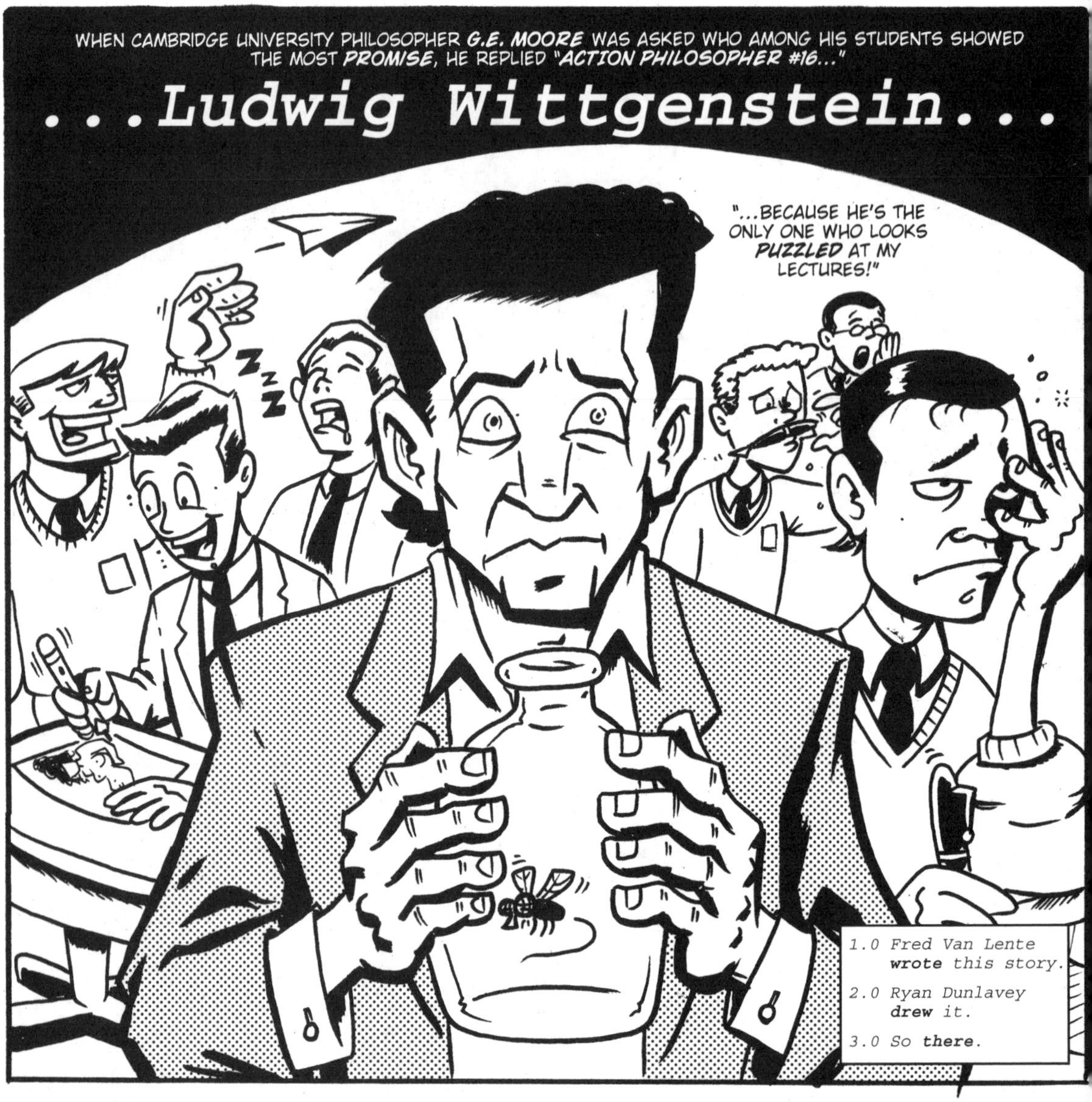
WHEN CAMBRIDGE UNIVERSITY PHILOSOPHER G.E. MOORE WAS ASKED WHO AMONG HIS STUDENTS SHOWED THE MOST PROMISE, HE REPLIED "ACTION PHILOSOPHER #16..."
...Ludwig Wittgenstein...
"...BECAUSE HE'S THE ONLY ONE WHO LOOKS PUZZLED AT MY LECTURES!"
ZZZ
1.0 Fred Van Lente wrote this story.
2.0 Ryan Dunlavey drew it.
3.0 So there.

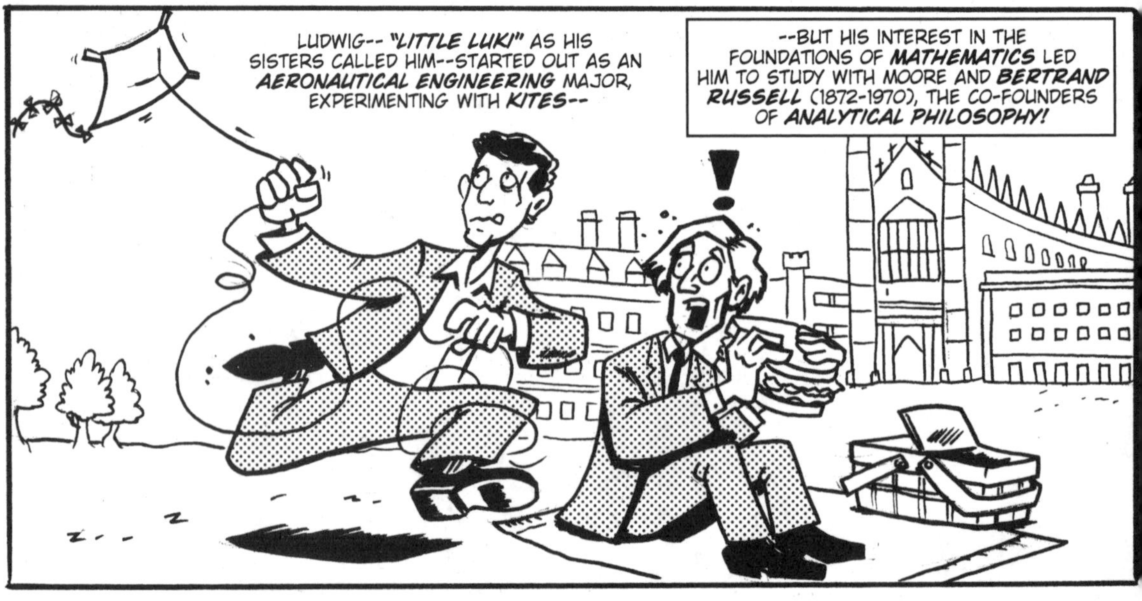
LUDWIG-- "LITTLE LUKI" AS HIS SISTERS CALLED HIM--STARTED OUT AS AN AERONAUTICAL ENGINEERING MAJOR, EXPERIMENTING WITH KITES--
--BUT HIS INTEREST IN THE FOUNDATIONS OF MATHEMATICS LED HIM TO STUDY WITH MOORE AND BERTRAND RUSSELL (1872-1970), THE CO-FOUNDERS OF ANALYTICAL PHILOSOPHY!
!

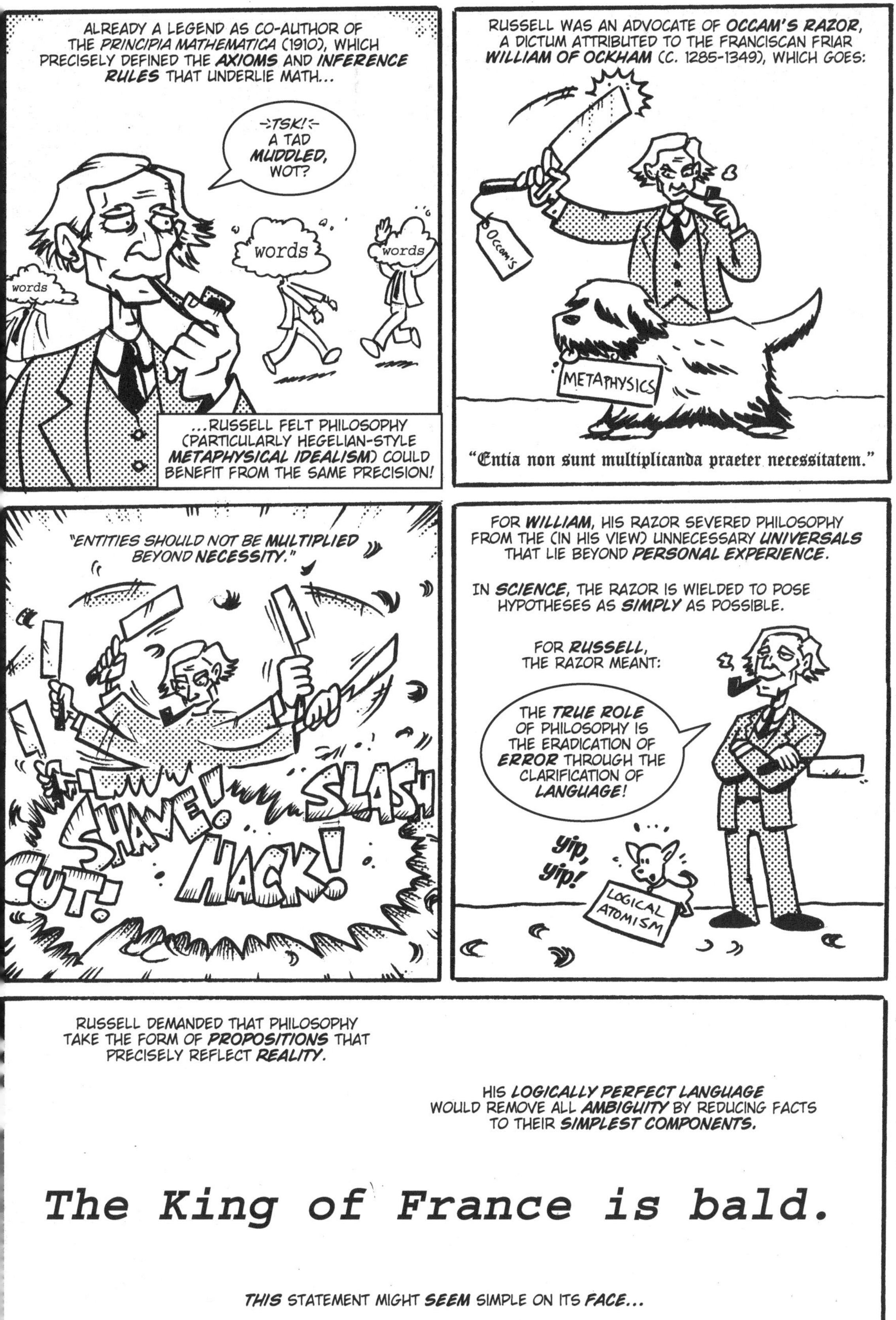

ALREADY A LEGEND AS CO-AUTHOR OF THE *PRINCIPIA MATHEMATICA* (1910), WHICH PRECISELY DEFINED THE ***AXIOMS*** AND ***INFERENCE RULES*** THAT UNDERLIE MATH...
-TSK!- A TAD ***MUDDLED,*** WOT?
words
words
words
...RUSSELL FELT PHILOSOPHY (PARTICULARLY HEGELIAN-STYLE ***METAPHYSICAL IDEALISM***) COULD BENEFIT FROM THE SAME PRECISION!
RUSSELL WAS AN ADVOCATE OF ***OCCAM'S RAZOR***, A DICTUM ATTRIBUTED TO THE FRANCISCAN FRIAR ***WILLIAM OF OCKHAM*** (C. 1285-1349), WHICH GOES:
Occam's
METAPHYSICS
"Entia non sunt multiplicanda praeter necessitatem."
*"ENTITIES SHOULD NOT BE **MULTIPLIED** BEYOND **NECESSITY**."*
SHAVE!
SLASH
CUT!
HACK!
FOR ***WILLIAM***, HIS RAZOR SEVERED PHILOSOPHY FROM THE (IN HIS VIEW) UNNECESSARY ***UNIVERSALS*** THAT LIE BEYOND ***PERSONAL EXPERIENCE***.
IN ***SCIENCE***, THE RAZOR IS WIELDED TO POSE HYPOTHESES AS ***SIMPLY*** AS POSSIBLE.
FOR ***RUSSELL***, THE RAZOR MEANT:
THE ***TRUE ROLE*** OF PHILOSOPHY IS THE ERADICATION OF ***ERROR*** THROUGH THE CLARIFICATION OF ***LANGUAGE!***
yip, yip!
LOGICAL ATOMISM
RUSSELL DEMANDED THAT PHILOSOPHY TAKE THE FORM OF ***PROPOSITIONS*** THAT PRECISELY REFLECT ***REALITY***.
HIS ***LOGICALLY PERFECT LANGUAGE*** WOULD REMOVE ALL ***AMBIGUITY*** BY REDUCING FACTS TO THEIR ***SIMPLEST COMPONENTS***.
The King of France is bald.
THIS STATEMENT MIGHT ***SEEM*** SIMPLE ON ITS ***FACE...***

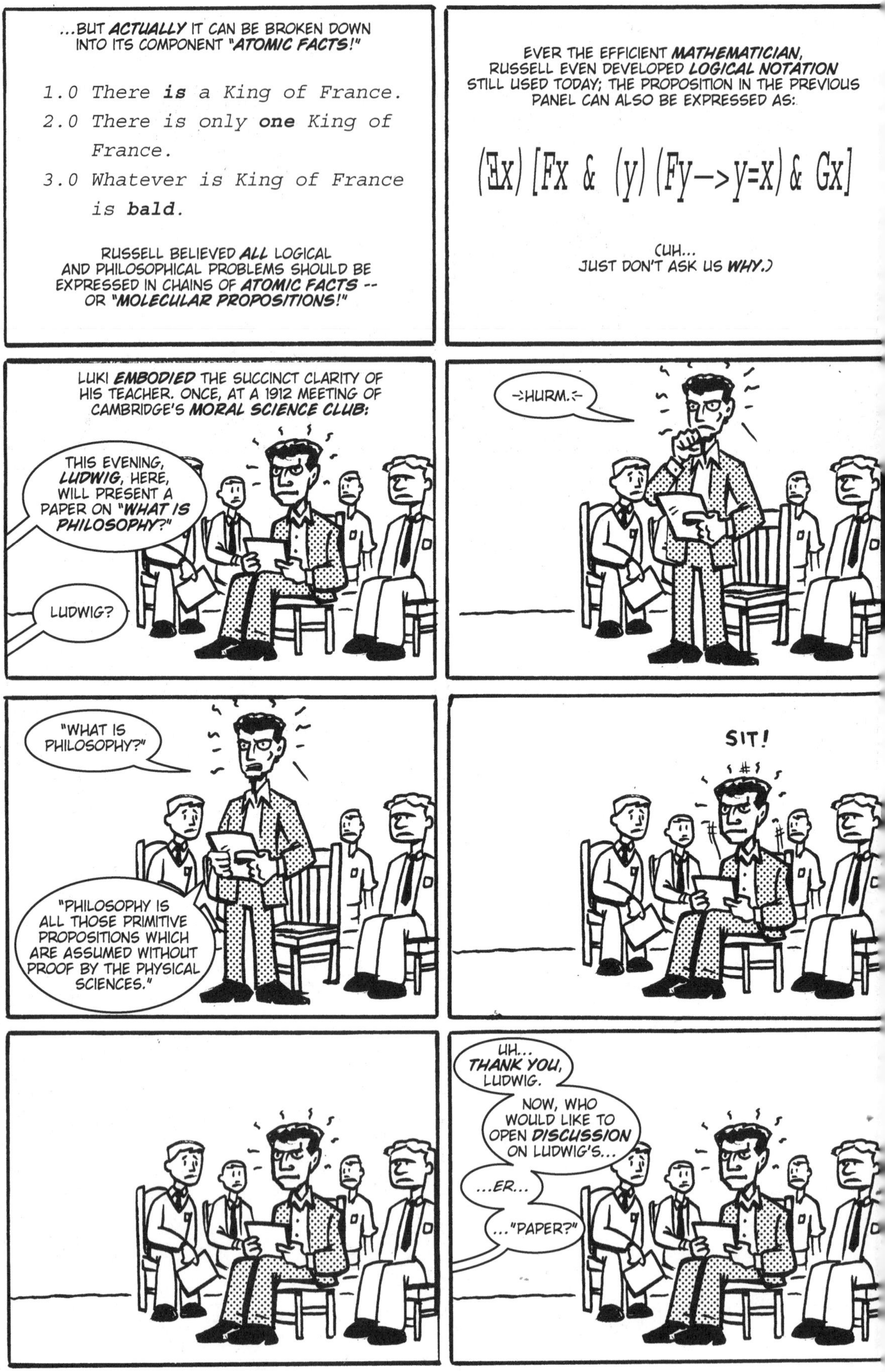
...BUT *ACTUALLY* IT CAN BE BROKEN DOWN INTO ITS COMPONENT "*ATOMIC FACTS!*"
1.0 There **is** a King of France.
2.0 There is only **one** King of France.
3.0 Whatever is King of France is **bald**.
RUSSELL BELIEVED *ALL* LOGICAL AND PHILOSOPHICAL PROBLEMS SHOULD BE EXPRESSED IN CHAINS OF *ATOMIC FACTS* -- OR "*MOLECULAR PROPOSITIONS!*"
EVER THE EFFICIENT *MATHEMATICIAN*, RUSSELL EVEN DEVELOPED *LOGICAL NOTATION* STILL USED TODAY; THE PROPOSITION IN THE PREVIOUS PANEL CAN ALSO BE EXPRESSED AS:
$(\exists x)\,[Fx\ \&\ (y)\,(Fy \rightarrow y=x)\ \&\ Gx]$
(UH... JUST DON'T ASK US *WHY*.)
LUKI *EMBODIED* THE SUCCINCT CLARITY OF HIS TEACHER. ONCE, AT A 1912 MEETING OF CAMBRIDGE'S *MORAL SCIENCE CLUB*:
THIS EVENING, *LUDWIG*, HERE, WILL PRESENT A PAPER ON "*WHAT IS PHILOSOPHY?*"
LUDWIG?
-HURM.-
"WHAT IS PHILOSOPHY?"
"PHILOSOPHY IS ALL THOSE PRIMITIVE PROPOSITIONS WHICH ARE ASSUMED WITHOUT PROOF BY THE PHYSICAL SCIENCES."
SIT!
UH... *THANK YOU*, LUDWIG.
NOW, WHO WOULD LIKE TO OPEN *DISCUSSION* ON LUDWIG'S...
...ER...
..."PAPER?"

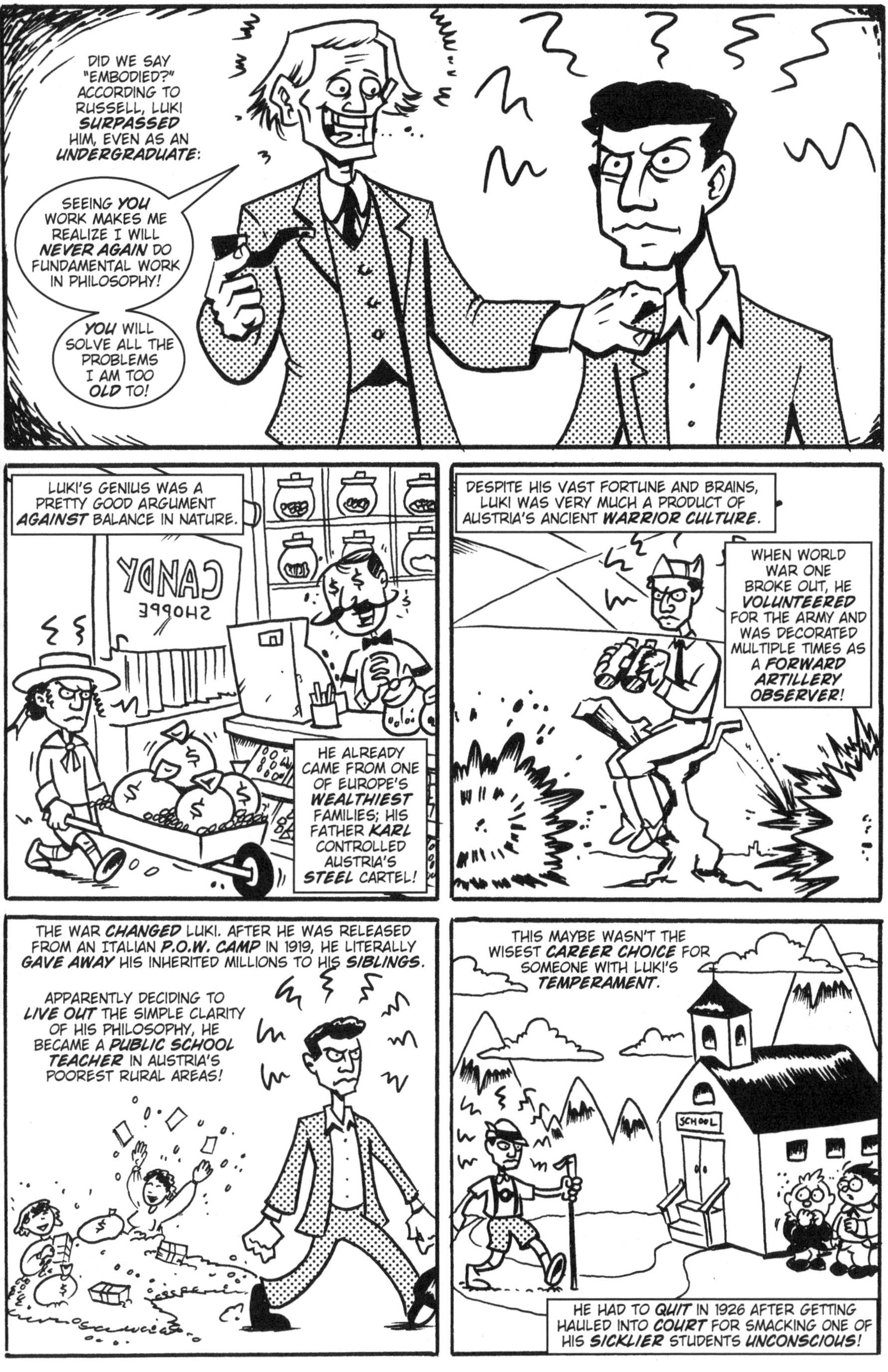
DID WE SAY "EMBODIED?" ACCORDING TO RUSSELL, LUKI SURPASSED HIM, EVEN AS AN UNDERGRADUATE:
SEEING YOU WORK MAKES ME REALIZE I WILL NEVER AGAIN DO FUNDAMENTAL WORK IN PHILOSOPHY!
YOU WILL SOLVE ALL THE PROBLEMS I AM TOO OLD TO!
LUKI'S GENIUS WAS A PRETTY GOOD ARGUMENT AGAINST BALANCE IN NATURE.
CANDY SHOPPE
HE ALREADY CAME FROM ONE OF EUROPE'S WEALTHIEST FAMILIES; HIS FATHER KARL CONTROLLED AUSTRIA'S STEEL CARTEL!
DESPITE HIS VAST FORTUNE AND BRAINS, LUKI WAS VERY MUCH A PRODUCT OF AUSTRIA'S ANCIENT WARRIOR CULTURE.
WHEN WORLD WAR ONE BROKE OUT, HE VOLUNTEERED FOR THE ARMY AND WAS DECORATED MULTIPLE TIMES AS A FORWARD ARTILLERY OBSERVER!
THE WAR CHANGED LUKI. AFTER HE WAS RELEASED FROM AN ITALIAN P.O.W. CAMP IN 1919, HE LITERALLY GAVE AWAY HIS INHERITED MILLIONS TO HIS SIBLINGS.
APPARENTLY DECIDING TO LIVE OUT THE SIMPLE CLARITY OF HIS PHILOSOPHY, HE BECAME A PUBLIC SCHOOL TEACHER IN AUSTRIA'S POOREST RURAL AREAS!
THIS MAYBE WASN'T THE WISEST CAREER CHOICE FOR SOMEONE WITH LUKI'S TEMPERAMENT.
SCHOOL
HE HAD TO QUIT IN 1926 AFTER GETTING HAULED INTO COURT FOR SMACKING ONE OF HIS SICKLIER STUDENTS UNCONSCIOUS!

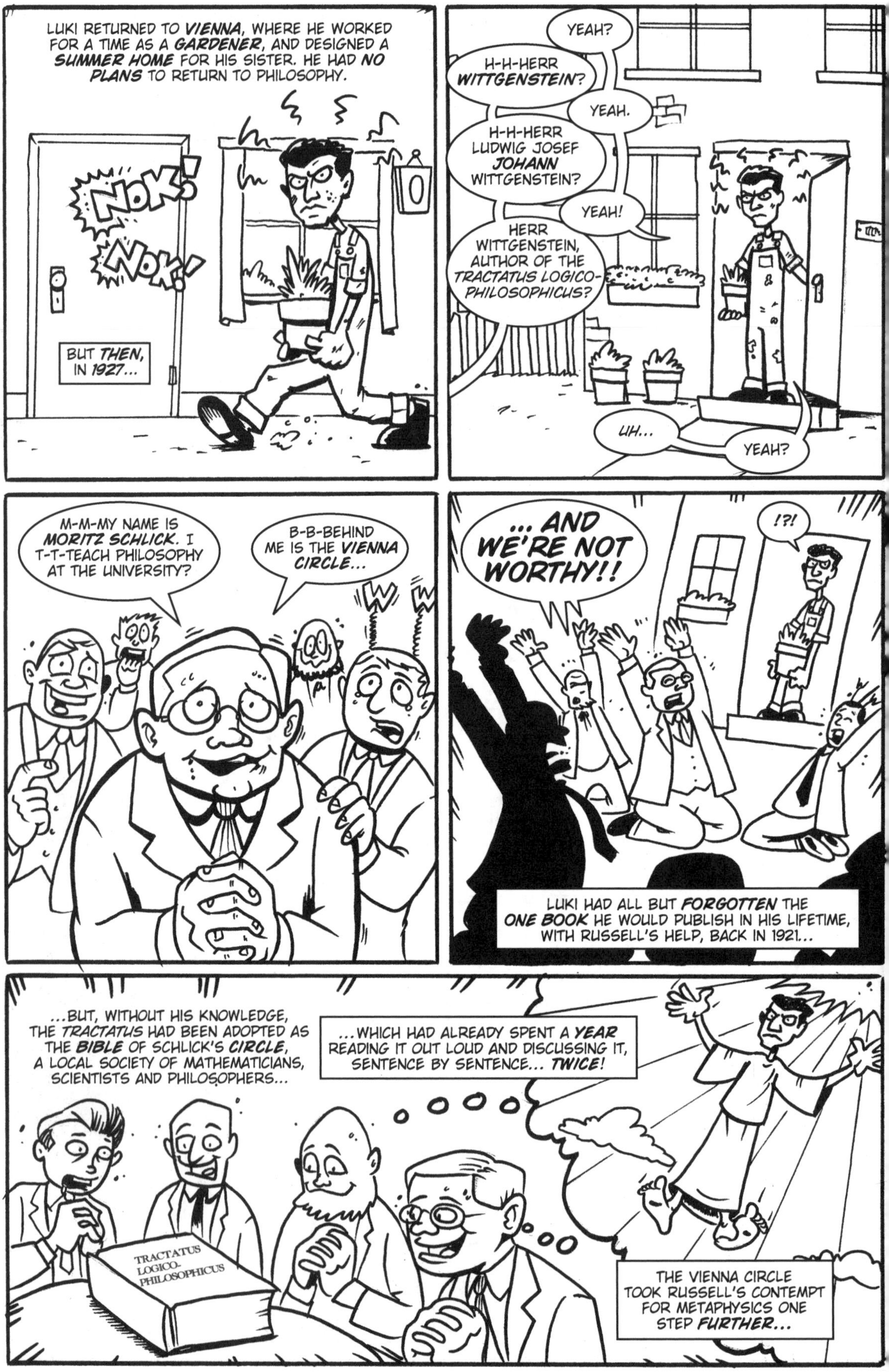
LUKI RETURNED TO VIENNA, WHERE HE WORKED FOR A TIME AS A GARDENER, AND DESIGNED A SUMMER HOME FOR HIS SISTER. HE HAD NO PLANS TO RETURN TO PHILOSOPHY.
NOK!
NOK!
BUT THEN, IN 1927...
H-H-HERR WITTGENSTEIN?
YEAH?
H-H-HERR LUDWIG JOSEF JOHANN WITTGENSTEIN?
YEAH.
HERR WITTGENSTEIN, AUTHOR OF THE TRACTATUS LOGICO-PHILOSOPHICUS?
YEAH!
UH...
YEAH?
M-M-MY NAME IS MORITZ SCHLICK. I T-T-TEACH PHILOSOPHY AT THE UNIVERSITY?
B-B-BEHIND ME IS THE VIENNA CIRCLE...
... AND WE'RE NOT WORTHY!!
!?!
LUKI HAD ALL BUT FORGOTTEN THE ONE BOOK HE WOULD PUBLISH IN HIS LIFETIME, WITH RUSSELL'S HELP, BACK IN 1921...
...BUT, WITHOUT HIS KNOWLEDGE, THE TRACTATUS HAD BEEN ADOPTED AS THE BIBLE OF SCHLICK'S CIRCLE, A LOCAL SOCIETY OF MATHEMATICIANS, SCIENTISTS AND PHILOSOPHERS...
...WHICH HAD ALREADY SPENT A YEAR READING IT OUT LOUD AND DISCUSSING IT, SENTENCE BY SENTENCE... TWICE!
TRACTATUS LOGICO-PHILOSOPHICUS
THE VIENNA CIRCLE TOOK RUSSELL'S CONTEMPT FOR METAPHYSICS ONE STEP FURTHER...

...ASSERTING THAT PHILOSOPHY'S *SOLE* FUNCTION WAS TO *CLARIFY* THE CONCEPTS EMPLOYED BY *SCIENCE*.

HERE COME SOME *WELL-ARMED GOONS*, PHILOSOPHY BOY!

YOU KEEP THEM *BUSY* WHILE *I* WAIT FOR THE *MAIN VILLAIN* TO APPEAR!

YOU *GOT IT*, SCIENCE MAN!

JIMINY JILLIKERS!

THE CIRCLE'S PHILOSOPHY, WHICH THEY DUBBED "*LOGICAL POSITIVISM*," ASSERTED THERE WERE ONLY *TWO* TYPES OF ACCEPTABLE PROPOSITIONS.

ONE WOULD BE *ANALYTIC*, A REFLECTIVE DEFINITION, LIKE *4=4*, OR "WHAT *COLOR* IS GEORGE WASHINGTON'S *WHITE* HORSE?"

WAIT... DON'T *TELL* ME...I CAN *GET* THIS...

THE OTHER KIND WOULD BE A *SYNTHETIC* STATEMENT THAT CAN BE *VERIFIED* (OR NOT) THROUGH SCIENTIFIC EXPERIMENTATION...

...SUCH AS "GEORGE WASHINGTON'S WHITE HORSE LIKES *CANNON*."

HMMM... I'M GONNA HAVE TO GO WITH "*NO*" ON THAT ONE...

YES / NO

THE LOGICAL POSITIVISTS HELD THAT ALL *OTHER* STATEMENTS--IN RELIGION, ETHICS, OR METAPHYSICS-- WERE "*EMOTIVE*" AND THEREFORE *NONSENSE!*

KUM BA YA, MY LORD...

THEIR GOAL WAS THE *UNIFICATION* OF THE SCIENCES BY IMPOSING THE SAME *BASIC CRITERIA FOR LOGIC* ONTO *ALL* OF THEM!

IN LUKI'S *TRACTATUS* THE VIENNA CIRCLE THOUGHT THEY FOUND THE PERFECT *RULEBOOK* TO GUIDE THEM THROUGH CONSISTENT APPLICATION OF THEIR *VERIFICATION PRINCIPLE*.

```
2 What is the case--a fact--is the existence of states of affairs.
    2.1 We make to ourselves pictures of facts.
            2.13 To the objects correspond in the picture the elements
                 of the picture.
                   2.131 The elements of the picture stand, in the picture,
                         for the objects.
```

THE BOOK IS A ARRANGED IN A SERIES OF SIMPLE, HIERARCHICAL--*MOLECULAR*--PROPOSITIONS, NUMBERED IN THEIR ORDER OF IMPORTANCE TO EACH OTHER.

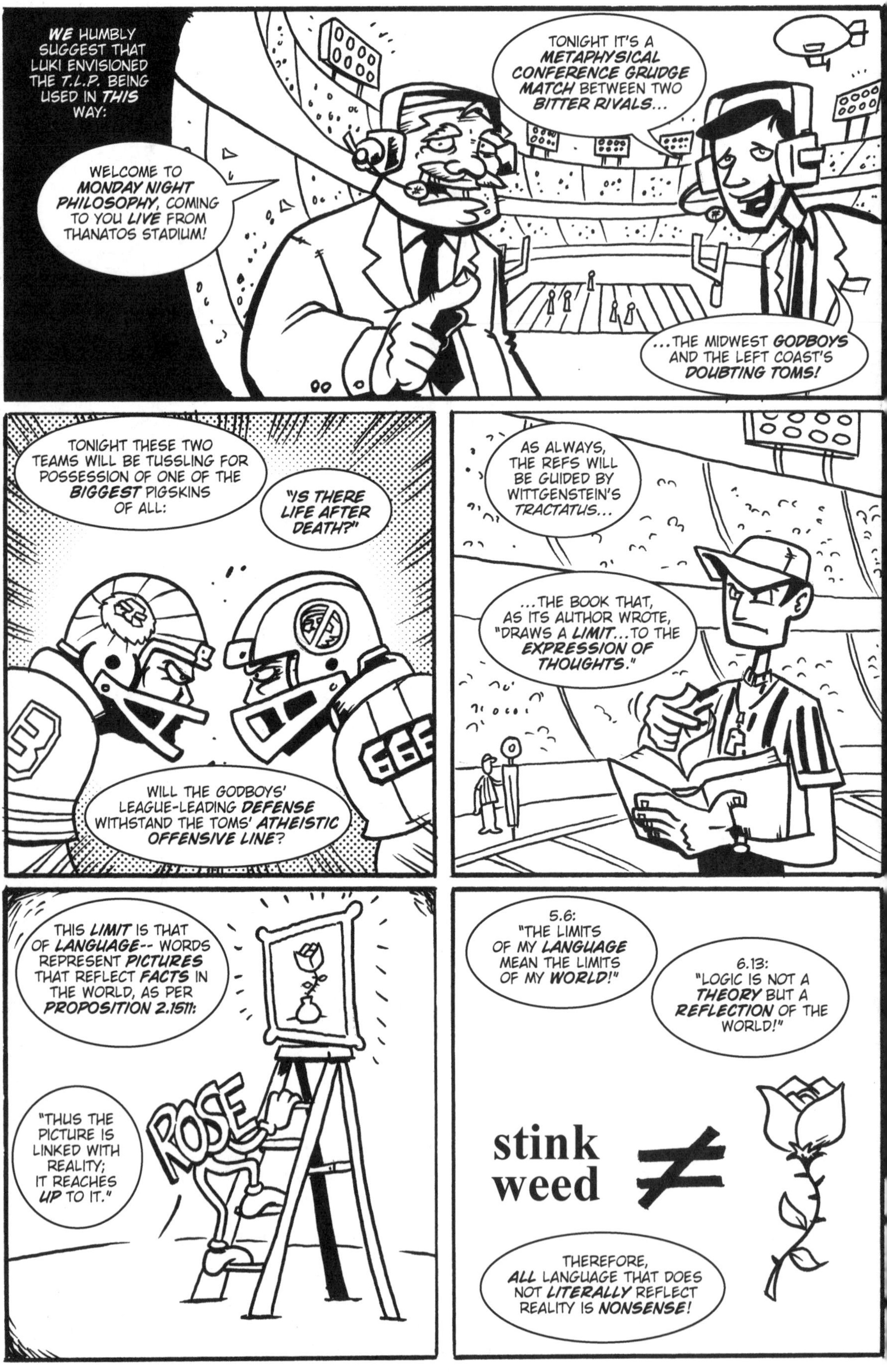
WE HUMBLY SUGGEST THAT LUKI ENVISIONED THE T.L.P. BEING USED IN THIS WAY:
WELCOME TO MONDAY NIGHT PHILOSOPHY, COMING TO YOU LIVE FROM THANATOS STADIUM!
TONIGHT IT'S A METAPHYSICAL CONFERENCE GRUDGE MATCH BETWEEN TWO BITTER RIVALS...
...THE MIDWEST GODBOYS AND THE LEFT COAST'S DOUBTING TOMS!
TONIGHT THESE TWO TEAMS WILL BE TUSSLING FOR POSSESSION OF ONE OF THE BIGGEST PIGSKINS OF ALL:
"IS THERE LIFE AFTER DEATH?"
666
WILL THE GODBOYS' LEAGUE-LEADING DEFENSE WITHSTAND THE TOMS' ATHEISTIC OFFENSIVE LINE?
AS ALWAYS, THE REFS WILL BE GUIDED BY WITTGENSTEIN'S TRACTATUS...
...THE BOOK THAT, AS ITS AUTHOR WROTE, "DRAWS A LIMIT...TO THE EXPRESSION OF THOUGHTS."
THIS LIMIT IS THAT OF LANGUAGE-- WORDS REPRESENT PICTURES THAT REFLECT FACTS IN THE WORLD, AS PER PROPOSITION 2.1511:
"THUS THE PICTURE IS LINKED WITH REALITY; IT REACHES UP TO IT."
ROSE
5.6: "THE LIMITS OF MY LANGUAGE MEAN THE LIMITS OF MY WORLD!"
6.13: "LOGIC IS NOT A THEORY BUT A REFLECTION OF THE WORLD!"
stink weed ≠
THEREFORE, ALL LANGUAGE THAT DOES NOT LITERALLY REFLECT REALITY IS NONSENSE!

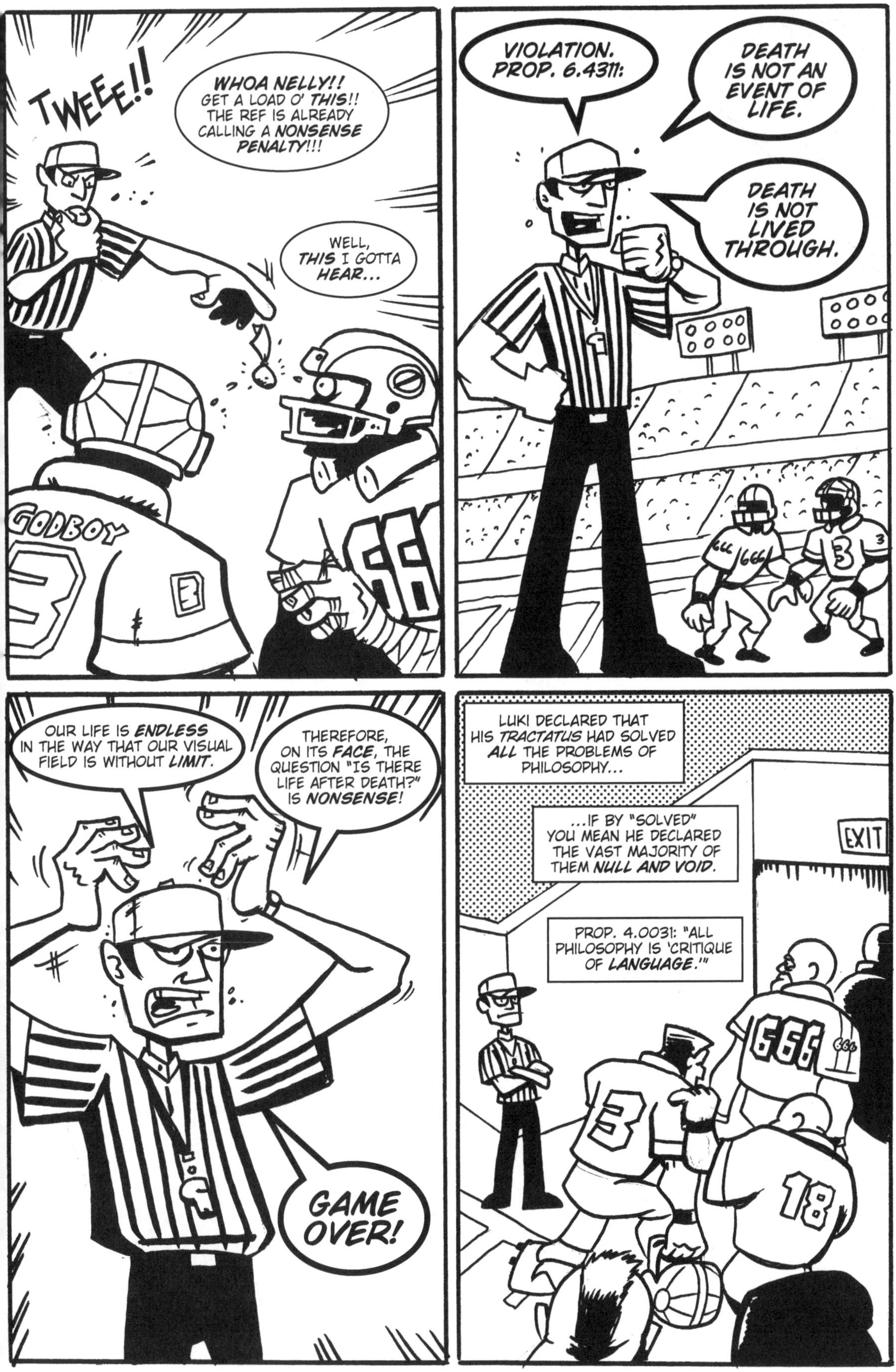
TWEEEE!!
WHOA NELLY!! GET A LOAD O' THIS!! THE REF IS ALREADY CALLING A NONSENSE PENALTY!!!
WELL, THIS I GOTTA HEAR...
GODBOY
VIOLATION. PROP. 6.4311:
DEATH IS NOT AN EVENT OF LIFE.
DEATH IS NOT LIVED THROUGH.
OUR LIFE IS ENDLESS IN THE WAY THAT OUR VISUAL FIELD IS WITHOUT LIMIT.
THEREFORE, ON ITS FACE, THE QUESTION "IS THERE LIFE AFTER DEATH?" IS NONSENSE!
GAME OVER!
LUKI DECLARED THAT HIS TRACTATUS HAD SOLVED ALL THE PROBLEMS OF PHILOSOPHY...
...IF BY "SOLVED" YOU MEAN HE DECLARED THE VAST MAJORITY OF THEM NULL AND VOID.
EXIT
PROP. 4.0031: "ALL PHILOSOPHY IS 'CRITIQUE OF LANGUAGE.'"

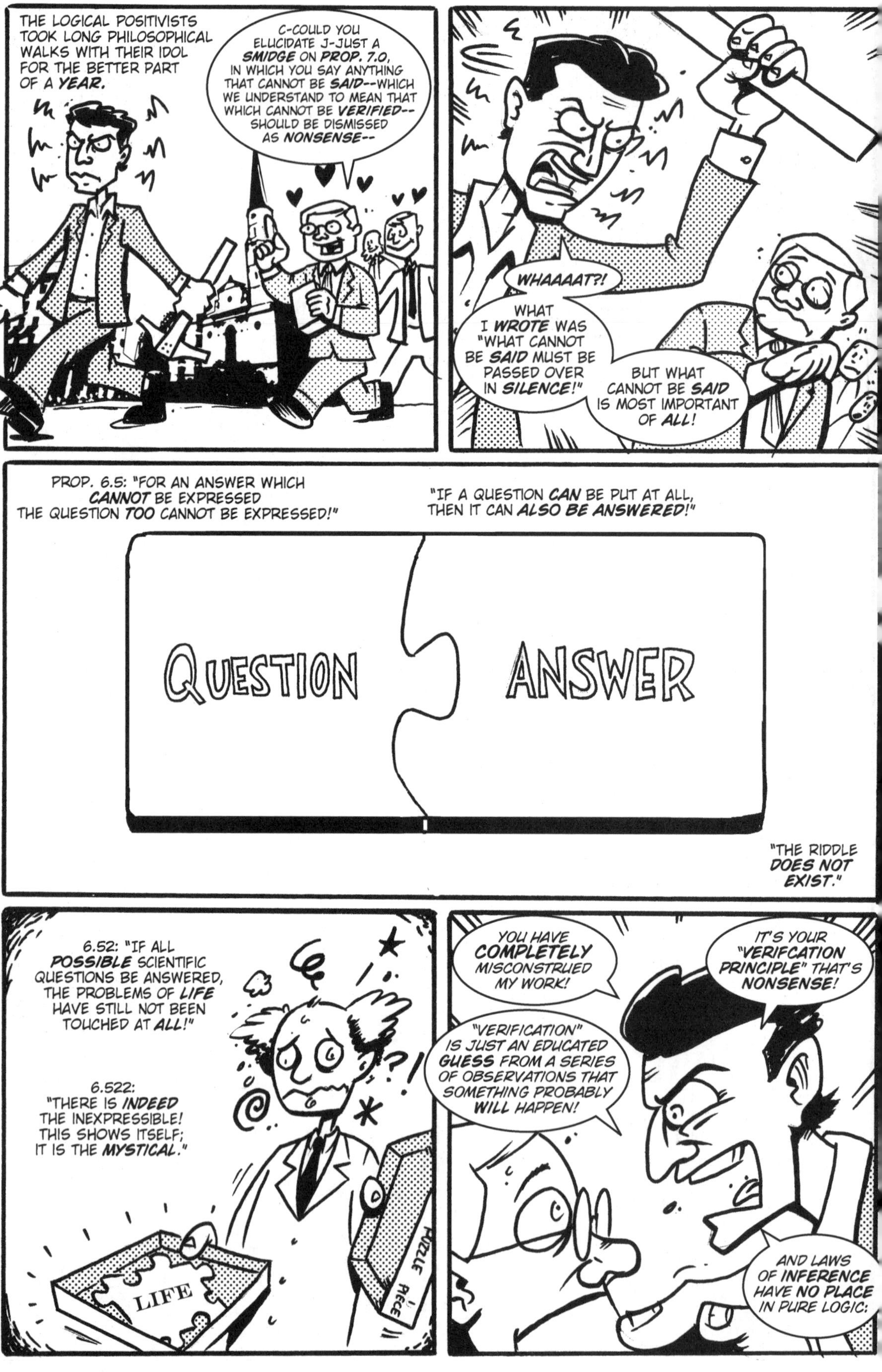
THE LOGICAL POSITIVISTS TOOK LONG PHILOSOPHICAL WALKS WITH THEIR IDOL FOR THE BETTER PART OF A YEAR.
C-COULD YOU ELUCIDATE J-JUST A SMIDGE ON PROP. 7.0, IN WHICH YOU SAY ANYTHING THAT CANNOT BE SAID--WHICH WE UNDERSTAND TO MEAN THAT WHICH CANNOT BE VERIFIED--SHOULD BE DISMISSED AS NONSENSE--
WHAAAAT?!
WHAT I WROTE WAS "WHAT CANNOT BE SAID MUST BE PASSED OVER IN SILENCE!"
BUT WHAT CANNOT BE SAID IS MOST IMPORTANT OF ALL!
PROP. 6.5: "FOR AN ANSWER WHICH CANNOT BE EXPRESSED THE QUESTION TOO CANNOT BE EXPRESSED!"
"IF A QUESTION CAN BE PUT AT ALL, THEN IT CAN ALSO BE ANSWERED!"
QUESTION
ANSWER
"THE RIDDLE DOES NOT EXIST."
6.52: "IF ALL POSSIBLE SCIENTIFIC QUESTIONS BE ANSWERED, THE PROBLEMS OF LIFE HAVE STILL NOT BEEN TOUCHED AT ALL!"
6.522: "THERE IS INDEED THE INEXPRESSIBLE! THIS SHOWS ITSELF; IT IS THE MYSTICAL."
LIFE
PUZZLE PIECE
YOU HAVE COMPLETELY MISCONSTRUED MY WORK!
IT'S YOUR "VERIFCATION PRINCIPLE" THAT'S NONSENSE!
"VERIFICATION" IS JUST AN EDUCATED GUESS FROM A SERIES OF OBSERVATIONS THAT SOMETHING PROBABLY WILL HAPPEN!
AND LAWS OF INFERENCE HAVE NO PLACE IN PURE LOGIC:

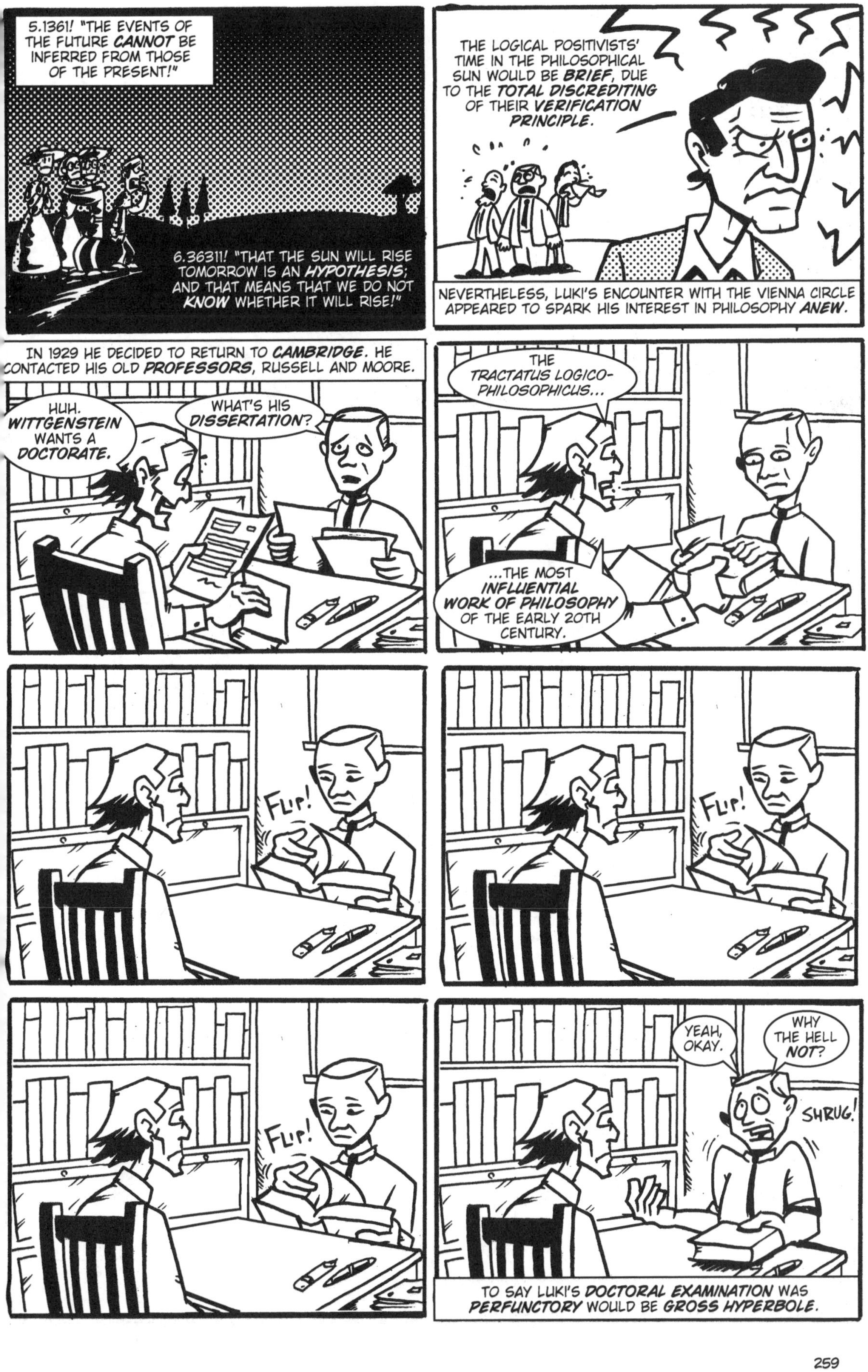
5.1361! "THE EVENTS OF THE FUTURE CANNOT BE INFERRED FROM THOSE OF THE PRESENT!"
6.36311! "THAT THE SUN WILL RISE TOMORROW IS AN HYPOTHESIS; AND THAT MEANS THAT WE DO NOT KNOW WHETHER IT WILL RISE!"
THE LOGICAL POSITIVISTS' TIME IN THE PHILOSOPHICAL SUN WOULD BE BRIEF, DUE TO THE TOTAL DISCREDITING OF THEIR VERIFICATION PRINCIPLE.
NEVERTHELESS, LUKI'S ENCOUNTER WITH THE VIENNA CIRCLE APPEARED TO SPARK HIS INTEREST IN PHILOSOPHY ANEW.
IN 1929 HE DECIDED TO RETURN TO CAMBRIDGE. HE CONTACTED HIS OLD PROFESSORS, RUSSELL AND MOORE.
HUH. WITTGENSTEIN WANTS A DOCTORATE.
WHAT'S HIS DISSERTATION?
THE TRACTATUS LOGICO-PHILOSOPHICUS...
...THE MOST INFLUENTIAL WORK OF PHILOSOPHY OF THE EARLY 20TH CENTURY.
FLIP!
FLIP!
FLIP!
YEAH, OKAY.
WHY THE HELL NOT?
SHRUG!
TO SAY LUKI'S DOCTORAL EXAMINATION WAS PERFUNCTORY WOULD BE GROSS HYPERBOLE.

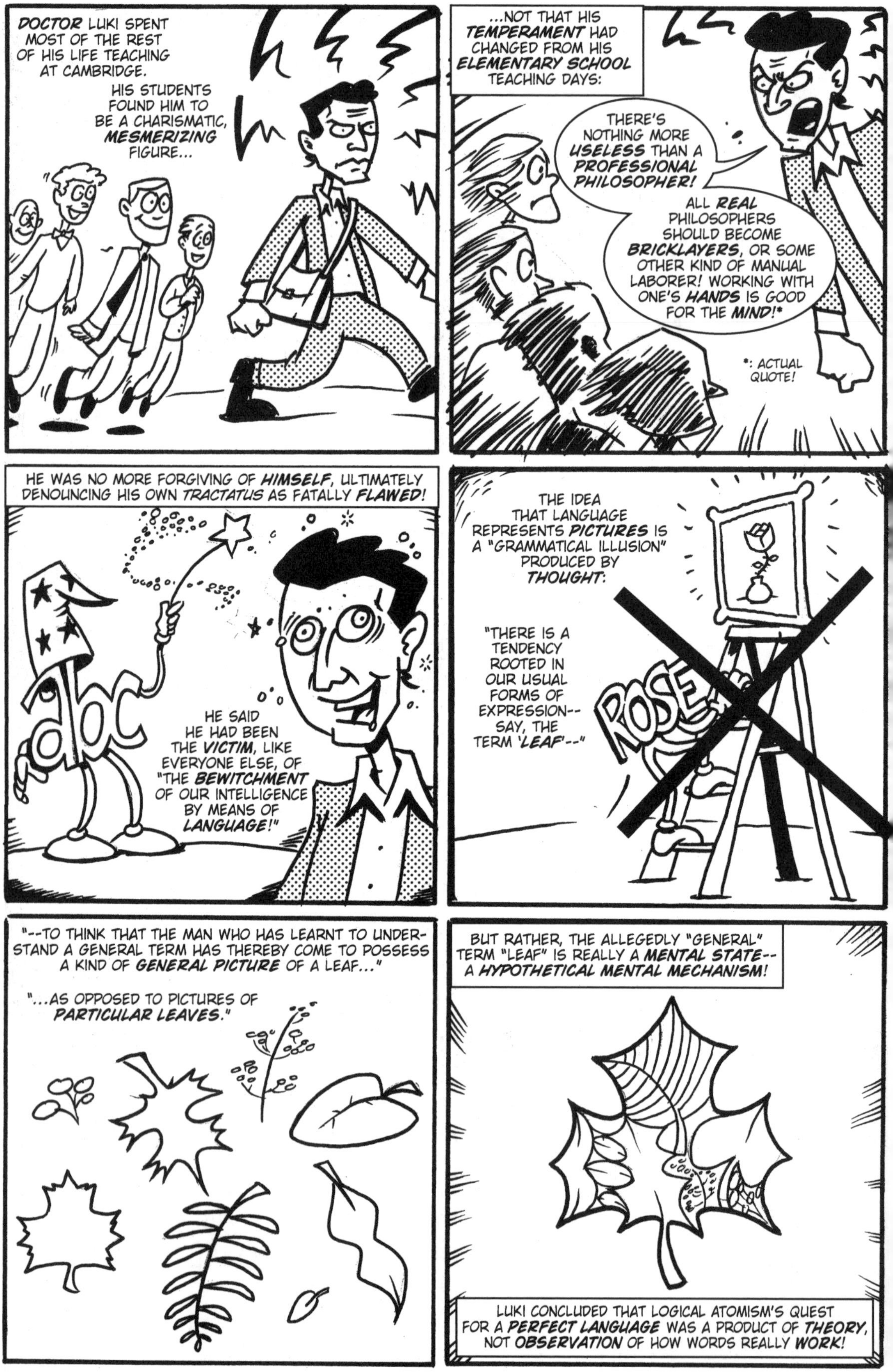
DOCTOR LUKI SPENT MOST OF THE REST OF HIS LIFE TEACHING AT CAMBRIDGE.
HIS STUDENTS FOUND HIM TO BE A CHARISMATIC, MESMERIZING FIGURE...
...NOT THAT HIS TEMPERAMENT HAD CHANGED FROM HIS ELEMENTARY SCHOOL TEACHING DAYS:
THERE'S NOTHING MORE USELESS THAN A PROFESSIONAL PHILOSOPHER!
ALL REAL PHILOSOPHERS SHOULD BECOME BRICKLAYERS, OR SOME OTHER KIND OF MANUAL LABORER! WORKING WITH ONE'S HANDS IS GOOD FOR THE MIND!*
*: ACTUAL QUOTE!
HE WAS NO MORE FORGIVING OF HIMSELF, ULTIMATELY DENOUNCING HIS OWN TRACTATUS AS FATALLY FLAWED!
abc
HE SAID HE HAD BEEN THE VICTIM, LIKE EVERYONE ELSE, OF "THE BEWITCHMENT OF OUR INTELLIGENCE BY MEANS OF LANGUAGE!"
THE IDEA THAT LANGUAGE REPRESENTS PICTURES IS A "GRAMMATICAL ILLUSION" PRODUCED BY THOUGHT:
"THERE IS A TENDENCY ROOTED IN OUR USUAL FORMS OF EXPRESSION--SAY, THE TERM 'LEAF'--"
ROSE
"--TO THINK THAT THE MAN WHO HAS LEARNT TO UNDERSTAND A GENERAL TERM HAS THEREBY COME TO POSSESS A KIND OF GENERAL PICTURE OF A LEAF..."
"...AS OPPOSED TO PICTURES OF PARTICULAR LEAVES."
BUT RATHER, THE ALLEGEDLY "GENERAL" TERM "LEAF" IS REALLY A MENTAL STATE--A HYPOTHETICAL MENTAL MECHANISM!
LUKI CONCLUDED THAT LOGICAL ATOMISM'S QUEST FOR A PERFECT LANGUAGE WAS A PRODUCT OF THEORY, NOT OBSERVATION OF HOW WORDS REALLY WORK!

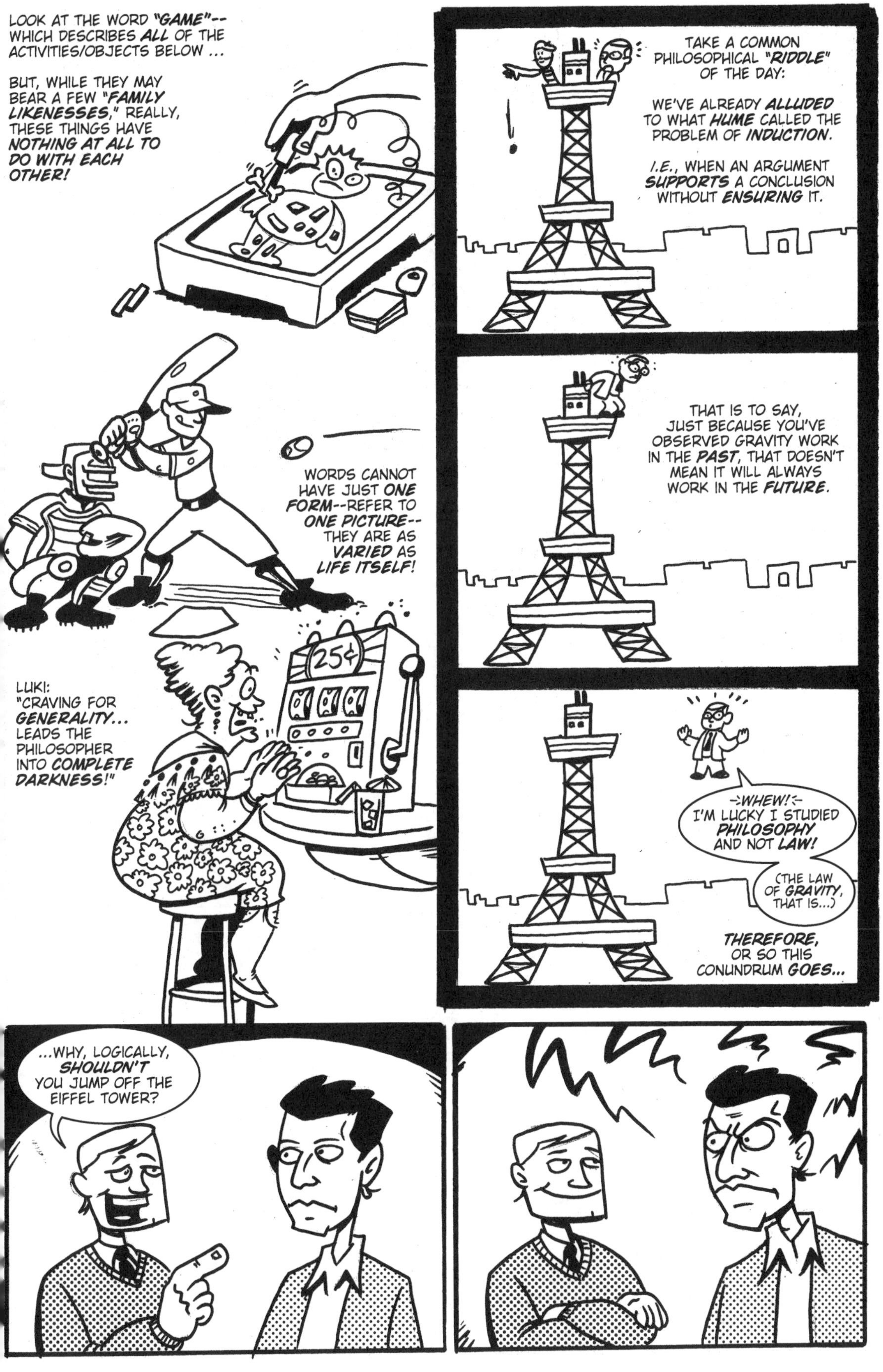

LOOK AT THE WORD "GAME"-- WHICH DESCRIBES ALL OF THE ACTIVITIES/OBJECTS BELOW ...
BUT, WHILE THEY MAY BEAR A FEW "FAMILY LIKENESSES," REALLY, THESE THINGS HAVE NOTHING AT ALL TO DO WITH EACH OTHER!
TAKE A COMMON PHILOSOPHICAL "RIDDLE" OF THE DAY:
WE'VE ALREADY ALLUDED TO WHAT HUME CALLED THE PROBLEM OF INDUCTION.
I.E., WHEN AN ARGUMENT SUPPORTS A CONCLUSION WITHOUT ENSURING IT.
THAT IS TO SAY, JUST BECAUSE YOU'VE OBSERVED GRAVITY WORK IN THE PAST, THAT DOESN'T MEAN IT WILL ALWAYS WORK IN THE FUTURE.
WORDS CANNOT HAVE JUST ONE FORM--REFER TO ONE PICTURE-- THEY ARE AS VARIED AS LIFE ITSELF!
25¢
LUKI: "CRAVING FOR GENERALITY... LEADS THE PHILOSOPHER INTO COMPLETE DARKNESS!"
WHEW! I'M LUCKY I STUDIED PHILOSOPHY AND NOT LAW!
(THE LAW OF GRAVITY, THAT IS...)
THEREFORE, OR SO THIS CONUNDRUM GOES...
...WHY, LOGICALLY, SHOULDN'T YOU JUMP OFF THE EIFFEL TOWER?

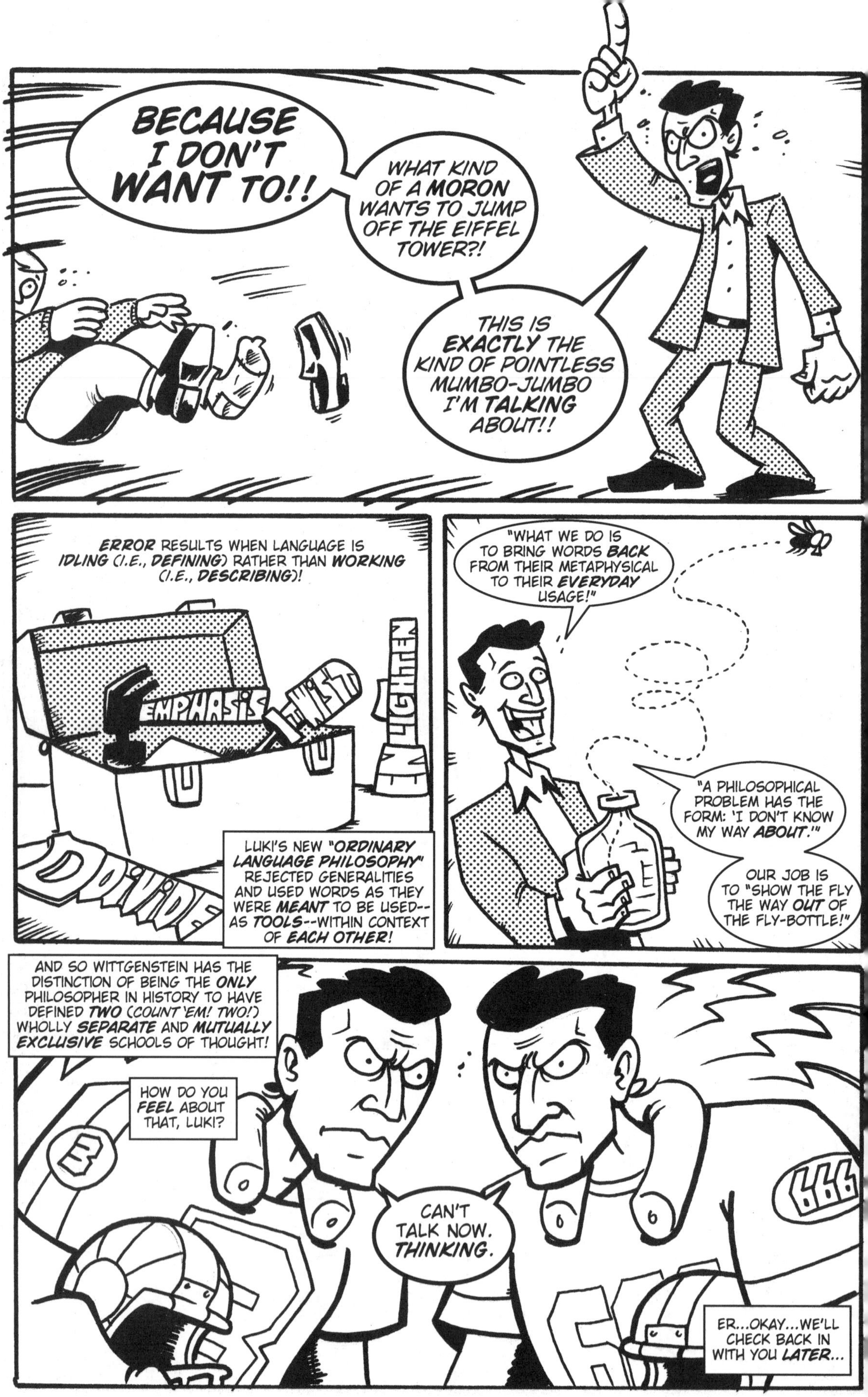
BECAUSE I DON'T WANT TO!!
WHAT KIND OF A MORON WANTS TO JUMP OFF THE EIFFEL TOWER?!
THIS IS EXACTLY THE KIND OF POINTLESS MUMBO-JUMBO I'M TALKING ABOUT!!
ERROR RESULTS WHEN LANGUAGE IS IDLING (I.E., DEFINING) RATHER THAN WORKING (I.E., DESCRIBING)!
EMPHASIS
TWIST
ENLIGHTEN
DIVIDE
LUKI'S NEW "ORDINARY LANGUAGE PHILOSOPHY" REJECTED GENERALITIES AND USED WORDS AS THEY WERE MEANT TO BE USED--AS TOOLS--WITHIN CONTEXT OF EACH OTHER!
"WHAT WE DO IS TO BRING WORDS BACK FROM THEIR METAPHYSICAL TO THEIR EVERYDAY USAGE!"
"A PHILOSOPHICAL PROBLEM HAS THE FORM: 'I DON'T KNOW MY WAY ABOUT.'"
OUR JOB IS TO "SHOW THE FLY THE WAY OUT OF THE FLY-BOTTLE!"
AND SO WITTGENSTEIN HAS THE DISTINCTION OF BEING THE ONLY PHILOSOPHER IN HISTORY TO HAVE DEFINED TWO (COUNT 'EM! TWO!) WHOLLY SEPARATE AND MUTUALLY EXCLUSIVE SCHOOLS OF THOUGHT!
HOW DO YOU FEEL ABOUT THAT, LUKI?
3
666
CAN'T TALK NOW. THINKING.
ER...OKAY...WE'LL CHECK BACK IN WITH YOU LATER...

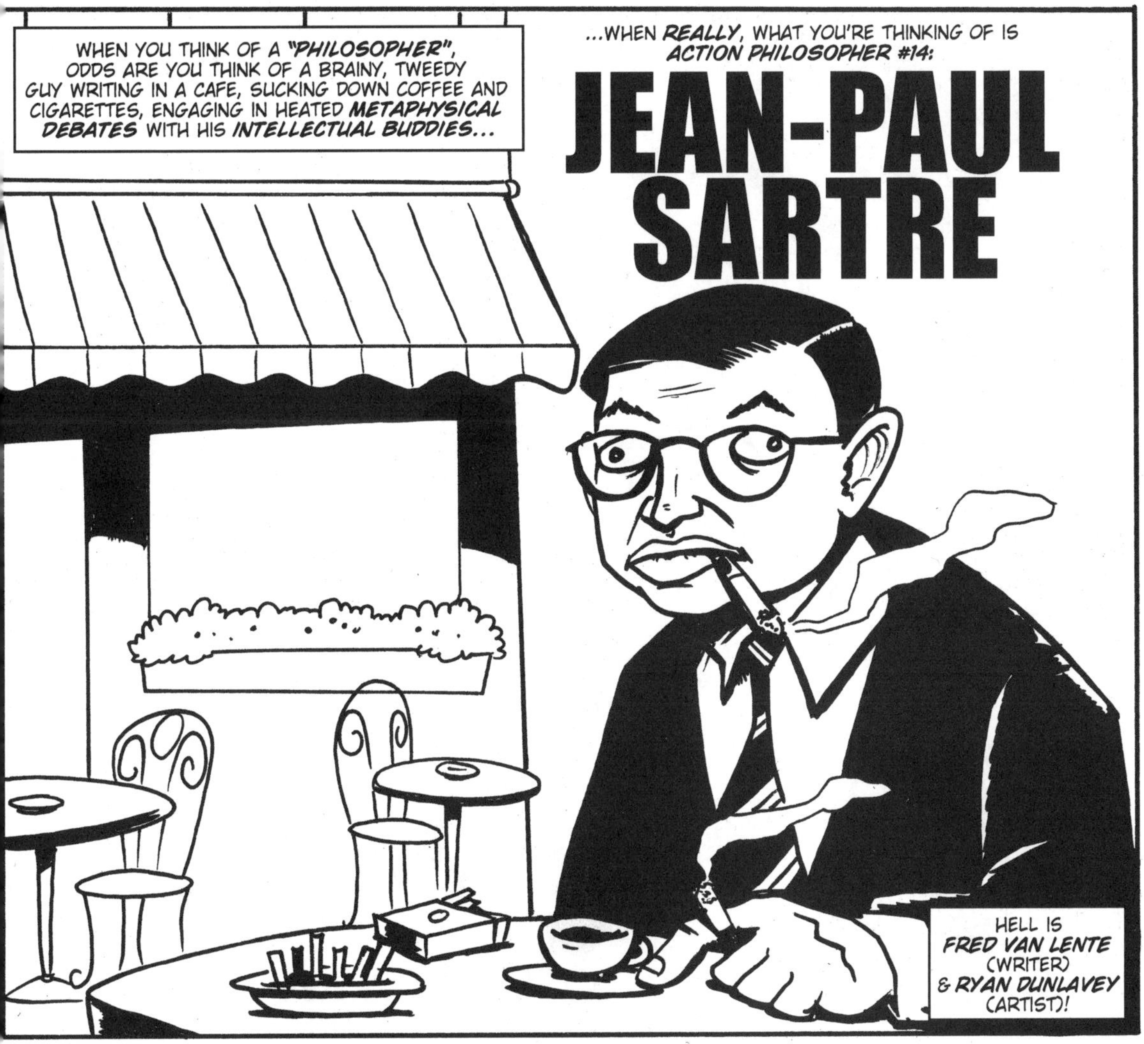
WHEN YOU THINK OF A "PHILOSOPHER", ODDS ARE YOU THINK OF A BRAINY, TWEEDY GUY WRITING IN A CAFE, SUCKING DOWN COFFEE AND CIGARETTES, ENGAGING IN HEATED METAPHYSICAL DEBATES WITH HIS INTELLECTUAL BUDDIES...
...WHEN REALLY, WHAT YOU'RE THINKING OF IS ACTION PHILOSOPHER #14:
JEAN-PAUL SARTRE
HELL IS FRED VAN LENTE (WRITER) & RYAN DUNLAVEY (ARTIST)!

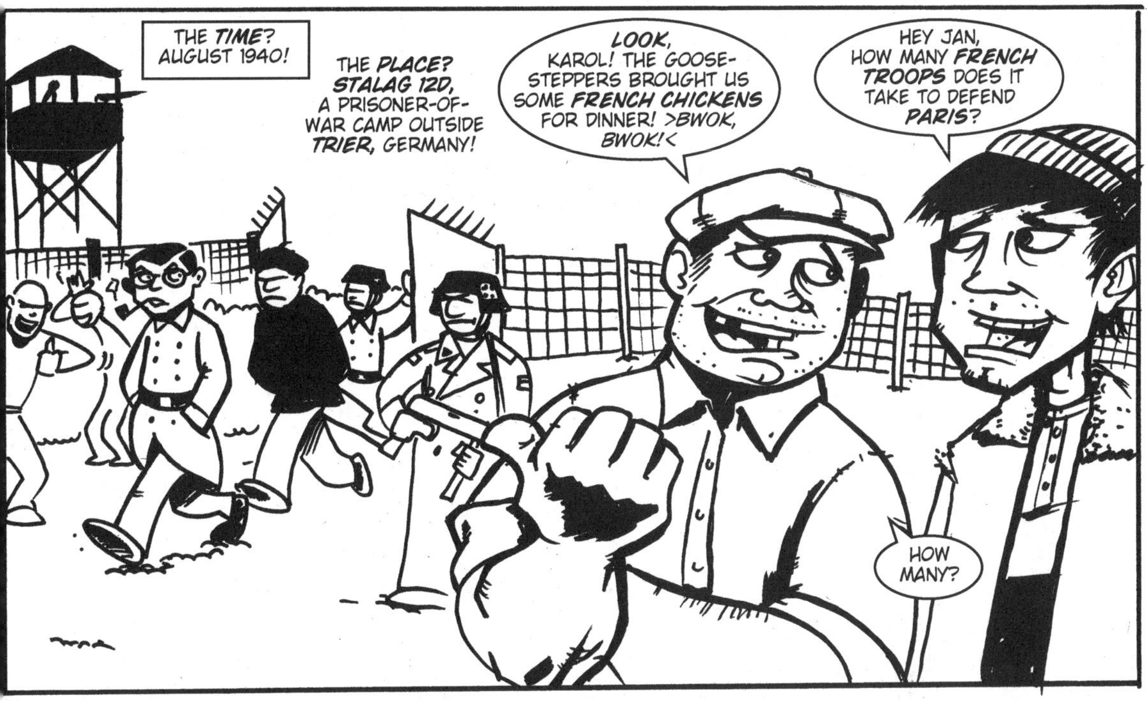
THE TIME? AUGUST 1940!
THE PLACE? STALAG 12D, A PRISONER-OF-WAR CAMP OUTSIDE TRIER, GERMANY!
LOOK, KAROL! THE GOOSE-STEPPERS BROUGHT US SOME FRENCH CHICKENS FOR DINNER! >BWOK, BWOK!<
HEY JAN, HOW MANY FRENCH TROOPS DOES IT TAKE TO DEFEND PARIS?
HOW MANY?

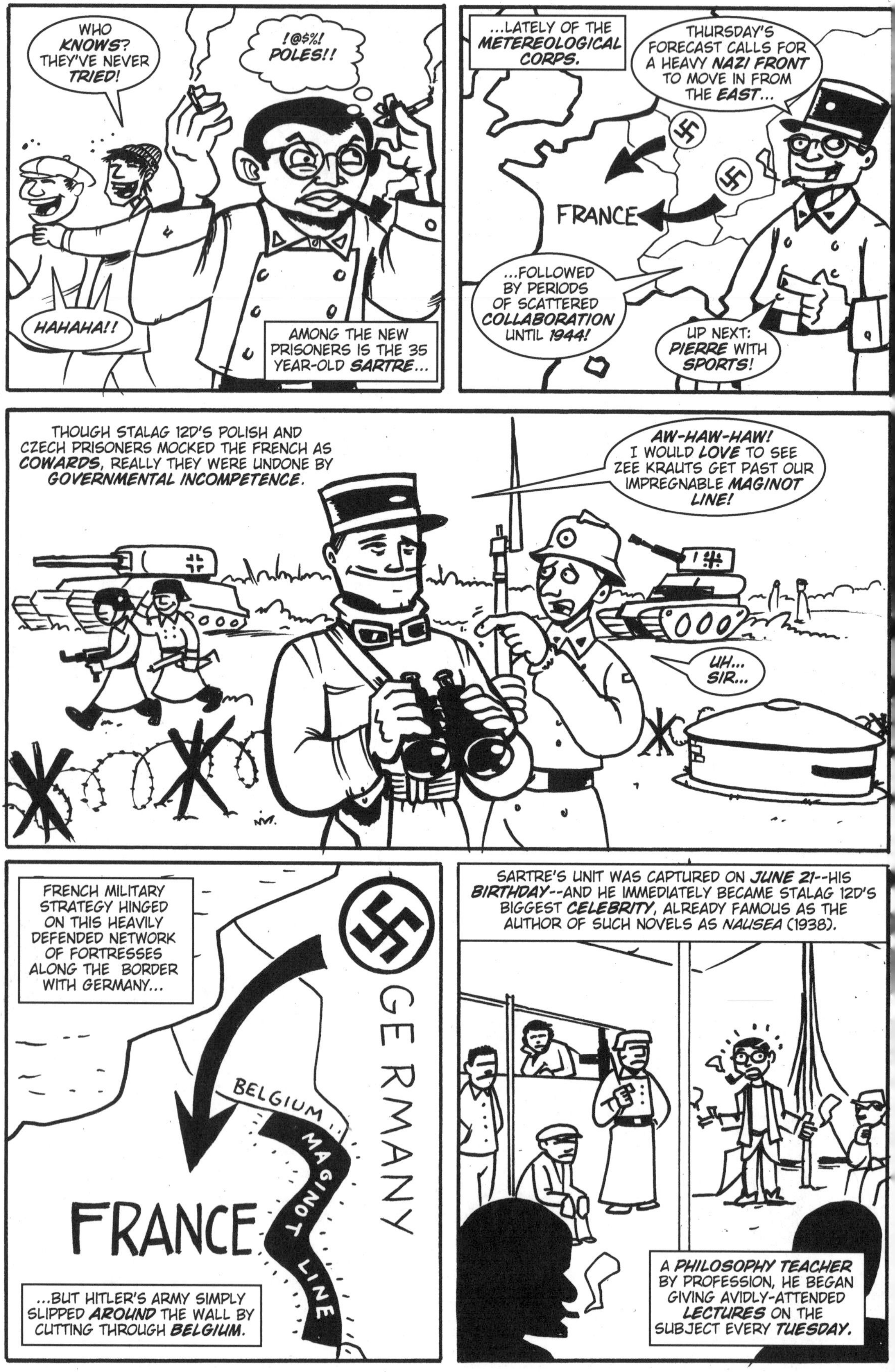
WHO KNOWS? THEY'VE NEVER TRIED!
!@$%! POLES!!
HAHAHA!!
AMONG THE NEW PRISONERS IS THE 35 YEAR-OLD SARTRE...
...LATELY OF THE METEREOLOGICAL CORPS.
THURSDAY'S FORECAST CALLS FOR A HEAVY NAZI FRONT TO MOVE IN FROM THE EAST...
FRANCE
...FOLLOWED BY PERIODS OF SCATTERED COLLABORATION UNTIL 1944!
UP NEXT: PIERRE WITH SPORTS!
THOUGH STALAG 12D'S POLISH AND CZECH PRISONERS MOCKED THE FRENCH AS COWARDS, REALLY THEY WERE UNDONE BY GOVERNMENTAL INCOMPETENCE.
AW-HAW-HAW! I WOULD LOVE TO SEE ZEE KRAUTS GET PAST OUR IMPREGNABLE MAGINOT LINE!
UH... SIR...
FRENCH MILITARY STRATEGY HINGED ON THIS HEAVILY DEFENDED NETWORK OF FORTRESSES ALONG THE BORDER WITH GERMANY...
GERMANY
BELGIUM
MAGINOT LINE
FRANCE
...BUT HITLER'S ARMY SIMPLY SLIPPED AROUND THE WALL BY CUTTING THROUGH BELGIUM.
SARTRE'S UNIT WAS CAPTURED ON JUNE 21--HIS BIRTHDAY--AND HE IMMEDIATELY BECAME STALAG 12D'S BIGGEST CELEBRITY, ALREADY FAMOUS AS THE AUTHOR OF SUCH NOVELS AS NAUSEA (1938).
A PHILOSOPHY TEACHER BY PROFESSION, HE BEGAN GIVING AVIDLY-ATTENDED LECTURES ON THE SUBJECT EVERY TUESDAY.

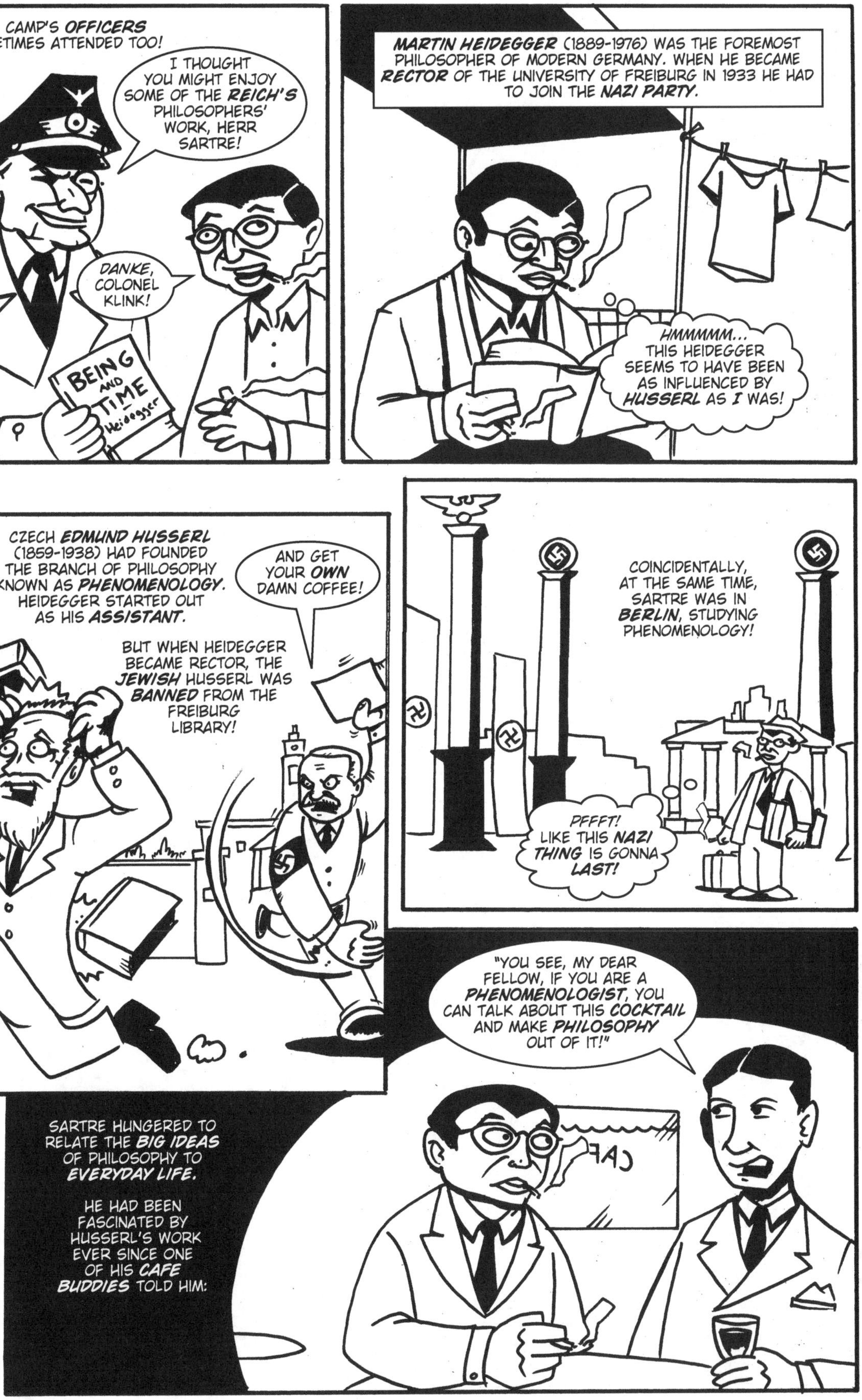
THE CAMP'S OFFICERS SOMETIMES ATTENDED TOO!
I THOUGHT YOU MIGHT ENJOY SOME OF THE REICH'S PHILOSOPHERS' WORK, HERR SARTRE!
DANKE, COLONEL KLINK!
BEING AND TIME Heidegger
MARTIN HEIDEGGER (1889-1976) WAS THE FOREMOST PHILOSOPHER OF MODERN GERMANY. WHEN HE BECAME RECTOR OF THE UNIVERSITY OF FREIBURG IN 1933 HE HAD TO JOIN THE NAZI PARTY.
HMMMMM... THIS HEIDEGGER SEEMS TO HAVE BEEN AS INFLUENCED BY HUSSERL AS I WAS!
CZECH EDMUND HUSSERL (1859-1938) HAD FOUNDED THE BRANCH OF PHILOSOPHY KNOWN AS PHENOMENOLOGY. HEIDEGGER STARTED OUT AS HIS ASSISTANT.
AND GET YOUR OWN DAMN COFFEE!
BUT WHEN HEIDEGGER BECAME RECTOR, THE JEWISH HUSSERL WAS BANNED FROM THE FREIBURG LIBRARY!
COINCIDENTALLY, AT THE SAME TIME, SARTRE WAS IN BERLIN, STUDYING PHENOMENOLOGY!
PFFFT! LIKE THIS NAZI THING IS GONNA LAST!
SARTRE HUNGERED TO RELATE THE BIG IDEAS OF PHILOSOPHY TO EVERYDAY LIFE.
HE HAD BEEN FASCINATED BY HUSSERL'S WORK EVER SINCE ONE OF HIS CAFE BUDDIES TOLD HIM:
"YOU SEE, MY DEAR FELLOW, IF YOU ARE A PHENOMENOLOGIST, YOU CAN TALK ABOUT THIS COCKTAIL AND MAKE PHILOSOPHY OUT OF IT!"

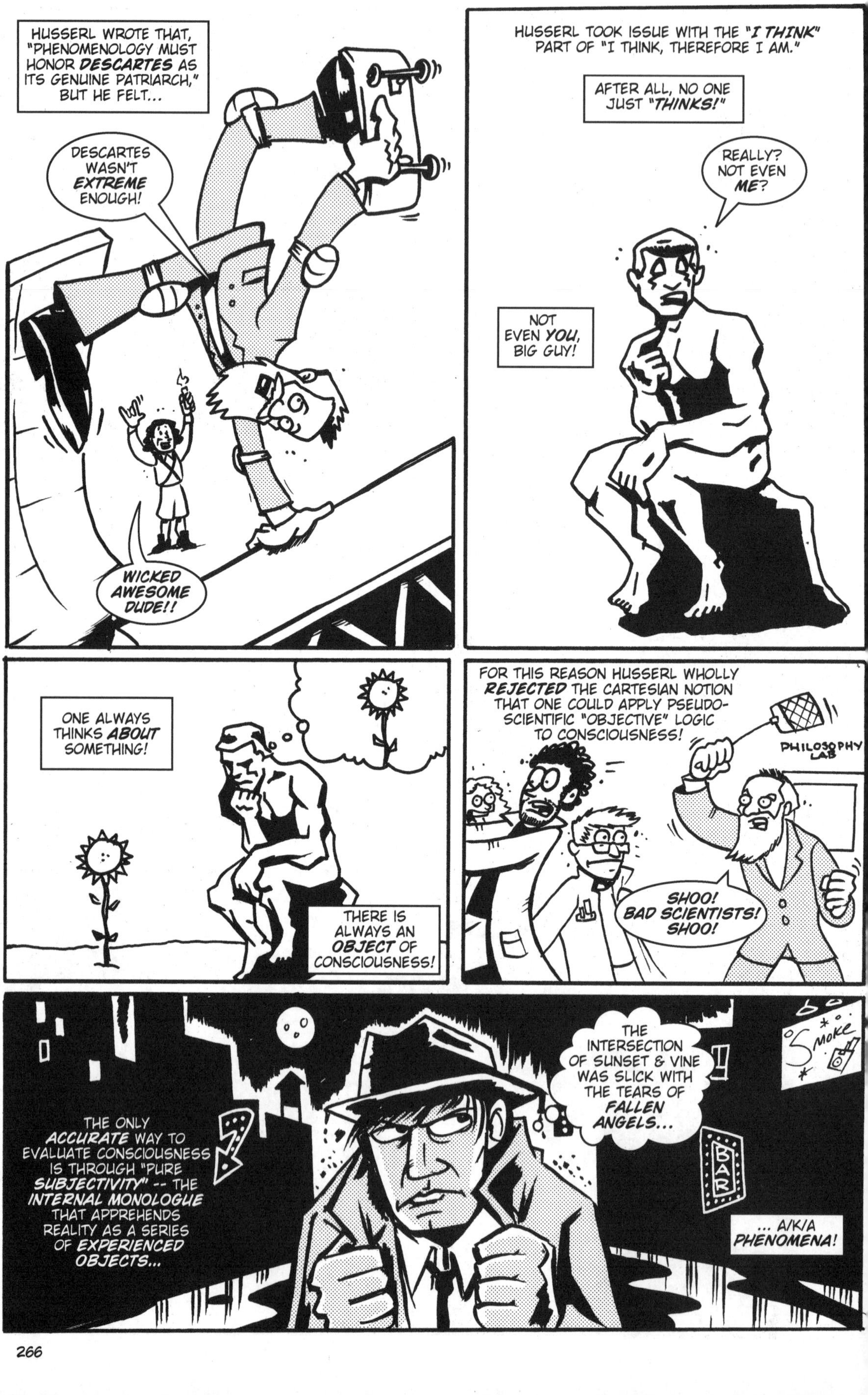

HUSSERL WROTE THAT, "PHENOMENOLOGY MUST HONOR DESCARTES AS ITS GENUINE PATRIARCH," BUT HE FELT...
DESCARTES WASN'T EXTREME ENOUGH!
WICKED AWESOME DUDE!!
HUSSERL TOOK ISSUE WITH THE "I THINK" PART OF "I THINK, THEREFORE I AM."
AFTER ALL, NO ONE JUST "THINKS!"
REALLY? NOT EVEN ME?
NOT EVEN YOU, BIG GUY!
ONE ALWAYS THINKS ABOUT SOMETHING!
THERE IS ALWAYS AN OBJECT OF CONSCIOUSNESS!
FOR THIS REASON HUSSERL WHOLLY REJECTED THE CARTESIAN NOTION THAT ONE COULD APPLY PSEUDO-SCIENTIFIC "OBJECTIVE" LOGIC TO CONSCIOUSNESS!
PHILOSOPHY LAB
SHOO! BAD SCIENTISTS! SHOO!
THE ONLY ACCURATE WAY TO EVALUATE CONSCIOUSNESS IS THROUGH "PURE SUBJECTIVITY" -- THE INTERNAL MONOLOGUE THAT APPREHENDS REALITY AS A SERIES OF EXPERIENCED OBJECTS...
THE INTERSECTION OF SUNSET & VINE WAS SLICK WITH THE TEARS OF FALLEN ANGELS...
Smoke
BAR
... A/K/A PHENOMENA!

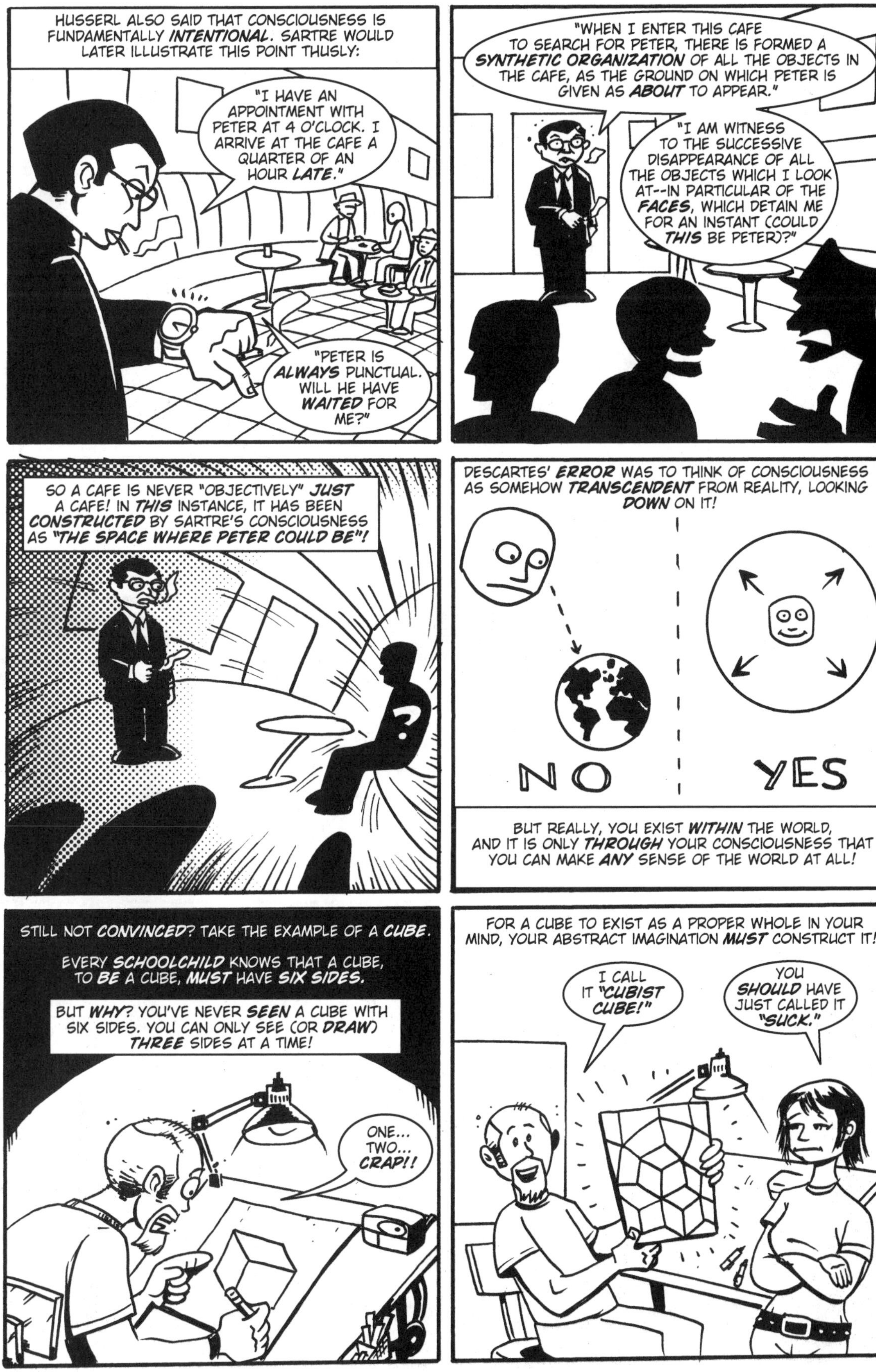
HUSSERL ALSO SAID THAT CONSCIOUSNESS IS FUNDAMENTALLY INTENTIONAL. SARTRE WOULD LATER ILLUSTRATE THIS POINT THUSLY:
"I HAVE AN APPOINTMENT WITH PETER AT 4 O'CLOCK. I ARRIVE AT THE CAFE A QUARTER OF AN HOUR LATE."
"PETER IS ALWAYS PUNCTUAL. WILL HE HAVE WAITED FOR ME?"
"WHEN I ENTER THIS CAFE TO SEARCH FOR PETER, THERE IS FORMED A SYNTHETIC ORGANIZATION OF ALL THE OBJECTS IN THE CAFE, AS THE GROUND ON WHICH PETER IS GIVEN AS ABOUT TO APPEAR."
"I AM WITNESS TO THE SUCCESSIVE DISAPPEARANCE OF ALL THE OBJECTS WHICH I LOOK AT--IN PARTICULAR OF THE FACES, WHICH DETAIN ME FOR AN INSTANT (COULD THIS BE PETER)?"
SO A CAFE IS NEVER "OBJECTIVELY" JUST A CAFE! IN THIS INSTANCE, IT HAS BEEN CONSTRUCTED BY SARTRE'S CONSCIOUSNESS AS "THE SPACE WHERE PETER COULD BE"!
DESCARTES' ERROR WAS TO THINK OF CONSCIOUSNESS AS SOMEHOW TRANSCENDENT FROM REALITY, LOOKING DOWN ON IT!
NO
YES
BUT REALLY, YOU EXIST WITHIN THE WORLD, AND IT IS ONLY THROUGH YOUR CONSCIOUSNESS THAT YOU CAN MAKE ANY SENSE OF THE WORLD AT ALL!
STILL NOT CONVINCED? TAKE THE EXAMPLE OF A CUBE.
EVERY SCHOOLCHILD KNOWS THAT A CUBE, TO BE A CUBE, MUST HAVE SIX SIDES.
BUT WHY? YOU'VE NEVER SEEN A CUBE WITH SIX SIDES. YOU CAN ONLY SEE (OR DRAW) THREE SIDES AT A TIME!
ONE... TWO... CRAP!!
FOR A CUBE TO EXIST AS A PROPER WHOLE IN YOUR MIND, YOUR ABSTRACT IMAGINATION MUST CONSTRUCT IT!
I CALL IT "CUBIST CUBE!"
YOU SHOULD HAVE JUST CALLED IT "SUCK."

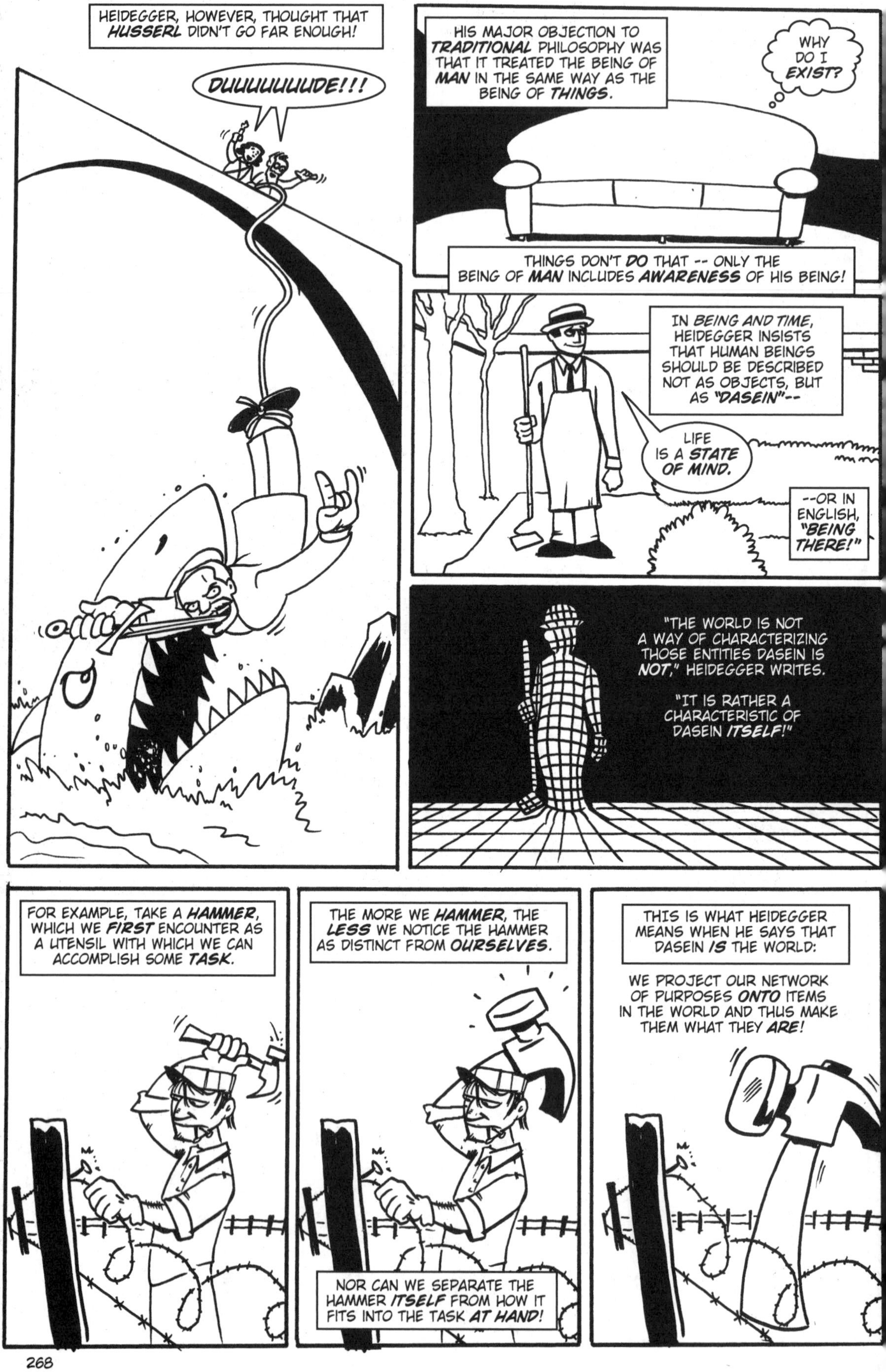
HEIDEGGER, HOWEVER, THOUGHT THAT **HUSSERL** DIDN'T GO FAR ENOUGH!
DUUUUUUUDE!!!
HIS MAJOR OBJECTION TO **TRADITIONAL** PHILOSOPHY WAS THAT IT TREATED THE BEING OF **MAN** IN THE SAME WAY AS THE BEING OF **THINGS**.
WHY DO I **EXIST?**
THINGS DON'T **DO** THAT -- ONLY THE BEING OF **MAN** INCLUDES **AWARENESS** OF HIS BEING!
IN *BEING AND TIME*, HEIDEGGER INSISTS THAT HUMAN BEINGS SHOULD BE DESCRIBED NOT AS OBJECTS, BUT AS **"DASEIN"**--
LIFE IS A **STATE OF MIND.**
--OR IN ENGLISH, **"BEING THERE!"**
"THE WORLD IS NOT A WAY OF CHARACTERIZING THOSE ENTITIES DASEIN IS **NOT**," HEIDEGGER WRITES.
"IT IS RATHER A CHARACTERISTIC OF DASEIN **ITSELF!**"
FOR EXAMPLE, TAKE A **HAMMER**, WHICH WE **FIRST** ENCOUNTER AS A UTENSIL WITH WHICH WE CAN ACCOMPLISH SOME **TASK**.
THE MORE WE **HAMMER**, THE **LESS** WE NOTICE THE HAMMER AS DISTINCT FROM **OURSELVES**.
NOR CAN WE SEPARATE THE HAMMER **ITSELF** FROM HOW IT FITS INTO THE TASK **AT HAND!**
THIS IS WHAT HEIDEGGER MEANS WHEN HE SAYS THAT DASEIN **IS** THE WORLD:
WE PROJECT OUR NETWORK OF PURPOSES **ONTO** ITEMS IN THE WORLD AND THUS MAKE THEM WHAT THEY **ARE!**

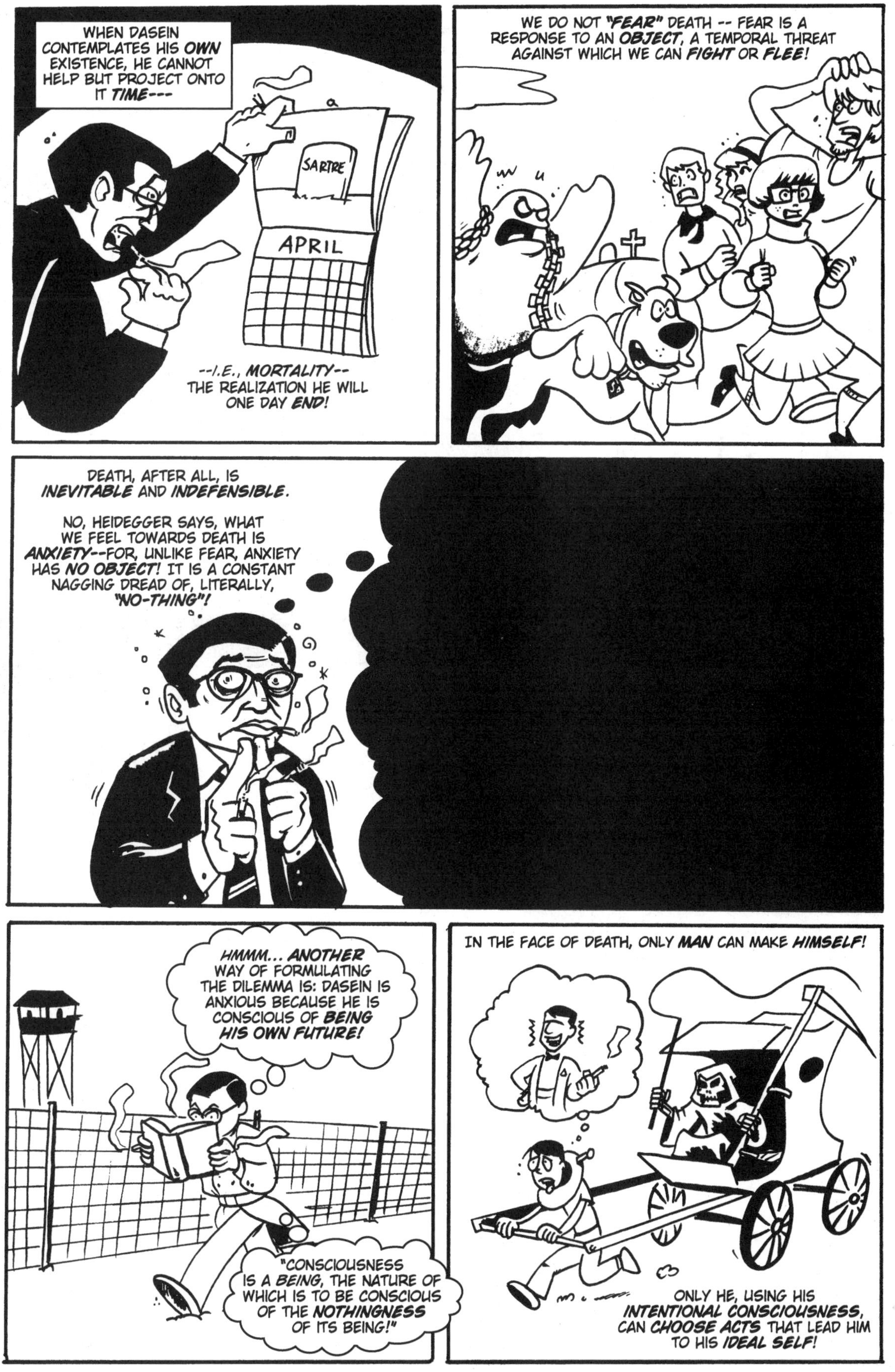
WHEN DASEIN CONTEMPLATES HIS OWN EXISTENCE, HE CANNOT HELP BUT PROJECT ONTO IT TIME---
SARTRE
APRIL
--I.E., MORTALITY-- THE REALIZATION HE WILL ONE DAY END!
WE DO NOT "FEAR" DEATH -- FEAR IS A RESPONSE TO AN OBJECT, A TEMPORAL THREAT AGAINST WHICH WE CAN FIGHT OR FLEE!
DEATH, AFTER ALL, IS INEVITABLE AND INDEFENSIBLE.
NO, HEIDEGGER SAYS, WHAT WE FEEL TOWARDS DEATH IS ANXIETY--FOR, UNLIKE FEAR, ANXIETY HAS NO OBJECT! IT IS A CONSTANT NAGGING DREAD OF, LITERALLY, "NO-THING"!
HMMM... ANOTHER WAY OF FORMULATING THE DILEMMA IS: DASEIN IS ANXIOUS BECAUSE HE IS CONSCIOUS OF BEING HIS OWN FUTURE!
"CONSCIOUSNESS IS A BEING, THE NATURE OF WHICH IS TO BE CONSCIOUS OF THE NOTHINGNESS OF ITS BEING!"
IN THE FACE OF DEATH, ONLY MAN CAN MAKE HIMSELF!
ONLY HE, USING HIS INTENTIONAL CONSCIOUSNESS, CAN CHOOSE ACTS THAT LEAD HIM TO HIS IDEAL SELF!

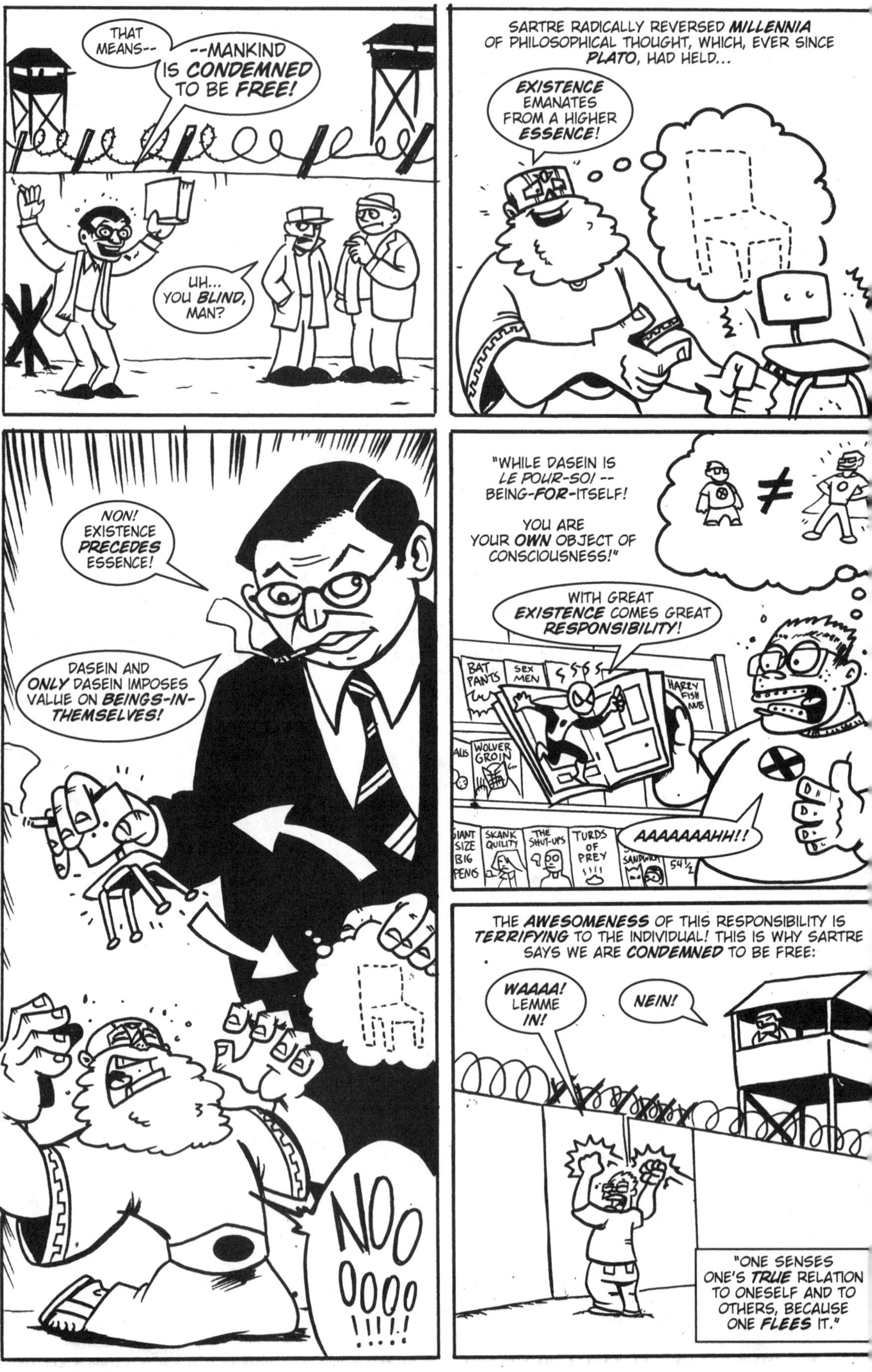
THAT MEANS--
--MANKIND IS CONDEMNED TO BE FREE!
UH... YOU BLIND, MAN?
SARTRE RADICALLY REVERSED MILLENNIA OF PHILOSOPHICAL THOUGHT, WHICH, EVER SINCE PLATO, HAD HELD...
EXISTENCE EMANATES FROM A HIGHER ESSENCE!
NON! EXISTENCE PRECEDES ESSENCE!
DASEIN AND ONLY DASEIN IMPOSES VALUE ON BEINGS-IN-THEMSELVES!
NOOOOOO!!!!!
"WHILE DASEIN IS LE POUR-SOI -- BEING-FOR-ITSELF!
YOU ARE YOUR OWN OBJECT OF CONSCIOUSNESS!"
WITH GREAT EXISTENCE COMES GREAT RESPONSIBILITY!
BAT PANTS
SEX MEN
HARRY FISH NUB
WOLVER GROIN
GIANT SIZE BIG PENIS
SKANK QUILITY
THE SHUT-UPS
TURDS OF PREY
54½
AAAAAAAHH!!
THE AWESOMENESS OF THIS RESPONSIBILITY IS TERRIFYING TO THE INDIVIDUAL! THIS IS WHY SARTRE SAYS WE ARE CONDEMNED TO BE FREE:
WAAAA! LEMME IN!
NEIN!
"ONE SENSES ONE'S TRUE RELATION TO ONESELF AND TO OTHERS, BECAUSE ONE FLEES IT."

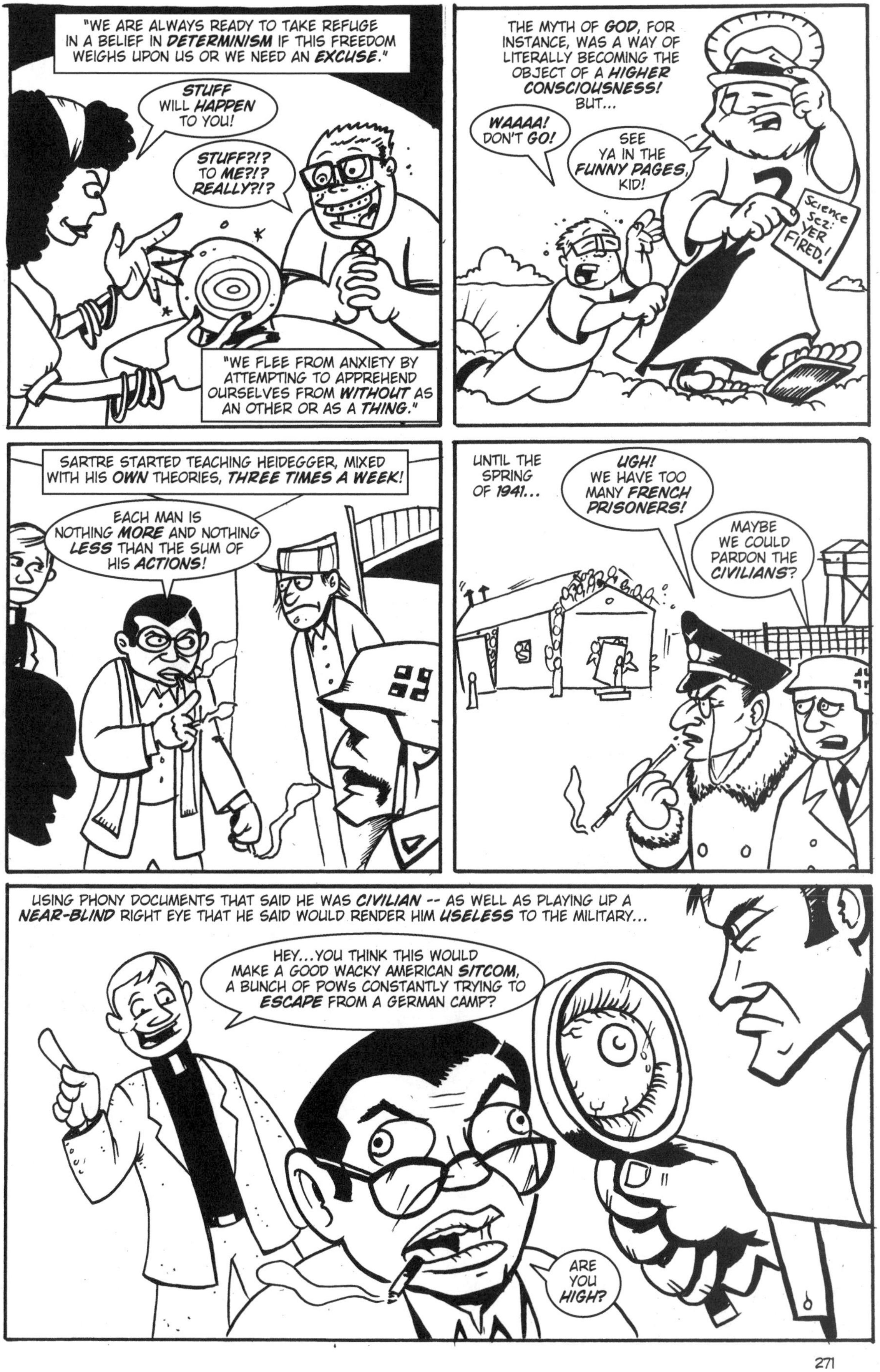
"WE ARE ALWAYS READY TO TAKE REFUGE IN A BELIEF IN DETERMINISM IF THIS FREEDOM WEIGHS UPON US OR WE NEED AN EXCUSE."
STUFF WILL HAPPEN TO YOU!
STUFF?!? TO ME?!? REALLY?!?
"WE FLEE FROM ANXIETY BY ATTEMPTING TO APPREHEND OURSELVES FROM WITHOUT AS AN OTHER OR AS A THING."
THE MYTH OF GOD, FOR INSTANCE, WAS A WAY OF LITERALLY BECOMING THE OBJECT OF A HIGHER CONSCIOUSNESS! BUT...
WAAAA! DON'T GO!
SEE YA IN THE FUNNY PAGES, KID!
Science Sez: YER FIRED!
SARTRE STARTED TEACHING HEIDEGGER, MIXED WITH HIS OWN THEORIES, THREE TIMES A WEEK!
EACH MAN IS NOTHING MORE AND NOTHING LESS THAN THE SUM OF HIS ACTIONS!
UNTIL THE SPRING OF 1941...
UGH! WE HAVE TOO MANY FRENCH PRISONERS!
MAYBE WE COULD PARDON THE CIVILIANS?
USING PHONY DOCUMENTS THAT SAID HE WAS CIVILIAN -- AS WELL AS PLAYING UP A NEAR-BLIND RIGHT EYE THAT HE SAID WOULD RENDER HIM USELESS TO THE MILITARY...
HEY...YOU THINK THIS WOULD MAKE A GOOD WACKY AMERICAN SITCOM, A BUNCH OF POWS CONSTANTLY TRYING TO ESCAPE FROM A GERMAN CAMP?
ARE YOU HIGH?

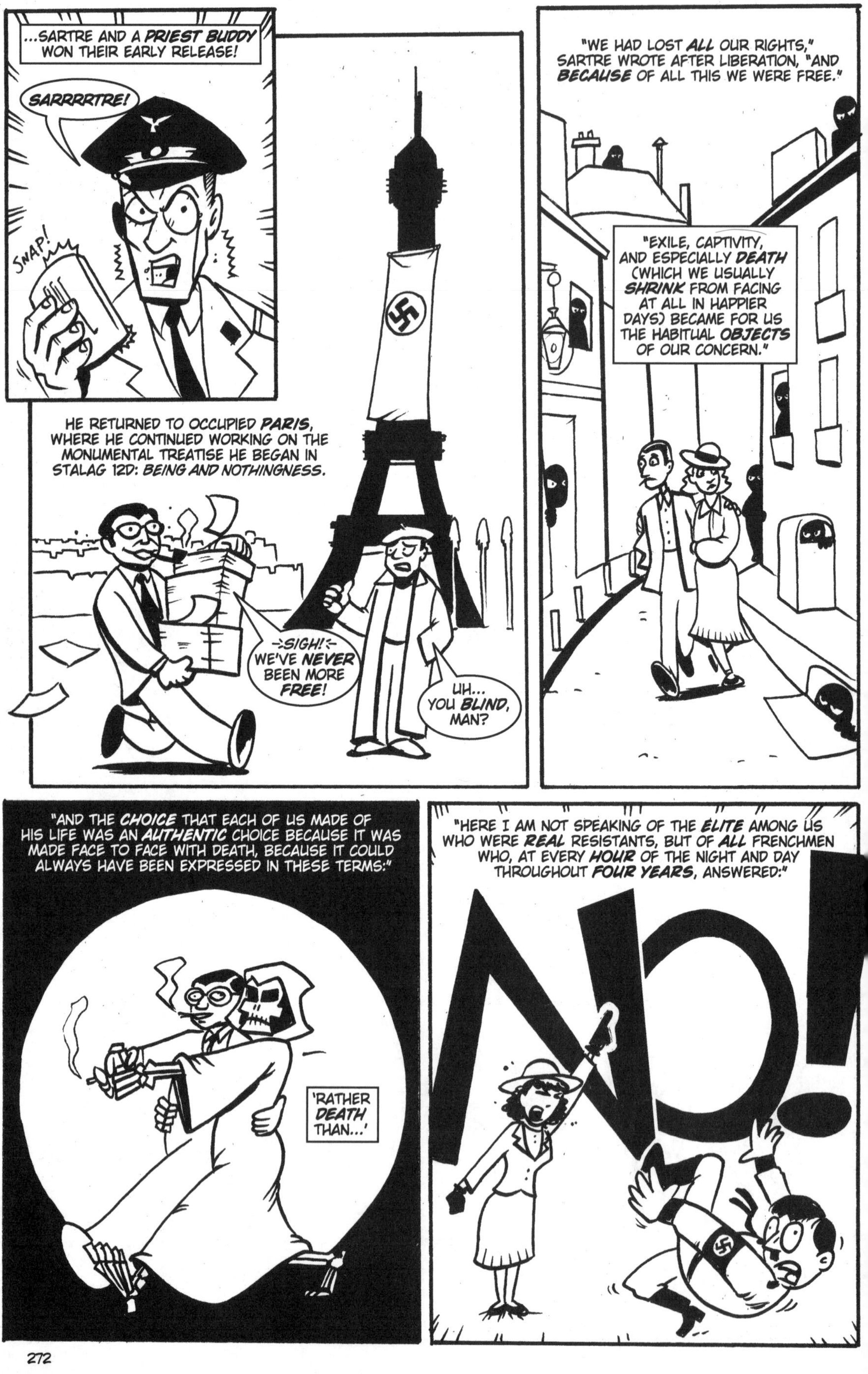

...SARTRE AND A PRIEST BUDDY WON THEIR EARLY RELEASE!
SARRRRTRE!
SNAP!
HE RETURNED TO OCCUPIED PARIS, WHERE HE CONTINUED WORKING ON THE MONUMENTAL TREATISE HE BEGAN IN STALAG 12D: BEING AND NOTHINGNESS.
SIGH! WE'VE NEVER BEEN MORE FREE!
UH... YOU BLIND, MAN?
"WE HAD LOST ALL OUR RIGHTS," SARTRE WROTE AFTER LIBERATION, "AND BECAUSE OF ALL THIS WE WERE FREE."
"EXILE, CAPTIVITY, AND ESPECIALLY DEATH (WHICH WE USUALLY SHRINK FROM FACING AT ALL IN HAPPIER DAYS) BECAME FOR US THE HABITUAL OBJECTS OF OUR CONCERN."
"AND THE CHOICE THAT EACH OF US MADE OF HIS LIFE WAS AN AUTHENTIC CHOICE BECAUSE IT WAS MADE FACE TO FACE WITH DEATH, BECAUSE IT COULD ALWAYS HAVE BEEN EXPRESSED IN THESE TERMS:"
'RATHER DEATH THAN...'
"HERE I AM NOT SPEAKING OF THE ELITE AMONG US WHO WERE REAL RESISTANTS, BUT OF ALL FRENCHMEN WHO, AT EVERY HOUR OF THE NIGHT AND DAY THROUGHOUT FOUR YEARS, ANSWERED:"
NO!

THOUGH IT'S FREQUENTLY ASSERTED THAT SARTRE WAS A MEMBER OF THE ***ARMED*** FRENCH RESISTANCE, THAT'S NOT TRUE.

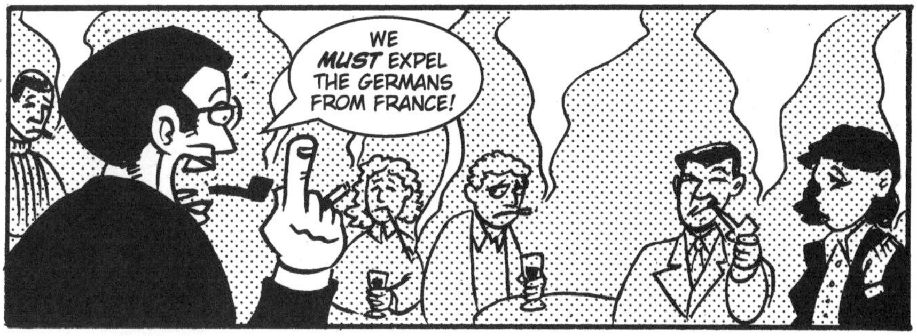
WE MUST EXPEL THE GERMANS FROM FRANCE!

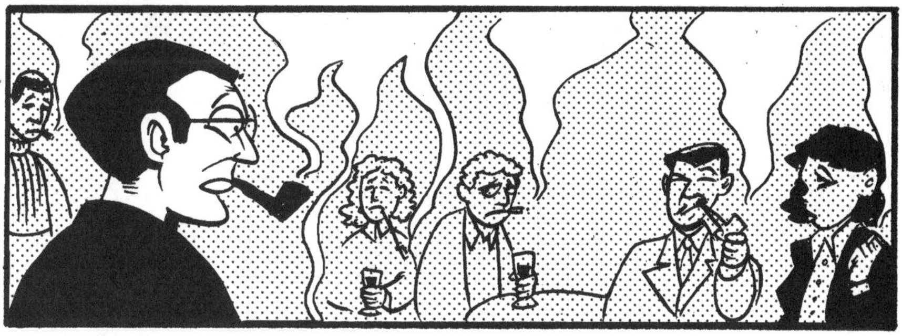

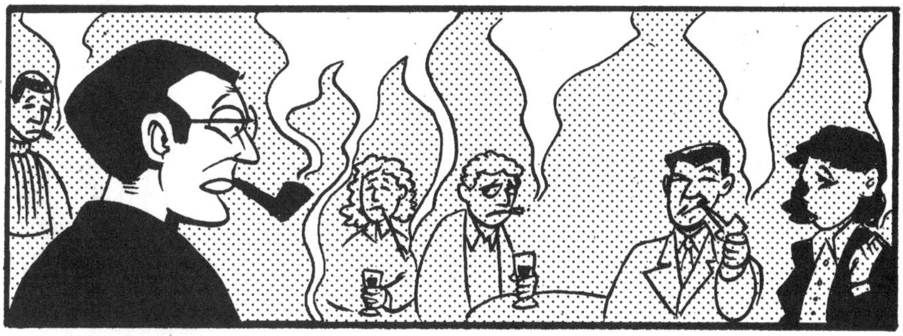

HIS OWN "NO" TOOK EFFECT ON THE ***STAGE.*** HE HAD WRITTEN A ***CHRISTMAS PAGEANT*** FOR STALAG 12D AND DISCOVERED HE ENJOYED ***PLAYWRITING.***

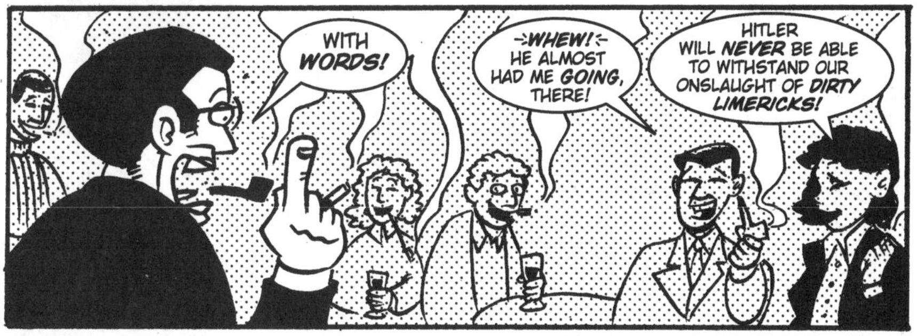
WITH WORDS!
WHEW! HE ALMOST HAD ME GOING, THERE!
HITLER WILL NEVER BE ABLE TO WITHSTAND OUR ONSLAUGHT OF DIRTY LIMERICKS!

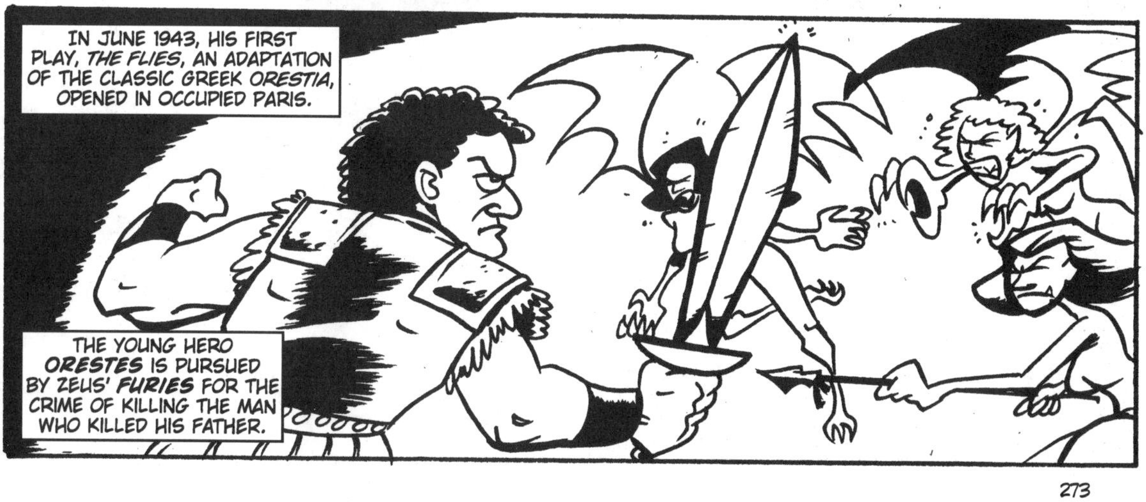
IN JUNE 1943, HIS FIRST PLAY, THE FLIES, AN ADAPTATION OF THE CLASSIC GREEK ORESTIA, OPENED IN OCCUPIED PARIS.
THE YOUNG HERO ORESTES IS PURSUED BY ZEUS' FURIES FOR THE CRIME OF KILLING THE MAN WHO KILLED HIS FATHER.

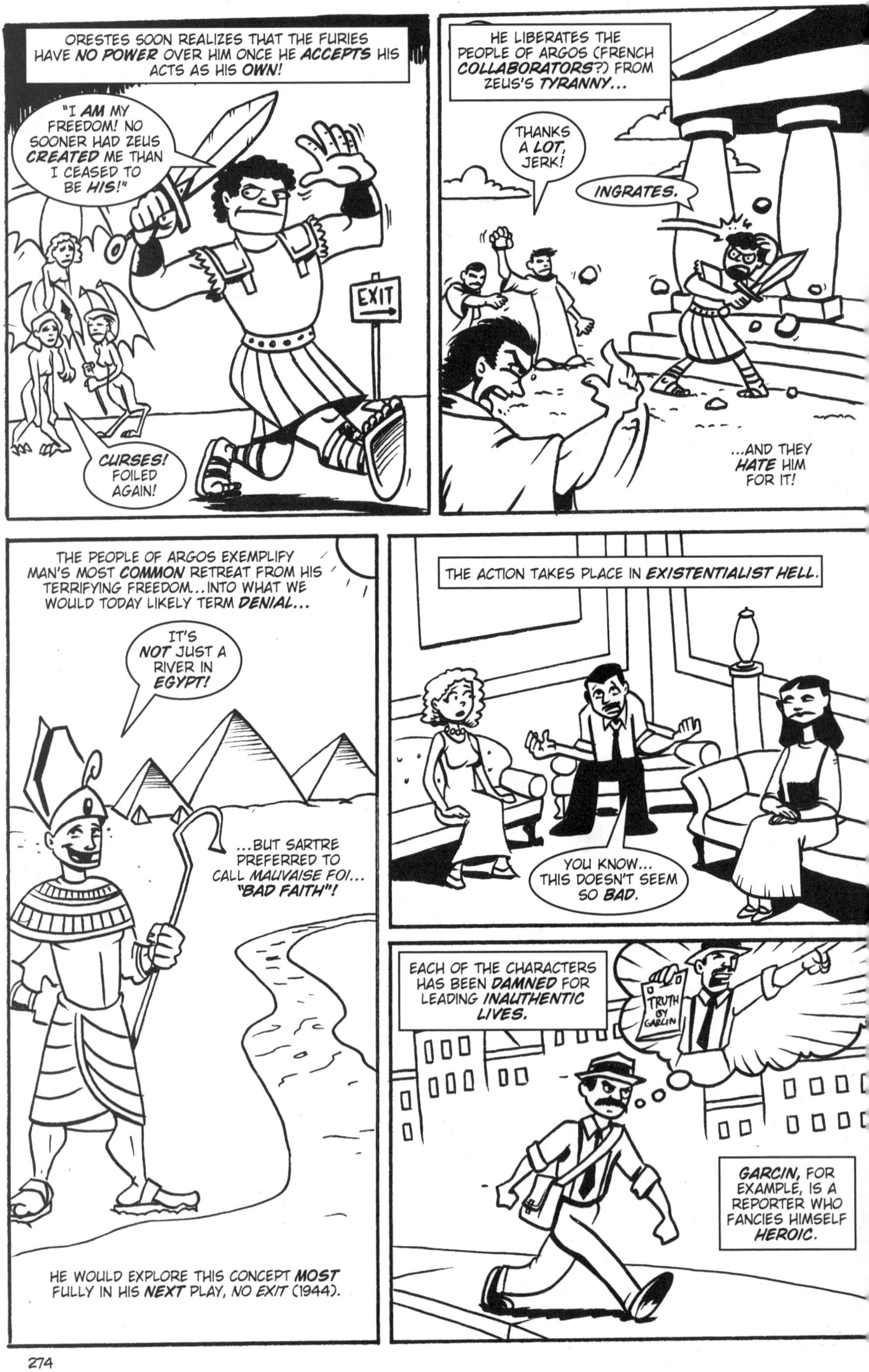
ORESTES SOON REALIZES THAT THE FURIES HAVE **NO POWER** OVER HIM ONCE HE **ACCEPTS** HIS ACTS AS HIS **OWN**!
"I **AM** MY FREEDOM! NO SOONER HAD ZEUS **CREATED** ME THAN I CEASED TO BE **HIS**!"
EXIT
CURSES! FOILED AGAIN!
HE LIBERATES THE PEOPLE OF ARGOS (FRENCH **COLLABORATORS**?) FROM ZEUS'S **TYRANNY**...
THANKS A **LOT**, JERK!
INGRATES.
...AND THEY **HATE** HIM FOR IT!
THE PEOPLE OF ARGOS EXEMPLIFY MAN'S MOST **COMMON** RETREAT FROM HIS TERRIFYING FREEDOM...INTO WHAT WE WOULD TODAY LIKELY TERM **DENIAL**...
IT'S **NOT** JUST A RIVER IN **EGYPT**!
...BUT SARTRE PREFERRED TO CALL *MAUVAISE FOI*... **"BAD FAITH"**!
HE WOULD EXPLORE THIS CONCEPT **MOST** FULLY IN HIS **NEXT** PLAY, *NO EXIT* (1944).
THE ACTION TAKES PLACE IN **EXISTENTIALIST HELL**.
YOU KNOW... THIS DOESN'T SEEM SO **BAD**.
EACH OF THE CHARACTERS HAS BEEN **DAMNED** FOR LEADING **INAUTHENTIC LIVES**.
TRUTH BY GARCIN
GARCIN, FOR EXAMPLE, IS A REPORTER WHO FANCIES HIMSELF **HEROIC**.

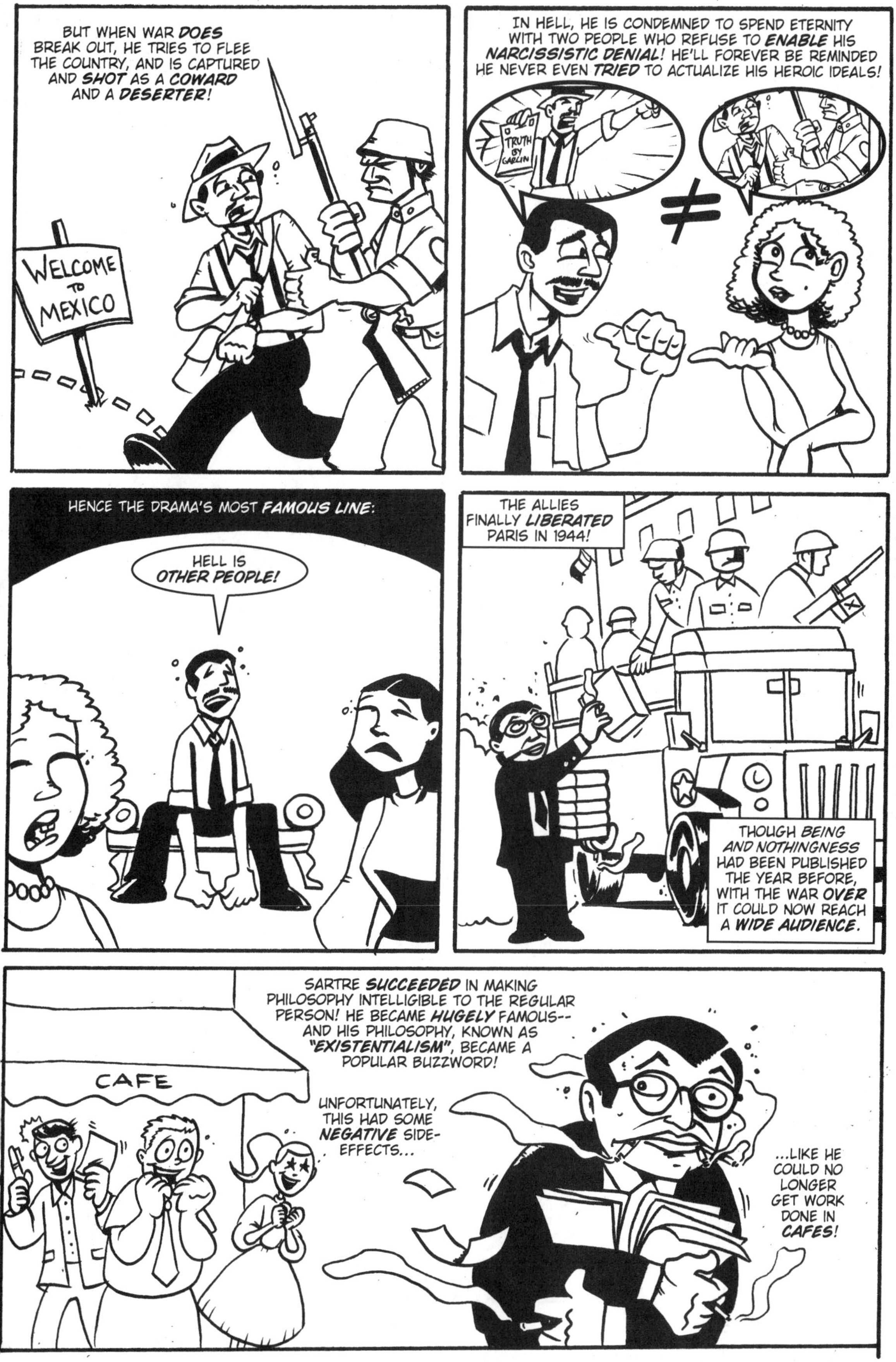
BUT WHEN WAR DOES BREAK OUT, HE TRIES TO FLEE THE COUNTRY, AND IS CAPTURED AND SHOT AS A COWARD AND A DESERTER!
WELCOME TO MEXICO
IN HELL, HE IS CONDEMNED TO SPEND ETERNITY WITH TWO PEOPLE WHO REFUSE TO ENABLE HIS NARCISSISTIC DENIAL! HE'LL FOREVER BE REMINDED HE NEVER EVEN TRIED TO ACTUALIZE HIS HEROIC IDEALS!
TRUTH BY GARCIN
≠
HENCE THE DRAMA'S MOST FAMOUS LINE:
HELL IS OTHER PEOPLE!
THE ALLIES FINALLY LIBERATED PARIS IN 1944!
THOUGH BEING AND NOTHINGNESS HAD BEEN PUBLISHED THE YEAR BEFORE, WITH THE WAR OVER IT COULD NOW REACH A WIDE AUDIENCE.
SARTRE SUCCEEDED IN MAKING PHILOSOPHY INTELLIGIBLE TO THE REGULAR PERSON! HE BECAME HUGELY FAMOUS-- AND HIS PHILOSOPHY, KNOWN AS "EXISTENTIALISM", BECAME A POPULAR BUZZWORD!
CAFE
UNFORTUNATELY, THIS HAD SOME NEGATIVE SIDE-EFFECTS...
...LIKE HE COULD NO LONGER GET WORK DONE IN CAFES!

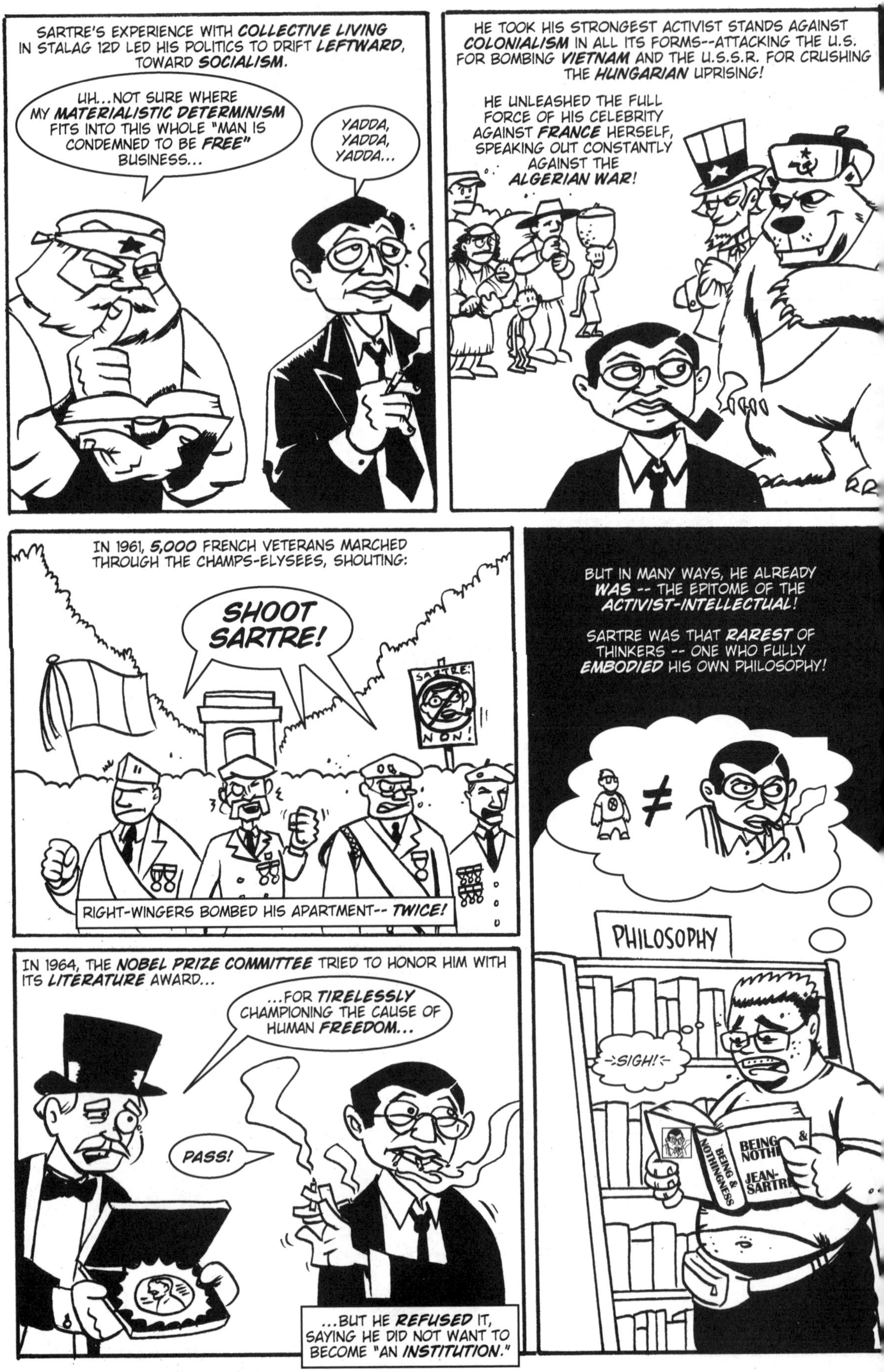
SARTRE'S EXPERIENCE WITH COLLECTIVE LIVING IN STALAG 12D LED HIS POLITICS TO DRIFT LEFTWARD, TOWARD SOCIALISM.
UH...NOT SURE WHERE MY MATERIALISTIC DETERMINISM FITS INTO THIS WHOLE "MAN IS CONDEMNED TO BE FREE" BUSINESS...
YADDA, YADDA, YADDA...
HE TOOK HIS STRONGEST ACTIVIST STANDS AGAINST COLONIALISM IN ALL ITS FORMS--ATTACKING THE U.S. FOR BOMBING VIETNAM AND THE U.S.S.R. FOR CRUSHING THE HUNGARIAN UPRISING!
HE UNLEASHED THE FULL FORCE OF HIS CELEBRITY AGAINST FRANCE HERSELF, SPEAKING OUT CONSTANTLY AGAINST THE ALGERIAN WAR!
IN 1961, 5,000 FRENCH VETERANS MARCHED THROUGH THE CHAMPS-ELYSEES, SHOUTING:
SHOOT SARTRE!
SARTRE: NON!
RIGHT-WINGERS BOMBED HIS APARTMENT-- TWICE!
BUT IN MANY WAYS, HE ALREADY WAS -- THE EPITOME OF THE ACTIVIST-INTELLECTUAL!
SARTRE WAS THAT RAREST OF THINKERS -- ONE WHO FULLY EMBODIED HIS OWN PHILOSOPHY!
PHILOSOPHY
-SIGH!-
BEING & NOTHINGNESS
BEING & NOTHI
JEAN-SARTR
IN 1964, THE NOBEL PRIZE COMMITTEE TRIED TO HONOR HIM WITH ITS LITERATURE AWARD...
...FOR TIRELESSLY CHAMPIONING THE CAUSE OF HUMAN FREEDOM...
PASS!
...BUT HE REFUSED IT, SAYING HE DID NOT WANT TO BECOME "AN INSTITUTION."

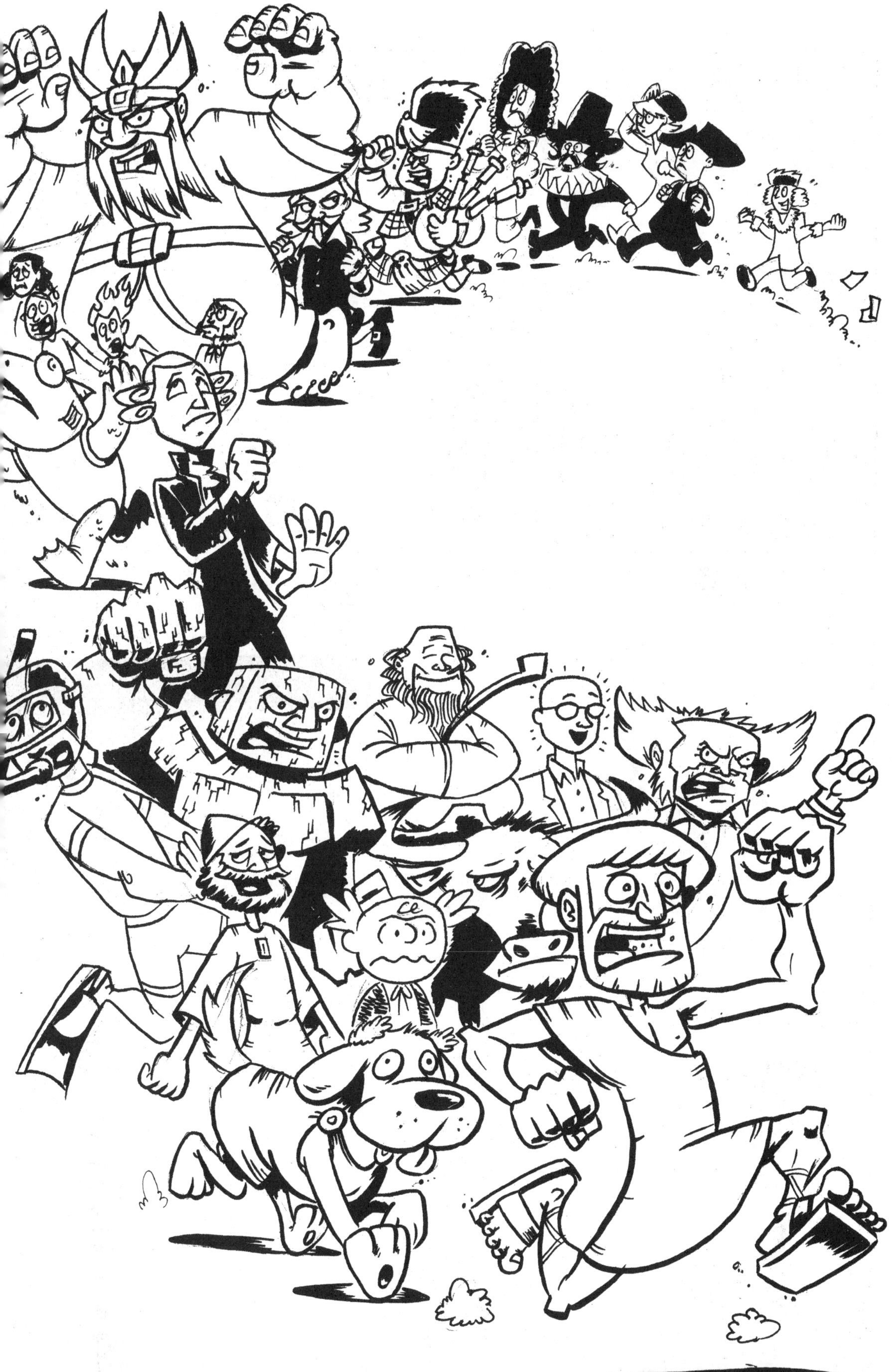

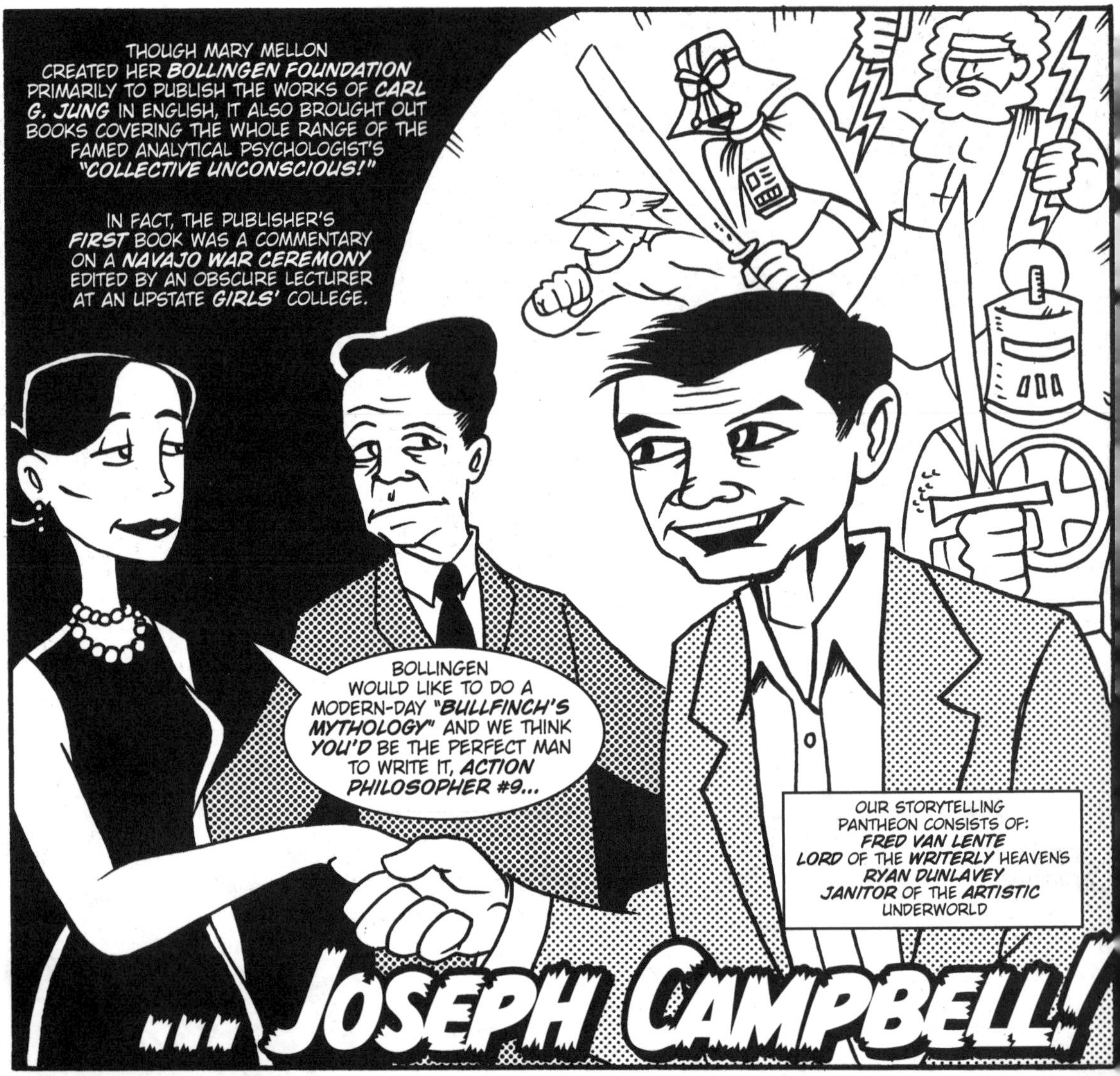
THOUGH MARY MELLON CREATED HER BOLLINGEN FOUNDATION PRIMARILY TO PUBLISH THE WORKS OF CARL G. JUNG IN ENGLISH, IT ALSO BROUGHT OUT BOOKS COVERING THE WHOLE RANGE OF THE FAMED ANALYTICAL PSYCHOLOGIST'S "COLLECTIVE UNCONSCIOUS!"
IN FACT, THE PUBLISHER'S FIRST BOOK WAS A COMMENTARY ON A NAVAJO WAR CEREMONY EDITED BY AN OBSCURE LECTURER AT AN UPSTATE GIRLS' COLLEGE.
BOLLINGEN WOULD LIKE TO DO A MODERN-DAY "BULLFINCH'S MYTHOLOGY" AND WE THINK YOU'D BE THE PERFECT MAN TO WRITE IT, ACTION PHILOSOPHER #9...
OUR STORYTELLING PANTHEON CONSISTS OF: FRED VAN LENTE LORD OF THE WRITERLY HEAVENS RYAN DUNLAVEY JANITOR OF THE ARTISTIC UNDERWORLD
...JOSEPH CAMPBELL!

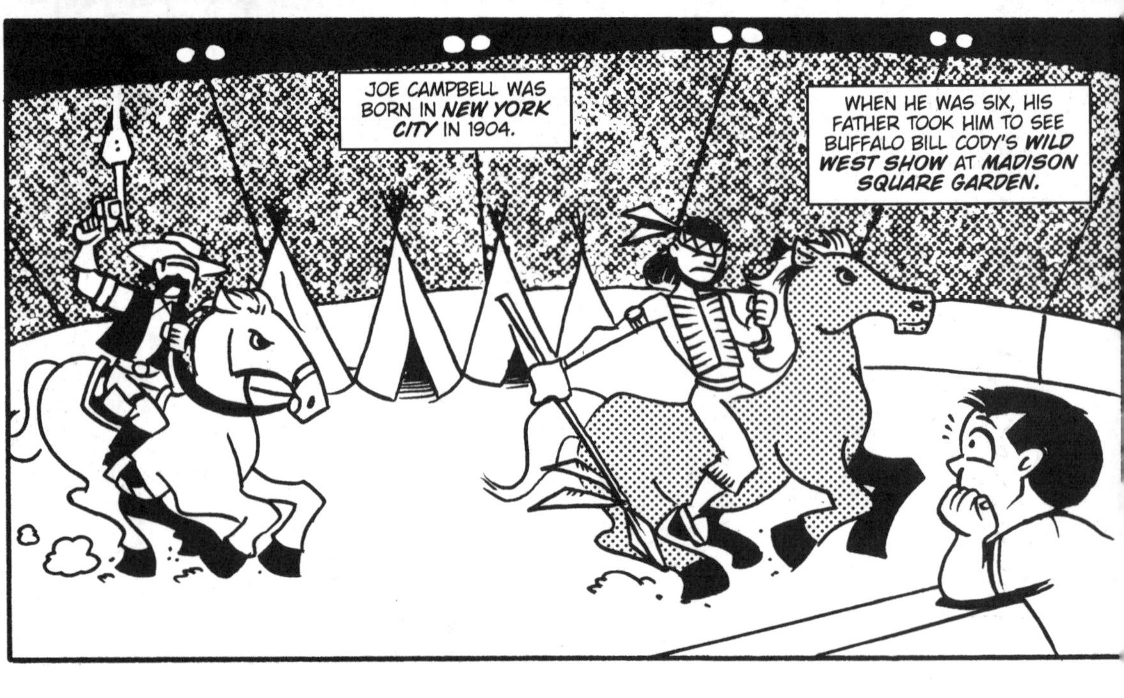
JOE CAMPBELL WAS BORN IN NEW YORK CITY IN 1904.
WHEN HE WAS SIX, HIS FATHER TOOK HIM TO SEE BUFFALO BILL CODY'S WILD WEST SHOW AT MADISON SQUARE GARDEN.

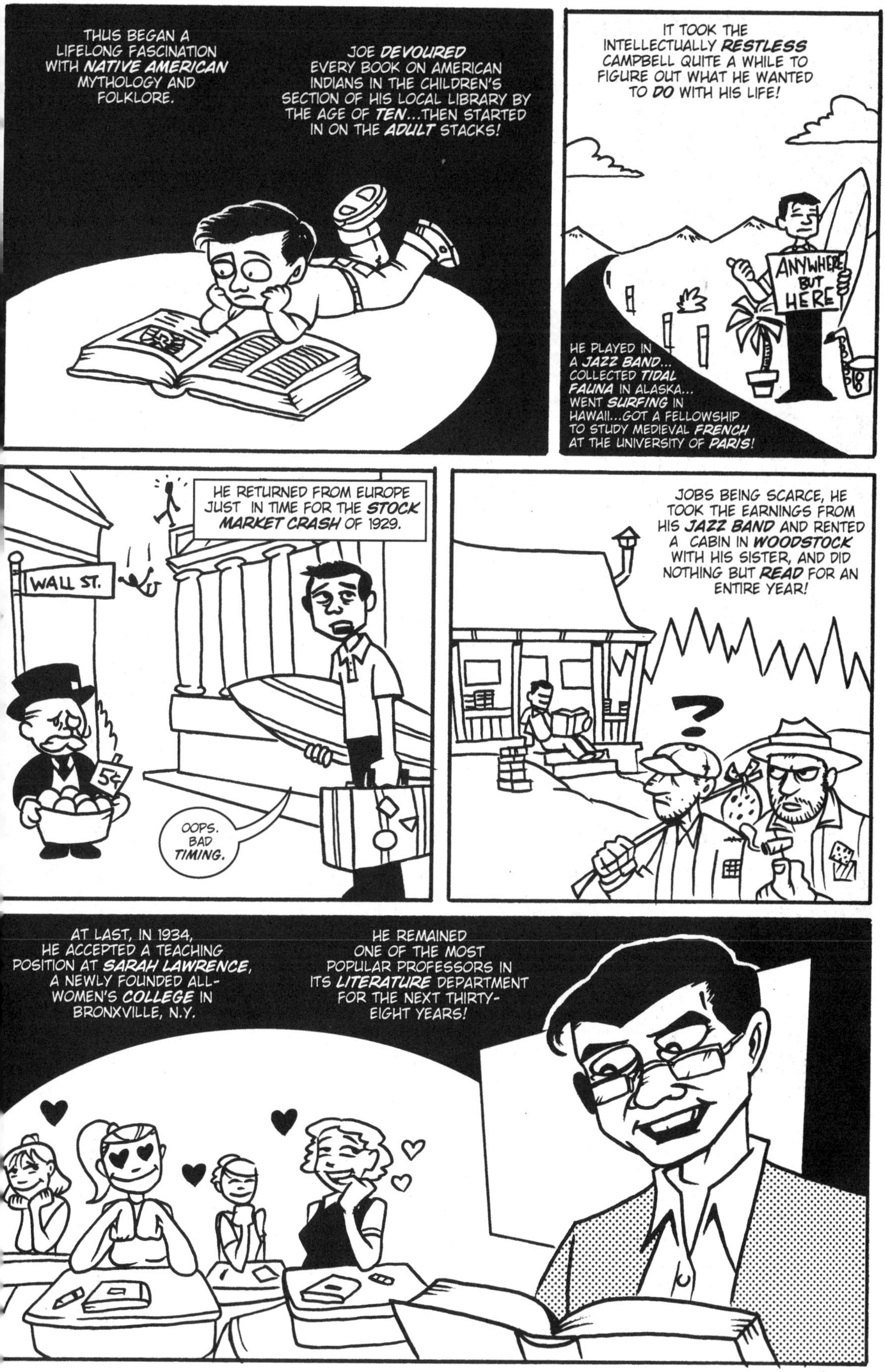
THUS BEGAN A LIFELONG FASCINATION WITH NATIVE AMERICAN MYTHOLOGY AND FOLKLORE.
JOE DEVOURED EVERY BOOK ON AMERICAN INDIANS IN THE CHILDREN'S SECTION OF HIS LOCAL LIBRARY BY THE AGE OF TEN...THEN STARTED IN ON THE ADULT STACKS!
IT TOOK THE INTELLECTUALLY RESTLESS CAMPBELL QUITE A WHILE TO FIGURE OUT WHAT HE WANTED TO DO WITH HIS LIFE!
ANYWHERE BUT HERE
HE PLAYED IN A JAZZ BAND... COLLECTED TIDAL FAUNA IN ALASKA... WENT SURFING IN HAWAII...GOT A FELLOWSHIP TO STUDY MEDIEVAL FRENCH AT THE UNIVERSITY OF PARIS!
HE RETURNED FROM EUROPE JUST IN TIME FOR THE STOCK MARKET CRASH OF 1929.
WALL ST.
5¢
OOPS. BAD TIMING.
JOBS BEING SCARCE, HE TOOK THE EARNINGS FROM HIS JAZZ BAND AND RENTED A CABIN IN WOODSTOCK WITH HIS SISTER, AND DID NOTHING BUT READ FOR AN ENTIRE YEAR!
?
AT LAST, IN 1934, HE ACCEPTED A TEACHING POSITION AT SARAH LAWRENCE, A NEWLY FOUNDED ALL-WOMEN'S COLLEGE IN BRONXVILLE, N.Y.
HE REMAINED ONE OF THE MOST POPULAR PROFESSORS IN ITS LITERATURE DEPARTMENT FOR THE NEXT THIRTY-EIGHT YEARS!

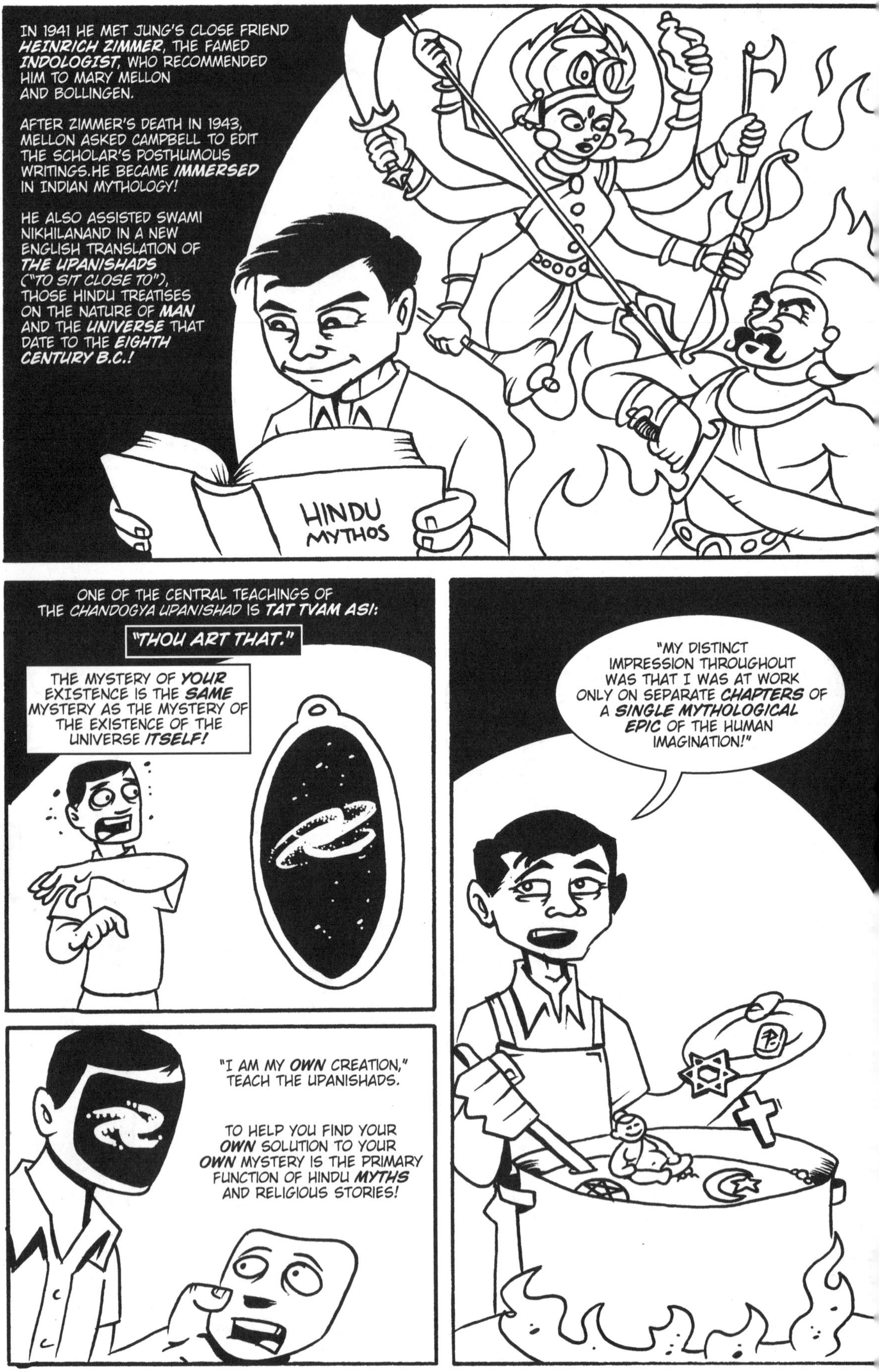
IN 1941 HE MET JUNG'S CLOSE FRIEND HEINRICH ZIMMER, THE FAMED INDOLOGIST, WHO RECOMMENDED HIM TO MARY MELLON AND BOLLINGEN.
AFTER ZIMMER'S DEATH IN 1943, MELLON ASKED CAMPBELL TO EDIT THE SCHOLAR'S POSTHUMOUS WRITINGS.HE BECAME IMMERSED IN INDIAN MYTHOLOGY!
HE ALSO ASSISTED SWAMI NIKHILANAND IN A NEW ENGLISH TRANSLATION OF THE UPANISHADS ("TO SIT CLOSE TO"), THOSE HINDU TREATISES ON THE NATURE OF MAN AND THE UNIVERSE THAT DATE TO THE EIGHTH CENTURY B.C.!
HINDU MYTHOS
ONE OF THE CENTRAL TEACHINGS OF THE CHANDOGYA UPANISHAD IS TAT TVAM ASI:
"THOU ART THAT."
THE MYSTERY OF YOUR EXISTENCE IS THE SAME MYSTERY AS THE MYSTERY OF THE EXISTENCE OF THE UNIVERSE ITSELF!
"MY DISTINCT IMPRESSION THROUGHOUT WAS THAT I WAS AT WORK ONLY ON SEPARATE CHAPTERS OF A SINGLE MYTHOLOGICAL EPIC OF THE HUMAN IMAGINATION!"
"I AM MY OWN CREATION," TEACH THE UPANISHADS.
TO HELP YOU FIND YOUR OWN SOLUTION TO YOUR OWN MYSTERY IS THE PRIMARY FUNCTION OF HINDU MYTHS AND RELIGIOUS STORIES!

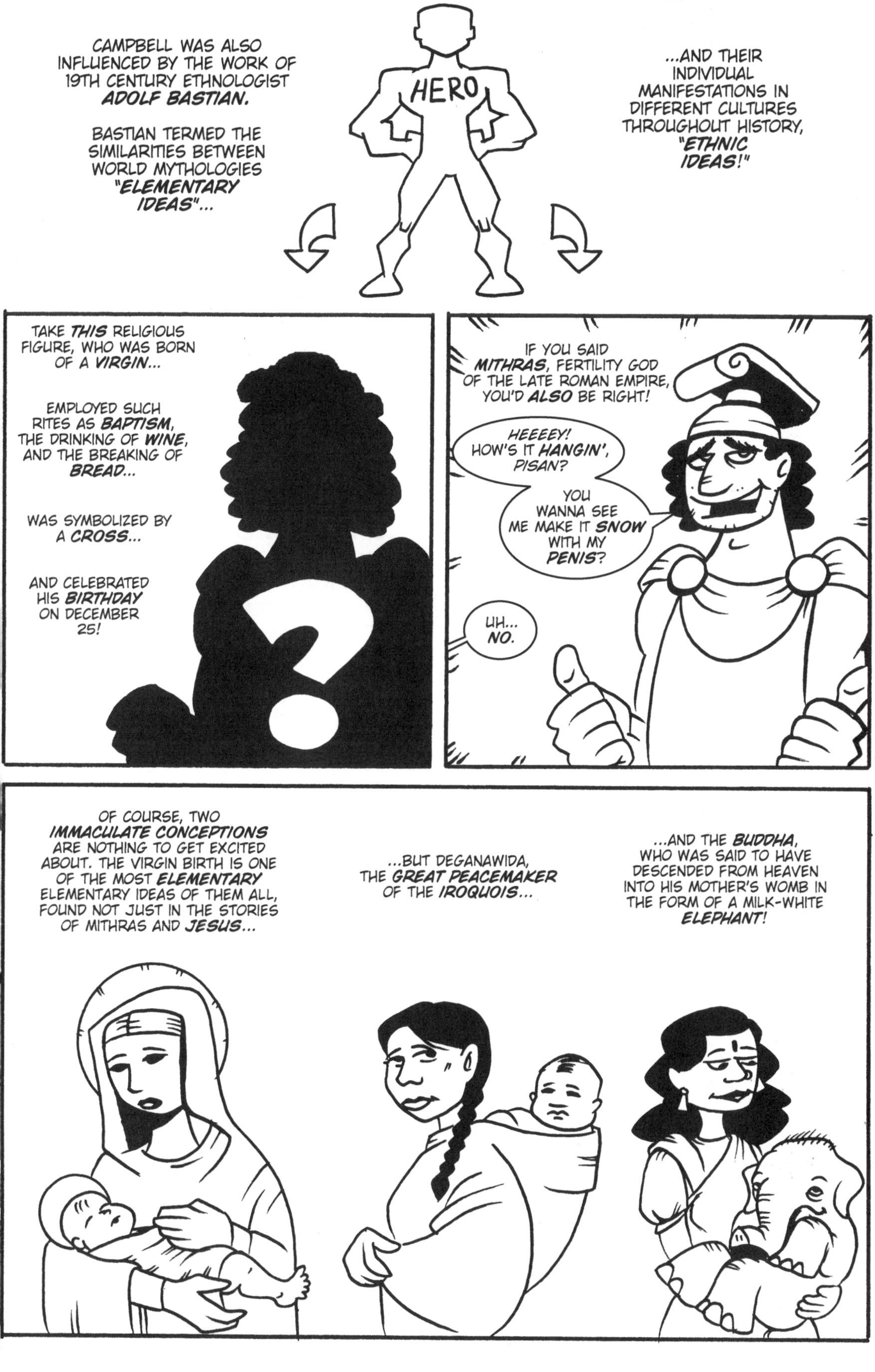
CAMPBELL WAS ALSO INFLUENCED BY THE WORK OF 19TH CENTURY ETHNOLOGIST ADOLF BASTIAN.
BASTIAN TERMED THE SIMILARITIES BETWEEN WORLD MYTHOLOGIES "ELEMENTARY IDEAS"...
HERO
...AND THEIR INDIVIDUAL MANIFESTATIONS IN DIFFERENT CULTURES THROUGHOUT HISTORY, "ETHNIC IDEAS!"
TAKE THIS RELIGIOUS FIGURE, WHO WAS BORN OF A VIRGIN...
EMPLOYED SUCH RITES AS BAPTISM, THE DRINKING OF WINE, AND THE BREAKING OF BREAD...
WAS SYMBOLIZED BY A CROSS...
AND CELEBRATED HIS BIRTHDAY ON DECEMBER 25!
IF YOU SAID MITHRAS, FERTILITY GOD OF THE LATE ROMAN EMPIRE, YOU'D ALSO BE RIGHT!
HEEEEY! HOW'S IT HANGIN', PISAN?
YOU WANNA SEE ME MAKE IT SNOW WITH MY PENIS?
UH... NO.
OF COURSE, TWO IMMACULATE CONCEPTIONS ARE NOTHING TO GET EXCITED ABOUT. THE VIRGIN BIRTH IS ONE OF THE MOST ELEMENTARY ELEMENTARY IDEAS OF THEM ALL, FOUND NOT JUST IN THE STORIES OF MITHRAS AND JESUS...
...BUT DEGANAWIDA, THE GREAT PEACEMAKER OF THE IROQUOIS...
...AND THE BUDDHA, WHO WAS SAID TO HAVE DESCENDED FROM HEAVEN INTO HIS MOTHER'S WOMB IN THE FORM OF A MILK-WHITE ELEPHANT!

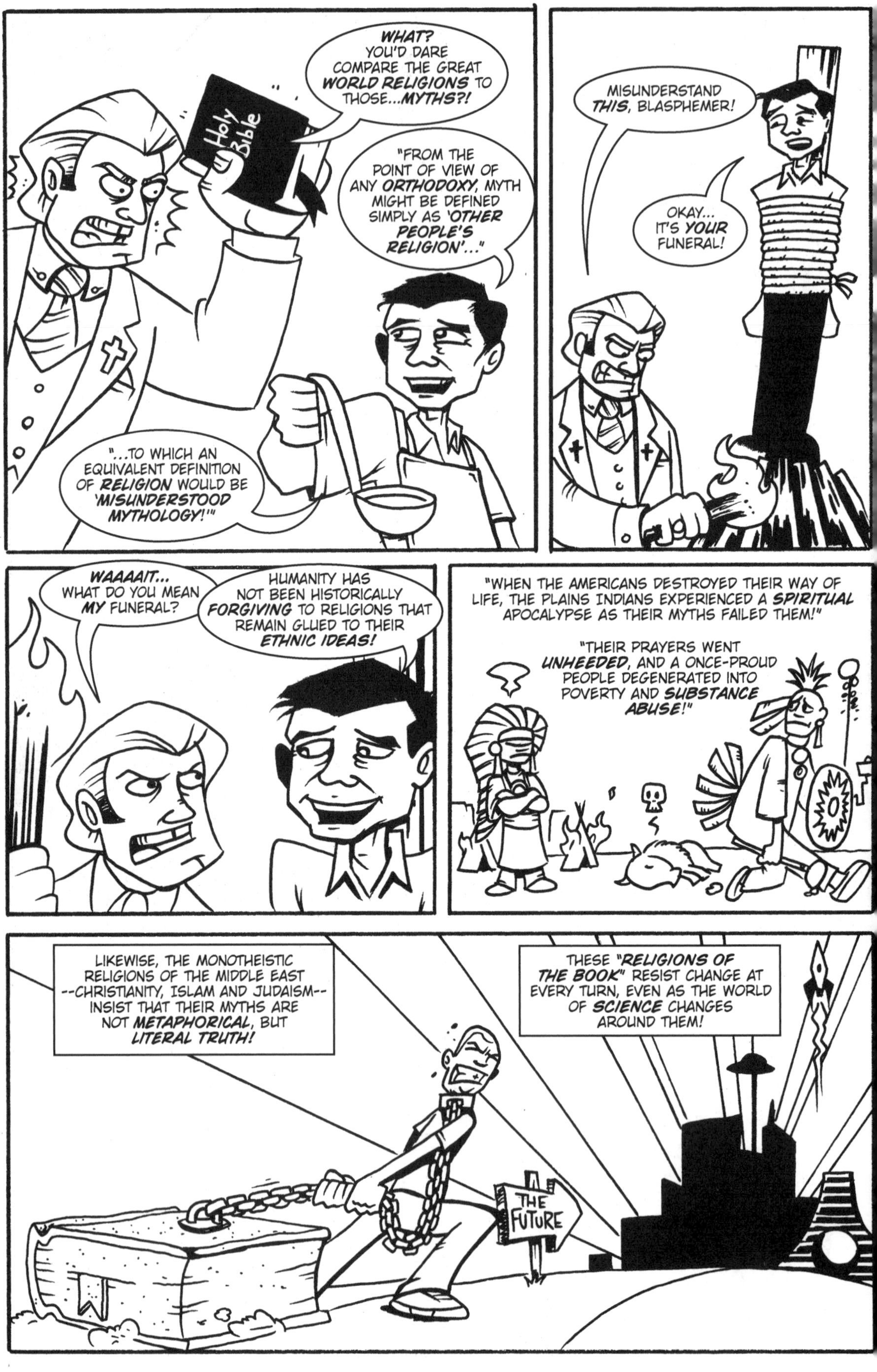
WHAT? YOU'D DARE COMPARE THE GREAT WORLD RELIGIONS TO THOSE...MYTHS?!
Holy Bible
"FROM THE POINT OF VIEW OF ANY ORTHODOXY, MYTH MIGHT BE DEFINED SIMPLY AS 'OTHER PEOPLE'S RELIGION'..."
"...TO WHICH AN EQUIVALENT DEFINITION OF RELIGION WOULD BE 'MISUNDERSTOOD MYTHOLOGY!'"
MISUNDERSTAND THIS, BLASPHEMER!
OKAY... IT'S YOUR FUNERAL!
WAAAAIT... WHAT DO YOU MEAN MY FUNERAL?
HUMANITY HAS NOT BEEN HISTORICALLY FORGIVING TO RELIGIONS THAT REMAIN GLUED TO THEIR ETHNIC IDEAS!
"WHEN THE AMERICANS DESTROYED THEIR WAY OF LIFE, THE PLAINS INDIANS EXPERIENCED A SPIRITUAL APOCALYPSE AS THEIR MYTHS FAILED THEM!"
"THEIR PRAYERS WENT UNHEEDED, AND A ONCE-PROUD PEOPLE DEGENERATED INTO POVERTY AND SUBSTANCE ABUSE!"
LIKEWISE, THE MONOTHEISTIC RELIGIONS OF THE MIDDLE EAST --CHRISTIANITY, ISLAM AND JUDAISM-- INSIST THAT THEIR MYTHS ARE NOT METAPHORICAL, BUT LITERAL TRUTH!
THESE "RELIGIONS OF THE BOOK" RESIST CHANGE AT EVERY TURN, EVEN AS THE WORLD OF SCIENCE CHANGES AROUND THEM!
THE FUTURE

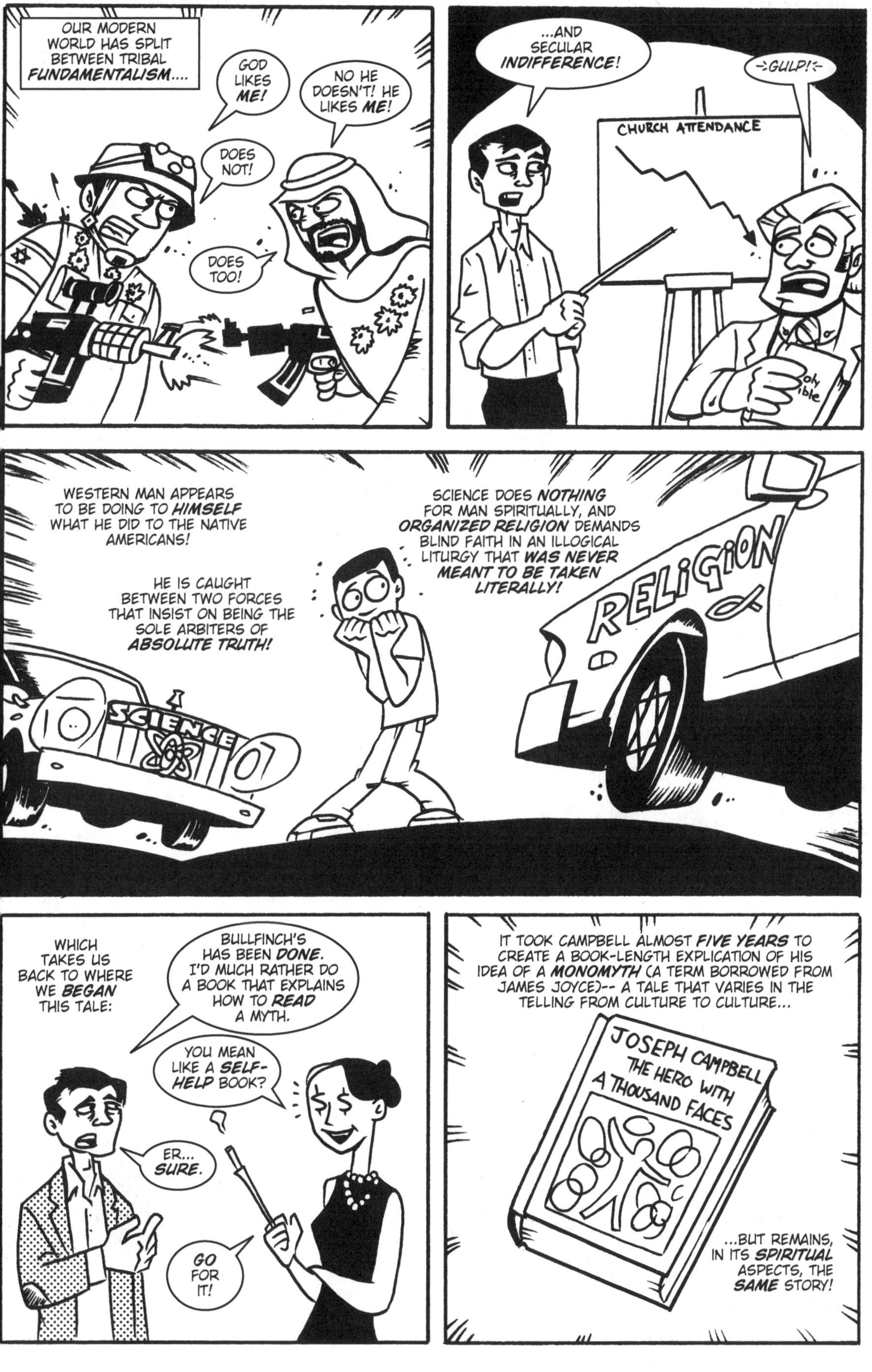
OUR MODERN WORLD HAS SPLIT BETWEEN TRIBAL **FUNDAMENTALISM**....
GOD LIKES **ME!**
NO HE DOESN'T! HE LIKES **ME!**
DOES NOT!
DOES TOO!
...AND SECULAR **INDIFFERENCE!**
CHURCH ATTENDANCE
-GULP!-
WESTERN MAN APPEARS TO BE DOING TO **HIMSELF** WHAT HE DID TO THE NATIVE AMERICANS!
HE IS CAUGHT BETWEEN TWO FORCES THAT INSIST ON BEING THE SOLE ARBITERS OF **ABSOLUTE TRUTH!**
SCIENCE DOES **NOTHING** FOR MAN SPIRITUALLY, AND **ORGANIZED RELIGION** DEMANDS BLIND FAITH IN AN ILLOGICAL LITURGY THAT **WAS NEVER MEANT TO BE TAKEN LITERALLY!**
SCIENCE
RELIGION
WHICH TAKES US BACK TO WHERE WE **BEGAN** THIS TALE:
BULLFINCH'S HAS BEEN **DONE.** I'D MUCH RATHER DO A BOOK THAT EXPLAINS HOW TO **READ** A MYTH.
YOU MEAN LIKE A **SELF-HELP** BOOK?
ER... **SURE.**
GO FOR IT!
IT TOOK CAMPBELL ALMOST **FIVE YEARS** TO CREATE A BOOK-LENGTH EXPLICATION OF HIS IDEA OF A **MONOMYTH** (A TERM BORROWED FROM JAMES JOYCE)-- A TALE THAT VARIES IN THE TELLING FROM CULTURE TO CULTURE...
JOSEPH CAMPBELL THE HERO WITH A THOUSAND FACES
...BUT REMAINS, IN ITS **SPIRITUAL** ASPECTS, THE **SAME** STORY!

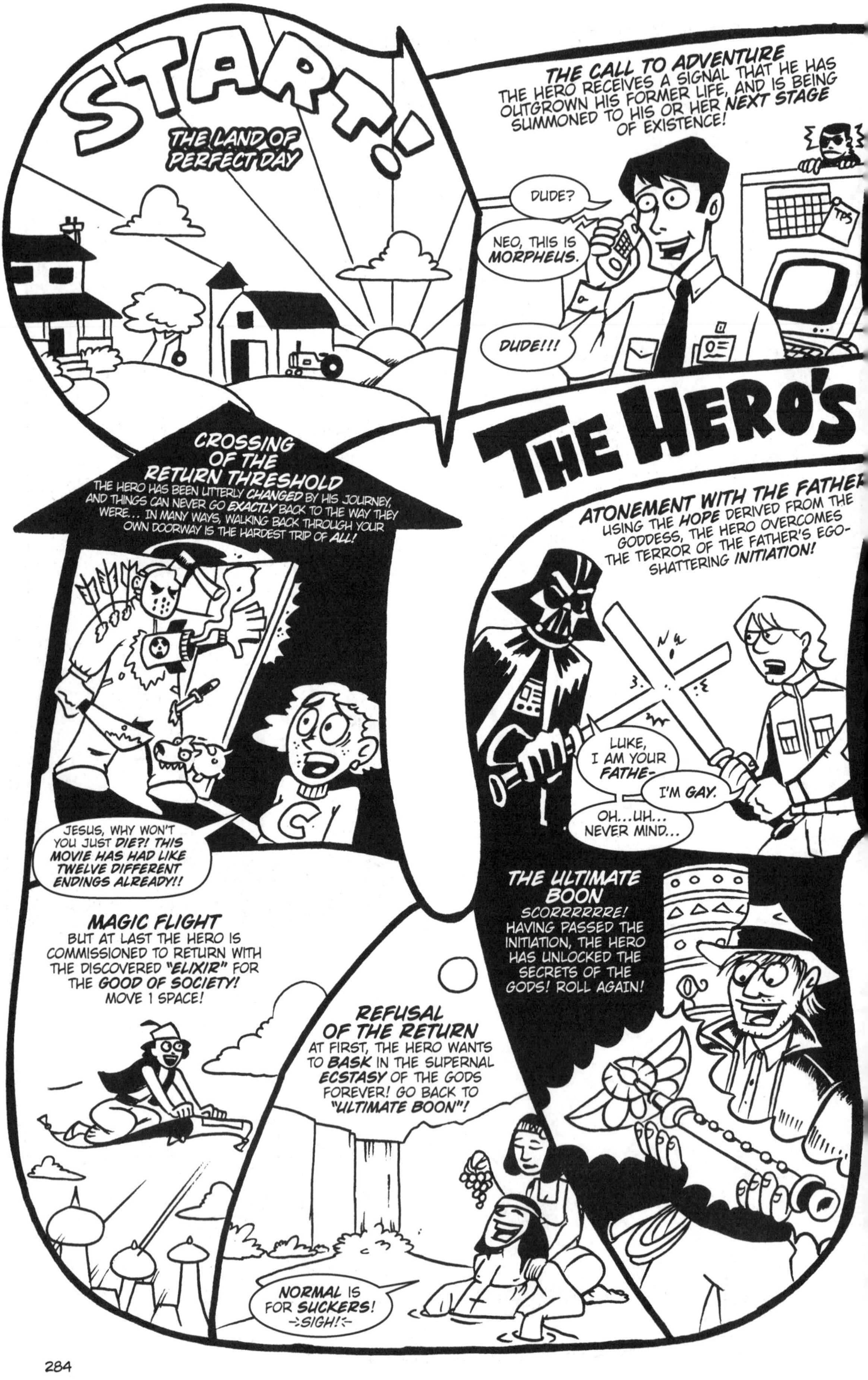

START!
THE LAND OF PERFECT DAY
THE CALL TO ADVENTURE
THE HERO RECEIVES A SIGNAL THAT HE HAS OUTGROWN HIS FORMER LIFE, AND IS BEING SUMMONED TO HIS OR HER NEXT STAGE OF EXISTENCE!
DUDE?
NEO, THIS IS MORPHEUS.
DUDE!!!
TPS
THE HERO'S
CROSSING OF THE RETURN THRESHOLD
THE HERO HAS BEEN UTTERLY CHANGED BY HIS JOURNEY, AND THINGS CAN NEVER GO EXACTLY BACK TO THE WAY THEY WERE... IN MANY WAYS, WALKING BACK THROUGH YOUR OWN DOORWAY IS THE HARDEST TRIP OF ALL!
JESUS, WHY WON'T YOU JUST DIE?! THIS MOVIE HAS HAD LIKE TWELVE DIFFERENT ENDINGS ALREADY!!
ATONEMENT WITH THE FATHER
USING THE HOPE DERIVED FROM THE GODDESS, THE HERO OVERCOMES THE TERROR OF THE FATHER'S EGO-SHATTERING INITIATION!
LUKE, I AM YOUR FATHE-
I'M GAY.
OH...UH... NEVER MIND...
THE ULTIMATE BOON
SCORRRRRRE! HAVING PASSED THE INITIATION, THE HERO HAS UNLOCKED THE SECRETS OF THE GODS! ROLL AGAIN!
MAGIC FLIGHT
BUT AT LAST THE HERO IS COMMISSIONED TO RETURN WITH THE DISCOVERED "ELIXIR" FOR THE GOOD OF SOCIETY! MOVE 1 SPACE!
REFUSAL OF THE RETURN
AT FIRST, THE HERO WANTS TO BASK IN THE SUPERNAL ECSTASY OF THE GODS FOREVER! GO BACK TO "ULTIMATE BOON"!
NORMAL IS FOR SUCKERS! -SIGH!-

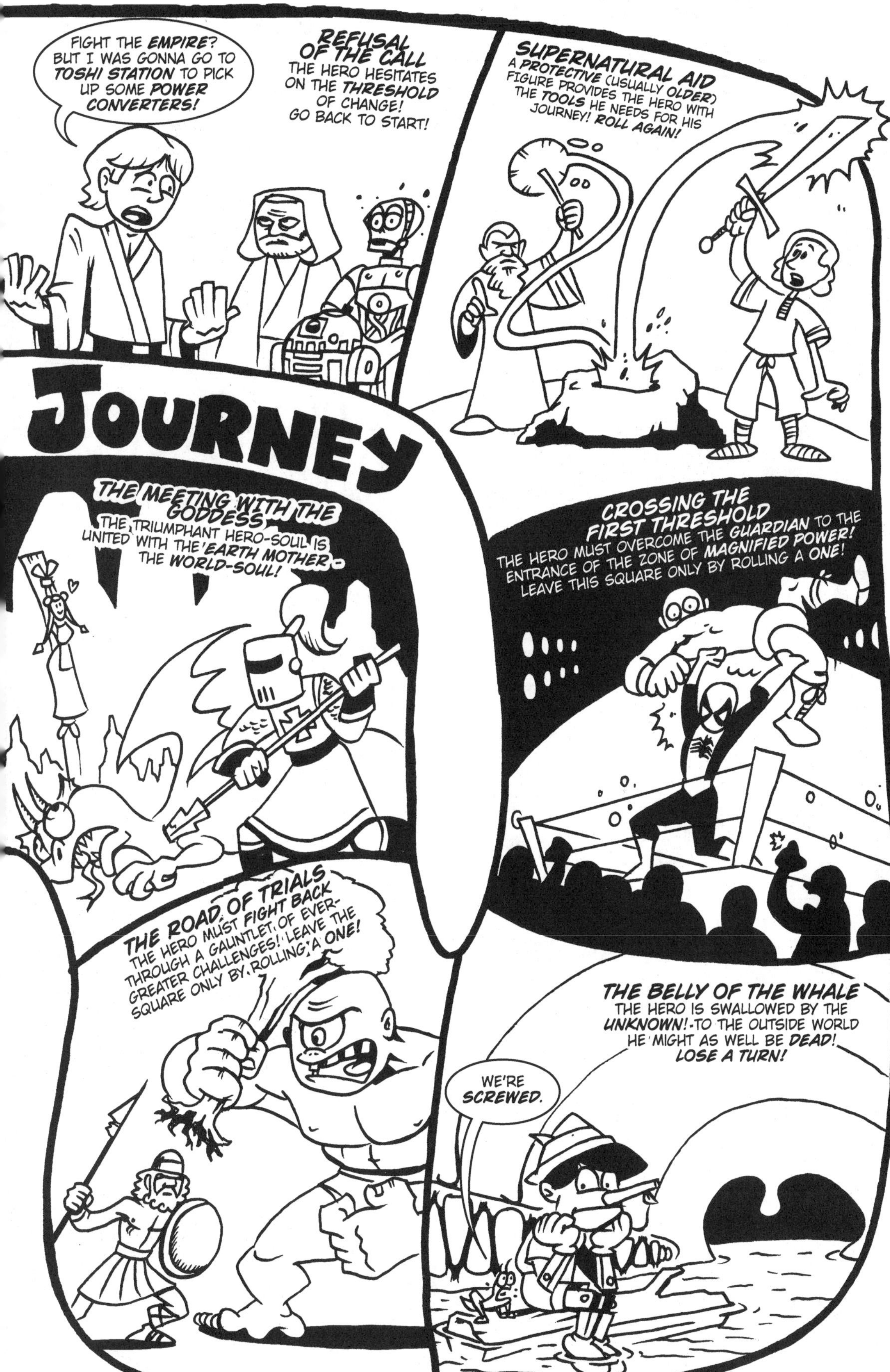

FIGHT THE EMPIRE? BUT I WAS GONNA GO TO TOSHI STATION TO PICK UP SOME POWER CONVERTERS!
REFUSAL OF THE CALL
THE HERO HESITATES ON THE THRESHOLD OF CHANGE! GO BACK TO START!
SUPERNATURAL AID
A PROTECTIVE (USUALLY OLDER) FIGURE PROVIDES THE HERO WITH THE TOOLS HE NEEDS FOR HIS JOURNEY! ROLL AGAIN!
JOURNEY
THE MEETING WITH THE GODDESS
THE TRIUMPHANT HERO-SOUL IS UNITED WITH THE EARTH MOTHER - THE WORLD-SOUL!
CROSSING THE FIRST THRESHOLD
THE HERO MUST OVERCOME THE GUARDIAN TO THE ENTRANCE OF THE ZONE OF MAGNIFIED POWER! LEAVE THIS SQUARE ONLY BY ROLLING A ONE!
THE ROAD OF TRIALS
THE HERO MUST FIGHT BACK THROUGH A GAUNTLET OF EVER-GREATER CHALLENGES! LEAVE THE SQUARE ONLY BY ROLLING A ONE!
THE BELLY OF THE WHALE
THE HERO IS SWALLOWED BY THE UNKNOWN! TO THE OUTSIDE WORLD HE MIGHT AS WELL BE DEAD! LOSE A TURN!
WE'RE SCREWED.

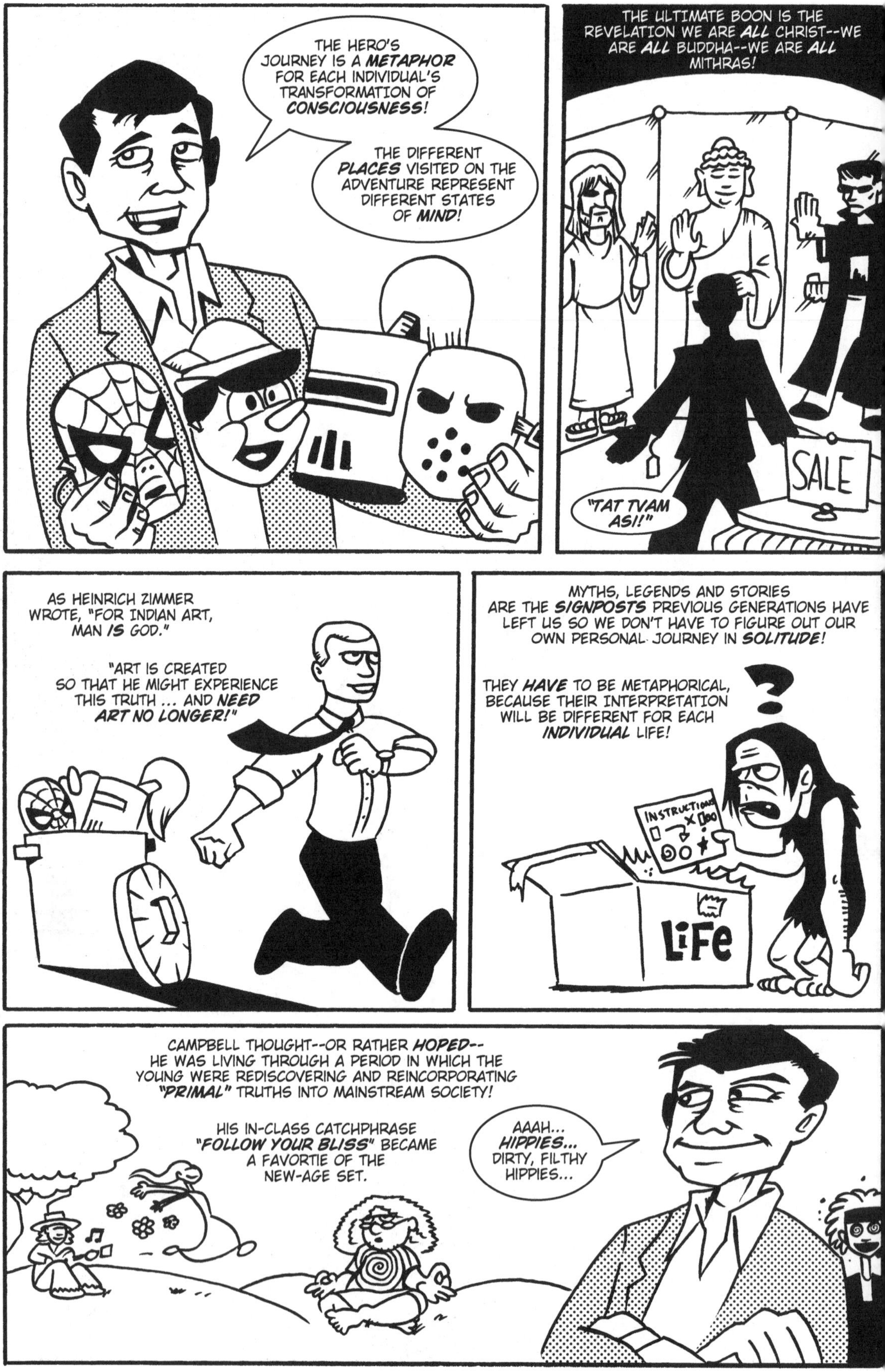
THE HERO'S JOURNEY IS A METAPHOR FOR EACH INDIVIDUAL'S TRANSFORMATION OF CONSCIOUSNESS!
THE DIFFERENT PLACES VISITED ON THE ADVENTURE REPRESENT DIFFERENT STATES OF MIND!
THE ULTIMATE BOON IS THE REVELATION WE ARE ALL CHRIST--WE ARE ALL BUDDHA--WE ARE ALL MITHRAS!
SALE
"TAT TVAM ASI!"
AS HEINRICH ZIMMER WROTE, "FOR INDIAN ART, MAN IS GOD."
"ART IS CREATED SO THAT HE MIGHT EXPERIENCE THIS TRUTH ... AND NEED ART NO LONGER!"
MYTHS, LEGENDS AND STORIES ARE THE SIGNPOSTS PREVIOUS GENERATIONS HAVE LEFT US SO WE DON'T HAVE TO FIGURE OUT OUR OWN PERSONAL JOURNEY IN SOLITUDE!
THEY HAVE TO BE METAPHORICAL, BECAUSE THEIR INTERPRETATION WILL BE DIFFERENT FOR EACH INDIVIDUAL LIFE!
INSTRUCTIONS
LiFe
CAMPBELL THOUGHT--OR RATHER HOPED--HE WAS LIVING THROUGH A PERIOD IN WHICH THE YOUNG WERE REDISCOVERING AND REINCORPORATING "PRIMAL" TRUTHS INTO MAINSTREAM SOCIETY!
HIS IN-CLASS CATCHPHRASE "FOLLOW YOUR BLISS" BECAME A FAVORTIE OF THE NEW-AGE SET.
AAAH... HIPPIES... DIRTY, FILTHY HIPPIES...

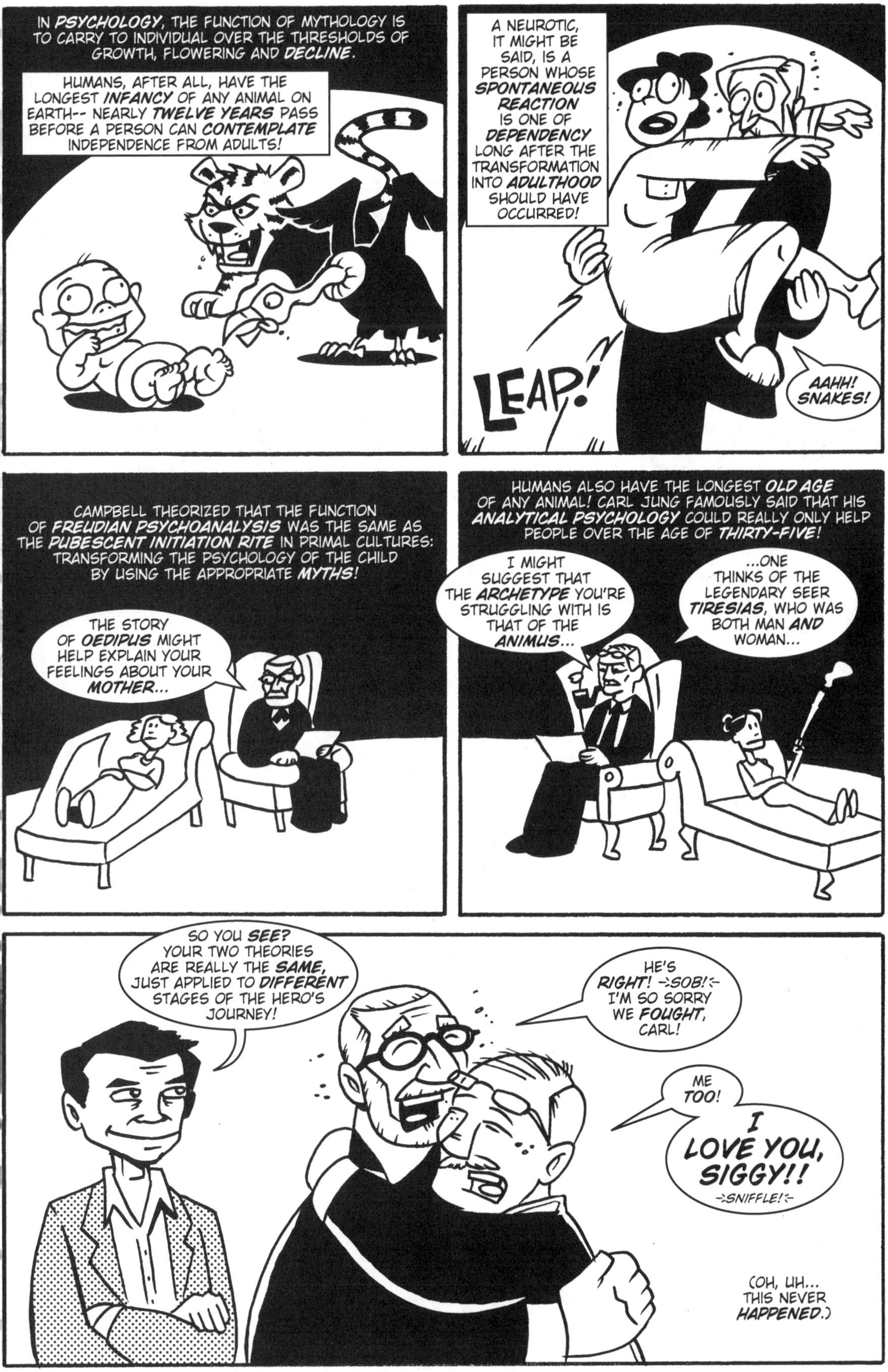
IN PSYCHOLOGY, THE FUNCTION OF MYTHOLOGY IS TO CARRY TO INDIVIDUAL OVER THE THRESHOLDS OF GROWTH, FLOWERING AND DECLINE.
HUMANS, AFTER ALL, HAVE THE LONGEST INFANCY OF ANY ANIMAL ON EARTH-- NEARLY TWELVE YEARS PASS BEFORE A PERSON CAN CONTEMPLATE INDEPENDENCE FROM ADULTS!
A NEUROTIC, IT MIGHT BE SAID, IS A PERSON WHOSE SPONTANEOUS REACTION IS ONE OF DEPENDENCY LONG AFTER THE TRANSFORMATION INTO ADULTHOOD SHOULD HAVE OCCURRED!
LEAP!
AAHH! SNAKES!
CAMPBELL THEORIZED THAT THE FUNCTION OF FREUDIAN PSYCHOANALYSIS WAS THE SAME AS THE PUBESCENT INITIATION RITE IN PRIMAL CULTURES: TRANSFORMING THE PSYCHOLOGY OF THE CHILD BY USING THE APPROPRIATE MYTHS!
THE STORY OF OEDIPUS MIGHT HELP EXPLAIN YOUR FEELINGS ABOUT YOUR MOTHER...
HUMANS ALSO HAVE THE LONGEST OLD AGE OF ANY ANIMAL! CARL JUNG FAMOUSLY SAID THAT HIS ANALYTICAL PSYCHOLOGY COULD REALLY ONLY HELP PEOPLE OVER THE AGE OF THIRTY-FIVE!
I MIGHT SUGGEST THAT THE ARCHETYPE YOU'RE STRUGGLING WITH IS THAT OF THE ANIMUS...
...ONE THINKS OF THE LEGENDARY SEER TIRESIAS, WHO WAS BOTH MAN AND WOMAN...
SO YOU SEE? YOUR TWO THEORIES ARE REALLY THE SAME, JUST APPLIED TO DIFFERENT STAGES OF THE HERO'S JOURNEY!
HE'S RIGHT! -SOB!- I'M SO SORRY WE FOUGHT, CARL!
ME TOO!
I LOVE YOU, SIGGY!! -SNIFFLE!-
(OH, UH... THIS NEVER HAPPENED.)

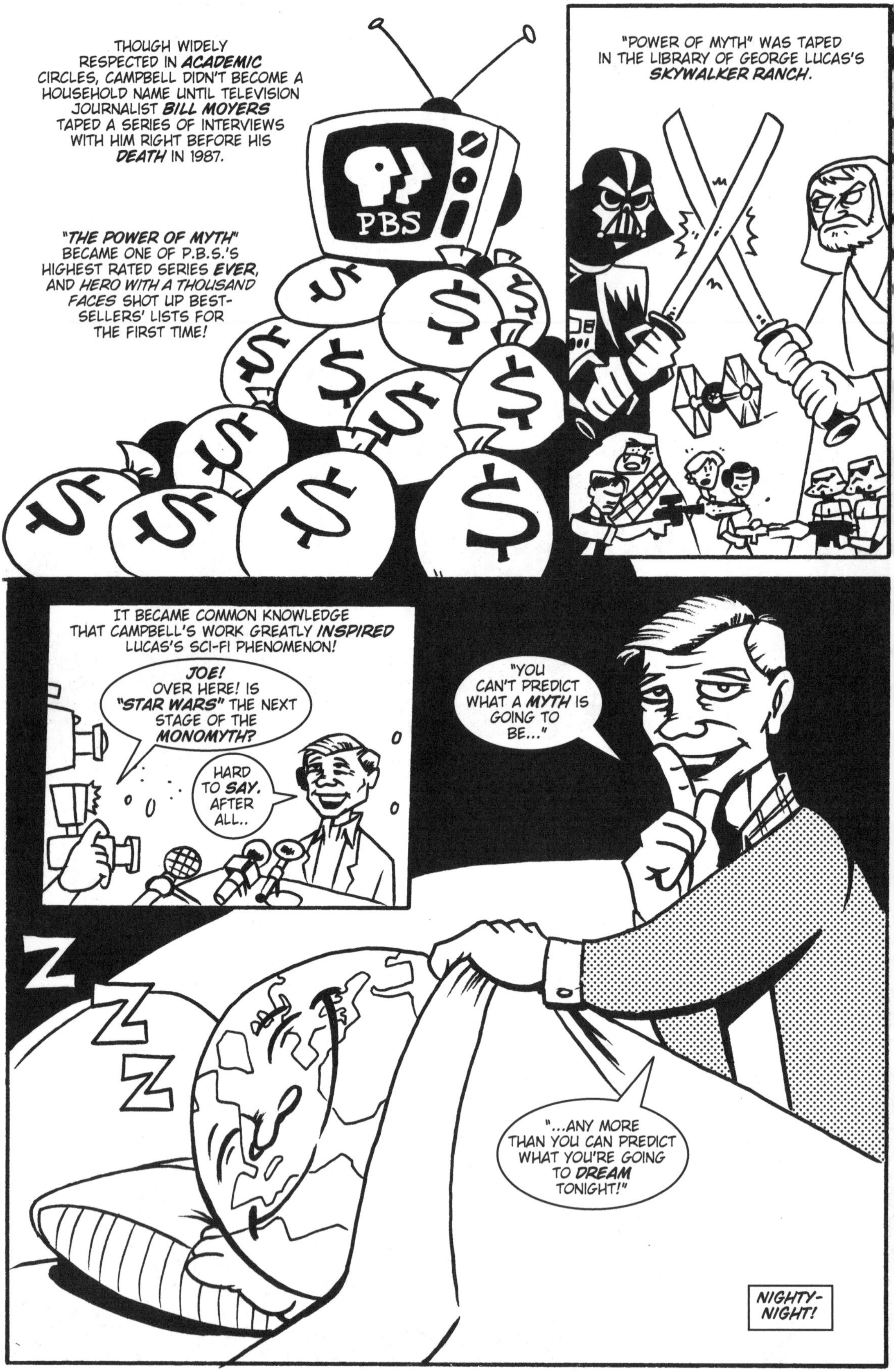
THOUGH WIDELY RESPECTED IN ACADEMIC CIRCLES, CAMPBELL DIDN'T BECOME A HOUSEHOLD NAME UNTIL TELEVISION JOURNALIST BILL MOYERS TAPED A SERIES OF INTERVIEWS WITH HIM RIGHT BEFORE HIS DEATH IN 1987.
PBS
"THE POWER OF MYTH" BECAME ONE OF P.B.S.'S HIGHEST RATED SERIES EVER, AND HERO WITH A THOUSAND FACES SHOT UP BEST-SELLERS' LISTS FOR THE FIRST TIME!
"POWER OF MYTH" WAS TAPED IN THE LIBRARY OF GEORGE LUCAS'S SKYWALKER RANCH.
IT BECAME COMMON KNOWLEDGE THAT CAMPBELL'S WORK GREATLY INSPIRED LUCAS'S SCI-FI PHENOMENON!
JOE! OVER HERE! IS "STAR WARS" THE NEXT STAGE OF THE MONOMYTH?
HARD TO SAY. AFTER ALL..
"YOU CAN'T PREDICT WHAT A MYTH IS GOING TO BE..."
"...ANY MORE THAN YOU CAN PREDICT WHAT YOU'RE GOING TO DREAM TONIGHT!"
Z Z Z
NIGHTY-NIGHT!

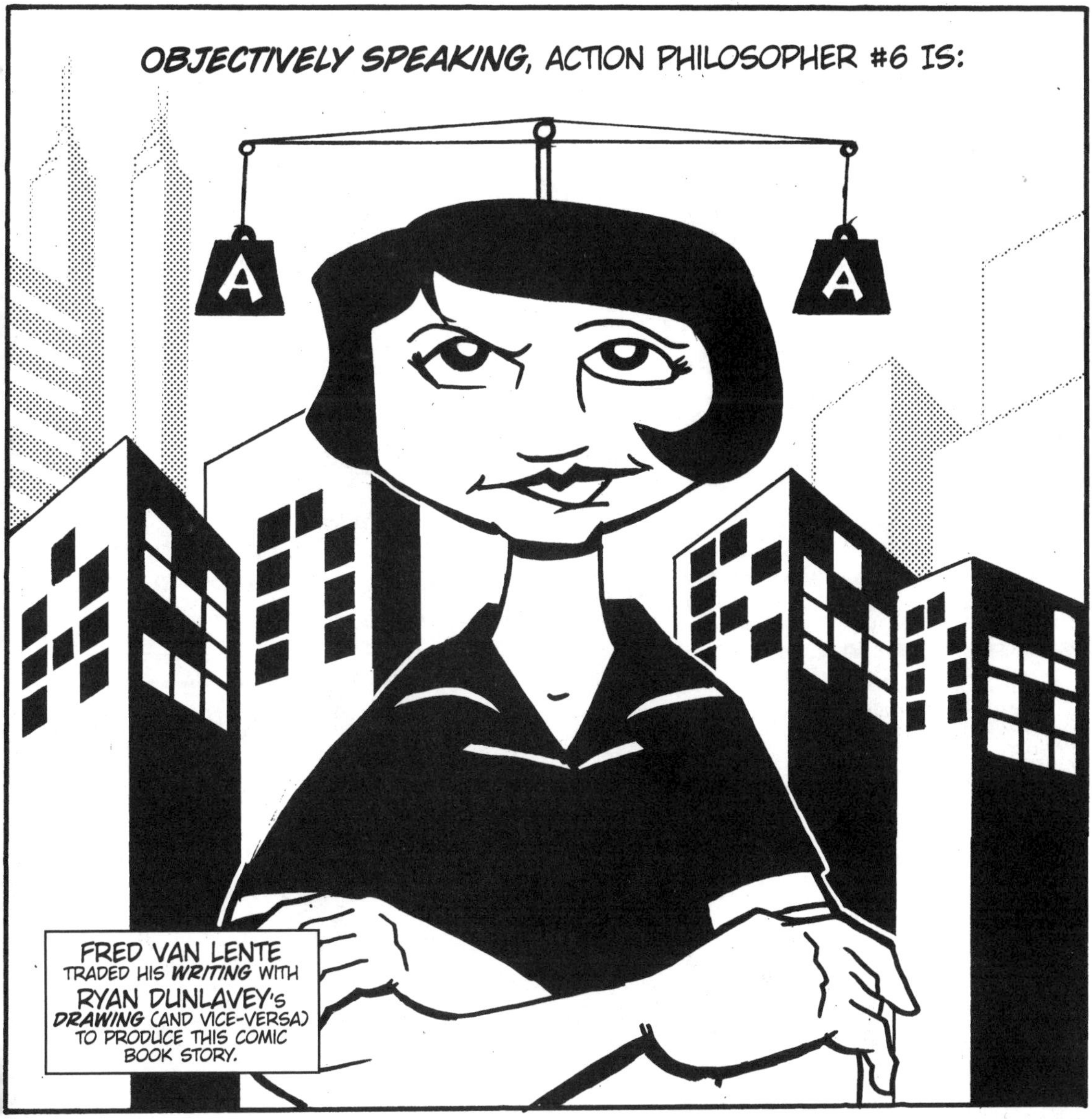
OBJECTIVELY SPEAKING, ACTION PHILOSOPHER #6 IS:
A
A
FRED VAN LENTE TRADED HIS WRITING WITH RYAN DUNLAVEY'S DRAWING (AND VICE-VERSA) TO PRODUCE THIS COMIC BOOK STORY.

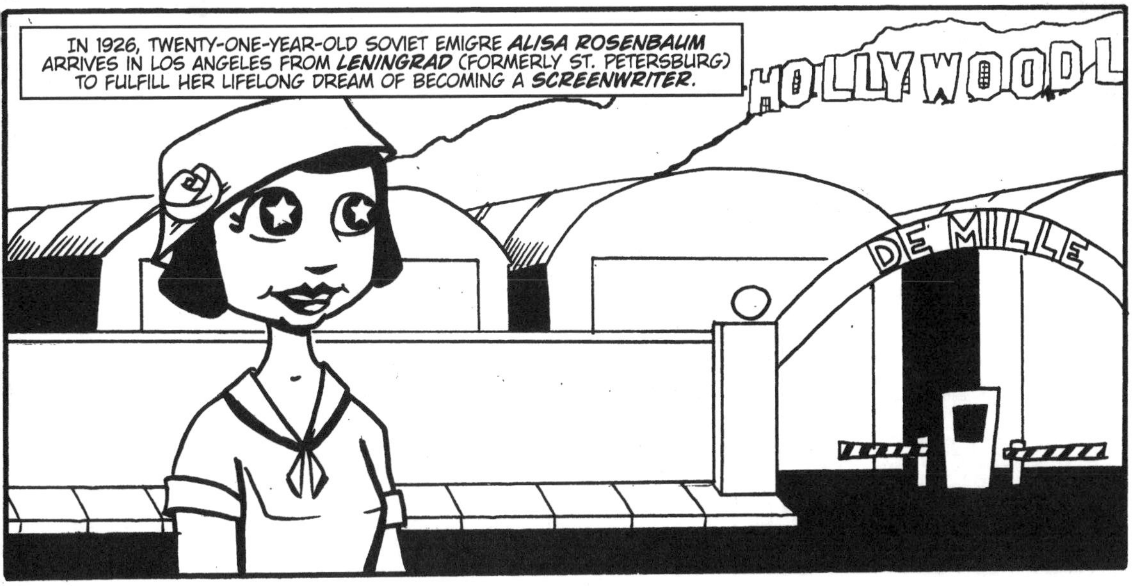
IN 1926, TWENTY-ONE-YEAR-OLD SOVIET EMIGRE ALISA ROSENBAUM ARRIVES IN LOS ANGELES FROM LENINGRAD (FORMERLY ST. PETERSBURG) TO FULFILL HER LIFELONG DREAM OF BECOMING A SCREENWRITER.
HOLLYWOODL
DE MILLE

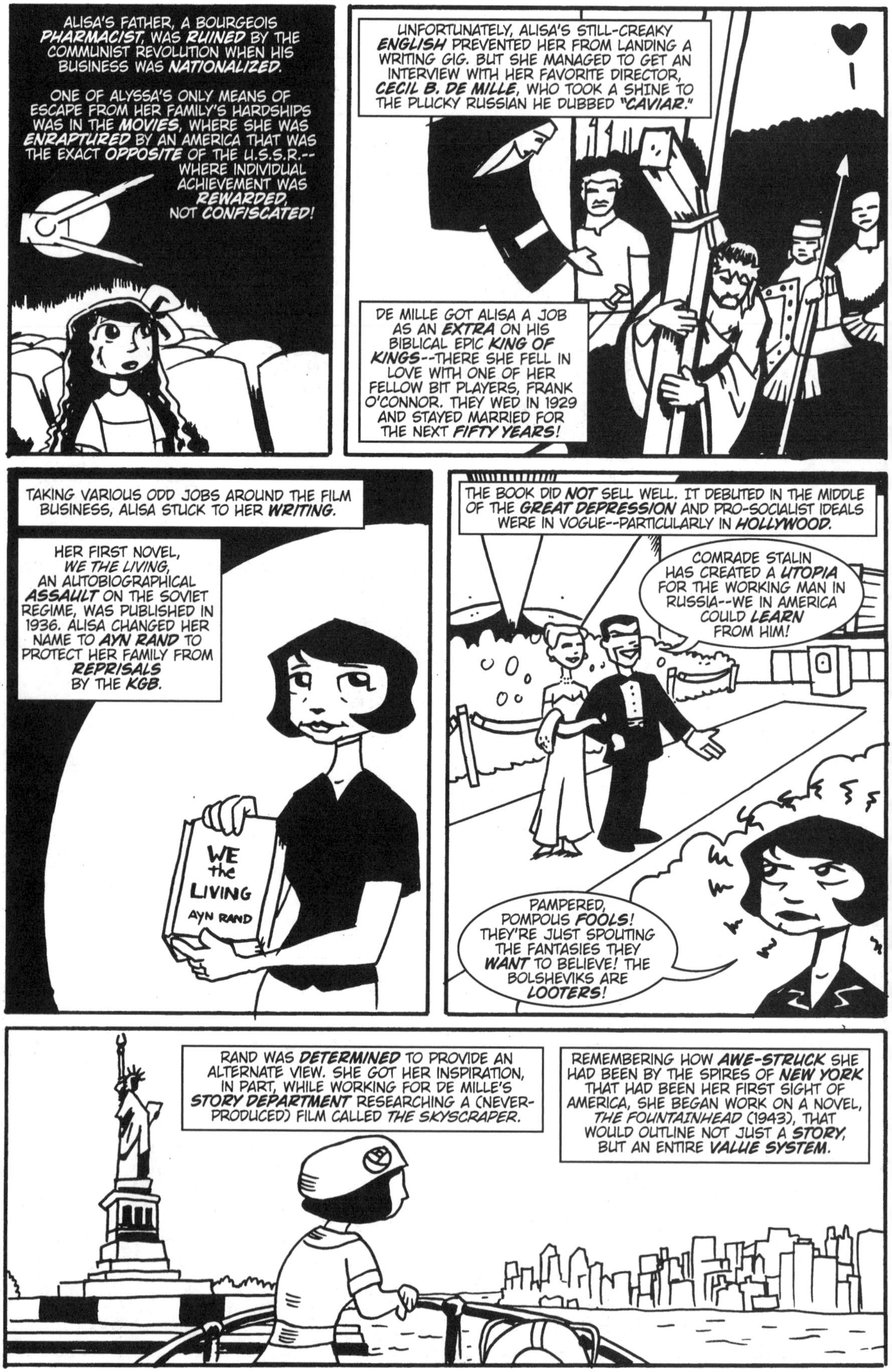
ALISA'S FATHER, A BOURGEOIS PHARMACIST, WAS RUINED BY THE COMMUNIST REVOLUTION WHEN HIS BUSINESS WAS NATIONALIZED.
ONE OF ALYSSA'S ONLY MEANS OF ESCAPE FROM HER FAMILY'S HARDSHIPS WAS IN THE MOVIES, WHERE SHE WAS ENRAPTURED BY AN AMERICA THAT WAS THE EXACT OPPOSITE OF THE U.S.S.R.--WHERE INDIVIDUAL ACHIEVEMENT WAS REWARDED, NOT CONFISCATED!
UNFORTUNATELY, ALISA'S STILL-CREAKY ENGLISH PREVENTED HER FROM LANDING A WRITING GIG. BUT SHE MANAGED TO GET AN INTERVIEW WITH HER FAVORITE DIRECTOR, CECIL B. DE MILLE, WHO TOOK A SHINE TO THE PLUCKY RUSSIAN HE DUBBED "CAVIAR."
DE MILLE GOT ALISA A JOB AS AN EXTRA ON HIS BIBLICAL EPIC KING OF KINGS--THERE SHE FELL IN LOVE WITH ONE OF HER FELLOW BIT PLAYERS, FRANK O'CONNOR. THEY WED IN 1929 AND STAYED MARRIED FOR THE NEXT FIFTY YEARS!
TAKING VARIOUS ODD JOBS AROUND THE FILM BUSINESS, ALISA STUCK TO HER WRITING.
HER FIRST NOVEL, WE THE LIVING, AN AUTOBIOGRAPHICAL ASSAULT ON THE SOVIET REGIME, WAS PUBLISHED IN 1936. ALISA CHANGED HER NAME TO AYN RAND TO PROTECT HER FAMILY FROM REPRISALS BY THE KGB.
WE the LIVING
AYN RAND
THE BOOK DID NOT SELL WELL. IT DEBUTED IN THE MIDDLE OF THE GREAT DEPRESSION AND PRO-SOCIALIST IDEALS WERE IN VOGUE--PARTICULARLY IN HOLLYWOOD.
COMRADE STALIN HAS CREATED A UTOPIA FOR THE WORKING MAN IN RUSSIA--WE IN AMERICA COULD LEARN FROM HIM!
PAMPERED, POMPOUS FOOLS! THEY'RE JUST SPOUTING THE FANTASIES THEY WANT TO BELIEVE! THE BOLSHEVIKS ARE LOOTERS!
RAND WAS DETERMINED TO PROVIDE AN ALTERNATE VIEW. SHE GOT HER INSPIRATION, IN PART, WHILE WORKING FOR DE MILLE'S STORY DEPARTMENT RESEARCHING A (NEVER-PRODUCED) FILM CALLED THE SKYSCRAPER.
REMEMBERING HOW AWE-STRUCK SHE HAD BEEN BY THE SPIRES OF NEW YORK THAT HAD BEEN HER FIRST SIGHT OF AMERICA, SHE BEGAN WORK ON A NOVEL, THE FOUNTAINHEAD (1943), THAT WOULD OUTLINE NOT JUST A STORY, BUT AN ENTIRE VALUE SYSTEM.

RAND CALLED THE FUNDAMENTAL PRINCIPLE OF HER ***OBJECTIVIST*** PHILOSOPHY THE ***LAW OF IDENTITY.***

A=A

"REALITY -- THE EXTERNAL WORLD -- EXISTS ***INDEPENDENT*** OF MAN'S CONSCIOUSNESS, INDEPENDENT OF ANY OBSERVER'S KNOWLEDGE, BELIEFS, FEELINGS, DESIRES OR FEARS... THE TASK OF MAN'S CONSCIOUSNESS IS TO ***PERCEIVE*** REALITY -- ***NOT*** TO CREATE OR INVENT IT!"

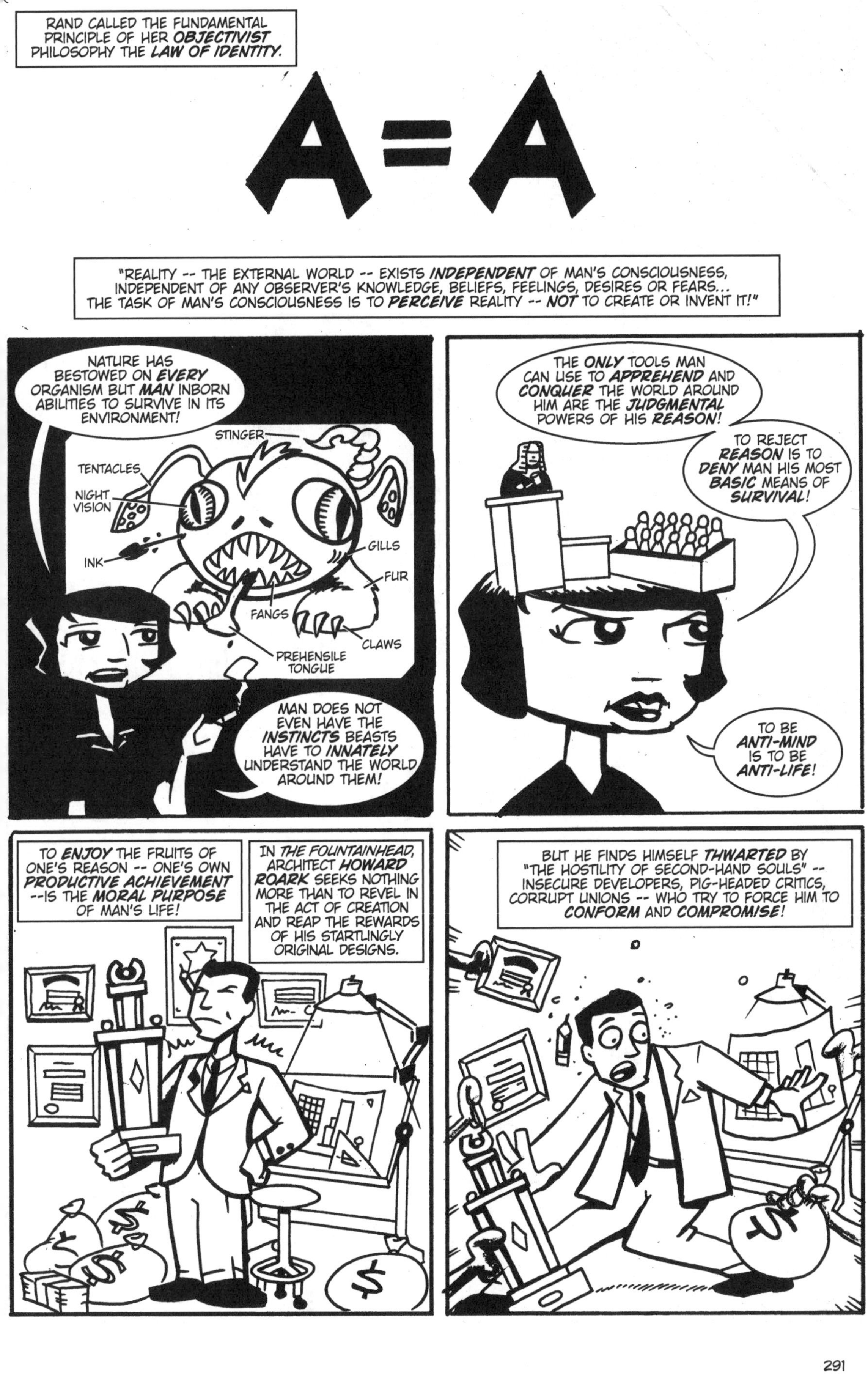

NATURE HAS BESTOWED ON EVERY ORGANISM BUT MAN INBORN ABILITIES TO SURVIVE IN ITS ENVIRONMENT!
STINGER
TENTACLES
NIGHT VISION
INK
GILLS
FUR
FANGS
CLAWS
PREHENSILE TONGUE
MAN DOES NOT EVEN HAVE THE INSTINCTS BEASTS HAVE TO INNATELY UNDERSTAND THE WORLD AROUND THEM!
THE ONLY TOOLS MAN CAN USE TO APPREHEND AND CONQUER THE WORLD AROUND HIM ARE THE JUDGMENTAL POWERS OF HIS REASON!
TO REJECT REASON IS TO DENY MAN HIS MOST BASIC MEANS OF SURVIVAL!
TO BE ANTI-MIND IS TO BE ANTI-LIFE!
TO ENJOY THE FRUITS OF ONE'S REASON -- ONE'S OWN PRODUCTIVE ACHIEVEMENT --IS THE MORAL PURPOSE OF MAN'S LIFE!
IN THE FOUNTAINHEAD, ARCHITECT HOWARD ROARK SEEKS NOTHING MORE THAN TO REVEL IN THE ACT OF CREATION AND REAP THE REWARDS OF HIS STARTLINGLY ORIGINAL DESIGNS.
BUT HE FINDS HIMSELF THWARTED BY "THE HOSTILITY OF SECOND-HAND SOULS" -- INSECURE DEVELOPERS, PIG-HEADED CRITICS, CORRUPT UNIONS -- WHO TRY TO FORCE HIM TO CONFORM AND COMPROMISE!

THESE ***LOOTERS*** HAVE BEEN TRYING TO GET PEOPLE TO ***SACRIFICE*** THEMSELVES FOR "SOCIETY'S" (I.E., ***THEIR***) GOOD WITH VARIOUS ***JUSTIFICATIONS*** AND TO VARIOUS DEGREES OF ***EVIL*** THROUGHOUT HISTORY!

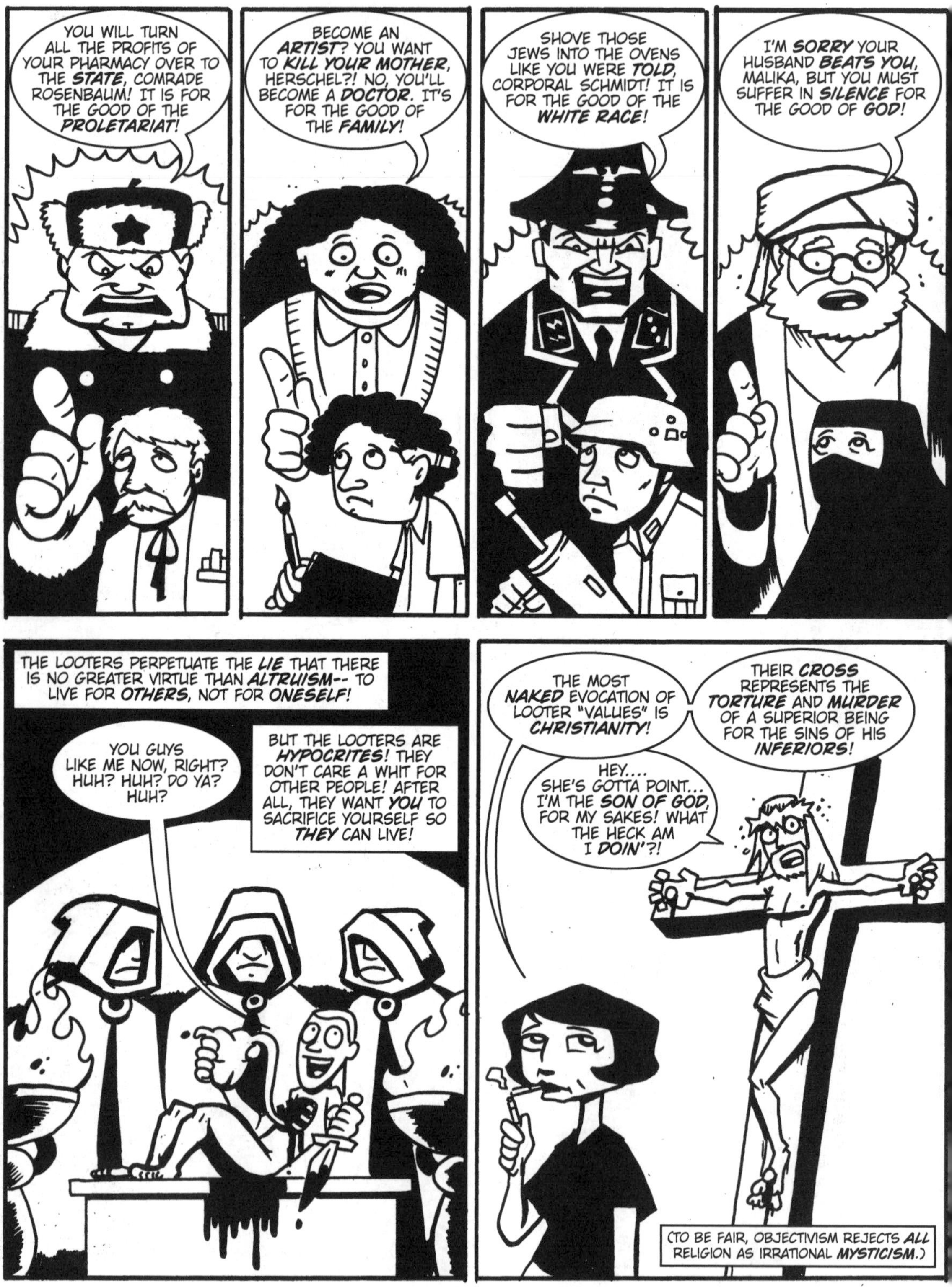
YOU WILL TURN ALL THE PROFITS OF YOUR PHARMACY OVER TO THE STATE, COMRADE ROSENBAUM! IT IS FOR THE GOOD OF THE PROLETARIAT!
BECOME AN ARTIST? YOU WANT TO KILL YOUR MOTHER, HERSCHEL?! NO, YOU'LL BECOME A DOCTOR. IT'S FOR THE GOOD OF THE FAMILY!
SHOVE THOSE JEWS INTO THE OVENS LIKE YOU WERE TOLD, CORPORAL SCHMIDT! IT IS FOR THE GOOD OF THE WHITE RACE!
I'M SORRY YOUR HUSBAND BEATS YOU, MALIKA, BUT YOU MUST SUFFER IN SILENCE FOR THE GOOD OF GOD!
THE LOOTERS PERPETUATE THE LIE THAT THERE IS NO GREATER VIRTUE THAN ALTRUISM-- TO LIVE FOR OTHERS, NOT FOR ONESELF!
YOU GUYS LIKE ME NOW, RIGHT? HUH? HUH? DO YA? HUH?
BUT THE LOOTERS ARE HYPOCRITES! THEY DON'T CARE A WHIT FOR OTHER PEOPLE! AFTER ALL, THEY WANT YOU TO SACRIFICE YOURSELF SO THEY CAN LIVE!
THE MOST NAKED EVOCATION OF LOOTER "VALUES" IS CHRISTIANITY!
THEIR CROSS REPRESENTS THE TORTURE AND MURDER OF A SUPERIOR BEING FOR THE SINS OF HIS INFERIORS!
HEY.... SHE'S GOTTA POINT... I'M THE SON OF GOD, FOR MY SAKES! WHAT THE HECK AM I DOIN'?!
(TO BE FAIR, OBJECTIVISM REJECTS ALL RELIGION AS IRRATIONAL MYSTICISM.)

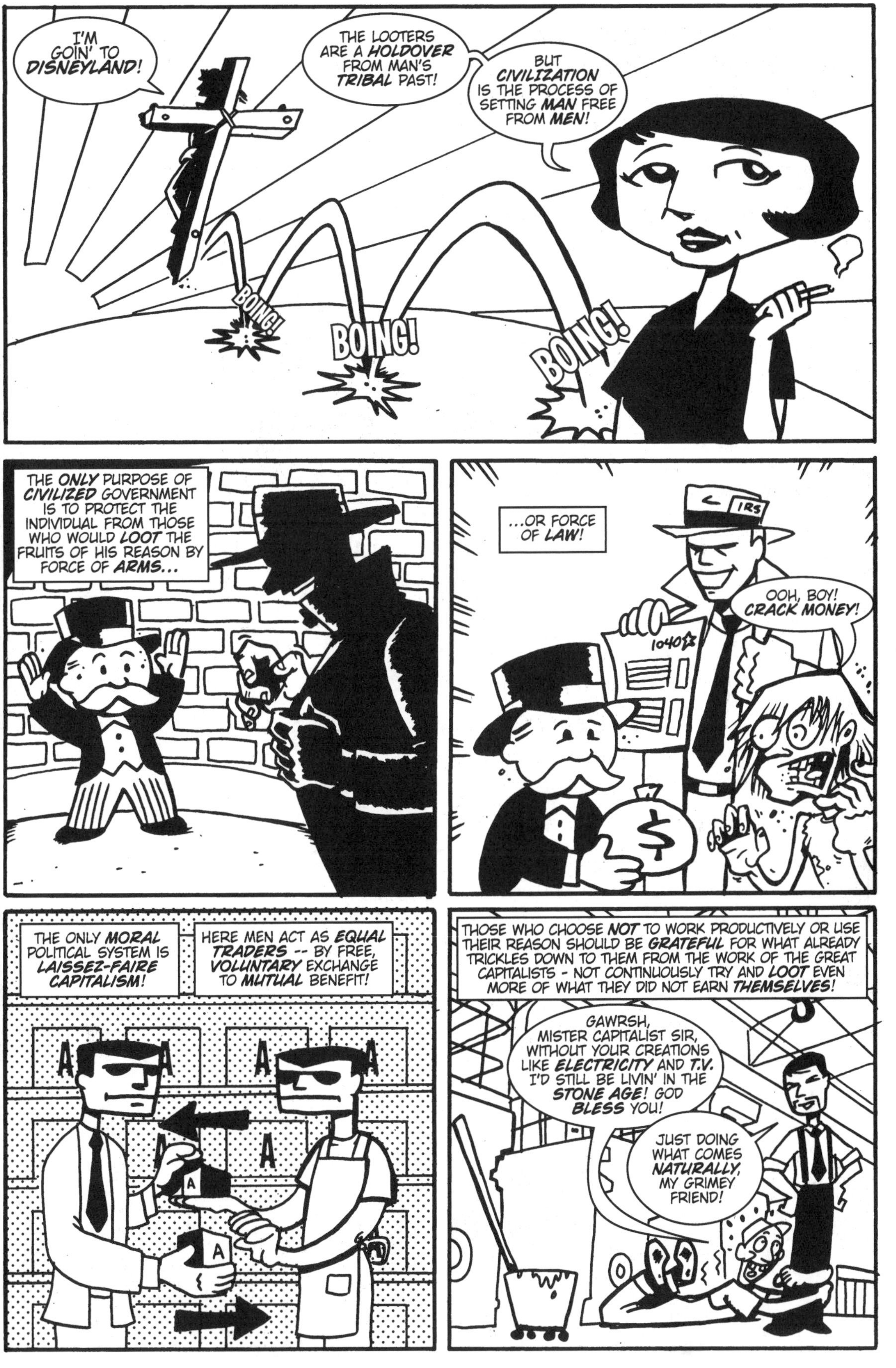
I'M GOIN' TO DISNEYLAND!
THE LOOTERS ARE A HOLDOVER FROM MAN'S TRIBAL PAST!
BUT CIVILIZATION IS THE PROCESS OF SETTING MAN FREE FROM MEN!
BOING!
BOING!
BOING!
THE ONLY PURPOSE OF CIVILIZED GOVERNMENT IS TO PROTECT THE INDIVIDUAL FROM THOSE WHO WOULD LOOT THE FRUITS OF HIS REASON BY FORCE OF ARMS...
...OR FORCE OF LAW!
IRS
OOH, BOY! CRACK MONEY!
1040
$
THE ONLY MORAL POLITICAL SYSTEM IS LAISSEZ-FAIRE CAPITALISM!
HERE MEN ACT AS EQUAL TRADERS -- BY FREE, VOLUNTARY EXCHANGE TO MUTUAL BENEFIT!
THOSE WHO CHOOSE NOT TO WORK PRODUCTIVELY OR USE THEIR REASON SHOULD BE GRATEFUL FOR WHAT ALREADY TRICKLES DOWN TO THEM FROM THE WORK OF THE GREAT CAPITALISTS - NOT CONTINUOUSLY TRY AND LOOT EVEN MORE OF WHAT THEY DID NOT EARN THEMSELVES!
GAWRSH, MISTER CAPITALIST SIR, WITHOUT YOUR CREATIONS LIKE ELECTRICITY AND T.V. I'D STILL BE LIVIN' IN THE STONE AGE! GOD BLESS YOU!
JUST DOING WHAT COMES NATURALLY, MY GRIMEY FRIEND!

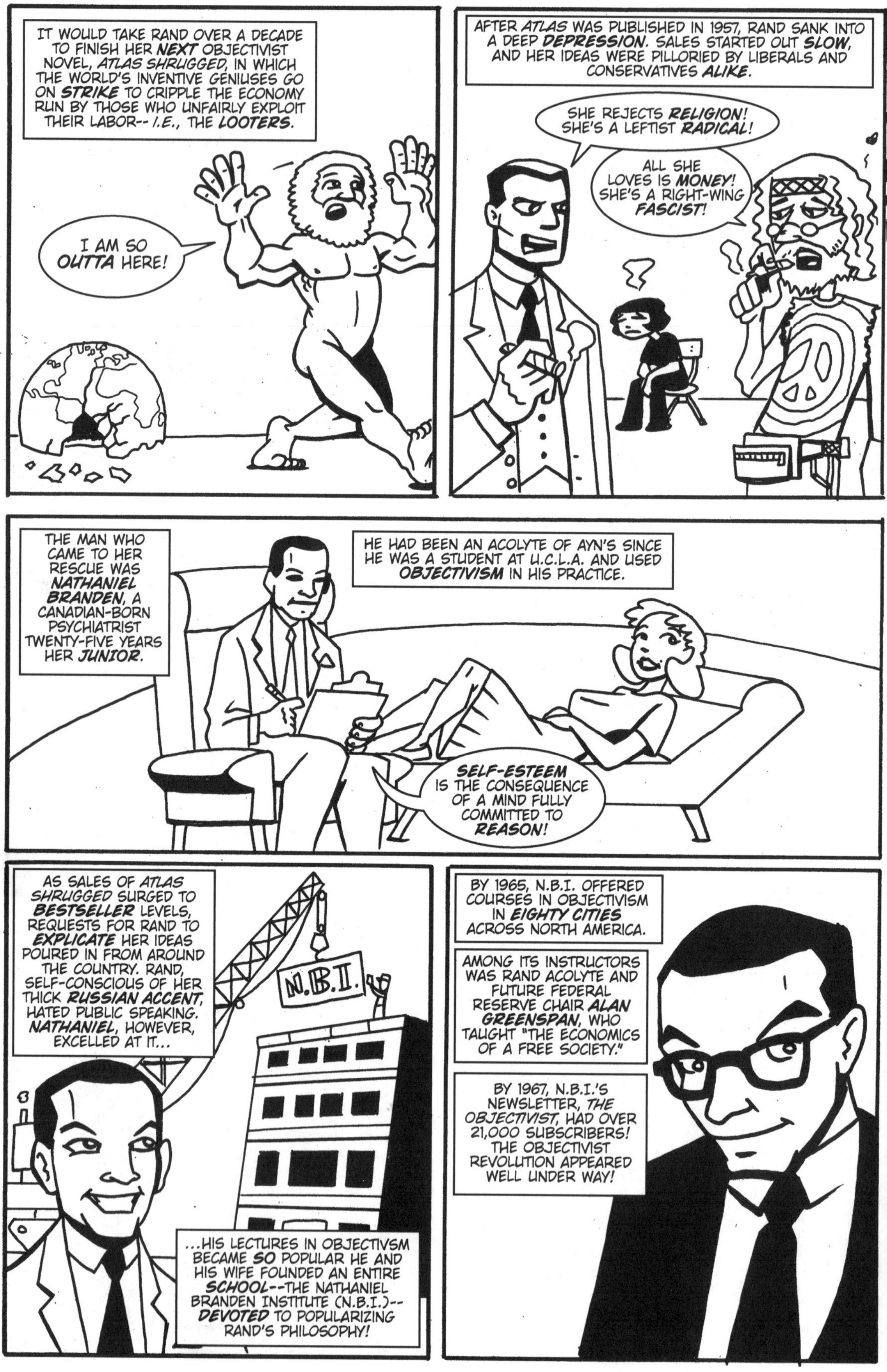
IT WOULD TAKE RAND OVER A DECADE TO FINISH HER NEXT OBJECTIVIST NOVEL, ATLAS SHRUGGED, IN WHICH THE WORLD'S INVENTIVE GENIUSES GO ON STRIKE TO CRIPPLE THE ECONOMY RUN BY THOSE WHO UNFAIRLY EXPLOIT THEIR LABOR-- I.E., THE LOOTERS.
I AM SO OUTTA HERE!
AFTER ATLAS WAS PUBLISHED IN 1957, RAND SANK INTO A DEEP DEPRESSION. SALES STARTED OUT SLOW, AND HER IDEAS WERE PILLORIED BY LIBERALS AND CONSERVATIVES ALIKE.
SHE REJECTS RELIGION! SHE'S A LEFTIST RADICAL!
ALL SHE LOVES IS MONEY! SHE'S A RIGHT-WING FASCIST!
THE MAN WHO CAME TO HER RESCUE WAS NATHANIEL BRANDEN, A CANADIAN-BORN PSYCHIATRIST TWENTY-FIVE YEARS HER JUNIOR.
HE HAD BEEN AN ACOLYTE OF AYN'S SINCE HE WAS A STUDENT AT U.C.L.A. AND USED OBJECTIVISM IN HIS PRACTICE.
SELF-ESTEEM IS THE CONSEQUENCE OF A MIND FULLY COMMITTED TO REASON!
AS SALES OF ATLAS SHRUGGED SURGED TO BESTSELLER LEVELS, REQUESTS FOR RAND TO EXPLICATE HER IDEAS POURED IN FROM AROUND THE COUNTRY. RAND, SELF-CONSCIOUS OF HER THICK RUSSIAN ACCENT, HATED PUBLIC SPEAKING. NATHANIEL, HOWEVER, EXCELLED AT IT...
N.B.I.
...HIS LECTURES IN OBJECTIVSM BECAME SO POPULAR HE AND HIS WIFE FOUNDED AN ENTIRE SCHOOL--THE NATHANIEL BRANDEN INSTITUTE (N.B.I.)--DEVOTED TO POPULARIZING RAND'S PHILOSOPHY!
BY 1965, N.B.I. OFFERED COURSES IN OBJECTIVISM IN EIGHTY CITIES ACROSS NORTH AMERICA.
AMONG ITS INSTRUCTORS WAS RAND ACOLYTE AND FUTURE FEDERAL RESERVE CHAIR ALAN GREENSPAN, WHO TAUGHT "THE ECONOMICS OF A FREE SOCIETY."
BY 1967, N.B.I.'S NEWSLETTER, THE OBJECTIVIST, HAD OVER 21,000 SUBSCRIBERS! THE OBJECTIVIST REVOLUTION APPEARED WELL UNDER WAY!

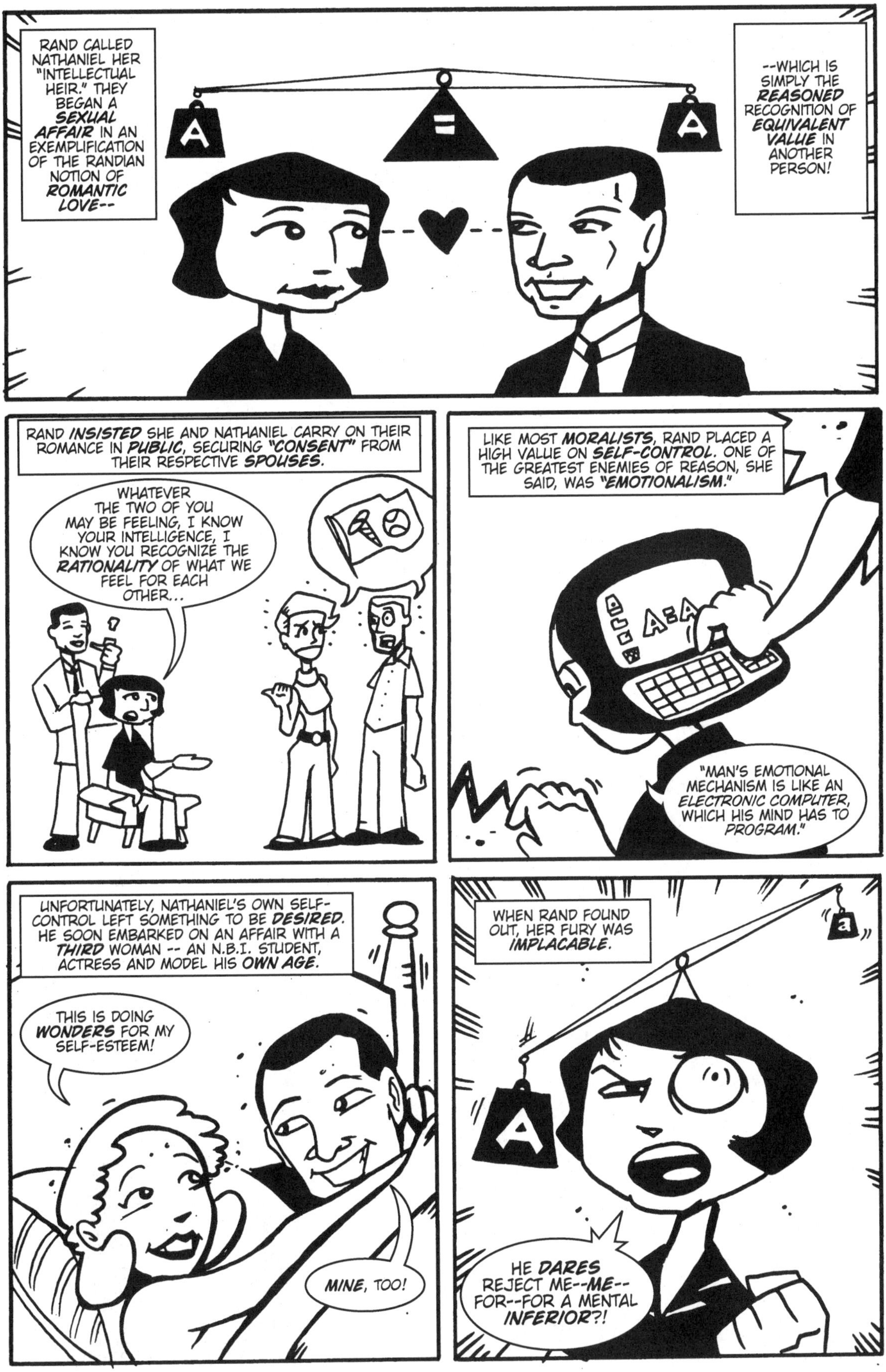
RAND CALLED NATHANIEL HER "INTELLECTUAL HEIR." THEY BEGAN A SEXUAL AFFAIR IN AN EXEMPLIFICATION OF THE RANDIAN NOTION OF ROMANTIC LOVE--
A
=
A
--WHICH IS SIMPLY THE REASONED RECOGNITION OF EQUIVALENT VALUE IN ANOTHER PERSON!
RAND INSISTED SHE AND NATHANIEL CARRY ON THEIR ROMANCE IN PUBLIC, SECURING "CONSENT" FROM THEIR RESPECTIVE SPOUSES.
WHATEVER THE TWO OF YOU MAY BE FEELING, I KNOW YOUR INTELLIGENCE, I KNOW YOU RECOGNIZE THE RATIONALITY OF WHAT WE FEEL FOR EACH OTHER...
LIKE MOST MORALISTS, RAND PLACED A HIGH VALUE ON SELF-CONTROL. ONE OF THE GREATEST ENEMIES OF REASON, SHE SAID, WAS "EMOTIONALISM."
A=A
"MAN'S EMOTIONAL MECHANISM IS LIKE AN ELECTRONIC COMPUTER, WHICH HIS MIND HAS TO PROGRAM."
UNFORTUNATELY, NATHANIEL'S OWN SELF-CONTROL LEFT SOMETHING TO BE DESIRED. HE SOON EMBARKED ON AN AFFAIR WITH A THIRD WOMAN -- AN N.B.I. STUDENT, ACTRESS AND MODEL HIS OWN AGE.
THIS IS DOING WONDERS FOR MY SELF-ESTEEM!
MINE, TOO!
WHEN RAND FOUND OUT, HER FURY WAS IMPLACABLE.
a
A
HE DARES REJECT ME--ME--FOR--FOR A MENTAL INFERIOR?!

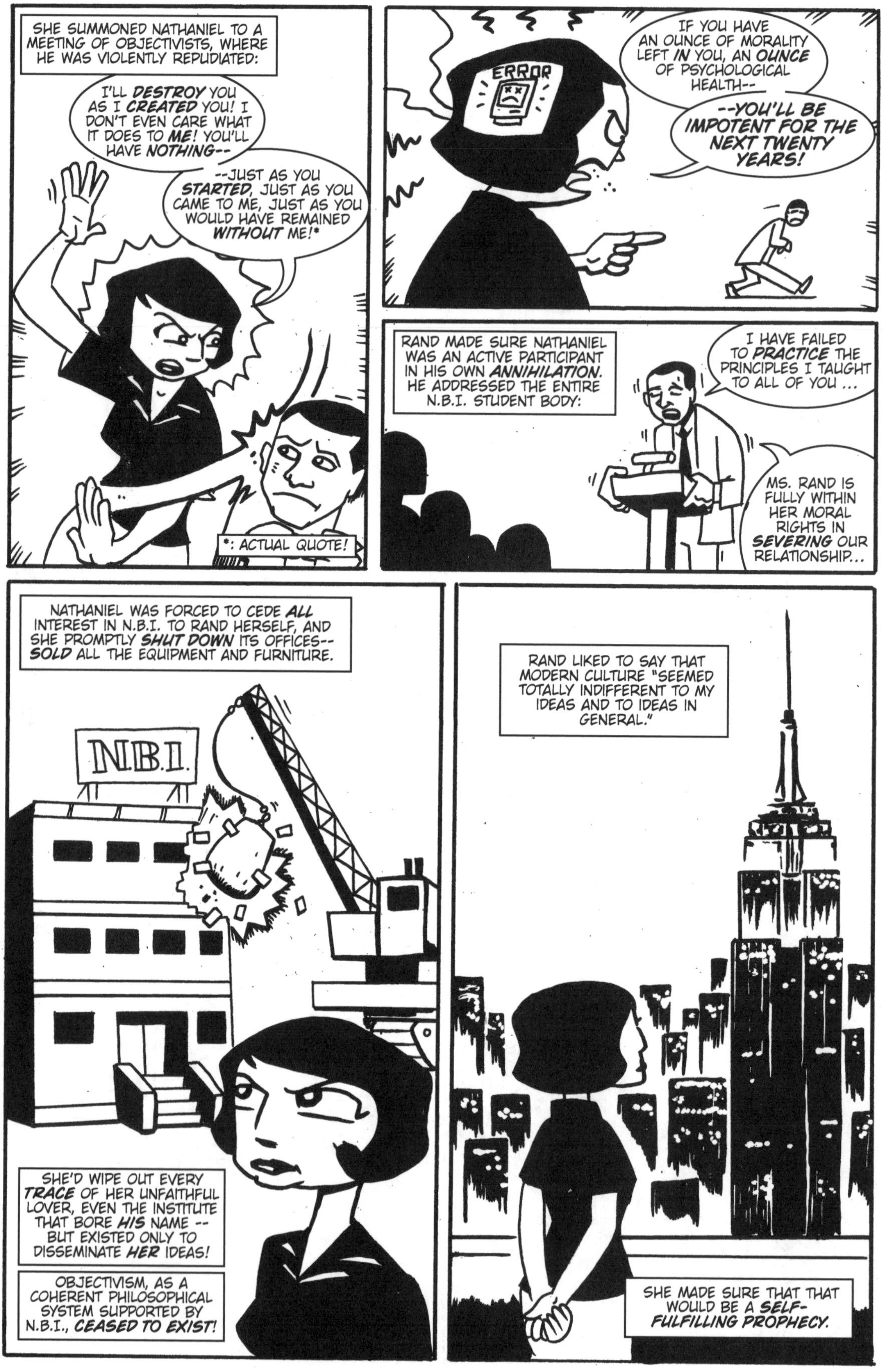
SHE SUMMONED NATHANIEL TO A MEETING OF OBJECTIVISTS, WHERE HE WAS VIOLENTLY REPUDIATED:
I'LL DESTROY YOU AS I CREATED YOU! I DON'T EVEN CARE WHAT IT DOES TO ME! YOU'LL HAVE NOTHING--
--JUST AS YOU STARTED, JUST AS YOU CAME TO ME, JUST AS YOU WOULD HAVE REMAINED WITHOUT ME!*
*: ACTUAL QUOTE!
ERROR
IF YOU HAVE AN OUNCE OF MORALITY LEFT IN YOU, AN OUNCE OF PSYCHOLOGICAL HEALTH--
--YOU'LL BE IMPOTENT FOR THE NEXT TWENTY YEARS!
RAND MADE SURE NATHANIEL WAS AN ACTIVE PARTICIPANT IN HIS OWN ANNIHILATION. HE ADDRESSED THE ENTIRE N.B.I. STUDENT BODY:
I HAVE FAILED TO PRACTICE THE PRINCIPLES I TAUGHT TO ALL OF YOU ...
MS. RAND IS FULLY WITHIN HER MORAL RIGHTS IN SEVERING OUR RELATIONSHIP...
NATHANIEL WAS FORCED TO CEDE ALL INTEREST IN N.B.I. TO RAND HERSELF, AND SHE PROMPTLY SHUT DOWN ITS OFFICES--SOLD ALL THE EQUIPMENT AND FURNITURE.
N.B.I.
SHE'D WIPE OUT EVERY TRACE OF HER UNFAITHFUL LOVER, EVEN THE INSTITUTE THAT BORE HIS NAME -- BUT EXISTED ONLY TO DISSEMINATE HER IDEAS!
OBJECTIVISM, AS A COHERENT PHILOSOPHICAL SYSTEM SUPPORTED BY N.B.I., CEASED TO EXIST!
RAND LIKED TO SAY THAT MODERN CULTURE "SEEMED TOTALLY INDIFFERENT TO MY IDEAS AND TO IDEAS IN GENERAL."
SHE MADE SURE THAT THAT WOULD BE A SELF-FULFILLING PROPHECY.

THE FOUCAULT CIRCUS

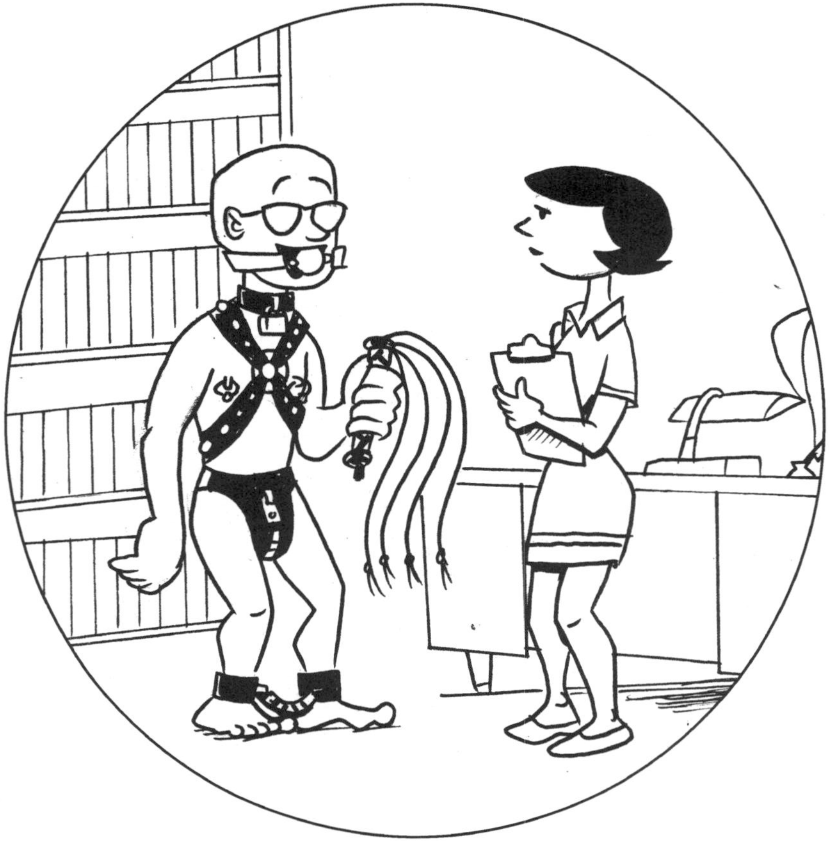

"Why yes, my new book *is* called ***Discipline & Punish***. How did you guess?"

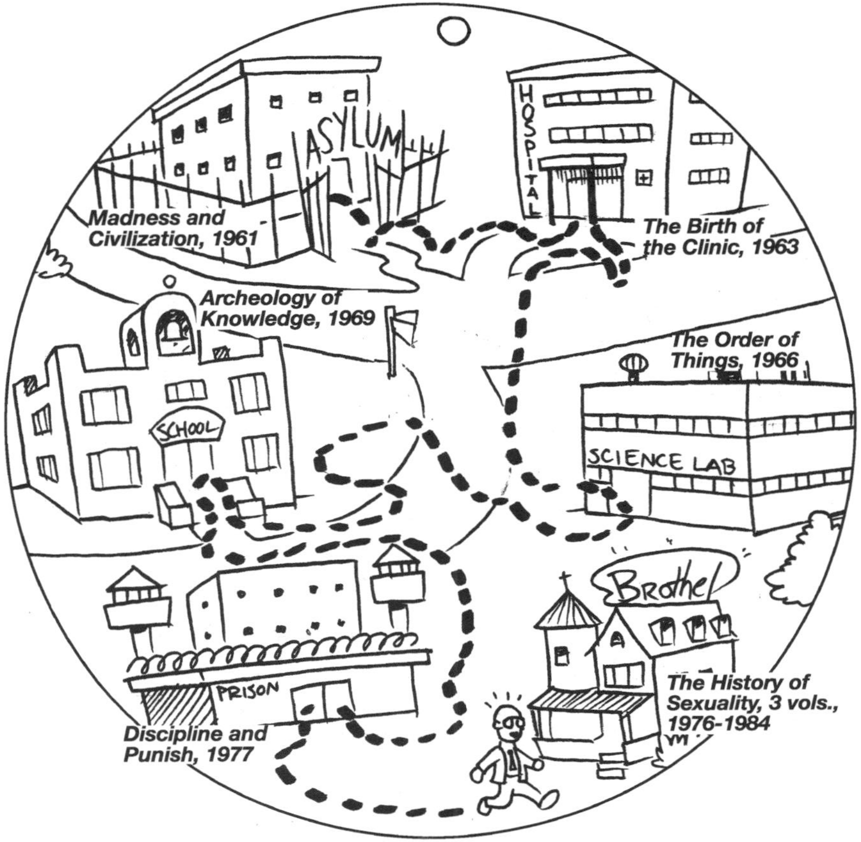
ASYLUM
HOSPITAL
Madness and Civilization, 1961
The Birth of the Clinic, 1963
Archeology of Knowledge, 1969
SCHOOL
The Order of Things, 1966
SCIENCE LAB
Brothel
PRISON
Discipline and Punish, 1977
The History of Sexuality, 3 vols., 1976-1984

Michel Foucault (1926-1984) held a chair called "The History of Systems of Thought" at the *Collège de France,* which aptly sums up his life's work of systematically examining and critiquing the logical structure of social institutions.

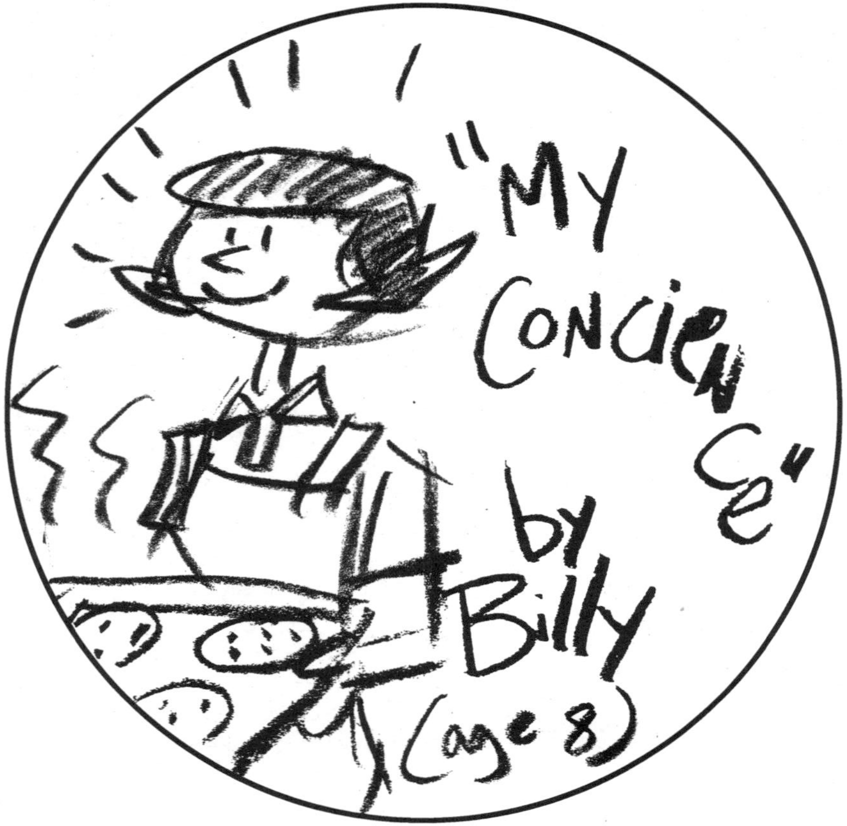
"My Concience"
by
Billy
(age 8)

Despite these institutions' claims of holding forth objective or essential knowledge, Foucault says, their assembled "truths" have in fact been subtly constructed by whatever elite happens to be in power at the time, to "reduce social agents to docile bodies" by forcing the powerless to unconsciously internalize the powerful's value system and structures of thought as their own. Furthermore, Foucault suggests that there is no knowledge other than what he calls "power-knowledge."

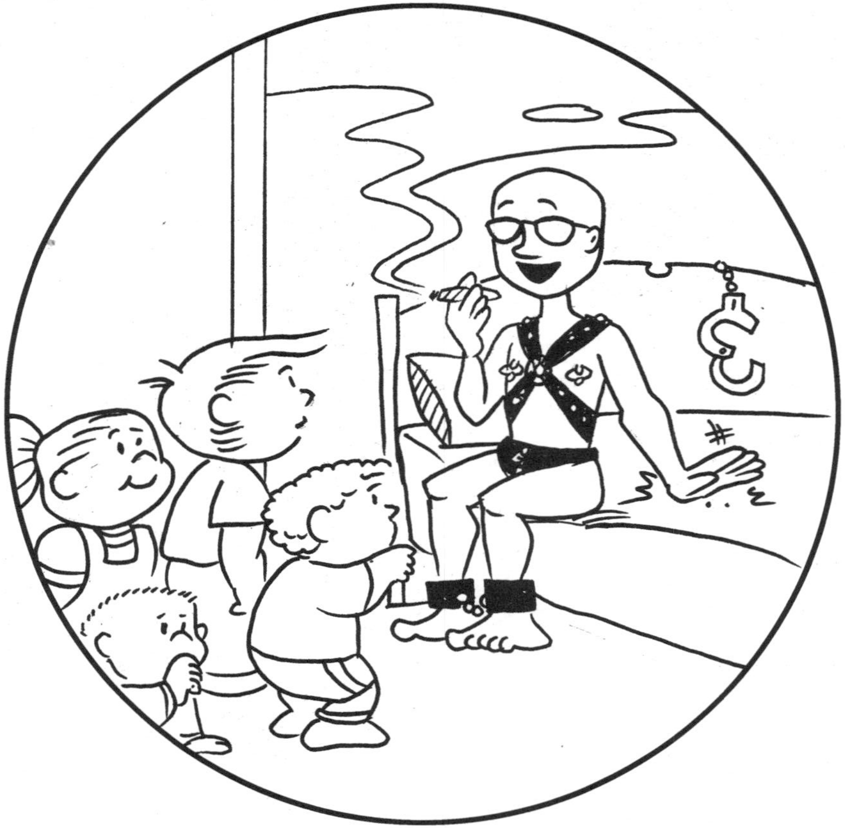

Not coincidentally, Foucault had some extreme ideas about social freedom, and garnered a reputation as something of a libertine: he was fond of anonymous gay S&M sex (which many believe contributed to his death from AIDS); he was once paid for a debate partially in hashish; and in 1977 he petitioned for France to abolish her age of consent laws (unsuccessfully).

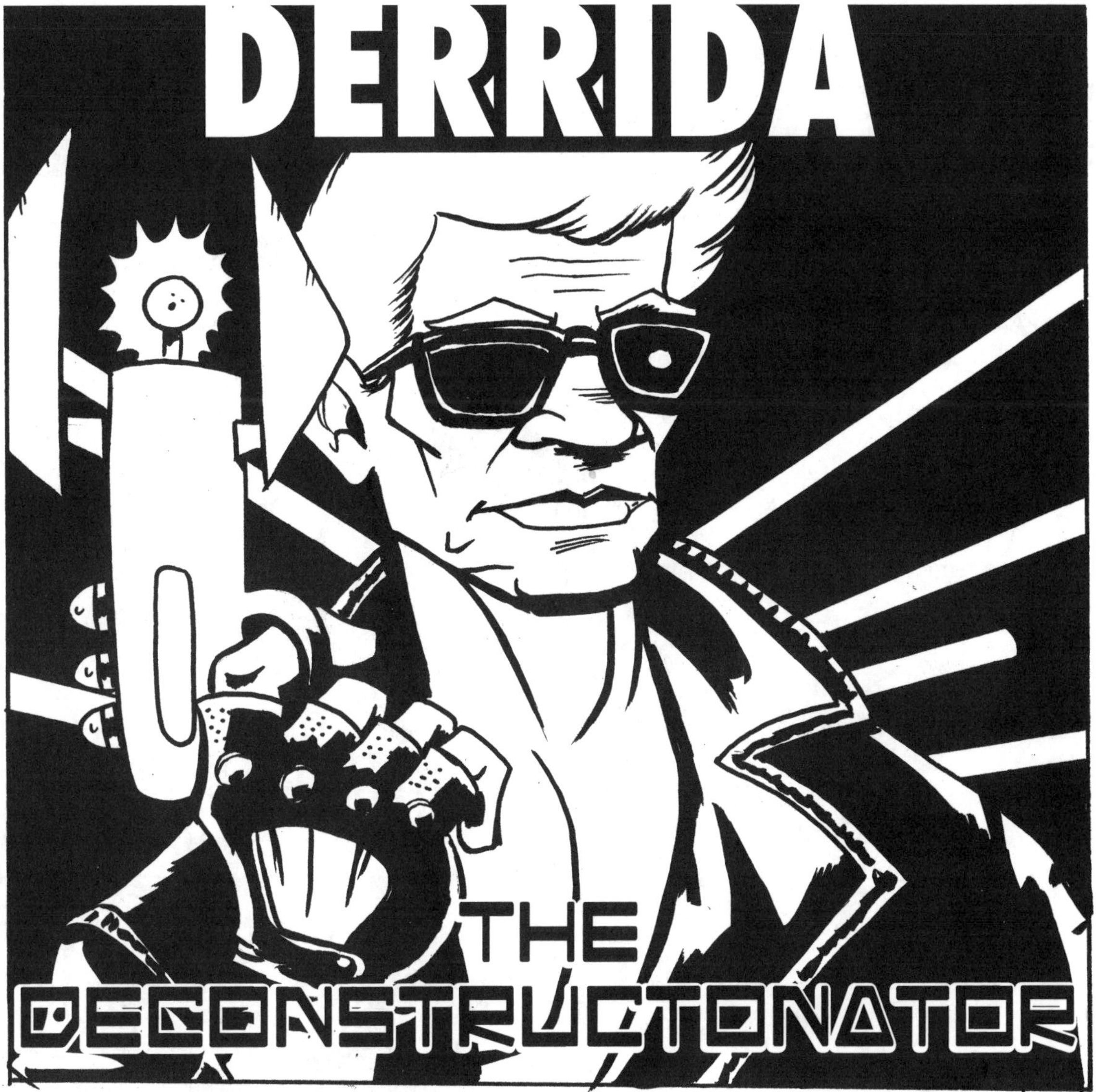
DERRIDA
THE
DECONSTRUCTONATOR

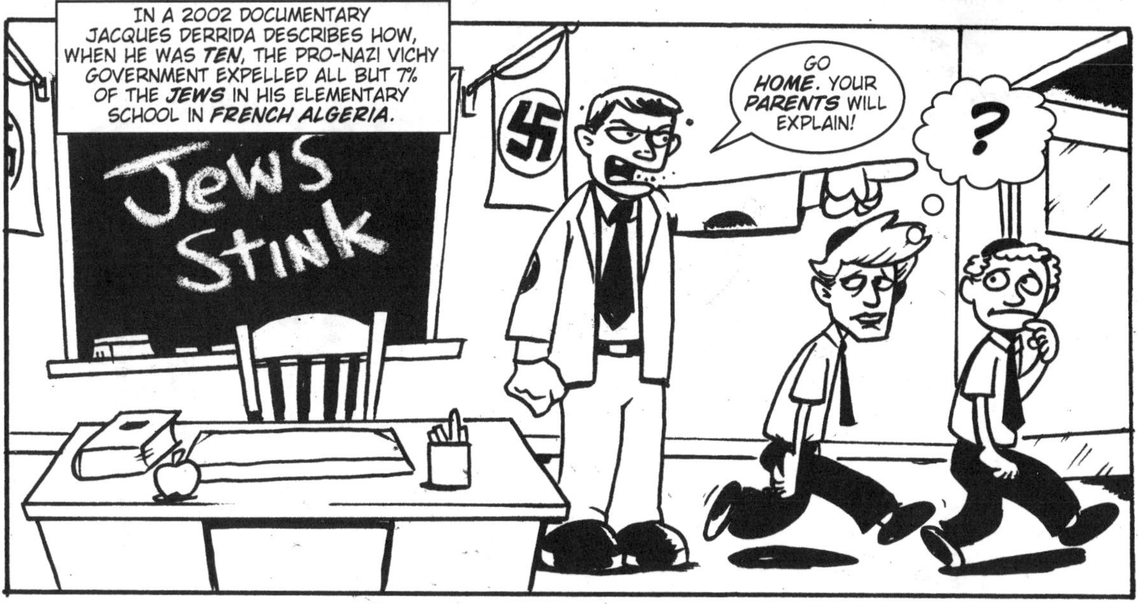
IN A 2002 DOCUMENTARY JACQUES DERRIDA DESCRIBES HOW, WHEN HE WAS **TEN**, THE PRO-NAZI VICHY GOVERNMENT EXPELLED ALL BUT 7% OF THE **JEWS** IN HIS ELEMENTARY SCHOOL IN **FRENCH ALGERIA**.
Jews Stink
GO **HOME**. YOUR **PARENTS** WILL EXPLAIN!
?

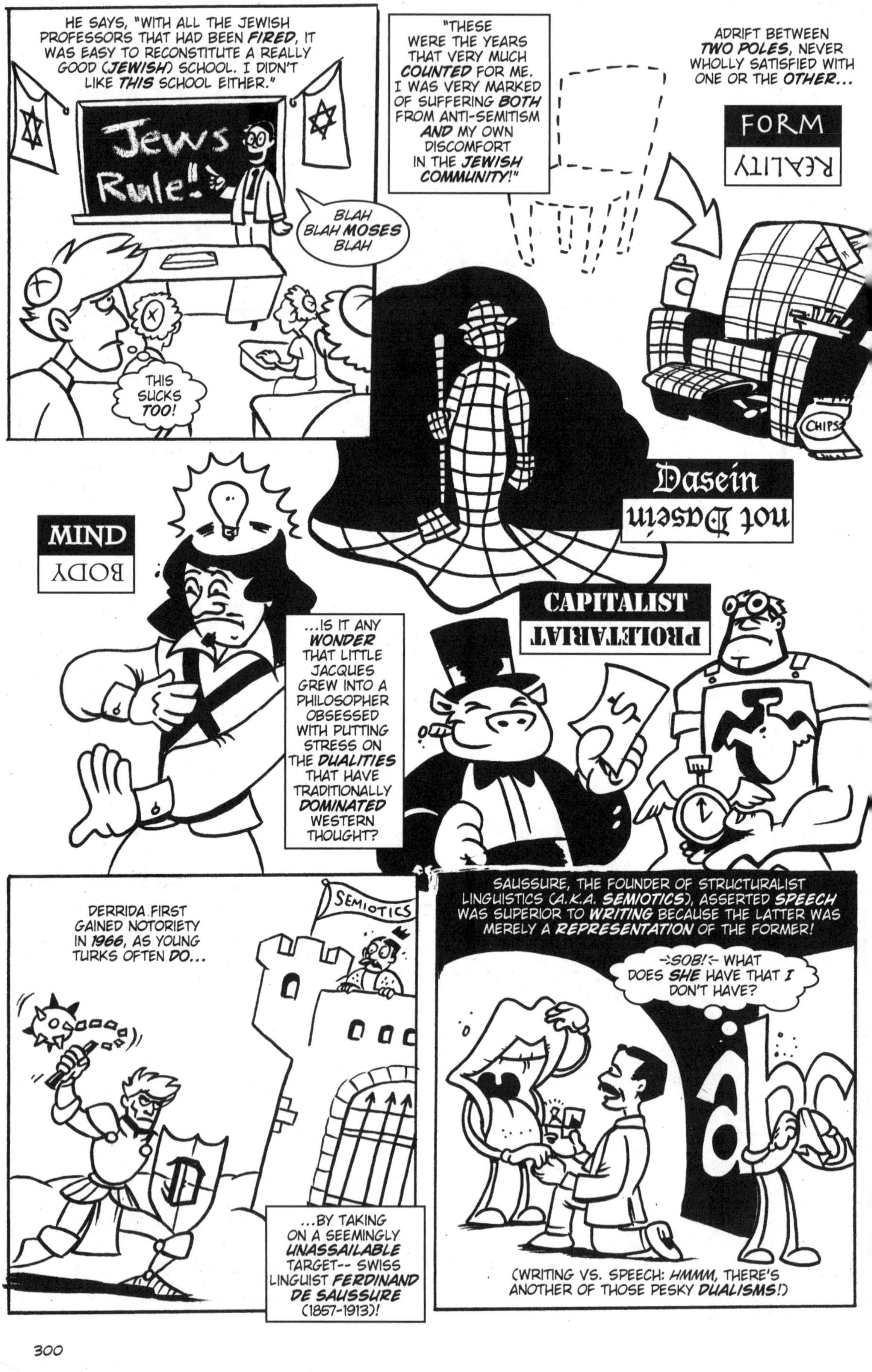
HE SAYS, "WITH ALL THE JEWISH PROFESSORS THAT HAD BEEN FIRED, IT WAS EASY TO RECONSTITUTE A REALLY GOOD (JEWISH) SCHOOL. I DIDN'T LIKE THIS SCHOOL EITHER."
Jews Rule!!
BLAH BLAH MOSES BLAH
THIS SUCKS TOO!
"THESE WERE THE YEARS THAT VERY MUCH COUNTED FOR ME. I WAS VERY MARKED OF SUFFERING BOTH FROM ANTI-SEMITISM AND MY OWN DISCOMFORT IN THE JEWISH COMMUNITY!"
ADRIFT BETWEEN TWO POLES, NEVER WHOLLY SATISFIED WITH ONE OR THE OTHER...
FORM
REALITY
CHIPS
Dasein
not Dasein
MIND
BODY
CAPITALIST
PROLETARIAT
...IS IT ANY WONDER THAT LITTLE JACQUES GREW INTO A PHILOSOPHER OBSESSED WITH PUTTING STRESS ON THE DUALITIES THAT HAVE TRADITIONALLY DOMINATED WESTERN THOUGHT?
DERRIDA FIRST GAINED NOTORIETY IN 1966, AS YOUNG TURKS OFTEN DO...
SEMIOTICS
...BY TAKING ON A SEEMINGLY UNASSAILABLE TARGET-- SWISS LINGUIST FERDINAND DE SAUSSURE (1857-1913)!
SAUSSURE, THE FOUNDER OF STRUCTURALIST LINGUISTICS (A.K.A. SEMIOTICS), ASSERTED SPEECH WAS SUPERIOR TO WRITING BECAUSE THE LATTER WAS MERELY A REPRESENTATION OF THE FORMER!
-SOB!- WHAT DOES SHE HAVE THAT I DON'T HAVE?
abc
(WRITING VS. SPEECH: HMMM, THERE'S ANOTHER OF THOSE PESKY DUALISMS!)

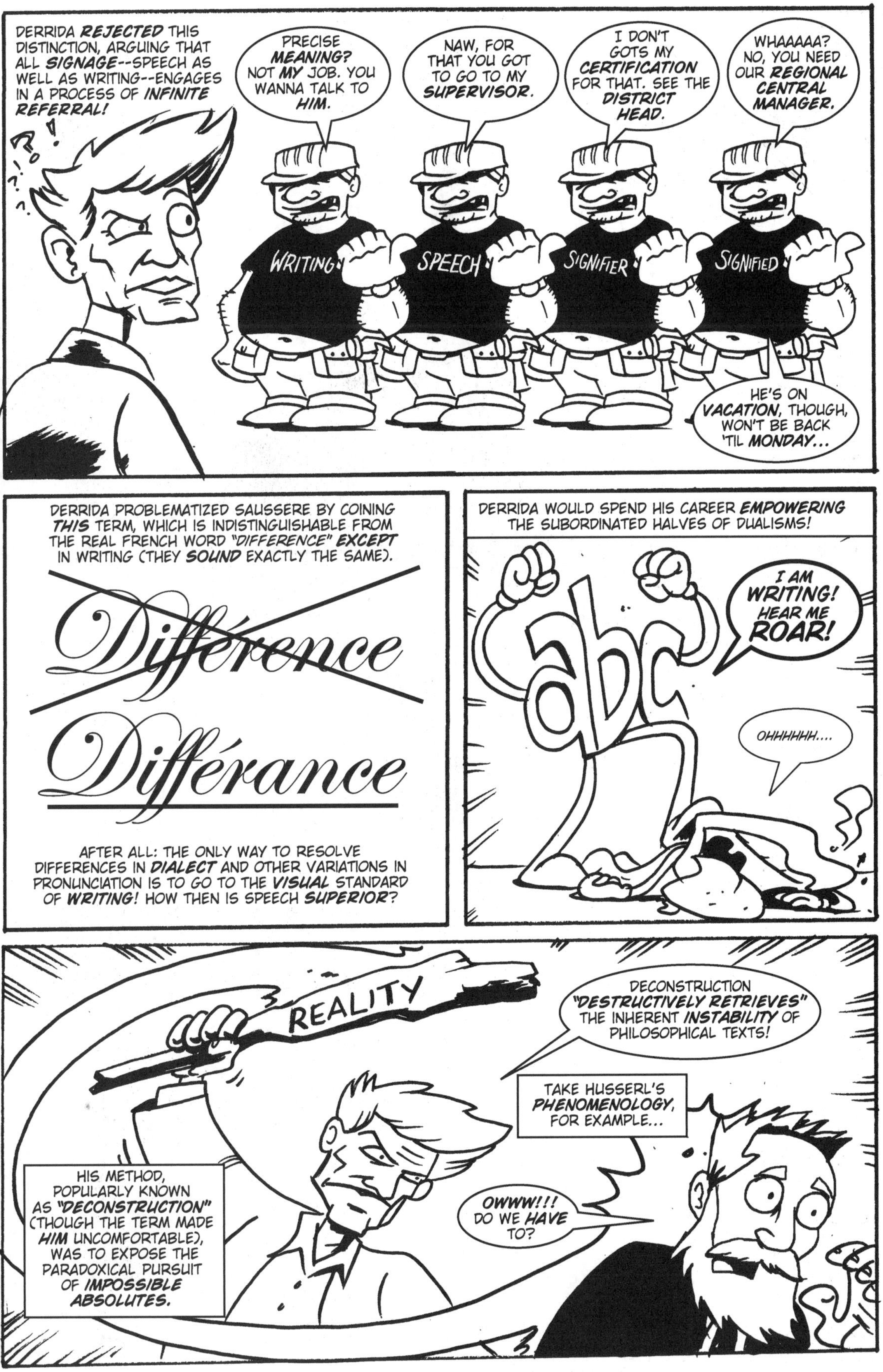
DERRIDA REJECTED THIS DISTINCTION, ARGUING THAT ALL SIGNAGE--SPEECH AS WELL AS WRITING--ENGAGES IN A PROCESS OF INFINITE REFERRAL!
?!
PRECISE MEANING? NOT MY JOB. YOU WANNA TALK TO HIM.
NAW, FOR THAT YOU GOT TO GO TO MY SUPERVISOR.
I DON'T GOTS MY CERTIFICATION FOR THAT. SEE THE DISTRICT HEAD.
WHAAAAA? NO, YOU NEED OUR REGIONAL CENTRAL MANAGER.
WRITING
SPEECH
SIGNIFIER
SIGNIFIED
HE'S ON VACATION, THOUGH, WON'T BE BACK 'TIL MONDAY...
DERRIDA PROBLEMATIZED SAUSSERE BY COINING THIS TERM, WHICH IS INDISTINGUISHABLE FROM THE REAL FRENCH WORD "DIFFERENCE" EXCEPT IN WRITING (THEY SOUND EXACTLY THE SAME).
Différence
Différance
AFTER ALL: THE ONLY WAY TO RESOLVE DIFFERENCES IN DIALECT AND OTHER VARIATIONS IN PRONUNCIATION IS TO GO TO THE VISUAL STANDARD OF WRITING! HOW THEN IS SPEECH SUPERIOR?
DERRIDA WOULD SPEND HIS CAREER EMPOWERING THE SUBORDINATED HALVES OF DUALISMS!
abc
I AM WRITING! HEAR ME ROAR!
OHHHHHH....
REALITY
DECONSTRUCTION "DESTRUCTIVELY RETRIEVES" THE INHERENT INSTABILITY OF PHILOSOPHICAL TEXTS!
TAKE HUSSERL'S PHENOMENOLOGY, FOR EXAMPLE...
HIS METHOD, POPULARLY KNOWN AS "DECONSTRUCTION" (THOUGH THE TERM MADE HIM UNCOMFORTABLE), WAS TO EXPOSE THE PARADOXICAL PURSUIT OF IMPOSSIBLE ABSOLUTES.
OWWW!!! DO WE HAVE TO?

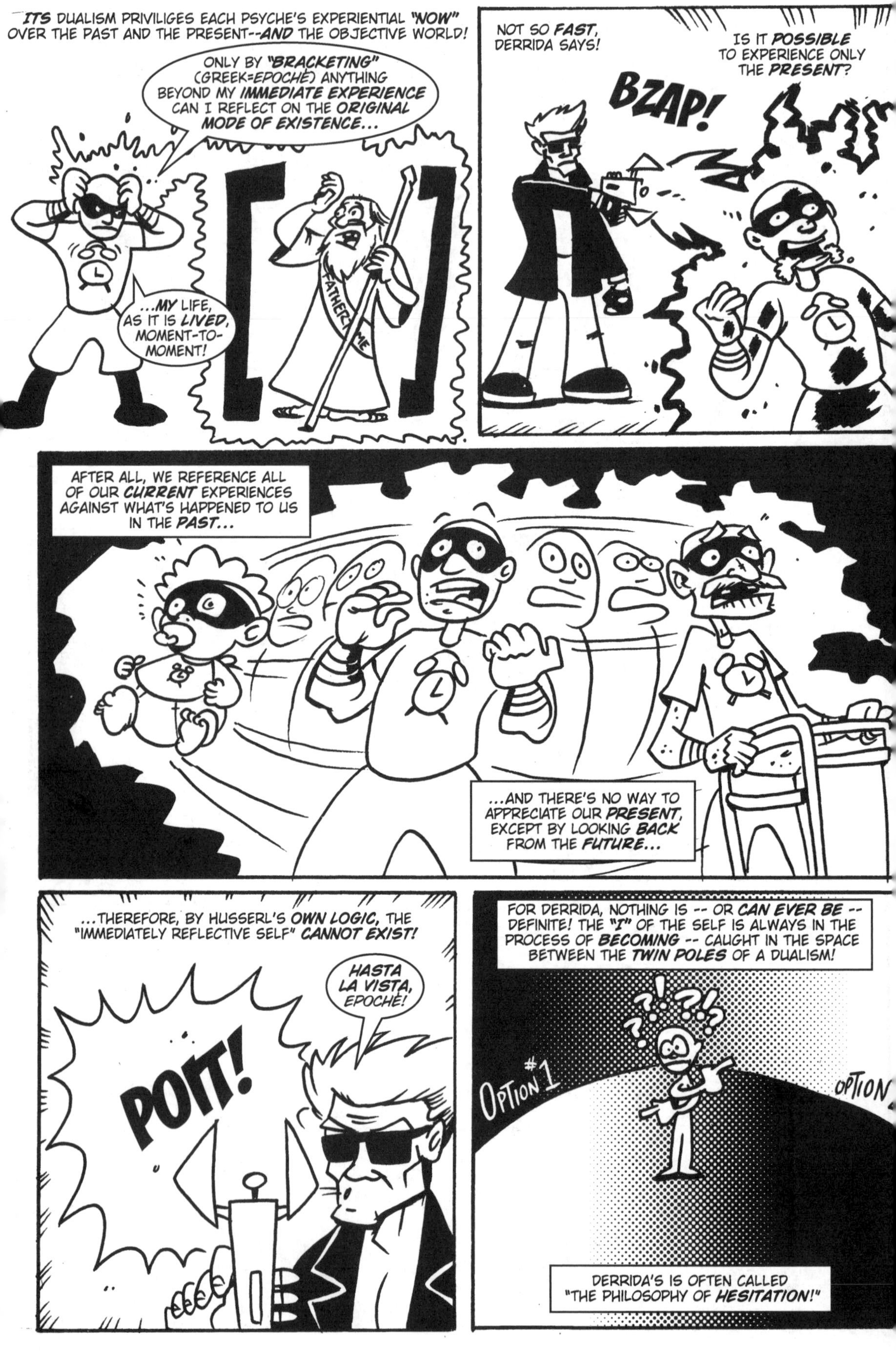
ITS DUALISM PRIVILIGES EACH PSYCHE'S EXPERIENTIAL "NOW" OVER THE PAST AND THE PRESENT--AND THE OBJECTIVE WORLD!
ONLY BY "BRACKETING" (GREEK=EPOCHÉ) ANYTHING BEYOND MY IMMEDIATE EXPERIENCE CAN I REFLECT ON THE ORIGINAL MODE OF EXISTENCE...
...MY LIFE, AS IT IS LIVED, MOMENT-TO-MOMENT!
FATHER TIME
NOT SO FAST, DERRIDA SAYS!
IS IT POSSIBLE TO EXPERIENCE ONLY THE PRESENT?
BZAP!
AFTER ALL, WE REFERENCE ALL OF OUR CURRENT EXPERIENCES AGAINST WHAT'S HAPPENED TO US IN THE PAST...
...AND THERE'S NO WAY TO APPRECIATE OUR PRESENT, EXCEPT BY LOOKING BACK FROM THE FUTURE...
...THEREFORE, BY HUSSERL'S OWN LOGIC, THE "IMMEDIATELY REFLECTIVE SELF" CANNOT EXIST!
HASTA LA VISTA, EPOCHÉ!
POIT!
FOR DERRIDA, NOTHING IS -- OR CAN EVER BE -- DEFINITE! THE "I" OF THE SELF IS ALWAYS IN THE PROCESS OF BECOMING -- CAUGHT IN THE SPACE BETWEEN THE TWIN POLES OF A DUALISM!
?!?!?
OPTION #1
OPTION
DERRIDA'S IS OFTEN CALLED "THE PHILOSOPHY OF HESITATION!"

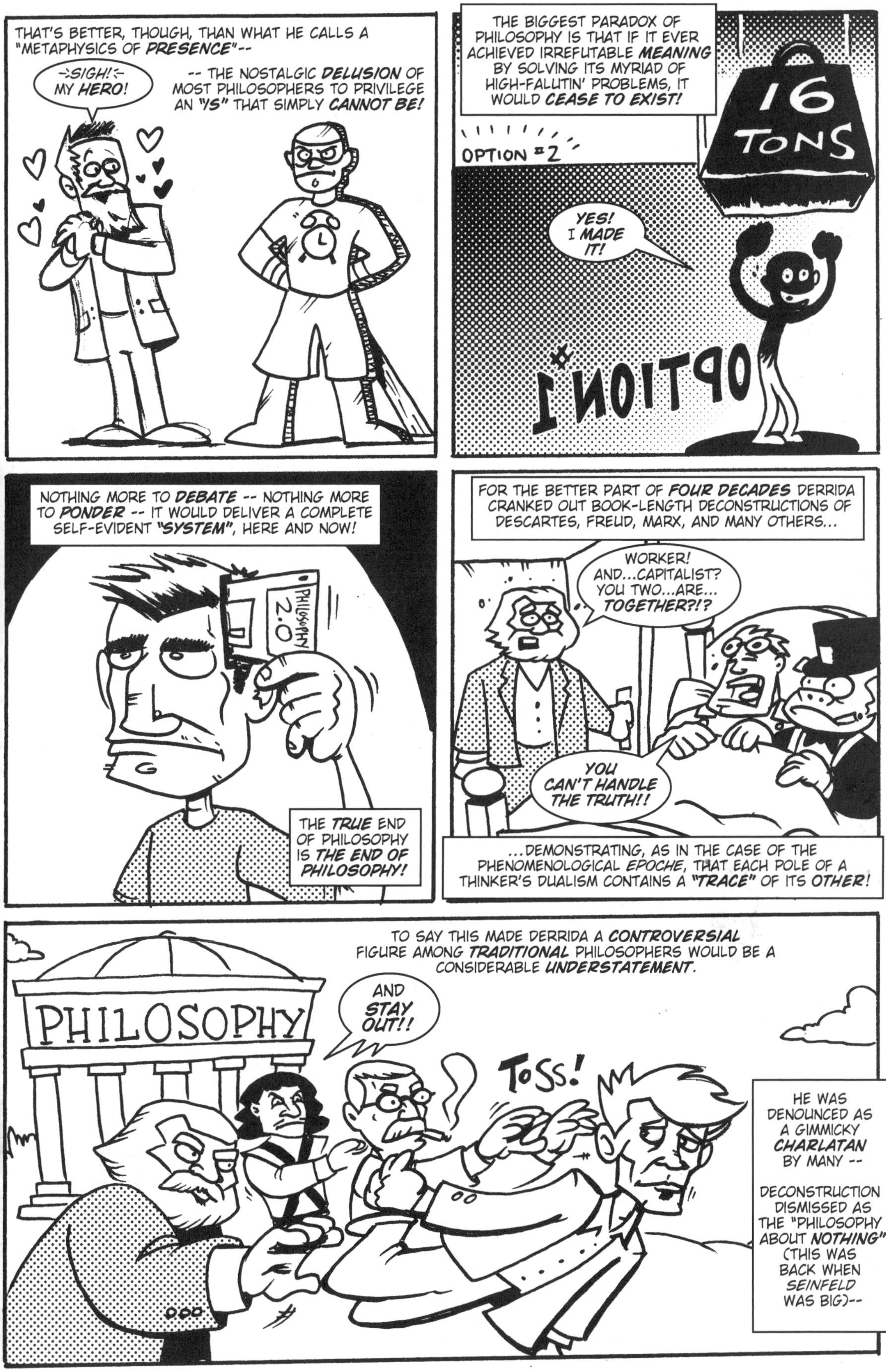
THAT'S BETTER, THOUGH, THAN WHAT HE CALLS A "METAPHYSICS OF PRESENCE"--
-SIGH!- MY HERO!
-- THE NOSTALGIC DELUSION OF MOST PHILOSOPHERS TO PRIVILEGE AN "IS" THAT SIMPLY CANNOT BE!
THE BIGGEST PARADOX OF PHILOSOPHY IS THAT IF IT EVER ACHIEVED IRREFUTABLE MEANING BY SOLVING ITS MYRIAD OF HIGH-FALUTIN' PROBLEMS, IT WOULD CEASE TO EXIST!
16 TONS
OPTION #2
YES! I MADE IT!
OPTION #1
NOTHING MORE TO DEBATE -- NOTHING MORE TO PONDER -- IT WOULD DELIVER A COMPLETE SELF-EVIDENT "SYSTEM", HERE AND NOW!
PHILOSOPHY 2.0
THE TRUE END OF PHILOSOPHY IS THE END OF PHILOSOPHY!
FOR THE BETTER PART OF FOUR DECADES DERRIDA CRANKED OUT BOOK-LENGTH DECONSTRUCTIONS OF DESCARTES, FREUD, MARX, AND MANY OTHERS...
WORKER! AND...CAPITALIST? YOU TWO...ARE... TOGETHER?!?
YOU CAN'T HANDLE THE TRUTH!!
...DEMONSTRATING, AS IN THE CASE OF THE PHENOMENOLOGICAL EPOCHE, THAT EACH POLE OF A THINKER'S DUALISM CONTAINS A "TRACE" OF ITS OTHER!
TO SAY THIS MADE DERRIDA A CONTROVERSIAL FIGURE AMONG TRADITIONAL PHILOSOPHERS WOULD BE A CONSIDERABLE UNDERSTATEMENT.
PHILOSOPHY
AND STAY OUT!!
TOSS!
HE WAS DENOUNCED AS A GIMMICKY CHARLATAN BY MANY --
DECONSTRUCTION DISMISSED AS THE "PHILOSOPHY ABOUT NOTHING" (THIS WAS BACK WHEN SEINFELD WAS BIG)--

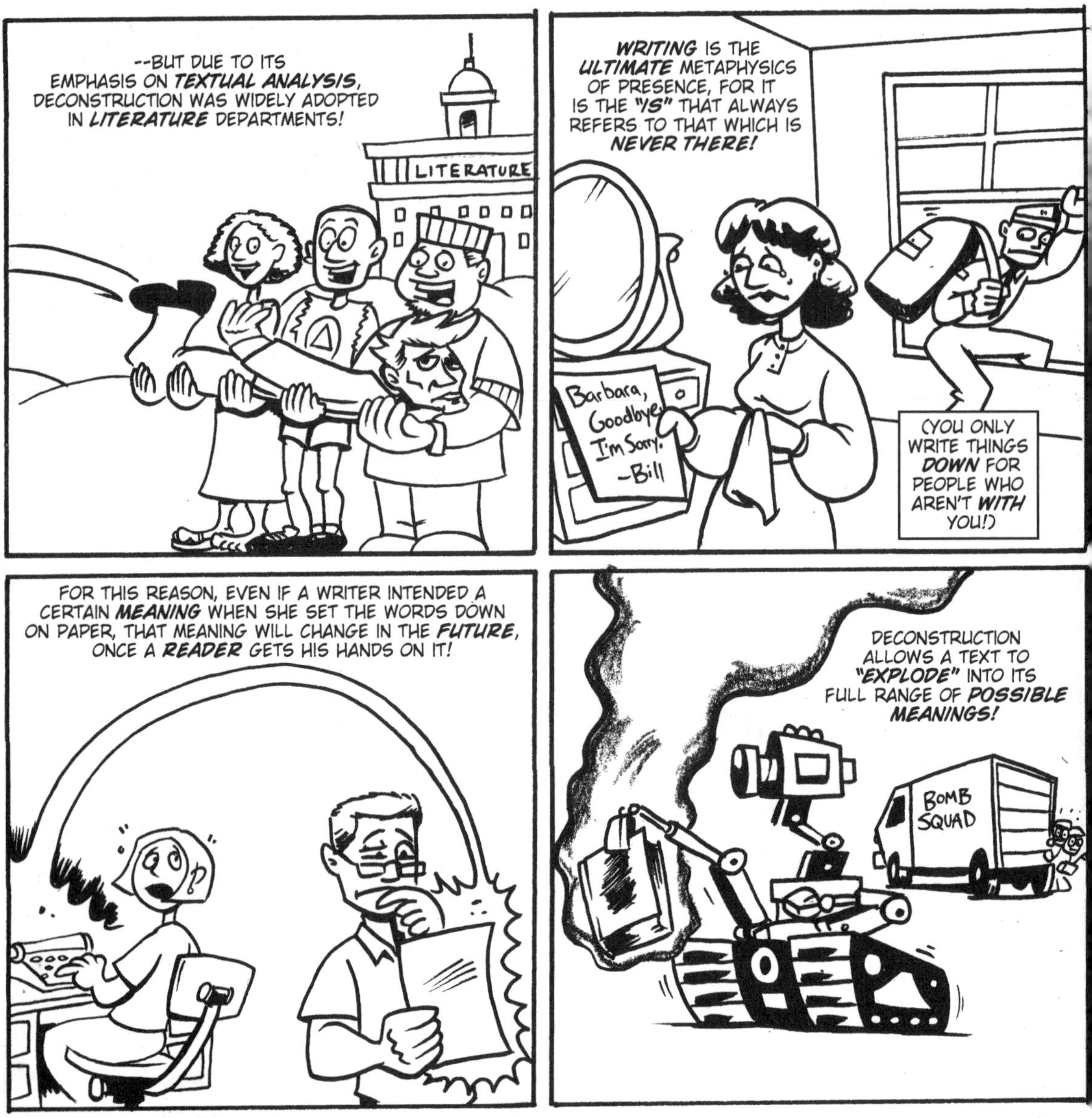
--BUT DUE TO ITS EMPHASIS ON *TEXTUAL ANALYSIS*, DECONSTRUCTION WAS WIDELY ADOPTED IN *LITERATURE* DEPARTMENTS!
LITERATURE
WRITING IS THE *ULTIMATE* METAPHYSICS OF PRESENCE, FOR IT IS THE *"IS"* THAT ALWAYS REFERS TO THAT WHICH IS *NEVER THERE!*
Barbara, Goodbye. I'm Sorry. -Bill
(YOU ONLY WRITE THINGS *DOWN* FOR PEOPLE WHO AREN'T *WITH* YOU!)
FOR THIS REASON, EVEN IF A WRITER INTENDED A CERTAIN *MEANING* WHEN SHE SET THE WORDS DOWN ON PAPER, THAT MEANING WILL CHANGE IN THE *FUTURE*, ONCE A *READER* GETS HIS HANDS ON IT!
DECONSTRUCTION ALLOWS A TEXT TO *"EXPLODE"* INTO ITS FULL RANGE OF *POSSIBLE MEANINGS!*
BOMB SQUAD

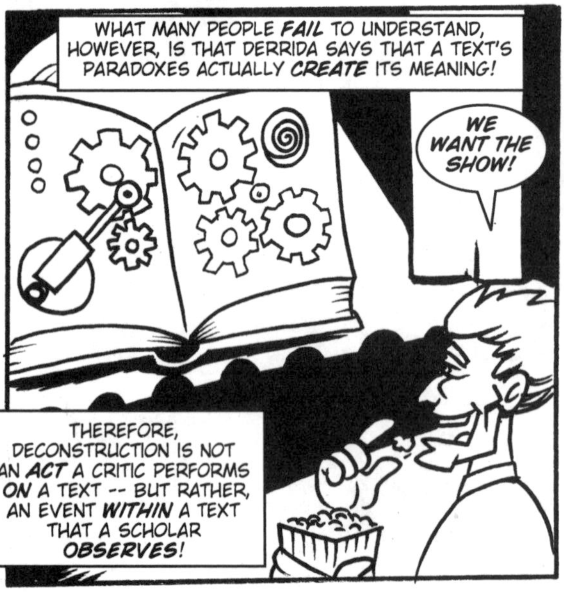
WHAT MANY PEOPLE *FAIL* TO UNDERSTAND, HOWEVER, IS THAT DERRIDA SAYS THAT A TEXT'S PARADOXES ACTUALLY *CREATE* ITS MEANING!
WE WANT THE SHOW!
THEREFORE, DECONSTRUCTION IS NOT AN *ACT* A CRITIC PERFORMS *ON* A TEXT -- BUT RATHER, AN EVENT *WITHIN* A TEXT THAT A SCHOLAR *OBSERVES!*

PAGE SIX

PANEL 6: CLOSE UP ON DERRIDA

DERRIDA: In order to be FAITHFUL to a text's true meaning we must invent NEW ONES for it!

DERRIDA: "Invent in your OWN language if you can or want to hear MINE; invent if you can or want to give my language to be understood."

DERRIDA: Any faithful INTERPRETATION of my work would require a student to go BEYOND it!

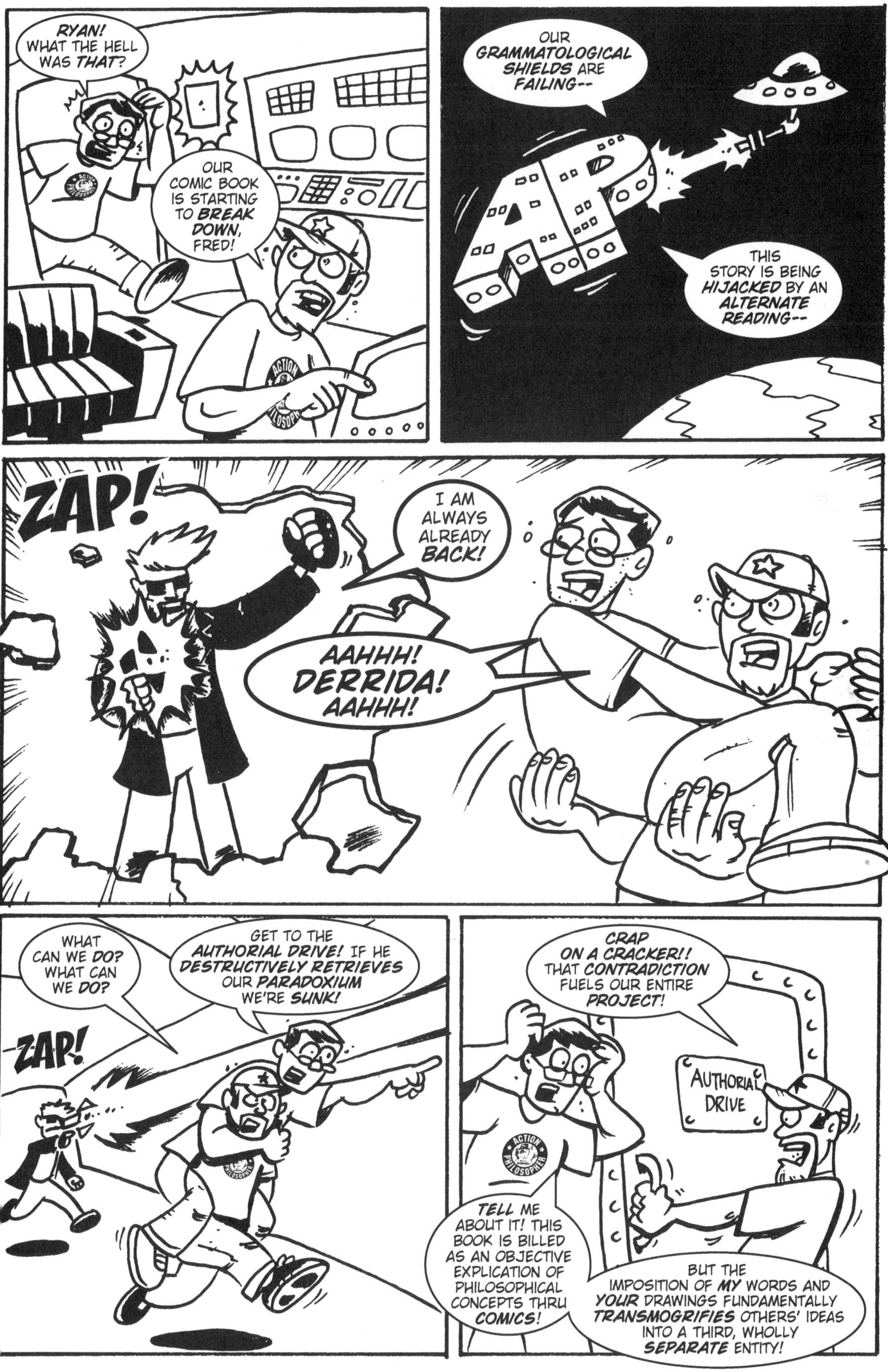
RYAN! WHAT THE HELL WAS THAT?
OUR COMIC BOOK IS STARTING TO BREAK DOWN, FRED!
ACTION PHILOSOPHER
OUR GRAMMATOLOGICAL SHIELDS ARE FAILING--
THIS STORY IS BEING HIJACKED BY AN ALTERNATE READING--
ZAP!
I AM ALWAYS ALREADY BACK!
AAHHH! DERRIDA! AAHHH!
WHAT CAN WE DO? WHAT CAN WE DO?
GET TO THE AUTHORIAL DRIVE! IF HE DESTRUCTIVELY RETRIEVES OUR PARADOXIUM WE'RE SUNK!
ZAP!
CRAP ON A CRACKER!! THAT CONTRADICTION FUELS OUR ENTIRE PROJECT!
AUTHORIAL DRIVE
TELL ME ABOUT IT! THIS BOOK IS BILLED AS AN OBJECTIVE EXPLICATION OF PHILOSOPHICAL CONCEPTS THRU COMICS!
BUT THE IMPOSITION OF MY WORDS AND YOUR DRAWINGS FUNDAMENTALLY TRANSMOGRIFIES OTHERS' IDEAS INTO A THIRD, WHOLLY SEPARATE ENTITY!

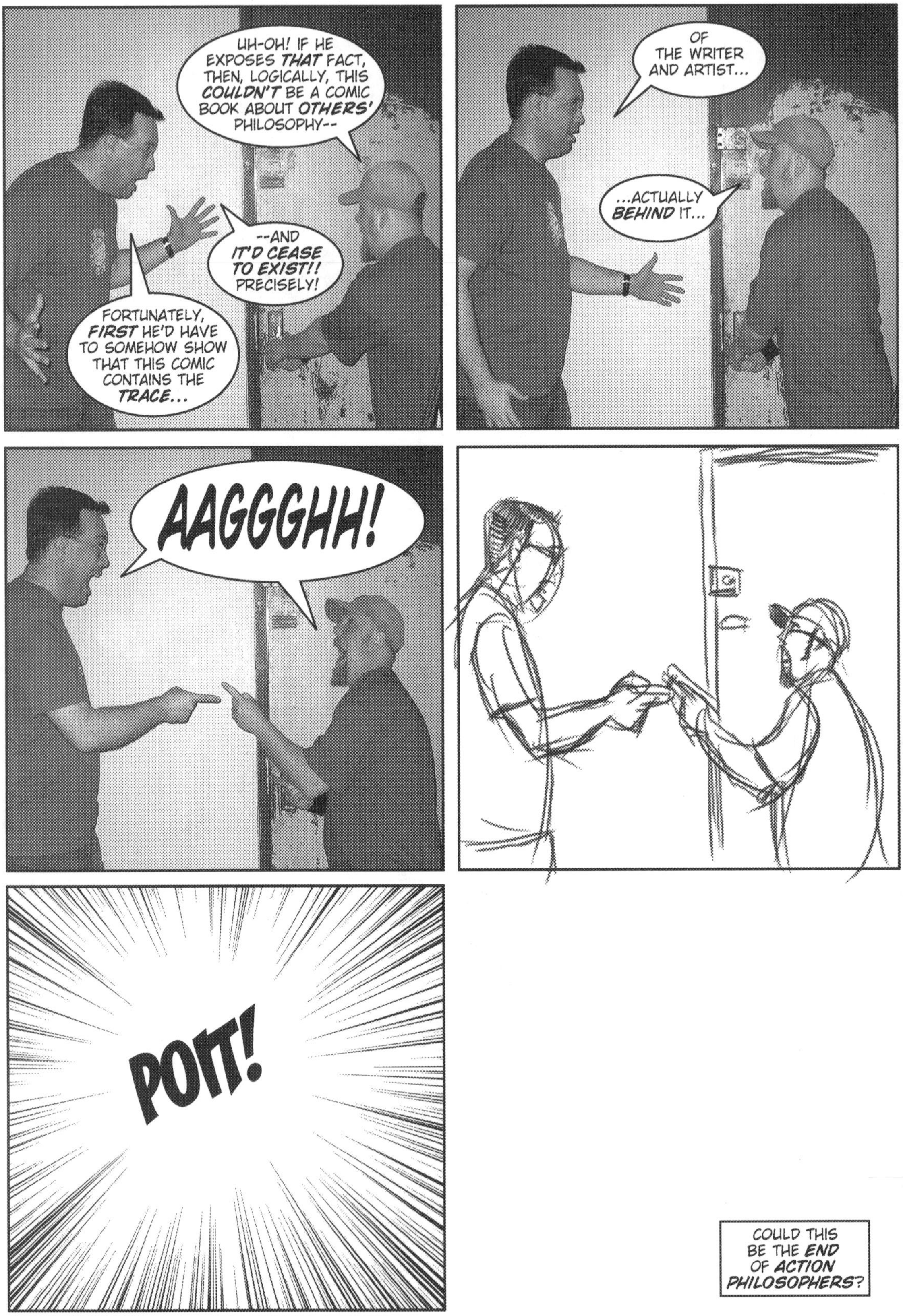

UH-OH! IF HE EXPOSES THAT FACT, THEN, LOGICALLY, THIS COULDN'T BE A COMIC BOOK ABOUT OTHERS' PHILOSOPHY--
--AND IT'D CEASE TO EXIST!! PRECISELY!
FORTUNATELY, FIRST HE'D HAVE TO SOMEHOW SHOW THAT THIS COMIC CONTAINS THE TRACE...
OF THE WRITER AND ARTIST...
...ACTUALLY BEHIND IT...
AAGGGHH!
POIT!
COULD THIS BE THE END OF ACTION PHILOSOPHERS?